Get the eBook FREE!
(PDF, ePub, Kindle, and liveBook all included)

We believe that once you buy a book from us, you should be able to read it in any format we have available. To get electronic versions of this book at no additional cost to you, purchase and then register this book at the Manning website.

Go to https://www.manning.com/freebook and follow the instructions to complete your pBook registration.

That's it!
Thanks from Manning!

Praise for the First Edition

Clear and succinct, this book provides the first hands-on map of the fertile ground between business acumen, statistics, and machine learning.
—Dwight Barry,
Group Health Cooperative

This is the book that I wish was available when I was first learning Data Science. The author presents a thorough and well-organized approach to the mechanics and mastery of Data Science, which is a conglomeration of statistics, data analysis, and computer science.
—Justin Fister, AI researcher,
PaperRater.com

The most comprehensive content I have seen on Data Science with R.
—Romit Singhai, SGI

Covers the process end to end, from data exploration to modeling to delivering the results.
—Nezih Yigitbasi,
Intel

Full of useful gems for both aspiring and experienced data scientists.
—Fred Rahmanian,
Siemens Healthcare

Hands-on data analysis with real-world examples. Highly recommended.
—Dr. Kostas Passadis,
IPTO

In working through the book, one gets the impression of being guided by knowledgeable and experienced professionals who are holding nothing back.
—Amazon reader

Practical Data Science
with R

SECOND EDITION

NINA ZUMEL
AND JOHN MOUNT

FOREWORD BY JEREMY HOWARD
AND RACHEL THOMAS

MANNING

SHELTER ISLAND

Manning Publications Co.
20 Baldwin Road
PO Box 761
Shelter Island, NY 11964

Development editor:	Dustin Archibald
Technical development editor:	Doug Warren
Review editor:	Aleksandar Dragosavljević
Project manager:	Lori Weidert
Copy editor:	Ben Berg
Proofreader:	Katie Tennant
Technical proofreader:	Taylor Dolezal
Typesetter:	Dottie Marsico
Cover designer:	Marija Tudor

ISBN 9781617295874
Printed in the United States of America

To our parents

Olive and Paul Zumel
Peggy and David Mount

brief contents

PART 1 INTRODUCTION TO DATA SCIENCE 1

1 ▪ The data science process   3
2 ▪ Starting with R and data   18
3 ▪ Exploring data   51
4 ▪ Managing data   88
5 ▪ Data engineering and data shaping   113

PART 2 MODELING METHODS 161

6 ▪ Choosing and evaluating models   163
7 ▪ Linear and logistic regression   215
8 ▪ Advanced data preparation   274
9 ▪ Unsupervised methods   311
10 ▪ Exploring advanced methods   353

PART 3 WORKING IN THE REAL WORLD 401

11 ▪ Documentation and deployment   403
12 ▪ Producing effective presentations   437

contents

foreword xv
preface xvi
acknowledgments xvii
about this book xviii
about the authors xxv
about the foreword authors xxvi
about the cover illustration xxvii

PART 1 INTRODUCTION TO DATA SCIENCE 1

1 The data science process   3

1.1   The roles in a data science project   4

Project roles   4

1.2   Stages of a data science project   6

*Defining the goal   7 ▪ Data collection and management   8
Modeling   10 ▪ Model evaluation and critique   12
Presentation and documentation   14 ▪ Model deployment
and maintenance   15*

1.3   Setting expectations   16

Determining lower bounds on model performance   16

2 Starting with R and data   18

2.1   Starting with R   19

Installing R, tools, and examples   20 ▪ R programming   20

ix

2.2 Working with data from files 29

Working with well-structured data from files or URLs 29
Using R with less-structured data 34

2.3 Working with relational databases 37

A production-size example 38

3 Exploring data 51

3.1 Using summary statistics to spot problems 53

Typical problems revealed by data summaries 54

3.2 Spotting problems using graphics and visualization 58

Visually checking distributions for a single variable 60
Visually checking relationships between two variables 70

4 Managing data 88

4.1 Cleaning data 88

Domain-specific data cleaning 89 ▪ Treating missing values 91 ▪ The vtreat package for automatically treating missing variables 95

4.2 Data transformations 98

Normalization 99 ▪ Centering and scaling 101 Log transformations for skewed and wide distributions 104

4.3 Sampling for modeling and validation 107

Test and training splits 108 ▪ Creating a sample group column 109 ▪ Record grouping 110 ▪ Data provenance 111

5 Data engineering and data shaping 113

5.1 Data selection 116

Subsetting rows and columns 116 ▪ Removing records with incomplete data 121 ▪ Ordering rows 124

5.2 Basic data transforms 128

Adding new columns 128 ▪ Other simple operations 133

5.3 Aggregating transforms 134

Combining many rows into summary rows 134

5.4 Multitable data transforms 137

Combining two or more ordered data frames quickly 137 Principal methods to combine data from multiple tables 143

5.5 Reshaping transforms 149

Moving data from wide to tall form 149 ▪ Moving data from tall to wide form 153 ▪ Data coordinates 158

PART 2   MODELING METHODS 161

6   *Choosing and evaluating models   163*

    6.1 Mapping problems to machine learning tasks   164
         Classification problems   165 ▪ Scoring problems   166
         Grouping: working without known targets   167
         Problem-to-method mapping   169

    6.2 Evaluating models   170
         Overfitting   170 ▪ Measures of model performance   174
         Evaluating classification models   175 ▪ Evaluating scoring
         models   185 ▪ Evaluating probability models   187

    6.3 Local interpretable model-agnostic explanations (LIME)
         for explaining model predictions   195
         LIME: Automated sanity checking   197 ▪ Walking through
         LIME: A small example   197 ▪ LIME for text classification   204
         Training the text classifier   208 ▪ Explaining the classifier's
         predictions   209

7   *Linear and logistic regression   215*

    7.1 Using linear regression   216
         Understanding linear regression   217 ▪ Building a
         linear regression model   221 ▪ Making predictions   222
         Finding relations and extracting advice   228 ▪ Reading the
         model summary and characterizing coefficient quality   230
         Linear regression takeaways   237

    7.2 Using logistic regression   237
         Understanding logistic regression   237 ▪ Building a
         logistic regression model   242 ▪ Making predictions   243
         Finding relations and extracting advice from logistic
         models   248 ▪ Reading the model summary and characterizing
         coefficients   249 ▪ Logistic regression takeaways   256

    7.3 Regularization   257
         An example of quasi-separation   257 ▪ The types of regularized
         regression   262 ▪ Regularized regression with glmnet   263

8   *Advanced data preparation   274*

    8.1 The purpose of the vtreat package   275

    8.2 KDD and KDD Cup 2009   277
         Getting started with KDD Cup 2009 data   278 ▪ The bull-in-
         the-china-shop approach   280

8.3   Basic data preparation for classification   282

*The variable score frame   284 ▪ Properly using the treatment
plan   288*

8.4   Advanced data preparation for classification   290

*Using mkCrossFrameCExperiment()   290 ▪ Building a
model   292*

8.5   Preparing data for regression modeling   297

8.6   Mastering the vtreat package   299

*The vtreat phases   299 ▪ Missing values   301
Indicator variables   303 ▪ Impact coding   304
The treatment plan   305 ▪ The cross-frame   306*

9 *Unsupervised methods   311*

9.1   Cluster analysis   312

*Distances   313 ▪ Preparing the data   316 ▪ Hierarchical
clustering with hclust   319 ▪ The k-means algorithm   332
Assigning new points to clusters   338 ▪ Clustering
takeaways   340*

9.2   Association rules   340

*Overview of association rules   340 ▪ The example problem   342
Mining association rules with the arules package   343
Association rule takeaways   351*

10 *Exploring advanced methods   353*

10.1   Tree-based methods   355

*A basic decision tree   356 ▪ Using bagging to improve
prediction   359 ▪ Using random forests to further improve
prediction   361 ▪ Gradient-boosted trees   368 ▪ Tree-based model
takeaways   376*

10.2   Using generalized additive models (GAMs)
to learn non-monotone relationships   376

*Understanding GAMs   376 ▪ A one-dimensional regression
example   378 ▪ Extracting the non-linear relationships   382
Using GAM on actual data   384 ▪ Using GAM for logistic
regression   387 ▪ GAM takeaways   388*

10.3   Solving "inseparable" problems using support vector
machines   389

*Using an SVM to solve a problem   390 ▪ Understanding support
vector machines   395 ▪ Understanding kernel functions   397
Support vector machine and kernel methods takeaways   399*

PART 3 WORKING IN THE REAL WORLD 401

11 *Documentation and deployment* 403

11.1 Predicting buzz   405

11.2 Using R markdown to produce milestone documentation   406

*What is R markdown?   407 ▪ knitr technical details   409
Using knitr to document the Buzz data and produce the model   411*

11.3 Using comments and version control for running
documentation   414

*Writing effective comments   414 ▪ Using version control to
record history   416 ▪ Using version control to explore your
project   422 ▪ Using version control to share work   424*

11.4 Deploying models   428

*Deploying demonstrations using Shiny   430 ▪ Deploying
models as HTTP services   431 ▪ Deploying models by
export   433 ▪ What to take away   435*

12 *Producing effective presentations* 437

12.1 Presenting your results to the project sponsor   439

*Summarizing the project's goals   440 ▪ Stating the project's
results   442 ▪ Filling in the details   444 ▪ Making
recommendations and discussing future work   446
Project sponsor presentation takeaways   446*

12.2 Presenting your model to end users   447

*Summarizing the project goals   447 ▪ Showing how the
model fits user workflow   448 ▪ Showing how to use the
model   450 ▪ End user presentation takeaways   452*

12.3 Presenting your work to other data scientists   452

*Introducing the problem   452 ▪ Discussing related work   453
Discussing your approach   454 ▪ Discussing results and future
work   455 ▪ Peer presentation takeaways   457*

appendix A   *Starting with R and other tools   459*
appendix B   *Important statistical concepts   484*
appendix C   *Bibliography   519*

index   523

foreword

Practical Data Science with R, Second Edition, is a hands-on guide to data science, with a focus on techniques for working with structured or tabular data, using the R language and statistical packages. The book emphasizes machine learning, but is unique in the number of chapters it devotes to topics such as the role of the data scientist in projects, managing results, and even designing presentations. In addition to working out how to code up models, the book shares how to collaborate with diverse teams, how to translate business goals into metrics, and how to organize work and reports. If you want to learn how to use R to work as a data scientist, get this book.

We have known Nina Zumel and John Mount for a number of years. We have invited them to teach with us at Singularity University. They are two of the best data scientists we know. We regularly recommend their original research on cross-validation and impact coding (also called target encoding). In fact, chapter 8 of *Practical Data Science with R* teaches the theory of impact coding and uses it through the author's own R package: `vtreat`.

Practical Data Science with R takes the time to describe what data science is, and how a data scientist solves problems and explains their work. It includes careful descriptions of classic supervised learning methods, such as linear and logistic regression. We liked the survey style of the book and extensively worked examples using contest-winning methodologies and packages such as random forests and `xgboost`. The book is full of useful, shared experience and practical advice. We notice they even include our own trick of using random forest variable importance for initial variable screening.

Overall, this is a great book, and we highly recommend it.

—Jeremy Howard
and Rachel Thomas

preface

This is the book we wish we'd had as we were teaching ourselves that collection of subjects and skills that has come to be referred to as *data science*. It's the book that we'd like to hand out to our clients and peers. Its purpose is to explain the relevant parts of statistics, computer science, and machine learning that are crucial to data science.

Data science draws on tools from the empirical sciences, statistics, reporting, analytics, visualization, business intelligence, expert systems, machine learning, databases, data warehousing, data mining, and big data. It's because we have so many tools that we need a discipline that covers them all. What distinguishes data science itself from the tools and techniques is the central goal of deploying effective decision-making models to a production environment.

Our goal is to present data science from a pragmatic, practice-oriented viewpoint. We work toward this end by concentrating on fully worked exercises on real data—altogether, this book works through over 10 significant datasets. We feel that this approach allows us to illustrate what we really want to teach and to demonstrate all the preparatory steps necessary in any real-world project.

Throughout our text, we discuss useful statistical and machine learning concepts, include concrete code examples, and explore partnering with and presenting to non-specialists. If perhaps you don't find one of these topics novel, we hope to shine a light on one or two other topics that you may not have thought about recently.

acknowledgments

We wish to thank our colleagues and others who read and commented on our early chapter drafts. Special appreciation goes to our reviewers: Charles C. Earl, Christopher Kardell, David Meza, Domingo Salazar, Doug Sparling, James Black, John MacKintosh, Owen Morris, Pascal Barbedo, Robert Samohyl, and Taylor Dolezal. Their comments, questions, and corrections have greatly improved this book. We especially would like to thank our development editor, Dustin Archibald, and Cynthia Kane, who worked on the first edition, for their ideas and support. The same thanks go to Nichole Beard, Benjamin Berg, Rachael Herbert, Katie Tennant, Lori Weidert, Cheryl Weisman, and all the other editors who worked hard to make this a great book.

In addition, we thank our colleague David Steier, Professor Doug Tygar from UC Berkeley's School of Information Science, Professor Robert K. Kuzoff from the Departments of Biological Sciences and Computer Science at the University of Wisconsin-Whitewater, as well as all the other faculty and instructors who have used this book as a teaching text. We thank Jim Porzak, Joseph Rickert, and Alan Miller for inviting us to speak at the R users groups, often on topics that we cover in this book. We especially thank Jim Porzak for having written the foreword to the first edition, and for being an enthusiastic advocate of our book. On days when we were tired and discouraged and wondered why we had set ourselves to this task, his interest helped remind us that there's a need for what we're offering and the way we're offering it. Without this encouragement, completing this book would have been much harder. Also, we'd like to thank Jeremy Howard and Rachel Thomas for writing the new foreword, inviting us to speak, and providing their strong support.

about this book

This book is about data science: a field that uses results from statistics, machine learning, and computer science to create predictive models. Because of the broad nature of data science, it's important to discuss it a bit and to outline the approach we take in this book.

What is data science?

The statistician William S. Cleveland defined data science as an interdisciplinary field larger than statistics itself. We define data science as managing the process that can transform hypotheses and data into actionable predictions. Typical predictive analytic goals include predicting who will win an election, what products will sell well together, which loans will default, and which advertisements will be clicked on. The data scientist is responsible for acquiring and managing the data, choosing the modeling technique, writing the code, and verifying the results.

Because data science draws on so many disciplines, it's often a "second calling." Many of the best data scientists we meet started as programmers, statisticians, business intelligence analysts, or scientists. By adding a few more techniques to their repertoire, they became excellent data scientists. That observation drives this book: we introduce the practical skills needed by the data scientist by concretely working through all of the common project steps on real data. Some steps you'll know better than we do, some you'll pick up quickly, and some you may need to research further.

Much of the theoretical basis of data science comes from statistics. But data science as we know it is strongly influenced by technology and software engineering methodologies, and has largely evolved in heavily computer science– and information technology–driven groups. We can call out some of the engineering flavor of data science by listing some famous examples:

- Amazon's product recommendation systems
- Google's advertisement valuation systems
- LinkedIn's contact recommendation system
- Twitter's trending topics
- Walmart's consumer demand projection systems

These systems share a lot of features:

- All of these systems are *built off large datasets.* That's not to say they're all in the realm of big data. But none of them could've been successful if they'd only used small datasets. To manage the data, these systems require concepts from computer science: database theory, parallel programming theory, streaming data techniques, and data warehousing.
- Most of these systems are *online or live.* Rather than producing a single report or analysis, the data science team deploys a decision procedure or scoring procedure to either directly make decisions or directly show results to a large number of end users. The production deployment is the last chance to get things right, as the data scientist can't always be around to explain defects.
- All of these systems are *allowed to make mistakes* at some non-negotiable rate.
- None of these systems are *concerned with cause.* They're successful when they find useful correlations and are not held to correctly sorting cause from effect.

This book teaches the principles and tools needed to build systems like these. We teach the common tasks, steps, and tools used to successfully deliver such projects. Our emphasis is on the whole process—project management, working with others, and presenting results to nonspecialists.

Roadmap

This book covers the following:

- Managing the data science process itself. The data scientist must have the ability to measure and track their own project.
- Applying many of the most powerful statistical and machine learning techniques used in data science projects. Think of this book as a series of explicitly worked exercises in using the R programming language to perform actual data science work.
- Preparing presentations for the various stakeholders: management, users, deployment team, and so on. You must be able to explain your work in concrete terms to mixed audiences with words in their common usage, *not in whatever technical definition is insisted on in a given field.* You can't get away with just throwing data science project results over the fence.

We've arranged the book topics in an order that we feel increases understanding. The material is organized as follows.

Part 1 describes the basic goals and techniques of the data science process, emphasizing collaboration and data. Chapter 1 discusses how to work as a data scientist. Chapter 2 works through loading data into R and shows how to start working with R.

Chapter 3 teaches what to first look for in data and the important steps in characterizing and understanding data. Data must be prepared for analysis, and data issues will need to be corrected. Chapter 4 demonstrates how to correct the issues identified in chapter 3.

Chapter 5 covers one more data preparation step: basic data wrangling. Data is not always available to the data scientist in a form or "shape" best suited for analysis. R provides many tools for manipulating and reshaping data into the appropriate structure; they are covered in this chapter.

Part 2 moves from characterizing and preparing data to building effective predictive models. Chapter 6 supplies a mapping of business needs to technical evaluation and modeling techniques. It covers the standard metrics and procedures used to evaluate model performance, and one specialized technique, LIME, for explaining specific predictions made by a model.

Chapter 7 covers basic linear models: linear regression, logistic regression, and regularized linear models. Linear models are the workhorses of many analytical tasks, and are especially helpful for identifying key variables and gaining insight into the structure of a problem. A solid understanding of them is immensely valuable for a data scientist.

Chapter 8 temporarily moves away from the modeling task to cover more advanced data treatment: how to prepare messy real-world data for the modeling step. Because understanding how these data treatment methods work requires some understanding of linear models and of model evaluation metrics, it seemed best to defer this topic until part 2.

Chapter 9 covers unsupervised methods: modeling methods that do not use labeled training data. Chapter 10 covers more advanced modeling methods that increase prediction performance and fix specific modeling issues. The topics covered include tree-based ensembles, generalized additive models, and support vector machines.

Part 3 moves away from modeling and back to process. We show how to deliver results. Chapter 11 demonstrates how to manage, document, and deploy your models. You'll learn how to create effective presentations for different audiences in chapter 12.

The appendixes include additional technical details about R, statistics, and more tools that are available. Appendix A shows how to install R, get started working, and work with other tools (such as SQL). Appendix B is a refresher on a few key statistical ideas.

The material is organized in terms of goals and tasks, bringing in tools as they're needed. The topics in each chapter are discussed in the context of a representative project with an associated dataset. You'll work through a number of substantial projects over the course of this book. All the datasets referred to in this book are at the book's GitHub repository, https://github.com/WinVector/PDSwR2. You can download the entire repository as a single zip file (one of GitHub's services), clone the repository to your machine, or copy individual files as needed.

Audience

To work the examples in this book, you'll need some familiarity with R and statistics. We recommend you have some good introductory texts already on hand. You don't need to be expert in R before starting the book, but you will need to be familiar with it.

To start with R, we recommend *Beyond Spreadsheets with R* by Jonathan Carroll (Manning, 20108) or *R in Action* by Robert Kabacoff (now available in a second edition: http://www.manning.com/kabacoff2/), along with the text's associated website, *Quick-R* (http://www.statmethods.net). For statistics, we recommend *Statistics,* Fourth Edition, by David Freedman, Robert Pisani, and Roger Purves (W. W. Norton & Company, 2007).

In general, here's what we expect from our ideal reader:

- *An interest in working examples.* By working through the examples, you'll learn at least one way to perform all steps of a project. You must be willing to attempt simple scripting and programming to get the full value of this book. For each example we work, you should try variations and expect both some failures (where your variations don't work) and some successes (where your variations outperform our example analyses).

- *Some familiarity with the R statistical system and the will to write short scripts and programs in R.* In addition to Kabacoff, we list a few good books in appendix C. We'll work specific problems in R; you'll need to run the examples and read additional documentation to understand variations of the commands we didn't demonstrate.

- *Some comfort with basic statistical concepts such as probabilities, means, standard deviations, and significance.* We'll introduce these concepts as needed, but you may need to read additional references as we work through examples. We'll define some terms and refer to some topic references and blogs where appropriate. But we expect you will have to perform some of your own internet searches on certain topics.

- *A computer (macOS, Linux, or Windows) to install R and other tools on, as well as internet access to download tools and datasets.* We strongly suggest working through the examples, examining R `help()` on various methods, and following up with some of the additional references.

What is not in this book?

- *This book is not an R manual.* We use R to concretely demonstrate the important steps of data science projects. We teach enough R for you to work through the examples, but a reader unfamiliar with R will want to refer to appendix A as well as to the many excellent R books and tutorials already available.

- *This book is not a set of case studies.* We emphasize methodology and technique. Example data and code is given only to make sure we're giving concrete, usable advice.

- *This book is not a big data book.* We feel most significant data science occurs at a database or file manageable scale (often larger than memory, but still small enough to be easy to manage). Valuable data that maps measured conditions to dependent outcomes tends to be expensive to produce, and that tends to bound its size. For some report generation, data mining, and natural language processing, you'll have to move into the area of big data.

- *This is not a theoretical book.* We don't emphasize the absolute rigorous theory of any one technique. The goal of data science is to be flexible, have a number of good techniques available, and be willing to research a technique more deeply if it appears to apply to the problem at hand. We prefer R code notation over beautifully typeset equations even in our text, as the R code can be directly used.

- *This is not a machine learning tinkerer's book.* We emphasize methods that are already implemented in R. For each method, we work through the theory of operation and show where the method excels. We usually don't discuss how to implement them (even when implementation is easy), as excellent R implementations are already available.

Code conventions and downloads

This book is example driven. We supply prepared example data at the GitHub repository (https://github.com/WinVector/PDSwR2), with R code and links back to original sources. You can explore this repository online or clone it onto your own machine. We also supply the code to produce all results and almost all graphs found in the book as a zip file (https://github.com/WinVector/PDSwR2/raw/master/CodeExamples.zip), since copying code from the zip file can be easier than copying and pasting from the book. Instructions on how to download, install, and get started with all the suggested tools and example data can be found in appendix A, in section A.1.

We encourage you to try the example R code as you read the text; even when we're discussing fairly abstract aspects of data science, we'll illustrate examples with concrete data and code. Every chapter includes links to the specific dataset(s) that it references.

In this book, code is set with a `fixed-width font like this` to distinguish it from regular text. Concrete variables and values are formatted similarly, whereas abstract math will be in *italic font like this*. R code is written without any command-line prompts such as > (which is often seen when displaying R code, but not to be typed in as new R code). Inline results are prefixed by R's comment character #. In many cases, the original source code has been reformatted; we've added line breaks and reworked indentation to accommodate the available page space in the book. In rare cases, even this was not enough, and listings include line-continuation markers (➥). Additionally, comments in the source code have often been removed from the listings when the code is described in the text. Code annotations accompany many of the listings, highlighting important concepts.

Working with this book

Practical Data Science with R is best read while working at least some of the examples. To do this we suggest you install R, RStudio, and the packages commonly used in the book. We share instructions on how to do this in section A.1 of appendix A. We also suggest you download all the examples, which include code and data, from our GitHub repository at https://github.com/WinVector/PDSwR2.

DOWNLOADING THE BOOK'S SUPPORTING MATERIALS/REPOSITORY

The contents of the repository can be downloaded as a zip file by using the "download as zip" GitHub feature, as shown in the following figure, from the GitHub URL https://github.com/WinVector/PDSwR2.

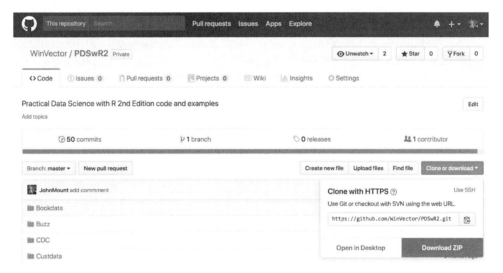

GitHub download example

Clicking on the "Download ZIP" link should download the compressed contents of the package (or you can try a direct link to the ZIP material: https://github.com/WinVector/PDSwR2/archive/master.zip). Or, if you are familiar with working with the Git source control system from the command line, you can do this with the following command from a Bash shell (not from R):

```
git clone https://github.com/WinVector/PDSwR2.git
```

In all examples, we assume you have either cloned the repository or downloaded and unzipped the contents. This will produce a directory named PDSwR2. Paths we discuss will start with this directory. For example, if we mention working with PDSwR2/UCI-Car, we mean to work with the contents of the UCICar subdirectory of wherever you unpacked PDSwR2. You can change R's working directory through the setwd() command (please type help(setwd) in the R console for some details). Or, if you are using RStudio, the file-browsing pane can also set the working directory from an option on the pane's gear/more menu. All of the code examples from this book are included in the directory PDSwR2/CodeExamples, so you should not need to type them in (though to run them you will have to be working in the appropriate data directory—not in the directory you find the code in).

The examples in this book are supplied in lieu of explicit exercises. We suggest working through the examples *and* trying variations. For example, in section 2.3.1, where we show how to relate expected income to schooling and gender, it makes sense to try relating income to employment status or even age. Data science requires curiosity about programming, functions, data, variables, and relations, and the earlier you find surprises in your data, the easier they are to work through.

Book forum

Purchase of *Practical Data Science with R* includes free access to a private web forum run by Manning Publications where you can make comments about the book, ask technical questions, and receive help from the author and from other users. To access the forum, go to https://forums.manning.com/forums/practical-data-science-with-r-second-edition. You can also learn more about Manning's forums and the rules of conduct at https://forums.manning.com/forums/about.

Manning's commitment to our readers is to provide a venue where a meaningful dialogue between individual readers and between readers and the authors can take place. It is not a commitment to any specific amount of participation on the part of the authors, whose contribution to the forum remains voluntary (and unpaid). We suggest you try asking them some challenging questions lest their interest stray! The forum and the archives of previous discussions will be accessible from the publisher's website as long as the book is in print.

about the authors

Nina Zumel has worked as a scientist at SRI International, an independent, nonprofit research institute. She has worked as chief scientist of a price optimization company and founded a contract research company. Nina is now a principal consultant at Win-Vector LLC. She can be reached at nzumel@win-vector.com.

John Mount has worked as a computational scientist in biotechnology and as a stock trading algorithm designer, and has managed a research team for Shopping.com. He is now a principal consultant at Win-Vector LLC. John can be reached at jmount@win-vector.com.

about the foreword authors

JEREMY HOWARD is an entrepreneur, business strategist, developer, and educator. Jeremy is a founding researcher at fast.ai, a research institute dedicated to making deep learning more accessible. He is also a faculty member at the University of San Francisco, and is chief scientist at doc.ai and platform.ai.

Previously, Jeremy was the founding CEO of Enlitic, which was the first company to apply deep learning to medicine, and was selected as one of the world's top 50 smartest companies by MIT Tech Review two years running. He was the president and chief scientist of the data science platform Kaggle, where he was the top-ranked participant in international machine learning competitions two years running.

RACHEL THOMAS is director of the USF Center for Applied Data Ethics and cofounder of fast.ai, which has been featured in *The Economist, MIT Tech Review,* and *Forbes.* She was selected by *Forbes* as one of 20 Incredible Women in AI, earned her math PhD at Duke, and was an early engineer at Uber. Rachel is a popular writer and keynote speaker. In her TEDx talk, she shares what scares her about AI and why we need people from all backgrounds involved with AI.

about the cover illustration

The figure on the cover of *Practical Data Science with R* is captioned "Habit of a Lady of China in 1703." The illustration is taken from Thomas Jefferys' *A Collection of the Dresses of Different Nations, Ancient and Modern* (four volumes), London, published between 1757 and 1772. The title page states that these are hand-colored copperplate engravings, heightened with gum arabic. Thomas Jefferys (1719–1771) was called "Geographer to King George III." He was an English cartographer who was the leading map supplier of his day. He engraved and printed maps for government and other official bodies and produced a wide range of commercial maps and atlases, especially of North America. His work as a mapmaker sparked an interest in local dress customs of the lands he surveyed and mapped; they are brilliantly displayed in this four-volume collection.

Fascination with faraway lands and travel for pleasure were relatively new phenomena in the eighteenth century, and collections such as this one were popular, introducing both the tourist as well as the armchair traveler to the inhabitants of other countries. The diversity of the drawings in Jefferys' volumes speaks vividly of the uniqueness and individuality of the world's nations centuries ago. Dress codes have changed, and the diversity by region and country, so rich at that time, has faded away. It is now often hard to tell the inhabitant of one continent from another. Perhaps, viewing it optimistically, we have traded a cultural and visual diversity for a more varied personal life—or a more varied and interesting intellectual and technical life.

At a time when it is hard to tell one computer book from another, Manning celebrates the inventiveness and initiative of the computer business with book covers based on the rich diversity of national costumes three centuries ago, brought back to life by Jefferys' pictures.

Part 1

Introduction
to data science

In part 1, we concentrate on the most essential tasks in data science: working with your partners, defining your problem, and examining your data.

Chapter 1 covers the lifecycle of a typical data science project. We look at the different roles and responsibilities of project team members, the different stages of a typical project, and how to define goals and set project expectations. This chapter serves as an overview of the material that we cover in the rest of the book, and is organized in the same order as the topics that we present.

Chapter 2 dives into the details of loading data into R from various external formats and transforming the data into a format suitable for analysis. It also discusses the most important R data structure for a data scientist: the data frame. More details about the R programming language are covered in appendix A.

Chapters 3 and 4 cover the data exploration and treatment that you should do before proceeding to the modeling stage. In chapter 3, we discuss some of the typical problems and issues that you'll encounter with your data and how to use summary statistics and visualization to detect those issues. In chapter 4, we discuss data treatments that will help you deal with the problems and issues in your data. We also recommend some habits and procedures that will help you better manage the data throughout the different stages of the project.

Chapter 5 covers how to wrangle or manipulate data into a ready-for-analysis shape.

On completing part 1, you'll understand how to define a data science project, and you'll know how to load data into R and prepare it for modeling and analysis.

The data science process

Data science is a cross-disciplinary practice that draws on methods from data engineering, descriptive statistics, data mining, machine learning, and predictive analytics. Much like operations research, data science focuses on implementing data-driven decisions and managing their consequences. For this book, we will concentrate on data science as applied to business and scientific problems, using these techniques.

The data scientist is responsible for guiding a data science project from start to finish. Success in a data science project comes not from access to any one exotic tool, but from having quantifiable goals, good methodology, cross-discipline interactions, and a repeatable workflow.

This chapter walks you through what a typical data science project looks like: the kinds of problems you encounter, the types of goals you should have, the tasks that you're likely to handle, and what sort of results are expected.

We'll use a concrete, real-world example to motivate the discussion in this chapter.[1]

Example   *Suppose you're working for a German bank. The bank feels that it's losing too much money to bad loans and wants to reduce its losses. To do so, they want a tool to help loan officers more accurately detect risky loans.*

This is where your data science team comes in.

1.1   *The roles in a data science project*

Data science is not performed in a vacuum. It's a collaborative effort that draws on a number of roles, skills, and tools. Before we talk about the process itself, let's look at the roles that must be filled in a successful project. Project management has been a central concern of software engineering for a long time, so we can look there for guidance. In defining the roles here, we've borrowed some ideas from Fredrick Brooks' "surgical team" perspective on software development, as described in *The Mythical Man-Month: Essays on Software Engineering* (Addison-Wesley, 1995). We also borrowed ideas from the agile software development paradigm.

1.1.1   *Project roles*

Let's look at a few recurring roles in a data science project in table 1.1.

Table 1.1   Data science project roles and responsibilities

Role	Responsibilities
Project sponsor	Represents the business interests; champions the project
Client	Represents end users' interests; domain expert
Data scientist	Sets and executes analytic strategy; communicates with sponsor and client
Data architect	Manages data and data storage; sometimes manages data collection
Operations	Manages infrastructure; deploys final project results

Sometimes these roles may overlap. Some roles—in particular, client, data architect, and operations—are often filled by people who aren't on the data science project team, but are key collaborators.

PROJECT SPONSOR

The most important role in a data science project is the project sponsor. The sponsor is the person who wants the data science result; generally, they represent the business interests.

---

[1] For this chapter, we'll use a credit dataset donated by Dr. Hans Hofmann, professor of integrative biology, to the UCI Machine Learning Repository in 1994. We've simplified some of the column names for clarity. The original dataset can be found at http://archive.ics.uci.edu/ml/datasets/Statlog+(German+Credit+Data). We'll show how to load this data and prepare it for analysis in chapter 2. Note that the German currency at the time of data collection was the deutsche mark (DM).

In the loan application example, the sponsor might be the bank's head of Consumer Lending. The sponsor is responsible for deciding whether the project is a success or failure. The data scientist may fill the sponsor role for their own project if they feel they know and can represent the business needs, but that's not the optimal arrangement. The ideal sponsor meets the following condition: if they're satisfied with the project outcome, then the project is by definition a success. *Getting sponsor sign-off becomes the central organizing goal of a data science project.*

> **KEEP THE SPONSOR INFORMED AND INVOLVED** It's critical to keep the sponsor informed and involved. Show them plans, progress, and intermediate successes or failures in terms they can understand. A good way to guarantee project failure is to keep the sponsor in the dark.

To ensure sponsor sign-off, you must get clear goals from them through directed interviews. You attempt to capture the sponsor's expressed goals as quantitative statements. An example goal might be "Identify 90% of accounts that will go into default at least two months before the first missed payment with a false positive rate of no more than 25%." This is a precise goal that allows you to check in parallel if meeting the goal is actually going to make business sense and whether you have data and tools of sufficient quality to achieve the goal.

CLIENT

While the sponsor is the role that represents the business interests, the client is the role that represents the model's end users' interests. Sometimes, the sponsor and client roles may be filled by the same person. Again, the data scientist may fill the client role if they can weight business trade-offs, but this isn't ideal.

The client is more hands-on than the sponsor; they're the interface between the technical details of building a good model and the day-to-day work process into which the model will be deployed. They aren't necessarily mathematically or statistically sophisticated, but are familiar with the relevant business processes and serve as the domain expert on the team. In the loan application example, the client may be a loan officer or someone who represents the interests of loan officers.

As with the sponsor, you should keep the client informed and involved. Ideally, you'd like to have regular meetings with them to keep your efforts aligned with the needs of the end users. Generally, the client belongs to a different group in the organization and has other responsibilities beyond your project. Keep meetings focused, present results and progress in terms they can understand, and take their critiques to heart. If the end users can't or won't use your model, then the project isn't a success, in the long run.

DATA SCIENTIST

The next role in a data science project is the data scientist, who's responsible for taking all necessary steps to make the project succeed, including setting the project strategy and keeping the client informed. They design the project steps, pick the data sources, and pick the tools to be used. Since they pick the techniques that will be tried, they have to be well informed about statistics and machine learning. They're also responsible for project planning and tracking, though they may do this with a project management partner.

At a more technical level, the data scientist also looks at the data, performs statistical tests and procedures, applies machine learning models, and evaluates results—the science portion of data science.

> **Domain empathy**
>
> It is often too much to ask for the data scientist to become a domain expert. However, in all cases the data scientist must develop strong *domain empathy* to help define and solve the right problems.

DATA ARCHITECT

The data architect is responsible for all the data and its storage. Often this role is filled by someone outside of the data science group, such as a database administrator or architect. Data architects often manage data warehouses for many different projects, and they may only be available for quick consultation.

OPERATIONS

The operations role is critical both in acquiring data and delivering the final results. The person filling this role usually has operational responsibilities outside of the data science group. For example, if you're deploying a data science result that affects how products are sorted on an online shopping site, then the person responsible for running the site will have a lot to say about how such a thing can be deployed. This person will likely have constraints on response time, programming language, or data size that you need to respect in deployment. The person in the operations role may already be supporting your sponsor or your client, so they're often easy to find (though their time may be already very much in demand).

1.2   Stages of a data science project

The ideal data science environment is one that encourages feedback and iteration between the data scientist and all other stakeholders. This is reflected in the lifecycle of a data science project. Even though this book, like other discussions of the data science process, breaks up the cycle into distinct stages, in reality the boundaries between the stages are fluid, and the activities of one stage will often overlap those of other stages.[2] Often, you'll loop back and forth between two or more stages before moving forward in the overall process. This is shown in figure 1.1.

---

[2] One common model of the machine learning process is the cross-industry standard process for data mining (CRISP-DM) (https://en.wikipedia.org/wiki/Cross-industry_standard_process_for_data_mining). The model we'll discuss here is similar, but emphasizes that back-and-forth is possible at any stage of the process.

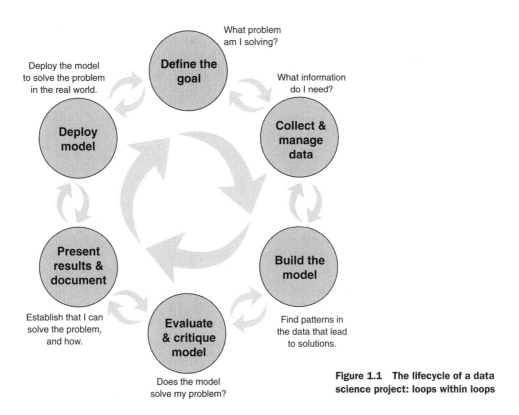

Figure 1.1 **The lifecycle of a data science project: loops within loops**

Even after you complete a project and deploy a model, new issues and questions can arise from seeing that model in action. The end of one project may lead into a follow-up project.

Let's look at the different stages shown in figure 1.1.

1.2.1 *Defining the goal*

The first task in a data science project is to define a measurable and quantifiable goal. At this stage, learn all that you can about the context of your project:

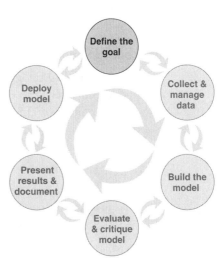

- Why do the sponsors want the project in the first place? What do they lack, and what do they need?
- What are they doing to solve the problem now, and why isn't that good enough?
- What resources will you need: what kind of data and how much staff? Will

you have domain experts to collaborate with, and what are the computational resources?

- How do the project sponsors plan to deploy your results? What are the constraints that have to be met for successful deployment?

Let's come back to our loan application example. The ultimate business goal is to reduce the bank's losses due to bad loans. Your project sponsor envisions a tool to help loan officers more accurately score loan applicants, and so reduce the number of bad loans made. At the same time, it's important that the loan officers feel that they have final discretion on loan approvals.

Once you and the project sponsor and other stakeholders have established preliminary answers to these questions, you and they can start defining the precise goal of the project. The goal should be specific and measurable; not "We want to get better at finding bad loans," but instead "We want to reduce our rate of loan charge-offs by at least 10%, using a model that predicts which loan applicants are likely to default."

A concrete goal leads to concrete stopping conditions and concrete acceptance criteria. The less specific the goal, the likelier that the project will go unbounded, because no result will be "good enough." If you don't know what you want to achieve, you don't know when to stop trying—or even what to try. When the project eventually terminates—because either time or resources run out—no one will be happy with the outcome.

Of course, at times there is a need for looser, more exploratory projects: "Is there something in the data that correlates to higher defaults?" or "Should we think about reducing the kinds of loans we give out? Which types might we eliminate?" In this situation, you can still scope the project with concrete stopping conditions, such as a time limit. For example, you might decide to spend two weeks, and no more, exploring the data, with the goal of coming up with candidate hypotheses. These hypotheses can then be turned into concrete questions or goals for a full-scale modeling project.

Once you have a good idea of the project goals, you can focus on collecting data to meet those goals.

1.2.2   *Data collection and management*

This step encompasses identifying the data you need, exploring it, and conditioning it to be suitable for analysis. This stage is often the most time-consuming step in the process. It's also one of the most important:

- What data is available to me?
- Will it help me solve the problem?
- Is it enough?
- Is the data quality good enough?

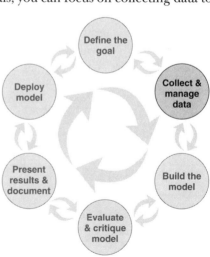

Imagine that, for your loan application problem, you've collected a sample of representative loans from the last decade. Some of the loans have defaulted; most of them (about 70%) have not. You've collected a variety of attributes about each loan application, as listed in table 1.2.

Table 1.2   Loan data attributes

```
Status_of_existing_checking_account (at time of application)
Duration_in_month (loan length)
Credit_history
Purpose (car loan, student loan, and so on)
Credit_amount (loan amount)
Savings_Account_or_bonds (balance/amount)
Present_employment_since
Installment_rate_in_percentage_of_disposable_income
Personal_status_and_sex
Cosigners
Present_residence_since
Collateral (car, property, and so on)
Age_in_years
Other_installment_plans (other loans/lines of credit—the type)
Housing (own, rent, and so on)
Number_of_existing_credits_at_this_bank
Job (employment type)
Number_of_dependents
Telephone (do they have one)
Loan_status (dependent variable)
```

In your data, `Loan_status` takes on two possible values: `GoodLoan` and `BadLoan`. For the purposes of this discussion, assume that a `GoodLoan` was paid off, and a `BadLoan` defaulted.

> **TRY TO DIRECTLY MEASURE THE INFORMATION YOU NEED**   As much as possible, try to use information that can be directly measured, rather than information that is inferred from another measurement. For example, you might be tempted to use income as a variable, reasoning that a lower income implies more difficulty paying off a loan. The ability to pay off a loan is more directly measured by considering the size of the loan payments relative to the borrower's disposable income. This information is more useful than income alone; you have it in your data as the variable `Installment_rate_in_percentage_of_disposable_income`.

This is the stage where you initially explore and visualize your data. You'll also clean the data: repair data errors and transform variables, as needed. In the process of exploring and cleaning the data, you may discover that it isn't suitable for your problem, or that you need other types of information as well. You may discover things in the data that raise issues more important than the one you originally planned to address. For example, the data in figure 1.2 seems counterintuitive.

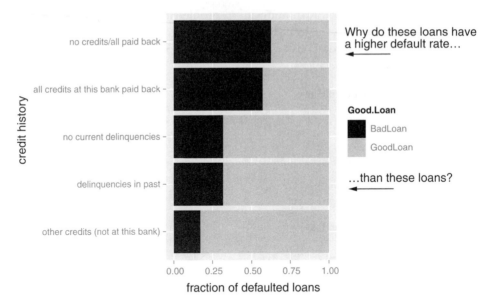

Figure 1.2　The fraction of defaulting loans by credit history category. The dark region of each bar represents the fraction of loans in that category that defaulted.

Why would some of the seemingly safe applicants (those who repaid all credits to the bank) default at a higher rate than seemingly riskier ones (those who had been delinquent in the past)? After looking more carefully at the data and sharing puzzling findings with other stakeholders and domain experts, you realize that this sample is inherently biased: *you only have loans that were actually made (and therefore already accepted).* A true unbiased sample of loan applications should include both loan applications that were accepted and ones that were rejected. Overall, because your sample only includes accepted loans, there are fewer risky-looking loans than safe-looking ones in the data. The probable story is that risky-looking loans were approved after a much stricter vetting process, a process that perhaps the safe-looking loan applications could bypass. This suggests that if your model is to be used downstream of the current application approval process, credit history is no longer a useful variable. It also suggests that even seemingly safe loan applications should be more carefully scrutinized.

Discoveries like this may lead you and other stakeholders to change or refine the project goals. In this case, you may decide to concentrate on the seemingly safe loan applications. It's common to cycle back and forth between this stage and the previous one, as well as between this stage and the modeling stage, as you discover things in the data. We'll cover data exploration and management in depth in chapters 3 and 4.

1.2.3　Modeling

You finally get to statistics and machine learning during the modeling, or analysis, stage. Here is where you try to extract useful insights from the data in order to achieve your goals. Since many modeling procedures make specific assumptions about data distribution and relationships, there may be overlap and back-and-forth between the modeling stage and the data-cleaning stage as you try to find the best way to represent the data and the best form in which to model it.

The most common data science modeling tasks are these:

- *Classifying*—Deciding if something belongs to one category or another
- *Scoring*—Predicting or estimating a numeric value, such as a price or probability
- *Ranking*—Learning to order items by preferences
- *Clustering*—Grouping items into most-similar groups
- *Finding relations*—Finding correlations or potential causes of effects seen in the data
- *Characterizing*—Very general plotting and report generation from data

For each of these tasks, there are several different possible approaches. We'll cover some of the most common approaches to the different tasks in this book.

The loan application problem is a classification problem: you want to identify loan applicants who are likely to default. Some common approaches in such cases are logistic regression and tree-based methods (we'll cover these methods in depth in chapters 7 and 10). You've been in conversation with loan officers and others who would be using your model in the field, so you know that they want to be able to understand the chain of reasoning behind the model's classification, and they want an indication of how confident the model is in its decision: is this applicant highly likely to default, or only somewhat likely? To solve this problem, you decide that a decision tree is most suitable. We'll cover decision trees more extensively in chapter 10, but for now we will just look at the resulting decision tree model.[3]

Let's suppose that you discover the model shown in figure 1.3. Let's trace an example path through the tree. Let's suppose that there is an application for a one-year loan of DM 10,000 (deutsche mark, the currency at the time of the study). At the top of the tree (node 1 in figure 1.3), the model checks if the loan is for longer than 34 months. The answer is "no," so the model takes the right branch down the tree. This is shown as the highlighted branch from node 1. The next question (node 3) is whether the loan is for more than DM 11,000. Again, the answer is "no," so the model branches right (as shown by the darker highlighted branch from node 3) and arrives at leaf 3.

---

[3] In this chapter, for clarity of illustration, we deliberately fit a small and shallow tree.

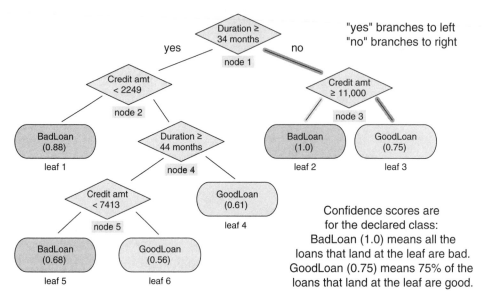

Figure 1.3 A decision tree model for finding bad loan applications. The outcome nodes show confidence scores.

Historically, 75% of loans that arrive at this leaf are good loans, so the model recommends that you approve this loan, as there is a high probability that it will be paid off.

On the other hand, suppose that there is an application for a one-year loan of DM 15,000. In this case, the model would first branch right at node 1, and then left at node 3, to arrive at leaf 2. Historically, all loans that arrive at leaf 2 have defaulted, so the model recommends that you reject this loan application.

We'll discuss general modeling strategies in chapter 6 and go into details of specific modeling algorithms in part 2.

1.2.4 Model evaluation and critique

Once you have a model, you need to determine if it meets your goals:

- Is it accurate enough for your needs? Does it generalize well?
- Does it perform better than "the obvious guess"? Better than whatever estimate you currently use?
- Do the results of the model (coefficients, clusters, rules, confidence intervals, significances, and diagnostics) make sense in the context of the problem domain?

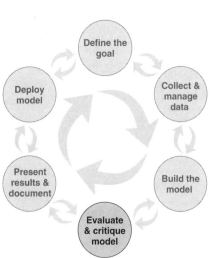

If you've answered "no" to any of these questions, it's time to loop back to the modeling step—or decide that the data doesn't support the goal you're trying to achieve. No one likes negative results, but understanding when you can't meet your success criteria with current resources will save you fruitless effort. Your energy will be better spent on crafting success. This might mean defining more-realistic goals or gathering the additional data or other resources that you need to achieve your original goals.

Returning to the loan application example, the first thing to check is whether the rules that the model discovered make sense. Looking at figure 1.3, you don't notice any obviously strange rules, so you can go ahead and evaluate the model's accuracy. A good summary of classifier accuracy is the *confusion matrix*, which tabulates actual classifications against predicted ones.[4]

In listing 1.1, you will create a confusion matrix where rows represent actual loan status, and columns represent predicted loan status. To improve legibility, the code references matrix elements by name rather than by index. For example, `conf_mat ["GoodLoan", "BadLoan"]` refers to the element `conf_mat[2, 1]`: the number of actual good loans that the model predicted were bad. The diagonal entries of the matrix represent correct predictions.

Listing 1.1 Calculating the confusion matrix

How to install all the packages needed to run examples in the book can be found here: https://github.com/WinVector/PDSwR2/blob/master/packages.R.

This file can be found at https://github.com/WinVector/PDSwR2/tree/master/Statlog.

```
library("rpart")
   load("loan_model_example.RData")
   conf_mat <-
       table(actual = d$Loan_status, pred = predict(model, type = 'class'))

##             pred
## actual    BadLoan GoodLoan
##    BadLoan      41      259
##    GoodLoan     13      687

(accuracy <- sum(diag(conf_mat)) / sum(conf_mat))
   ## [1] 0.728
(precision <- conf_mat["BadLoan", "BadLoan"] / sum(conf_mat[, "BadLoan"]))
   ## [1] 0.7592593
(recall <- conf_mat["BadLoan", "BadLoan"] / sum(conf_mat["BadLoan", ]))
   ## [1] 0.1366667

(fpr <- conf_mat["GoodLoan","BadLoan"] / sum(conf_mat["GoodLoan", ]))
   ## [1] 0.01857143
```

Creates the confusion matrix

Overall model accuracy: 73% of the predictions were correct.

False positive rate: 2% of the good applicants were mistakenly identified as bad.

Model precision: 76% of the applicants predicted as bad really did default.

Model recall: the model found 14% of the defaulting loans.

---

[4] Normally, we'd evaluate the model against a test set (data that wasn't used to build the model). In this example, for simplicity, we'll evaluate the model against the training data (data that was used to build the model). Also note we are following a convention that we will use when plotting: predictions are the x-axis, which for tables means predictions are the column names. Be aware that there are other conventions for confusion matrices.

The model predicted loan status correctly 73% of the time—better than chance (50%). In the original dataset, 30% of the loans were bad, so guessing `GoodLoan` all the time would be 70% accurate (though not very useful). So you know that the model does better than random and somewhat better than obvious guessing.

Overall accuracy is not enough. You want to know what kind of mistakes are being made. Is the model missing too many bad loans, or is it marking too many good loans as bad? *Recall* measures how many of the bad loans the model can actually find. *Precision* measures how many of the loans identified as bad really are bad. *False positive rate* measures how many of the good loans are mistakenly identified as bad. Ideally, you want the recall and the precision to be high, and the false positive rate to be low. What constitutes "high enough" and "low enough" is a decision that you make together with the other stakeholders. Often, the right balance requires some trade-off between recall and precision.

There are other measures of accuracy and other measures of the quality of a model, as well. We'll talk about model evaluation in chapter 6.

1.2.5   *Presentation and documentation*

Once you have a model that meets your success criteria, you'll present your results to your project sponsor and other stakeholders. You must also document the model for those in the organization who are responsible for using, running, and maintaining the model once it has been deployed.

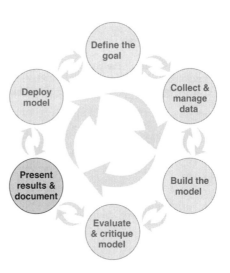

Different audiences require different kinds of information. Business-oriented audiences want to understand the impact of your findings in terms of business metrics. In the loan example, the most important thing to present to business audiences is how your loan application model will reduce charge-offs (the money that the bank loses to bad loans). Suppose your model identified a set of bad loans that amounted to 22% of the total money lost to defaults. Then your presentation or executive summary should emphasize that the model can potentially reduce the bank's losses by that amount, as shown in figure 1.4.

You also want to give this audience your most interesting findings or recommendations, such as that new car loans are much riskier than used car loans, or that most losses are tied to bad car loans and bad equipment loans (assuming that the audience didn't already know these facts). Technical details of the model won't be as interesting to this audience, and you should skip them or only present them at a high level.

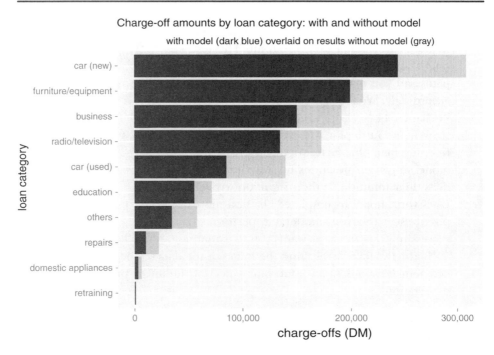

Figure 1.4 Example slide from an executive presentation

A presentation for the model's end users (the loan officers) would instead emphasize how the model will help them do their job better:

- How should they interpret the model?
- What does the model output look like?
- If the model provides a trace of which rules in the decision tree executed, how do they read that?
- If the model provides a confidence score in addition to a classification, how should they use the confidence score?
- When might they potentially overrule the model?

Presentations or documentation for operations staff should emphasize the impact of your model on the resources that they're responsible for. We'll talk about the structure of presentations and documentation for various audiences in part 3.

1.2.6 *Model deployment and maintenance*

Finally, the model is put into operation. In many organizations, this means the data scientist no longer has primary responsibility for the day-to-day operation of the model. But you still should ensure that the model will run smoothly and won't make

disastrous unsupervised decisions. You also
want to make sure that the model can be
updated as its environment changes. And in
many situations, the model will initially be
deployed in a small pilot program. The test
might bring out issues that you didn't anticipate, and you may have to adjust the model
accordingly. We'll discuss model deployment
in chapter 11.

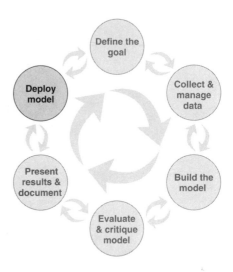

When you deploy the model, you might
find that loan officers frequently override the
model in certain situations because it contradicts their intuition. Is their intuition wrong?
Or is your model incomplete? Or, in a more
positive scenario, your model may perform so
successfully that the bank wants you to extend it to home loans as well.

Before we dive deeper into the stages of the data science lifecycle, in the following
chapters, let's look at an important aspect of the initial project design stage: setting
expectations.

1.3   Setting expectations

Setting expectations is a crucial part of defining the project goals and success criteria.
The business-facing members of your team (in particular, the project sponsor) probably already have an idea of the performance required to meet business goals: for
example, the bank wants to reduce their losses from bad loans by at least 10%. Before
you get too deep into a project, you should make sure that the resources you have are
enough for you to meet the business goals.

This is an example of the fluidity of the project lifecycle stages. You get to know the
data better during the exploration and cleaning phase; after you have a sense of the
data, you can get a sense of whether the data is good enough to meet desired performance thresholds. If it's not, then you'll have to revisit the project design and goal-
setting stage.

1.3.1   Determining lower bounds on model performance

Understanding how well a model *should* do for acceptable performance is important
when defining acceptance criteria.

The *null model* represents the lower bound on model performance that you should
strive for. You can think of the null model as being "the obvious guess" that your model
must do better than. In situations where there's a working model or solution already in
place that you're trying to improve, the null model is the existing solution. In situations
where there's no existing model or solution, the null model is the simplest possible

model: for example, always guessing GoodLoan, or always predicting the mean value of the output when you're trying to predict a numerical value.

In our loan application example, 70% of the loan applications in the dataset turned out to be good loans. A model that labels all loans as GoodLoan (in effect, using only the existing process to classify loans) would be correct 70% of the time. So you know that any actual model that you fit to the data should be better than 70% accurate to be useful—if accuracy were your only metric. Since this is the simplest possible model, its error rate is called the *base error rate*.

How much better than 70% should you be? In statistics there's a procedure called *hypothesis testing*, or *significance testing*, that tests whether your model is equivalent to a null model (in this case, whether a new model is basically only as accurate as guessing GoodLoan all the time). You want your model accuracy to be "significantly better"—in statistical terms—than 70%. We will discuss significance testing in chapter 6.

Accuracy is not the only (or even best) performance metric. As we saw previously, the *recall* measures the fraction of true bad loans that a model identifies. In our example, the null model that always guesses GoodLoan would have zero recall in identifying bad loans, which obviously is not what you want. Generally, if there is an existing model or process in place, you'd like to have an idea of its precision, recall, and false positive rates; improving one of these metrics is almost always more important than considering accuracy alone. If the purpose of your project is to improve the existing process, then the current model must be unsatisfactory for at least one of these metrics. Knowing the limitations of the existing process helps you determine useful lower bounds on desired performance.

Summary

The data science process involves a lot of back-and-forth—between the data scientist and other project stakeholders, and between the different stages of the process. Along the way, you'll encounter surprises and stumbling blocks; this book will teach you procedures for overcoming some of these hurdles. It's important to keep all the stakeholders informed and involved; when the project ends, no one connected with it should be surprised by the final results.

In the next chapters, we'll look at the stages that follow project design: loading, exploring, and managing the data. Chapter 2 covers a few basic ways to load the data into R, in a format that's convenient for analysis.

In this chapter you have learned

- A successful data science project involves more than just statistics. It also requires a variety of roles to represent business and client interests, as well as operational concerns.
- You should make sure you have a clear, verifiable, quantifiable goal.
- Make sure you've set realistic expectations for all stakeholders.

Starting with R and data

This chapter works through how to start working with R and how to import data into R from diverse sources. This will prepare you to work examples throughout the rest of the book.

Figure 2.1 is a diagram representing a mental model for the book that has been reshaded to emphasize the purpose of this chapter: starting to work with R and importing data into R. The overall diagram shows the data science process diagram from chapter 1 combined with a rebus form of the book title. In each chapter, we will reshade this mental model to indicate the parts of the data science process we are emphasizing. For example: in this chapter, we are mastering the initial steps of collecting and managing data, and touching on issues of practicality, data, and R (but not yet the art of science).

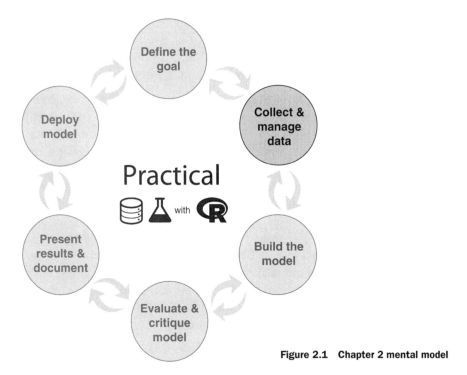

Figure 2.1   Chapter 2 mental model

Many data science projects start when someone points the analyst toward a bunch of data, and the analyst is left to make sense of it.[5] Your first thought may be to use ad hoc tools and spreadsheets to sort through it, but you will quickly realize that you're taking more time tinkering with the tools than actually analyzing the data. Luckily, there's a better way: using R. By the end of the chapter, you'll be able to confidently use R to extract, transform, and load data for analysis.

> *R without data is like going to the theater to watch the curtain go up and down.*
>
> —Adapted from Ben Katchor's
> *Julius Knipl, Real Estate Photographer: Stories*

2.1   Starting with R

R is open source software that runs well on Unix, Linux, Apple's macOS, and Microsoft Windows. This book will concentrate on how to work as a data scientist. However, to work the examples, the reader must be familiar with R programming. If you want to pick up some prerequisite knowledge, we suggest consulting free manuals from CRAN (the main R package repository: https://cran.r-project.org/manuals.html) and other online materials. A number of good books for starting with R include these:

---

[5] We assume the reader is interested in working as an analyst, statistician, or data scientist, so we will alternate using these terms to represent people similar to the reader.

- *R in Action, Second Edition*, Robert Kabacoff, Manning, 2015
- *Beyond Spreadsheets with R*, Jonathan Carroll, Manning, 2018
- *The Art of R Programming*, Norman Matloff, No Starch Press, 2011
- *R for Everyone, Second Edition*, Jared P. Lander, Addison-Wesley, 2017

Each book has a different teaching style, and some include material on statistics, machine learning, and data engineering. A little research may tell you which books work well for you. This book will concentrate on working substantial data science examples, demonstrating the steps needed to overcome typical issues found in your own future real-world applications.

It is our opinion that data science is repeatable: the same job rerun on the same data should give a similar quality result (the exact result may vary due to numeric issues, timing issues, issues arising from parallelism, and issues around pseudo-random numbers). In fact, we should insist on repeatability. This is why we are discussing programming in a data science book. Programming is the reliable way to specify a reusable sequence of operations. With this in mind, one should always consider a data refresh (getting newer, corrected, or larger data) as a good thing, because rerunning an analysis should be, by design, very easy. An analysis that has a number of steps performed by hand is never going to be easy to repeat.

2.1.1 Installing R, tools, and examples

We suggest you follows the steps in section A.1 of appendix A to install R, packages, tools, and the book examples.

> **LOOK FOR HELP**   R includes a very nice help system. To get help on an R command, just run the `help()` command in the R console. For example, to see details about how to change directories, you would type `help(setwd)`. You must know the name of the function to get help, so we strongly recommend keeping notes. For some simple functions, we will not explain the function and leave it to the reader to call `help()` to work out what the function does.

2.1.2 R programming

In this section, we will briefly describe some R programming conventions, semantics, and style issues. Details can be found in package-specific documentation, the R `help()` system, and by trying variations of the examples we present here. Here, we'll concentrate on aspects that differ from other common programming languages, and conventions that we emphasize in the book. This should help you get into an R frame of mind.

There are a number of common R coding style guides. *Coding style* is an attempt to make things more consistent, clear, and readable. This book will follow a style variation we have found to be very effective in teaching and code maintenance. Obviously, our style is just one among many, and is in no way mandatory. Good starting references include these:

- The Google R Style Guide (https://google.github.io/styleguide/Rguide.html)
- Hadley Wickham's style guide from *Advanced R* (http://adv-r.had.co.nz/Style.html)

We will try to minimize differences from current convention and call out where we have such differences. We also recommend "R tips and tricks" from the author's blog.[6]

R is a rich and broad language, often with many ways to accomplish the same task. This represents a bit of an initial learning curve, as the meaning of R programs can be hard to discern until you get familiar with the notation. However, time spent reviewing some of the basic notation is well rewarded, as it will make working through the coming substantial examples much easier. We understand the grammar of R is itself uninteresting to the reader coming here to learn data science methods and practices (our exact target audience!), but this small initial exertion prevents a lot of confusion later. We will use this section to describe a bit of R's notation and meaning, concentrating on that which is particularly useful and surprising. All the following are small and basic points, but many of them are subtle and worth experimenting with.

> **PREFER WORKING CODE**   Prefer programs, scripts, or code that works but does not yet do what you want. Instead of writing a large, untested program or script that embodies every desired step of analysis, write a program that performs a step correctly, and then iteratively revise the script to perform more steps correctly. This discipline of moving from a working revision usually gets to final correct results much faster than attempting to debug a large, faulty system into correctness.

EXAMPLES AND THE COMMENT CHARACTER (#)

In examples, we will show R commands as free text, with the results prefixed by the hash mark, #, which is R's comment character. In many examples, we will include the results after the commands, prefixed with the comment character. R printing usually includes array cell indices in square braces and often involves line wrapping. For example, printing the integers 1 through 25 looks like the following:

```
print(seq_len(25))
# [1]  1  2  3  4  5  6  7  8  9 10 11 12
# [13] 13 14 15 16 17 18 19 20 21 22 23 24
# [25] 25
```

Notice the numbers were wrapped to three lines, and each line starts with the index of the first cell reported on the line inside square brackets. Sometimes we will not show results, an extra encouragement to work these particular examples.

PRINTING

R has a number of rules that turn implicit or automatic printing on and off. Some packages such as `ggplot2` use printing to trigger their intended operations. Typing a value usually triggers printing the value. Care must be taken in a function or a for loop, as in

---

[6] See http://www.win-vector.com/blog/tag/r-tips/.

these contexts, R's automatic printing of results is disabled. Printing of very large objects can be a problem, so you want to avoid printing objects of unknown size. Implicit printing can often be forced by adding extra parentheses such as in " (x <- 5) ".

VECTORS AND LISTS

Vectors (sequential arrays of values) are fundamental R data structures. Lists can hold different types in each slot; vectors can only hold the same primitive or atomic type in each slot. In addition to numeric indexing, both vectors and lists support name-keys. Retrieving items from a list or vector can be done by the operators shown next.

> **VECTOR INDEXING**   R vectors and lists are indexed from 1, and not from 0 as with many other programming languages.

Builds an example vector. c() is R's concatenate operator—it builds longer vectors and lists from shorter ones without nesting. For example, c(1) is just the number 1, and c(1, c(2, 3)) is equivalent to c(1, 2, 3), which in turn is the integers 1 through 3 (though stored in a floating-point format).

```
example_vector <- c(10, 20, 30)
example_list <- list(a = 10, b = 20, c = 30)    ◁——— Builds an example list

example_vector[1]       ◁——┐   Demonstrates vector and list use of
 ## [1] 10                  │   [ ]. Notice that for the list, [ ] returns
example_list[1]             │   a new short list, not the item.
## $a
## [1] 10

example_vector[[2]]     ◁——┐   Demonstrates vector and list use of [[ ]]. In common cases,
 ## [1] 20                  │   [[ ]] forces a single item to be returned, though for nested
example_list[[2]]           │   lists of complex type, this item itself could be a list.
## [1] 20

example_vector[c(FALSE, TRUE, TRUE)]   ◁——┐  Vectors and lists can be indexed by vectors
 ## [1] 20 30                              │  of logicals, integers, and (if the vector or
example_list[c(FALSE, TRUE, TRUE)]         │  list has names) characters.
## $b
## [1] 20
##
## $c
## [1] 30

example_list$b          ◁——┐   For named examples, the syntax example_list$b is
 ## [1] 20                  │   essentially a short-hand for example_list[["b"]] (the
                            │   same is true for named vectors).
example_list[["b"]]
## [1] 20
```

We will not always share so many notes for every example, but we invite the reader to work as if there were such notes by calling `help()` on every function or command used. Also, we very much encourage trying variations. In R "errors " are just R's way of saying it safely refused to complete an ill-formed operation (an error does not indicate "crash," and results are not corrupted). So fear of errors should not limit experiments.

```
x <- 1:5
print(x)
# [1] 1 2 3 4 5

x <- cumsumMISSPELLED(x)
# Error in cumsumMISSPELLED(x) : could not find function "cumsumMISSPELLED"

print(x)
# [1] 1 2 3 4 5

x <- cumsum(x)
print(x)
# [1]  1  3  6 10 15
```

Defines a value we are interested in and stores it in the variable x

Attempts, and fails, to assign a new result to x

Notice that in addition to supplying a useful error message, R preserves the original value of x.

Tries the operation again, using the correct spelling of cumsum(). cumsum(), short for cumulative sum, is a useful function that computes running totals quickly.

Another aspect of vectors in R is that most R operations are *vectorized*. A function or operator is called vectorized when applying it to a vector is shorthand for applying a function to each entry of the vector independently. For example, the function nchar() counts how many characters are in a string. In R this function can be used on a single string, or on a vector of strings.

LISTS AND VECTORS ARE R'S MAP STRUCTURES Lists and vectors are R's map structures. They can map strings to arbitrary objects. The primary list operations [], match (), and %in% are *vectorized*. This means that, when applied to a vector of values, they return a vector of results by performing one lookup per entry. For pulling individual elements out of a list, use the double-bracket notation [[]].

```
nchar("a string")
# [1] 8

nchar(c("a", "aa", "aaa", "aaaa"))
# [1] 1 2 3 4
```

LOGICAL OPERATIONS R's logical operators come in two flavors. R has standard infix scalar-valued operators that expect only one value and have the same behavior and same names as you would see in C or Java: && and ||. R also has vectorized infix operators that work on vectors of logical values: & and |. Be sure to always use the scalar versions (&& and ||) in situations such as if statements, and the vectorized versions (& and |) when processing logical vectors.

NULL AND NANA (NOT AVAILABLE) VALUES

In R NULL is just a synonym for the empty or length-zero vector formed by using the concatenate operator c() with no arguments. For example, when we type c() into the R console, we will see the value NULL returned. In R NULL is not any sort of invalid pointer (as it is in most C/Java-related languages). NULL is simply a length-zero vector. Concatenating NULL is a safe and well-defined operation (in fact it's a "no operation" or "no-op" that does nothing). For example, `c(c(), 1, NULL)` is perfectly valid and returns the value 1.

NA stands for "not available" and is fairly unique to R. Most any simple type can take on the value NA. For example, the vector `c("a", NA, "c")` is a vector of three character strings where we do not know the value of the second entry. Having NA is a great convenience as it allows us to annotate missing or unavailable values in place, which can be critical in data processing. NA behaves a little bit like the NaN value in floating-point arithmetic,[7] except we are not restricted to using it only with floating-point types. Also, NA means "not available," not invalid (as NaN denotes), so NA has some convenient rules such as the logical expression `FALSE & NA` simplifying to `FALSE`.

IDENTIFIERS

Identifiers or symbol names are how R refers to variables and functions. The Google R Style Guide insists on writing symbol names in what is called "CamelCase" (word boundaries in names are denoted by uppercase letters, as in "CamelCase" itself). The Advanced R guide recommends an underscore style where names inside identifiers are broken up with underscores (such as "day_one" instead of "DayOne"). Also, many R users use a dot to break up names with identifiers (such as "day.one"). In particular, important built-in R types such as `data.frame` and packages such as `data.table` use the dot notation convention.

We recommend using the underscore notation, but find we often must switch between conventions when working with others. If possible, avoid the dot convention, as this notation is usually used for other purposes in object-oriented languages and databases, and so needlessly confuses others.[8]

LINE BREAKS

It is generally recommended to keep R source code lines at 80 columns or fewer. R accepts multiple-line statements as long as where the statement ends is unambiguous. For example, to break the single statement "1 + 2" into multiple lines, write the code as follows:

```
1 +
  2
```

Do not write code like the following, as the first line is itself a valid statement, creating ambiguity:

```
1
  + 2
```

---

[7] The limits of *floating-point arithmetic*, or how real numbers are commonly *approximated* in computers, is a common source of confusion and problems when working with numeric data. To appreciate the issues of working with numeric data, we recommend data scientists read David Goldberg's 1991 *Computing Surveys*. "What Every Computer Scientist Should Know About Floating-Point Arithmetic" has been publicly shared from this issue (https://docs.oracle.com/cd/E19957-01/806-3568/ncg_goldberg.html).

[8] The dot notation likely comes from the Lisp world (which strongly influenced R) and the aversion to underscores likely is a holdover from when "_" was one of the usable assignment operators in R (it is no longer used as an assignment operator in R).

The rule is this: force a syntax error every time reading the statement across multiple lines terminates early.

SEMICOLONS

R allows semicolons as end-of-statement markers, but does not require them. Most style guides recommend not using semicolons in R code and certainly not using them at ends of lines.

ASSIGNMENT

R has many assignment operators (see table 2.1); the preferred one is <-. = can be used for assignment in R, but is also used to bind argument values to argument names by name during function calls (so there is some potential ambiguity in using =).

Table 2.1   Primary R assignment operators

Operator	Purpose	Example
<-	Assign the value on the right to the symbol on the left.	`x <- 5 # assign the value of 5 to the symbol x`
=	Assign the value on the right to the symbol on the left.	`x = 5 # assign the value of 5 to the symbol x`
->	Assign left to right, instead of the traditional right to left.	`5 -> x # assign the value of 5 to the symbol x`

LEFT-HAND SIDES OF ASSIGNMENTS

Many popular programming languages only allow assignment of values into variable name or symbols. R allows slice expressions on the left-hand sides of assignments, and both numeric and logical array indexing. This allows for very powerful array-slicing commands and coding styles. For example, we can replace all the missing values (denoted by "NA") in a vector with zero as shown in the following example:

```
d <- data.frame(x = c(1, NA, 3))
print(d)
#   x
# 1 1
# 2 NA
# 3 3

d$x[is.na(d$x)] <- 0
print(d)
#   x
# 1 1
# 2 0
# 3 3
```

"data.frame" is R's tabular data type, and the most important data type in R. A data.frame holds data organized in rows and columns.

When printing data.frames, row numbers are shown in the first (unnamed) column, and column values are shown under their matching column names.

We can place a slice or selection of the x column of d on the left-hand side of an assignment to easily replace all NA values with zero.

FACTORS

R can handle many kinds of data: numeric, logical, integer, strings (called *character* types), and *factors*. Factors are an R type that encodes a fixed set of strings as integers. Factors can save a lot on storage while appearing to behave as strings. However, factors can have potentially confusing interactions with the as.numeric() command (which returns the factor codes for factors, but parses text for character types). Factors also encode the entire set of allowed values, which is useful—but can make combining data from different sources (that saw different sets of values) a bit of a chore. To avoid issues, we suggest delaying conversion of strings to factors until late in an analysis. This is usually accomplished by adding the argument stringsAsFactors = FALSE to functions such as data.frame() or read.table(). We, however, do encourage using factors when you have a reason, such as wanting to use summary() or preparing to produce dummy indicators (see "A bit more on factor coding" after listing 2.10 for more details on dummy indicators and their relation to factors).

NAMED ARGUMENTS

R is centered around applying functions to data. Functions that take a large number of arguments rapidly become confusing and illegible. This is why R includes a named argument feature. As an example, if we wanted to set our working directory to "/tmp" we would usually use the setwd() command like so: setwd("/tmp"). However, help(setwd) shows us the first argument to setwd() has the name dir, so we could also write this as setwd(dir = "/tmp"). This becomes useful for functions that have a large number of arguments, and for setting optional function arguments. Note: named arguments must be set by =, and not by an assignment operator such as <-.

> *If you have a procedure with 10 parameters, you probably missed some.*

> —Alan Perlis, "Epigrams on Programming,"
> ACM SIGPLAN Notices 17

PACKAGE NOTATION

In R there are two primary ways to use a function from a package. The first is to attach the package with the library() command and then use the function name. The second is to use the package name and then :: to name the function. An example of this second method is stats::sd(1:5). The :: notation is good to avoid ambiguity or to leave a reminder of which package the function came from for when you read your own code later.

VALUE SEMANTICS

R is unusual in that it efficiently simulates "copy by value" semantics. Any time a user has two references to data, each evolves independently: changes to one do not affect the other. This is very desirable for part-time programmers and eliminates a large class of possible aliasing bugs when writing code. We give a quick example here:

```
d <- data.frame(x = 1, y = 2)        ◁             Creates some example
d2 <- d             ◁                              data and refers to it
d$x <- 5  ◁─┐                  Creates an          by the name d
            │ Alters the value  additional reference
print(d)    └ referred to by d  d2 to the same data
#   x y
# 1 5 2

print(d2)
#   x y
# 1 1 2
```

Notice d2 keeps the old value of 1 for x. This feature allows for very convenient and safe coding. Many programming languages protect references or pointers in function calls in this manner; however, R protects complex values and does so in all situations (not just function calls). Some care has to be taken when you want to share back changes, such as invoking a final assignment such as d2 <- d after all desired changes have been made. In our experience, R's value isolation semantics prevents far more issues than the copy-back inconvenience it introduces.

ORGANIZING INTERMEDIATE VALUES

Long sequences of calculations can become difficult to read, debug, and maintain. To avoid this, we suggest reserving the variable named "." to store intermediate values. The idea is this: work slow to move fast. For example: a common data science problem is to sort revenue records and then calculate what fraction of total revenue is achieved up to a given sorting key. In R this can be done easily by breaking this task into small steps:

```
data <- data.frame(revenue = c(2, 1, 2),        Our notional, or
                   sort_key = c("b", "c", "a"),  example, data.
                   stringsAsFactors = FALSE)
print(data)

#   revenue sort_key     Assign our data to a temporary variable named ".".
# 1       2        b     The original values will remain available in the "data"
# 2       1        c     variable, making it easy to restart the calculation from
# 3       2        a     the beginning if necessary.

. <- data
. <- .[order(.$sort_key), , drop = FALSE]
.$ordered_sum_revenue <- cumsum(.$revenue)
.$fraction_revenue_seen <- .$ordered_sum_revenue/sum(.$revenue)
result <- .          Assigns the result away from "." to
                     a more memorable variable name
print(result)

#   revenue sort_key ordered_sum_revenue fraction_revenue_seen
# 3       2        a                   2                   0.4
# 1       2        b                   4                   0.8
# 2       1        c                   5                   1.0
```

Use the order command to sort the rows. drop = FALSE is not strictly needed, but it is good to get in the habit of including it. For single-column data.frames without the drop = FALSE argument, the [,] indexing operator will convert the result to a vector, which is almost never the R user's true intent. The drop = FALSE argument turns off this conversion, and it is a good idea to include it "just in case" and a definite requirement when either the data.frame has a single column or when we don't know if the data.frame has more than one column (as the data.frame comes from somewhere else).

The R package dplyr replaces the dot notation with what is called *piped notation* (supplied by a another package named magrittr, and similar to the JavaScript method, chaining). Because the dplyr is very popular, you are likely to see code written in this style, and we will use this style from time to time to help prepare you for such code.

However, it is important to remember that dplyr is merely a popular alternative to standard R code, and not a superior alternative.

```
library("dplyr")

result <- data %>%
  arrange(., sort_key) %>%
  mutate(., ordered_sum_revenue = cumsum(revenue)) %>%
  mutate(., fraction_revenue_seen = ordered_sum_revenue/sum(revenue))
```

Each step of this example has been replaced by the corresponding dplyr equivalent. arrange() is dplyr's replacement for order(), and mutate() is dplyr's replacement for assignment. The code translation is line by line, with the minor exception that assignment is written first (even though it happens after all other steps). The calculation steps are sequenced by the magrittr pipe symbol %>%.

The magrittr pipe allows you to write any of x %>% f, x %>% f(), or x %>% f(.) in place of f(x). Typically, x %>% f is the notation taught: however, we feel x %>% f(.) is the most explicit in representing what is happening.[9]

The details of the dplyr notation can be found here: http://dplyr.tidyverse.org/articles/dplyr.html. Be aware that debugging long dplyr pipelines is difficult, and during development and experimentation it makes sense to break dplyr pipelines into smaller steps, storing intermediate results into temporary variables.

The intermediate result notation has the advantages that it is easy to both restart and step-debug. In this book, we will use different notations as convenient.

THE DATA.FRAME CLASS

The R data.frame class is designed to store data in a very good "ready for analysis" format. data.frames are two-dimensional arrays where each column represents a variable, measurement, or fact, and each row represents an individual or instance. In this format, an individual cell represents what is known about a single fact or variable for a single instance. data.frames are implemented as a named list of column vectors (list columns are possible, but they are more of the exception than the rule for data.frames). In a data.frame, all columns have the same length, and this means we can think of the kth entry of all columns as forming a row.

Operations on data.frame columns tend to be efficient and vectorized. Adding, looking up, and removing columns is fast. Operations per row on a data.frame can be expensive, so you should prefer vectorized column notations for large data.frame processing.

R's data.frame is much like a database table in that it has schema-like information: an explicit list of column names and column types. Most analyses are best expressed in terms of transformations over data.frame columns.

---

[9] For our own work, we actual prefer to use the "dot pipe" %.>% from the wrapr package that enforces more notational consistency.

LET R DO THE WORK FOR YOU

Most common statistical or data processing operations already have a good implementation either in "base R" (R itself and its core packages such as `utils` and `stats`) or in an extension package. If you do not delegate to R, you end up fighting R. For example, a programmer coming from Java might expect to have to use a for loop to add every row of values from two data columns. In R, adding two data columns is considered fundamental and achieved as follows:

```
d <- data.frame(col1 = c(1, 2, 3), col2 = c(-1, 0, 1))
d$col3 <- d$col1 + d$col2
print(d)
#   col1 col2 col3
# 1    1   -1    0
# 2    2    0    2
# 3    3    1    4
```

`data.frames` are in fact named lists of columns. We will use them throughout the book. In R one tends to work over columns and let R's vectorized nature perform the specified operation over every row at once. If you find yourself iterating over rows in R, you are fighting the language.

> **SEARCH FOR READY-MADE SOLUTIONS** Searching for the right R function can be tedious, but it is well worth the time (especially if you keep searchable notes). R was designed for data analysis, so the most common steps needed in a data analysis have already been implemented well in R, though possibly under an obscure name and possibly with odd default settings. It is as chemist Frank Westheimer said, "A couple of months in the laboratory can frequently save a couple of hours in the library."[10] This is a deliberately ironic restatement of the move-fast-by-working-slow principle: researching available solutions costs time, but often saves far more direct coding time.

2.2 Working with data from files

The most common ready-to-go data format is in fact a family of tabular formats called *structured values*. Most of the data you find will be in (or nearly in) one of these formats. When you can read such files into R, you can analyze data from an incredible range of public and private data sources. In this section, we'll work on two examples of loading data from structured files, and one example of loading data directly from a relational database. The point is to get data quickly into R so we can then use R to perform interesting analyses.

2.2.1 Working with well-structured data from files or URLs

The easiest data format to read is table-structured data with headers. As shown in figure 2.2, this data is arranged in rows and columns with a header showing the column names. Each column represents a different fact or measurement; each row represents

---

[10] See https://en.wikiquote.org/wiki/Frank_Westheimer.

an instance or datum about which we know the set of facts. A lot of public data is in this format, so being able to read it opens up a lot of opportunities.

Before we load the German credit data we used in the previous chapter, let's demonstrate the basic loading commands with a simple dataset originally from the University of California Irvine Machine Learning Repository (http://archive.ics .uci.edu/ml/). The UCI data files tend to come without headers, so to save steps (and to keep things simple) we've pre-prepared our first data example from the UCI car dataset: http://archive.ics.uci.edu/ml/machine-learning-databases/car/. Our pre-prepared file is included in the book support directory PDSwR2/UCICar (please see section FM.5.6 for instructions) and looks like the following:

```
buying,maint,doors,persons,lug_boot,safety,rating
vhigh,vhigh,2,2,small,low,unacc
vhigh,vhigh,2,2,small,med,unacc
vhigh,vhigh,2,2,small,high,unacc
vhigh,vhigh,2,2,med,low,unacc
. . .
```

The data rows are in the same format as the header row, but each row contains actual data values. In this case, the first row represents the set of name/value pairs: buying=vhigh, maintenance=vhigh, doors=2, persons=2, and so on.

The header row contains the names of the data columns, in this case separated by commas. When the separators are commas, the format is called comma-separated values, or .csv.

> **AVOID "BY HAND" STEPS OUTSIDE OF R** We strongly encourage you to avoid performing steps "by hand" outside of R when importing data. It's tempting to use an editor to add a header line to a file, as we did in our example. A better strategy is to write an R script to perform any necessary reformatting. Automating these steps greatly reduces the amount of trauma and work during the inevitable data refresh. Receiving new, better data should always feel like good news, and writing automated and replicable procedures is a big step in this direction.
>
> Our example in section 2.2.2 will show how to add headers without editing files by hand as we did in this example.

Notice that this presentation is structured like a spreadsheet with easy-to-identify rows and columns. Each (non-header) row represents a review of a different model of car. The columns represent facts about each car model. Most of the columns are objective measurements (purchase cost, maintenance cost, number of doors, and so on), and the final subjective column "rating" is marked with the overall rating (vgood, good, acc, and unacc). These sorts of details come from the documentation found with the original data, and are key to projects (so we suggest keeping a lab book or notes).

LOADING WELL-STRUCTURED DATA

Loading data of this type into R is a one-liner: we use the R command utils::read .table() and we're done.[11] To work this exercise, we assume that you have downloaded

---

[11] Another option is using functions from the readr package.

and unpacked the contents of this book's GitHub repository https://github.com/ WinVector/PDSwR2 and changed your working directory to PDSwR2/UCICar as explained in section "Working with this book" in the front matter (to do this, you will use the setwd() R function, and you will need to type in the full path to where you have saved PDSwR2, not just the text fragment we have shown). Once R is in the PDS-wR2/UCICar directory, reading the data is done as shown in the following listing.

Listing 2.1 Reading the UCI car data

Command to read from a file or URL and store the result in a new data frame object called uciCar

Filename or URL to get the data from

Specifies the column or field separator as a comma

```
uciCar <- read.table(
    'car.data.csv',
    sep = ',',
    header = TRUE,
    stringsAsFactor = TRUE
    )

View(uciCar)
```

Tells R to expect a header line that defines the data column names

Tells R to convert string values to factors. This is the default behavior, so we are just using this argument to document intent.

Examines the data with R's built-in table viewer

Listing 2.1 loads the data and stores it in a new R data frame object called uciCar, which we show a View() of in figure 2.2.

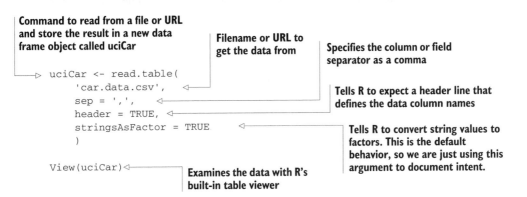

	buying	maint	doors	persons	lug_boot	safety	rating
1	vhigh	vhigh	2	2	small	low	unacc
2	vhigh	vhigh	2	2	small	med	unacc
3	vhigh	vhigh	2	2	small	high	unacc
4	vhigh	vhigh	2	2	med	low	unacc
5	vhigh	vhigh	2	2	med	med	unacc
6	vhigh	vhigh	2	2	med	high	unacc
7	vhigh	vhigh	2	2	big	low	unacc
8	vhigh	vhigh	2	2	big	med	unacc
9	vhigh	vhigh	2	2	big	high	unacc
10	vhigh	vhigh	2	4	small	low	unacc
11	vhigh	vhigh	2	4	small	med	unacc

Showing 1 to 12 of 1,728 entries

Figure 2.2 Car data viewed as a table

The read.table() command is powerful and flexible; it can accept many different types of data separators (commas, tabs, spaces, pipes, and others), and it has many options for controlling quoting and escaping data. read.table() can read from local files or remote URLs. If a resource name ends with the *.gz* suffix, read.table() assumes the file has been compressed in gzip style and will automatically decompress it while reading.

EXAMINING OUR DATA

Once we've loaded the data into R, we'll want to examine it. These are the commands to always try first:

- class()—Tells you what kind of R object you have. In our case, class(uciCar) tells us the object uciCar is of class data.frame. Class is an object-oriented concept, which describes how an object is going to behave. R also has a (less useful) typeof() command, which reveals how the object's storage is implemented.
- dim()—For data frames, this command shows how many rows and columns are in the data.
- head()—Shows the top few rows (or "head") of the data. Example: head(uciCar).
- help()—Provides the documentation for a class. In particular, try help(class (uciCar)).
- str()—Gives you the structure for an object. Try str(uciCar).
- summary()—Provides a summary of almost any R object. summary(uciCar) shows us a lot about the distribution of the UCI car data.
- print()—Prints all the data. Note: for large datasets, this can take a very long time and is something you want to avoid.
- View()—Displays the data in a simple spreadsheet-like grid viewer.

MANY R FUNCTIONS ARE GENERIC Many R functions are generic in that they work much the same on many data types, or even object-oriented in that they pick a correct behavior depending on the runtime class of the object they are working with. We suggest that if you see a function used in an example on one object or class, try it on others. Common R functions that can be used on many different classes and types include length(), print(), saveRDS(), str(), and summary(). The R runtime is very robust and rewards experimentation. Most common errors are caught and cannot corrupt your data or crash the R interpreter. So please, experiment!

We show the results of a few of these steps next (R results are shown prefixed by "##" after each step).

Listing 2.2 Exploring the car data

```
class(uciCar)
## [1] "data.frame"                    The loaded object uciCar
summary(uciCar)                        is of type data.frame.
##     buying        maint         doors
```

```
##   high :432    high :432    2    :432
##   low  :432    low  :432    3    :432
##   med  :432    med  :432    4    :432
##   vhigh:432    vhigh:432    5more:432
##
##   persons      lug_boot     safety
##   2   :576     big  :576    high:576
##   4   :576     med  :576    low :576
##   more:576     small:576    med :576
##
##      rating
##   acc  : 384
##   good :  69
##   unacc:1210
##   vgood:  65

dim(uciCar)
## [1] 1728    7
```

[1] is merely an output sequence marker. The actual information is this: uciCar has 1728 rows and 7 columns. Always try to confirm you got a good parse by at least checking that the number of rows is exactly one fewer than the number of lines of text in the original file. The difference of one is because the column header counts as a line of text, but not as a data row.

The `summary()` command shows us the distribution of each variable in the dataset. For example, we know each car in the dataset was declared to seat 2, 4, or more persons, and we know there were 576 two-seater cars in the dataset. Already we've learned a lot about our data, without having to spend a lot of time manually building pivot tables as we would have to in a spreadsheet.

WORKING WITH OTHER DATA FORMATS

.csv is not the only common data file format you'll encounter. Other formats include .tsv (tab-separated values), pipe-separated (vertical bar) files, Microsoft Excel workbooks, JSON data, and XML. R's built-in `read.table()` command can be made to read most separated value formats. Many of the deeper data formats have corresponding R packages:

- *CSV/TSV/FWF*—The package `reader` (http://readr.tidyverse.org) supplies tools for reading "separated data" such as comma-separated values (CSV), tab-separated values (TSV), and fixed-width files (FWF).
- *SQL*—https://CRAN.R-project.org/package=DBI
- *XLS/XLSX*—http://readxl.tidyverse.org
- *.RData/.RDS*—R has binary data formats (which can avoid complications of parsing, quoting, escaping, and loss of precision in reading and writing numeric or floating-point data as text). The .RData format is for saving sets of objects and object names, and is used through the `save()`/`load()` commands. The .RDS format is for saving single objects (without saving the original object name) and is used through the `saveRDS()`/`readRDS()` commands. For ad hoc work, .RData is more convenient (as it can save the entire R workspace), but for reusable work, the .RDS format is to be preferred as it makes saving and restoring a bit more explicit. To save multiple objects in .RDS format, we suggest using a *named list*.
- *JSON*—https://CRAN.R-project.org/package=rjson

- *XML*—https://CRAN.R-project.org/package=XML
- *MongoDB*—https://CRAN.R-project.org/package=mongolite

2.2.2 *Using R with less-structured data*

Data isn't always available in a ready-to-go format. Data curators often stop just short of producing a ready-to-go machine-readable format. The German bank credit dataset discussed in chapter 1 is an example of this. This data is stored as tabular data without headers; it uses a cryptic coding of values that requires the dataset's accompanying documentation to untangle. This isn't uncommon and is often due to habits or limitations of other tools that commonly work with the data. Instead of reformatting the data before we bring it into R, as we did in the last example, we'll now show how to reformat the data using R. This is a much better practice, as we can save and reuse the R commands needed to prepare the data.

Details of the German bank credit dataset can be found at http://mng.bz/mZbu, and we have included a copy of this data in the directory PDSwR2/Statlog. We'll show how to transform this data into something meaningful using R. After these steps, you can perform the analysis already demonstrated in chapter 1. As we can see in our file excerpt, the data appears to initially be an incomprehensible block of codes:

```
A11 6 A34 A43 1169 A65 A75 4 A93 A101 4 ...
A12 48 A32 A43 5951 A61 A73 2 A92 A101 2 ...
A14 12 A34 A46 2096 A61 A74 2 A93 A101 3 ...
 ...
```

TRANSFORMING DATA IN R

Data often needs a bit of transformation before it makes sense. In order to decrypt troublesome data, you need what's called the *schema documentation* or a *data dictionary*. In this case, the included dataset description says the data is 20 input columns followed by one result column. In this example, there's no header in the data file. The column definitions and the meaning of the cryptic A-* codes are all in the accompanying data documentation. Let's start by loading the raw data into R. Start a copy of R or RStudio and type in the commands in the following listing.

Listing 2.3   Loading the credit dataset

```
setwd("PDSwR2/Statlog")          <─
 d <- read.table('german.data', sep=' ',
   stringsAsFactors = FALSE, header = FALSE)
```

Replace this path with the actual path where you have saved PDSwR2.

As there was no column header in the file, our data.frame d will have useless column names of the form V#. We can change the column names to something meaningful with the c() command, as shown in the following listing.

Listing 2.4   Setting column names

```
d <- read.table('german.data',
               sep = " ",
               stringsAsFactors = FALSE, header = FALSE)
```

```
colnames(d) <- c('Status_of_existing_checking_account', 'Duration_in_month',
                 'Credit_history', 'Purpose', 'Credit_amount', 'Savings_accou
      nt_bonds',
                 'Present_employment_since',
                 'Installment_rate_in_percentage_of_disposable_income',
                 'Personal_status_and_sex', 'Other_debtors_guarantors',
                 'Present_residence_since', 'Property', 'Age_in_years',
                 'Other_installment_plans', 'Housing',
                 'Number_of_existing_credits_at_this_bank', 'Job',
                 'Number_of_people_being_liable_to_provide_maintenance_for',
                 'Telephone', 'foreign_worker', 'Good_Loan')
str(d)
## 'data.frame':    1000 obs. of  21 variables:
##  $ Status_of_existing_checking_account                    : chr  "A11" "A
      12" "A14" "A11" ...
##  $ Duration_in_month                                      : int  6 48 12
      42 24 36 24 36 12 30 ...
##  $ Credit_history                                         : chr  "A34" "A
      32" "A34" "A32" ...
##  $ Purpose                                                : chr  "A43" "A
      43" "A46" "A42" ...
##  $ Credit_amount                                          : int  1169 595
      1 2096 7882 4870 9055 2835 6948 3059 5234 ...
##  $ Savings_account_bonds                                  : chr  "A65" "A
      61" "A61" "A61" ...
##  $ Present_employment_since                               : chr  "A75" "A
      73" "A74" "A74" ...
##  $ Installment_rate_in_percentage_of_disposable_income    : int  4 2 2 2
      3 2 3 2 2 4 ...
##  $ Personal_status_and_sex                                : chr  "A93" "A
      92" "A93" "A93" ...
##  $ Other_debtors_guarantors                               : chr  "A101" "
      A101" "A101" "A103" ...
##  $ Present_residence_since                                : int  4 2 3 4
      4 4 4 2 4 2 ...
##  $ Property                                               : chr  "A121" "
      A121" "A121" "A122" ...
##  $ Age_in_years                                           : int  67 22 49
       45 53 35 53 35 61 28 ...
##  $ Other_installment_plans                                : chr  "A143" "
      A143" "A143" "A143" ...
##  $ Housing                                                : chr  "A152" "
      A152" "A152" "A153" ...
##  $ Number_of_existing_credits_at_this_bank                : int  2 1 1 1
      2 1 1 1 1 2 ...
##  $ Job                                                    : chr  "A173" "
      A173" "A172" "A173" ...
##  $ Number_of_people_being_liable_to_provide_maintenance_for: int  1 1 2 2
      2 2 1 1 1 1 ...
##  $ Telephone                                              : chr  "A192" "
      A191" "A191" "A191" ...
##  $ foreign_worker                                         : chr  "A201" "
      A201" "A201" "A201" ...
##  $ Good_Loan                                              : int  1 2 1 1
      2 1 1 1 1 2 ...
```

The `c()` command is R's method to construct a vector.[12] We copied the column names directly from the dataset documentation. By assigning our vector of names into the data frame's `colnames()`, we've reset the data frame's column names to something sensible.

> **ASSIGNING TO ACCESSORS** In R the data frame class has a number of data accessors such as `colnames()` and `names()`. Many of these data accessors can be assigned to, as we saw when we assigned new names in listing 2.3 with `colnames(d) <- c('Status_of_existing_checking_account', ...)`. This ability to assign into accessors is a bit unusual, but a very useful feature of R.

The data documentation further tells us the column names, and also has a code dictionary of the meanings of all of the cryptic A-* codes. For example, it says in column 4 (now called *Purpose*, meaning the purpose of the loan) that the code `A40` is a "new car loan," `A41` is a "used car loan," and so on. We can use R's list-mapping capabilities to remap the values to more descriptive terms. The file PDSwR2/Statlog/GCD-Steps.Rmd is an R Markdown that includes all the steps up through now and also remaps the values from the A# forms to clearer names. The file first implements the dataset documentation's value mapping as an R named vector. This allows us to change the illegible names (such as A11) into somewhat meaningful descriptions (such as ... < 0 DM, which itself is presumably shorthand for "zero or fewer deutsche marks reported").[13] The first few lines of this map definition look like the following:

```
mapping <- c('A11' = '... < 0 DM',
             'A12' = '0 <= ... < 200 DM',
             'A13' = '... >= 200 DM / salary assignments for at least 1 year',
             ...
                )
```

Note: In building a named map, you must use the argument binding symbol =, and not any of the assignment operators such as <-.

With the mapping list defined, we can then use the following for loop to convert values in each column that was of type `character` from the original cryptic A-* codes into short level descriptions taken directly from the data documentation. We, of course, skip any such transform for columns that contain numeric data.

Listing 2.5 Transforming the car data

Prefer using column names to column indices.

```
source("mapping.R")                              ◁───── This file can be found at https://github.com/
  ┌─▷ for(ci in colnames(d)) {                           WinVector/PDSwR2/blob/master/Statlog/mapping.R.
  │       if(is.character(d[[ci]])) {
  │         d[[ci]] <- as.factor(mapping[d[[ci]]]) ◁───────────────────────────────────────┐
  │       }               The [ [ ] ] notation is using the fact that data.frames are named lists of
  │     }                 columns. So we are working on each column in turn. Notice the mapping
  │                       lookup is vectorized: it is applied to all elements in the column in one step.
```

---

[12] `c()` also concatenates lists or vectors, without introducing additional nesting.
[13] German currency at the time of data collection was the deutsche mark (DM).

As we mentioned, the complete set of column preparations for this is in the R Markdown file PDSwR2/Statlog/GCDSteps.Rmd. We encourage readers to examine this file and try all of these steps themselves. For convenience, the prepared data is saved in PDSwR2/Statlog/creditdata.RDS.

EXAMINING OUR NEW DATA

We can now easily examine the purpose of the first three loans with the command `print(d[1:3, 'Purpose'])`. We can look at the distribution of loan purpose with `summary(d$Purpose)`. This summary is why we converted the values into factors, as `summary()` does not report much for string/character types, though we could also use `table(d$Purpose, useNA = "always")` directly on character types. We can also start to investigate the relation of loan type to loan outcome, as shown in the following listing.

Listing 2.6 Summary of `Good_Loan` and `Purpose`

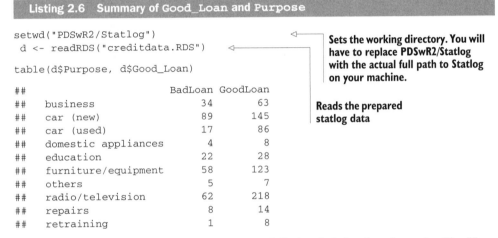

```
setwd("PDSwR2/Statlog")
  d <- readRDS("creditdata.RDS")

table(d$Purpose, d$Good_Loan)

##                        BadLoan GoodLoan
##    business                34       63
##    car (new)               89      145
##    car (used)              17       86
##    domestic appliances      4        8
##    education               22       28
##    furniture/equipment     58      123
##    others                   5        7
##    radio/television        62      218
##    repairs                  8       14
##    retraining               1        8
```

Sets the working directory. You will have to replace PDSwR2/Statlog with the actual full path to Statlog on your machine.

Reads the prepared statlog data

From the output, we can see we have successfully loaded the data from the file. However, as mentioned, a lot of data is in other sources such as Excel spreadsheets (with the `readxl` package, these can be treated much like the way one works with files) and in databases (including big data systems such as Apache Spark). We will next discuss working with relational databases through the SQL query language and the DBI package.

2.3 Working with relational databases

In many production environments, the data you want lives in a relational or SQL database, not in files. Public data is often in files (as they are easier to share), but your most important client data is often in databases. Relational databases scale easily to hundreds of millions of records and supply important production features such as parallelism, consistency, transactions, logging, and audits. Relational databases are designed to support online transaction processing (OLTP), so they're likely where transactions you need to know about were actually produced.

Often you can export the data into a structured file and use the methods from our previous sections to then transfer the data into R. But this is generally not the right way to do things. Exporting from databases to files is often unreliable and idiosyncratic due to loss of schema information, escaping, quoting, and character-encoding issues. The best way to work with data found in databases is to connect R directly to the database, which is what we'll demonstrate in this section.

As a step of the demonstration, we'll first show how to load data into a database. Relational databases are a good place for transformations such as joins or sampling (though packages such as `sqldf` and `dplyr` give R similar capabilities), which will be the topic of chapter 5. We will start working with data in a database for our next example.

2.3.1   *A production-size example*

For our production-size example, we'll use the 2016 United States Census American Community Survey (ACS) Public Use Microdata Sample (PUMS) data, often called "ACS PUMS." We have documentation on how to download and prepare a sample of this data in the dictionary `PDSwR2/PUMS/download`. We also have a ready-to-work-with recoded sample in the R-data file PDSwR2/PUMS/PUMSsample.RDS, allowing you to skip the initial download and processing steps.

The PUMS data is ideal for setting up somewhat realistic data science scenarios: summarizing data and building models predicting one column of the data from other columns. We will return to this dataset later in this book.

The PUMS is a remarkable set of data involving around 3 million individuals and 1.5 million households. It is one of the few shared United States Census datasets that deals with individual people and households (instead of per-region summaries). This is important, as most common data science tasks are designed to use detailed per-individual records, so this is public data that is most like the private data a data scientist would work with. Each row contains over 200 facts about each individual or household (income, employment, education, number of rooms, and so on). The data has household cross-reference IDs so individuals can be joined to the household they're in. The size of the dataset is interesting: a few gigabytes when compressed. So it's small enough to store on a good network or thumb drive, but larger than is convenient to work with on a laptop with R in memory (which is more comfortable when working in the range of hundreds of thousands of rows).

> **SUMMARIES OR MARGINALS**   Moving from individual-oriented data to summaries or marginals is an easy process called *summary statistics* or *basic analytics*. Converting the other way is often not possible, or at best a deep statistical problem (beyond the scope of basic data science). Most United States Census data is shared as regional summaries, so it often requires sophisticated statistical imputation methodology to generate useful individual-level predictive models. The PUMS data is very useful because it is individually oriented.

Tens of millions of rows is a sweet spot size for relational database or SQL-assisted analysis on a single machine. We're not yet forced to move into a database cluster or a Apache Spark cluster to do our work.

CURATING THE DATA

A hard rule of science is that you must be able to reproduce your results. At the very least, you should be able to repeat your own successful work through your recorded steps. Everything must either have directions on how to produce it or clear documentation on where it came from. We call this the "no alien artifacts" discipline. For example, when we said we're using PUMS American Community Survey data, this statement isn't precise enough for anybody to know what data we specifically mean. Our actual notebook entry (which we keep online, so we can search it) on the PUMS data is shown in the next listing.

> Listing 2.7 **PUMS data provenance documentation**
> **(PDSwR2/PUMS/download/LoadPUMS.Rmd)**

Where we found the data documentation. This is important to record, as many data files don't contain links back to the documentation.

When we downloaded the data

```
Data downloaded 4/21/2018 from:Reduce Zoom

    https://www.census.gov/data/developers/data-sets/acs-1year.2016.html
     https://www.census.gov/programs-surveys/acs/
technical-documentation/pums.html
    http://www2.census.gov/programs-
        surveys/acs/tech_docs/pums/data_dict/PUMSDataDict16.txt
    https://www2.census.gov/programs-surveys/acs/data/pums/2016/1-Year/


First in a `bash` shell perform the following steps:

wget https://www2.census.gov/programs-surveys/acs/data/
pums/2016/1-Year/csv_hus.zip                        The exact steps we took
 md5 csv_hus.zip
# MD5 (csv_hus.zip) = c81d4b96a95d573c1b10fc7f230d5f7a
 wget https://www2.census.gov/programs-surveys/acs/data/pums/2016/1-
        Year/csv_pus.zip
md5 csv_pus.zip
# MD5 (csv_pus.zip) = 06142320c3865620b0630d74d74181db
wget http://www2.census.gov/programs-
        surveys/acs/tech_docs/pums/data_dict/PUMSDataDict16.txt
md5 PUMSDataDict16.txt
# MD5 (PUMSDataDict16.txt) = 56b4e8fcc7596cc8b69c9e878f2e699aunzip csv_hus.zip
```

Cryptographic hashes of the file contents we downloaded. These are very short summaries (called hashes) that are highly unlikely to have the same value for different files. These summaries can later help us determine if another researcher in our organization is using the same data.

KEEP NOTES   A big part of being a data scientist is being able to defend your results and repeat your work. We strongly advise keeping local copies of data and keeping a notebook. Notice that in listing 2.7 we not only show how and when we got the data, we also show what cryptographic hash the download had at the time. This is important to help ensure reproducible results and also to diagnose if and where something has changed. We also strongly advise keeping all of your scripts and code under version control, as we'll discuss in chapter 11. You absolutely need to be able to answer exactly what code and which data were used to build results you presented last week.

A particularly important form of note maintenance is using Git source control, which we will discuss in chapter 11.

STARTING WITH THE PUMS DATA

It is important to at least skim the downloaded PUMS data documentation: PDSwR2/PUMS/ACS2016_PUMS_README.pdf (a file that was in the downloaded zip container) and PDSwR2/PUMS/PUMSDataDict16.txt (one of the files we downloaded). Three things stand out: the data is distributed as comma-separated structured files with column headers, the values are coded as indecipherable integers (much like our earlier `Statlog` example), and the individuals are weighted to represent varying numbers of additional households. The R Markdown[14] script PDSwR2/PUMS/download/LoadPUMS.Rmd reads the CSV files (from a compressed intermediate file), recodes the values to more-meaningful strings, and takes a pseudo-random sample of the data with probabilities proportional to the specified household sampling weights. The proportional sampling both cuts the file size down to around 10 megabytes (a size easy to be distributed through GitHub) and builds a sample that can be used in a statistically correct manner, without further reference to the Census weights.

SAMPLING   When we say "pseudo-random sample," we simply mean a sample built from R's pseudo-random number generator. R's random number generator is called "pseudo-random" as it is actually a deterministic sequence of choices that are hoped to be hard to predict and thus behave much like a truly random unpredictable sample. Pseudo-random samples are good to work with as they are repeatable: start the pseudo-random generator with the same seed, and you get the same sequences of choices. Prior to the widespread availability of digital computers, statisticians used to achieve this repeatability by using pre-prepared tables such as Rand Corporation's 1955 book *A Million Random Digits with 100,000 Normal Deviates*. The intent is that a random sample should have properties very similar to the total population. The more common the feature you are working with, the more often this is in fact true.

---

[14] We will discuss R Markdown later in this book. It is an important format for storing both R code and text documentation together.

Note: Some care must be taken around the repeatability of pseudo-random experiments. A number of things can interfere with the exact reproduction of pseudo-random samples and results. For example, using a different order of operation can produce different results (especially in the case of parallel algorithms), and R itself changed details of its pseudo-random number when it moved from version 3.5.* (used in the preparation of this book) to 3.6.* (the next version of R). As with things like floating-point representations, one must sometimes accept equivalent results in place of exactly identical results.

Structured data at a scale of millions of rows is best handled in a database, though R and the `data.table` package also work well at this scale. We will simulate working with data that lives in a database by copying our PUMS sample into an in-memory database, as shown next.

Listing 2.8 Loading data into R from a relational database

Loads the data from the compressed RDS disk format into R memory. Note: You will need to change the path PUMSsample to where you have saved the contents of PDSwR2/PUMS.

Copies the data from the in-memory structure dlist into the database

Attaches some packages we wish to use commands and functions from.

Connects to a new RSQLite in-memory database. We will use RSQLite for our examples. In practice you would connect to a preexisting database, such as PostgreSQL or Spark, with preexisting tables.

```
library("DBI")
library("dplyr")
library("rquery")

dlist <- readRDS("PUMSsample.RDS")
db <- dbConnect(RSQLite::SQLite(), ":memory:")
dbWriteTable(db, "dpus", as.data.frame(dlist$ss16pus))
dbWriteTable(db, "dhus", as.data.frame(dlist$ss16hus))
rm(list = "dlist")

dbGetQuery(db, "SELECT * FROM dpus LIMIT 5")

dpus <- tbl(db, "dpus")
dhus <- tbl(db, "dhus")

print(dpus)
glimpse(dpus)

View(rsummary(db, "dpus"))
```

Builds dplyr handles that refer to the remote database data

Uses dplyr to examine and work with the remote data

Uses the SQL query language for a quick look at up to five rows of our data

Uses the rquery package to get a summary of the remote data

Removes our local copy of the data, as we are simulating having found the data in the database

In this listing, we have deliberately not shown any of the results the commands produce, as we would like you to try this example yourself.

> **CODE EXAMPLES**   All code examples from this book are available in the directory PDSwR2/CodeExamples. Taking code from this directory can be easier than retyping it and more reliable than copying and pasting from an electronic copy of the book (avoiding issues of page breaks, character encodings, and formatting glitches such as smart quotes).

Note that this data, while small, is out of the range where using spreadsheets is convenient. Using `dim(dlist$ss16hus)` and `dim(dlist$ss16pus)` (before the `rm()` step, or after reloading the data), we see that our household sample has 50,000 rows and 149 columns, and the people sample has 109,696 rows and 203 columns. All columns and value codes are defined in the Census documentation. Such documentation is critical, and we supply links to the documentation in PDSwR2/PUMS.

EXAMINING AND CONDITIONING THE PUMS DATA

The point of loading data into R is to facilitate modeling and analysis. Data analysts should always have their "hands in the data" and always take a quick look at their data after loading it. As our example, we'll demonstrate how to perform a quick examination of some of the PUMS columns or fields.

Each row of PUMS data represents a single anonymized person or household. Personal data recorded includes occupation, level of education, personal income, and many other demographics variables. We loaded the data in listing 2.8, but before we continue, let's discuss a few of the columns found in the dataset and its documentation:

- *Age*—An integer found in column AGEP
- *Employment class*—Examples: for-profit company, nonprofit company, and so on, found in column COW
- *Education level*—Examples: no high school diploma, high school, college, and so on, found in column SCHL
- *Total person's income*—Found in column PINCP
- *Sex of worker*—Found in column SEX

We will make our example problem to relate income (represented in US dollars in the field) to these variables. This is a typical predictive modeling task: relating some variables we know the values of (age, employment, and so on) to a variable we wish to know (in this case, income). This task is an example of supervised learning, meaning we use a dataset where both the observable variables (denoted "independent variables" in statistics) and the unobserved outcome (or the "dependent variable") are both available at the same time. You usually get such labeled data by buying data, employing annotators, or using older data where you have had time to observe the desired outcome.

DON'T BE TOO PROUD TO SAMPLE Many data scientists spend too much time adapting algorithms to work directly with big data. Often this is wasted effort, as for many model types you would get almost exactly the same results on a reasonably sized data sample. You only need to work with "all of your data" when what you're modeling isn't well served by sampling, such as when characterizing rare events or performing linkage calculations over social networks.

We don't want to spend too much on time on the artificial aspects of the example problem; our goal is to illustrate modeling and data-handling procedures. Conclusions are very dependent on choices of data conditioning (what subset of the data you use) and data coding (how you map records to informative symbols). This is why empirical scientific papers have a mandatory "materials and methods" section describing how data was chosen and prepared. Our data treatment is to select a subset of "typical full-time workers" by restricting the subset to data that meets all of the following conditions:

- Workers self-described as full-time employees
- Workers reporting at least 30 hours a week of activity
- Workers 18–65 years of age
- Workers with an annual income between $1,000 and $250,000.

The following listing shows the code to limit to our desired subset of the data. Continuing with our data from listing 2.8, we work as shown in listing 2.9. As our data is small (just a sample from PUMS), we use the DBI package to bring the data into R where we can work with it.

> **Listing 2.9 Loading data from a database**

Copies data from the database into R memory. This assumes we are continuing from the previous example, so the packages we have attached are still available and the database handle db is still valid.

All the columns in this copy of PUMS data are stored as the character type to preserve features such as leading zeros from the original data. Here we are converting columns we wish to treat as numeric to the numeric type. Non-numeric values, often missing entries, get coded with the symbol NA, which stands for not available.

Selects a subset of columns we want to work with. Restricting columns is not required, but improves legibility of later printing.

```
dpus <- dbReadTable(db, "dpus")

dpus <- dpus[, c("AGEP", "COW", "ESR", "PERNP",
            "PINCP","SCHL", "SEX", "WKHP")]

for(ci in c("AGEP", "PERNP", "PINCP", "WKHP")) {
   dpus[[ci]] <- as.numeric(dpus[[ci]])
}

dpus$COW <- strtrim(dpus$COW, 50)

str(dpus)
```

Looks at the first few rows of data in a column orientation.

The PUMS level names are very long (which is one of the reasons these columns are distributed as integers), so for this dataset that has level names instead of level codes, we are shortening the employment codes to no more than 50 characters.

WATCH OUT FOR NAs   R's representation for blank or missing data is *NA*. Unfortunately, a lot of R commands quietly skip NAs without warning. The command `table(dpus$COW, useNA = 'always')` will show NAs much like `summary(dpus$COW)` does.

We have now performed a few standard data analysis steps: loading the data, reprocessing a few columns, and taking a look at the data. These steps have been performed using what we call "base R," which means using features and functions coming from the R language itself and the basic packages that are automatically attached (such as `base`, `stats`, and `utils`). R is well suited to data processing tasks, as this is what most users come to R to do. There are extension packages such as `dplyr` that have their own data processing notation and can perform many steps directly against data in a database in addition to being able to work on data held in memory. We share examples showing how to perform the same data processing steps using base R in the R Markdown example PDSwR2/PUMS/PUMS1.Rmd, or using `dplyr` in PDSwR2/PUMS/PUMS1_dplyr.Rmd, or using the advanced query generation package `rquery` in PDSwR2/PUMS/PUMS1_rquery.Rmd.

We are now ready to work our notional problem in listing 2.10: characterizing income with relation to other facts known about individuals. We will start with some domain-specific steps: we will remap some level names and convert the levels to factors, each with a chosen reference level. Factors are strings taken from a specified set (much like an enumerate type in other languages). Factors also have one special level called the *reference level*; it is convention that each level is considered to be a difference from the reference level. For example, we will set all less-than-bachelors-degree education levels to a new level called *No Advanced Degree* and make No Advanced Degree our reference level. Some R modeling functions will then score education levels such as Master's Degree as how they differ from the reference level No Advanced Degree. This will be made clear in our example.

Listing 2.10   Remapping values and selecting rows from data

```
target_emp_levs <- c(                          ⊲        Defines a vector of
  "Employee of a private for-profit company or busine",   employment
  "Employee of a private not-for-profit, tax-exempt, ",   definitions we
  "Federal government employee",                          consider "standard"
  "Local government employee (city, county, etc.)",
  "Self-employed in own incorporated business, profes",
  "Self-employed in own not incorporated business, pr",
  "State government employee")


complete <- complete.cases(dpus)    ⊲
```

Builds a new logical vector indicating which rows have valid values in all of our columns of interest. In real applications, dealing with missing values is important and cannot always be handled by skipping incomplete rows. We will return to the issue of properly dealing with missing values when we discuss managing data.

Builds a new logical vector indicating which workers we consider typical full-time employees. All of these column names are the ones we discussed earlier. The results of any analysis will be heavily influenced by this definition, so, in a real task, we would spend a lot of time researching the choices in this step. It literally controls who and what we are studying. Notice that to keep things simple and homogeneous, we restricted this study to civilians, which would be an unacceptable limitation in a complete work.

```
stdworker <- with(dpus,
                   (PINCP>1000) &
                   (ESR=="Civilian employed, at work") &
                   (PINCP<=250000) &
                   (PERNP>1000) & (PERNP<=250000) &
                   (WKHP>=30) &
                   (AGEP>=18) & (AGEP<=65) &
                   (COW %in% target_emp_levs))
```

Restricts to only rows or examples that meet our definition of a typical worker

```
dpus <- dpus[complete & stdworker, , drop = FALSE]

no_advanced_degree <- is.na(dpus$SCHL) |
   (!(dpus$SCHL %in% c("Associate's degree",
                       "Bachelor's degree",
                       "Doctorate degree",
                       "Master's degree",
                       "Professional degree beyond a bachelor's degree")))
dpus$SCHL[no_advanced_degree] <- "No Advanced Degree"
```

Recodes education, merging the less-than-bachelor's-degree levels to the single level No Advanced Degree

```
dpus$SCHL <- relevel(factor(dpus$SCHL),
                     "No Advanced Degree")
dpus$COW <- relevel(factor(dpus$COW),
                    target_emp_levs[[1]])
dpus$ESR <- relevel(factor(dpus$ESR),
                    "Civilian employed, at work")
dpus$SEX <- relevel(factor(dpus$SEX),
                    "Male")
```

Converts our string-valued columns to factors, picking the reference level with the relevel() function

Save this data to a file so we can use it in later examples. This file is also already available at the path PDSwR2/PUMS/dpus_std_employee.RDS.

```
saveRDS(dpus, "dpus_std_employee.RDS")

summary(dpus)
```

Takes a look at our data. One of the advantages of factors is that summary() builds up useful counts for them. However, it was best to delay having string codes as factors until after we finished with remapping level codes.

A BIT MORE ON FACTOR CODING

R's factor type encodes strings as integer indices into a known set of possible strings. For example, our SCHL column is represented in R as follows:

Shows the possible levels for SCHL

```
levels(dpus$SCHL)
## [1] "No Advanced Degree"              "Associate's degree"
## [3] "Bachelor's degree"               "Doctorate degree"
## [5] "Master's degree"                 "Professional degree
     beyond a bachelor's degree"
```

Shows how the first few levels are represented as codes

```
head(dpus$SCHL)
## [1] Associate's degree Associate's degree Associate's degree No Advanced D
      egree Doctorate degree Associate's degree
##   6 Levels: No Advanced Degree Associate's degree Bachelor's degree Doctor
      ate degree ... Professional degree beyond a bachelor's degree
```

Shows the first few string values for SCHL

```
str(dpus$SCHL)
##   Factor w/ 6 levels "No Advanced Degree",..: 2 2 2 1 4 2 1 5 1 1 ...
```

Non-statisticians are often surprised that you can use non-numeric columns (such as strings or factors) as inputs to or variables in models. This can be accomplished a number of ways, and the most common one is a method called *introducing indicators* or *dummy variables*. In R this encoding is often automatic and unseen. In other systems (such as Python's scikit-learn), the analyst must specify an encoding (through a method name such as "one-hot"). In this book, we will use this encoding and additional, more sophisticated encodings from the vtreat package. The SCHL column can be explicitly converted into basic dummy variables as we show next. This recoding strategy will be used both implicitly and explicitly in the book, so we will demonstrate it here:

The cbind operator combines two data frames by columns, or each row is built by matching columns from rows in each data frame.

Builds a data.frame with the SCHL column recoded as character strings instead of as a factor

Builds a matrix with dummy variables generated from the SCHL factor column

```
d <- cbind(
    data.frame(SCHL = as.character(dpus$SCHL),
               stringsAsFactors = FALSE),
    model.matrix(~SCHL, dpus)
  )
d$'(Intercept)' <- NULL
  str(d)

## 'data.frame':    41305 obs. of  6 variables:
## $ SCHL                                            : chr  "Associate's d
    egree" "Associate's degree" "Associate's degree" "No Advanced Degree" ..
    .
## $ SCHLAssociate's degree                          : num  1 1 1 0 0 1 0
    0 0 0 ...
## $ SCHLBachelor's degree                           : num  0 0 0 0 0 0 0
    0 0 0 ...
## $ SCHLDoctorate degree                            : num  0 0 0 0 1 0 0
    0 0 0 ...
## $ SCHLMaster's degree                             : num  0 0 0 0 0 0 0
    1 0 0 ...
## $ SCHLProfessional degree beyond a bachelor's degree: num  0 0 0 0 0 0 0
    0 0 0 ...
```

Removes a column named "(Intercept)" from the data.frame, as it is a side effect of model.matrix that we are not interested in at this time.

Shows the structure that presents the original SCHL string form along with the indicators. str() presents the first few rows in transpose format (flipped so rows are now up and down and columns are across).

Notice that the reference level No Advanced Degree did not get a column, and new indicator columns have a 1, which reveals which value is in the original SCHL column. The No Advanced Degree columns have all-zero dummies, so we can also tell which examples had that value. This coding can be read as "all-zero rows are the base or normal case and other rows differ from the all-zero case by having one indicator on (showing which case we are talking about)." Notice that this encoding contains all the information of the original string form, but all columns are now numeric (which is a format many machine learning and modeling procedures require). This format is implicitly used in many R machine learning and modeling functions, and the user may not even be aware of the conversion.

WORKING WITH THE PUMS DATA

At this point, we are ready to practice working on our problem with data. As we have seen, summary(dpus) already gives us information about the distribution of every variable in our dataset. We can also look at relations between variables with one of the tabulating commands: tapply() or table(). For example, to see a count of examples simultaneously broken down by level of schooling and sex, we could type in the command table(schooling = dpus$SCHL, sex = dpus$SEX). To get the mean income broken down the same way, we could use the command tapply(dpus$PINCP, list(dpus$SCHL, dpus$SEX), FUN = mean).

Uses the table command to count how often each pair of SCHL and SEX occurs

```
table(schooling = dpus$SCHL, sex = dpus$SEX)

##                                                      sex
## schooling                                            Male Female
##    No Advanced Degree                                13178   9350
##    Associate's degree                                 1796   2088
##    Bachelor's degree                                  4927   4519
##    Doctorate degree                                    361    269
##    Master's degree                                    1792   2225
##    Professional degree beyond a bachelor's degree      421    379
```

```
tapply(
    dpus$PINCP,
    list(dpus$SCHL, dpus$SEX),
    FUN = mean
    )
```

This argument list specifies how we are grouping the data, in this case simultaneously by SCHL and SEX.

```
##                                                         Male    Female
## No Advanced Degree                                  44304.21  33117.37
## Associate's degree                                  56971.93  42002.06
## Bachelor's degree                                   76111.84  57260.44
## Doctorate degree                                   104943.33  89336.99
## Master's degree                                     94663.41  69104.54
## Professional degree beyond a bachelor's degree     111047.26  92071.56
```

This argument is the vector of data we are aggregating or summarizing in the tapply.

Uses tapply to tally how often each pair of SCHL of SEX occurs

This argument specifies how we are aggregating values; in this case, we are taking the mean or average using the mean function.

The same calculation in `dplyr` idiom is as follows:

```
library("dplyr")

dpus %>%
  group_by(., SCHL, SEX)  %>%
  summarize(.,
          count = n(),
          mean_income = mean(PINCP)) %>%
  ungroup(.) %>%
  arrange(., SCHL, SEX)
```

```
## # A tibble: 12 x 4
##    SCHL                                              SEX     count mean_income
##    <fct>                                             <fct>   <int>       <dbl>
##  1 No Advanced Degree                                Male    13178      44304.
##  2 No Advanced Degree                                Female   9350      33117.
##  3 Associate's degree                                Male     1796      56972.
##  4 Associate's degree                                Female   2088      42002.
##  5 Bachelor's degree                                 Male     4927      76112.
##  6 Bachelor's degree                                 Female   4519      57260.
##  7 Doctorate degree                                  Male      361     104943.
##  8 Doctorate degree                                  Female    269      89337.
##  9 Master's degree                                   Male     1792      94663.
## 10 Master's degree                                   Female   2225      69105.
## 11 Professional degree beyond a bachelor's degree Male        421     111047.
## 12 Professional degree beyond a bachelor's degree Female      379      92072.
```

`dplyr` pipelines express tasks as sequences of basic data transformations. Also, notice that the `tapply()` result was in a so-called wide format (data cells keyed by row and column), and the `dplyr` output is in a tall format (data cells keyed by key columns in each row).

We can even graph relations, as shown in listing 2.11. Finally, if we want a model estimating income as a joint function of all of our other variables simultaneously, we can try a regression, which is the topic of chapter 8. Converting between such formats is one of the key topics covered in chapter 5.

Listing 2.11 Plotting the data

```
WVPlots::ScatterHist(
  dpus, "AGEP", "PINCP",
  "Expected income (PINCP) as function age (AGEP)",
  smoothmethod = "lm",
  point_alpha = 0.025)
```

This is a moment to celebrate, as we have finally achieved a data science goal. In figure 2.3, we are looking at the data and relations in the data. The technical task of explaining the summary information in the graph will be covered in chapter 8.

We'll return to the Census data and demonstrate more-sophisticated modeling techniques a few times in this book. In all cases, we are working these examples to demonstrate the basic challenges one encounters in working with their hands on the data, and to introduce some of the R tools that are ready to help. As a follow-up, we

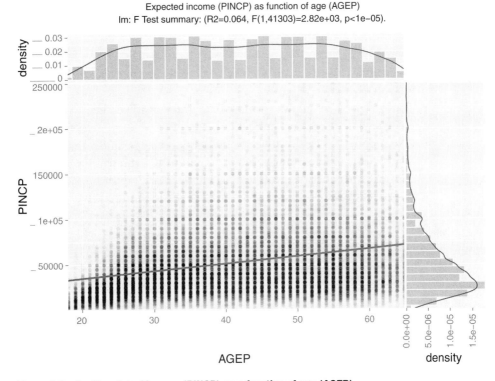

Figure 2.3   **Scatter plot of income (PINCP) as a function of age (AGEP)**

strongly advise running these examples, consulting the `help()` on all of these functions, and also searching online for official documentation and user guides.

Summary

In this chapter, we've worked through the basics of how to initially extract, transform, and load data for analysis. For smaller datasets, we perform the transformations using R and in memory. For larger datasets, we advise using a SQL database or even a big data system such as Spark (via the `sparklyr` package plus SQL, `dplyr`, or `rquery`). In any case, we save *all* the transformation steps as code (either in SQL or in R) that can be reused in the event of a data refresh. The intent of this chapter was to prepare for the actual interesting work in our next chapters: exploring, managing, correcting, and modeling data.

R is built to work with data, and the purpose of loading data into R is to examine and work with it. In chapter 3, we'll demonstrate how to characterize your data through summaries, exploration, and graphing. These are key steps early in any modeling effort because it is through these steps that you learn the actual details and nature of the problem you're hoping to model.

In this chapter you have learned

- Data frames, with their discipline of each row being an instance and each column being a variable or measurement, are a preferred data structure for data analysis.
- Use `utils::read.table()` or the `readr` package to load small, structured datasets into R.
- The `DBI` package allows you to work directly with databases or Apache Spark using any of `SQL`, `dplyr`, or `rquery`.
- R is designed to work with data in high-level steps, and has many ready-made, data-transforming commands and functions. Generally, if a task becomes difficult in R, it is because you are accidentally attempting to reimplement high-level data transforms in terms of low-level programming steps.

Exploring data 3

This chapter covers

- Using summary statistics to explore data
- Exploring data using visualization
- Finding problems and issues during data exploration

In the last two chapters, you learned how to set the scope and goal of a data science project, and how to start working with your data in R. In this chapter, you'll start to get your hands into the data. As shown in the mental model (figure 3.1), this chapter emphasizes the science of exploring the data, prior to the model-building step. Your goal is to have data that is as clean and useful as possible.

> **Example**   *Suppose your goal is to build a model to predict which of your customers don't have health insurance. You've collected a dataset of customers whose health insurance status you know. You've also identified some customer properties that you believe help predict the probability of insurance coverage: age, employment status, income, information about residence and vehicles, and so on.*

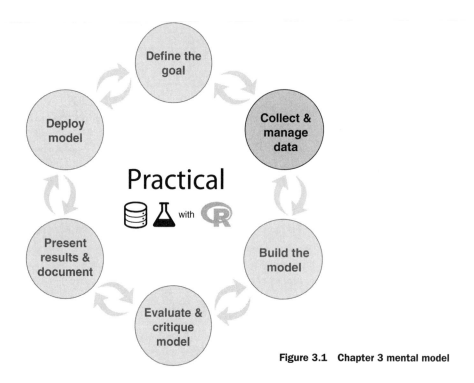

Figure 3.1   Chapter 3 mental model

You've put all your data into a single data frame called customer_data that you've input into R.[1] Now you're ready to start building the model to identify the customers you're interested in.

It's tempting to dive right into the modeling step without looking very hard at the dataset first, especially when you have a lot of data. Resist the temptation. No dataset is perfect: you'll be missing information about some of your customers, and you'll have incorrect data about others. Some data fields will be dirty and inconsistent. If you don't take the time to examine the data before you start to model, you may find yourself redoing your work repeatedly as you discover bad data fields or variables that need to be transformed before modeling. In the worst case, you'll build a model that returns incorrect predictions—and you won't be sure why.

GET TO KNOW YOUR DATA BEFORE MODELING   By addressing data issues early, you can save yourself some unnecessary work, and a lot of headaches!

---

[1] We have a copy of this synthetic dataset available for download from https://github.com/WinVector/ PDSwR2/tree/master/Custdata, and once it's saved, you can load it into R with the command customer_data <- readRDS("custdata.RDS"). This dataset is derived from the census data that you saw in chapter 2. We have introduced a little noise to the age variable to reflect what is typically seen in real-world noisy datasets. We have also included some columns not necessarily relevant to our example scenario, but which exhibit some important data anomalies.

You'd also like to get a sense of who your customers are. Are they young, middle-aged, or seniors? How affluent are they? Where do they live? Knowing the answers to these questions can help you build a better model, because you'll have a more specific idea of what information most accurately predicts the probability of insurance coverage.

In this chapter, we'll demonstrate some ways to get to know your data, and discuss some of the potential issues that you're looking for as you explore. Data exploration uses a combination of *summary statistics*—means and medians, variances, and counts—and *visualization*, or graphs of the data. You can spot some problems just by using summary statistics; other problems are easier to find visually.

> ## Organizing data for analysis
>
> For most of this book, we'll assume that the data you're analyzing is in a single data frame. This is not how data is usually stored. In a database, for example, data is usually stored in *normalized form* to reduce redundancy: information about a single customer is spread across many small tables. In log data, data about a single customer can be spread across many log entries, or sessions. These formats make it easy to add (or, in the case of a database, modify) data, but are not optimal for analysis. You can often join all the data you need into a single table in the database using SQL, but in chapter 5, we'll discuss commands like `join` that you can use within R to further consolidate data.

3.1 Using summary statistics to spot problems

In R, you'll typically use the `summary()` command to take your first look at the data. The goal is to understand whether you have the kind of customer information that can potentially help you predict health insurance coverage, and whether the data is of good enough quality to be informative.[1]

> **Listing 3.1 The `summary()` command**

Change this to your actual path to the directory where you unpacked PDSwR2

The variable is_employed is missing for about a third of the data. The variable income has negative values, which are potentially invalid.

```
setwd("PDSwR2/Custdata")
customer_data = readRDS("custdata.RDS")
summary(customer_data)
##      custid              sex        is_employed       income
##   Length:73262      Female:37837   FALSE: 2351    Min.   :  -6900
##   Class :character   Male  :35425   TRUE :45137    1st Qu.:  10700
##   Mode  :character                  NA's :25774    Median :  26200
##                                                    Mean   :  41764
##                                                    3rd Qu.:  51700
##                                                    Max.   :1257000
##
```

---

[1] If you haven't already done so, we suggest you follow the steps in section A.1 of appendix A to install R, packages, tools, and the book examples.

```
##              marital_status   health_ins
## Divorced/Separated:10693   Mode :logical
## Married           :38400   FALSE:7307
## Never married     :19407   TRUE :65955
## Widowed           : 4762
##
##
##
##                              housing_type   recent_move        num_vehicles
## Homeowner free and clear        :16763   Mode :logical   Min.   :0.000
## Homeowner with mortgage/loan:31387   FALSE:62418   1st Qu.:1.000
## Occupied with no rent           : 1138   TRUE :9123    Median :2.000
## Rented                          :22254   NA's :1721    Mean   :2.066
## NA's                            : 1720                 3rd Qu.:3.000
##                                                        Max.   :6.000
##                                                        NA's   :1720
##       age               state_of_res        gas_usage
## Min.   :   0.00   California  : 8962   Min.   :   1.00
## 1st Qu.: 34.00   Texas       : 6026   1st Qu.:   3.00
## Median : 48.00   Florida     : 4979   Median :  10.00
## Mean   : 49.16   New York    : 4431   Mean   :  41.17
## 3rd Qu.: 62.00   Pennsylvania: 2997   3rd Qu.:  60.00
## Max.   :120.00   Illinois    : 2925   Max.   : 570.00
##                  (Other)     :42942   NA's   :1720
```

> **About 90% of the customers have health insurance.**

> **The variables housing_type, recent_move, num_vehicles, and gas_usage are each missing 1720 or 1721 values.**

> **The average value of the variable age seems plausible, but the minimum and maximum values seem unlikely. The variable state_of_res is a categorical variable; summary() reports how many customers are in each state (for the first few states).**

The summary() command on a data frame reports a variety of summary statistics on the numerical columns of the data frame, and count statistics on any categorical columns (if the categorical columns have already been read in as factors[1]).

As you see from listing 3.1, the summary of the data helps you quickly spot potential problems, like missing data or unlikely values. You also get a rough idea of how categorical data is distributed. Let's go into more detail about the typical problems that you can spot using the summary.

3.1.1 *Typical problems revealed by data summaries*

At this stage, you're looking for several common issues:

- Missing values
- Invalid values and outliers
- Data ranges that are too wide or too narrow
- The units of the data

Let's address each of these issues in detail.

---

[1] Categorical variables are of class factor in R. They can be represented as strings (class character), and some analytical functions will automatically convert string variables to factor variables. To get a useful summary of a categorical variable, it needs to be a factor.

MISSING VALUES

A few missing values may not really be a problem, but if a particular data field is largely unpopulated, it shouldn't be used as an input without some repair (as we'll discuss in section 4.1.2). In R, for example, many modeling algorithms will, by default, quietly drop rows with missing values. As you see in the following listing, all the missing values in the is_employed variable could cause R to quietly ignore more than a third of the data.

Listing 3.2   Will the variable `is_employed` be useful for modeling?

```
## is_employed
## FALSE: 2321
## TRUE :44887
## NA's :24333
```
◁── The variable is_employed is missing for more than a third of the data. Why? Is employment status unknown? Did the company start collecting employment data only recently? Does NA mean "not in the active workforce" (for example, students or stay-at-home parents)?

```
##                               housing_type   recent_move
## Homeowner free and clear    :16763         Mode :logical
## Homeowner with mortgage/loan:31387         FALSE:62418
## Occupied with no rent       : 1138         TRUE :9123
## Rented                      :22254         NA's :1721
## NA's                        : 1720
##
##
##    num_vehicles      gas_usage
## Min.   :0.000    Min.   :  1.00
## 1st Qu.:1.000    1st Qu.:  3.00
## Median :2.000    Median : 10.00
## Mean   :2.066    Mean   : 41.17
## 3rd Qu.:3.000    3rd Qu.: 60.00
## Max.   :6.000    Max.   :570.00
## NA's   :1720     NA's   :1720
```
◁── The variables housing_type, recent_move, num_vehicles, and gas_usage are missing relatively few values— about 2% of the data. It's probably safe to just drop the rows that are missing values, especially if the missing values are all in the same 1720 rows.

If a particular data field is largely unpopulated, it's worth trying to determine why; sometimes the fact that a value is missing is informative in and of itself. For example, why is the is_employed variable missing so many values? There are many possible reasons, as we noted in listing 3.2.

Whatever the reason for missing data, you must decide on the most appropriate action. Do you include a variable with missing values in your model, or not? If you decide to include it, do you drop all the rows where this field is missing, or do you convert the missing values to 0 or to an additional category? We'll discuss ways to treat missing data in chapter 4. In this example, you might decide to drop the data rows where you're missing data about housing or vehicles, since there aren't many of them. You probably don't want to throw out the data where you're missing employment information, since employment status is probably highly predictive of having health insurance; you might instead treat the NAs as a third employment category. You will likely encounter missing values when model scoring, so you should deal with them during model training.

INVALID VALUES AND OUTLIERS

Even when a column or variable isn't missing any values, you still want to check that the values that you do have make sense. Do you have any invalid values or outliers? Examples of invalid values include negative values in what should be a non-negative numeric data field (like age or income) or text where you expect numbers. Outliers are data points that fall well out of the range of where you expect the data to be. Can you spot the outliers and invalid values in the next listing?

Listing 3.3 Examples of invalid values and outliers

```
summary(customer_data$income)
##     Min. 1st Qu.  Median   Mean 3rd Qu.     Max.
##    -6900   11200   27300  42522   52000 1257000

summary(customer_data$age)
##     Min. 1st Qu.  Median   Mean 3rd Qu.     Max.
##     0.00   34.00   48.00  49.17   62.00  120.00
```

Negative values for income could indicate bad data. They might also have a special meaning, like "amount of debt." Either way, you should check how prevalent the issue is, and decide what to do. Do you drop the data with negative income? Do you convert negative values to zero?

Customers of age zero, or customers of an age greater than about 110, are outliers. They fall out of the range of expected customer values. Outliers could be data input errors. They could be special sentinel values: zero might mean "age unknown" or "refuse to state." And some of your customers might be especially long-lived.

Often, invalid values are simply bad data input. A negative number in a field like age, however, could be a *sentinel value* to designate "unknown." Outliers might also be data errors or sentinel values. Or they might be valid but unusual data points—people do occasionally live past 100.

As with missing values, you must decide the most appropriate action: drop the data field, drop the data points where this field is bad, or convert the bad data to a useful value. For example, even if you feel certain outliers are valid data, you might still want to omit them from model construction, if the outliers interfere with the model-fitting process. Generally, the goal of modeling is to make good predictions on typical cases, and a model that is highly skewed to predict a rare case correctly may not always be the best model overall.

DATA RANGE

You also want to pay attention to how much the values in the data vary. If you believe that age or income helps to predict the probability of health insurance coverage, then you should make sure there is enough variation in the age and income of your customers for you to see the relationships. Let's look at income again, in the next listing. Is the data range wide? Is it narrow?

Listing 3.4 Looking at the data range of a variable

```
summary(customer_data$income)
##    Min. 1st Qu.  Median    Mean 3rd Qu.     Max.
##   -6900   10700   26200   41764   51700 1257000
```
Income ranges from zero to over a million dollars, a very wide range.

Even ignoring negative income, the `income` variable in listing 3.4 ranges from zero to over a million dollars. That's pretty wide (though typical for income). Data that ranges over several orders of magnitude like this can be a problem for some modeling methods. We'll talk about mitigating data range issues when we talk about logarithmic transformations in chapter 4.

Data can be too narrow, too. Suppose all your customers are between the ages of 50 and 55. It's a good bet that age range wouldn't be a very good predictor of the probability of health insurance coverage for that population, since it doesn't vary much at all.

How narrow is "too narrow" for a data range?

Of course, the term *narrow* is relative. If we were predicting the ability to read for children between the ages of 5 and 10, then age probably is a useful variable as is. For data including adult ages, you may want to transform or bin ages in some way, as you don't expect a significant change in reading ability between ages 40 and 50. You should rely on information about the problem domain to judge if the data range is narrow, but a rough rule of thumb relates to the ratio of the standard deviation to the mean. If that ratio is very small, then the data isn't varying much.

We'll revisit data range in section 3.2, when we talk about examining data graphically.

One factor that determines apparent data range is the unit of measurement. To take a nontechnical example, we measure the ages of babies and toddlers in weeks or in months, because developmental changes happen at that time scale for very young children. Suppose we measured babies' ages in years. It might appear numerically that there isn't much difference between a one-year-old and a two-year-old. In reality, there's a dramatic difference, as any parent can tell you! Units can present potential issues in a dataset for another reason, as well.

UNITS

Does the income data in listing 3.5 represent hourly wages, or yearly wages in units of $1000? As a matter of fact, it's yearly wages in units of $1000, but what if it were hourly wages? You might not notice the error during the modeling stage, but down the line someone will start inputting hourly wage data into the model and get back bad predictions in return.

Listing 3.5   Checking units; mistakes can lead to spectacular errors

```
IncomeK = customer_data$income/1000
summary(IncomeK)        ◁
 ##    Min. 1st Qu.  Median    Mean 3rd Qu.     Max.
 ##   -6.90   10.70   26.20   41.76   51.70 1257.00
```

> The variable IncomeK is defined as IncomeK = customer_data$income/1000. But suppose you didn't know that. Looking only at the summary, the values could plausibly be interpreted to mean either "hourly wage" or "yearly income in units of $1000."

Are time intervals measured in days, hours, minutes, or milliseconds? Are speeds in kilometers per second, miles per hour, or knots? Are monetary amounts in dollars, thousands of dollars, or 1/100 of a penny (a customary practice in finance, where calculations are often done in fixed-point arithmetic)? This is actually something that you'll catch by checking data definitions in data dictionaries or documentation, rather than in the summary statistics; the difference between hourly wage data and annual salary in units of $1000 may not look that obvious at a casual glance. But it's still something to keep in mind while looking over the value ranges of your variables, because often you can spot when measurements are in unexpected units. Automobile speeds in knots look a lot different than they do in miles per hour.

3.2   *Spotting problems using graphics and visualization*

As you've seen, you can spot plenty of problems just by looking over the data summaries. For other properties of the data, pictures are better than text.

> *We cannot expect a small number of numerical values [summary statistics] to consistently convey the wealth of information that exists in data. Numerical reduction methods do not retain the information in the data.*
>
> —William Cleveland,
> *The Elements of Graphing Data*

Figure 3.2 shows a plot of how customer ages are distributed. We'll talk about what the y-axis of the graph means later; for now, just know that the height of the graph corresponds to how many customers in the population are of that age. As you can see, information like the peak age of distribution, the range of the data, and the presence of outliers is easier to absorb visually than it is to determine textually.

The use of graphics to examine data is called *visualization*. We try to follow William Cleveland's principles for scientific visualization. Details of specific plots aside, the key points of Cleveland's philosophy are these:

- A graphic should display as much information as it can, with the lowest possible cognitive strain to the viewer.
- Strive for clarity. Make the data stand out. Specific tips for increasing clarity include these:

- Avoid too many superimposed elements, such as too many curves in the same graphing space.
- Find the right aspect ratio and scaling to properly bring out the details of the data.
- Avoid having the data all skewed to one side or the other of your graph.
- Visualization is an iterative process. Its purpose is to answer questions about the data.

During the visualization stage, you graph the data, learn what you can, and then regraph the data to answer the questions that arise from your previous graphic. Different graphics are best suited for answering different questions. We'll look at some of them in this section.

In this book, we'll demonstrate the visualizations and graphics using the R graphing package ggplot2 (the R realization of Leland Wilkinson's *Grammar of Graphics*, Springer, 1999), as well as some prepackaged ggplot2 visualizations from the package WVPlots. You may also want to check out the ggpubr and ggstatsplot packages for more prepackaged ggplot2 graphs. And, of course, other R visualization packages, such as base graphics or the lattice package, can produce similar plots.

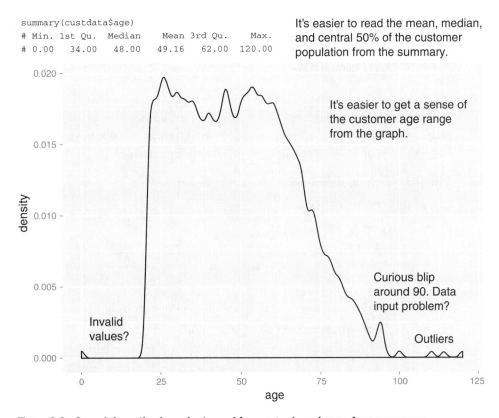

Figure 3.2 Some information is easier to read from a graph, and some from a summary.

A note on ggplot2

The theme of this section is how to use visualization to explore your data, not how to use `ggplot2`. The `ggplot2` package is based on Leland Wilkinson's book, *Grammar of Graphics*. We chose `ggplot2` because it excels at combining multiple graphical elements together, but its syntax can take some getting used to. Here are the key points to understand when looking at our code snippets:

- Graphs in `ggplot2` can only be defined on data frames. The variables in a graph—the *x* variable, the *y* variable, the variables that define the color or the size of the points—are called *aesthetics*, and are declared by using the `aes` function.
- The `ggplot()` function declares the graph object. The arguments to `ggplot()` can include the data frame of interest and the aesthetics. The `ggplot()` function doesn't itself produce a visualization; visualizations are produced by *layers*.
- Layers produce the plots and plot transformations and are added to a given graph object using the + operator. Each layer can also take a data frame and aesthetics as arguments, in addition to plot-specific parameters. Examples of layers are `geom_point` (for a scatter plot) or `geom_line` (for a line plot).

This syntax will become clearer in the examples that follow. For more information, we recommend Hadley Wickham's reference site https://ggplot2.tidyverse.org/reference/, which has pointers to online documentation; the Graphs section of Winston Chang's site http://www.cookbook-r.com/; and Winston Chang's *R Graphics Cookbook* (O'Reilly, 2012).

In the next two sections, we'll show how to use pictures and graphs to identify data characteristics and issues. In section 3.2.2, we'll look at visualizations for two variables. But let's start by looking at visualizations for single variables.

3.2.1   *Visually checking distributions for a single variable*

In this section we will look at

- Histograms
- Density plots
- Bar charts
- Dot plots

The visualizations in this section help you answer questions like these:

- What is the peak value of the distribution?
- How many peaks are there in the distribution (unimodality versus bimodality)?
- How normal (or lognormal) is the data? We'll discuss normal and lognormal distributions in appendix B.
- How much does the data vary? Is it concentrated in a certain interval or in a certain category?

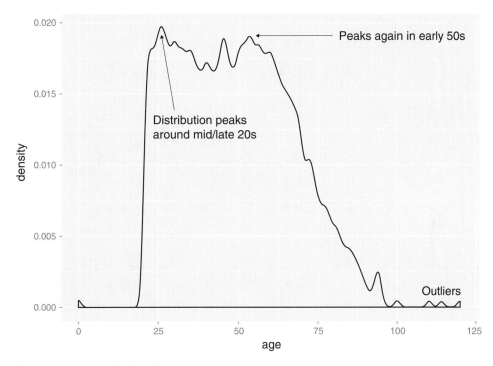

Figure 3.3 The density plot of age

One of the things that's easy to grasp visually is the shape of the data distribution. The graph in figure 3.3 is somewhat flattish between the ages of about 25 and about 60, falling off slowly after 60. However, even within this range, there seems to be a peak at around the late-20s to early 30s range, and another in the early 50s. This data has multiple peaks: it is not *unimodal*.[1]

Unimodality is a property you want to check in your data. Why? Because (roughly speaking) a unimodal distribution corresponds to one population of subjects. For the solid curve in figure 3.4, the mean customer age is about 50, and 50% of the customers are between 34 and 64 (the first and third quartiles, shown shaded). So you can say that a "typical" customer is middle-aged and probably possesses many of the demographic qualities of a middle-aged person—though, of course, you have to verify that with your actual customer information.

The dashed curve in figure 3.4 shows what can happen when you have two peaks, or a *bimodal distribution*. (A distribution with more than two peaks is *multimodal*.) This set of customers has about the same mean age as the customers represented by the solid curve—but a 50-year-old is hardly a "typical" customer! This (admittedly exaggerated)

---

[1] The strict definition of *unimodal* is that a distribution has a unique maximum value; in that sense, figure 3.3 is unimodal. However, most people use the term "unimodal" to mean that a distribution has a unique peak (local maxima); the customer age distribution has multiple peaks, and so we will call it *multimodal*.

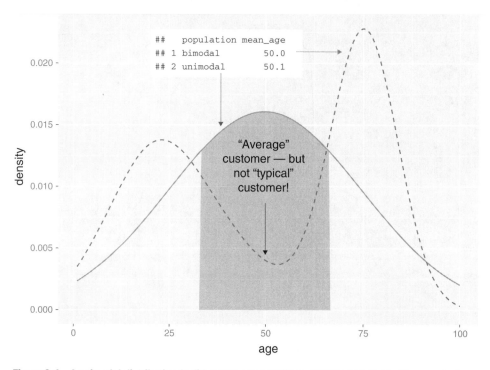

Figure 3.4   A unimodal distribution (solid curve) can usually be modeled as coming from a single population of users. With a bimodal distribution (dashed curve), your data often comes from two populations of users.

example corresponds to two populations of customers: a fairly young population mostly in their teens to late twenties, and an older population mostly in their 70s. These two populations probably have very different behavior patterns, and if you want to model whether a customer probably has health insurance or not, it wouldn't be a bad idea to model the two populations separately.

The histogram and the density plot are two visualizations that help you quickly examine the distribution of a numerical variable. Figures 3.1 and 3.3 are density plots. Whether you use histograms or density plots is largely a matter of taste. We tend to prefer density plots, but histograms are easier to explain to less quantitatively-minded audiences.

HISTOGRAMS

A basic histogram bins a variable into fixed-width buckets and returns the number of data points that fall into each bucket as a height. For example, suppose you wanted a sense of how much your customers pay in monthly gas heating bills. You could group the gas bill amounts in intervals of $10: $0–10, $10–20, $20–30, and so on. Customers at a boundary go into the higher bucket: people who pay around $20 a month go into the $20–30 bucket. For each bucket, you then count how many customers are in that bucket. The resulting histogram is shown in figure 3.5.

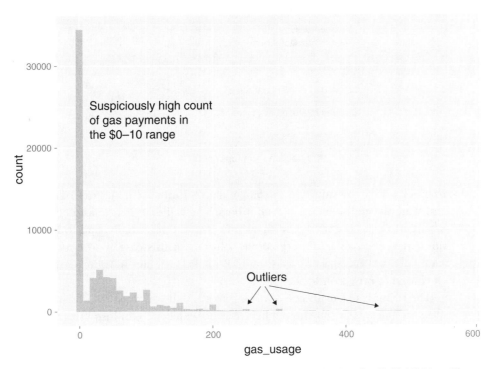

Figure 3.5 A histogram tells you where your data is concentrated. It also visually highlights outliers and anomalies.

You create the histogram in figure 3.5 in ggplot2 with the geom_histogram layer.

Listing 3.6 Plotting a histogram

```
library(ggplot2)
ggplot(customer_data, aes(x=gas_usage)) +
  geom_histogram(binwidth=10, fill="gray")
```

Load the ggplot2 library, if you haven't already done so.

The binwidth parameter tells the geom_histogram call how to make bins of $10 intervals (default is datarange/30). The fill parameter specifies the color of the histogram bars (default: black).

With the proper binwidth, histograms visually highlight where the data is concentrated, and point out the presence of potential outliers and anomalies. In figure 3.5, for example, you see that some outlier customers have much larger gas bills than is typical, so you may possibly want to drop those customers from any analysis that uses gas heating bills as an input. You also see an unusually high concentration of people who pay $0–10/month in gas. This could mean that most of your customers don't have gas heating, but on further investigation you notice this in the data dictionary (table 3.1).

Table 3.1 Data dictionary entry for `gas_usage`

Value	Definition
NA	Unknown or not applicable
001	Included in rent or condo fee
002	Included in electricity payment
003	No charge or gas not used
004-999	$4 to $999 (rounded and top-coded)

In other words, the values in the `gas_usage` column are a mixture of numerical values and symbolic codes encoded as numbers. The values 001, 002, and 003 are *sentinel values,* and to treat them as numerical values could potentially lead to incorrect conclusions in your analysis. One possible solution in this case is to convert the numeric values 1-3 into NA, and add additional Boolean variables to indicate the possible cases (included in rent/condo fee, and so on).

The primary disadvantage of histograms is that you must decide ahead of time how wide the buckets are. If the buckets are too wide, you can lose information about the shape of the distribution. If the buckets are too narrow, the histogram can look too noisy to read easily. An alternative visualization is the density plot.

DENSITY PLOTS

You can think of a *density plot* as a *continuous histogram* of a variable, except the area under the density plot is rescaled to equal one. A point on a density plot corresponds to the fraction of data (or the percentage of data, divided by 100) that takes on a particular value. This fraction is usually very small. When you look at a density plot, you're more interested in the overall shape of the curve than in the actual values on the y-axis. You've seen the density plot of age; figure 3.6 shows the density plot of income.

You produce figure 3.6 with the `geom_density` layer, as shown in the following listing.

Listing 3.7 Producing a density plot

```
library(scales)          ◁─────────────────────────────────   The scales package
                                                               brings in the dollar
ggplot(customer_data, aes(x=income)) + geom_density() +        scale notation.
    scale_x_continuous(labels=dollar)   ◁─────────
                                          Sets the x-axis
                                          labels to dollars
```

When the data range is very wide and the mass of the distribution is heavily concentrated to one side, like the distribution in figure 3.6, it's difficult to see the details of its shape. For instance, it's hard to tell the exact value where the income distribution has its peak. If the data is non-negative, then one way to bring out more detail is to plot the distribution on a logarithmic scale, as shown in figure 3.7. This is equivalent to plotting the density plot of `log10(income)`.

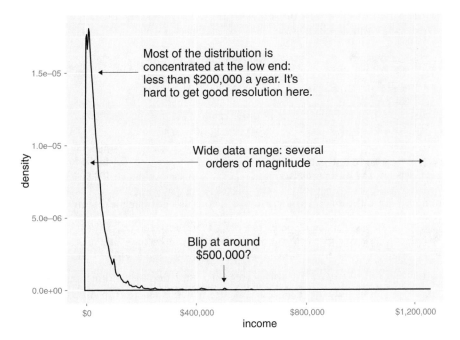

Figure 3.6 Density plots show where data is concentrated.

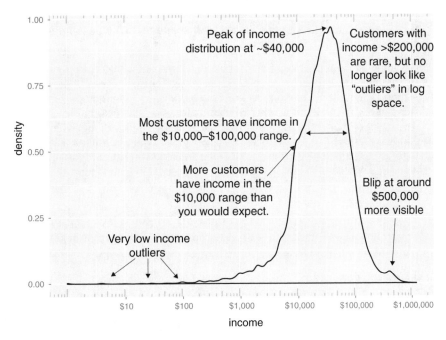

Figure 3.7 The density plot of income on a log10 scale highlights details of the income distribution that are harder to see in a regular density plot.

In ggplot2, you can plot figure 3.7 with the geom_density and scale_x_log10 layers, such as in the following listing.

Listing 3.8   Creating a log-scaled density plot

```
ggplot(customer_data, aes(x=income)) +
  geom_density() +
  scale_x_log10(breaks = c(10, 100, 1000, 10000, 100000, 1000000),
    ⮡labels=dollar) +
    annotation_logticks(sides="bt", color="gray")
```

> Sets the x-axis to be in log10 scale, with manually set tick points and labels as dollars

> Adds log-scaled tick marks to the top and bottom of the graph

When you issue the preceding command, you also get back a warning message:

```
## Warning in self$trans$transform(x): NaNs produced
## Warning: Transformation introduced infinite values in continuous x-axis
## Warning: Removed 6856 rows containing non-finite values (stat_density).
```

This tells you that ggplot2 ignored the zero- and negative-valued rows (since log(0) = Infinity), and that there were 6856 such rows. Keep that in mind when evaluating the graph.

When should you use a logarithmic scale ?

You should use a logarithmic scale when percent change, or change in orders of magnitude, is more important than changes in absolute units. You should also use a log scale to better visualize data that is heavily skewed.

For example, in income data, a difference in income of $5,000 means something very different in a population where the incomes tend to fall in the tens of thousands of dollars than it does in populations where income falls in the hundreds of thousands or millions of dollars. In other words, what constitutes a "significant difference" depends on the order of magnitude of the incomes you're looking at. Similarly, in a population like that in figure 3.7, a few people with very high income will cause the majority of the data to be compressed into a relatively small area of the graph. For both those reasons, plotting the income distribution on a logarithmic scale is a good idea.

In log space, income is distributed as something that looks like a "normalish" distribution, as will be discussed in appendix B. It's not exactly a normal distribution (in fact, it appears to be at least two normal distributions mixed together).

BAR CHARTS AND DOTPLOTS

A *bar chart* is a histogram for discrete data: it records the frequency of every value of a categorical variable. Figure 3.8 shows the distribution of marital status in your customer dataset. If you believe that marital status helps predict the probability of health insurance coverage, then you want to check that you have enough customers with different marital statuses to help you discover the relationship between being married (or not) and having health insurance.

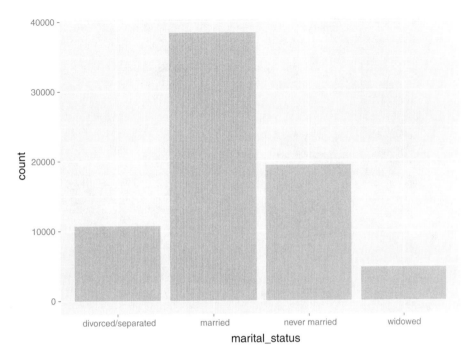

Figure 3.8   Bar charts show the distribution of categorical variables.

The ggplot2 command to produce figure 3.8 uses geom_bar:

```
ggplot(customer_data, aes(x=marital_status)) + geom_bar(fill="gray")
```

This graph doesn't really show any more information than summary(customer_data$marital.stat) would show, but some people find the graph easier to absorb than the text. Bar charts are most useful when the number of possible values is fairly large, like state of residence. In this situation, we often find that a horizontal graph like that shown in figure 3.9 is more legible than a vertical graph.

The ggplot2 command to produce figure 3.9 is shown in the next listing.

Listing 3.9   Producing a horizontal bar chart

```
ggplot(customer_data, aes(x=state_of_res)) +
   geom_bar(fill="gray") +        ⊲
      coord_flip()    ⊲
```

Plots bar chart as before: state_of_res is on x-axis, count is on y-axis

Flips the x and y axes: state_of_res is now on the y-axis

Cleveland[1] prefers the *dot plot* to the bar chart for visualizing discrete counts. This is because bars are two dimensional, so that a difference in counts looks like a difference

---

[1] See William S. Cleveland, *The Elements of Graphing Data*, Hobart Press, 1994.

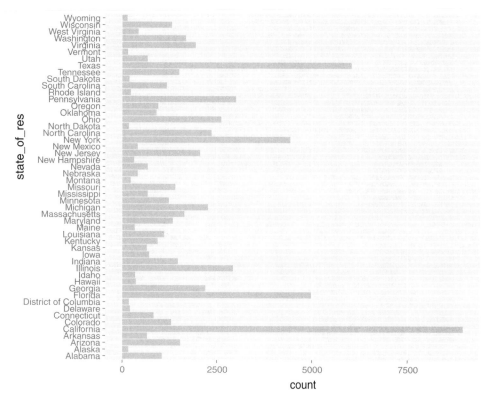

Figure 3.9   A horizontal bar chart can be easier to read when there are several categories with long names.

in bar *areas*, rather than merely in bar heights. This can be perceptually misleading. Since the dot-and-line of a dot plot is not two dimensional, the viewer considers only the height difference when comparing two quantities, as they should.

Cleveland also recommends that the data in a bar chart or dot plot be sorted, to more efficiently extract insight from the data. This is shown in figure 3.10. Now it is easy to see in which states the most customers—or the fewest—live.

A sorted visualization requires a bit more manipulation, at least in `ggplot2`, because by default, `ggplot2` will plot the categories of a factor variable in alphabetical order. Fortunately, much of the code is already wrapped in the `ClevelandDotPlot` function from the `WVPlots` package.

Listing 3.10   Producing a dot plot with sorted categories

```
library(WVPlots)                          ⟵──────────────  Loads the WVPlots library
ClevelandDotPlot(customer_data, "state_of_res",   ⟵┐
    sort = 1, title="Customers by state") +   ⟵──┐│
 ▷ coord_flip()                                  ││   Plots the state_of_res
                                                 ││   column of the
                                                 ││   customer_data data frame
```

Flips the axes as before ⟶

"sort = 1" sorts the categories in increasing order (most frequent last).

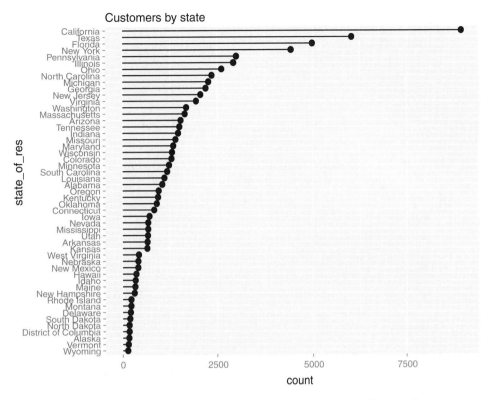

Figure 3.10   **Using a dot plot and sorting by count makes the data even easier to read.**

Before we move on to visualizations for two variables, we'll summarize the visualizations that we've discussed in this section in table 3.2.

Table 3.2   **Visualizations for one variable**

Graph type	Uses	Examples
Histogram or density plot	Examine data range Check number of modes Check if distribution is normal/ lognormal Check for anomalies and outliers	Examine the distribution of customer age to get the typical customer age range Examine the distribution of customer income to get typical income range
Bar chart or dot plot	Compare frequencies of the values of a categorical variable	Count the number of customers from different states of residence to determine which states have the largest or smallest customer base

3.2.2 *Visually checking relationships between two variables*

In addition to examining variables in isolation, you'll often want to look at the relationship between two variables. For example, you might want to answer questions like these:

- Is there a relationship between the two inputs *age* and *income* in my data?
- If so, what kind of relationship, and how strong?
- Is there a relationship between the input *marital status* and the output *health insurance*? How strong?

You'll precisely quantify these relationships during the modeling phase, but exploring them now gives you a feel for the data and helps you determine which variables are the best candidates to include in a model.

This section explores the following visualizations:

- Line plots and scatter plots for comparing two continuous variables
- Smoothing curves and hexbin plots for comparing two continuous variables at high volume
- Different types of bar charts for comparing two discrete variables
- Variations on histograms and density plots for comparing a continuous and discrete variable

First, let's consider the relationship between two continuous variables. The first plot you might think of (though it's not always the best) is the line plot.

LINE PLOTS

Line plots work best when the relationship between two variables is relatively clean: each *x* value has a unique (or nearly unique) *y* value, as in figure 3.11. You plot figure 3.11 with `geom_line`.

> **Listing 3.11 Producing a line plot**

```
x <- runif(100)              The y variable is a
y <- x^2 + 0.2*x       ◁─── quadratic function of x.
ggplot(data.frame(x=x,y=y), aes(x=x,y=y)) + geom_line()   ◁─────── Plots the line plot
```

**First, generate the data for this example. The
x variable is uniformly randomly distributed
between 0 and 1.**

When the data is not so cleanly related, line plots aren't as useful; you'll want to use the scatter plot instead, as you'll see in the next section.

SCATTER PLOTS AND SMOOTHING CURVES

You'd expect there to be a relationship between age and health insurance, and also a relationship between income and health insurance. But what is the relationship between age and income? If they track each other perfectly, then you might not want

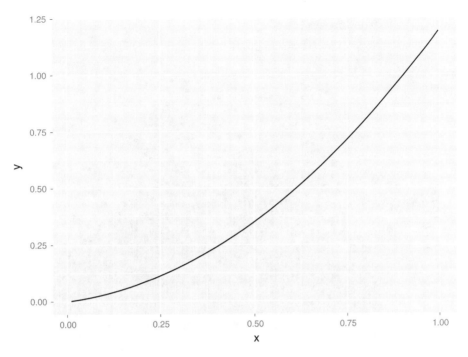

Figure 3.11 Example of a line plot

to use both variables in a model for health insurance. The appropriate summary statistic is the correlation, which we compute on a safe subset of our data.

Listing 3.12 Examining the correlation between age and income

```
customer_data2 <- subset(customer_data,                    Only consider a subset of
                 0 < age & age < 100 &                     data with reasonable age
                 0 < income & income < 200000)  ◁          and income values.

cor(customer_data2$age, customer_data2$income)  ◁          Gets correlation of
  ## [1] 0.005766697   ◁          Resulting correlation is  age and income
                                  positive but nearly zero.
```

The correlation is positive, as you might expect, but nearly zero, meaning there is apparently not much relation between age and income. A visualization gives you more insight into what's going on than a single number can. Let's try a scatter plot first (figure 3.12). Because our dataset has over 64,000 rows, which is too large for a legible scatterplot, we will sample the dataset down before plotting. You plot figure 3.12 with geom_point, as shown in listig 3.13.

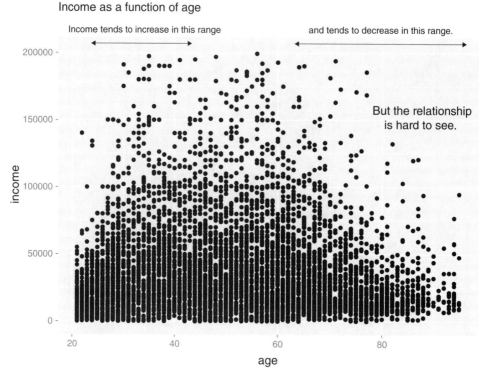

Figure 3.12   A scatter plot of income versus age

```
set.seed(245566)
customer_data_samp <-
    dplyr::sample_frac(customer_data2, size=0.1, replace=FALSE)

ggplot(customer_data_samp, aes(x=age, y=income)) +
    geom_point() +
    ggtitle("Income as a function of age")
```

Make the random sampling reproducible by setting the random seed.

Creates the scatterplot

For legibility, only plot a 10% sample of the data. We will show how to plot all the data in a following section.

The relationship between age and income isn't easy to see. You can try to make the relationship clearer by also plotting a smoothing curve through the data, as shown in figure 3.13.

The smoothing curve makes it easier to see that in this population, income tends to increase with age from a person's twenties until their mid-thirties, after which income

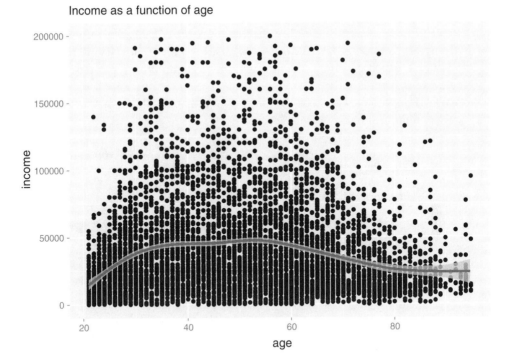

Figure 3.13   A scatter plot of income versus age, with a smoothing curve

increases at a slower, almost flat, rate until about a person's mid-fifties. Past the mid-fifties, income tends to decrease with age.

In ggplot2, you can plot a smoothing curve to the data by using geom_smooth :

```
ggplot(customer_data_samp, aes(x=age, y=income)) +
  geom_point() + geom_smooth() +
  ggtitle("Income as a function of age")
```

For datasets with a small number of points, the geom_smooth function uses the loess (or lowess) function to calculate smoothed local linear fits of the data. For larger datasets, like this one, geom_smooth uses a spline fit.

By default, geom_smooth also plots a "standard error" ribbon around the smoothing curve. This ribbon is wider where there are fewer data points and narrower where the data is dense. It's meant to indicate where the smoothing curve estimate is more uncertain. For the plot in figure 3.13, the scatterplot is so dense that the smoothing ribbon isn't visible, except at the extreme right of the graph. Since the scatterplot already gives you the same information that the standard error ribbon does, you can turn it off with the argument se=FALSE, as we will see in a later example.

A scatter plot with a smoothing curve also makes a useful visualization of the relationship between a continuous variable and a Boolean. Suppose you're considering using age as an input to your health insurance model. You might want to plot health insurance coverage as a function of age, as shown in figure 3.14.

The variable `health_ins` has the value `1` (for TRUE) when the person has health insurance, and `0` (for FALSE) otherwise. A scatterplot of the data will have all the y-values at `0` or `1`, which may not seem informative, but a smoothing curve of the data estimates the average value of the `0/1` variable `health_ins` as a function of age. The average value of `health_ins` for a given age is simply the probability that a person of that age in your dataset has health insurance.

Figure 3.14 shows you that the probability of having health insurance increases as customer age increases, from about 80% at age 20 to nearly 100% after about age 75.

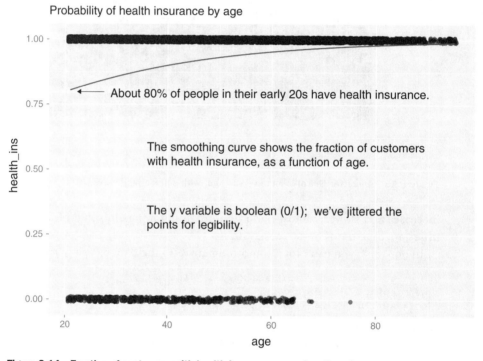

Figure 3.14   Fraction of customers with health insurance, as a function of age

Why keep the scatterplot?

You might ask, why bother to plot the points? Why not just plot the smoothing curve? After all, the data only takes on the values `0` and `1`, so the scatterplot doesn't seem informative.

> This is a matter of taste, but we like to keep the scatterplot because it gives us a visual estimate of how much data there is in different ranges of the x variable. For example, if your data has only a dozen or so customers in the 70–100 age range, then you know that estimates of the probability of health insurance in that age range may not be very good. Conversely, if you have hundreds of customers spread over that age range, then you can have more confidence in the estimate.
>
> The standard error ribbon that `geom_smooth` plots around the smoothing curve gives equivalent information, but we find the scatterplot more helpful.

An easy way to plot figure 3.14 is with the `BinaryYScatterPlot` function from WVPlots:

```
BinaryYScatterPlot(customer_data_samp, "age", "health_ins",
                title = "Probability of health insurance by age")
```

By default, `BinaryYScatterPlot` fits a logistic regression curve through the data. You will learn more about logistic regression in chapter 8, but for now just know that a logistic regression tries to estimate the probability that the Boolean outcome y is true, as a function of the data x.

If you tried to plot all the points from the `customer_data2` dataset, the scatter plot would turn into an illegible smear. To plot all the data in higher volume situations like this, try an aggregated plot, like a hexbin plot.

HEXBIN PLOTS

A *hexbin plot* is like a two-dimensional histogram. The data is divided into bins, and the number of data points in each bin is represented by color or shading. Let's go back to the income versus age example. Figure 3.15 shows a hexbin plot of the data. Note how the smoothing curve traces out the shape formed by the densest region of data.

To make a hexbin plot in R, you must have the `hexbin` package installed. We'll discuss how to install R packages in appendix A. Once `hexbin` is installed and the library loaded, you create the plots using the `geom_hex` layer, or use the convenience function `HexBinPlot` from WVPlots, as we do here. `HexBinPlot` predefines a color scale where denser cells are colored darker; the default `ggplot2` color scale colors denser cells lighter.

Listing 3.14   Producing a hexbin plot

```
library(WVPlots)   ◁————— Loads the WVPlots library

HexBinPlot(customer_data2, "age", "income", "Income as a function of age") +
    geom_smooth(color="black", se=FALSE)   ◁—┐ Adds the smoothing line in
                                              │ black; suppresses standard
                                              │ error ribbon (se=FALSE)
```

Plots the hexbin of income
as a function of age

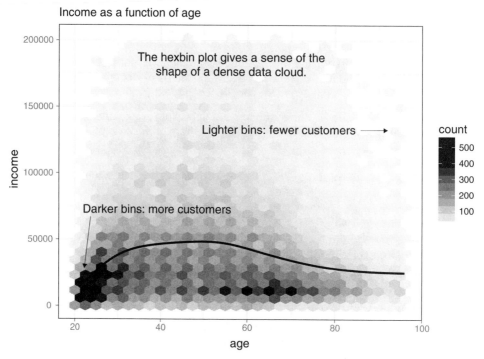

Figure 3.15   Hexbin plot of income versus age, with a smoothing curve superimposed

In this section and the previous section, we've looked at plots where at least one of the variables is numerical. But in our health insurance example, the output is categorical, and so are many of the input variables. Next we'll look at ways to visualize the relationship between two categorical variables.

BAR CHARTS FOR TWO CATEGORICAL VARIABLES

Let's examine the relationship between marital status and the probability of health insurance coverage. The most straightforward way to visualize this is with a *stacked bar chart*, as shown in figure 3.16.

The stacked bar chart makes it easy to compare the total number of people in each marital category, and to compare the number of uninsured people in each marital category. However, you can't directly compare the number of insured people in each category, because the bars don't all start at the same level. So some people prefer the *side-by-side bar chart*, shown in figure 3.17, which makes it easier to compare the number of both insured and uninsured across categories—but not the total number of people in each category.

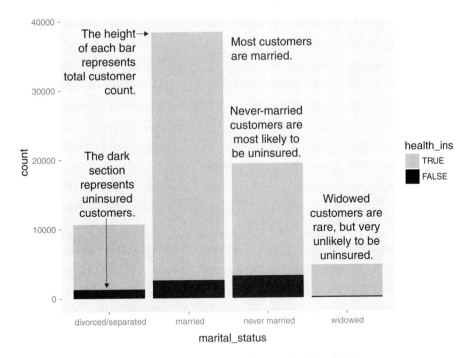

Figure 3.16 Health insurance versus marital status: stacked bar chart

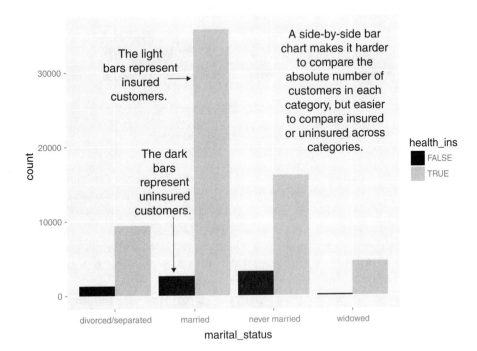

Figure 3.17 Health insurance versus marital status: side-by-side bar chart

If you want to compare the number of insured and uninsured people across categories, while keeping a sense of the total number of people in each category, one plot to try is what we call a *shadow plot*. A shadow plot of this data creates two graphs, one for the insured population and one for the uninsured population. Both graphs are superimposed against a "shadow graph" of the total population. This allows comparison both across and within marital status categories, while maintaining information about category totals. This is shown in figure 3.18.

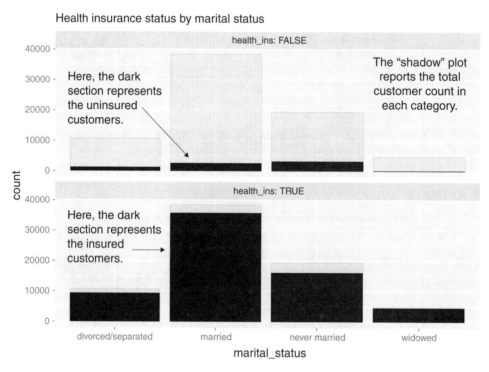

Figure 3.18   Health insurance versus marital status: shadow plot

The main shortcoming of all the preceding charts is that you can't easily compare the ratios of insured to uninsured across categories, especially for rare categories like Widowed. You can use what ggplot2 calls a *filled bar chart* to plot a visualization of the ratios directly, as in figure 3.19.

The filled bar chart makes it obvious that divorced customers are slightly more likely to be uninsured than married ones. But you've lost the information that being widowed, though highly predictive of insurance coverage, is a rare category.

Which bar chart you use depends on what information is most important for you to convey. The code to generate each of these plots is given next. Note the use of the fill aesthetic in the ggplot2 commands; this tells ggplot2 to color (fill) the bars

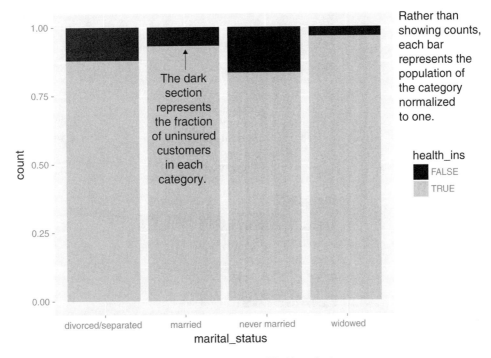

Figure 3.19 Health insurance versus marital status: filled bar chart

according to the value of the variable health_ins. The position argument to geom_bar specifies the bar chart style.

```
ggplot(customer_data, aes(x=marital_status, fill=health_ins)) +
                    geom_bar()    ⟵———————— Stacked bar chart, the default

ggplot(customer_data, aes(x=marital_status, fill=health_ins)) +
                geom_bar(position = "dodge") ⟵——————— Side-by-side bar chart

ShadowPlot(customer_data, "marital_status", "health_ins",
                    title = "Health insurance status by marital status") ⟵┐
ggplot(customer_data, aes(x=marital_status, fill=health_ins)) +
                    geom_bar(position = "fill")  ⟵┐
```

**Uses the ShadowPlot
command from the WVPlots
Filled bar chart   package for the shadow plot**

In the preceding examples, one of the variables was binary; the same plots can be applied to two variables that each have several categories, but the results are harder to read. Suppose you're interested in the distribution of marriage status across housing types. Some find the side-by-side bar chart easiest to read in this situation, but it's not perfect, as you see in figure 3.20.

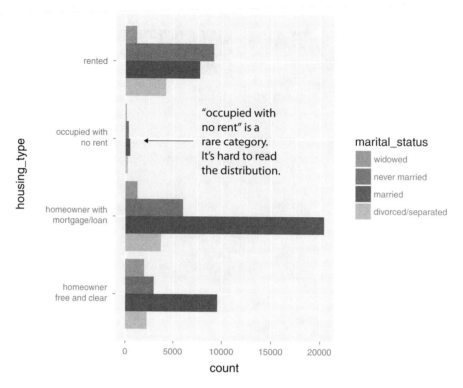

Figure 3.20   Distribution of marital status by housing type: side-by-side bar chart

A graph like figure 3.20 gets cluttered if either of the variables has a large number of categories. A better alternative is to break the distributions into different graphs, one for each housing type. In ggplot2 this is called *faceting* the graph, and you use the facet_wrap layer. The result is shown in figure 3.21.

The code for figures 3.20 and 3.21 looks like the next listing.

Listing 3.16   Plotting a bar chart with and without facets

Side-by-side bar chart

```
cdata <- subset(customer_data, !is.na(housing_type))
ggplot(cdata, aes(x=housing_type, fill=marital_status)) +
   geom_bar(position = "dodge") +
   scale_fill_brewer(palette = "Dark2") +
   coord_flip()
```

Restricts to the data where housing_type is known

The faceted bar chart

```
ggplot(cdata, aes(x=marital_status)) +
   geom_bar(fill="darkgray") +
   facet_wrap(~housing_type, scale="free_x") +
   coord_flip()
```

Uses coord_flip () to rotate the graph so that marital_status is legible

Uses coord_flip() to rotate the graph

Facets the graph by housing.type. The scales="free_x" argument specifies that each facet has an independently scaled x-axis; the default is that all facets have the same scales on both axes. The argument "free_y" would free the y-axis scaling, and the argument "free" frees both axes.

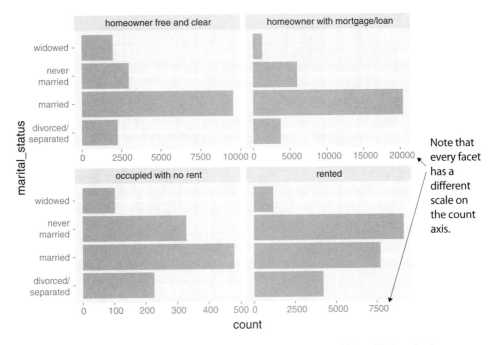

Figure 3.21　**Distribution of marital status by housing type: faceted side-by-side bar chart**

COMPARING A CONTINUOUS AND CATEGORICAL VARIABLE

Suppose you want to compare the age distributions of people of different marital statuses in your data. You saw in section 3.2.1 that you can use histograms or density plots to look at the distribution of continuous variables like age. Now you want multiple distribution plots: one for each category of marital status. The most straightforward way to do this is to superimpose these plots in the same graph.

Figure 3.22 compares the age distributions of the widowed (dashed line) and never married (solid line) populations in the data. You can quickly see that the two populations are distributed quite differently: the widowed population skews older, and the never married population skews younger.

The code to produce figure 3.22 is as follows.

Listing 3.17　Comparing population densities across categories

```
customer_data3 = subset(customer_data2, marital_status %in%
    c("Never married", "Widowed"))
ggplot(customer_data3, aes(x=age, color=marital_status,
    linetype=marital_status)) +
    geom_density() + scale_color_brewer(palette="Dark2")
```

Restricts to the data for widowed or never married people

Differentiates the color and line style of the plots by marital_status

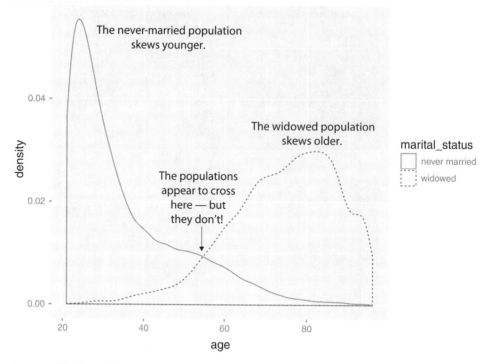

Figure 3.22   Comparing the distribution of marital status for widowed and never married populations

Overlaid density plots give you good information about distribution shape: where populations are dense and where they are sparse, whether the populations are separated or overlap. However, they lose information about the relative size of each population. This is because each individual density plot is scaled to have unit area. This has the advantage of improving the legibility of each individual distribution, but can fool you into thinking that all the populations are about the same size. In fact, the superimposed density plots in figure 3.22 can also fool you into thinking that the widowed population becomes greater than the never married population after age 55, which is actually not true.

To retain information about the relative size of each population, use histograms. Histograms don't superimpose well, so you can use the `facet_wrap()` command with `geom_histogram()`, as you saw with bar charts in listing 3.16. You can also produce a histogram version of the shadow plot, using the `ShadowHist()` function from `WVPlots`, as shown next.

Listing 3.18 Comparing population densities across categories with `ShadowHist()`

```
ShadowHist(customer_data3, "age", "marital_status",
  "Age distribution for never married vs. widowed populations", binwidth=5)
```

Sets the bin widths of the histogram to 5

The result is shown in figure 3.23. Now you can see that the widowed population is quite small, and doesn't exceed the never married population until after about age 65—10 years later than the crossover point in figure 3.22.

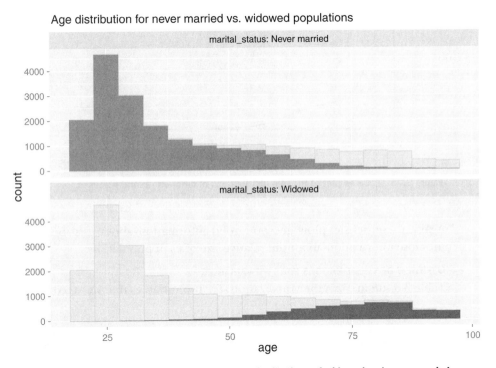

Figure 3.23 `ShadowHist` comparison of the age distributions of widowed and never married populations

You should also use faceting when comparing distributions across more than two categories, because too many overlaid plots are hard to read. Try examining the age distributions for all four categories of marital status; the plot is shown in figure 3.24.

```
ggplot(customer_data2, aes(x=age)) +
  geom_density() + facet_wrap(~marital_status)
```

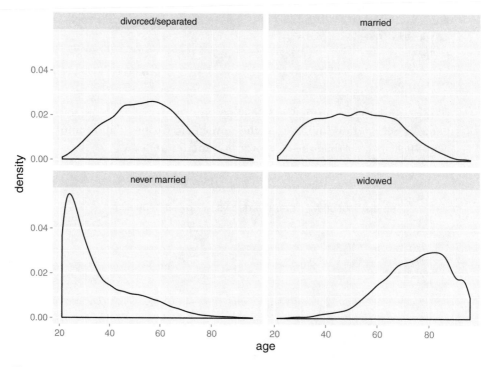

Figure 3.24   Faceted plot of the age distributions of different marital statuses

Again, these density plots give you good information about distribution shape, but they lose information about the relative size of each population.

OVERVIEW OF VISUALIZATIONS FOR TWO VARIABLES

Table 3.3 summarizes the visualizations for two variables that we've covered.

Table 3.3   Visualizations for two variables

Graph type	Uses	Examples
Line plot	Shows the relationship between two continuous variables. Best when that relationship is functional, or nearly so.	Plot $y = f(x)$.
Scatter plot	Shows the relationship between two continuous variables. Best when the relationship is too loose or cloud-like to be easily seen on a line plot.	Plot income vs. years in the work-force (income on the y-axis).

Table 3.3 Visualizations for two variables *(continued)*

Graph type	Uses	Examples
Smoothing curve	Shows underlying "average" relationship, or trend, between two continuous variables. Can also be used to show the relationship between a continuous and a binary or Boolean variable: the fraction of `true` values of the discrete variable as a function of the continuous variable.	Estimate the "average" relationship of income to years in the workforce.
Hexbin plot	Shows the relationship between two continuous variables when the data is very dense.	Plot income vs. years in the workforce for a large population.
Stacked bar chart	Shows the relationship between two categorical variables (`var1` and `var2`). Highlights the frequencies of each value of `var1`. Works best when `var2` is binary.	Plot insurance coverage (`var2`) as a function of marital status (`var1`) when you wish to retain information about the number of people in each marital category.
Side-by-side bar chart	Shows the relationship between two categorical variables (`var1` and `var2`). Good for comparing the frequencies of each value of `var2` across the values of `var1`. Works best when `var2` is binary.	Plot insurance coverage (`var2`) as a function of marital status (`var1`) when you wish to directly compare the number of insured and uninsured people in each marital category.
Shadow plot	Shows the relationship between two categorical variables (`var1` and `var2`). Displays the frequency of each value of `var1`, while allowing comparison of `var2` values both within and across the categories of `var1`.	Plot insurance coverage (`var2`) as a function of marital status (`var1`) when you wish to directly compare the number of insured and uninsured people in each marital category *and* still retain information about the total number of people in each marital category.
Filled bar chart	Shows the relationship between two categorical variables (`var1` and `var2`). Good for comparing the relative frequencies of each value of `var2` within each value of `var1`. Works best when `var2` is binary.	Plot insurance coverage (`var2`) as a function of marital status (`var1`) when you wish to compare the *ratio* of uninsured to insured people in each marital category.
Bar chart with faceting	Shows the relationship between two categorical variables (`var1` and `var2`). Best for comparing the relative frequencies of each value of `var2` within each value of `var1` when `var2` takes on more than two values.	Plot the distribution of marital status (`var2`) as a function of housing type (`var1`).

Table 3.3   Visualizations for two variables *(continued)*

Graph type	Uses	Examples
Overlaid density plot	Compares the distribution of a continuous variable over different values of a categorical variable. Best when the categorical variable has only two or three categories. Shows whether the continuous variable is distributed differently or similarly across the categories.	Compare the age distribution of married vs. divorced populations.
Faceted density plot	Compares the distribution of a continuous variable over different values of a categorical variable. Suitable for categorical variables with more than three or so categories. Shows whether the continuous variable is distributed differently or similarly across the categories.	Compare the age distribution of several marital statuses (never married, married, divorced, widowed).
Faceted histogram or shadow histogram	Compares the distribution of a continuous variable over different values of a categorical variable while retaining information about the relative population sizes.	Compare the age distribution of several marital statuses (never married, married, divorced, widowed), while retaining information about relative population sizes.

There are many other variations and visualizations you could use to explore the data; the preceding set covers some of the most useful and basic graphs. You should try different kinds of graphs to get different insights from the data. It's an interactive process. One graph will raise questions that you can try to answer by replotting the data again, with a different visualization.

Eventually, you'll explore your data enough to get a sense of it and to spot most major problems and issues. In the next chapter, we'll discuss some ways to address common problems that you may discover in the data.

Summary

At this point, you've gotten a feel for your data. You've explored it through summaries and visualizations; you now have a sense of the quality of your data, and of the relationships among your variables. You've caught and are ready to correct several kinds of data issues—although you'll likely run into more issues as you progress.

Maybe some of the things you've discovered have led you to reevaluate the question you're trying to answer, or to modify your goals. Maybe you've decided that you need more or different types of data to achieve your goals. This is all good. As we mentioned in the previous chapter, the data science process is made of loops within loops. The data exploration and data cleaning stages (we'll discuss cleaning in the next chapter) are two of the more time-consuming—and also the most important—stages of the process. Without good data, you can't build good models. Time you spend here is time you don't waste elsewhere.

In the next chapter, we'll talk about fixing the issues that you've discovered in the data.

In this chapter you have learned

- Take the time to examine and understand your data before diving into the modeling.
- The summary command helps you spot issues with data range, units, data type, and missing or invalid values.
- The various visualization techniques have different benefits and applications.
- Visualization is an iterative process and helps answer questions about the data. Information you learn from one visualization may lead to more questions—that you might try to answer with another visualization. If one visualization doesn't work, try another. Time spent here is time not wasted during the modeling process.

Managing data 4

This chapter covers

- Fixing data quality problems
- Transforming data before modeling
- Organizing your data for the modeling process

In chapter 3, you learned how to explore your data and how to identify common data issues. In this chapter, you'll see how to fix the data issues that you've discovered. After that, we'll talk about transforming and organizing the data for the modeling process. Most of the examples in this chapter use the same customer data that you used in the previous chapter.[1]

As shown in the mental model (figure 4.1), this chapter again emphasizes the science of managing the data in a statistically valid way, prior to the model-building step.

4.1 Cleaning data

In this section, we'll address issues that you discovered during the data exploration/visualization phase, in particular, invalid and missing values. Missing values in data happen quite commonly, and the way you treat them is generally the same

---

[1] The data can be loaded by saving the file custdata.RDS from https://github.com/WinVector/PDSwR2/tree/master/Custdata and then running `readRDS("custdata.RDS")` in R.

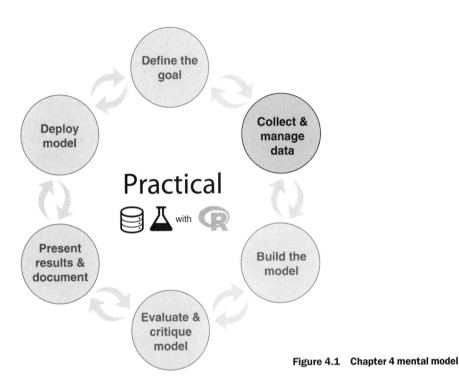

Figure 4.1   Chapter 4 mental model

from project to project. Handling invalid values is often *domain-specific*: which values are invalid, and what you do about them, depends on the problem that you are trying to solve.

> **Example**   *Suppose you have a numeric variable called* credit_score. *Domain knowledge will tell you what the valid range for that variable should be. If the credit score is supposed to be a customer's "classic FICO score," then any value outside the range 300–850 should be treated as invalid. Other types of credit scores will have different ranges of valid values.*

We'll look at an example of domain-specific data cleaning first.

4.1.1   Domain-specific data cleaning

From our data exploration in the previous chapter, we know of some issues with our data:

- The variable gas_usage mixes numeric and symbolic data: values greater than 3 are monthly gas_bills, but values from 1 to 3 are special codes. In addition, gas_usage has some missing values.
- The variable age has the problematic value 0, which probably means that the age is unknown. In addition, there are a few customers with ages older than 100

years, which may also be an error. However, for this project, we'll treat the value 0 as invalid, and assume ages older than 100 years are valid.

- The variable income has negative values. We'll assume for this discussion that those values are invalid.

These sorts of issues are quite common. In fact, most of the preceding problems were already in the actual census data that our notional customer data example is based on.

A quick way to treat the age and income variables is to convert the invalid values to NA, as if they were missing variables. You can then treat the NAs using the automatic missing-value treatment discussed in section 4.1.2.[2]

Listing 4.1   Treating the age and income variables

```
library(dplyr)
customer_data = readRDS("custdata.RDS")    ◁────── Loads the data

customer_data <- customer_data %>%
    mutate(age = na_if(age, 0),
           income = ifelse(income < 0, NA, income))  ◁─┐
```

The function mutate() from the dplyr package adds columns to a data frame, or modifies existing columns. The function na_if (), also from dplyr, turns a specific problematic value (in this case, 0) to NA.

Converts negative incomes to NA

The gas_usage variable has to be treated specially. Recall from chapter 3 that the values 1, 2, and 3 aren't numeric values, but codes:

- The value 1 means "Gas bill included in rent or condo fee."
- The value 2 means "Gas bill included in electricity payment."
- The value 3 means "No charge or gas not used."

One way to treat gas_usage is to convert all the special codes (1, 2, 3) to NA, and to add three new *indicator variables*, one for each code. For example, the indicator variable gas_with_electricity will have the value 1 (or TRUE) whenever the original gas_usage variable had the value 2, and the value 0 otherwise. In the following listing, you will create the three new indicator variables, gas_with_rent, gas_with_electricity, and no_gas_bill.

Listing 4.2   Treating the gas_usage variable

```
customer_data <- customer_data %>%
    mutate(gas_with_rent = (gas_usage == 1),
           gas_with_electricity = (gas_usage == 2),
           no_gas_bill = (gas_usage == 3) ) %>%
    mutate(gas_usage = ifelse(gas_usage < 4, NA, gas_usage))  ◁─┘
```

Creates the three indicator variables

Converts the special codes in the gas_usage column to NA

---

[2] If you haven't already done so, we suggest you follows the steps in section A.1 of appendix A to install R, packages, tools, and the book examples.

4.1.2 Treating missing values

Let's take another look at some of the variables with missing values in our customer dataset from the previous chapter. One way to find these variables programmatically is to count how many missing values are in each column of the customer data frame, and look for the columns where that count is greater than zero. The next listing counts the number of missing values in each column of the dataset.

> **Listing 4.3 Counting the missing values in each variable**

```
count_missing = function(df) {
    sapply(df, FUN=function(col) sum(is.na(col)) )      ◁────┐   Defines a function that counts
}                                                             the number of NAs in each
                                                              column of a data frame

nacounts <- count_missing(customer_data)          ┐   Applies the function to customer_data,
hasNA = which(nacounts > 0)           ◁───────────┤   identifies which columns have missing
nacounts[hasNA]                                   ┘   values, and prints the columns and counts

##        is_employed              income          housing_type
##              25774                  45                  1720
##        recent_move         num_vehicles                   age
##               1721                 1720                    77
##          gas_usage       gas_with_rent  gas_with_electricity
##              35702                 1720                  1720
##        no_gas_bill
##               1720
```

Fundamentally, there are two things you can do with these variables: drop the rows with missing values, or convert the missing values to a meaningful value. For variables like income or age that have very few missing values relative to the size of the data (customer_data has 73,262 rows), it could be safe to drop the rows. It wouldn't be safe to drop rows from variables like is_employed or gas_usage, where a large fraction of the values is missing.

In addition, remember that many modeling algorithms in R (and in other languages) will quietly drop rows that have missing values. So if you have wide data, and many columns have missing values, it may not be safe to drop rows with missing values. This is because the fraction of rows with at least one missing value can be high in that situation, and you can lose most of your data, as figure 4.2 shows. So for this discussion, we will convert all the missing values to meaningful values.

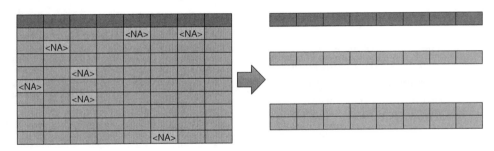

Figure 4.2 Even a few missing values can lose all your data.

MISSING DATA IN CATEGORICAL VARIABLES

When the variable with missing values is categorical, an easy solution is to create a new category for the variable, called, for instance, `missing` or `_invalid_`. This is shown schematically for the variable `housing_type` in figure 4.3.

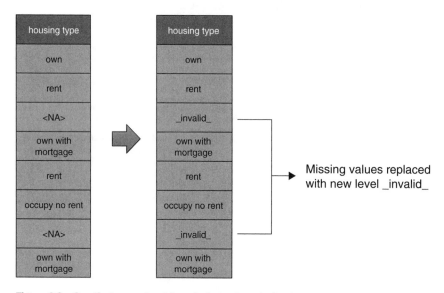

Figure 4.3   Creating a new level for missing categorical values

MISSING VALUES IN NUMERIC OR LOGICAL VARIABLES

Suppose your income variable were missing substantial data, as in figure 4.4. You believe that income is still an important predictor of the probability of health insurance coverage, so you still want to use the variable. What do you do? This can depend on *why* you think the data is missing.

THE NATURE OF MISSING VALUES

You might believe that the data is missing because the data collection failed at random, independent of the situation and of the other values. In this case, you can replace the missing values with a "reasonable estimate," or *imputed value.* Statistically, one commonly used estimate is the expected, or mean, income, as shown in figure 4.5.

Assuming that the customers with missing income are distributed the same way as the others, replacing missing values with the mean will be correct on average. It's also an easy fix to implement.

income
80,000
270,000
<NA>
50,000
54,000
<NA>
<NA>
80,000
68,400
42,000
<NA>
<NA>
<NA>
80,000

Figure 4.4   Income data with missing values

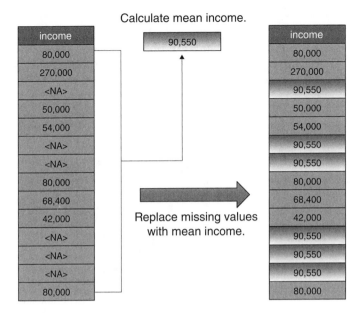

Figure 4.5 Replacing missing values with the mean

You can improve this estimate when you remember that income is related to other variables in your data—for instance, you know from your data exploration in the previous chapter that there's a relationship between age and income. There might be a relationship between state of residence or marital status and income, as well. If you have this information, you can use it. The method of imputing a missing value of an input variable based on the other input variables can be applied to categorical data, as well.[3]

It's important to remember that replacing missing values by the mean, as well as other more sophisticated methods for imputing missing values, assumes that the customers with missing income are in some sense typical. It's possible that the customers with missing income data are *systematically* different from the others. For instance, it could be the case that the customers with missing income information truly have no income, because they are full-time students or stay-at-home spouses or otherwise not in the active workforce. If this is so, then "filling in" their income information by using one of the preceding methods is an insufficient treatment, and may lead to false conclusions.

---

[3] The text *R in Action*, Second Edition (Robert Kabacoff, 2014, http://mng.bz/ybS4) includes an extensive discussion of several value imputation methods available in R.

TREATING MISSING VALUES AS INFORMATION

You still need to replace the NAs with a stand-in value, perhaps the mean. But the modeling algorithm should know that these values are possibly different from the others. A trick that has worked well for us is to replace the NAs with the mean, and add an additional indicator variable to keep track of which data points have been altered. This is shown in figure 4.6.

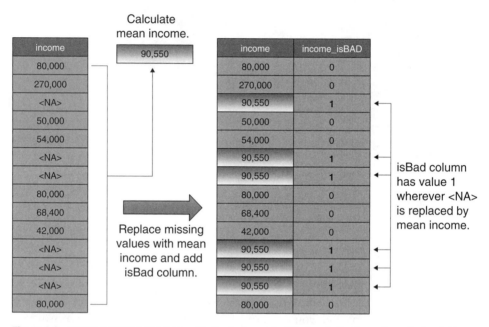

Figure 4.6   Replacing missing values with the mean and adding an indicator column to track the altered values

The income_isBAD variable lets you differentiate the two kinds of values in the data: the ones that you are about to add, and the ones that were already there.

You've seen a variation of this approach already, in another example of systematic missing values: the gas_usage variable. Most of the customers with missing gas_usage values aren't random: they either pay for gas together with another bill, such as electricity or rent, or they don't use gas. You identified those customers by adding additional indicator variables: no_gas_bill, gas_with_rent, and so on. Now you can fill in the "missing" values in gas_usage with a stand-in value, such as zero, or the average value of gas_usage.

The idea is that at the modeling step, you give all the variables—income, income_isBAD, gas_usage, no_gas_bill, and so on—to the modeling algorithm, and it can determine how to best use the information to make predictions. If the missing values really are missing randomly, then the indicator variables that you added are uninformative, and the model should ignore them. If the missing values are missing systematically, then the indicator variables provide useful additional information to the modeling algorithm.

> **MISSINGNESS INDICATORS CAN BE USEFUL** We've observed in many situations that the isBAD variables are sometimes even *more* informative and useful than the original variables!

If you don't know whether the missing values are random or systematic, we recommend assuming that the difference is systematic, rather than working hard to impute values to the variables based on the random missingness assumption. As we said earlier, treating missing values as if they are missing at random when they really indicate a systematic difference in some of the datums may lead to false conclusions.

4.1.3 *The vtreat package for automatically treating missing variables*

Since missing values are such a common problem with data, it's useful to have an automatic and repeatable process for dealing with them. We recommend using the vtreat variable treatment package. The vtreat process creates a *treatment plan* that records all the information needed to repeat the data treatment process: for example, the average observed income, or all the observed values of a categorical variable like housing_type. You then use this treatment plan to "prepare" or treat your training data before you fit a model, and then again to treat new data before feeding it into the model. The idea is that treated data is "safe," with no missing or unexpected values, and shouldn't ruin the model.

You'll see more-sophisticated examples of using vtreat in later chapters, but for now you will just create a simple treatment plan to manage the missing values in customer_data. Figure 4.7 shows the processes of creating and applying this simple treatment plan. First, you have to designate which columns of the data are the input variables: all of them except health_ins (which is the outcome to be predicted) and custid:

```
varlist <- setdiff(colnames(customer_data), c("custid", "health_ins"))
```

Then, you create the treatment plan, and "prepare" the data.

> **Listing 4.4 Creating and applying a treatment plan**

```
library(vtreat)
treatment_plan <-
     design_missingness_treatment(customer_data, varlist = varlist)
training_prepared <- prepare(treatment_plan, customer_data)
```

Model Training

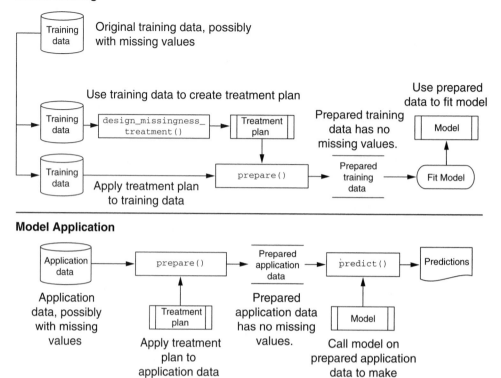

Model Application

Figure 4.7   Creating and applying a simple treatment plan

The data frame `training_prepared` is the treated data that you would use to train a model. Let's compare it to the original data.

Listing 4.5   Comparing the treated data to the original

```
colnames(customer_data)
##   [1] "custid"            "sex"                  "is_employed"
##   [4] "income"            "marital_status"       "health_ins"
##   [7] "housing_type"      "recent_move"          "num_vehicles"
##  [10] "age"               "state_of_res"         "gas_usage"
##  [13] "gas_with_rent"     "gas_with_electricity" "no_gas_bill"

colnames(training_prepared)
##   [1] "custid"            "sex"
##   [3] "is_employed"       "income"
##   [5] "marital_status"    "health_ins"
##   [7] "housing_type"      "recent_move"
##   [9] "num_vehicles"      "age"
##  [11] "state_of_res"      "gas_usage"
##  [13] "gas_with_rent"     "gas_with_electricity"
```

The prepared data has additional columns that are not in the original data, most importantly those with the _isBAD designation.

```
## [15] "no_gas_bill"                "is_employed_isBAD"
## [17] "income_isBAD"               "recent_move_isBAD"
## [19] "num_vehicles_isBAD"         "age_isBAD"
## [21] "gas_usage_isBAD"            "gas_with_rent_isBAD"
## [23] "gas_with_electricity_isBAD" "no_gas_bill_isBAD"


nacounts <- sapply(training_prepared, FUN=function(col) sum(is.na(col)) )
sum(nacounts)
## [1] 0
```

The prepared data has no missing values.

Now examine a few columns that you know had missing values.

Listing 4.6 Examining the data treatment

Finds the rows where   **Looks at a few columns from**
housing_type was missing   **those rows in the original data**

```
htmissing <- which(is.na(customer_data$housing_type))

columns_to_look_at <- c("custid", "is_employed", "num_vehicles",
                        "housing_type", "health_ins")

customer_data[htmissing, columns_to_look_at] %>% head()
##            custid is_employed num_vehicles housing_type health_ins
## 55  000082691_01        TRUE           NA         <NA>      FALSE
## 65  000116191_01        TRUE           NA         <NA>       TRUE
## 162 000269295_01          NA           NA         <NA>      FALSE
## 207 000349708_01          NA           NA         <NA>      FALSE
## 219 000362630_01          NA           NA         <NA>       TRUE
## 294 000443953_01          NA           NA         <NA>       TRUE

columns_to_look_at = c("custid", "is_employed", "is_employed_isBAD",
                       "num_vehicles","num_vehicles_isBAD",
                       "housing_type", "health_ins")

training_prepared[htmissing, columns_to_look_at] %>%  head()
##            custid is_employed is_employed_isBAD num_vehicles
## 55  000082691_01   1.0000000                 0       2.0655
## 65  000116191_01   1.0000000                 0       2.0655
## 162 000269295_01   0.9504928                 1       2.0655
## 207 000349708_01   0.9504928                 1       2.0655
## 219 000362630_01   0.9504928                 1       2.0655
## 294 000443953_01   0.9504928                 1       2.0655
##      num_vehicles_isBAD housing_type health_ins
## 55                    1     _invalid_      FALSE
## 65                    1     _invalid_       TRUE
## 162                   1     _invalid_      FALSE
## 207                   1     _invalid_      FALSE
## 219                   1     _invalid_       TRUE
## 294                   1     _invalid_       TRUE
```

Looks at those
rows and
columns in the
treated data
(along with the
isBADs)

```
customer_data %>%
    summarize(mean_vehicles = mean(num_vehicles, na.rm = TRUE),
      mean_employed = mean(as.numeric(is_employed), na.rm = TRUE))
##    mean_vehicles mean_employed
## 1        2.0655     0.9504928
```

Verifies the expected
number of vehicles
and the expected
unemployment
rate in the dataset

You see that `vtreat` replaced missing values of the categorical variable `housing_type` with the token _invalid_, and missing values of the numerical column `num_vehicles` with its average value in the original data. It also converted the logical variable `is_employed` to a numeric variable, and replaced missing values with its average value in the original data.

In addition to fixing missing data, there are other ways that you can transform the data to address issues that you found during the exploration phase. In the next section, we'll examine some additional common transformations.

4.2   *Data transformations*

The purpose of data transformation is to make data easier to model, and easier to understand. Machine learning works by learning meaningful patterns in training data, and then making predictions by exploiting those patterns in new data. Therefore, a data transformation that makes it easier to match patterns in the training data to patterns in new data can be a benefit.

> **Example**   *Suppose you are considering the use of income as an input to your insurance model. The cost of living will vary from state to state, so what would be a high salary in one region could be barely enough to scrape by in another. Because of this, it might be more meaningful to normalize a customer's income by the typical income in the area where they live. This is an example of a relatively simple (and common) transformation.*

For this example, you have external information about the median income in each state, in a file called median_income.RDS. Listing 4.7 uses this information to normalize the incomes. The code uses a join operation to match the information from median_income.RDS to the existing customer data. We will discuss joining tables in the next chapter, but for now, you should understand joining as copying data into a data frame from another data frame with matching rows.

Listing 4.7   Normalizing income by state

```
library(dplyr)
median_income_table <-
     readRDS("median_income.RDS")       ◁     If you have downloaded the PDSwR2 code
head(median_income_table)                     example directory, then median_income.RDS
                                              is in the directory PDSwR2/Custdata. We
##    state_of_res median_income             assume that this is your working directory.
## 1      Alabama          21100
## 2       Alaska          32050
## 3      Arizona          26000          Joins median_income_table into the
## 4     Arkansas          22900          customer data, so you can normalize
## 5   California          25000          each person's income by the median
## 6     Colorado          32000                   income of their state

training_prepared <-  training_prepared %>%
  left_join(., median_income_table, by="state_of_res") %>%     ◁
   mutate(income_normalized = income/median_income)
```

```
head(training_prepared[, c("income", "median_income", "income_normalized")])
```
**Compares the values
of income and
income_normalized**

```
##   income median_income income_normalized
## 1  22000         21100         1.0426540
## 2  23200         21100         1.0995261
## 3  21000         21100         0.9952607
## 4  37770         21100         1.7900474
## 5  39000         21100         1.8483412
## 6  11100         21100         0.5260664
```

```
summary(training_prepared$income_normalized)
```

```
##    Min. 1st Qu.  Median    Mean 3rd Qu.    Max.
##  0.0000  0.4049  1.0000  1.5685  1.9627 46.5556
```

Looking at the results in listing 4.7, you see that customers with an income higher than the median income of their state have an income_normalized value larger than 1, and customers with an income lower than the median income of their state have an income_normalized value less than 1. Because customers in different states get a different normalization, we call this a *conditional* transform. A long way to say this is that "the normalization is conditioned on the customer's state of residence." We would call scaling all the customers by the same value an *unconditioned* transform.

The need for data transformation can also depend on which modeling method you plan to use. For linear and logistic regression, for example, you ideally want to make sure that the relationship between the input variables and the output variable is approximately linear, and that the output variable is constant variance (the variance of the output variable is independent of the input variables). You may need to transform some of your input variables to better meet these assumptions.

In this section, we'll look at some useful data transformations and when to use them:

- Normalization
- Centering and scaling
- Log transformations

4.2.1 Normalization

Normalization (or rescaling) is useful when absolute quantities are less meaningful than relative ones. You've already seen an example of normalizing income relative to another meaningful quantity (median income). In that case, the meaningful quantity was external (it came from outside information), but it can also be internal (derived from the data itself).

For example, you might be less interested in a customer's absolute age than you are in how old or young they are relative to a "typical" customer. Let's take the mean age of your customers to be the typical age. You can normalize by that, as shown in the following listing.

Listing 4.8   Normalizing by mean age

```
summary(training_prepared$age)

##    Min. 1st Qu.  Median   Mean 3rd Qu.    Max.
##   21.00   34.00   48.00  49.22   62.00  120.00

mean_age <- mean(training_prepared$age)
age_normalized <- training_prepared$age/mean_age
summary(age_normalized)

##    Min. 1st Qu.  Median   Mean 3rd Qu.    Max.
##  0.4267  0.6908  0.9753  1.0000  1.2597  2.4382
```

A value for `age_normalized` that is much less than 1 signifies an unusually young customer; much greater than 1 signifies an unusually old customer. But what constitutes "much less" or "much greater" than 1? That depends on how wide an age spread your customers tend to have. See figure 4.8 for an example.

The average customer in both populations is 50. The *population 1* group has a fairly wide age spread, so a 35-year-old still seems fairly typical (perhaps a little young). That same 35-year-old seems unusually young in *population 2*, which has a narrow age spread. The typical age spread of your customers is summarized by the standard deviation. This leads to another way of expressing the relative ages of your customers.

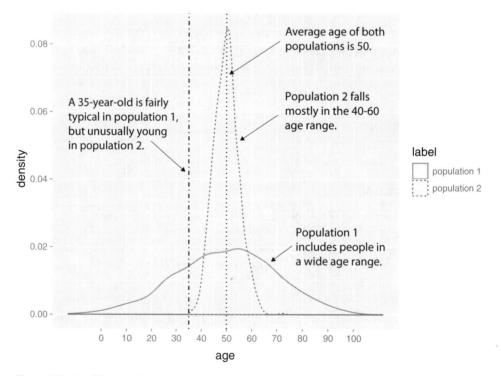

Figure 4.8   Is a 35-year-old young?

4.2.2 Centering and scaling

You can rescale your data by using the standard deviation as a unit of distance. A customer who is within one standard deviation of the mean age is considered not much older or younger than typical. A customer who is more than one or two standard deviations from the mean can be considered much older, or much younger. To make the relative ages even easier to understand, you can also center the data by the mean, so a customer of "typical age" has a centered age of 0.

Listing 4.9 Centering and scaling age

```
(mean_age <- mean(training_prepared$age))      ◁──────── Takes the mean
  ## [1] 49.21647

(sd_age <- sd(training_prepared$age))      ◁──────── Takes the standard deviation
  ## [1] 18.0124

print(mean_age + c(-sd_age, sd_age))                    ◁
  ## [1] 31.20407 67.22886                                   The typical age range for
                                                             this population is from
training_prepared$scaled_age <- (training_prepared$age -   about 31 to 67.
    mean_age) / sd_age            ◁
                                                   Uses the mean value as the
training_prepared %>%                              origin (or reference point) and
  filter(abs(age - mean_age) < sd_age) %>%         rescales the distance from the
  select(age, scaled_age) %>%                      mean by the standard deviation
  head()

##    age scaled_age               ◁
## 1  67  0.9872942                   Customers in the typical age
## 2  54  0.2655690                   range have a scaled_age with
## 3  61  0.6541903                   magnitude less than 1.
## 4  64  0.8207422
## 5  57  0.4321210
## 6  55  0.3210864

training_prepared %>%
  filter(abs(age - mean_age) > sd_age) %>%
  select(age, scaled_age) %>%
  head()

##    age scaled_age               ◁
## 1  24  -1.399951                   Customers outside the typical
## 2  82   1.820054                   age range have a scaled_age
## 3  31  -1.011329                   with magnitude greater than 1.
## 4  93   2.430745
## 5  76   1.486950
## 6  26  -1.288916
```

Now, values less than -1 signify customers younger than typical; values greater than 1 signify customers older than typical.

A technicality

The common interpretation of standard deviation as a unit of distance implicitly assumes that the data is distributed normally. For a normal distribution, roughly two-thirds of the data (about 68%) is within plus/minus one standard deviation from the mean. About 95% of the data is within plus/minus two standard deviations from the mean. In figure 4.8 (reproduced as a faceted graph in figure 4.9), a 35-year-old is within one standard deviation from the mean in *population 1*, but more than one (in fact, more than two) standard deviations from the mean in *population 2*.

You can still use this transformation if the data isn't normally distributed, but the standard deviation is most meaningful as a unit of distance if the data is unimodal and roughly symmetric around the mean.

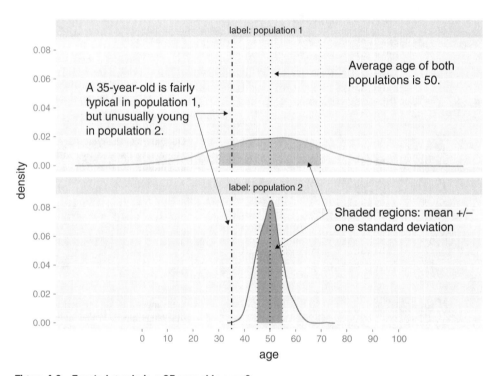

Figure 4.9   Faceted graph: is a 35-year-old young?

When you have multiple numeric variables, you can use the scale() function to center and scale all of them simultaneously. This has the advantage that the numeric variables now all have similar and more-compatible ranges. To make this concrete, compare the variable *age* in years to the variable *income* in dollars. A 10-year difference in age between two customers could be a lot, but a 10-dollar difference in income is quite small. If you center and scale both variables, then the value 0 means the same thing for both scaled variables: the mean age or mean income. And the value 1.5 also means the same thing: a person who is 1.5 standard deviations older than the mean age, or who makes 1.5 standard deviations more than the mean income. In both situations, the value 1.5 can be considered a big difference from the average.

The following listing demonstrates centering and scaling four numerical variables from the data with `scale()`.

Listing 4.10 Centering and scaling multiple numeric variables

```
dataf <- training_prepared[, c("age", "income", "num_vehicles", "gas_usage")]
summary(dataf)

##       age              income          num_vehicles       gas_usage
##  Min.   : 21.00   Min.   :       0   Min.   :0.000   Min.   :   4.00
##  1st Qu.: 34.00   1st Qu.:   10700   1st Qu.:1.000   1st Qu.:  50.00
##  Median : 48.00   Median :   26300   Median :2.000   Median :  76.01
##  Mean   : 49.22   Mean   :   41792   Mean   :2.066   Mean   :  76.01
##  3rd Qu.: 62.00   3rd Qu.:   51700   3rd Qu.:3.000   3rd Qu.:  76.01
##  Max.   :120.00   Max.   : 1257000   Max.   :6.000   Max.   : 570.00
```

```
dataf_scaled <- scale(dataf, center=TRUE, scale=TRUE)

summary(dataf_scaled)
##       age               income            num_vehicles        gas_usage
##  Min.   :-1.56650   Min.   :-0.7193   Min.   :-1.78631   Min.   :-1.4198
##  1st Qu.:-0.84478   1st Qu.:-0.5351   1st Qu.:-0.92148   1st Qu.:-0.5128
##  Median :-0.06753   Median :-0.2666   Median :-0.05665   Median : 0.0000
##  Mean   : 0.00000   Mean   : 0.0000   Mean   : 0.00000   Mean   : 0.0000
##  3rd Qu.: 0.70971   3rd Qu.: 0.1705   3rd Qu.: 0.80819   3rd Qu.: 0.0000
##  Max.   : 3.92971   Max.   :20.9149   Max.   : 3.40268   Max.   : 9.7400
```

```
(means <- attr(dataf_scaled, 'scaled:center'))
 ##          age         income num_vehicles      gas_usage
 ##     49.21647    41792.51062      2.06550       76.00745

(sds <- attr(dataf_scaled, 'scaled:scale'))
 ##          age         income num_vehicles      gas_usage
 ##     18.012397   58102.481410     1.156294      50.717778
```

Centers the data by its mean and scales it by its standard deviation

Gets the means and standard deviations of the original data, which are stored as attributes of dataf_scaled

Because the `scale()` transformation puts all the numeric variables in compatible units, it's a recommended preprocessing step for some data analysis and machine learning techniques like principal component analysis and deep learning.

KEEP THE TRAINING TRANSFORMATION

When you use parameters derived from the data (like means, medians, or standard deviations) to transform the data before modeling, you generally should keep those parameters and use them when transforming new data that will be input to the model. When you used the `scale()` function in listing 4.10, you kept the values of the scaled:center and scaled:scale attributes as the variables means and sds, respectively. This is so that you can use these values to scale new data, as shown in listing 4.11. This makes sure that the new scaled data is in the same units as the training data.

The same principle applies when cleaning missing values using the design_ missingness_treatment() function from the vtreat package, as you did in section 4.1.3. The resulting treatment plan (called treatment_plan in listing 4.1.3) keeps the information from the training data in order to clean missing values from new data, as you saw in listing 4.5.

Listing 4.11 Treating new data before feeding it to a model

```
newdata <- customer_data  ◁────────  Simulates having a new customer dataset

library(vtreat)                                         ◁─┐ Cleans it using the treatment
newdata_treated <- prepare(treatment_plan, newdata)       │ plan from the original dataset

new_dataf <- newdata_treated[, c("age", "income",   ◁───────┐
    "num_vehicles", "gas_usage")]                           │

dataf_scaled <- scale(new_dataf, center=means, scale=sds)   │
```

Scales age, income, num_vehicles, and
gas_usage using the means and standard
deviations from the original dataset

However, there are some situations when you may wish to use new parameters. For example, if the important information in the model is how a subject's income relates to the *current* median income, then when preparing new data for modeling, you would want to normalize income by the current median income, rather than the median income from the time when the model was trained. The implication here is that the characteristics of someone who earns three times the median income will be different from those of someone who earns less than the median income, and that these differences are the same independent of the actual dollar amount of the income.

4.2.3 *Log transformations for skewed and wide distributions*

Normalizing by mean and standard deviation, as you did in section 4.2.2, is most meaningful when the data distribution is roughly symmetric. Next, we'll look at a transformation that can make some distributions more symmetric.

Monetary amounts—incomes, customer value, account values, or purchase sizes— are some of the most commonly encountered sources of skewed distributions in data science applications. In fact, as we'll discuss in appendix B, monetary amounts are often *lognormally distributed*: the log of the data is normally distributed. This leads us to the idea that taking the log of monetary data can restore symmetry and scale to the data, by making it look "more normal." We demonstrate this in figure 4.11.

For the purposes of modeling, it's generally not too critical which logarithm you use, whether the natural logarithm, log base 10, or log base 2. In regression, for example, the choice of logarithm affects the magnitude of the coefficient that corresponds to the logged variable, but it doesn't affect the structure of the model. We like to use

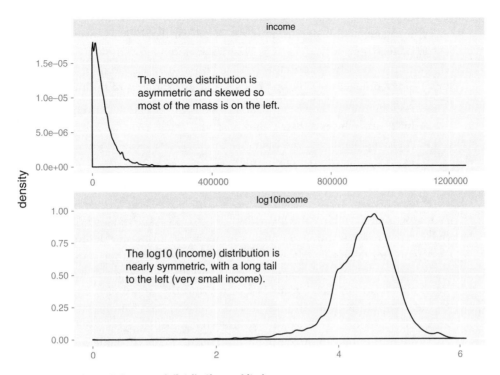

Figure 4.10 **A nearly lognormal distribution and its log**

log base 10 for monetary amounts, because orders of ten seem natural for money: $100, $1000, $10,000, and so on. The transformed data is easy to read.

AN ASIDE ON GRAPHING Notice that the bottom panel of figure 4.10 has the same shape as figure 3.7. The difference between using the `ggplot` layer `scale_x_log10` on a density plot of *income* and plotting a density plot of *log10(income)* is primarily axis labeling. Using `scale_x_log10` will label the x-axis in dollar amounts, rather than in logs.

It's also generally a good idea to log transform data containing values that range over several orders of magnitude, for example, the population of towns and cities, which may range from a few hundred to several million. One reason for this is that modeling techniques often have a difficult time with very wide data ranges. Another reason is because such data often comes from multiplicative processes rather than from an additive one, so log units are in some sense more natural.

As an example of an *additive* process, suppose you are studying weight loss. If you weigh 150 pounds and your friend weighs 200, you're equally active, and you both go on the exact same restricted-calorie diet, then you'll probably both lose about the same number of pounds. How much weight you lose doesn't depend on how much you weighed in the first place, only on calorie intake. The natural unit of measurement in this situation is absolute pounds (or kilograms) lost.

As an example of a *multiplicative* process, consider salary increases. If management gives everyone in the department a raise, it probably isn't giving everyone $5,000 extra. Instead, everyone gets a 2% raise: how much extra money ends up in your paycheck depends on your initial salary. In this situation, the natural unit of measurement is percentage, not absolute dollars. Other examples of multiplicative processes:

- A change to an online retail site increases conversion (purchases) for each item by 2% (not by exactly two purchases).
- A change to a restaurant menu increases patronage every night by 5% (not by exactly five customers every night).

When the process is multiplicative, log transforming the process data can make modeling easier.

Unfortunately, taking the logarithm only works if the data is non-negative, because the log of zero is –Infinity and the log of negative values isn't defined (R marks the log of negative numbers as NaN: not a number). There are other transforms, such as *arcsinh*, that you can use to decrease data range if you have zero or negative values. We don't always use *arcsinh*, because we don't find the values of the transformed data to be meaningful. In applications where the skewed data is monetary (like account balances or customer value), we instead use what we call a *signed logarithm*. A signed logarithm takes the logarithm of the absolute value of the variable and multiplies by the appropriate sign. Values strictly between -1 and 1 are mapped to zero. The difference between log and signed log is shown in figure 4.11.

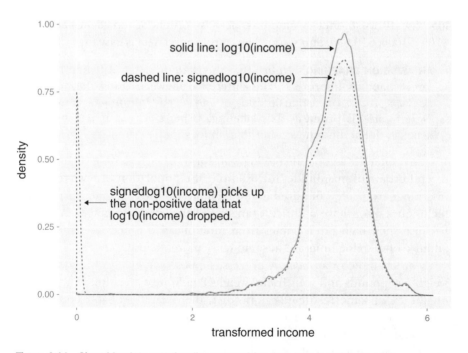

Figure 4.11 Signed log lets you visualize non-positive data on a logarithmic scale.

Here's how to calculate signed log base 10 in R:

```
signedlog10 <- function(x) {
    ifelse(abs(x) <= 1, 0, sign(x)*log10(abs(x)))
}
```

This maps all datums between -1 and 1 to zero, so clearly this transformation isn't useful if values with magnitude less than 1 are important. But with many monetary variables (in US currency), values less than a dollar aren't much different from zero (or 1), for all practical purposes. So, for example, mapping account balances that are less than or equal to $1 (the equivalent of every account always having a minimum balance of $1) is probably okay. You can also pick a larger threshold for "small," such as $100. This would map the small accounts of less than $100 to the same value, and eliminate the long left tail in figures 4.10 and 4.11. In some situations, eliminating this long tail can be desirable—for one thing, it makes a graph of the data less visually skewed.[4]

Once you've got the data suitably cleaned and transformed, you're almost ready to start the modeling stage. Before we get there, we have one more step.

4.3 *Sampling for modeling and validation*

Sampling is the process of selecting a subset of a population to represent the whole during analysis and modeling. In the current era of big datasets, some people argue that computational power and modern algorithms let us analyze the entire large dataset without the need to sample. But keep in mind even "big data" is usually itself a sample from a larger universe. So some understanding of sampling is always needed to work with data.

We can certainly analyze larger datasets than we could before, but sampling is still a useful tool. When you're in the middle of developing or refining a modeling procedure, it's easier to test and debug the code on small subsamples before training the model on the entire dataset. Visualization can be easier with a subsample of the data; ggplot runs faster on smaller datasets, and too much data will often obscure the patterns in a graph, as we mentioned in chapter 3. And often it's not feasible to use your entire customer base to train a model.

It's important that the dataset that you do use is an accurate representation of your population as a whole. For example, your customers might come from all over the United States. When you collect your customer data, it might be tempting to use all the customers from one state, say Connecticut, to train the model. But if you plan to use the model to make predictions about customers all over the country, it's a good idea to pick customers randomly from all the states, because what predicts health insurance coverage for Texas customers might be different from what predicts health insurance coverage in Connecticut. This might not always be possible (perhaps only

---

[4] There are methods other than capping to deal with signed logarithms, such as the arcsinh function (see http://mng.bz/ZWQa), but they also distort data near zero and make almost any data appear to be bimodal, which can be deceiving.

your Connecticut and Massachusetts branches currently collect the customer health insurance information), but the shortcomings of using a nonrepresentative dataset should be kept in mind.

Another reason to sample your data is to create test and training splits.

4.3.1   *Test and training splits*

When you're building a model to make predictions, like our model to predict the probability of health insurance coverage, you need data to build the model. You also need data to test whether the model makes correct predictions on new data. The first set is called the *training set*, and the second set is called the *test* (or *holdout*) set. Figure 4.12 shows the splitting process (along with an optional split for a calibration set, which is discussed in the sidebar "Train/calibration/test splits").

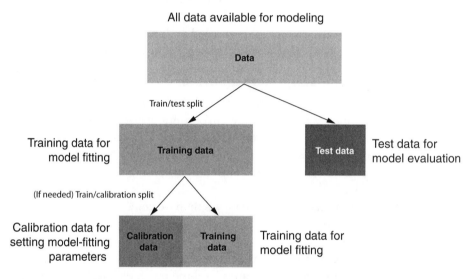

Figure 4.12   Splitting data into training and test (or training, calibration, and test) sets

The training set is the data that you feed to the model-building algorithm (we'll cover specific algorithms in part 2) so that the algorithm can fit the correct structure to best predict the outcome variable. The test set is the data that you feed into the resulting model, to verify that the model's predictions will be accurate on new data. We'll go into detail about the kinds of modeling issues that you can detect by

Train/calibration/test splits

Many writers recommend train/calibration/test splits, where the *calibration set* is used to set parameters that the model-fitting algorithm needs, and the training set is used to fit the model. This is also good advice. Our philosophy is this: split the data into train/test early, don't look at test until final evaluation, and if you need calibration data, resplit it from your training subset.

using holdout data in chapter 6. For now, we'll get our data ready for doing holdout experiments at a later stage.

4.3.2   *Creating a sample group column*

A convenient way to manage random sampling is to add a sample group column to the data frame. The sample group column contains a number generated uniformly from zero to one, using the runif() function. You can draw a random sample of arbitrary size from the data frame by using the appropriate threshold on the sample group column.

For example, once you've labeled all the rows of your data frame with your sample group column (let's call it gp), then the set of all rows such that gp < 0.4 will be about four-tenths, or 40%, of the data. The set of all rows where gp is between 0.55 and 0.70 is about 15% of the data ($0.7 - 0.55 = 0.15$). So you can repeatably generate a random sample of the data of any size by using gp.

Listing 4.12   Splitting into test and training using a random group mark

```
set.seed(25643)              ◁────────── Sets the random seed so this example is reproducible
customer_data$gp <- runif(nrow(customer_data))
customer_test <- subset(customer_data, gp <= 0.1)    ◁─────
customer_train <- subset(customer_data, gp > 0.1)    ◁──┐

dim(customer_test)
## [1] 7463     16

dim(customer_train)
## [1] 65799    16
```

Creates the grouping column → (points to `customer_data$gp <- runif(...)`)

Here we generate a training set using the remaining data. (points to `customer_train` line)

Here we generate a test set of about 10% of the data. (points to `customer_test` line)

Listing 4.12 generates a test set of approximately 10% of the data and allocates the remaining 90% of the data to the training set.

The dplyr package also has functions called sample_n() and sample_frac() that draw a random sample (a uniform random sample, by default) from a data frame. Why not just use one of these to draw training and test sets? You could, but you should make sure to set the random seed via the set.seed() command (as we did in listing 4.12) to guarantee that you'll draw the same sample group every time. Reproducible sampling is essential when you're debugging code. In many cases, code will crash because of a corner case that you forgot to guard against. This corner case might show up in your random sample. If you're using a different random input sample every time you run the code, you won't know if you will tickle the bug again. This makes it hard to track down and fix errors.

You also want repeatable input samples for what software engineers call *regression testing* (not to be confused with statistical regression). In other words, when you make changes to a model or to your data treatment, you want to make sure you don't break what was already working. If model version 1 was giving "the right answer" for a certain input set, you want to make sure that model version 2 does so also.

We find that storing a sample group column with the data is a more reliable way to guarantee reproducible sampling during development and testing.

> **REPRODUCIBLE SAMPLING IS NOT JUST A TRICK FOR R** If your data is in a database or other external store, and you only want to pull a subset of the data into R for analysis, you can draw a reproducible random sample by generating a sample group column in an appropriate table in the database, using the SQL command RAND.

4.3.3　Record grouping

One caveat is that the preceding trick works if every object of interest (every customer, in this case) corresponds to a unique row. But what if you're interested less in which customers don't have health insurance, and more in which households have uninsured members? If you're modeling a question at the household level rather than the customer level, then every member of a household should be in the same group (test or training). In other words, the random sampling also has to be at the household level.

Suppose your customers are marked both by a household ID and a customer ID. This is shown in figure 4.13. We want to split the households into a training set and a test set. Listing 4.13 shows one way to generate an appropriate sample group column.

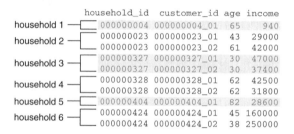

Figure 4.13　Example of a dataset with customers and households

---

Listing 4.13　Ensuring test/train split doesn't split inside a household

If you have downloaded the PDSwR2 code example directory, then the household dataset is in the directory PDSwR2/Custdata. We assume that this is your working directory.

```
household_data <- readRDS("hhdata.RDS")
hh <- unique(household_data$household_id)          ⬅ Gets the unique household IDs

set.seed(243674)
households <- data.frame(household_id = hh,         ⬅ Generates a unique sampling
                  gp = runif(length(hh)),              group ID per household, and
                  stringsAsFactors=FALSE)              puts in a column named gp

household_data <- dplyr::left_join(household_data,  ⬅ Joins the household
                  households,                           IDs back into the
                  by = "household_id")                  original data
```

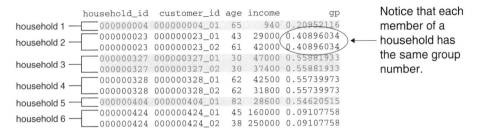

Figure 4.14   Sampling the dataset by household rather than customer

The resulting sample group column is shown in figure 4.14. Everyone in a household has the same sampling group number.

Now we can generate the test and training sets as before. This time, however, the threshold 0.1 doesn't represent 10% of the data rows, but 10% of the households, which may be more or less than 10% of the data, depending on the sizes of the households.

4.3.4   Data provenance

You'll also want to add a column (or columns) to record data provenance: when your dataset was collected, perhaps what version of your data-cleaning procedure was used on the data before modeling, and so on. This metadata is akin to version control for data. It's handy information to have, to make sure that you're comparing apples to apples when you're in the process of improving your model, or comparing different models or different versions of a model.

data_source_id	data_collection_date	data_treatment_date	custid	health_ins	income	is_employed
data_pull 8/2/18	2018-08-02	2018-08-03	000006646_03	TRUE	22000	TRUE
data_pull 8/2/18	2018-08-02	2018-08-03	000007827_01	TRUE	23200	NA
data_pull 8/2/18	2018-08-02	2018-08-03	000008359_04	TRUE	21000	TRUE
data_pull 8/2/18	2018-08-02	2018-08-03	000008529_01	TRUE	37770	NA
data_pull 8/2/18	2018-08-02	2018-08-03	000008744_02	TRUE	39000	TRUE
data_pull 8/2/18	2018-08-02	2018-08-03	000011466_01	TRUE	11100	NA

Figure 4.15   Recording the data source, collection date, and treatment date with data

Figure 4.15 shows an example of some possible metadata added to training data. In this example, you have recorded the original data source (called "data pull 8/2/18"), when the data was collected, and when it was treated. If, for example, the treatment date on the data is earlier than the most recent version of your data treatment procedures, then you know that this treated data is possibly obsolete. Thanks to the metadata, you can go back to the original data source and treat it again.

Summary

At some point, you'll have data quality that is as good as you can make it. You've fixed problems with missing data and performed any needed transformations. You're ready to go on to the modeling stage.

Remember, though, that data science is an iterative process. You may discover during the modeling process that you have to do additional data cleaning or transformation. You may have to go back even further and collect different types of data. That's why we recommend adding columns for sample groups and data provenance to your datasets (and, later, to the models and model output), so you can keep track of the data management steps as the data and the models evolve.

In this chapter you have learned

- Different ways of handling missing values may be more suitable for a one purpose or another.
- You can use the `vtreat` package to manage missing values automatically.
- How to normalize or rescale data, and when normalization/rescaling are appropriate.
- How to log transform data, and when log transformations are appropriate.
- How to implement a reproducible sampling scheme for creating test/train splits of your data.

Data engineering
and data shaping

This chapter covers
- Becoming comfortable with applying data transforms
- Starting with important data manipulation packages including `data.table` and `dplyr`
- Learning to control the layout of your data

This chapter will show you how to use R to organize or wrangle data into a shape useful for analysis. Data shaping is a set of steps you have to take if your data is not found all in one table or in an arrangement ready for analysis.

Figure 5.1 is the mental model for this chapter: working with data. Previous chapters have assumed the data is in a ready-to-go form, or we have pre-prepared the data to be in such a form for you. This chapter will prepare you to take these steps yourself. The basic concept of data wrangling is to visualize your data being structured to make your task easier, and then take steps to add this structure to your data. To teach this, we'll work a number of examples, each with a motivating task, and then work a transform that solves the problem. We'll concentrate on a set of transforms that are powerful and useful, and that cover most common situations.

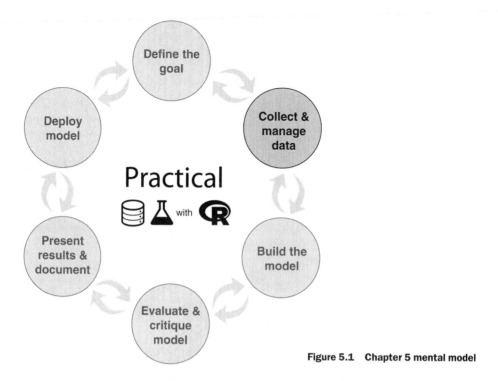

Figure 5.1   Chapter 5 mental model

We will show data wrangling solutions using base R, data.table, and dplyr.[1] Each of these has its advantages, which is why we are presenting more than one solution. Throughout this book, we are deliberately using a polyglot approach to data wrangling: mixing base R, data.table, and dplyr, as convenient. Each of these systems has its strengths:

- *Base R*—This is code written in R that directly manipulates data.frames using R's built-in capabilities. Breaking complex transforms into base R primitives can be a puzzle, but we will give you the tools to solve the puzzle in this chapter.

- *data.table*—data.table is the package for fast and memory-efficient data manipulation in R. It differs from normal R semantics in that data.table uses *reference semantics* where changes are made directly in a shared data structure (visible to all references to the same structure) instead of R's more typical *value semantics* (where changes made in one reference do not become visible to other references). data.table notation specifies powerful transforms through a variation of the []-indexing operator, and is well explained in help(data .table, package="data.table") and vignette("datatable-intro", package= "data.table").

---

[1] For database tasks, we suggest using dbplyr or rquery, which we will touch on briefly in appendix A.

- *dplyr*—dplyr is a popular data manipulation package that emphasizes data manipulations through sequences of SQL-like (or Codd-style) operators. dplyr is usually not as fast (or space efficient) as data.table, but the notations are convenient.

Some good places to start on manipulating data in R are the following free guides:

- Getting Started in R, data.table version: https://eddelbuettel.github.io/gsir-te/Getting-Started-in-R.pdf
- Getting Started in R, tidyverse version: https://github.com/saghirb/Getting-Started-in-R

We want to improve your ability to write R code (to translate intent into implementation) and to read R code (to infer intent from existing code). To this end, this chapter, like much of this book, is designed as a sequence of worked examples. We strongly encourage you try running the examples yourself (they are available here: https://github.com/WinVector/PDSwR2). It is key to get into the habit of planning (even drawing) your data transformation before coding. Finish clarifying your intent before getting bogged down by the details of coding. Trust that there are easy-to-find methods for most common data wrangling tasks in R, and plan with the assumption that you can find them when needed. The principle is this: make your analysis simpler by transforming your data into a simple "data matrix" format where each row is an observation, and each column is a measurement type. Fix issues, such as odd column names, early, and then you don't have to write complicated code to work around them.

This chapter is organized in terms of the type of transform needed. For variety, we will bring in a number of small notional datasets, and spend a little time looking at each dataset. This task-to-example organization will give you a quick introduction to data transforms in R. The transforms we are going to cover include these:

- Choosing a subset of columns
- Choosing a subset of rows
- Reordering rows
- Creating new columns
- Dealing with missing values
- Combining two datasets by row
- Combining two datasets by column
- Joining two datasets
- Aggregating rows
- General data reshaping (tall versus wide forms)

The idea is that this list will give you enough tools for a very large number of tasks. We'll work from problems to solutions. We will show which command solves a given problem, and leave details of the command's syntax to R's help system and the guides and tutorials we suggest in this chapter. Please think of this chapter as a Rosetta Stone for data wrangling: each concept is explained once and then executed three times (usually in base R, `data.table`, and `dplyr`).

Our first application (subsetting rows and columns) will set up the general pattern of the applications, so it is worth reading through even if you are already confidently subsetting data in R.

> **DATA SOURCES**   In this chapter, we'll use small, toy-sized datasets to make it easier to examine data before and after the transforms. We strongly suggest you run all the examples along with us. All examples are either built-in data that comes with R or available from the book's GitHub site: https://github .com/WinVector/PDSwR2. Also, all code examples can be found in the `Code-Examples` at the same location. We suggest cloning or downloading this material to help working with this book.

For more information on R's built-in examples, try the command `help(datasets)`.

5.1 Data selection

This section covers removing rows, removing columns, reordering columns, removing missing data, and reordering data rows. In the era of big data, you often have too much to look at, so limiting your data to what you need can greatly speed up your work.

5.1.1 Subsetting rows and columns

A common task when working with a dataset is selecting a subset of rows or columns.

SITUATION

For our first example, we will use the `iris` dataset : measurements of sepal length and width and petal length and width for three species of iris.

First we will look at some aspects of the data. We suggest always doing this and making it part of an "eyes on the data" work discipline. For example, figure 5.2 shows the petal dimensions of our example irises:

```
library("ggplot2")        ⟵——  Attaches the ggplot2 package
                                 for later plotting

summary(iris)             ⟵————— Takes a look at the built-in iris data

##    Sepal.Length    Sepal.Width     Petal.Length    Petal.Width
##   Min.   :4.300   Min.   :2.000   Min.   :1.000   Min.   :0.100
##   1st Qu.:5.100   1st Qu.:2.800   1st Qu.:1.600   1st Qu.:0.300
##   Median :5.800   Median :3.000   Median :4.350   Median :1.300
##   Mean   :5.843   Mean   :3.057   Mean   :3.758   Mean   :1.199
##   3rd Qu.:6.400   3rd Qu.:3.300   3rd Qu.:5.100   3rd Qu.:1.800
##   Max.   :7.900   Max.   :4.400   Max.   :6.900   Max.   :2.500
##
##         Species
##   setosa    :50
##   versicolor:50
##   virginica :50
```

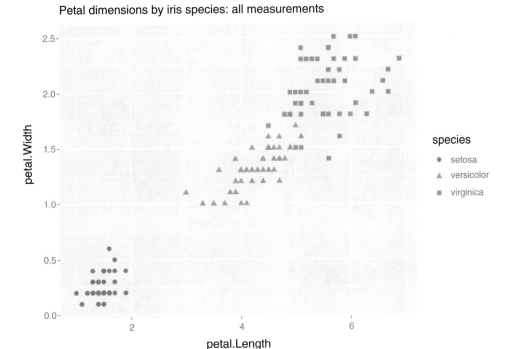

Figure 5.2 **Example iris plot**

ATTACHING PACKAGES It is good practice to attach packages early. If a package won't attach, try installing it with a command such as `install.packages` (`"ggplot2"`).

```
head(iris)
```

```
##   Sepal.Length Sepal.Width Petal.Length Petal.Width Species
## 1          5.1         3.5          1.4         0.2  setosa
## 2          4.9         3.0          1.4         0.2  setosa
## 3          4.7         3.2          1.3         0.2  setosa
## 4          4.6         3.1          1.5         0.2  setosa
## 5          5.0         3.6          1.4         0.2  setosa
## 6          5.4         3.9          1.7         0.4  setosa
```

```
ggplot(iris,
       aes(x = Petal.Length, y = Petal.Width,
           shape = Species, color = Species)) +
  geom_point(size =2 ) +
  ggtitle("Petal dimensions by iris species: all measurements")
```

The `iris` data comes preinstalled with R and is part of the `datasets` package. We will deliberately use small examples in this chapter so it is easy to look at results.

SCENARIO

Suppose we are assigned to generate a report on only petal length and petal width, by iris species, for irises where the petal length is greater than 2. To accomplish this, we need to select a subset of columns (variables) or a subset of rows (instances) from a data frame.

Column and row selections look like figure 5.3.

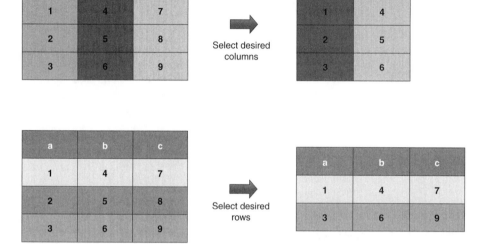

Figure 5.3 Selecting columns and rows

THE DIAGRAMS   The diagrams in this chapter are meant to be mnemonic cartoons of the transform. We suggest looking at the actual data before and after the transform to get more details on what the data transforms are doing. We also suggest reviewing them again after working the solutions and noticing how they abstract the arrangement of the data before and after the transforms. Think of these diagrams as a visual index of transforms.

SOLUTION 1: BASE R

The base R solution works by using the `[,]` indexing operator.

DROP = FALSE   When working with `[,]` always add a third argument `drop = FALSE` to get around the issue that the default behavior when selecting a single column from an R `data.frame` returns a vector and not a `data.frame` containing the column. In many cases, we know we have more than one column, and don't strictly need the command. But it is good to get in the habit of adding this argument to avoid unpleasant surprises.

The solution strategy is this:

- Get desired columns by name or column index in the second position of [,].
- Get desired rows by Boolean per-row selection in the first position of [,].

```
columns_we_want <- c("Petal.Length", "Petal.Width", "Species")
rows_we_want <- iris$Petal.Length > 2

# before
head(iris)

##   Sepal.Length Sepal.Width Petal.Length Petal.Width Species
## 1          5.1         3.5          1.4         0.2  setosa
## 2          4.9         3.0          1.4         0.2  setosa
## 3          4.7         3.2          1.3         0.2  setosa
## 4          4.6         3.1          1.5         0.2  setosa
## 5          5.0         3.6          1.4         0.2  setosa
## 6          5.4         3.9          1.7         0.4  setosa

iris_base <- iris[rows_we_want, columns_we_want, drop = FALSE]

# after
head(iris_base)

##    Petal.Length Petal.Width    Species
## 51          4.7         1.4 versicolor
## 52          4.5         1.5 versicolor
## 53          4.9         1.5 versicolor
## 54          4.0         1.3 versicolor
## 55          4.6         1.5 versicolor
## 56          4.5         1.3 versicolor
```

Notice column selection is also a good way to reorder columns. An advantage of base R is it tends to be fast and has very stable APIs: code written this year in base R is most likely to work next year (tidyverse packages, unfortunately, tend to have less-stable APIs). The one disadvantage is that a few base R defaults are irritating. For example, we included the drop=FALSE notation to work around the fact that base R would return a vector instead of a data.frame if we tried to select only one column.

SOLUTION 2: DATA.TABLE

Row and column selection in data.table is performed similarly to base R. data .table uses a very powerful set of index notations. In this case, we use a .. notation to tell data.table that we are using the second index position to specify column names (and not to specify calculations, as we will demonstrate later).

```
library("data.table")

iris_data.table <- as.data.table(iris)        ◁──── Converts to data.table class
                                                     to get data.table semantics
columns_we_want <- c("Petal.Length", "Petal.Width", "Species")
rows_we_want <- iris_data.table$Petal.Length > 2

iris_data.table <- iris_data.table[rows_we_want , ..columns_we_want]    ◁───┐

head(iris_data.table)               The .. notation tells data.table that
                            columns_we_want isn't itself the name of a column
                                but a variable referring to names of columns.
```

```
##    Petal.Length Petal.Width    Species
## 1:          4.7         1.4 versicolor
## 2:          4.5         1.5 versicolor
## 3:          4.9         1.5 versicolor
## 4:          4.0         1.3 versicolor
## 5:          4.6         1.5 versicolor
## 6:          4.5         1.3 versicolor
```

The advantage of data.table is that it is the fastest and most memory efficient solution for data wrangling in R at a wide range of scales. data.table has a very helpful FAQ, and there is a nice cheat sheet:

- https://cran.r-project.org/web/packages/data.table/vignettes/datatable-faq .html
- https://www.datacamp.com/community/tutorials/data-table-cheat-sheet

Both of these will make more sense if you approach them after working some examples from the data.table vignette accessible in R with the command vignette ("datatable-intro", package = "data.table").

Taking care when using data.table

data.table works like data.frames for packages that are not data.table-aware. This means you can use data.tables with just about any package, even those that predate data.table. In a data.table-aware situation (using data.table at the command line, or using a package that depends on data.table), data.table implements slightly enhanced semantics. We show a quick example here:

```
library("data.table")                          Example data.frame
df <- data.frame(x = 1:2, y = 3:4)

df[, x]                                         Notice that writing
## Error in `[.data.frame`(df, , x) : object 'x' not found    df[, x] instead of
                                                df[, "x"] is an error
x <- "y"          Sets up data.table example   (assuming x is not
dt <- data.table(df)                            bound to a value in
                                                our environment).
dt[, x]
## [1] 1 2         Notice that this returns the
                  column x much like d$x would.

dt[, ..x]         This uses data.table's "look up"
##     y           idiom to get a data.table of columns
## 1: 3            referred to by the variable x.
## 2: 4
```

SOLUTION 3: DPLYR

The dplyr solution is written in terms of select and filter:

- dplyr::select to select desired columns
- dplyr::filter to select desired rows

It is traditional to chain dplyr steps with the magrittr pipe operator %>%, but assigning to temporary variables works just as well. While teaching here, we'll use *explicit dot* notation, where the data pipeline is written as iris %>% select(., column) instead of the more-common implicit first-argument notation (iris %>% select(column)). Explicit dot notation was discussed in chapter 2 and is the topic of the following R Tip: http://www.win-vector.com/blog/2018/03/r-tip-make-arguments-explicit-in-magrittr-dplyr-pipelines/.[2]

```
library("dplyr")

iris_dplyr <- iris %>%
  select(.,
         Petal.Length, Petal.Width, Species) %>%
  filter(.,
         Petal.Length > 2)

head(iris_dplyr)

##   Petal.Length Petal.Width    Species
## 1          4.7         1.4 versicolor
## 2          4.5         1.5 versicolor
## 3          4.9         1.5 versicolor
## 4          4.0         1.3 versicolor
## 5          4.6         1.5 versicolor
## 6          4.5         1.3 versicolor
```

The advantage of dplyr is the emphasis of data processing as a sequence of operations broken down into a visible pipeline.

There is a nice cheat sheet for dplyr available from https://www.rstudio.com/wp-content/uploads/2015/02/data-wrangling-cheatsheet.pdf. Cheat sheets are always going to be a bit brief, so the sheet will become very useful after you have tried a few examples.

5.1.2 *Removing records with incomplete data*

An important variation of subsetting data is removing rows of data that have missing values. We will also deal with some simple strategies for replacing missing values by moving values across rows (using na.locf()) or moving values across columns (called *coalescing*).[3]

In this section, we will show how to quickly select only rows that have no missing data or values. This is only an example; we generally suggest using the methodologies in chapters 4 and 8 for treating missing values in real-world applications.

SITUATION

As our preceding example does not have missing values, we will move to another example: the msleep dataset of sleep times of animals with different characteristics. In this dataset, several rows have missing values. An additional goal of this example is to

---

[2] A powerful alternate pipe called the *dot arrow pipe* (written as %.>%) that insists on explicit dot notation and supplies additional capabilities can be found in the wrapr package. For most of this book, we will stick to the magrittr pipe, but we encourage curious readers to check out the wrapr pipe in their own work.

[3] There is actually an entire science devoted to imputing values for missing data. A good resource on this topic is https://CRAN.R-project.org/view=MissingData.

familiarize you with a number of common practice datasets. These are the datasets that you should break out to try a new data wrangling method.

First, as always, let's look at the data:

```
library("ggplot2")
data(msleep)
```
Copies the msleep from the ggplot2
package into our workspace

```
str(msleep)
```

```
## Classes 'tbl_df', 'tbl' and 'data.frame':    83 obs. of  11 variables:
##  $ name        : chr  "Cheetah" "Owl monkey" "Mountain beaver" "Greater sh
##    ort-tailed shrew" ...
##  $ genus       : chr  "Acinonyx" "Aotus" "Aplodontia" "Blarina" ...
##  $ vore        : chr  "carni" "omni" "herbi" "omni" ...
##  $ order       : chr  "Carnivora" "Primates" "Rodentia" "Soricomorpha" ...
##  $ conservation: chr  "lc" NA "nt" "lc" ...
##  $ sleep_total : num  12.1 17 14.4 14.9 4 14.4 8.7 7 10.1 3 ...
##  $ sleep_rem   : num  NA 1.8 2.4 2.3 0.7 2.2 1.4 NA 2.9 NA ...
##  $ sleep_cycle : num  NA NA NA 0.133 0.667 ...
##  $ awake       : num  11.9 7 9.6 9.1 20 9.6 15.3 17 13.9 21 ...
##  $ brainwt     : num  NA 0.0155 NA 0.00029 0.423 NA NA NA 0.07 0.0982 ...
##  $ bodywt      : num  50 0.48 1.35 0.019 600 ...
```

```
summary(msleep)
```

```
##      name               genus               vore
##  Length:83          Length:83          Length:83
##  Class :character   Class :character   Class :character
##  Mode  :character   Mode  :character   Mode  :character
##
##
##
##
##     order            conservation        sleep_total       sleep_rem
##  Length:83          Length:83          Min.   : 1.90     Min.   :0.100
##  Class :character   Class :character   1st Qu.: 7.85     1st Qu.:0.900
##  Mode  :character   Mode  :character   Median :10.10     Median :1.500
##                                        Mean   :10.43     Mean   :1.875
##                                        3rd Qu.:13.75     3rd Qu.:2.400
##                                        Max.   :19.90     Max.   :6.600
##                                                          NA's   :22
##   sleep_cycle         awake            brainwt           bodywt
##  Min.   :0.1167    Min.   : 4.10    Min.   :0.00014   Min.   :   0.005
##  1st Qu.:0.1833    1st Qu.:10.25    1st Qu.:0.00290   1st Qu.:   0.174
##  Median :0.3333    Median :13.90    Median :0.01240   Median :   1.670
##  Mean   :0.4396    Mean   :13.57    Mean   :0.28158   Mean   : 166.136
##  3rd Qu.:0.5792    3rd Qu.:16.15    3rd Qu.:0.12550   3rd Qu.:  41.750
##  Max.   :1.5000    Max.   :22.10    Max.   :5.71200   Max.   :6654.000
##  NA's   :51                         NA's   :27
```

SCENARIO

We have been asked to build an extract of the `msleep` data that has no missing values. To accomplish this, we will remove all rows that have missing values. The cartoon of the transform is shown in figure 5.4.

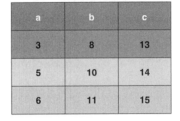

Figure 5.4 Removing rows with missing values

Base R solution

- `complete.cases()` returns a vector with one entry for each row of the data frame, which is TRUE if and only if the row has no missing entries. Once we know what rows we want, it is just a matter of selecting those rows (which we have seen earlier).
- `na.omit()` performs the whole task in one step.

```
clean_base_1 <- msleep[complete.cases(msleep), , drop = FALSE]

summary(clean_base_1)

##       name                genus               vore
##  Length:20          Length:20          Length:20
##  Class :character   Class :character   Class :character
##  Mode  :character   Mode  :character   Mode  :character
##
##
##
##      order            conservation        sleep_total         sleep_rem
##  Length:20          Length:20          Min.   : 2.900     Min.   :0.600
##  Class :character   Class :character   1st Qu.: 8.925     1st Qu.:1.300
##  Mode  :character   Mode  :character   Median :11.300     Median :2.350
##                                        Mean   :11.225     Mean   :2.275
##                                        3rd Qu.:13.925     3rd Qu.:3.125
##                                        Max.   :19.700     Max.   :4.900
##   sleep_cycle          awake            brainwt             bodywt
##  Min.   :0.1167   Min.   : 4.30   Min.   :0.00014   Min.   :  0.0050
##  1st Qu.:0.1792   1st Qu.:10.07   1st Qu.:0.00115   1st Qu.:  0.0945
##  Median :0.2500   Median :12.70   Median :0.00590   Median :  0.7490
##  Mean   :0.3458   Mean   :12.78   Mean   :0.07882   Mean   : 72.1177
##  3rd Qu.:0.4167   3rd Qu.:15.07   3rd Qu.:0.03670   3rd Qu.:  6.1250
##  Max.   :1.0000   Max.   :21.10   Max.   :0.65500   Max.   :600.0000

nrow(clean_base_1)

## [1] 20

clean_base_2 = na.omit(msleep)
```

```
nrow(clean_base_2)
```

```
## [1] 20
```

data.table solution

The `complete.cases()` solution also works with `data.table`:

```
library("data.table")
```

```
msleep_data.table <- as.data.table(msleep)
```

```
clean_data.table = msleep_data.table[complete.cases(msleep_data.table), ]
```

```
nrow(clean_data.table)
```

```
## [1] 20
```

dplyr solution

`dplyr::filter` can also be used with `complete.cases()`.

With `magrittr` pipe notation, a `.` is taken to mean the item being piped. So we can use `.` to refer to our data multiple times conveniently, such as telling the `dplyr::filter` to use the data both as the object to be filtered and as the object to pass to `complete.cases()`.

```
library("dplyr")
```

```
clean_dplyr <- msleep %>%
filter(., complete.cases(.))
```

```
nrow(clean_dplyr)
```

```
## [1] 20
```

5.1.3 Ordering rows

In this section, we want to sort or control what order our data rows are in. Perhaps the data came to us unsorted, or sorted for a purpose other than ours.

SCENARIO

We are asked to build a running or cumulative sum of sales by time, but the data came to us out of order:

```
purchases <- wrapr::build_frame(         <----┐   Uses wrapr::build_frame
   "day", "hour", "n_purchase" |                │   to type data in directly in
   1     , 9      , 5             |                │   legible column order
   2     , 9      , 3             |
   2     , 11     , 5             |
   1     , 13     , 1             |
   2     , 13     , 3             |
   1     , 14     , 1             )
```

PROBLEM

Reorder the rows by day and then hour and compute a running sum. The abstract diagram is shown in figure 5.5.

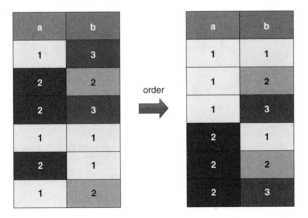

Figure 5.5 Ordering rows

Base R solution

```
order_index <- with(purchases, order(day, hour))

purchases_ordered <- purchases[order_index, , drop = FALSE]
purchases_ordered$running_total <- cumsum(purchases_ordered$n_purchase)

purchases_ordered

##   day hour n_purchase running_total
## 1   1    9          5             5
## 4   1   13          1             6
## 6   1   14          1             7
## 2   2    9          3            10
## 3   2   11          5            15
## 5   2   13          3            18
```

Computes the running sum

**with() executes the code in its second argument
as if the columns of the first argument were variables.
This lets us write x instead of purchases_ordered$x.**

data.table solution

```
library("data.table")

DT_purchases <- as.data.table(purchases)

order_cols <- c("day", "hour")         Reorders data
setorderv(DT_purchases, order_cols)

DT_purchases[ , running_total := cumsum(n_purchase)]

# print(DT_purchases)
```

:= AND []   Operations that alter data in place (such as :=) annotate the result
to suppress printing. This is important, as often you are working with large
structures and do not want intermediate data to print. [] is a no-operation
that as a side effect restores printing.

setorderv() reorders data in place and takes a list of ordering column names to specify the order. This is much more convenient than the base R solution that takes

multiple ordering columns as multiple arguments. `wrapr::orderv()` tries to bridge this gap by allowing the user to specify ordering constraints with a list of columns (column values, not column names).

dplyr solution

dplyr uses the word `arrange` to order data, and `mutate` to add a new column:

```
library("dplyr")

res <- purchases %>%
  arrange(., day, hour) %>%
  mutate(., running_total = cumsum(n_purchase))

# print(res)
```

ADVANCED USE OF ORDERING

For our advanced example, suppose we want the cumulative sum of sales to be per-day—that is, to reset the sum at the start of each day.

Base R solution

This easiest base R solution is a split and recombine strategy:

First sorts the data

Now splits the data into a list of groups

```
order_index <- with(purchases, order(day, hour))
purchases_ordered <- purchases[order_index, , drop = FALSE]

data_list <- split(purchases_ordered, purchases_ordered$day)

data_list <- lapply(
  data_list,
  function(di) {
    di$running_total <- cumsum(di$n_purchase)
    di
  })

purchases_ordered <- do.call(base::rbind, data_list)
rownames(purchases_ordered) <- NULL

purchases_ordered

##   day hour n_purchase running_total
## 1   1    9          5             5
## 2   1   13          1             6
## 3   1   14          1             7
## 4   2    9          3             3
## 5   2   11          5             8
## 6   2   13          3            11
```

Applies the cumsum to each group

Puts the results back together into a single data.frame

R often keeps annotations in rownames(). In this case, it is storing the original row numbers of the pieces we are assembling. This can confuse users when printing, so it is good practice to remove these annotations, as we do here.

data.table solution

The `data.table` solution is particularly concise. We order the data and then tell `data.table` to calculate the new running sum per-group with the `by` argument. The idea that the grouping is a property of the calculation, and not a property of the data, is similar to SQL and helps minimize errors.

:= VERSUS = In data.table, := means "assign in place"—it is used to alter or create a column in the incoming data.table. Conversely, = is used to mean "create in new data.table," and we wrap these sorts of assignments in a .() notation so that column names are not confused with arguments to data.table.

```
library("data.table")

# new copy for result solution
DT_purchases <- as.data.table(purchases)[order(day, hour),
            .(hour = hour,
              n_purchase = n_purchase,
              running_total = cumsum(n_purchase)),
            by = "day"]
# print(DT_purchases)
```

> Adding the by keyword converts the calculation into a per-group calculation.

> First solution: result is a second copy of the data .(=) notation. Only columns used in the calculation (such as day) and those explicitly assigned to are in the result.

```
# in-place solution
DT_purchases <- as.data.table(purchases)
order_cols <- c("day", "hour")
setorderv(DT_purchases, order_cols)
DT_purchases[ , running_total := cumsum(n_purchase), by = day]
# print(DT_purchases)
```

> Second solution: result is computed in place by ordering the table before the grouped calculation.

```
# don't reorder the actual data variation!
DT_purchases <- as.data.table(purchases)
DT_purchases[order(day, hour),
            `:=`(hour = hour,
              n_purchase = n_purchase,
              running_total = cumsum(n_purchase)),
            by = "day"]
# print(DT_purchases)
```

> Third solution: result is in the same order as the original table, but the cumulative sum is computed as if we sorted the table, computed the grouped running sum, and then returned the table to the original order.

SEQUENCING DATA.TABLE OPERATIONS Sequencing data.table operations is achieved either by writing in-place operations one after the other (as we did in these examples) or by starting a new open-[right after a close-] for operations that create new copies (this is called *method chaining* and is equivalent to using a pipe operator).

dplyr solution

The dplyr solution works because the command mutate() (which we will discuss in the next section) works per-group if the data is grouped. We can make the data grouped by using the group_by() command :

```
library("dplyr")

res <- purchases %>%
  arrange(., day, hour) %>%
  group_by(., day) %>%
  mutate(., running_total = cumsum(n_purchase)) %>%
  ungroup(.)

# print(res)
```

UNGROUP()   In `dplyr` it is important to always `ungroup` your data when you are done performing per-group operations. This is because the presence of a `dplyr` grouping annotation can cause many downstream steps to calculate unexpected and incorrect results. We advise doing this even after a `summarize()` step, as `summarize()` removes one key from the grouping, leaving it unclear to a code reader if the data remains grouped or not.

5.2   Basic data transforms

This section covers adding and renaming columns.

5.2.1   Adding new columns

The section covers adding new variables (columns) to a data frame, or applying transformations to existing columns (see figure 5.6).

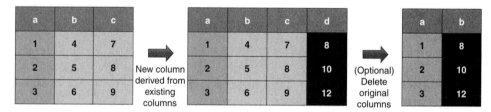

Figure 5.6   Adding or altering columns

EXAMPLE DATA

For our example data, we will use air quality measurements with missing data and non-standard date formatting, for the year 1973:

```
library("datasets")
library("ggplot2")

summary(airquality)
```

```
##      Ozone           Solar.R          Wind            Temp
##  Min.   :  1.00   Min.   :  7.0   Min.   : 1.700   Min.   :56.00
##  1st Qu.: 18.00   1st Qu.:115.8   1st Qu.: 7.400   1st Qu.:72.00
##  Median : 31.50   Median :205.0   Median : 9.700   Median :79.00
##  Mean   : 42.13   Mean   :185.9   Mean   : 9.958   Mean   :77.88
##  3rd Qu.: 63.25   3rd Qu.:258.8   3rd Qu.:11.500   3rd Qu.:85.00
##  Max.   :168.00   Max.   :334.0   Max.   :20.700   Max.   :97.00
##  NA's   :37       NA's   :7
##      Month            Day
##  Min.   :5.000   Min.   : 1.0
##  1st Qu.:6.000   1st Qu.: 8.0
##  Median :7.000   Median :16.0
##  Mean   :6.993   Mean   :15.8
##  3rd Qu.:8.000   3rd Qu.:23.0
##  Max.   :9.000   Max.   :31.0
##
```

SCENARIO

We are asked to convert this non-standard date representation into a new, more useful date column for queries and plotting.

```
library("lubridate")
library("ggplot2")

# create a function to make the date string.
datestr = function(day, month, year) {
  paste(day, month, year, sep="-")
}
```

Base R solution

In base R, we create new columns by assigning to them:

Builds a copy of the data

Adds the date column, using with () to refer to columns without needing the table name

```
airquality_with_date <- airquality

airquality_with_date$date <- with(airquality_with_date,
                              dmy(datestr(Day, Month, 1973)))

airquality_with_date <- airquality_with_date[,
                                  c("Ozone", "date"),
                                  drop = FALSE]
```

Limits down to the columns of interest

```
head(airquality_with_date)    ⟵—— Shows the results

##   Ozone       date
## 1    41 1973-05-01
## 2    36 1973-05-02
## 3    12 1973-05-03
## 4    18 1973-05-04
## 5    NA 1973-05-05
## 6    28 1973-05-06

ggplot(airquality_with_date, aes(x = date, y = Ozone)) +   ⟵—— Plots the results
  geom_point() +
  geom_line() +
  xlab("Date") +
  ggtitle("New York ozone readings, May 1 - Sept 30, 1973")
```

The preceding code produces figure 5.7.

Base R has had transform-style (or pipeable) versions of these basic operators for quite some time (just no pipe!). Let's work the example again in that style:

```
library("wrapr")

airquality %.>%
  transform(., date = dmy(datestr(Day, Month, 1973))) %.>%
  subset(., !is.na(Ozone), select = c("Ozone", "date")) %.>%
  head(.)

##   Ozone       date
## 1    41 1973-05-01
## 2    36 1973-05-02
## 3    12 1973-05-03
## 4    18 1973-05-04
## 6    28 1973-05-06
## 7    23 1973-05-07
```

Attaches the wrapr package to define the wrapr dot arrow pipe: %.>%. The dot arrow pipe is another R pipe and is described in the R Journal at https://journal.r-project.org/archive/2018/RJ-2018-042/index.html.

Runs all the steps as before using transform() and subset(), adding an extra step of filtering down to rows that do not have missing Ozone values

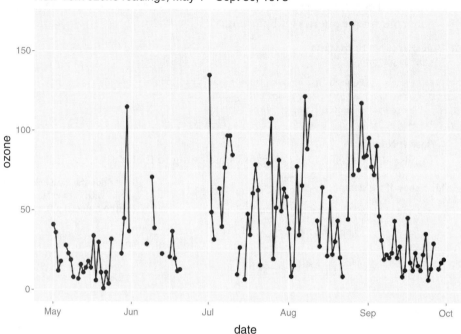

Figure 5.7   Ozone plot example

data.table solution

`data.table` uses `:=` to show column alterations or creations that are supposed to happen "in place" (the `data.table` at hand gets altered, instead of a new one being created).

```
library("data.table")

DT_airquality <-
  as.data.table(airquality)[
    , date := dmy(datestr(Day, Month, 1973)) ][
    , c("Ozone", "date")]

head(DT_airquality)

##    Ozone       date
## 1:    41 1973-05-01
## 2:    36 1973-05-02
## 3:    12 1973-05-03
## 4:    18 1973-05-04
## 5:    NA 1973-05-05
## 6:    28 1973-05-06
```

Builds a data.table copy of the data

Adds the date column

Limits down to the columns of interest

Notice how the open-[steps work a lot like pipes, connecting one data.table stage to another. This is one of the reasons data.table places so many operations inside the []: in R the [] naturally chains operations left to right.

dplyr solution

dplyr users will remember that in dplyr, new columns are produced with the mutate() command :

```
library("dplyr")

airquality_with_date2 <- airquality %>%
  mutate(., date = dmy(datestr(Day, Month, 1973))) %>%
  select(., Ozone, date)

head(airquality_with_date2)

##   Ozone       date
## 1    41 1973-05-01
## 2    36 1973-05-02
## 3    12 1973-05-03
## 4    18 1973-05-04
## 5    NA 1973-05-05
## 6    28 1973-05-06
```

THE SCENARIO CONTINUED

Notice the original Ozone graph had holes in the data, due to missing values. We will try to fix this by propagating the last known Ozone reading forward to the dates with missing values. This "the task was finished ... until we looked at the results" situation is typical of data science. So always look, and look for problems.

Filling in missing values from earlier in a column is illustrated in figure 5.8.

The zoo package supplies a function called na.locf(), which is designed to solve our issue. We will show how to apply this function now.

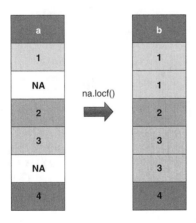

Figure 5.8 Filling in missing values

Base R solution

```
library("zoo")

airquality_corrected <- airquality_with_date
airquality_corrected$OzoneCorrected <-
  na.locf(airquality_corrected$Ozone, na.rm = FALSE)

summary(airquality_corrected)

##      Ozone             date              OzoneCorrected
## Min.   :  1.00   Min.   :1973-05-01   Min.   :  1.00
## 1st Qu.: 18.00   1st Qu.:1973-06-08   1st Qu.: 16.00
## Median : 31.50   Median :1973-07-16   Median : 30.00
## Mean   : 42.13   Mean   :1973-07-16   Mean   : 39.78
## 3rd Qu.: 63.25   3rd Qu.:1973-08-23   3rd Qu.: 52.00
## Max.   :168.00   Max.   :1973-09-30   Max.   :168.00
## NA's   :37

ggplot(airquality_corrected, aes(x = date, y = Ozone)) +
  geom_point(aes(y=Ozone)) +
  geom_line(aes(y=OzoneCorrected)) +
  ggtitle("New York ozone readings, May 1 - Sept 30, 1973",
          subtitle = "(corrected)") +
  xlab("Date")
```

This produces figure 5.9.

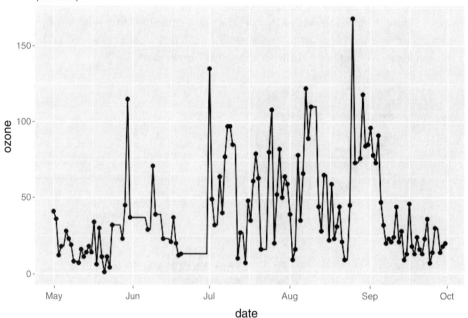

Figure 5.9   Ozone plot again

USE NA.RM = FALSE Always use `na.rm = FALSE` with `na.locf()`; otherwise, it may delete initial `NA` elements from your data.

data.table solution

```
library("data.table")
library("zoo")

DT_airquality[, OzoneCorrected := na.locf(Ozone, na.rm=FALSE)]

summary(DT_airquality)

##      Ozone              date            OzoneCorrected
## Min.   :  1.00   Min.   :1973-05-01   Min.   :  1.00
## 1st Qu.: 18.00   1st Qu.:1973-06-08   1st Qu.: 16.00
## Median : 31.50   Median :1973-07-16   Median : 30.00
## Mean   : 42.13   Mean   :1973-07-16   Mean   : 39.78
## 3rd Qu.: 63.25   3rd Qu.:1973-08-23   3rd Qu.: 52.00
## Max.   :168.00   Max.   :1973-09-30   Max.   :168.00
## NA's   :37
```

Notice that `data.table` performed the correction "in place," in `DT_airquality` instead of producing a new `data.frame`.

dplyr solution

```
library("dplyr")
library("zoo")

airquality_with_date %>%
  mutate(.,
         OzoneCorrected = na.locf(Ozone, na.rm = FALSE)) %>%
  summary(.)

##      Ozone              date            OzoneCorrected
## Min.   :  1.00   Min.   :1973-05-01   Min.   :  1.00
## 1st Qu.: 18.00   1st Qu.:1973-06-08   1st Qu.: 16.00
## Median : 31.50   Median :1973-07-16   Median : 30.00
## Mean   : 42.13   Mean   :1973-07-16   Mean   : 39.78
## 3rd Qu.: 63.25   3rd Qu.:1973-08-23   3rd Qu.: 52.00
## Max.   :168.00   Max.   :1973-09-30   Max.   :168.00
## NA's   :37
```

5.2.2 *Other simple operations*

A number of additional simple operations commonly used in working with data are available—in particular, renaming columns by altering the column names directly, and also removing columns by assigning `NULL`. We will show these briefly:

```
d <- data.frame(x = 1:2, y = 3:4)
print(d)
#>   x y
#> 1 1 3
#> 2 2 4

colnames(d) <- c("BIGX", "BIGY")
print(d)
#>   BIGX BIGY
#> 1    1    3
```

```
#> 2    2    4

d$BIGX <- NULL
print(d)
#>   BIGY
#> 1    3
#> 2    4
```

5.3   Aggregating transforms

This section covers transforms that combine multiple rows or multiple columns.

5.3.1   Combining many rows into summary rows

Here we address the situation where there are multiple observations or measurements of a single subject, in this case species of Iris, that we wish to aggregate into a single observation.

SCENARIO

We have been asked to make a report summarizing iris petals by species.

PROBLEM

Summarize measurements by category, as shown in figure 5.10.

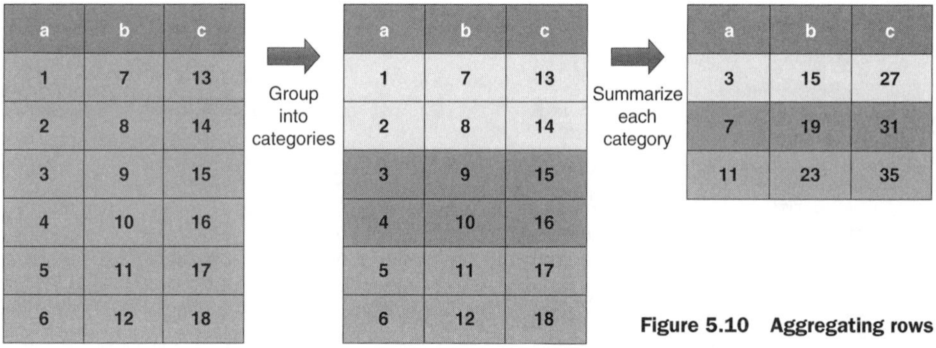

Figure 5.10   Aggregating rows

EXAMPLE DATA

Again, we use measurements of petal length and width, by iris species, from the iris dataset :

```
library("datasets")
library("ggplot2")

head(iris)

##   Sepal.Length Sepal.Width Petal.Length Petal.Width Species
## 1          5.1         3.5          1.4         0.2  setosa
## 2          4.9         3.0          1.4         0.2  setosa
## 3          4.7         3.2          1.3         0.2  setosa
## 4          4.6         3.1          1.5         0.2  setosa
## 5          5.0         3.6          1.4         0.2  setosa
## 6          5.4         3.9          1.7         0.4  setosa
```

Base R solution

```
iris_summary <- aggregate(
  cbind(Petal.Length, Petal.Width) ~ Species,
  data = iris,
  FUN = mean)

print(iris_summary)

#       Species Petal.Length Petal.Width
# 1      setosa        1.462       0.246
# 2 versicolor        4.260       1.326
# 3  virginica        5.552       2.026

library(ggplot2)
ggplot(mapping = aes(x = Petal.Length, y = Petal.Width,
                     shape = Species, color = Species)) +
  geom_point(data = iris, # raw data
             alpha = 0.5) +
  geom_point(data = iris_summary, # per-group summaries
             size = 5) +
  ggtitle("Average Petal dimensions by iris species\n(with raw data for refer
    ence)")
```

This produces figure 5.11, a new iris plot with group mean annotations.

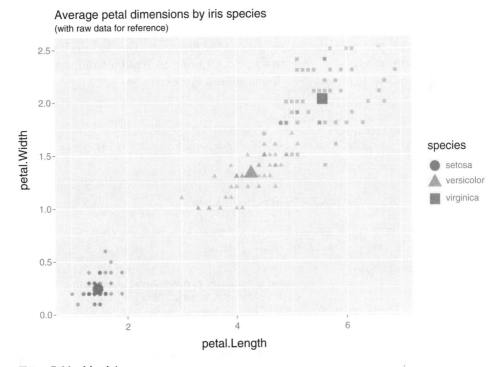

Figure 5.11 Iris plot

data.table solution

```
library("data.table")

iris_data.table <- as.data.table(iris)
iris_data.table <- iris_data.table[,
                                .(Petal.Length = mean(Petal.Length),
                                  Petal.Width = mean(Petal.Width)),
                                by = .(Species)]

# print(iris_data.table)
```

dplyr solution

- dplyr::group_by
- dplyr::summarize
- A one-argument aggregation function, for example sum or mean

```
library("dplyr")

iris_summary <- iris %>% group_by(., Species) %>%
  summarize(.,
            Petal.Length = mean(Petal.Length),
            Petal.Width = mean(Petal.Width)) %>%
  ungroup(.)

# print(iris_summary)
```

Window functions

Both data.table and dplyr have grouped versions of the preceding operations (similar to what relational databases call *window functions*). This lets each row include the per-group summary in each row without having to build a summary table and join (the usual way to compute such quantities). For example:

```
iris_copy <- iris
iris_copy$mean_Petal.Length <-
    ave(iris$Petal.Length, iris$Species, FUN = mean)
iris_copy$mean_Petal.Width <- ave(iris$Petal.Width, iris$Species, FUN = mean)

# head(iris_copy)
# tail(iris_copy)
```

In data.table, the task looks like the following:

```
library("data.table")

iris_data.table <- as.data.table(iris)

iris_data.table[ ,
                 `:=`(mean_Petal.Length = mean(Petal.Length),
                      mean_Petal.Width = mean(Petal.Width)),
                 by = "Species"]

# print(iris_data.table)
```

Please run the preceding code and print iris_data.table to see that the computed means are per-group.

dplyr has similar functionality:

```
library("dplyr")

iris_dplyr <- iris %>%
  group_by(., Species) %>%
  mutate(.,
         mean_Petal.Length = mean(Petal.Length),
         mean_Petal.Width = mean(Petal.Width)) %>%
  ungroup(.)

# head(iris_dplyr)
```

Again, it is critical to ungroup() when applying per-group transforms. Also, be aware that dplyr grouped operations (in particular, row selection through filter()) can be much slower than ungrouped operations, so you want to make your group()/ungroup() intervals as short as possible. And dplyr grouped operations are usually much slower than data.table grouped operations in general.

5.4 Multitable data transforms

This section covers operations between multiple tables. This includes the tasks of splitting tables, concatenating tables, and joining tables.

5.4.1 Combining two or more ordered data frames quickly

Here we discuss combining two data frames, with the same number of rows or columns (and same order!). A more involved, but more general way to combine data is demonstrated in section 5.4.2.

SCENARIO

We have been asked to draw information about products from a sales database and produce a report. Typically, different facts (in this case, price and units sold) are stored in different tables, so to produce our report, we will have to combine data from more than one table.

For example, suppose our example data was the following:

```
productTable <- wrapr::build_frame(
    "productID", "price" |
    "p1"        , 9.99   |
    "p2"        , 16.29  |
    "p3"        , 19.99  |
    "p4"        , 5.49   |
    "p5"        , 24.49  )

salesTable <- wrapr::build_frame(
    "productID", "sold_store", "sold_online" |
    "p1"        , 6           , 64           |
    "p2"        , 31          , 1            |
    "p3"        , 30          , 23           |
    "p4"        , 31          , 67           |
    "p5"        , 43          , 51           )

productTable2 <- wrapr::build_frame(
    "productID", "price" |
    "n1"        , 25.49  |
```

```
    "n2"        , 33.99   |
    "n3"        , 17.99   )
productTable$productID <- factor(productTable$productID)
productTable2$productID <- factor(productTable2$productID)
```

PROBLEM 1: APPENDING ROWS

When two tables have the exact same column structure, we can concatenate them to get a larger table, as in figure 5.12.

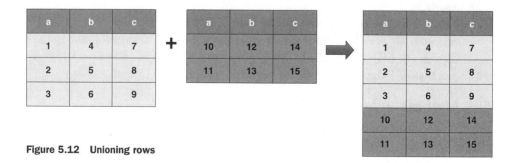

Figure 5.12   Unioning rows

Base R solution

rbind

```
rbind_base = rbind(productTable,
                   productTable2)
```

Note that rbind creates a new factor variable when merging incompatible factor variables:

```
str(rbind_base)

## 'data.frame':    8 obs. of  2 variables:
##  $ productID: Factor w/ 8 levels "p1","p2","p3",..: 1 2 3 4 5 6 7 8
##  $ price    : num  9.99 16.29 19.99 5.49 24.49 ...
```

data.table solution

```
library("data.table")

rbindlist(list(productTable,
               productTable2))

##     productID price
## 1:         p1  9.99
## 2:         p2 16.29
## 3:         p3 19.99
## 4:         p4  5.49
## 5:         p5 24.49
## 6:         n1 25.49
## 7:         n2 33.99
## 8:         n3 17.99
```

data.table also correctly merges factor types.

dplyr solution

dplyr::bind_rows

```
library("dplyr")

bind_rows(list(productTable,
               productTable2))

## Warning in bind_rows_(x, .id): Unequal factor levels: coercing to character

## Warning in bind_rows_(x, .id): binding character and factor vector,
## coercing into character vector

## Warning in bind_rows_(x, .id): binding character and factor vector,
## coercing into character vector

##   productID price
## 1        p1  9.99
## 2        p2 16.29
## 3        p3 19.99
## 4        p4  5.49
## 5        p5 24.49
## 6        n1 25.49
## 7        n2 33.99
## 8        n3 17.99
```

Notice that bind_rows coerces incompatible factor variables to character.

PROBLEM 2: SPLITTING TABLES

The inverse of row binding is *splitting*. Many difficult calculations can be made easy by splitting a data frame into a family of data frames, then working on each data frame, and finally rebinding them together. The best implementation is the one found in data.table, which has some priority (being one of the first). na.rm = FALSE only simulates splitting and recombining data (so tends to be very fast).

Base R solution

```
# add an extra column telling us which table
# each row comes from
productTable_marked <- productTable
productTable_marked$table <- "productTable"
productTable2_marked <- productTable2
productTable2_marked$table <- "productTable2"

# combine the tables
rbind_base <- rbind(productTable_marked,
                    productTable2_marked)
rbind_base

##   productID price         table
## 1        p1  9.99  productTable
## 2        p2 16.29  productTable
## 3        p3 19.99  productTable
## 4        p4  5.49  productTable
## 5        p5 24.49  productTable
## 6        n1 25.49 productTable2
## 7        n2 33.99 productTable2
## 8        n3 17.99 productTable2
```

```
# split them apart
tables <- split(rbind_base, rbind_base$table)
tables

## $productTable
##    productID price        table
## 1         p1  9.99 productTable
## 2         p2 16.29 productTable
## 3         p3 19.99 productTable
## 4         p4  5.49 productTable
## 5         p5 24.49 productTable
##
## $productTable2
##    productID price         table
## 6         n1 25.49 productTable2
## 7         n2 33.99 productTable2
## 8         n3 17.99 productTable2
```

data.table solution

data.table combines the split, apply, and recombine steps into a single, very efficient operation. We will continue our example with the rbind_base object to show the effect. data.table is willing to call a user function or execute a user expression for each data group and supplies special variables to work per-group:

- .*BY*—A named list of the grouping variables and values per group. .BY is a list of scalars, as by definition grouping variables do not vary per group.
- .*SD*—A data.table representation of the set of rows for the given group with the grouping columns removed.

For instance, to compute a max price per group, we can do the following:

```
library("data.table")

# convert to data.table
dt <- as.data.table(rbind_base)

# arbitrary user defined function
f <- function(.BY, .SD) {
  max(.SD$price)
}

# apply the function to each group
# and collect results
dt[ , max_price := f(.BY, .SD), by = table]

print(dt)

##    productID price        table max_price
## 1:        p1  9.99 productTable     24.49
## 2:        p2 16.29 productTable     24.49
## 3:        p3 19.99 productTable     24.49
## 4:        p4  5.49 productTable     24.49
## 5:        p5 24.49 productTable     24.49
## 6:        n1 25.49 productTable2    33.99
## 7:        n2 33.99 productTable2    33.99
## 8:        n3 17.99 productTable2    33.99
```

Note that the preceding is a powerful general form not needed for such a simple task. Simple per-group aggregation of values is usually achieved by naming the columns:

```
library("data.table")

dt <- as.data.table(rbind_base)
grouping_column <- "table"
dt[ , max_price := max(price), by = eval(grouping_column)]

print(dt)

##    productID price          table max_price
## 1:        p1  9.99   productTable     24.49
## 2:        p2 16.29   productTable     24.49
## 3:        p3 19.99   productTable     24.49
## 4:        p4  5.49   productTable     24.49
## 5:        p5 24.49   productTable     24.49
## 6:        n1 25.49  productTable2     33.99
## 7:        n2 33.99  productTable2     33.99
## 8:        n3 17.99  productTable2     33.99
```

In this example, we took the liberty of showing how we would group by a column chosen by a variable.

dplyr solution

dplyr doesn't have its own split implementation. dplyr tries to simulate working on subtables with its group_by() notation. For example, to compute the maximum price per group in dplyr, we would write code like the following:

```
rbind_base %>%
  group_by(., table) %>%
  mutate(., max_price = max(price)) %>%
  ungroup(.)

## # A tibble: 8 x 4
##    productID price table         max_price
##    <fct>     <dbl> <chr>             <dbl>
## 1 p1          9.99 productTable       24.5
## 2 p2         16.3  productTable       24.5
## 3 p3         20.0  productTable       24.5
## 4 p4          5.49 productTable       24.5
## 5 p5         24.5  productTable       24.5
## 6 n1         25.5  productTable2      34.0
## 7 n2         34.0  productTable2      34.0
## 8 n3         18.0  productTable2      34.0
```

This is not going to be as powerful as calling an arbitrary function per data group.

PROBLEM 3: APPENDING COLUMNS

Append a data frame as columns to another data frame. The data frames must have the same number of rows and same row order (with respect to what we consider to be row-keys). This is illustrated in figure 5.13.

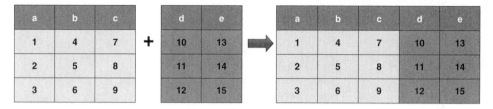

Figure 5.13   Unioning columns

Create a table of product information (price and units sold), from `productTable` and `salesTable`. This assumes that the products are sorted in the same order in both tables. If they are not, then sort them, or use a join command to merge the tables together (please see section 5.4.2).

Base R solution

cbind

```
cbind(productTable, salesTable[, -1])

##   productID price sold_store sold_online
## 1        p1  9.99          6          64
## 2        p2 16.29         31           1
## 3        p3 19.99         30          23
## 4        p4  5.49         31          67
## 5        p5 24.49         43          51
```

data.table solution

For binding columns, `data.table` methods require the data to already be of type `data.table`.

```
library("data.table")

cbind(as.data.table(productTable),
      as.data.table(salesTable[, -1]))

##    productID price sold_store sold_online
## 1:        p1  9.99          6          64
## 2:        p2 16.29         31           1
## 3:        p3 19.99         30          23
## 4:        p4  5.49         31          67
## 5:        p5 24.49         43          51
```

dplyr solution

dplyr::bind_cols

```
library("dplyr")

# list of data frames calling convention
dplyr::bind_cols(list(productTable, salesTable[, -1]))

##    productID price sold_store sold_online
## 1         p1  9.99          6          64
## 2         p2 16.29         31           1
## 3         p3 19.99         30          23
## 4         p4  5.49         31          67
## 5         p5 24.49         43          51
```

5.4.2 *Principal methods to combine data from multiple tables*

Join is the relational name for the process of combining two tables to create a third. The join results in a table that possibly has a new row for every pair of rows from the original two tables (plus possibly rows from each table that did not have matches from the other table). Rows are matched on key-values, matching from one table to another. The simplest case is when each table has a set of columns that uniquely determine each row (a unique key), and this is the case we will discuss here.

SCENARIO

Our example data is information about products in a sales database. Various facts (in this case, price and units sold) are stored in different tables. Missing values are allowed. We are tasked with combining these tables to produce a report.

First let's set up some example data:

```
productTable <- wrapr::build_frame(
   "productID", "price" |
   "p1"        , 9.99   |
   "p3"        , 19.99  |
   "p4"        , 5.49   |
   "p5"        , 24.49  )

salesTable <- wrapr::build_frame(
   "productID", "unitsSold" |
   "p1"        , 10          |
   "p2"        , 43          |
   "p3"        , 55          |
   "p4"        , 8           )
```

LEFT JOIN

The most important join for the data scientist is likely the *left join*. This join keeps every row from the left table and adds columns coming from matching rows in the right table. When there are no matching rows, NA values are substituted in. Usually, you design the right table (the second argument to your join command) to have unique keys; otherwise, the number of rows may grow (there is no need for the left table to have unique keys).

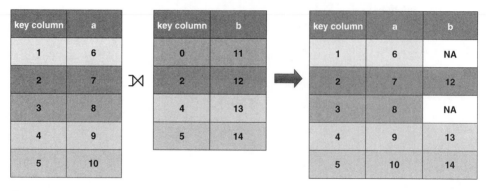

Figure 5.14   Left join

The operation is typically used to adjoin data from the second (or right) table into a copy of the first or left table, as shown in figure 5.14.

Base R solution

merge with argument `all.x = TRUE`

```
merge(productTable, salesTable, by = "productID", all.x = TRUE)

##    productID price unitsSold
## 1        p1  9.99        10
## 2        p3 19.99        55
## 3        p4  5.49         8
## 4        p5 24.49        NA
```

data.table solution

```
library("data.table")

productTable_data.table <- as.data.table(productTable)
salesTable_data.table <- as.data.table(salesTable)

# index notation for join
# idea is rows are produced for each row inside the []
salesTable_data.table[productTable_data.table, on = "productID"]

##    productID unitsSold price
## 1:        p1        10  9.99
## 2:        p3        55 19.99
## 3:        p4         8  5.49
## 4:        p5        NA 24.49

# data.table also overrides merge()
merge(productTable, salesTable, by = "productID", all.x = TRUE)

##    productID price unitsSold
## 1        p1  9.99        10
## 2        p3 19.99        55
## 3        p4  5.49         8
## 4        p5 24.49        NA
```

Base R indexing solution

The data.table index notation reminds us that there is another very good Base R way to use one table to add a single column to another: vectorized lookup through the match() and [] methods.

```
library("data.table")

joined_table <- productTable
joined_table$unitsSold <- salesTable$unitsSold[match(joined_table$productID,
salesTable$productID)]
print(joined_table)

##   productID price unitsSold
## 1        p1  9.99        10
## 2        p3 19.99        55
## 3        p4  5.49         8
## 4        p5 24.49        NA
```

match() found the matching indices, and [] used the indices to retrieve the data. Please see help(match) for more details.

dplyr solution

```
library("dplyr")

left_join(productTable, salesTable, by = "productID")

##   productID price unitsSold
## 1        p1  9.99        10
## 2        p3 19.99        55
## 3        p4  5.49         8
## 4        p5 24.49        NA
```

Right join

There is also a join called *right join* that is just the left join with the arguments reversed. As the right join is so similar to the left, we will forgo any right join examples.

INNER JOIN

In an *inner join*, you merge two tables into a single table, keeping only the rows where the key exists in both tables. This produces an intersection of the two tables, as shown in figure 5.15.

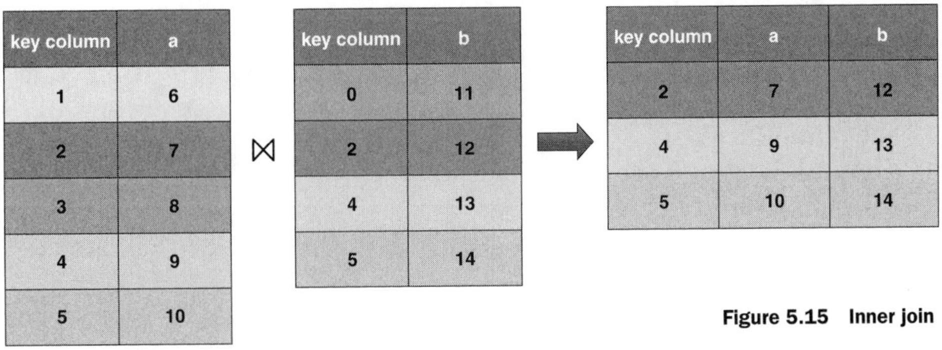

Figure 5.15 Inner join

Base R solution

merge

```
merge(productTable, salesTable, by = "productID")

##    productID price unitsSold
## 1         p1  9.99        10
## 2         p3 19.99        55
## 3         p4  5.49         8
```

data.table solution

```
library("data.table")

productTable_data.table <- as.data.table(productTable)
salesTable_data.table <- as.data.table(salesTable)

merge(productTable, salesTable, by = "productID")

##    productID price unitsSold
## 1         p1  9.99        10
## 2         p3 19.99        55
## 3         p4  5.49         8
```

dplyr solution

inner_join

```
library("dplyr")

inner_join(productTable, salesTable, by = "productID")

##    productID price unitsSold
## 1         p1  9.99        10
## 2         p3 19.99        55
## 3         p4  5.49         8
```

FULL JOIN

In a *full join*, you merge two tables into a single table, keeping rows for all key values. Notice that the two tables have equal importance here. We show the result in figure 5.16.

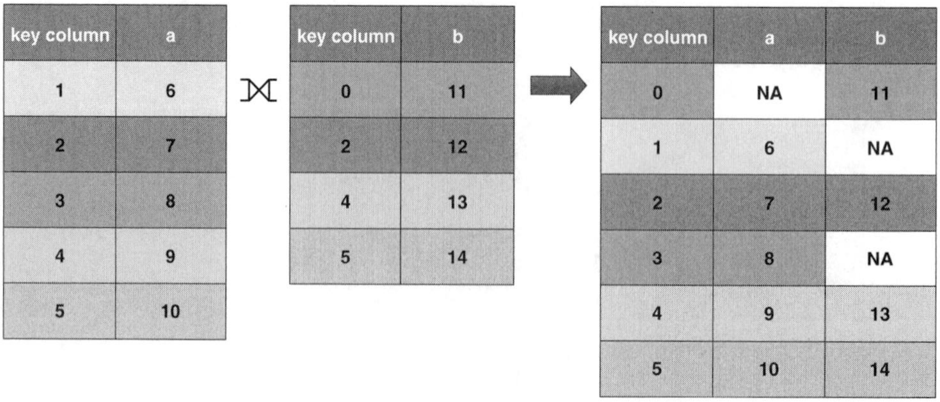

Figure 5.16   Full join

Base R solution

merge with argument all=TRUE

```
# note that merge orders the result by key column by default
# use sort=FALSE to skip the sorting
merge(productTable, salesTable, by = "productID", all=TRUE)
```

```
##    productID price unitsSold
## 1         p1  9.99        10
## 2         p2    NA        43
## 3         p3 19.99        55
## 4         p4  5.49         8
## 5         p5 24.49        NA
```

data.table solution

```
library("data.table")
```

```
productTable_data.table <- as.data.table(productTable)
salesTable_data.table <- as.data.table(salesTable)
```

```
merge(productTable_data.table, salesTable_data.table,
      by = "productID", all = TRUE)
```

```
##    productID price unitsSold
## 1:        p1  9.99        10
## 2:        p2    NA        43
## 3:        p3 19.99        55
## 4:        p4  5.49         8
## 5:        p5 24.49        NA
```

dplyr solution

dplyr::full_join

```
library("dplyr")
```

```
full_join(productTable, salesTable, by = "productID")
```

```
##    productID price unitsSold
## 1         p1  9.99        10
## 2         p3 19.99        55
## 3         p4  5.49         8
## 4         p5 24.49        NA
## 5         p2    NA        43
```

A HARDER JOIN PROBLEM

The examples we have given up to now do not use row order. Some problems can be solved much more efficiently with methods that do use row order, such as data.table's powerful rolling join operation.

Scenario

You are given historic stock trade and quote (bid/ask) data. You are asked to perform the following analyses on the stock data: find what the bid and ask price were current when each trade was performed. This involves using row order to indicate time, and sharing information between rows.

Example data

In stock markets, the *bid* is the highest price somebody has declared they are willing to pay for a stock, and the *ask* is the lowest price that somebody has declared they are willing to sell a stock for. Bid and ask data are called *quotes*, and they usually are in an irregular time series (as new quotes can be formed at arbitrary times, not just at regular intervals), such as the following example:

```
library("data.table")

quotes <- data.table(
  bid = c(5, 5, 7, 8),
  ask = c(6, 6, 8, 10),
  bid_quantity = c(100, 100, 100, 100),
  ask_quantity = c(100, 100, 100, 100),
  when = as.POSIXct(strptime(
    c("2018-10-18 1:03:17",
      "2018-10-18 2:12:23",
      "2018-10-18 2:15:00",
      "2018-10-18 2:17:51"),
    "%Y-%m-%d %H:%M:%S")))

print(quotes)

##    bid ask bid_quantity ask_quantity                when
## 1:   5   6          100          100 2018-10-18 01:03:17
## 2:   5   6          100          100 2018-10-18 02:12:23
## 3:   7   8          100          100 2018-10-18 02:15:00
## 4:   8  10          100          100 2018-10-18 02:17:51
```

Another irregular time series is *trades*. These are after-the-fact reports about exchanges of quantities of stock at a given price at a given time.

```
trades <- data.table(
  trade_id = c(32525, 32526),
  price = c(5.5, 9),
  quantity = c(100, 200),
  when = as.POSIXct(strptime(
    c("2018-10-18 2:13:42",
      "2018-10-18 2:19:20"),
    "%Y-%m-%d %H:%M:%S")))

print(trades)

##    trade_id price quantity                when
## 1:    32525   5.5      100 2018-10-18 02:13:42
## 2:    32526   9.0      200 2018-10-18 02:19:20
```

Rolling joins

The data.table rolling join is perfect for finding what was the most recent quote information for each trade. A *rolling join* is a type of join on an ordered column that gives us the most recent data available at the lookup time.

```
quotes[, quote_time := when]
    trades[ , trade_time := when ]
      quotes[ trades, on = "when", roll = TRUE ][
        , .(quote_time, bid, price, ask, trade_id, trade_time) ]
```

```
##               quote_time bid price ask trade_id       trade_time
## 1: 2018-10-18 02:12:23   5   5.5   6     32525 2018-10-18 02:13:42
## 2: 2018-10-18 02:17:51   8   9.0  10     32526 2018-10-18 02:19:20
```

We read the preceding as "for each trade, look up the appropriate quote." In the join, the when field comes from the trades, which is why we added a quote_time field so we could also see when the quote was established. The data.table rolling join is very fast, and also not easy to efficiently simulate in base R, SQL, or dplyr.

Rolling joins are unique to data.table. In R there are a number of tasks, such as matching most recent records, that are easily expressed as moving indexes across rows. However, moving indexes across rows tends to be inefficient in R, as it can't be vectorized like column operations can. A rolling join is a direct way of solving such problems, and has an efficient implementation.

5.5   *Reshaping transforms*

This section covers moving data between rows and columns. This is often called *pivoting*, a name from Pito Salas's work that combines data summarization and shape transforms. Examples will be worked in three packages: data.table, cdata (which only reshapes data, and does not summarize data), and tidyr. Base R does have notations for these transforms (such as stack() and unstack()), but the package versions are significantly better tools.

5.5.1   *Moving data from wide to tall form*

We will show how to move data records where all measurements are in single rows to a new record set where data is in multiple rows. We call this moving from a wide form to a thin or tall form.

DATA EXAMPLE

Let's work with measurements of vehicle drivers/passengers injured or killed, by month. The data includes additional information about fuel price and whether seatbelts are required by law.

Relevant variables for this example:

- date—Year and month of measurement (numeric representation)
- DriversKilled—Car drivers killed
- front—Front seat passengers killed or seriously injured
- rear—Rear seat passengers killed or seriously injured
- law—Whether or not seatbelt law was in effect (0/1)

```
library("datasets")
library("xts")

# move the date index into a column
dates <- index(as.xts(time(Seatbelts)))
Seatbelts <- data.frame(Seatbelts)
Seatbelts$date <- dates

# restrict down to 1982 and 1983
```

```
Seatbelts <- Seatbelts[ (Seatbelts$date >= as.yearmon("Jan 1982")) &
                        (Seatbelts$date <= as.yearmon("Dec 1983")),
                       , drop = FALSE]
Seatbelts$date <- as.Date(Seatbelts$date)
# mark if the seatbelt law was in effect
Seatbelts$law <- ifelse(Seatbelts$law==1, "new law", "pre-law")
# limit down to the columns we want
Seatbelts <- Seatbelts[, c("date", "DriversKilled", "front", "rear", "law")]

head(Seatbelts)

##             date DriversKilled front rear     law
## 157 1982-01-01            115   595  238 pre-law
## 158 1982-02-01            104   673  285 pre-law
## 159 1982-03-01            131   660  324 pre-law
## 160 1982-04-01            108   676  346 pre-law
## 161 1982-05-01            103   755  410 pre-law
## 162 1982-06-01            115   815  411 pre-law
```

To get our data into a presentable format, we have performed transforms described in earlier sections of this chapter: selecting rows, selecting columns, adding new derived columns, and so on. The data now has one row per date (we think of the date as the row-key) and contains information such as how many people were killed in each of three seating positions (driver, front, rear) and if the new seatbelt law was in effect.

We want to see if the new seatbelt law saves lives. Notice that we are missing a key bit of information: a normalizing factor such as number of cars owned per date, driving population size by date, or total miles driven per date (risks make more sense as rates than as absolute counts). This is an example of true data science being an iterative process: we are going to do the best job we can with the data at hand, but in a real project, we would also go back to sources and partners to try to get the critical missing data (or at least an estimate or proxy for the missing data).

Let's plot the data conditioned on the law:

```
# let's give an example of the kind of graph we have in mind,
# using just driver deaths
library("ggplot2")

ggplot(Seatbelts,
       aes(x = date, y = DriversKilled, color = law, shape = law)) +
  geom_point() +
  geom_smooth(se=FALSE) +
  ggtitle("UK car driver deaths by month")
```

This code produces figure 5.17.

From the chart, it looks like the introduction of the seatbelt law produced a drop in deaths that is non-trivial when compared to the normal variation in deaths. It also looks like the effect may have reverted quickly.

Suppose our follow-up question is to break down this data further to seating position (as types of seatbelts differ quite a bit by seating position).

To make such a plot with ggplot2, we need to move the data from all facts being in each row to having one row per seating position. This is an example of moving from a

UK car driver deaths by month

Figure 5.17 Passenger deaths plot

wide or denormalized format, the natural format for machine learning tasks, to a tall or multiline record format.

PROBLEM

Plot deaths conditioned on date and seating position, using ggplot2. ggplot2 requires the data to be in a long, rather than wide, format. So we will concentrate on how to perform this transform. We call this sort of transform moving data from row-oriented records to blocks of rows, as shown in figure 5.18.

Figure 5.18 Wide-to-tall conversion

Solution 1: data.table::melt.data.table()

We can solve this with `data.table::melt.data.table()`. Specify the columns of the original table that the values are to be taken from with the `measure.vars` argument. Specify the pair of columns the information is to be written into in the transformed table with the arguments `variable.name` (the new key column) and `value.name` (the new value column).

```
library("data.table")

seatbelts_long2 <-
  melt.data.table(as.data.table(Seatbelts),
                  id.vars = NULL,
                  measure.vars = c("DriversKilled", "front", "rear"),
                  variable.name = "victim_type",
                  value.name = "nvictims")
```

These new graphs do show us something more: the law had essentially no effect on people in the rear seats. This could be perhaps because the law didn't cover these seats, perhaps enforcing rear seat compliance was difficult, or perhaps rear-seat seatbelts were lap belts (instead of three-point restraints) and were not effective. The strongest benefit seems to be to front-seat passengers, and that is not too unusual, as they tend to have high-quality seatbelts and are not sitting in front of the steering column (a primary source of fatal injuries).

Solution 2: cdata::unpivot_to_blocks()

```
library("cdata")

seatbelts_long3 <- unpivot_to_blocks(
  Seatbelts,
  nameForNewKeyColumn = "victim_type",
  nameForNewValueColumn = "nvictims",
  columnsToTakeFrom = c("DriversKilled", "front", "rear
"))
```

cdata has simple methods to specify the coordinated conversions of many columns at once. A good introduction can be found at http://www.win-vector.com/blog/2018/10/faceted-graphs-with-cdata-and-ggplot2/.

We encourage you to try all three solutions and convince yourself they produce the equivalent results. We prefer the `cdata` solution, but it is new and not as well known as the `data.table` or `tidyr` solutions.

Solution 3: tidyr::gather()

```
library("tidyr")

seatbelts_long1 <- gather(
  Seatbelts,
  key = victim_type,
  value = nvictims,
  DriversKilled, front, rear)

head(seatbelts_long1)
```

```
##           date      law    victim_type nvictims
## 1 1982-01-01 pre-law DriversKilled      115
## 2 1982-02-01 pre-law DriversKilled      104
## 3 1982-03-01 pre-law DriversKilled      131
## 4 1982-04-01 pre-law DriversKilled      108
## 5 1982-05-01 pre-law DriversKilled      103
## 6 1982-06-01 pre-law DriversKilled      115
```

```
ggplot(seatbelts_long1,
       aes(x = date, y = nvictims, color = law, shape = law)) +
  geom_point() +
  geom_smooth(se=FALSE) +
  facet_wrap(~victim_type, ncol=1, scale="free_y") +
  ggtitle("UK auto fatalities by month and seating position")
```

And we now have the passenger death data faceted by seating position in figure 5.19.

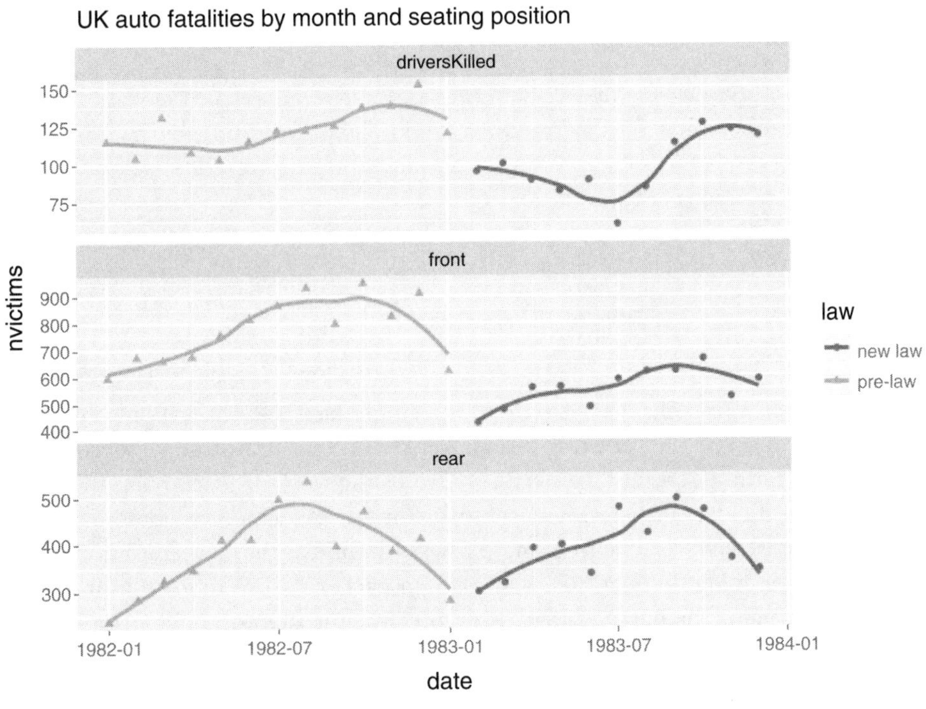

Figure 5.19 Faceted passenger death plot

5.5.2   *Moving data from tall to wide form*

We have been given data in a log style, where each detail of a measurement is written in a separate row. Colloquially, we call this a *tall* or *thin* data form (formally, it is related to information storage ideas such as RDF triples). The operation of moving to a wide form is very much like what Microsoft Excel users call *pivoting*, except aggregations (sums, averages, counts) are not strictly part of moving from tall to wide form (we suggest aggregating first before transforming). Also, moving from tall to wide form is, of course, the inverse of the moving from wide to tall form conversion we discussed earlier.

THE DATA

For our example, we have taken the ChickWeight data from R's datasets package. Please try these commands along with the book and take extra steps to examine the data (using commands such as View(), head(), summary() and so on):

```
library("datasets")
library("data.table")
library("ggplot2")

ChickWeight <- data.frame(ChickWeight) # get rid of attributes
ChickWeight$Diet <- NULL # remove the diet label
# pad names with zeros
padz <- function(x, n=max(nchar(x))) gsub(" ", "0", formatC(x, width=n))
# append "Chick" to the chick ids
ChickWeight$Chick <- paste0("Chick", padz(as.character(ChickWeight$Chick)))

head(ChickWeight)

##    weight Time    Chick
## 1      42    0 Chick01
## 2      51    2 Chick01
## 3      59    4 Chick01
## 4      64    6 Chick01
## 5      76    8 Chick01
## 6      93   10 Chick01
```

This data is organized so each row is a single fact (weight) about a given chick at a given time. The is a very easy format to produce and transmit, which is why it is popular in scientific settings. To perform interesting work or learn from the data, we need to bring the data into a wider structure. For our problem, we would like all the weight facts about a chick to be in a single row, with time as the new column name.

Before doing that, let's use some of our earlier lessons to get a look at the data. We can aggregate the data to move from information about individuals to overall trends.

```
# aggregate count and mean weight by time
ChickSummary <- as.data.table(ChickWeight)
ChickSummary <- ChickSummary[,
                .(count = .N,
                  weight = mean(weight),
                  q1_weight = quantile(weight, probs = 0.25),
                  q2_weight = quantile(weight, probs = 0.75)),
                by = Time]
head(ChickSummary)

##    Time count    weight q1_weight q2_weight
## 1:    0    50  41.06000        41        42
## 2:    2    50  49.22000        48        51
## 3:    4    49  59.95918        57        63
```

```
## 4:      6    49   74.30612          68          80
## 5:      8    49   91.24490          83         102
## 6:     10    49  107.83673          93         124
```

In ChickSummary the only key is Time (specified by the data.tableby argument) and we can now see how many chicks are surviving at a given time and the distribution of surviving chick weights at a given time.

We can present this table graphically. To use ggplot2 to do this, we need to move the summarized data to a tall form (as ggplot2 prefers to work with tall data). We use cdata::unpivot_to_blocks:

```
library("ggplot2")                                    │ Unpivots into tall
                                                      │ form for plotting
ChickSummary <- cdata::unpivot_to_blocks(   ◁─────────┘
    ChickSummary,
  nameForNewKeyColumn = "measurement",
  nameForNewValueColumn = "value",                Makes sure we have the exact set
  columnsToTakeFrom = c("count", "weight"))        of columns needed for plotting

ChickSummary$q1_weight[ChickSummary$measurement=="count"] <- NA    ◁
 ChickSummary$q2_weight[ChickSummary$measurement=="count"] <- NA
CW <- ChickWeight
CW$measurement <- "weight"

ggplot(ChickSummary, aes(x = Time, y = value, color = measurement)) + ◁
  geom_line(data = CW, aes(x = Time, y = weight, group = Chick),
          color="LightGray") +                             Makes the plot
  geom_line(size=2) +
  geom_ribbon(aes(ymin = q1_weight, ymax = q2_weight),
            alpha = 0.3, colour = NA) +
  facet_wrap(~measurement, ncol=1, scales = "free_y") +
  theme(legend.position = "none") +
  ylab(NULL) +
  ggtitle("Chick Weight and Count Measurements by Time",
        subtitle = "25% through 75% quartiles of weight shown shaded around
    mean")
```

This gives the chick weights organized by time and chick, as shown in figure 5.20.

Here we have plotted the total count of surviving chicks as a function of time, plus the weight trajectory of each individual check, and the summary statistics (mean weight, and 25% through 75% quartiles of weight).

PROBLEM

We can now return to the example task of this section: putting all the information about each chick into a single row.

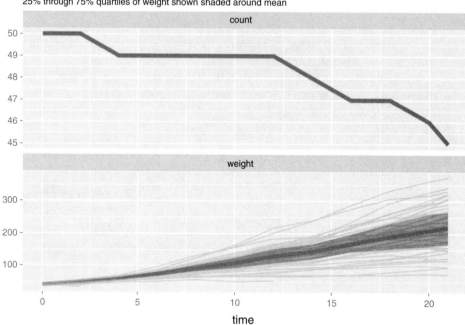

Figure 5.20   Chick count and weight over time

Diagrammatically, it looks like the following: one column's (meastype) values are used as new column headers and a second column (meas) supplies values. We call this moving data from blocks to wide row records, as illustrated in figure 5.21.

Figure 5.21   Moving from tall to wide form

Solution 1: data.table::dcast.data.table()

To move data to a wide form using `dcast.data.table()`, we specify the rows and columns of a result matrix using a formula with the ~notation. We then say how to populate the cells of this matrix with the `value.var` argument. In our case, to get a data frame with a row per chick, a column per time, and weight in the cells, we use the following step:

```
library("data.table")

ChickWeight_wide2 <- dcast.data.table(
  as.data.table(ChickWeight),
  Chick ~ Time,
  value.var = "weight")
```

This table is a matrix where the row is identified by the chick, and the column is time. The cells contain the weight for the given chick and time (and NA if the chick did not survive to a given time). Notice that this format is much easier to read and may be required for reporting.

   `data.table`'s implementation of `dcast` also allows more-powerful transforms, such as casting to multiple variables and aggregations at the same time.

Solution 2: cdata::pivot_to_rowrecs()

`cdata::pivot_to_rowrecs()` describes the intended table by row-keys, column to take new column keys from, and column to take values from :

```
library("cdata")

ChickWeight_wide3 <- pivot_to_rowrecs(
  ChickWeight,
  columnToTakeKeysFrom = "Time",
  columnToTakeValuesFrom = "weight",
  rowKeyColumns = "Chick")
```

Solution 3: tidyr::spread()

```
library("tidyr")

ChickWeight_wide1 <- spread(ChickWeight,
                     key = Time,
                     value = weight)

head(ChickWeight_wide1)
##     Chick  0  2  4  6  8  10  12  14  16  18  20  21
## 1 Chick01 42 51 59 64 76  93 106 125 149 171 199 205
## 2 Chick02 40 49 58 72 84 103 122 138 162 187 209 215
## 3 Chick03 43 39 55 67 84  99 115 138 163 187 198 202
## 4 Chick04 42 49 56 67 74  87 102 108 136 154 160 157
## 5 Chick05 41 42 48 60 79 106 141 164 197 199 220 223
## 6 Chick06 41 49 59 74 97 124 141 148 155 160 160 157
```

5.5.3   *Data coordinates*

There are a lot of details to data transforms. The important concept to retain is this: data has coordinates such as name of table, name of column, and identity of row. The exact way the coordinates are specified is an implementation detail to be overcome or transformed to a convenient state. All of this is a consequence of Codd's second rule of database design: "Each and every datum (atomic value) in a relational database is guaranteed to be logically accessible by resorting to a combination of table name, primary key value, and column name."[4] What we hope you have learned is this: what parts of the coordinates (or access plan) happen to be the table name, versus row-keys, versus the column name is an alterable implementation detail.

> **PREFER SIMPLE CODE**   Building temporary tables, adding columns, and correcting column names early is much better than having complicated analysis code. This follows Raymond's "Rule of Representation."

Raymond's "Rule of Representation"

> *Fold knowledge into data, so program logic can be stupid and robust.*
>
> *—The Art of Unix Programming,*
> Erick S. Raymond, Addison-Wesley, 2003

We suggest transforming your data to fix problems (correct column names, change the data layout) early, to make later steps easier. The format you should try to move to for predictive modeling is what database designers call a *denormalized form*, or what statisticians call a *multivariate data matrix*, or *model matrix*: a regular array where rows are individuals, and columns are possible observations.[5]

The interested reader may want to pursue cdata's powerful diagrammatic system of data layout, which is being broadly adopted, and is discussed here: https://github .com/WinVector/cdata.

Summary

In this chapter, we've worked through the basic examples of transform data for analysis and presentation.

At this point, we have worked through a great number of data transforms. Natural questions to ask are these: are these enough transforms? Can we quickly decompose any task into a small sequence of these transforms?

The answer is "no and yes." There are more-specialized transforms such as "rolling window" functions and other time-series operations that are hard to express in terms of these transforms, but do in fact have their own efficient implementations in R and data.table. However, toward the "yes" answer, there are good reasons to consider the set of transforms we have learned as substantial. The basic manipulation transforms

---

[4] See https://en.wikipedia.org/wiki/Edgar_F._Codd.
[5] See W. J. Krzanowski and F. H. C. Marriott, *Multivariate Analysis, Part 1*, Edward Arnold, 1994.

pretty much cover all of Edgar F. Codd's relational algebra: a set of transforms that has been driving data engineering since 1970.

In this chapter you have learned

- How to use a catalog of powerful data-reshaping transforms
- How to apply these transforms to solve data organization issues

In part 2 of the book, we'll talk about the process of building and evaluating models to meet your stated objectives.

Part 2

Modeling methods

In part 1, we discussed the initial stages of a data science project. After you've defined more precisely the questions you want to answer and the scope of the problem you want to solve, it's time to analyze the data and find the answers. In part 2, we work with powerful modeling methods from statistics and machine learning.

Chapter 6 covers how to identify appropriate modeling methods to address your specific business problem. It also discusses how to evaluate the quality and effectiveness of models that you or others have discovered.

Chapter 7 covers basic linear models: linear regression, logistic regression, and regularized linear models. Linear models are the workhorses of many analytical tasks, and are especially helpful for identifying key variables and gaining insight into the structure of a problem. A solid understanding of them is immensely valuable for a data scientist.

Chapter 8 temporarily moves away from the modeling task to cover advanced data preparation with the `vtreat` package. `vtreat` prepares messy real-world data for the modeling step. Because understanding how `vtreat` works requires some understanding of linear models and of model evaluation metrics, it seemed best to defer this topic until part 2.

Chapter 9 covers unsupervised methods: clustering and association rule mining. Unsupervised methods don't make explicit outcome predictions; they discover relationships and hidden structure in the data. Chapter 10 touches on some more-advanced modeling algorithms. We discuss bagged decision trees, random forests, gradient boosted trees, generalized additive models, and support vector machines.

We work through every method that we cover with a specific data science problem along with a nontrivial dataset. Where appropriate, we also discuss additional model evaluation and interpretation procedures that are specific to the methods we cover.

On completing part 2, you'll be familiar with the most popular modeling methods, and you'll have a sense of which methods are most appropriate for answering different types of questions.

Choosing and evaluating models

6

This chapter covers

- Mapping business problems to machine learning tasks
- Evaluating model quality
- Explaining model predictions

In this chapter, we will discuss the modeling process (figure 6.1). We discuss this process before getting into the details of specific machine learning approaches, because the topics in this chapter apply generally to any kind of model. First, let's discuss choosing an appropriate model approach.

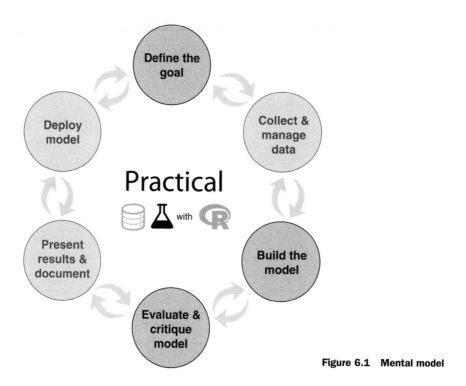

Figure 6.1   **Mental model**

6.1   *Mapping problems to machine learning tasks*

As a data scientist, your task is to map a business problem to a good machine learning method. Let's look at a real-world situation. Suppose that you're a data scientist at an online retail company. There are a number of business problems that your team might be called on to address:

- Predicting what customers might buy, based on past transactions
- Identifying fraudulent transactions
- Determining price elasticity (the rate at which a price increase will decrease sales, and vice versa) of various products or product classes
- Determining the best way to present product listings when a customer searches for an item
- Customer segmentation: grouping customers with similar purchasing behavior
- AdWord valuation: how much the company should spend to buy certain AdWords on search engines
- Evaluation of marketing campaigns
- Organizing new products into a product catalog

Your intended uses of the model have a big influence on what methods you should use. If you want to know how small variations in input variables affect outcome, then you likely want to use a regression method. If you want to know what single variable drives most of a categorization, then decision trees might be a good choice. Also, each business problem suggests a statistical approach to try. For the purposes of this discussion, we will group the different kinds of problems that a data scientist typically solves into these categories:

- *Classification*—Assigning labels to datums
- *Scoring*—Assigning numerical values to datums
- *Grouping*—Discovering patterns and commonalities in data

In this section, we'll describe these problem classes and list some typical approaches to each.

6.1.1 Classification problems

Let's try the following example.

> **Example** *Suppose your task is to automate the assignment of new products to your company's product categories, as shown in figure 6.2.*

This can be more complicated than it sounds. Products that come from different sources may have their own product classification that doesn't coincide with the one that you use on your retail site, or they may come without any classification at all. Many large online retailers use teams of human taggers to hand categorize their products. This is not only labor intensive, but inconsistent and error prone. Automation is an attractive option; it's labor saving, and can improve the quality of the retail site.

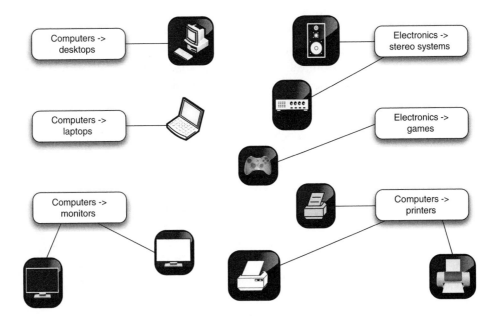

Figure 6.2 Assigning products to product categories

Product categorization based on product attributes and/or text descriptions of the product is an example of *classification*: deciding how to assign (known) labels to an object. Classification itself is an example of what is called *supervised learning*: in order to learn how to classify objects, you need a dataset of objects that have already been classified (called the *training set*). Building training data is the major expense for most classification tasks, especially text-related ones.

Multicategory vs. two-category classification

Product classification is an example of *multicategory* or *multinomial* classification. Most classification problems and most classification algorithms are specialized for two-category, or binomial, classification. There are tricks to using binary classifiers to solve multicategory problems (for example, building one classifier for each category, called a *one-versus-rest* classifier). But in most cases it's worth the effort to find a suitable multiple-category implementation, as they tend to work better than multiple binary classifiers (for example, using the package `mlogit` instead of the base method `glm()` for logistic regression).

Common classification methods that we will cover in this book include logistic regression (with a threshold) and decision tree ensembles.

6.1.2 *Scoring problems*

Scoring can be explained as follows.

Example   *Suppose that your task is to help evaluate how different marketing campaigns can increase valuable traffic to the website. The goal is not only to bring more people to the site, but to bring more people who buy.*

In this situation, you may want to consider a number of different factors: the communication channel (ads on websites, YouTube videos, print media, email, and so on); the traffic source (Facebook, Google, radio stations, and so on); the demographic targeted; the time of year, and so on. You want to measure if these factors increase sales, and by how much.

Predicting the increase in sales from a particular marketing campaign based on factors such as these is an example of *regression*, or *scoring*. In this case, a regression model would map the different factors being measured into a numerical value: sales, or the increase in sales from some baseline.

Predicting the probability of an event (like belonging to a given class) can also be considered scoring. For example, you might think of fraud detection as classification: is this event fraud or not? However, if you are trying to estimate the probability that an event is fraud, this can be considered scoring. This is shown in figure 6.3. Scoring is also an instance of supervised learning.

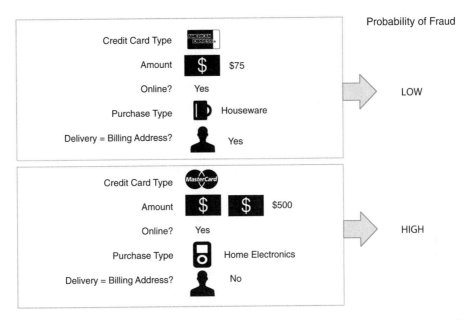

Figure 6.3 **Notional example of determining the probability that a transaction is fraudulent**

6.1.3 *Grouping: working without known targets*

The preceding methods require that you have a training dataset of situations with known outcomes. In some situations, there's not (yet) a specific outcome that you want to predict. Instead, you may be looking for patterns and relationships in the data that will help you understand your customers or your business better.

These situations correspond to a class of approaches called *unsupervised learning*: rather than predicting outputs based on inputs, the objective of unsupervised learning is to discover similarities and relationships in the data. Some common unsupervised tasks include these:

- *Clustering*—Grouping similar objects together
- *Association rules*—Discovering common behavior patterns, for example, items that are always bought together, or library books that are always checked out together

Let's expand on these two types of unsupervised methods.

WHEN TO USE BASIC CLUSTERING

A good clustering example is the following.

> **Example** *Suppose you want to segment your customers into general categories of people with similar buying patterns. You might not know in advance what these groups should be.*

This problem is a good candidate for *k-means clustering*. K-means clustering is one way to sort the data into groups such that members of a cluster are more similar to each other than they are to members of other clusters.

Suppose that you find (as in figure 6.4) that your customers cluster into those with young children, who make more family-oriented purchases, and those with no children or with adult children, who make more leisure- and social-activity-related purchases. Once you have assigned a customer into one of those clusters, you can make general statements about their behavior. For example, a customer in the with-young-children cluster is likely to respond more favorably to a promotion on attractive but durable glassware than to a promotion on fine crystal wine glasses.

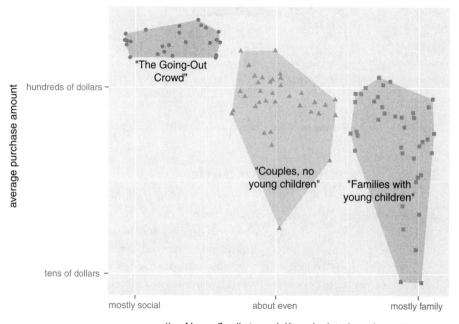

Figure 6.4   Notional example of clustering your customers by purchase pattern and purchase amount

We will cover k-means and other clustering approaches in more detail in section 9.1.

WHEN TO USE ASSOCIATION RULES

You might be interested in directly determining which products tend to be purchased together. For example, you might find that bathing suits and sunglasses are frequently purchased at the same time, or that people who purchase certain cult movies, like *Repo Man*, will often buy the movie soundtrack at the same time.

This is a good application for association rules (or even recommendation systems). You can mine useful product recommendations: whenever you observe that someone

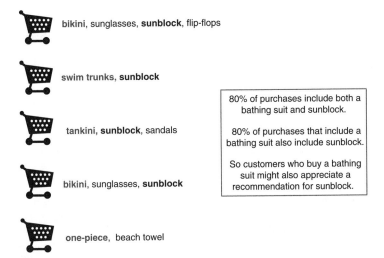

Figure 6.5   Notional example of finding purchase patterns in your data

has put a bathing suit into their shopping cart, you can recommend suntan lotion, as well. This is shown in figure 6.5. We'll cover the Apriori algorithm for discovering association rules in section 9.2.

6.1.4   *Problem-to-method mapping*

To summarize the preceding, table 6.1 maps some typical business problems to their corresponding machine learning tasks.

Table 6.1   From problem to approach

Example tasks	Machine learning terminology
Identifying spam email Sorting products in a product catalog Identifying loans that are about to default Assigning customers to preexisting customer clusters	*Classification* —Assigning known labels to objects. Classification is a supervised method, so you need preclassified data in order to train a model.
Predicting the value of AdWords Estimating the probability that a loan will default Predicting how much a marketing campaign will increase traffic or sales Predicting the final price of an auction item based on the final prices of similar products that have been auctioned in the past	*Regression* —Predicting or forecasting numerical values. Regression is also a supervised method, so you need data where the output is known, in order to train a model.
Finding products that are purchased together Identifying web pages that are often visited in the same session Identifying successful (often-clicked) combinations of web pages and AdWords	*Association rules* —Finding objects that tend to appear in the data together. Association rules are an unsupervised method; you do not need data where you already know the relationships, but are trying to discover the relationships within your data.

Table 6.1   From problem to approach *(continued)*

Example tasks	Machine learning terminology
Identifying groups of customers with the same buying patterns Identifying groups of products that are popular in the same regions or with the same customer clusters Identifying news items that are all discussing similar events	*Clustering* —Finding groups of objects that are more similar to each other than to objects in other groups. Clustering is also an unsupervised method; you do not need pregrouped data, but are trying to discover the groupings within your data.

Prediction vs. forecasting

In everyday language, we tend to use the terms *prediction* and *forecasting* interchangeably. Technically, to predict is to pick an outcome, such as "It will rain tomorrow," and to forecast is to assign a probability: "There's an 80% chance it will rain tomorrow." For unbalanced class applications (such as predicting credit default), the difference is important. Consider the case of modeling loan defaults, and assume the overall default rate is 5%. Identifying a group that has a 30% default rate is an inaccurate prediction (you don't know who in the group will default, and most people in the group won't default), but potentially a very useful forecast (this group defaults at six times the overall rate).

6.2   *Evaluating models*

When building a model, you must be able to estimate model quality in order to ensure that your model will perform well in the real world. To attempt to estimate future model performance, we often split our data into training data and test data, as illustrated in figure 6.6. *Test data* is data not used during training, and is intended to give us some experience with how the model will perform on new data.

One of the things the test set can help you identify is *overfitting*: building a model that memorizes the training data, and does not generalize well to new data. A lot of modeling problems are related to overfitting, and looking for signs of overfit is a good first step in diagnosing models.

6.2.1   *Overfitting*

An overfit model looks great on the training data and then performs poorly on new data. A model's prediction error on the data that it trained from is called *training error*. A model's prediction error on new data is called *generalization error*. Usually, training error will be smaller than generalization error (no big surprise). Ideally, though, the two error rates should be close. If generalization error is large, and your model's test performance is poor, then your model has probably *overfit*—it's memorized the training data instead of discovering generalizable rules or patterns. You want to avoid overfitting by preferring (as long as possible) simpler models which do in fact tend to

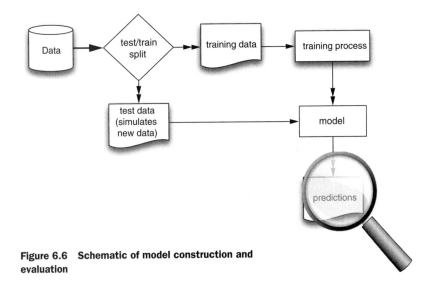

Figure 6.6 Schematic of model construction and evaluation

generalize better.[1] Figure 6.7 shows the typical appearance of a reasonable model and an overfit model.

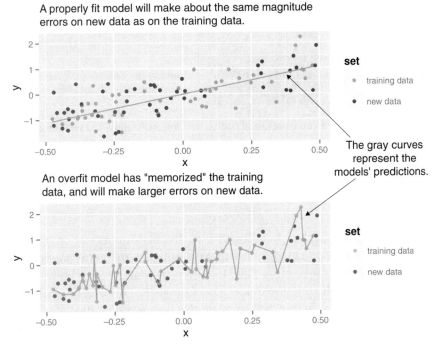

Figure 6.7 A notional illustration of overfitting

---

[1] Other techniques to prevent overfitting include regularization (preferring small effects from model variables) and bagging (averaging different models to reduce variance).

An overly complicated and overfit model is bad for at least two reasons. First, an overfit model may be much more complicated than anything useful. For example, the extra wiggles in the overfit part of figure 6.7 could make optimizing with respect to x needlessly difficult. Also, as we mentioned, overfit models tend to be less accurate in production than during training, which is embarrassing.

TESTING ON HELD-OUT DATA

In section 4.3.1 we introduced the idea of splitting your data into test-train or test-train-calibration sets, as shown in figure 6.8. Here we'll go into more detail about why you want to split your data this way.

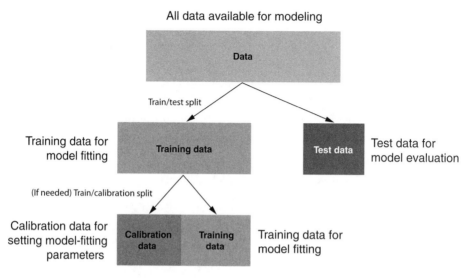

Figure 6.8   Splitting data into training and test (or training, calibration, and test) sets

> **Example**   *Suppose you are building models to predict used car prices, based on various features of the car. You fit both a linear regression model and a random forest model, and you wish to compare the two.[2]*

If you do not split your data, but instead use all available data to both train and evaluate each model, then you might think that you will pick the better model, because the model evaluation has seen more data. However, the data used to build a model is not the best data for evaluating the model's performance. This is because there's an optimistic *measurement bias* in this data, because this data was seen during model construction. Model construction is optimizing your performance measure (or at least something related to your performance measure), so you tend to get exaggerated estimates of performance on your training data.

---

[2] Both these modeling techniques will be covered in later chapters of the book.

In addition, data scientists naturally tend to tune their models to get the best possible performance out of them. This also leads to exaggerated measures of performance. This is often called *multiple comparison bias*. And since this tuning might sometimes take advantage of quirks in the training data, it can potentially lead to overfit.

A recommended precaution for this optimistic bias is to split your available data into test and training. Perform all of your clever work on the training data alone, and delay measuring your performance with respect to your test data until as late as possible in your project (as all choices you make after seeing your test or holdout performance introduce a modeling bias). The desire to keep the test data secret for as long as possible is why we often actually split data into training, calibration, and test sets (as we'll demonstrate in section 8.2.1).

When partitioning your data, you want to balance the trade-off between keeping enough data to fit a good model, and holding out enough data to make good estimates of the model's performance. Some common splits are 70% training to 30% test, or 80% training to 20% test. For large datasets, you may even sometimes see a 50–50 split.

K-FOLD CROSS-VALIDATION

Testing on holdout data, while useful, uses each example only once: either as part of the model construction or as part of the held-out model evaluation set. This is not *statistically efficient*,[3] because the test set is often much smaller than our whole dataset. This means we are losing some precision in our estimate of model performance by partitioning our data so simply. In our example scenario, suppose you were not able to collect a very large dataset of historical used car prices. Then you might feel that you do not have enough data to split into training and test sets that are large enough to both build good models *and* evaluate them properly. In this situation, you might choose to use a more thorough partitioning scheme called *k-fold cross-validation*.

The idea behind k-fold cross-validation is to repeat the construction of a model on different subsets of the available training data and then evaluate that model only on data not seen during construction. This allows us to use each and every example in both training and evaluating models (just never the same example in both roles at the same time). The idea is shown in figure 6.9 for $k = 3$.

In the figure, the data is split into three non-overlapping partitions, and the three partitions are arranged to form three test-train splits. For each split, a model is trained on the training set and then applied to the corresponding test set. The entire set of predictions is then evaluated, using the appropriate evaluation scores that we will discuss later in the chapter. This simulates training a model and then evaluating it on a holdout set that is the same size as the entire dataset. Estimating the model's performance on all the data gives us a more precise estimate of how a model of a given type would perform on new data. Assuming that this performance estimate is satisfactory, then you would go back and train a final model, using *all* the training data.

---

[3] An estimator is called statistically efficient when it has minimal variance for a given dataset size.

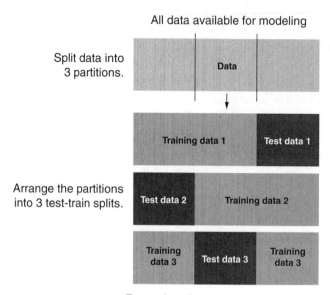

All data available for modeling

Split data into
3 partitions.

Data

Arrange the partitions
into 3 test-train splits.

Training data 1   Test data 1

Test data 2   Training data 2

Training
data 3   Test data 3   Training
data 3

For each split, train a model on the training set,
and then predict on the corresponding test set.

Figure 6.9   Partitioning data for 3-fold cross-validation

For big data, a test-train split tends to be good enough and is much quicker to implement. In data science applications, cross-validation is generally used for tuning modeling parameters, which is basically trying many models in succession. Cross-validation is also used when nesting models (using one model as input to another model). This is an issue that can arise when transforming data for analysis, and is discussed in chapter 7.

6.2.2   *Measures of model performance*

In this section, we'll introduce some quantitative measures of model performance. From an evaluation point of view, we group model types this way:

- Classification
- Scoring
- Probability estimation
- Clustering

For most model evaluations, we just want to compute one or two summary scores that tell us if the model is effective. To decide if a given score is high or low, we generally compare our model's performance to a few baseline models.

THE NULL MODEL

The null model is the best version of a very simple model you're trying to outperform. The most typical null model is a model that returns the same answer for all situations (a constant model). We use null models as a lower bound on desired performance. For example, in a categorical problem, the null model would always return the most popular category, as this is the easy guess that is least often wrong. For a score model, the null model is often the average of all the outcomes, as this has the least square deviation from all the outcomes.

The idea is that if you're not outperforming the null model, you're not delivering value. Note that it can be hard to do as good as the best null model, because even though the null model is simple, it's privileged to know the overall distribution of the items it will be quizzed on. We always assume the null model we're comparing to is the best of all possible null models

SINGLE-VARIABLE MODELS

We also suggest comparing any complicated model against the best single-variable model you have available (please see chapter 8 for how to convert single variables into single-variable models). A complicated model can't be justified if it doesn't outperform the best single-variable model available from your training data. Also, business analysts have many tools for building effective single-variable models (such as pivot tables), so if your client is an analyst, they're likely looking for performance above this level.

We'll present the standard measures of model quality, which are useful in model construction. In all cases, we suggest that in addition to the standard model quality assessments, you try to design your own custom business-oriented metrics with your project sponsor or client. Usually this is as simple as assigning a notional dollar value to each outcome and then seeing how your model performs under that criterion. Let's start with how to evaluate classification models and then continue from there.

6.2.3 *Evaluating classification models*

A classification model places examples into one of two or more categories. For measuring classifier performance, we'll first introduce the incredibly useful tool called the *confusion matrix* and show how it can be used to calculate many important evaluation scores. The first score we'll discuss is accuracy.

> **Example** *Suppose we want to classify email into spam (email we in no way want) and non-spam (email we want).*

A ready-to-go example (with a good description) is the "Spambase Data Set" (http://mng.bz/e8Rh). Each row of this dataset is a set of features measured for a specific email and an additional column telling whether the mail was spam (unwanted) or non-spam (wanted). We'll quickly build a spam classification model using logistic regression so we have results to evaluate. We will discuss logistic regression in section 7.2, but for right now you can just download the file Spambase/spamD.tsv from the book's GitHub site (https://github.com/WinVector/PDSwR2/tree/master/Spambase) and then perform the steps shown in the following listing.

Listing 6.1 Building and applying a logistic regression spam model

```
spamD <- read.table('spamD.tsv',header=T,sep='\t')   ⟵──── Reads in the data

spamTrain <-
      subset(spamD,spamD$rgroup  >= 10)                ⟵─┐
spamTest <- subset(spamD,spamD$rgroup < 10)              ├ Splits the data into
                                                           training and test sets

spamVars <- setdiff(colnames(spamD), list('rgroup','spam'))  ⟵─┐
spamFormula <- as.formula(paste('spam == "spam"',              │ Creates a
paste(spamVars, collapse = ' + '),sep = ' ~ '))               │ formula that
                                                                │ describes
spamModel <- glm(spamFormula,family = binomial(link = 'logit'),│ the model
                             data = spamTrain)

spamTrain$pred <- predict(spamModel,newdata = spamTrain,   ⟵─┐
                          type = 'response')                  ├ Makes predictions
spamTest$pred <- predict(spamModel,newdata = spamTest,        │ on the training and
                         type = 'response')                     test sets
```

Fits the logistic regression model — (annotation pointing to spamModel line)

The spam model predicts the probability that a given email is spam. A sample of the results of our simple spam classifier is shown in the next listing.

Listing 6.2 Spam classifications

```
sample <- spamTest[c(7,35,224,327), c('spam','pred')]
print(sample)
##            spam          pred    ⟵─┐
## 115        spam 0.9903246227       │ The first column gives the actual class label
## 361        spam 0.4800498077       │ (spam or non-spam). The second column gives
## 2300   non-spam 0.0006846551       │ the predicted probability that an email is spam.
## 3428   non-spam 0.0001434345       │ If the probability > 0.5, the email is labeled
                                        "spam;" otherwise, it is "non-spam."
```

THE CONFUSION MATRIX

The absolute most interesting summary of classifier performance is the confusion matrix. This matrix is just a table that summarizes the classifier's predictions against the actual known data categories.

The confusion matrix is a table counting how often each combination of known outcomes (the truth) occurred in combination with each prediction type. For our email spam example, the confusion matrix is calculated by the R command in the following listing.

Listing 6.3 Spam confusion matrix

```
confmat_spam <- table(truth = spamTest$spam,
                      prediction = ifelse(spamTest$pred > 0.5,
                      "spam", "non-spam"))
print(confmat_spam)
##          prediction
## truth    non-spam spam
##    non-spam  264    14
##    spam       22   158
```

The rows of the table (labeled *truth*) correspond to the actual labels of the datums: whether they are really spam or not. The columns of the table (labeled *prediction*) correspond to the predictions that the model makes. So the first cell of the table (*truth = non-spam* and *prediction = non-spam*) corresponds to the 264 emails in the test set that are not spam, and that the model (correctly) predicts are not spam. These correct negative predictions are called *true negatives*.

> **CONFUSION MATRIX CONVENTIONS**   A number of tools, as well as Wikipedia, draw confusion matrices with the actual truth values controlling the x-axis in the figure. This is likely due to the math convention that the first coordinate in matrices and tables names the row (vertical offset), and not the column (horizontal offset). It is our feeling that direct labels, such as "pred" and "actual," are much clearer than *any* convention. Also note that in residual graphs the prediction is always the x-axis, and being visually consistent with this important convention is a benefit. So in this book, we will plot predictions on the x-axis (regardless how that is named).

It is standard terminology to refer to datums that are in the class of interest as *positive* instances, and those not in the class of interest as *negative* instances. In our scenario, spam emails are positive instances, and non-spam emails are negative instances.

In a two-by-two confusion matrix, every cell has a special name, as illustrated in table 6.2.

Table 6.2   Two-by-two confusion matrix

	Prediction=NEGATIVE (predicted as non-spam)	Prediction=POSITIVE (predicted as spam)
Truth mark=NEGATIVE (non-spam)	True negatives (TN) `confmat_spam[1,1]=264`	False positives (FP) `confmat_spam[1,2]=14`
Truth mark=POSITIVE (spam)	False negatives (FN) `confmat_spam[2,1]=22`	True positives (TP) `confmat_spam[2,2]=158`

Using this summary, we can now start to calculate various performance metrics of our spam filter.

> **CHANGING A SCORE TO A CLASSIFICATION**   Note that we converted the numerical prediction score into a decision by checking if the score was above or below 0.5. This means that if the model returned a probability higher than 50% that an email is spam, we classify it as spam. For some scoring models (like logistic regression) the 0.5 score is likely a threshold that gives a classifier with reasonably good accuracy. However, accuracy isn't always the end goal, and for unbalanced training data, the 0.5 threshold won't be good. Picking thresholds other than 0.5 can allow the data scientist to trade *precision* for *recall* (two terms that we'll define later in this chapter). You can start at 0.5, but consider trying other thresholds and looking at the ROC curve (see section 6.2.5).

ACCURACY

Accuracy answers the question, "When the spam filter says this email is or is not spam, what's the probability that it's correct?" For a classifier, accuracy is defined as the number of items categorized correctly divided by the total number of items. It's simply what fraction of classifications the classifier makes is correct. This is shown in figure 6.10.

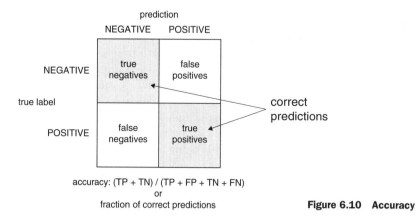

Figure 6.10   Accuracy

At the very least, you want a classifier to be accurate. Let's calculate the accuracy of the spam filter:

```
(confmat_spam[1,1] + confmat_spam[2,2]) / sum(confmat_spam)
## [1] 0.9213974
```

The error of around 8% is unacceptably high for a spam filter, but is good for illustrating different sorts of model evaluation criteria.

Before we move on, we'd like to share the confusion matrix of a good spam filter. In the next listing, we create the confusion matrix for the Akismet comment spam filter from the Win-Vector blog.[4]

Listing 6.4   Entering the Akismet confusion matrix by hand

```
confmat_akismet <- as.table(matrix(data=c(288-1,17,1,13882-17),nrow=2,ncol=2))
rownames(confmat_akismet) <- rownames(confmat_spam)
colnames(confmat_akismet) <- colnames(confmat_spam)
print(confmat_akismet)
##          non-spam  spam
## non-spam    287       1
## spam         17  13865
```

Because the Akismet filter uses link destination clues and determination from other websites (in addition to text features), it achieves a more acceptable accuracy:

```
(confmat_akismet[1,1] + confmat_akismet[2,2]) / sum(confmat_akismet)
## [1] 0.9987297
```

---

[4]   See http://www.win-vector.com/blog/.

More importantly, Akismet seems to have suppressed fewer good comments. Our next section on precision and recall will help quantify this distinction.

ACCURACY IS AN INAPPROPRIATE MEASURE FOR UNBALANCED CLASSES Suppose we have a situation where we have a rare event (say, severe complications during childbirth). If the event we're trying to predict is rare (say, around 1% of the population), the null model that says the rare event never happens is *very* (99%) accurate. The null model is in fact more accurate than a useful (but not perfect model) that identifies 5% of the population as being "at risk" and captures all of the bad events in the 5%. This is not any sort of paradox. It's just that accuracy is not a good measure for events that have unbalanced distribution or unbalanced costs.

PRECISION AND RECALL

Another evaluation measure used by machine learning researchers is a pair of numbers called precision and recall. These terms come from the field of information retrieval and are defined as follows.

Precision answers the question, "If the spam filter says this email is spam, what's the probability that it's really spam?" Precision is defined as the ratio of true positives to predicted positives. This is shown in figure 6.11.

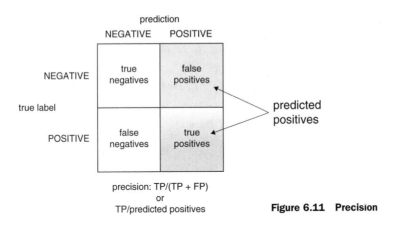

Figure 6.11 Precision

We can calculate the precision of our spam filter as follows:

```
confmat_spam[2,2] / (confmat_spam[2,2]+ confmat_spam[1,2])
## [1] 0.9186047
```

It is only a coincidence that the precision is so close to the accuracy number we reported earlier. Again, precision is how often a positive indication turns out to be correct. It's important to remember that precision is a function of the combination of the classifier and the dataset. It doesn't make sense to ask how precise a classifier is in isolation; it's only sensible to ask how precise a classifier is for a given dataset. The hope is that the classifier will be similarly precise on the overall population that the dataset is drawn from—a population with the same distribution of positives instances as the dataset.

In our email spam example, 92% precision means 8% of what was flagged as spam was in fact not spam. This is an unacceptable rate for losing possibly important messages. Akismet, on the other hand, had a precision of over 99.99%, so it throws out very little non-spam email.

```
confmat_akismet[2,2] / (confmat_akismet[2,2] + confmat_akismet[1,2])
## [1] 0.9999279
```

The companion score to precision is *recall*. Recall answers the question, "Of all the spam in the email set, what fraction did the spam filter detect?" Recall is the ratio of true positives over all actual positives, as shown in figure 6.12.

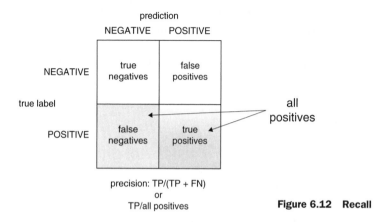

Figure 6.12   Recall

Let's compare the recall of the two spam filters.

```
confmat_spam[2,2] / (confmat_spam[2,2] + confmat_spam[2,1])
## [1] 0.8777778
```

```
confmat_akismet[2,2] / (confmat_akismet[2,2] + confmat_akismet[2,1])
## [1] 0.9987754
```

For our email spam filter, this is 88%, which means about 12% of the spam email we receive will still make it into our inbox. Akismet has a recall of 99.88%. In both cases, most spam is in fact tagged (we have high recall) and precision is emphasized over recall. This is appropriate for a spam filter, because it's more important to not lose non-spam email than it is to filter every single piece of spam out of our inbox.

It's important to remember this: precision is a measure of confirmation (when the classifier indicates positive, how often it is in fact correct), and recall is a measure of utility (how much the classifier finds of what there actually is to find). Precision and recall tend to be relevant to business needs and are good measures to discuss with your project sponsor and client.

F1

Example   *Suppose that you had multiple spam filters to choose from, each with different values of precision and recall. How do you pick which spam filter to use?*

In situations like this, some people prefer to have just one number to compare all the different choices by. One such score is the *F1 score*. The F1 score measures a trade-off between precision and recall. It is defined as the harmonic mean of the precision and recall. This is most easily shown with an explicit calculation:

```
precision <- confmat_spam[2,2] / (confmat_spam[2,2]+ confmat_spam[1,2])
recall <- confmat_spam[2,2] / (confmat_spam[2,2] + confmat_spam[2,1])

(F1 <- 2 * precision * recall / (precision + recall) )
## [1] 0.8977273
```

Our spam filter with 0.93 precision and 0.88 recall has an F1 score of 0.90. F1 is 1.00 when a classifier has perfect precision and recall, and goes to 0.00 for classifiers that have either very low precision or recall (or both). Suppose you think that your spam filter is losing too much real email, and you want to make it "pickier" about marking email as spam; that is, you want to increase its precision. Quite often, increasing the precision of a classifier will also lower its recall: in this case, a pickier spam filter may also mark fewer real spam emails as spam, and allow it into your inbox. If the filter's recall falls too low as its precision increases, this will result in a lower F1. This possibly means that you have traded too much recall for better precision.

SENSITIVITY AND SPECIFICITY

Example   *Suppose that you have successfully trained a spam filter with acceptable precision and recall, using your work email as training data. Now you want to use that same spam filter on a personal email account that you use primarily for your photography hobby. Will the filter work as well?*

It's possible the filter will work just fine on your personal email as is, since the nature of spam (the length of the email, the words used, the number of links, and so on) probably doesn't change much between the two email accounts. However, the *proportion* of spam you get on the personal email account may be different than it is on your work email. This can change the performance of the spam filter on your personal email.[5]

Let's see how changes in the proportion of spam can change the performance metrics of the spam filter. Here we simulate having email sets with both higher and lower proportions of email than the data that we trained the filter on.

---

[5]   The spam filter performance can also change because the nature of the non-spam will be different, too: the words commonly used will be different; the number of links or images in a legitimate email may be different; the email domains of people you correspond with may be different. For this discussion, we will assume that the proportion of spam email is the main reason that a spam filter's performance will be different.

Listing 6.5   Seeing filter performance change when spam proportions change

```
set.seed(234641)

N <- nrow(spamTest)
pull_out_ix <- sample.int(N, 100, replace=FALSE)
removed = spamTest[pull_out_ix,]        ◁

get_performance <- function(sTest) {     ◁
  proportion <- mean(sTest$spam == "spam")
  confmat_spam <- table(truth = sTest$spam,
                        prediction = ifelse(sTest$pred>0.5,
                                            "spam",
                                            "non-spam"))

  precision <- confmat_spam[2,2]/sum(confmat_spam[,2])
  recall <- confmat_spam[2,2]/sum(confmat_spam[2,])
  list(spam_proportion = proportion,
       confmat_spam = confmat_spam,
       precision = precision, recall = recall)
}

sTest <- spamTest[-pull_out_ix,]         ◁
get_performance(sTest)

## $spam_proportion
## [1] 0.3994413
##
## $confmat_spam
##            prediction
## truth       non-spam spam
##    non-spam      204   11
##    spam           17  126
##
## $precision
## [1] 0.919708
##
## $recall
## [1] 0.8811189

get_performance(rbind(sTest, subset(removed, spam=="spam")))    ◁

## $spam_proportion
## [1] 0.4556962
##
## $confmat_spam
##            prediction
## truth       non-spam spam
##    non-spam      204   11
##    spam           22  158
##
## $precision
## [1] 0.9349112
##
## $recall
## [1] 0.8777778
```

Pulls 100 emails out of the test set at random

A convenience function to print out the confusion matrix, precision, and recall of the filter on a test set.

Looks at performance on a test set with the same proportion of spam as the training data

Adds back only additional spam, so the test set has a higher proportion of spam than the training set

```
get_performance(rbind(sTest, subset(removed, spam=="non-spam")))  ⊲
```
Adds back only non-spam, so the test set has a lower proportion of spam than the training set

```
## $spam_proportion
## [1] 0.3396675
##
## $confmat_spam
##            prediction
## truth       non-spam spam
##   non-spam        264   14
##   spam             17  126
##
## $precision
## [1] 0.9
##
## $recall
## [1] 0.8811189
```

Note that the recall of the filter is the same in all three cases: about 88%. When the data has more spam than the filter was trained on, the filter has higher precision, which means it throws a lower proportion of non-spam email out. This is good! However, when the data has less spam than the filter was trained on, the precision is lower, meaning the filter will throw out a higher fraction of non-spam email. This is undesirable.

Because there are situations where a classifier or filter may be used on populations where the prevalence of the positive class (in this example, spam) varies, it's useful to have performance metrics that are independent of the class prevalence. One such pair of metrics is *sensitivity* and *specificity*. This pair of metrics is common in medical research, because tests for diseases and other conditions will be used on different populations, with different prevalence of a given disease or condition.

Sensitivity is also called the *true positive rate* and is exactly equal to recall. *Specificity* is also called the *true negative rate*: it is the ratio of true negatives to all negatives. This is shown in figure 6.13.

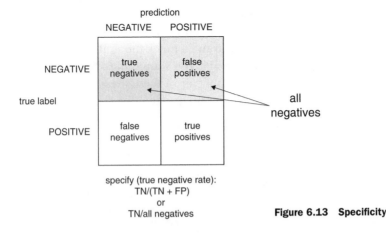

Figure 6.13 Specificity

Sensitivity and recall answer the question, "What fraction of spam does the spam filter find?" Specificity answers the question, "What fraction of non-spam does the spam filter find?"

We can calculate specificity for our spam filter:

```
confmat_spam[1,1] / (confmat_spam[1,1] + confmat_spam[1,2])
## [1] 0.9496403
```

One minus the specificity is also called the *false positive rate*. False positive rate answers the question, "What fraction of non-spam will the model classify as spam?" You want the false positive rate to be low (or the specificity to be high), and the sensitivity to also be high. Our spam filter has a specificity of about 0.95, which means that it will mark about 5% of non-spam email as spam.

An important property of sensitivity and specificity is this: if you flip your labels (switch from *spam* being the class you're trying to identify to *non-spam* being the class you're trying to identify), you just switch sensitivity and specificity. Also, a trivial classifier that always says positive or always says negative will always return a zero score on either sensitivity or specificity. So useless classifiers always score poorly on at least one of these measures.

Why have both precision/recall and sensitivity/specificity? Historically, these measures come from different fields, but each has advantages. Sensitivity/specificity is good for fields, like medicine, where it's important to have an idea how well a classifier, test, or filter separates positive from negative instances independently of the distribution of the different classes in the population. But precision/recall gives you an idea how well a classifier or filter will work on a specific population. If you want to know the probability that an email identified as spam is really spam, you have to know how common spam is in that person's email box, and the appropriate measure is precision.

SUMMARY: USING COMMON CLASSIFICATION PERFORMANCE MEASURES

You should use these standard scores while working with your client and sponsor to see which measure most models their business needs. For each score, you should ask them if they need that score to be high, and then run a quick thought experiment with them to confirm you've gotten their business need. You should then be able to write a project goal in terms of a minimum bound on a pair of these measures. Table 6.3 shows a typical business need and an example follow-up question for each measure.

Table 6.3 Classifier performance measures business stories.

Measure	Typical business need	Follow-up question
Accuracy	"We need most of our decisions to be correct."	"Can we tolerate being wrong 5% of the time? And do users see mistakes like spam marked as non-spam or non-spam marked as spam as being equivalent?"

Table 6.3 Classifier performance measures business stories. *(continued)*

Measure	Typical business need	Follow-up question
Precision	"Most of what we marked as spam had darn well better be spam."	"That would guarantee that most of what is in the spam folder is in fact spam, but it isn't the best way to measure what fraction of the user's legitimate email is lost. We could cheat on this goal by sending all our users a bunch of easy-to-identify spam that we correctly identify. Maybe we really want good specificity."
Recall	"We want to cut down on the amount of spam a user sees by a factor of 10 (eliminate 90% of the spam)."	"If 10% of the spam gets through, will the user see mostly non-spam mail or mostly spam? Will this result in a good user experience?"
Sensitivity	"We have to cut a lot of spam; otherwise, the user won't see a benefit."	"If we cut spam down to 1% of what it is now, would that be a good user experience?"
Specificity	"We must be at least *three nines* on legitimate email; the user must see at least 99.9% of their non-spam email."	"Will the user tolerate missing 0.1% of their legitimate email, and should we keep a spam folder the user can look at?"

One conclusion for this dialogue process on spam classification could be to recommend writing the business goals as maximizing sensitivity while maintaining a specificity of at least 0.999.

6.2.4 *Evaluating scoring models*

Let's demonstrate evaluation on a simple example.

Example *Suppose you've read that the rate at which crickets chirp is proportional to the temperature, so you have gathered some data and fit a model that predicts temperature (in Fahrenheit) from the chirp rate (chirps/sec) of a striped ground cricket. Now you want to evaluate this model.*

You can fit a linear regression model to this data, and then make predictions, using the following listing. We will discuss linear regression in detail in chapter 8. Make sure you have the dataset crickets.csv in your working directory.[6]

Listing 6.6 Fitting the cricket model and making predictions

```
crickets <- read.csv("cricketchirps/crickets.csv")

cricket_model <- lm(temperatureF ~ chirp_rate, data=crickets)
crickets$temp_pred <- predict(cricket_model, newdata=crickets)
```

---

6 George W. Pierce, *The Song of Insects*, Harvard University Press, 1948. You can find the dataset here: https://github.com/WinVector/PDSwR2/tree/master/cricketchirps

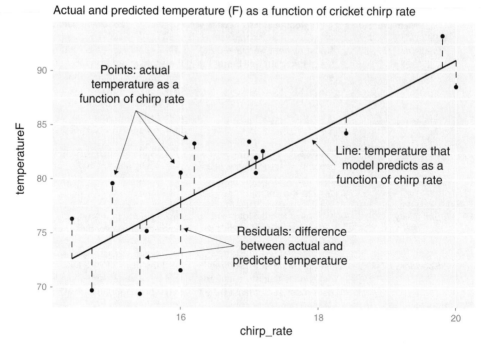

Actual and predicted temperature (F) as a function of cricket chirp rate

Figure 6.14   Scoring residuals

Figure 6.14 compares the actual data (points) to the model's predictions (the line). The differences between the predictions of temperatureF and temp_pred are called the *residuals* or *error* of the model on the data. We will use the residuals to calculate some common performance metrics for scoring models.

ROOT MEAN SQUARE ERROR

The most common goodness-of-fit measure is called *root mean square error (RMSE)*. The RMSE is the square root of the average squared residuals (also called the mean squared error). RMSE answers the question, "How much is the predicted temperature typically off?" We calculate the RMSE as shown in the following listing.

> **Listing 6.7   Calculating RMSE**

```
error_sq <- (crickets$temp_pred - crickets$temperatureF)^2
( RMSE <- sqrt(mean(error_sq)) )
## [1] 3.564149
```

The RMSE is in the same units as the outcome: since the outcome (temperature) is in degrees Fahrenheit, the RMSE is also in degrees Fahrenheit. Here the RMSE tells you that the model's predictions will typically (that is, on average) be about 3.6 degrees off from the actual temperature. Suppose that you consider a model that typically predicts the temperature to within 5 degrees to be "good." Then, congratulations! You have fit a model that meets your goals.

RMSE is a good measure, because it is often what the fitting algorithms you're using are explicitly trying to minimize. In a business setting, a good RMSE-related goal would be "We want the RMSE on account valuation to be under $1,000 per account."

The quantity `mean(error_sq)` is called the *mean squared error*. We will call the quantity `sum(error_sq)` the *sum squared error*, and also refer to it as the model's *variance*.

R-SQUARED

Another important measure of fit is called *R-squared* (or *R2*, or the *coefficient of determination*). We can motivate the definition of R-squared as follows.

For the data that you've collected, the simplest baseline prediction of the temperature is simply the average temperature in the dataset. This is the *null model*; it's not a very good model, but you have to perform at least better than it does. The data's *total variance* is the sum squared error of the null model. You want the sum squared error of your actual model to be much smaller than the data's variance—that is, you want the ratio of your model's sum squared error to the total variance to be near zero. R-squared is defined as one minus this ratio, so we want R-squared to be close to one. This leads to the following calculation for R-squared.

Listing 6.8 Calculating R-squared

Calculates the squared error terms → **Sums them to get the model's sum squared error, or variance**

```
error_sq <- (crickets$temp_pred - crickets$temperatureF)^2
numerator <- sum(error_sq)

delta_sq <- (mean(crickets$temperatureF) - crickets$temperatureF)^2
denominator = sum(delta_sq)

(R2 <- 1 - numerator/denominator)
## [1] 0.6974651
```

Calculates the data's total variance — Calculates the squared error terms from the null model

Calculates R-squared

As R-squared is formed from a ratio comparing your model's variance to the total variance, you can think of R-squared as a measure of how much variance your model "explains." R-squared is also sometimes referred to as a measure of how well the model "fits" the data, or its "goodness of fit."

The best possible R-squared is 1.0, with near-zero or negative R-squareds being horrible. Some other models (such as logistic regression) use deviance to report an analogous quantity called *pseudo R-squared*.

Under certain circumstances, R-squared is equal to the square of another measure called the *correlation* (see http://mng.bz/ndYf). A good statement of a R-squared business goal would be "We want the model to explain at least 70% of variation in account value."

6.2.5 *Evaluating probability models*

Probability models are models that both decide if an item is in a given class and return an estimated probability (or confidence) of the item being in the class. The modeling techniques of logistic regression and decision trees are fairly famous for being able to return good probability estimates. Such models can be evaluated on their final decisions, as we've already shown in section 6.2.3, but they can also be evaluated in terms of their estimated probabilities.

In our opinion, most of the measures for probability models are very technical and very good at comparing the qualities of different models on the same dataset. It's important to know them, because data scientists generally use these criteria among themselves. But these criteria aren't easy to precisely translate into businesses needs. So we recommend tracking them, but not using them with your project sponsor or client.

To motivate the use of the different metrics for probability models, we'll continue the spam filter example from section 6.2.3.

Example   *Suppose that, while building your spam filter, you try several different algorithms and modeling approaches and come up with several models, all of which return the probability that a given email is spam. You want to compare these different models quickly and identify the one that will make the best spam filter.*

In order to turn a probability model into a classifier, you need to select a threshold: items that score higher than that threshold will be classified as spam; otherwise, they are classified as non-spam. The easiest (and probably the most common) threshold for a probability model is 0.5, but the "best possible" classifier for a given probability model may require a different threshold. This optimal threshold can vary from model to model. The metrics in this section compare probability models directly, without having turned them into classifiers. If you make the reasonable assumption that the best probability model will make the best classifier, then you can use these metrics to quickly select the most appropriate probability model, and then spend some time tuning the threshold to build the best classifier for your needs.

THE DOUBLE DENSITY PLOT

When thinking about probability models, it's useful to construct a double density plot (illustrated in figure 6.15).

> **Listing 6.9   Making a double density plot**

```
library(WVPlots)
DoubleDensityPlot(spamTest,
                  xvar = "pred",
                  truthVar = "spam",
                  title = "Distribution of scores for spam filter")
```

The x-axis in the figure corresponds to the prediction scores returned by the spam filter. Figure 6.15 illustrates what we're going to try to check when evaluating estimated probability models: examples in the class should mostly have high scores, and examples not in the class should mostly have low scores.

Double density plots can be useful when picking classifier thresholds, or the threshold score where the classifier switches from labeling an email as non-spam to spam. As we mentioned earlier, the standard classifier threshold is 0.5, meaning that

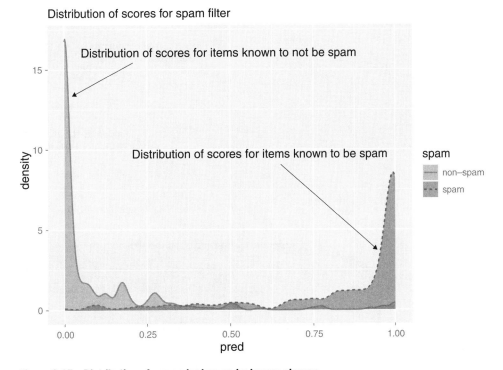

Figure 6.15 **Distribution of scores broken up by known classes**

if the probability that an email is spam is greater than one-half, then we label the email as spam. This is the threshold that you used in section 6.2.3. However, in some circumstances you may choose to use a different threshold. For instance, using a threshold of 0.75 for the spam filter will produce a classifier with higher precision (but lower recall), because a higher fraction of emails that scored higher than 0.75 are actually spam.

THE RECEIVER OPERATING CHARACTERISTIC CURVE AND THE AUC

The *receiver operating characteristic curve* (or *ROC curve*) is a popular alternative to the double density plot. For each different classifier we'd get by picking a different score threshold between spam and not-spam, we plot both the true positive (TP) rate and the false positive (FP) rate. The resulting curve represents every possible trade-off between true positive rate and false positive rate that is available for classifiers derived from this model. Figure 6.16 shows the ROC curve for our spam filter, as produced in the next listing. In the last line of the listing, we compute the *AUC* or *area under the curve*, which is another measure of the quality of the model.

Listing 6.10   Plotting the receiver operating characteristic curve

```
library(WVPlots)
ROCPlot(spamTest,                    ◁·········   Plots the receiver operating
        xvar = 'pred',                            characteristic (ROC ) curve
        truthVar = 'spam',
        truthTarget = 'spam',
        title = 'Spam filter test performance')

library(sigr)
calcAUC(spamTest$pred, spamTest$spam=='spam')  ◁──   Calculates the area under the
  ## [1] 0.9660072                                    ROC curve explicitly
```

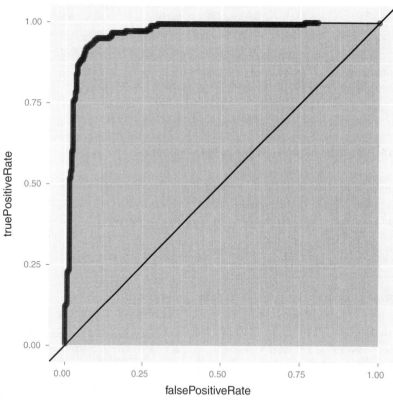

Figure 6.16   ROC curve for the email spam example

The reasoning behind the AUC

At one end of the spectrum of models is the ideal perfect model that would return a score of 1 for spam emails and a score of 0 for non-spam. This ideal model would form an ROC with three points:

- (0,0)—Corresponding to a classifier defined by the threshold p = 1: nothing gets classified as spam, so this classifier has a zero false positive rate and a zero true positive rate.
- (1,1)—Corresponding to a classifier defined by the threshold p = 0: everything gets classified as spam, so this classifier has a false positive rate of 1 and a true positive rate of 1.
- (0,1)—Corresponding to any classifier defined by a threshold between 0 and 1: everything is classified correctly, so this classifier has a false positive rate of 0 and a true positive rate of 1.

The shape of the ROC for the ideal model is shown in figure 6.17. The area under the curve for this model is 1. A model that returns random scores would have an ROC that is the diagonal line from the origin to the point (1,0): the true positive rate is proportional to the threshold. The area under the curve for the random model is 0.5. So you want a model whose AUC is close to 1, and greater than 0.5.

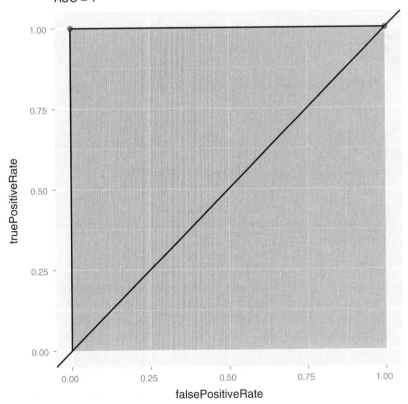

Figure 6.17 **ROC curve for an ideal model that classifies perfectly**

When comparing multiple probability models, you generally want to prefer models that have a higher AUC. However, you also want to examine the shape of the ROC to explore possible project goal trade-offs. Each point on the curve shows the trade-off between achievable true positive and false positive rates with this model. If you share the information from the ROC curve with your client, they may have an opinion about the acceptable trade-offs between the two.

LOG LIKELIHOOD

Log likelihood is a measure of how well the model's predictions "match" the true class labels. It is a non-positive number, where a log likelihood of 0 means a perfect match: the model scores all the spam as being spam with a probability of 1, and all the non-spam as having a probability 0 of being spam. The larger the magnitude of the log likelihood, the worse the match.

The log likelihood of a model's prediction on a specific instance is the logarithm of the probability that the model assigns to the instance's actual class. As shown in figure 6.18, for a spam email with an estimated probability of p of being spam, the log likelihood is `log(p)`; for a non-spam email, the same score of p gives a log likelihood of `log(1 - p)`.

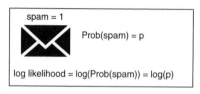

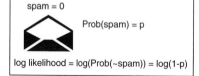

Figure 6.18   Log likelihood of a spam filter prediction

The log likelihood of a model's predictions on an entire dataset is the sum of the individual log likelihoods:

```
log_likelihood = sum(y * log(py) + (1-y) * log(1 - py))
```

Here `y` is the true class label (0 for non-spam and 1 for spam) and `py` is the probability that an instance is of class 1 (spam). We are using multiplication to select the correct logarithm. We also use the convention that `0 * log(0) = 0` (though for simplicity, this isn't shown in the code).

Figure 6.19 shows how log likelihood rewards matches and penalizes mismatches between the actual label of an email and the score assigned by the model. For positive instances (spam), the model should predict a value close to 1, and for negative instances (non-spam), the model should predict a value close to 0. When the prediction and the

Figure 6.19   Log likelihood penalizes mismatches between the prediction and the true class label.

class label match, the contribution to the log likelihood is a small negative number. When they don't match, the contribution to the log likelihood is a larger negative number. The closer to 0 the log likelihood is, the better the prediction.

The next listing shows one way to calculate the log likelihood of the spam filter's predictions.

Listing 6.11   Calculating log likelihood

```
ylogpy <- function(y, py) {
   logpy = ifelse(py > 0, log(py), 0)
  y*logpy
}

y <- spamTest$spam == 'spam'

sum(ylogpy(y, spamTest$pred) +
      ylogpy(1-y, 1-spamTest$pred))
## [1] -134.9478
```

A function to calculate y * log(py), with the convention that 0 * log(0) = 0

Gets the class labels of the test set as TRUE/FALSE, which R treats as 1/0 in arithmetic operations

Calculates the log likelihood of the model's predictions on the test set

The log likelihood is useful for comparing multiple probability models *on the same test dataset*—because the log likelihood is an unnormalized sum, its magnitude implicitly depends on the size of the dataset, so you can't directly compare log likelihoods that were computed on different datasets. When comparing multiple models, you generally want to prefer models with a larger (that is, smaller magnitude) log likelihood.

At the very least, you want to compare the model's performance to the null model of predicting the same probability for every example. The best observable single estimate of the probability of being spam is the observed rate of spam on the training set.

Listing 6.12   Computing the null model's log likelihood

```
(pNull <- mean(spamTrain$spam == 'spam'))
## [1] 0.3941588

sum(ylogpy(y, pNull) + ylogpy(1-y, 1-pNull))
## [1] -306.8964
```

The spam model assigns a log likelihood of -134.9478 to the test set, which is much better than the null model's -306.8964.

DEVIANCE

Another common measure when fitting probability models is the *deviance*. The deviance is defined as -2*(logLikelihood-S), where S is a technical constant called "the log likelihood of the saturated model." In most cases, the saturated model is a perfect model that returns probability 1 for items in the class and probability 0 for items not in the class (so S=0). The lower the deviance, the better the model.

We're most concerned with ratios of deviance, such as the ratio between the null deviance and the model deviance. These deviances can be used to calculate a pseudo R-squared (see http://mng.bz/j338). Think of the null deviance as how much variation there is to explain, and the model deviance as how much was left unexplained by the model. You want a pseudo R-squared that is close to 1.

In the next listing, we show a quick calculation of deviance and pseudo R-squared using the sigr package.

Listing 6.13   Computing the deviance and pseudo R-squared

```
library(sigr)

(deviance <- calcDeviance(spamTest$pred, spamTest$spam == 'spam'))
## [1] 253.8598
(nullDeviance <- calcDeviance(pNull, spamTest$spam == 'spam'))
## [1] 613.7929

(pseudoR2 <- 1 - deviance/nullDeviance)
## [1] 0.586408
```

Like the log likelihood, deviance is unnormalized, so you should only compare deviances that are computed over the same dataset. When comparing multiple models, you will generally prefer models with smaller deviance. The pseudo R-squared is normalized (it's a function of a ratio of deviances), so in principle you can compare pseudo R-squareds even when they were computed over different test sets. When comparing multiple models, you will generally prefer models with larger pseudo R-squareds.

AIC

An important variant of deviance is the *Akaike information criterion (AIC)*. This is equivalent to `deviance + 2*numberOfParameters` used in the model. The more parameters in the model, the more complex the model is; the more complex a model is, the more likely it is to overfit. Thus, AIC is deviance penalized for model complexity. When comparing models (on the same test set), you will generally prefer the model with the smaller AIC. The AIC is useful for comparing models with different measures of complexity and modeling variables with differing numbers of levels. However, adjusting for model complexity is often more reliably achieved using the holdout and cross-validation methods discussed in section 6.2.1.

So far, we have evaluated models on how well they perform *in general*: the overall rates at which a model returns correct or incorrect predictions on test data. In the next section, we look at one method for evaluating a model on *specific* examples, or *explaining* why a model returns a specific prediction on a given example.

6.3 Local interpretable model-agnostic explanations (LIME) for explaining model predictions

In many people's opinion, the improved prediction performance of modern machine learning methods like deep learning or gradient boosted trees comes at the cost of decreased explanation. As you saw in chapter 1, a human domain expert can review the if-then structure of a decision tree and compare it to their own decision-making processes to decide if the decision tree will make reasonable decisions. Linear models also have an easily explainable structure, as you will see in chapter 8. However, other methods have far more complex structures that are difficult for a human to evaluate. Examples include the multiple individual trees of a random forest (as in figure 6.20), or the highly connected topology of a neural net.

If a model evaluates well on holdout data, that is an indication that the model will perform well in the wild—but it's not foolproof. One potential issue is that the holdout set generally comes from the same source as the training data, and has all the same quirks and idiosyncrasies of the training data. How do you know whether your

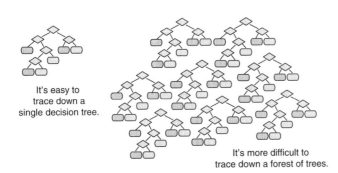

It's easy to trace down a single decision tree.

It's more difficult to trace down a forest of trees.

Figure 6.20 Some kinds of models are easier to manually inspect than others.

model is learning the actual concept of interest, or simply the quirks in the data? Or, putting it another way, will the model work on similar data from a different source?

Example *Suppose you want to train a classifier to distinguish documents about Christianity from documents about atheism.*

One such model was trained using a corpus of postings from the 20 Newsgroups Dataset, a dataset frequently used for research in machine learning on text. The resulting random forest model was 92% accurate on holdout.[7] On the surface, this seems pretty good.

However, delving deeper into the model showed that it was exploiting idiosyncrasies in the data, using the distribution of words like "There" or "Posting" or "edu" to decide whether a post was about Christianity or about atheism. In other words, the model was looking at the wrong features in the data. An example of a classification by this model is shown in figure 6.21.[8]

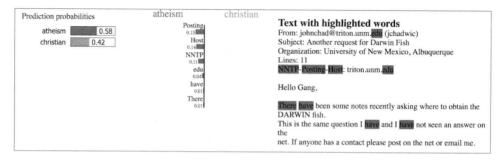

Figure 6.21   Example of a document and the words that most strongly contributed to its classification as "atheist" by the model

In addition, since the documents in the corpus seem to have included the names of specific posters, this model could also potentially be learning whether a *person* who posts frequently in the training corpus is a Christian or an atheist, which is not the same as learning if a *text* is Christian or atheist, especially when trying to apply the model to a document from a different corpus, with different authors.

Another real-world example is Amazon's recent attempt to automate resume reviews, using the resumes of people hired by Amazon over a 10-year period as training data.[9] As Reuters reported, the company discovered that their model was discriminating against women. It penalized resumes that included words like "women's," and downvoted applicants who had graduated from two particular all-women's colleges. Researchers also discovered that the algorithm ignored common terms that referred to

[7] The experiment is described in Ribeiro, Singh, and Guestrin, "'Why Should I Trust You?' Explaining the Predictions of Any Classifier," https://arxiv.org/pdf/1602.04938v1.pdf.

[8] Source: https://homes.cs.washington.edu/~marcotcr/blog/lime/

[9] Jeffrey Dastin, "Amazon scraps secret AI recruiting tool that showed bias against women," Reuters, October 9, 2018, https://www.reuters.com/article/us-amazon-com-jobs-automation-insight/amazon-scraps-secret-ai-recruiting-tool-that-showed-bias-against-women-idUSKCN1MK08G.

specific skills (such as the names of computer programming languages), and favored words like *executed* or *captured* that were disproportionately used by male applicants.

In this case, the flaw was not in the machine learning algorithm, but in the training data, which had apparently captured existing biases in Amazon's hiring practices—which the model then codified. Prediction explanation techniques like LIME can potentially discover such issues.

6.3.1 *LIME: Automated sanity checking*

In order to detect whether a model is really learning the concept, and not just data quirks, it's not uncommon for domain experts to manually sanity-check a model by running some example cases through and looking at the answers. Generally, you would want to try a few typical cases, and a few extreme cases, just to see what happens. You can think of LIME as one form of automated sanity checking.

LIME produces an "explanation" of a model's prediction on a specific datum. That is, LIME tries to determine which features of that datum contributed the most to the model's decision about it. This helps data scientists attempt to understand the behavior of black-box machine learning models.

To make this concrete, we will demonstrate LIME on two tasks: classifying iris species, and classifying movie reviews.

6.3.2 *Walking through LIME: A small example*

The first example is iris classification.

Example   *Suppose you have a dataset of petal and sepal measurements for three varieties of iris. The object is to predict whether a given iris is a setosa based on its petal and sepal dimensions.*

Let's get the data and split it into test and training.

```
Listing 6.14  Loading the iris dataset
```

```
iris <- iris                                                         Setosa is the
                                                                     positive class.
iris$class <- as.numeric(iris$Species == "setosa")    <-

set.seed(2345)
intrain <- runif(nrow(iris)) < 0.75    <-          Uses 75% of the data for
                                                   training, the remainder as
train <- iris[intrain,]                            holdout (test data)
test <- iris[!intrain,]

head(train)

##   Sepal.Length Sepal.Width Petal.Length Petal.Width Species class
## 1          5.1         3.5          1.4         0.2  setosa     1
## 2          4.9         3.0          1.4         0.2  setosa     1
## 3          4.7         3.2          1.3         0.2  setosa     1
## 4          4.6         3.1          1.5         0.2  setosa     1
## 5          5.0         3.6          1.4         0.2  setosa     1
## 6          5.4         3.9          1.7         0.4  setosa     1
```

The variables are the length and width of the sepals and petals. The outcome you want to predict is class, which is 1 when the iris is *setosa*, and 0 otherwise. You will fit a gradient boosting model (from the package xgboost) to predict class.

You will learn about gradient boosting models in detail in chapter 10; for now, we have wrapped the fitting procedure into the function fit_iris_example() that takes as input a matrix of inputs and a vector of class labels, and returns a model that predicts class.[10] The source code for fit_iris_example() is in https://github.com/WinVector/PDSwR2/tree/master/LIME_iris/lime_iris_example.R; in chapter 10, we will unpack how the function works in detail.

To get started, convert the training data to a matrix and fit the model. Make sure that lime_iris_example.R is in your working directory.

Listing 6.15   Fitting a model to the iris training data

```
source("lime_iris_example.R")     ◁──────── Loads the convenience function


input <- as.matrix(train[, 1:4])        ◁
model <- fit_iris_example(input, train$class)
```

The input to the model is the first four columns of the training data, converted to a matrix.

After you fit the model, you can evaluate the model on the test data. The model's predictions are the probability that a given iris is *setosa*.

Listing 6.16   Evaluating the iris model

```
predictions <- predict(model, newdata=as.matrix(test[,1:4]))  ◁

teframe <- data.frame(isSetosa = ifelse(test$class == 1,
                                        "setosa",
                                        "not setosa"),
                      pred = ifelse(predictions > 0.5,
                                    "setosa",
                                    "not setosa"))
with(teframe, table(truth=isSetosa, pred=pred))  ◁

##              pred
## truth        not setosa setosa
##   not setosa         25      0
##   setosa              0     11
```

A data frame of predictions and actual outcome

Makes predictions on the test data. The predictions are the probability that an iris is a setosa.

Examines the confusion matrix

Note that all the datums in the test set fall into the diagonals of the confusion matrix: the model correctly labels all *setosa* examples as "*setosa*" and all the others as "not *setosa*." This model predicts perfectly on the test set! However, you might still want to know which features of an iris are most important when classifying it with

[10] The xgboost package requires that the input be a numeric matrix, and the class labels be a numeric vector.

your model. Let's take a specific example from the `test` dataset and explain it, using the `lime` package.[11]

First, use the training set and the model to build an *explainer*: a function that you will use to explain the model's predictions.

Listing 6.17 Building a LIME explainer from the model and training data

```
library(lime)
explainer <- lime(train[,1:4],                    ◁········ Builds the explainer
                  model = model,                            from the training data
                  bin_continuous = TRUE,       ◁
Uses 10 bins ·······▷ n_bins = 10)                  Bins the continuous variables
                                                    when making explanations
```

Now pick a specific example from the test set.

Listing 6.18 An example iris datum

```
(example <- test[5, 1:4, drop=FALSE])           ◁·······  A single row
##    Sepal.Length Sepal.Width Petal.Length Petal.Width   data frame
## 30          4.7         3.2          1.6         0.2

test$class[5]
## [1] 1          ◁········  This example is a setosa.

round(predict(model, newdata = as.matrix(example)))    And the model predicts
## [1] 1                                                 that it is a setosa.
```

Now explain the model's prediction on `example`. Note that the `dplyr` package also has a function called `explain()`, so if you have `dplyr` in your namespace, you may get a conflict trying to call `lime`'s `explain()` function. To prevent this ambiguity, specify the function using namespace notation: `lime::explain(...)`.

Listing 6.19 Explaining the iris example

```
explanation <- lime::explain(example,
                             explainer,            The number of labels to explain;
                             n_labels = 1,    ◁┘   use 1 for binary classification.
                             n_features = 4)
      The number of features to use  ┌·▷
        when fitting the explanation  │
```

You can visualize the explanation using `plot_features()`, as shown in figure 6.22.

```
plot_features(explanation)
```

---

[11] The `lime` package does not support every type of model out of the box. See `help(model_support)` for the list of model classes that it does support (`xgboost` is one), and how to add support for other types of models. See also LIME's README (https://cran.r-project.org/web/packages/lime/README.html) for other examples.

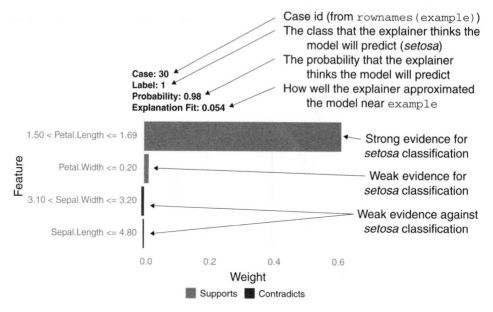

Figure 6.22   **Visualize the explanation of the model's prediction.**

The explainer expects the model will predict that this example is a *setosa* (Label = 1), and that the example's value of Petal.Length is strong evidence supporting this prediction.

HOW LIME WORKS

In order to better understand LIME's explanations, and to diagnose when the explanations are trustworthy or not, it helps to understand how LIME works at a high level. Figure 6.23 sketches out the LIME procedure for a classifier at a high level. The figure shows these points:

- *The model's decision surface.* A classifier's *decision surface* is the surface in variable space that separates where the model classifies datums as positive (in our example, as "*setosa*") from where it classifies them as negative (in our example, as "not *setosa*").

- *The datum we want to explain* marked as the circled plus in the figure. In the figure, the datum is a positive example. In the explanation that follows, we'll call this point "the original example," or example.

- *Synthetic data points* that the algorithm creates and gives to the model to evaluate. We'll detail how the synthetic examples come about.

- *LIME's estimate of the decision surface* near the example we are trying to explain. We'll detail how LIME comes up with this estimate.

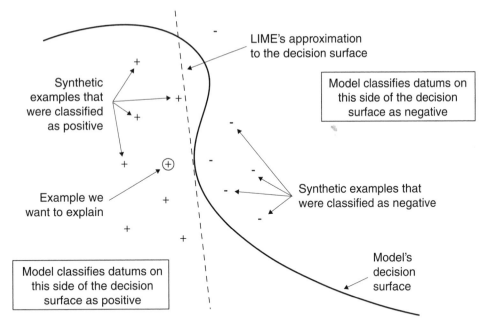

Figure 6.23   Notional sketch of how LIME works

The procedure is as follows:

1   "Jitter" the original example to generate synthetic examples that are similar to it.
    You can think of each jittered point as the original example with the value of each variable changed slightly. For example, if the original example is

```
Sepal.Length Sepal.Width Petal.Length Petal.Width
         5.1         3.5          1.4         0.2
```

then a jittered point might be

```
Sepal.Length Sepal.Width Petal.Length Petal.Width
    5.505938    3.422535       1.3551   0.4259682
```

To make sure that the synthetic examples are plausible, LIME uses the distributions of the data in the training set to generate the jittered data. For our discussion, we'll call the set of synthetic examples {s_i}. Figure 6.23 shows the synthetic data as the additional pluses and minuses.

Note that the jittering is randomized. This means that running `explain()` on the same example multiple times will produce different results each time. If LIME's explanation is strong, the results should not be too different, so that the explanations remain quantitatively similar. In our case, it's likely that `Petal.Length` will always show up as the variable with the most weight; it's just the exact value of `Petal.Length`'s weight and its relationship to the other variables that will vary.

2   Use the model to make predictions {y_i} on all the synthetic examples.

In figure 6.23, the pluses indicate synthetic examples that the model classified as positive, and the minuses indicate synthetic examples that the model classified as negative.

LIME will use the values of {y_i} to get an idea of what the decision surface of the model looks like near the original example. In figure 6.23, the decision surface is the large curvy structure that separates the regions where the model classifies datums as positive from the regions where it classifies datums as negative.

3   Fit an *m*-dimensional linear model for {y_i} as a function of {s_i}.

The linear model is LIME's estimate of the original model's decision surface near example, shown as a dashed line in figure 6.23. Using a linear model means that LIME assumes that the model's decision surface is locally linear (flat) in a small neighborhood around example. You can think of LIME's estimate as the flat surface (in the figure, it's a line) that separates the positive synthetic examples from the negative synthetic examples most accurately.

The R^2 of the linear model (reported as the "explanation fit" in figure 6.22) indicates how well this assumption is met. If the explanation fit is close to 0, then there isn't a flat surface that separates the positive examples from the negative examples well, and LIME's explanation is probably not reliable.

You specify the value of *m* with the n_features parameter in the function explain(). In our case, we are using four features (all of them) to fit the linear model. When there is a large number of features (as in text processing), LIME tries to pick the best *m* features to fit the model.

The coefficients of the linear model give us the weights of the features in the explanation. For classification, a large positive weight means that the corresponding feature is strong evidence in favor of the model's prediction, and a large negative weight means that the corresponding feature is strong evidence against it.

TAKING THE STEPS AS A WHOLE

This may seem like a lot of steps, but they are all supplied in a convenient wrapper by the lime package. Altogether, the steps are implementing a solution to a simple counter-factual question: how would a given example score differently if it had different attributes? The summaries emphasize what are the most important plausible variations.

BACK TO THE IRIS EXAMPLE

Let's pick a couple more examples and explain the model's predictions on them.

Listing 6.20   More iris examples

```
(example <- test[c(13, 24), 1:4])

##      Sepal.Length Sepal.Width Petal.Length Petal.Width
## 58            4.9         2.4          3.3         1.0
## 110           7.2         3.6          6.1         2.5
```

```
test$class[c(13,24)]
## [1] 0 0
```

> Both examples are
> negative (not setosa).

```
round(predict(model, newdata=as.matrix(example)))
## [1] 0 0
```

> The model predicts
> that both examples
> are negative.

```
explanation <- explain(example,
                       explainer,
                       n_labels = 1,
                       n_features = 4,
                       kernel_width = 0.5)
```

```
plot_features(explanation)
```

The explainer expects that the model will predict that both these examples are not *setosa* (Label = 0). For case 110 (the second row of example and the right side plot of figure 6.24), this is again because of Petal.Length. Case 58 (the left side plot of figure 6.24) seems strange: most of the evidence seems to contradict the expected classification! Note that the explanation fit for case 58 is quite small: it's an order of magnitude less than the fit for case 110. This tells you that you may not want to trust this explanation.

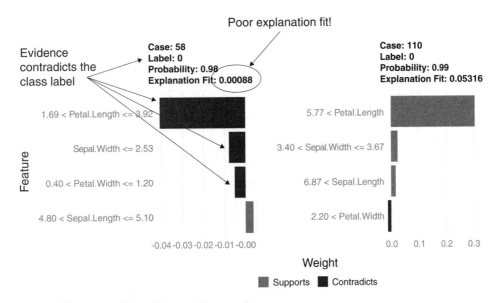

Figure 6.24   Explanations of the two iris examples

Let's look at how these three examples compare to the rest of the iris data. Figure 6.25 shows the distribution of petal and sepal dimensions in the data, with the three sample cases marked.

It's clear from figure 6.25 that petal length strongly differentiates *setosa* from the other species of iris. With respect to petal length, case 30 is obviously *setosa*, and case

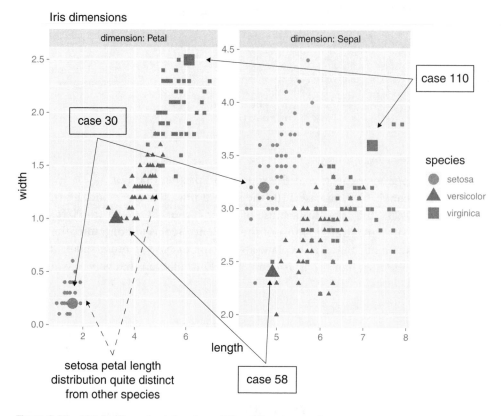

Figure 6.25 Distributions of petal and sepal dimensions by species

110 is obviously not. Case 58 appears to be not *setosa* due to petal length, but as noted earlier, the entire explanation of case 58 is quite poor, probably because case 58 sits at some sort of kink on the model's decision surface.

Now let's try LIME on a larger example.

6.3.3 *LIME for text classification*

Example   *For this example, you will classify movie reviews from the Internet Movie Database (IMDB). The task is to identify positive reviews.*

For convenience, we've converted the data from the original archive[12] into two RDS files, IMDBtrain.RDS and IMDBtest.RDS, found at https://github.com/WinVector/ PDSwR2/tree/master/IMDB. Each RDS object is a list with two elements: a character vector representing 25,000 reviews, and a vector of numeric labels where 1 means a

---

[12] The original data can be found at http://s3.amazonaws.com/text-datasets/aclImdb.zip.

positive review and 0 a negative review.[13] You will again fit an xgboost model to classify the reviews.

You might wonder how LIME jitters a text datum. It does so by randomly removing words from the document, and then converting the resulting new text into the appropriate representation for the model. If removing a word tends to change the classification of a document, then that word is probably important to the model.

First, load the training set. Make sure you have downloaded the RDS files into your working directory.

Listing 6.21 Loading the IMDB training data

```
library(zeallot)

c(texts, labels) %<-% readRDS("IMDBtrain.RDS")
```

Loads the zeallot library. Calls install.packages("zeallot") if this fails.

The command read(IMDBtrain.RDS) returns a list object. The zeallot assignment arrow %<-% unpacks the list into two elements: texts is a character vector of reviews, and labels is a 0/1 vector of class labels. The label 1 designates a positive review.

You can examine the reviews and their corresponding labels. Here's a positive review:

```
list(text = texts[1], label = labels[1])
## $text
## train_21317
## train_21317
## "Forget depth of meaning, leave your logic at the door, and have a
## great time with this maniacally funny, totally absurdist, ultra-
## campy live-action \"cartoon\". MYSTERY MEN is a send-up of every
## superhero flick you've ever seen, but its unlikelysuper-wannabes
## are so interesting, varied, and well-cast that they are memorable
## characters in their own right. Dark humor, downright silliness,
## bona fide action, and even a touchingmoment or two, combine to
## make this comic fantasy about lovable losers a true winner. The
## comedic talents of the actors playing the Mystery Men --
## including one Mystery Woman -- are a perfect foil for Wes Studi
## as what can only be described as a bargain-basement Yoda, and
## Geoffrey Rush as one of the most off-the-wall (and bizarrely
## charming) villains ever to walk off the pages of a Dark Horse
## comic book and onto the big screen. Get ready to laugh, cheer,
## and say \"huh?\" more than once.... enjoy!"
##
## $label
## train_21317
##             1
```

---

[13] The extraction/conversion script we used to create the RDS files can be found at https://github.com/WinVector/PDSwR2/tree/master/IMDB/getIMDB.R.

Here's a negative review:

```
list(text = texts[12], label = labels[12])
## $text
## train_385
## train_385
## "Jameson Parker And Marilyn Hassett are the screen's most unbelievable
## couple since John Travolta and Lily Tomlin. Larry Peerce's direction
## wavers uncontrollably between black farce and Roman tragedy. Robert
## Klein certainly think it's the former and his self-centered  performance
## in a minor role underscores the total lack of balance and chemistry
## between the players in the film. Normally, I don't like to let myself
## get so ascerbic, but The Bell Jar is one of my all-time favorite books,
## and to watch what they did with it makes me literally crazy."
##
## $label
## train_385
##         0
```

REPRESENTING DOCUMENTS FOR MODELING

For our text model, the features are the individual words, and there are a lot of them. To use xgboost to fit a model on texts, we have to build a finite feature set, or the *vocabulary*. The words in the vocabulary are the only features that the model will consider.

We don't want to use words that are too common, because common words that show up in both positive reviews and negative reviews won't be informative. We also don't want to use words that are too rare, because a word that rarely shows up in a review is not that useful. For this task, let's define "too common" as words that show up in more than half the training documents, and "too rare" as words that show up in fewer than 0.1% of the documents.

We'll build a vocabulary of 10,000 words that are not too common or too rare, using the package text2vec. For brevity, we've wrapped the procedure in the function create_pruned_vocabulary(), which takes a vector of documents as input and returns a vocabulary object. The source code for create_pruned_vocabulary() is in https://github.com/WinVector/PDSwR2/tree/master/IMDB/lime_imdb_example.R.

Once we have the vocabulary, we have to convert the texts (again using text2vec) into a numeric representation that xgboost can use. This representation is called a *document-term matrix*, where the rows represent each document in the corpus, and each column represents a word in the vocabulary. For a document-term matrix dtm, the entry dtm[i, j] is the number of times that the vocabulary word w[j] appeared in document texts[i]. See figure 6.26. Note that this representation loses the order of the words in the documents.

The document-term matrix will be quite large: 25,000 rows by 10,000 columns. Luckily, most words in the vocabulary won't show up in a given document, so each row will be mostly zeros. This means that we can use a special representation called a *sparse*

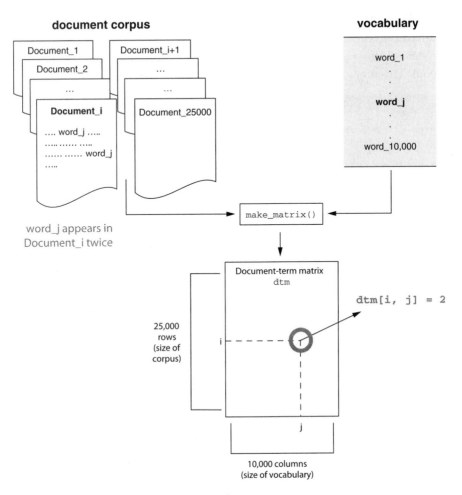

Figure 6.26   Creating a document-term matrix

matrix, of class `dgCMatrix`, that represents large, mostly zero matrices in a space-efficient way.

We've wrapped this conversion in the function `make_matrix()` that takes as input a vector of texts and a vocabulary, and returns a sparse matrix. As in the iris example, we've also wrapped the model fitting into a function `fit_imdb_model()` that takes as input a document term matrix and the numeric document labels, and returns an `xgboost` model. The source code for these functions is also in https://github.com/WinVector/PDSwR2/tree/master/IMDB/lime_imdb_example.R.

6.3.4 *Training the text classifier*

After you download `lime_imdb_example.R` into your working directory, you can create the vocabulary and a document-term matrix from the training data, and fit the model. This may take a while.

Listing 6.22 Converting the texts and fitting the model

```
source("lime_imdb_example.R")

vocab <- create_pruned_vocabulary(texts)
dtm_train <- make_matrix(texts, vocab)
model <- fit_imdb_model(dtm_train, labels)
```

Trains the model ┄┄▷

Creates the vocabulary from the training data ◁┄┄

Creates the document-term matrix of the training corpus ◁┄┄

Now load the test corpus and evaluate the model.

Listing 6.23 Evaluate the review classifier

```
c(test_txt, test_labels) %<-% readRDS("IMDBtest.RDS")   ◁─ Reads in the test corpus
dtm_test <- make_matrix(test_txt, vocab)   ◁─

predicted <- predict(model, newdata=dtm_test)   ◁─

teframe <- data.frame(true_label = test_labels,
                      pred = predicted)

(cmat <- with(teframe, table(truth=true_label, pred=pred > 0.5)))   ◁─

##       pred
## truth FALSE   TRUE
##     0 10836   1664
##     1  1485  11015

sum(diag(cmat))/sum(cmat)   ◁────── Computes the accuracy
## [1] 0.87404

library(WVPlots)
DoubleDensityPlot(teframe, "pred", "true_label",
                  "Distribution of test prediction scores")   ◁─
```

Converts the corpus to a document-term matrix

Makes predictions (probabilities) on the test corpus

Creates a frame with true and predicted labels ┄┄▷

Computes the confusion matrix

Plots the distribution of predictions

Based on its performance on the test set, the model does a good, but not perfect, job at classifying reviews. The distribution of test prediction scores (figure 6.27) shows that most negative (class 0) reviews have low scores, and most positive (class 1) reviews have high scores. However, there are some positive reviews that get scores near 0, and some negative reviews get scores near 1. And some reviews have scores near 0.5, meaning the model isn't sure about them at all. You would like to improve the classifier to do a better job on these seemingly ambiguous reviews.

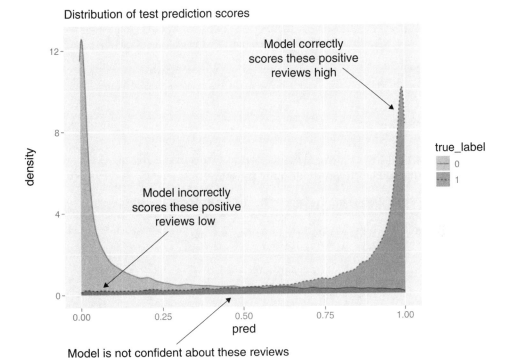

Figure 6.27   **Distribution of test prediction scores**

6.3.5 *Explaining the classifier's predictions*

Try explaining the predictions for a few example reviews to get some insight into the model. First, build the explainer from the training data and the model. For text models, the `lime()` function takes a preprocessor function that converts the training texts and the synthetic examples to a document-term matrix for the model.

Listing 6.24   Building an explainer for a text classifier

```
explainer <- lime(texts, model = model,
                  preprocess = function(x) make_matrix(x, vocab))
```

Now take a short sample text from the test corpus. This review is positive, and the model predicts that it is positive.

Listing 6.25   Explaining the model's prediction on a review

```
casename <- "test_19552";
sample_case <- test_txt[casename]
pred_prob <- predict(model, make_matrix(sample_case, vocab))
list(text = sample_case,
     label = test_labels[casename],
     prediction = round(pred_prob) )
```

```
## $text
## test_19552
## "Great story, great music. A heartwarming love story that's beautiful to
## watch and delightful to listen to. Too bad there is no soundtrack CD."
##
## $label
## test_19552
##           1
##
## $prediction
## [1] 1
```

Now explain the model's classification in terms of the five most evidential words. The words that affect the prediction the most are shown in figure 6.28.

Listing 6.26   Explaining the model's prediction

```
explanation <- lime::explain(sample_case,
                    explainer,
                    n_labels = 1,
                    n_features = 5)

plot_features(explanation)
```

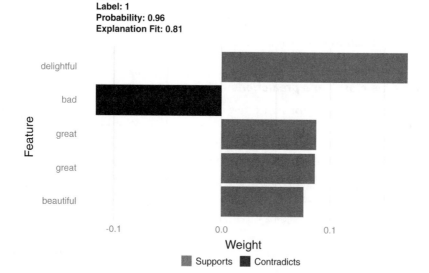

Figure 6.28   Explanation of the prediction on the sample review

In listing 6.26, you used `plot_features()` to visualize the explanation, as you did in the `iris` example, but `lime` also has a special visualization for text, `plot_text_explanations()`.

As shown in figure 6.29, `plot_text_explanations()` highlights the key words within the text, green for supporting evidence, and red for contradictory. The stronger the evidence, the darker the color. Here, the explainer expects that the model will predict that this review is positive, based on the words *delightful*, *great*, and *beautiful*, and in spite of the word *bad*.

```
plot_text_explanations(explanation)
```

supports   supports   supports   supports   contradicts

Great story, great music. A heartwarming love story that's beautiful to watch and delightful to listen to. Too bad there is no soundtrack CD.

Label predicted: 1 (96.31%)

Explainer fit: 0.81

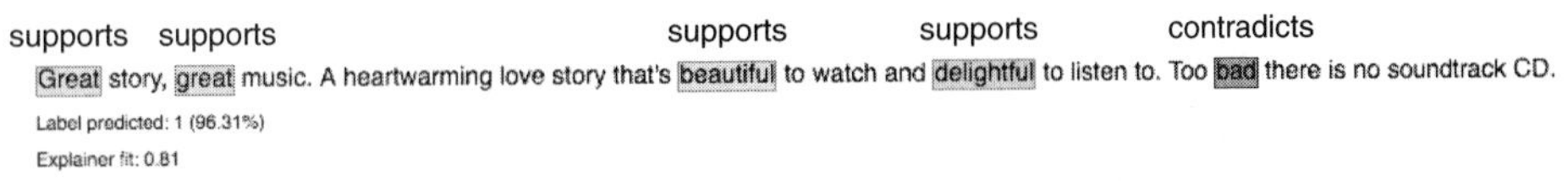

Figure 6.29   Text explanation of the prediction in listing 6.26

Let's look at a couple more reviews, including one that the model misclassified.

Listing 6.27   Examining two more reviews

```
casenames <-  c("test_12034", "test_10294")
sample_cases <- test_txt[casenames]
pred_probs <- predict(model, newdata=make_matrix(sample_cases, vocab))
list(texts = sample_cases,
     labels = test_labels[casenames],
     predictions = round(pred_probs))

## $texts
## test_12034
## "I don't know why I even watched this film. I think it was because
## I liked the idea of the scenery and was hoping the film would be
## as good. Very boring and pointless."
##
## test_10294
## "To anyone who likes the TV series: forget the movie. The jokes
## are bad and some topics are much too sensitive to laugh about it.
## <br /><br />We have seen much better acting by R. Dueringer in
## \"Hinterholz 8\"".
##
## $labels
## test_12034 test_10294        ⟵────── Both these reviews are negative.
##          0          0
##
## $predictions                ⟵────────┐ The model misclassified
## [1] 0 1                               │ the second review.

explanation <- lime::explain(sample_cases,
                             explainer,
                             n_labels = 1,
                             n_features = 5)

plot_features(explanation)
plot_text_explanations(explanation)
```

As shown in figure 6.30, the explainer expects that the model will classify the first review as negative, based mostly on the words *pointless* and *boring*. It expects that the model will classify the second review as positive, based on the words *8*, *sensitive*, and *seen*, and in spite of the words *bad* and (somewhat surprisingly) *better*.

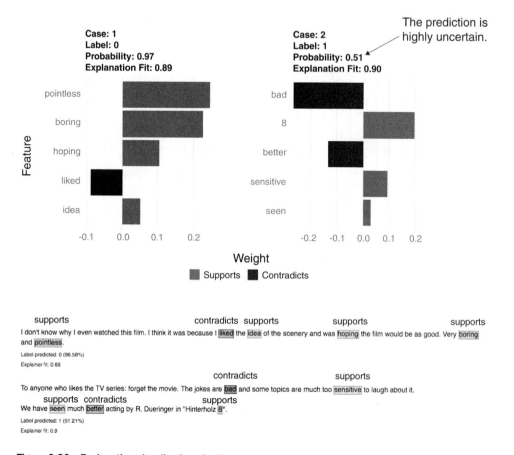

Figure 6.30   Explanation visualizations for the two sample reviews in listing 6.27

Note that according to figure 6.30, the probability of the classification of the second review appears to be 0.51—in other words, the explainer expects that the model won't be sure of its prediction at all. Let's compare this to what the model predicted in reality:

```
predict(model, newdata=make_matrix(sample_cases[2], vocab))
## [1] 0.6052929
```

The model actually predicts the label 1 with probability 0.6: not a confident prediction, but slightly more confident than the explainer estimated (though still wrong). The discrepancy is because the label and probability that the explainer returns are from the predictions of the linear approximation to the model, *not* from the model itself. You may occasionally even see cases where the explainer and the model return different labels for the same example. This will usually happen when the explanation fit is poor, so you don't want to trust those explanations, anyway.

As the data scientist responsible for classifying reviews, you may wonder about the seemingly high importance of the number *8*. On reflection, you might remember that some movie reviews include the ratings "8 out of 10," or "8/10." This may lead you to consider extracting apparent ratings out of the reviews before passing them to the text processor, and adding them to the model as an additional special feature. You may also not like using words like *seen* or *idea* as features.

As a simple experiment, you can try removing the numbers 1 through 10 from the vocabulary,[14] and then refitting the model. The new model correctly classifies test_10294 and returns a more reasonable explanation, as shown in figure 6.31.

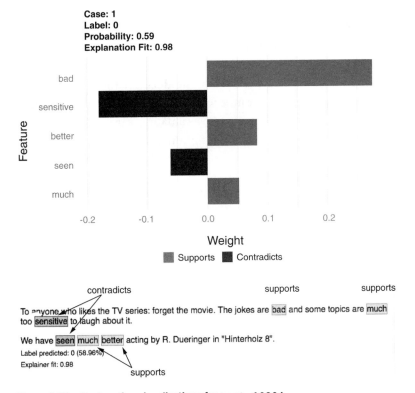

Figure 6.31   Explanation visualizations for test_10294

---

[14] This involves adding the numbers 1 through 10 as strings to the stopword list in the function create_pruned_vocabulary() in the file lime_imdb_example.R. We leave recreating the vocabulary and document-term matrices, and refitting the review classifier, as an exercise for the reader.

Looking at the explanations of other reviews that the model misclassifies can lead you to improved feature engineering or data preprocessing that can potentially improve your model. You may decide that sequences of words (*good idea*, rather than just *idea*) make better features. Or you may decide that you want a text representation and model that looks at the order of the words in the document rather than just word frequencies. In any case, looking at explanations of a model's predictions on corner cases can give you insight into your model, and help you decide how to better achieve your modeling goals.

Summary

You now have some solid ideas on how to choose among modeling techniques. You also know how to evaluate the quality of data science work, be it your own or that of others. The remaining chapters of part 2 of the book will go into more detail on how to build, test, and deliver effective predictive models. In the next chapter, we'll actually start building predictive models.

In this chapter you have learned

- How to match the problem you want to solve to appropriate modeling approaches.
- How to partition your data for effective model evaluation.
- How to calculate various measures for evaluating classification models.
- How to calculate various measures for evaluating scoring (regression) models.
- How to calculate various measures for evaluating probability models.
- How to use the `lime` package to explain individual predictions from a model.

7
Linear and logistic regression

This chapter covers

- Using linear regression to predict quantities
- Using logistic regression to predict probabilities or categories
- Extracting relations and advice from linear models
- Interpreting the diagnostics from R's `lm()` call
- Interpreting the diagnostics from R's `glm()` call
- Using regularization via the `glmnet` package to address issues that can arise with linear models.

In the previous chapter, you learned how to evaluate models. Now that we have the ability to discuss if a model is good or bad, we'll move on to the modeling step, as shown in the mental model (figure 7.1). In this chapter, we'll cover fitting and interpreting *linear models* in R.

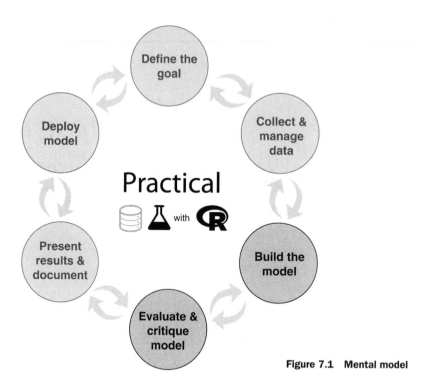

Figure 7.1   Mental model

Linear models are especially useful when you don't want only to predict an outcome, but also to know the relationship between the input variables and the outcome. This knowledge can prove useful because this relationship can often be used as *advice* on how to get the outcome that you want.

We'll first define *linear regression* and then use it to predict customer income. Later, we will use *logistic regression* to predict the probability that a newborn baby will need extra medical attention. We'll also walk through the diagnostics that R produces when you fit a linear or logistic model.

Linear methods can work well in a surprisingly wide range of situations. However, there can be issues when the inputs to the model are correlated or *collinear*. In the case of logistic regression, there can also be issues (ironically) when a subset of the variables predicts a classification output perfectly in a subset of the training data. The last section of the chapter will show how to address these issues by a technique called *regularization*.

7.1   Using linear regression

Linear regression is the bread and butter prediction method for statisticians and data scientists. If you're trying to predict a numerical quantity like profit, cost, or sales volume, you should always try linear regression first. If it works well, you're done; if it fails, the detailed diagnostics produced can give you a good clue as to what methods you should try next.

7.1.1   *Understanding linear regression*

Example   *Suppose you want to predict how many pounds a person on a diet and exercise plan will lose in a month. You will base that prediction on other facts about that person, like how much they reduce their average daily caloric intake over that month and how many hours a day they exercised. In other words, for every person* i, *you want to predict* pounds_lost[i] *based on* daily_cals_down[i] *and* daily_exercise[i].

Linear regression assumes that the outcome pounds_lost is linearly related to each of the inputs daily_cals_down[i] and daily_exercise[i]. This means that the relationship between (for instance) daily_cals_down[i] and pounds_lost looks like a (noisy) straight line, as shown in figure 7.2.[1]

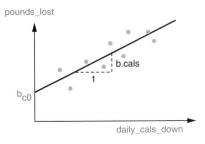

pounds_lost ~ b.cals * daily_cals_down
(plus an offset)

Figure 7.2   The linear relationship between daily_cals_down and pounds_lost

The relationship between daily_exercise and pounds_lost would similarly be a straight line. Suppose that the equation of the line shown in figure 7.2 is

```
pounds_lost = bc0 + b.cals * daily_cals_down
```

This means that for every unit change in daily_cals_down (every calorie reduced), the value of pounds_lost changes by b.cals, no matter what the starting value of daily_cals_down was. To make it concrete, suppose pounds_lost = 3 + 2 * daily_cals_down. Then increasing daily_cals_down by one increases pounds_lost by 2, no matter what value of daily_cals_down you start with. This would not be true for, say, pounds_lost = 3 + 2 * (daily_cals_down^2).

Linear regression further assumes that the total pounds lost is a *linear combination* of our variables daily_cals_down[i] and daily_exercise[i], or the sum of the pounds lost due to reduced caloric intake, and the pounds lost due to exercise. This gives us the following form for the linear regression model of pounds_lost:

```
pounds_lost[i] = b0 + b.cals * daily_cals_down[i] +
        b.exercise * daily_exercise[i]
```

---

[1] It is tempting to hope that b0J = bC0 + be0 or that b.calsJ = b.cals; however, a joint regression does not ensure this.

The goal of linear regression is to find the values of b0, b.cals, and b.exercise so that the linear combination of daily_cals_lost[i] and daily_exercise[i] (plus some offset b0) comes very close to pounds_lost[i] for all persons i in the training data.

Let's put this in more general terms. Suppose that y[i] is the numeric quantity you want to predict (called the *dependent* or *response* variable), and x[i,] is a row of inputs that corresponds to output y[i] (the x[i,] are the *independent* or *explanatory* variables). Linear regression attempts to find a function *f(x)* such that

```
y[i] ~ f(x[i,]) + e[i] = b[0] + b[1] * x[i,1] + ... + b[n] * x[i,n] + e[i]
```

Equation 7.1   The expression for a linear regression model

You want numbers b[0],...,b[n] (called the *coefficients* or *betas*) such that f(x[i,]) is as near as possible to y[i] for all (x[i,],y[i]) pairs in the training data. R supplies a one-line command to find these coefficients: lm().

The last term in equation 7.1, e[i], represents what are called *unsystematic errors*, or noise. Unsystematic errors are defined to all have a mean value of 0 (so they don't represent a net upward or net downward bias) and are defined as uncorrelated with x[i,]. In other words, x[i,] should not encode information about e[i] (or vice versa).

By assuming that the noise is unsystematic, linear regression tries to fit what is called an "unbiased" predictor. This is another way of saying that the predictor gets the right answer "on average" over the entire training set, or that it underpredicts about as much as it overpredicts. In particular, unbiased estimates tend to get totals correct.

Example *Suppose you have fit a linear regression model to predict weight loss based on reduction of caloric intake and exercise. Now consider the set of subjects in the training data,* LowExercise, *who exercised between zero and one hour a day. Together, these subjects lost a total of 150 pounds over the course of the study. How much did the model predict they would lose?*

With a linear regression model, if you take the predicted weight loss for all the subjects in LowExercise and sum them up, that total will sum to 150 pounds, which means that the model predicts the *average* weight loss of a person in the LowExercise group correctly, even though some of the individuals will have lost more than the model predicted, and some of them will have lost less. In a business setting, getting sums like this correct is critical, particularly when summing up monetary amounts.

Under these assumptions (linear relationships and unsystematic noise), linear regression is absolutely relentless in finding the best coefficients b[i]. If there's some advantageous combination or cancellation of features, it'll find it. One thing that linear regression doesn't do is reshape variables to be linear. Oddly enough, linear regression often does an excellent job, even when the actual relation is not in fact linear.

THINKING ABOUT LINEAR REGRESSION   When working with linear regression, you'll go back and forth between "Adding is too simple to work," and "How is it even possible to estimate the coefficients?" This is natural and comes from the fact that the method is both simple and powerful. Our friend Philip Apps sums it up: "You have to get up pretty early in the morning to beat linear regression."

WHEN THE ASSUMPTIONS OF LINEAR REGRESSION ARE VIOLATED

As a toy example, consider trying to fit the squares of the integers 1–10 using only a linear function plus a constant. We're asking for coefficients b[0] and b[1] such that

```
x[i]^2 nearly equals b[0] + b[1] * x[i]
```

This is clearly not a fair thing to ask, since we know that what we are trying to predict is not linear. In this case, however, linear regression still does a pretty good job. It picks the following fit:

```
x[i]^2 nearly equals -22 + 11 * x[i]
```

As figure 7.3 shows, this is a good fit in the region of values we trained on.

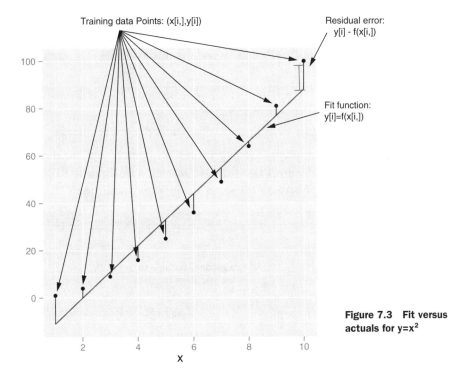

Figure 7.3   Fit versus actuals for $y=x^2$

The example in figure 7.3 is typical of how linear regression is "used in the field"— we're using a linear model to predict something that is itself not linear. Be aware that this is a minor sin. In particular, note that the errors between the model's predictions and the true y are not random, but systematic: the model underpredicts for specific ranges of x and overpredicts for others. This isn't ideal, but often the best we can do. Note also that, in this example, the predictions veer further away from the true outcome near the endpoints of the fit, which indicates that this model is probably not safe to use outside the range of x that the model observed in the training data.

EXTRAPOLATION IS NOT AS SAFE AS INTERPOLATION   In general, you should try to use a model only for *interpolation*: predicting for new data that falls inside the range of your training data. *Extrapolation* (predicting for new data outside the range observed during training) is riskier for any model. It's especially risky for linear models, unless you know that the system that you are modeling is truly linear.

Next we'll work through an example of how to apply linear regression on more-interesting real data.

INTRODUCING THE PUMS DATASET

Example   *Suppose you want to predict personal income of any individual in the general public, within some relative percent, given their age, education, and other demographic variables. In addition to predicting income, you also have a secondary goal: to determine the effect of a bachelor's degree on income, relative to having no degree at all.*

For this task, you will use the 2016 US Census PUMS dataset. For simplicity, we have prepared a small sample of PUMS data to use for this example. The data preparation steps include these:

- Restricting the data to full-time employees between 20 and 50 years of age, with an income between \$1,000 and \$250,000.
- Dividing the data into a training set, dtrain, and a test set, dtest.

We can continue the example by loading psub.RDS (which you can download from https://github.com/WinVector/PDSwR2/raw/master/PUMS/psub.RDS) into your working directory, and performing the steps in the following listing.[1]

Listing 7.1   Loading the PUMS data and fitting a model

```
psub <- readRDS("psub.RDS")

set.seed(3454351)              Makes a random variable to
gp <- runif(nrow(psub))    ◁── group and partition the data

dtrain <- subset(psub, gp >= 0.5)    ◁········· Splits 50–50 into training and test sets
 dtest <- subset(psub, gp < 0.5)

 model <- lm(log10(PINCP) ~ AGEP + SEX + COW + SCHL, data = dtrain)
    dtest$predLogPINCP <- predict(model, newdata = dtest)    ◁─────────────
    dtrain$predLogPINCP <- predict(model, newdata = dtrain)

Fits a linear model                          Gets the predicted log(income)
to log(income)                                  on the test and training sets
```

---

[1]   The script for preparing the data sample can be found at https://github.com/WinVector/PDSwR2/blob/master/PUMS/makeSubSample.Rmd.

Each row of PUMS data represents a single anonymized person or household. Personal data recorded includes occupation, level of education, personal income, and many other demographic variables.

For this example we have decided to predict `log10(PINCP)`, or the logarithm of income. Fitting logarithm-transformed data typically gives results with smaller relative error, emphasizing smaller errors on smaller incomes. But this improved relative error comes at a cost of introducing a bias: on average, predicted incomes are going to be below actual training incomes. An unbiased alternative to predicting `log(income)` would be to use a type of generalized linear model called *Poisson regression*. We will discuss generalized linear models (specifically, logistic regression) in section 7.2. The Poisson regression is unbiased, but typically at the cost of larger relative errors.[1]

For the analysis in this section, we'll consider the input variables age (`AGEP`), sex (`SEX`), class of worker (`COW`), and level of education (`SCHL`). The output variable is personal income (`PINCP`). We'll also set the *reference level*, or "default" sex to `M` (male); the reference level of class of worker to `Employee of a private for-profit`; and the reference level of education level to `no high school diploma`. We'll discuss reference levels later in this chapter.

Reference levels are baselines, not value judgments

When we say that the default sex is male and the default educational level is `no high school diploma`, we are not implying that you should expect that a typical worker is male, or that a typical worker has no high school diploma. The reference level of a variable is the baseline that other values of the variable are compared to. So we are saying that at some point in this analysis, we may want to compare the income of female workers to that of male workers with equivalent characteristics, or that we may want to compare the income of workers with a high school degree or a bachelor's degree to that of a worker with no high school diploma (but otherwise equivalent characteristics).

By default, R selects the alphabetically first value of a categorical variable as the reference level.

Now on to the model building.

7.1.2 *Building a linear regression model*

The first step in either prediction or finding relations (advice) is to build the linear regression model. The function to build the linear regression model in R is `lm()`, supplied by the `stats` package. The most important argument to `lm()` is a formula with ~ used in place of an equals sign. The formula specifies what column of the data frame

---

[1] For a series of articles discussing these issues, please see http://www.win-vector.com/blog/2019/07/link-functions-versus-data-transforms/.

is the quantity to be predicted, and what columns are to be used to make the predictions.

Statisticians call the quantity to be predicted the *dependent variable* and the variables/columns used to make the prediction the *independent variables*. We find it is easier to call the quantity to be predicted the *y* and the variables used to make the predictions the *x*s. Our formula is this: `log10(PINCP) ~ AGEP + SEX + COW + SCHL`, which is read "Predict the log base 10 of income as a function of age, sex, employment class, and education."[1] The overall method is demonstrated in figure 7.4.

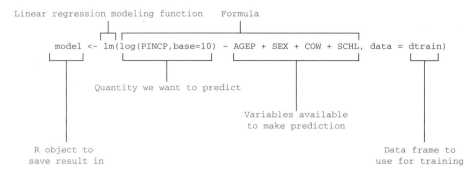

Figure 7.4   **Building a linear model using `lm()`**

The statement in figure 7.4 builds the linear regression model and stores the results in the new object called `model`. This model is able to make predictions, and to extract important advice from the data.

> **R STORES TRAINING DATA IN THE MODEL**   R holds a copy of the training data in its model to supply the residual information seen in `summary(model)`. Holding a copy of the data this way is not strictly necessary, and can needlessly run you out of memory. If you're running low on memory (or swapping), you can dispose of R objects like `model` using the `rm()` command. In this case, you'd dispose of the model by running `rm("model")`.

7.1.3   *Making predictions*

Once you've called `lm()` to build the model, your first goal is to predict income. This is easy to do in R. To predict, you pass data into the `predict()` method. Figure 7.5 demonstrates this using both the test and training data frames `dtest` and `dtrain`.

---

[1]   Recall from the discussion of the lognormal distribution in section 4.2 that it's often useful to log transform monetary quantities. The log transform is also compatible with our original task of predicting incomes with a relative error (meaning large errors count more against small incomes). The `glm()` methods of section 7.2 can be used to avoid the log transform and predict in such a way as to minimize square errors (so being off by $50,000 would be considered the same error for both large and small incomes).

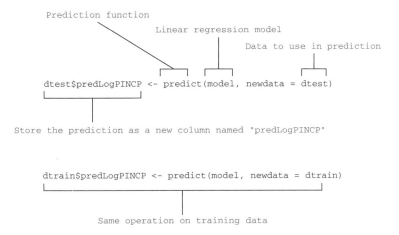

Figure 7.5 **Making predictions with a linear regression model**

The data frame columns `dtest$predLogPINCP` and `dtrain$predLogPINCP` now store the predictions for the test and training sets, respectively. We have now both produced and applied a linear regression model.

CHARACTERIZING PREDICTION QUALITY

Before publicly sharing predictions, you want to inspect both the predictions and model for quality. We recommend plotting the actual y (in this case, predicted income) that you're trying to predict as if it were a function of your prediction. In this case, plot `log10(PINCP)` as if it were a function of `predLogPINCP`. If the predictions are very good, then the plot will be dots arranged near the line y=x, which we call *the line of perfect prediction* (the phrase is not standard terminology; we use it to make talking about the graph easier). The steps to produce this, illustrated in figure 7.6, are shown in the next listing.

Listing 7.2   Plotting log income as a function of predicted log income

```
library('ggplot2')
ggplot(data = dtest, aes(x = predLogPINCP, y = log10(PINCP))) +
   geom_point(alpha = 0.2, color = "darkgray") +
   geom_smooth(color = "darkblue") +
   geom_line(aes(x = log10(PINCP),        <─── Plots the line x=y
                 y = log10(PINCP)),
             color = "blue", linetype = 2) +
   coord_cartesian(xlim = c(4, 5.25),     <─┐ Limits the range of the
                   ylim = c(3.5, 5.5))      ─┘ graph for legibility
```

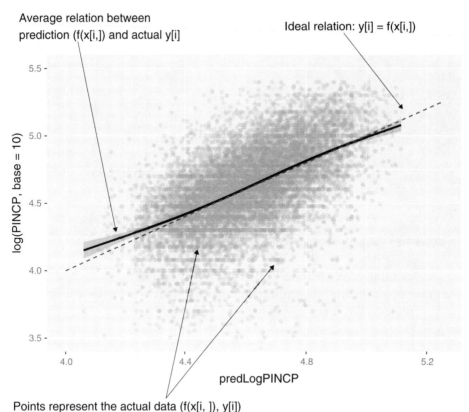

Figure 7.6   Plot of actual log income as a function of predicted log income

Statisticians prefer the residual plot shown in figure 7.7, where the residual errors (in this case, `predLogPINCP - log10(PINCP)`) are plotted as a function of `predLogPINCP`. In this case, the line of perfect prediction is the line y=0. Notice that the points are scattered widely from this line (a possible sign of low-quality fit). The residual plot in figure 7.7 is prepared with the R steps in the next listing.

Listing 7.3   Plotting residuals income as a function of predicted log income

```
ggplot(data = dtest, aes(x = predLogPINCP,
                     y = predLogPINCP - log10(PINCP))) +
   geom_point(alpha = 0.2, color = "darkgray") +
   geom_smooth(color = "darkblue") +
   ylab("residual error (prediction - actual)")
```

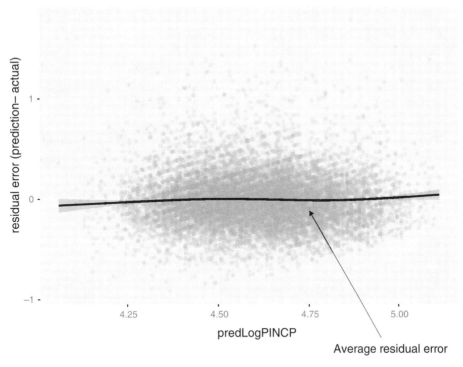

Figure 7.7 **Plot of residual error as a function of prediction**

Why are the predictions, not the true values, on the x-axis?

A graph that plots predictions on the x-axis and either true values (as in figure 7.6) or residuals (as in figure 7.7) on the y-axis answers different questions than a graph that puts true values on the x-axis and predictions (or residuals) on the y-axis. Statisticians tend to prefer the graph as shown in figure 7.7. A residual graph with *predictions* on the x-axis gives you a sense of when the model may be under- or overpredicting, based on the model's output.

A residual graph with the *true outcome* on the x-axis and residuals on the y-axis would almost always appear to have undesirable residual structure, even when there is no modeling problem. This illusion is due to an effect called *regression to the mean* or *reversion to mediocrity*.

When you look at the true-versus-fitted or residual graphs, you're looking for some specific things that we'll discuss next.

On average, are the predictions correct?

Does the smoothing curve lie more or less along the line of perfect prediction? Ideally, the points will all lie very close to that line, but you may instead get a wider cloud of points (as we do in figures 7.6 and 7.7) if your input variables don't explain the output too closely. But if the smoothing curve lies along the line of perfect prediction and "down the middle" of the cloud of points, then the model predicts correctly on average: it underpredicts about as much as it overpredicts.

Are there systematic errors?

If the smoothing curve veers off the line of perfect prediction too much, as in figure 7.8, this is a sign of systematic under- or overprediction in certain ranges: the error is correlated with the prediction. Systematic errors indicate that the system is not "linear enough" for a linear model to be a good fit, so you should try one of the different modeling approaches that we will discuss later in this book.

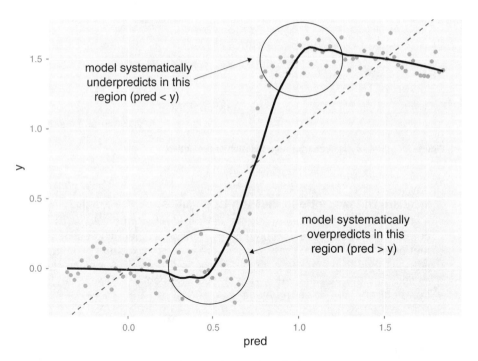

Figure 7.8   An example of systematic errors in model predictions

R-squared and RMSE

In addition to inspecting graphs, you should produce quantitative summaries of the quality of the predictions and the residuals. One standard measure of quality of a prediction is called *R-squared*, which we covered in section 6.2.4. R-squared is a measure of how well the model "fits" the data, or its "goodness of fit." You can compute the R-squared between the prediction and the actual y with the R steps in the following listing.

Listing 7.4 Computing R-squared

```
rsq <- function(y, f) { 1 - sum((y - f)^2)/sum((y - mean(y))^2) }

rsq(log10(dtrain$PINCP), dtrain$predLogPINCP)     R-squared of the model
 ## [1] 0.2976165                                  on the training data

rsq(log10(dtest$PINCP), dtest$predLogPINCP)       R-squared of the model
 ## [1] 0.2911965                                   on the test data
```

R-squared can be thought of as what fraction of the y variation is explained by the model. You want R-squared to be fairly large (1.0 is the largest you can achieve) and R-squareds that are similar on test and training. A significantly lower R-squared on test data is a symptom of an overfit model that looks good in training and won't work in production. In this case, the R-squareds were about 0.3 for both the training and test data. We'd like to see R-squareds higher than this (say, 0.7–1.0). So the model is of low quality, but not overfit.

For well-fit models, R-squared is also equal to the square of the correlation between the predicted values and actual training values.[1]

R-squared can be overoptimistic

In general, R-squared on training data will be higher for models with more input parameters, independent of whether the additional variables actually improve the model or not. That's why many people prefer the adjusted R-squared (which we'll discuss later in this chapter).

Also, R-squared is related to correlation, and the correlation can be artificially inflated if the model correctly predicts a few outliers. This is because the increased data range makes the overall data cloud appear "tighter" against the line of perfect prediction. Here's a toy example. Let y <- c(1,2,3,4,5,9,10) and pred <- c(0.5,0.5,0.5, 0.5,0.5,9,10). This corresponds to a model that's completely uncorrelated to the true outcome for the first five points, and perfectly predicts the last two points, which are somewhat far away from the first five. You can check for yourself that this obviously poor model has a correlation cor(y, pred) of about 0.926, with a corresponding R-squared of 0.858. So it's an excellent idea to look at the true-versus-fitted graph on test data, in addition to checking R-squared.

Another good measure to consider is *root mean square error* (RMSE).

Listing 7.5 Calculating root mean square error

```
rmse <- function(y, f) { sqrt(mean( (y-f)^2 )) }       RMSE of the model
                                                        on the training data
rmse(log10(dtrain$PINCP), dtrain$predLogPINCP)
 ## [1] 0.2685855

rmse(log10(dtest$PINCP), dtest$predLogPINCP)            RMSE of the model
 ## [1] 0.2675129                                        on the test data
```

---

[1] See http://www.win-vector.com/blog/2011/11/correlation-and-r-squared/.

You can think of the RMSE as a measure of the width of the data cloud around the line of perfect prediction. We'd like RMSE to be small, and one way to achieve this is to introduce more useful, explanatory variables.

7.1.4 *Finding relations and extracting advice*

Recall that your other goal, beyond predicting income, is to find the value of having a bachelor's degree. We'll show how this value, and other relations in the data, can be read directly off a linear regression model.

All the information in a linear regression model is stored in a block of numbers called the *coefficients*. The coefficients are available through the coefficients(model) function. The coefficients of our income model are shown in figure 7.9.

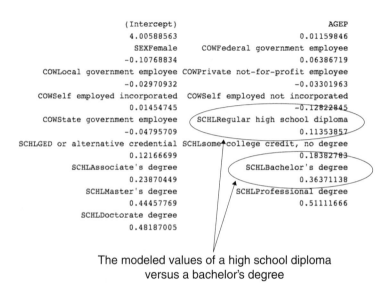

The modeled values of a high school diploma
versus a bachelor's degree

Figure 7.9   The model coefficients

REPORTED COEFFICIENTS

Our original modeling variables were only AGEP, SEX, COW (class of work), and SCHL (schooling/education); yet the model reports many more coefficients than these four. We'll explain what all the reported coefficients are.

In figure 7.9, there are eight coefficients that start with SCHL. The original variable SCHL took on these eight string values plus one more not shown: no high school diploma. Each of these possible strings is called a *level*, and SCHL itself is called a *categorical* or *factor* variable. The level that isn't shown is called the *reference level*; the coefficients of the other levels are measured with respect to the reference level.

For example, in SCHLBachelor's degree we find the coefficient 0.36, which is read as "The model gives a 0.36 bonus to log base 10 income for having a bachelor's degree, relative to not having a high school degree." You can solve for the income ratio between someone with a bachelor's degree and the equivalent person (same sex, age, and class of work) without a high school degree as follows:

```
log10(income_bachelors) = log10(income_no_hs_degree) + 0.36
log10(income_bachelors) - log10(income_no_hs_degree) = 0.36
        (income_bachelors) / (income_no_hs_degree)  = 10^(0.36)
```

This means that someone with a bachelor's degree will tend to have an income about $10^{0.36}$, or 2.29 times higher than the equivalent person without a high school degree.

And under `SCHLRegular high school diploma`, we find the coefficient 0.11. This is read as "The model believes that having a bachelor's degree tends to add 0.36–0.11 units to the predicted log income, relative to having a high school degree."

```
log10(income_bachelors) - log10(income_no_hs_degree) = 0.36      Subtracts the
        log10(income_hs) - log10(income_no_hs_degree) = 0.11     second equation
                                                                 from the first
log10(income_bachelors) - log10(income_hs) = 0.36 - 0.11    ⬑
        (income_bachelors) / (income_hs)   = 10^(0.36 - 0.11)
```

The modeled relation between the bachelor's degree holder's expected income and the high school graduate's (all other variables being equal) is $10^{(0.36 - 0.11)}$, or about 1.8 times greater. The advice: college is worth it if you can find a job (remember that we limited the analysis to the fully employed, so this is assuming you can find a job).

SEX and COW are also discrete variables, with reference levels `Male` and `Employee of a private for profit` [company], respectively. The coefficients that correspond to the different levels of SEX and COW can be interpreted in a manner similar to the education level. AGEP is a continuous variable with coefficient 0.0116. You can interpret this as saying that a one-year increase in age adds a 0.0116 bonus to log income; in other words, an increase in age of one year corresponds to an increase of income of $10^{0.0116}$, or a factor of 1.027—about a 2.7% increase in income (all other variables being equal).

The coefficient (Intercept) corresponds to a variable that always has a value of 1, which is implicitly added to linear regression models unless you use the special 0+ notation in the formula during the call to `lm()`. One way to interpret the intercept is to think of it as "the prediction for the reference subject"—that is, the subject who takes on the values of all the reference levels for the categorical inputs, and zero for the continuous variables. Note that this may not be a physically plausible subject.

In our example, the reference subject would be a male employee of a private for-profit company, with no high school degree, who is zero years old. If such a person could exist, the model would predict their log base 10 income to be about 4.0, which corresponds to an income of $10,000.

> ## Indicator variables
>
> Most modeling methods handle a string-valued (categorical) variable with n possible levels by converting it to n (or n-1) binary variables, or *indicator variables*. R has commands to explicitly control the conversion of string-valued variables into well-behaved indicators: `as.factor()` creates categorical variables from string variables; `relevel()` allows the user to specify the reference level.
>
> But beware of variables with a very large number of levels, like ZIP codes. The runtime of linear (and logistic) regression increases as roughly the cube of the number of coefficients. Too many levels (or too many variables in general) will bog the algorithm down and require much more data for reliable inference. In chapter 8, we will discuss methods for dealing with such high cardinality variables, such as effects coding or impact coding.

The preceding interpretations of the coefficients assume that the model has provided good estimates of the coefficients. We'll see how to check that in the next section.

7.1.5   *Reading the model summary and characterizing coefficient quality*

In section 7.1.3, we checked whether our income predictions were to be trusted. We'll now show how to check whether model coefficients are reliable. This is especially important, as we've been discussing showing coefficients' relations to others as advice.

Most of what we need to know is already in the model summary, which is produced using the `summary()` command: `summary(model)`. This produces the output shown in figure 7.10.

This figure looks intimidating, but it contains a lot of useful information and diagnostics. You're likely to be asked about elements of figure 7.10 when presenting results, so we'll demonstrate how all of these fields are derived and what the fields mean.

We'll first break down the `summary()` into pieces.

THE ORIGINAL MODEL CALL

The first part of the `summary()` is how the `lm()` model was constructed:

```
Call:
lm(formula = log10(PINCP) ~ AGEP + SEX + COW + SCHL,
    data = dtrain)
```

This is a good place to double-check whether you used the correct data frame, performed your intended transformations, and used the right variables. For example, you can double-check whether you used the data frame `dtrain` and not the data frame `dtest`.

THE RESIDUALS SUMMARY

The next part of the `summary()` is the residuals summary:

```
Residuals:
    Min      1Q  Median      3Q     Max
-1.5038 -0.1354  0.0187  0.1710  0.9741
```

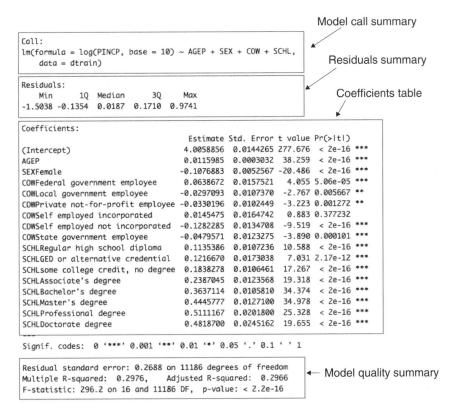

```
Call:
lm(formula = log(PINCP, base = 10) ~ AGEP + SEX + COW + SCHL,
    data = dtrain)

Residuals:
    Min      1Q  Median      3Q     Max
-1.5038 -0.1354  0.0187  0.1710  0.9741

Coefficients:
                                          Estimate Std. Error t value Pr(>|t|)
(Intercept)                              4.0058856  0.0144265 277.676  < 2e-16 ***
AGEP                                     0.0115985  0.0003032  38.259  < 2e-16 ***
SEXFemale                               -0.1076883  0.0052567 -20.486  < 2e-16 ***
COWFederal government employee           0.0638672  0.0157521   4.055 5.06e-05 ***
COWLocal government employee            -0.0297093  0.0107370  -2.767 0.005667 **
COWPrivate not-for-profit employee      -0.0330196  0.0102449  -3.223 0.001272 **
COWSelf employed incorporated            0.0145475  0.0164742   0.883 0.377232
COWSelf employed not incorporated       -0.1282285  0.0134708  -9.519  < 2e-16 ***
COWState government employee            -0.0479571  0.0123275  -3.890 0.000101 ***
SCHLRegular high school diploma          0.1135386  0.0107236  10.588  < 2e-16 ***
SCHLGED or alternative credential        0.1216670  0.0173038   7.031 2.17e-12 ***
SCHLsome college credit, no degree       0.1838278  0.0106461  17.267  < 2e-16 ***
SCHLAssociate's degree                   0.2387045  0.0123568  19.318  < 2e-16 ***
SCHLBachelor's degree                    0.3637114  0.0105810  34.374  < 2e-16 ***
SCHLMaster's degree                      0.4445777  0.0127100  34.978  < 2e-16 ***
SCHLProfessional degree                  0.5111167  0.0201800  25.328  < 2e-16 ***
SCHLDoctorate degree                     0.4818700  0.0245162  19.655  < 2e-16 ***

Signif. codes:  0 '***' 0.001 '**' 0.01 '*' 0.05 '.' 0.1 ' ' 1

Residual standard error: 0.2688 on 11186 degrees of freedom
Multiple R-squared:  0.2976,     Adjusted R-squared:  0.2966
F-statistic: 296.2 on 16 and 11186 DF,  p-value: < 2.2e-16
```

Model call summary

Residuals summary

Coefficients table

← Model quality summary

Figure 7.10 Model summary

Recall that the residuals are the errors in prediction: `log10(dtrain$PINCP) - predict(model,newdata=dtrain)`. In linear regression, the residuals are everything. Most of what you want to know about the quality of your model fit is in the residuals. You can calculate useful summaries of the residuals for both the training and test sets, as shown in the following listing.

Listing 7.6 Summarizing residuals

```
( resids_train <- summary(log10(dtrain$PINCP) -
      predict(model, newdata = dtrain)) )
##    Min. 1st Qu.  Median    Mean 3rd Qu.    Max.
## -1.5038 -0.1354  0.0187  0.0000  0.1710  0.9741

( resids_test <- summary(log10(dtest$PINCP) -
      predict(model, newdata = dtest)) )
##       Min.   1st Qu.    Median      Mean   3rd Qu.      Max.
## -1.789150 -0.130733  0.027413  0.006359  0.175847  0.912646
```

In linear regression, the coefficients are chosen to minimize the sum of squares of the residuals. This is why the method is also often called the *least squares method*. So for good models, you expect the residuals to be small.

In the residual summary, you're given the Min. and Max., which are the smallest and largest residuals seen. You're also given the quartiles of the residuals: 1st. Qu., or the value that upper bounds the first 25% of the data; the Median, or the value that upper bounds the first 50% of the data; and 3rd Qu., or the value that upper bounds the first 75% of the data (the Max is the 4th quartile: the value that upper bounds 100% of the data). The quartiles give you a rough idea of the data's distribution.

What you hope to see in the residual summary is that the median is near 0 (as it is in our example), and that the 1st. Qu. and the 3rd Qu. are roughly equidistant from the median (with neither too large). In our example, the 1st. Qu. and 3rd Qu. of the training residuals (resids_train) are both about 0.15 from the median. They are slightly less symmetric for the test residuals (0.16 and 0.15 from the median), but still within bounds.

The 1st. Qu. and 3rd Qu. quantiles are interesting because exactly half of the training data has a residual in this range. In our example, if you drew a random training datum, its residual would be in the range –0.1354 to 0.1710 exactly half the time. So you really expect to commonly see prediction errors of these magnitudes. If these errors are too big for your application, you don't have a usable model.

THE COEFFICIENTS TABLE

The next part of the summary(model) is the coefficients table, as shown in figure 7.11. A matrix form of this table can be retrieved as summary(model)$coefficients.

Each model coefficient forms a row of the summary coefficients table. The columns report the estimated coefficient, the uncertainty of the estimate, how large the

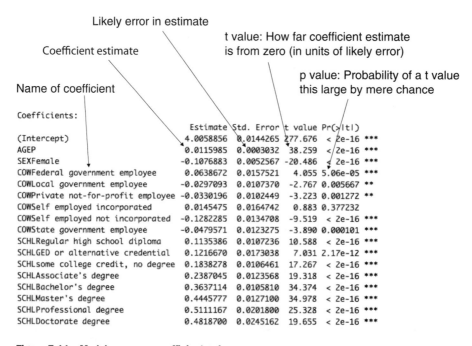

Figure 7.11   Model summary coefficient columns

coefficient is relative to the uncertainty, and how likely such a ratio would be due to mere chance. Figure 7.11 gives the names and interpretations of the columns.

Insignificant coefficients

Notice in figure 7.11 the coefficient `COWSelf employed incorporated` is "not significant." This means there is not enough evidence with respect to this model design to determine if the coefficient is non-zero.

Some recommend stepwise regression to remove such variables, or add a useful inductive bias of the form, "If we can't tell it is non-zero, force it to zero." In this case, this wouldn't be convenient as the variable is just a level of a categorical variable (so it's a bit harder to treat independently). We do not recommend stepwise regression, as stepwise regression introduces *multiple comparison* problems that bias the estimates of the remaining coefficients.[a] We recommend either living with the non-significant estimates (as even replacing them with zero is still trading one uncertain estimate for another), or prefiltering the variables for utility, or regularized methods (such as `glmnet`/lasso). All of these ideas are covered throughout this book.

A point to remember: in terms of prediction (our primary goal), it's not a problem to have a small number of insignificant coefficients with small effects sizes. Problems arise when we have insignificant coefficients with large coefficients/effects or a great number of insignificant coefficients.

---

[a] See Robert Tibshirani, "Regression shrinkage and selection via the lasso." *Journal of the Royal Statistical Society*, Series B 58: 267–288, 1996.

You set out to study income and the impact that getting a bachelor's degree has on income. But you must look at all the coefficients to check for interfering effects.

For example, the coefficient of –0.108 for `SEXF` means that your model learned a penalty of –0.108 to `log10(PINCP)` for being female. The ratio of female income to male income is modeled to be `10^(-0.108)`: women earn 78% of what men earn, all other model parameters being equal. Note we said "all other model parameters being equal" not "all other things being equal." That's because we're not modeling the number of years in the workforce (which age may not be a reliable proxy for) or occupation/industry type (which has a big impact on income). This model is not, with the features it was given, capable of testing if, on average, a female in the same job with the same number of years of experience is paid less.

Statistics as an attempt to correct bad experimental design

The absolute best experiment to test if there's a sex-driven difference in income distribution would be to compare incomes of individuals who were identical in all possible variables (age, education, years in industry, performance reviews, race, region, and so on) but differ only in sex. We're unlikely to have access to such data, so we'd settle for a good experimental design: a population where there's no correlation

(continued)

between any other feature and sex. Random selection can help in experimental design, but it's not a complete panacea. Barring a good experimental design, the usual pragmatic strategy is this: introduce extra variables to represent effects that may have been interfering with the effect we were trying to study. Thus a study of the effect of sex on income may include other variables like education and age to try to disentangle the competing effects.

The p-value and significance

The *p-value* (also called the *significance*) is one of the most important diagnostic columns in the coefficient summary. The p-value estimates the probability of seeing a coefficient with a magnitude as large as you observed if the true coefficient is really zero (if the variable has no effect on the outcome). So don't trust the estimate of any coefficient with a large p-value. Generally, people pick a threshold, and call all the coefficients with a p-value below that threshold *statistically significant*, meaning that those coefficients are likely not zero. A common threshold is $p < 0.05$; however, this is an arbitrary level.

Note that lower p-values aren't always "better" once they're good enough. There's no reason to prefer a coefficient with a p-value of 1e-23 to one with a p-value of 1e-08 as long as both p-values are below your chosen threshold; at this point, you know both coefficients are likely good estimates and you should prefer the ones that explain the most variance. Also note that high p-values don't always tell you which of the coefficients are bad, as we discuss in the sidebar.

Collinearity also lowers significance

Sometimes, a predictive variable won't appear significant because it's collinear (or correlated) with another predictive variable. For example, if you did try to use both age and number of years in the workforce to predict income, neither variable may appear significant. This is because age tends to be correlated with number of years in the workforce. If you remove one of the variables and the other one gains significance, this is a good indicator of correlation.

If you see coefficients that seem unreasonably large (often of opposite signs), or unusually large standard errors on the coefficients, that may indicate collinear variables.

Another possible indication of collinearity in the inputs is seeing coefficients with an unexpected sign: for example, seeing that income is *negatively* correlated with years in the workforce.

The overall model can still predict income quite well, even when the inputs are correlated; it just can't determine which variable deserves the credit for the prediction.

> Using regularization can be helpful in collinear situations, as we will discuss in section 7.3. Regularization prefers small coefficients, which can be less hazardous when used on new data.
>
> If you want to use the coefficient values as advice as well as to make good predictions, try to avoid collinearity in the inputs as much as possible.

OVERALL MODEL QUALITY SUMMARIES

The last part of the `summary(model)` report is the overall model quality statistics. It's a good idea to check the overall model quality before sharing any predictions or coefficients. The summaries are as follows:

```
Residual standard error: 0.2688 on 11186 degrees of freedom
Multiple R-squared:  0.2976,    Adjusted R-squared:  0.2966
F-statistic: 296.2 on 16 and 11186 DF,  p-value: < 2.2e-16
```

Let's explain each of the summaries in a little more detail.

Degrees of freedom

The *degrees of freedom* is the number of data rows minus the number of coefficients fit, in our case, this:

```
(df <-  nrow(dtrain) - nrow(summary(model)$coefficients))
## [1] 11186
```

The degrees of freedom is the number of training data rows you have after correcting for the number of coefficients you tried to solve for. You want the number of datums in the training set to be large compared to the number of coefficients you are solving for; in other words, you want the degrees of freedom to be high. A low degree of freedom indicates that the model you are trying to fit is too complex for the amount of data that you have, and your model is likely to be overfit. Overfitting is when you find chance relations in your training data that aren't present in the general population. Overfitting is bad: you think you have a good model when you don't.

Residual standard error

The *residual standard error* is the sum of the square of the residuals (or the sum of squared error) divided by the degrees of freedom. So it's similar to the RMSE (root mean squared error) that we discussed earlier, except with the number of data rows adjusted to be the degrees of freedom; in R, this is calculated as follows:

```
(modelResidualError <- sqrt(sum(residuals(model)^2) / df))
## [1] 0.2687895
```

The residual standard error is a more conservative estimate of model performance than the RMSE, because it's adjusted for the complexity of the model (the degrees of freedom is less than the number of rows of training data, so the residual standard error is larger than the RMSE). Again, this tries to compensate for the fact that more-complex models have a higher tendency to overfit the data.

> ## Degrees of freedom on test data
>
> On test data (data not used during training), the degrees of freedom equal the number of rows of data. This differs from the case of training data, where, as we have said, the degrees of freedom equal the number of rows of data minus the number of parameters of the model.
>
> The difference arises from the fact that model training "peeks at" the training data, but not the test data.

Multiple and adjusted R-squared

Multiple R-squared is just the R-squared of the model on the training data (discussed in section 7.1.3).

The *adjusted R-squared* is the multiple R-squared penalized for the number of input variables. The reason for this penalty is that, in general, increasing the number of input variables will improve the R-squared on the training data, even if the added variables aren't actually informative. This is another way of saying that more-complex models tend to look better on training data due to overfitting, so the adjusted R-squared is a more conservative estimate of the model's goodness of fit.

If you do not have test data, it's a good idea to rely on the adjusted R-squared when evaluating your model. But it's even better to compute the R-squared between predictions and actuals on holdout test data. In section 7.1.3, we showed the R-squared on test data was 0.29, which in this case is about the same as the reported adjusted R-squared of 0.3. However, we still advise preparing both training and test datasets; the test dataset estimates can be more representative of production model performance than statistical formulas.

The F-statistic and its p-value

The *F-statistic* is similar to the t-values for coefficients that you saw earlier in figure 7.11. Just as the t-values are used to calculate p-values on the coefficients, the F-statistic is used to calculate a p-value on the model fit. It gets its name from the F-test, which is the technique used to check if two variances—in this case, the variance of the residuals from the constant model and the variance of the residuals from the linear model—are significantly different. The corresponding p-value is the estimate of the probability that we would've observed an F-statistic this large or larger if the two variances in question were in reality the same. So you want the p-value to be small (a common threshold: less that 0.05).

In our example, the F-statistic p-value is quite small ($< 2.2e\text{-}16$): the model explains more variance than the constant model does, and the improvement is incredibly unlikely to have arisen only from sampling error.

> **INTERPRETING MODEL SIGNIFICANCES**   Most of the tests of linear regression, including the tests for coefficient and model significance, are based on the assumption that the error terms or residuals are normally distributed. It's important to examine graphically or use quantile analysis to determine if the regression model is appropriate.

7.1.6 Linear regression takeaways

Linear regression is the go-to statistical modeling method for predicting quantities. It is simple and has the advantage that the coefficients of the model can often function as advice. Here are a few points you should remember about linear regression:

- Linear regression assumes that the outcome is a linear combination of the input variables. Naturally, it works best when that assumption is nearly true, but it can predict surprisingly well even when it isn't.
- If you want to use the coefficients of your model for advice, you should only trust the coefficients that appear statistically significant.
- Overly large coefficient magnitudes, overly large standard errors on the coefficient estimates, and the wrong sign on a coefficient could be indications of correlated inputs.
- Linear regression can predict well even in the presence of correlated variables, but correlated variables lower the quality of the advice.
- Linear regression will have trouble with problems that have a very large number of variables, or categorical variables with a very large number of levels.
- Linear regression packages have some of the best built-in diagnostics available, but rechecking your model on test data is still your most effective safety check.

7.2 Using logistic regression

Logistic regression is the most important (and probably most used) member of a class of models called *generalized linear models*. Unlike linear regression, logistic regression can directly predict values that are restricted to the (0, 1) interval, such as probabilities. It's the go-to method for predicting probabilities or rates, and like linear regression, the coefficients of a logistic regression model can be treated as *advice*. It's also a good first choice for binary classification problems.

In this section, we'll use a medical classification example (predicting whether a newborn will need extra medical attention) to work through all the steps of producing and using a logistic regression model.[1]

As we did with linear regression, we'll take a quick overview of logistic regression before tackling the main example.

7.2.1 Understanding logistic regression

> **Example** *Suppose you want to predict whether or not a flight will be delayed, based on facts like the flight's origin and destination, weather, and air carrier. For every flight* i, *you want to predict* flight_delayed[i] *based on* origin[i], destination[i], weather[i], *and* air_carrier[i].

We'd like to use linear regression to predict the probability that a flight i will be delayed, but probabilities are strictly in the range 0:1, and linear regression doesn't restrict its prediction to that range.

---

[1] Logistic regression is usually used to perform classification, but logistic regression and its close cousin *beta regression* are also useful in estimating *rates*. In fact, R's standard glm() call will work with predicting numeric values between 0 and 1 in addition to predicting classifications.

One idea is to find a function of probability that is in the range `-Infinity:Infinity`, fit a linear model to predict that quantity, and then solve for the appropriate probabilities from the model predictions. So let's look at a slightly different problem: instead of predicting the probability that a flight is delayed, consider the *odds* that the flight is delayed, or the ratio of the probability that the flight is delayed over the probability that it is not.

```
odds[flight_delayed] = P[flight_delayed == TRUE] / P[flight_delayed == FALSE]
```

The range of the odds function isn't `-Infinity:Infinity`; it's restricted to be a non-negative number. But we can take the log of the odds—the *log-odds*—to get a function of the probabilities that *is* in the range `-Infinity:Infinity`.

```
log_odds[flight_delayed] = log(P[flight_delayed == TRUE] / P[flight_delayed =
    = FALSE])

Let: p = P[flight_delayed == TRUE]; then
log_odds[flight_delayed] = log(p / (1 - p))
```

Note that if it's more likely that a flight will be delayed than on time, the odds ratio will be greater than one; if it's less likely that a flight will be delayed than on time, the odds ratio will be less than one. So the log-odds is positive if it's more likely that the flight will be delayed, negative if it's more likely that the flight will be on time, and zero if the chances of delay are 50-50. This is shown in figure 7.12.

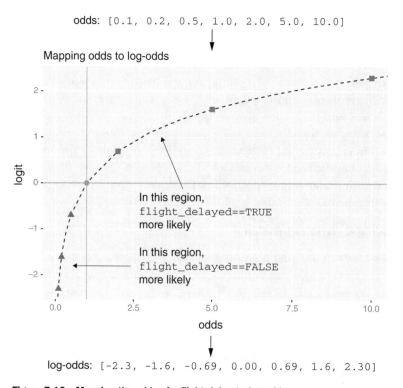

Figure 7.12 Mapping the odds of a flight delay to log-odds

The log-odds of a probability p is also known as *logit(p)*. The inverse of *logit(p)* is the *sigmoid* function, shown in figure 7.13. The sigmoid function maps values in the range from `-Infinity:Infinity` to the range `0:1`—in this case, the sigmoid maps unbounded log-odds ratios to a probability value that is between 0 and 1.

```
logit <- function(p) { log(p/(1-p)) }
s <- function(x) { 1/(1 + exp(-x))}

s(logit(0.7))
# [1] 0.7

logit(s(-2))
# -2
```

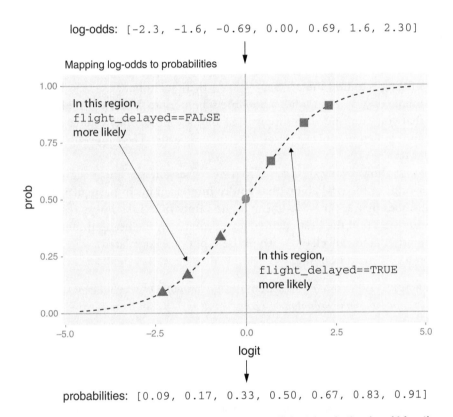

log-odds: `[-2.3, -1.6, -0.69, 0.00, 0.69, 1.6, 2.30]`

probabilities: `[0.09, 0.17, 0.33, 0.50, 0.67, 0.83, 0.91]`

Figure 7.13 Mapping log-odds to the probability of a flight delay via the sigmoid function

Now we can try to fit a linear model to the log-odds of a flight being delayed:

```
logit(P[flight_delayed[i] == TRUE]) = b0 + b_origin * origin[i] + ...
```

But what we are really interested in is the *probability* that a flight is delayed. To get that, take the sigmoid `s()` of both sides:

```
P[flight_delayed[i] == TRUE] =  s(b0 + b_origin * origin[i] + ...)
```

This is the *logistic regression model* for the probability that a flight will be delayed. The preceding derivation may seem ad hoc, but using the `logit` function to transform the probabilities is known to have a number of favorable properties. For instance, like linear regression, it gets totals right (as we will see in section 7.2.3).

More generally, suppose `y[i]` is the class of object i: TRUE or FALSE; delayed or on_time. Also, suppose that `x[i,]` is a row of inputs, and call one of the classes the "class of interest " or *target class* —that is, the class you are trying to predict (you want to predict whether something is TRUE or whether the flight is in the class delayed). Then logistic regression attempts to a fit function `f(x)` such that

```
P[y[i] in class of interest] ~ f(x[i,]) = s(a + b[1] * x[i,1] + ... + b[n] *
x[i,n])
```

Equation 7.2   The expression for a logistic regression model

If the `y[i]` are the probabilities that the `x[i,]` belong to the class of interest, then the task of fitting is to find the a, `b[1]`, ..., `b[n]` such that `f(x[i,])` is the best possible estimate of `y[i]`. R supplies a one-line statement to find these coefficients: `glm()`.[1] Note that you don't need to supply `y[i]` that are probability estimates to run `glm()`; the training method only requires `y[i]` that say which class a given training example belongs to.

As we've shown, you can think of logistic regression as a linear regression that finds the log-odds of the probability that you're interested in. In particular, logistic regression assumes that `logit(y)` is linear in the values of x. Like linear regression, logistic regression will find the best coefficients to predict y, including finding advantageous combinations and cancellations when the inputs are correlated.

Now to the main example.

Example   *Imagine that you're working at a hospital. The overall goal is to design a plan that provisions neonatal emergency equipment to delivery rooms. Newborn babies are assessed at one and five minutes after birth using what's called the Apgar test, which is designed to determine if a baby needs immediate emergency care or extra medical attention. A baby who scores below 7 (on a scale from 0 to 10) on the Apgar scale needs extra attention.*

Such at-risk babies are rare, so the hospital doesn't want to provision extra emergency equipment for every delivery. On the other hand, at-risk babies may need attention quickly, so provisioning resources proactively to appropriate deliveries can save lives. Your task is to build a model to identify ahead of time situations with a higher probability of risk, so that resources can be allocated appropriately.

---

[1] Logistic regression can be used for classifying into any number of categories (as long as the categories are disjoint and cover all possibilities: every x has to belong to one of the given categories). But `glm()` only handles the two-category case, so our discussion will focus on this case.

We'll use a sample dataset from the 2010 CDC natality public-use data file (http://mng.bz/pnGy). This dataset records statistics for all US births registered in the 50 states and the District of Columbia, including facts about the mother and father, and about the delivery. The sample has just over 26,000 births in a data frame called sdata.[1] The data is split into training and test sets, using a random grouping column that we added, which allows for repeatable experiments with the split ratio.

Listing 7.7 Loading the CDC data

```
load("NatalRiskData.rData")
train <- sdata[sdata$ORIGRANDGROUP <= 5 , ]
test <- sdata[sdata$ORIGRANDGROUP > 5, ]
```

Table 7.1 lists the columns of the dataset that you will use. Because the goal is to anticipate at-risk infants ahead of time, we'll restrict variables to those whose values are known before delivery or can be determined during labor. For example, facts about the mother's weight and health history are valid inputs, but post-birth facts like infant birth weight are not. We can include in-labor complications like breech birth by reasoning that the model can be updated in the delivery room (via a protocol or checklist) in time for emergency resources to be allocated before delivery.

Table 7.1 Some variables in the natality dataset

Variable	Type	Description
atRisk	Logical	TRUE if 5-minute Apgar score < 7; FALSE otherwise
PWGT	Numeric	Mother's prepregnancy weight
UPREVIS	Numeric (integer)	Number of prenatal medical visits
CIG_REC	Logical	TRUE if smoker; FALSE otherwise
GESTREC3	Categorical	Two categories: <37 weeks (premature) and >=37 weeks
DPLURAL	Categorical	Birth plurality, three categories: single/twin/triplet+
ULD_MECO	Logical	TRUE if moderate/heavy fecal staining of amniotic fluid
ULD_PRECIP	Logical	TRUE for unusually short labor (< three hours)
ULD_BREECH	Logical	TRUE for breech (pelvis first) birth position
URF_DIAB	Logical	TRUE if mother is diabetic
URF_CHYPER	Logical	TRUE if mother has chronic hypertension

---

[1] Our pre-prepared file is at https://github.com/WinVector/PDSwR2/tree/master/CDC/NatalRiskData .rData; we also provide a script file (https://github.com/WinVector/PDSwR2/blob/master/CDC/PrepNatal-RiskData.R), which prepares the data frame from an extract of the full natality dataset. Details found at https://github.com/WinVector/PDSwR2/blob/master/CDC/README.md.

Table 7.1   Some variables in the natality dataset *(continued)*

Variable	Type	Description
URF_PHYPER	Logical	TRUE if mother has pregnancy-related hypertension
URF_ECLAM	Logical	TRUE if mother experienced eclampsia: pregnancy-related seizures

Now we're ready to build the model.

7.2.2   *Building a logistic regression model*

The function to build a logistic regression model in R is `glm()`, supplied by the `stats` package. In our case, the dependent variable y is the logical (or Boolean) atRisk; all the other variables in table 7.1 are the independent variables x. The formula for building a model to predict atRisk using these variables is rather long to type in by hand; you can generate the formula using the `mk_formula()` function from the `wrapr` package, as shown next.

Listing 7.8   Building the model formula

```
complications <- c("ULD_MECO","ULD_PRECIP","ULD_BREECH")
riskfactors <- c("URF_DIAB", "URF_CHYPER", "URF_PHYPER",
                 "URF_ECLAM")
y <- "atRisk"
x <- c("PWGT",
       "UPREVIS",
       "CIG_REC",
       "GESTREC3",
       "DPLURAL",
       complications,
       riskfactors)
library(wrapr)
fmla <- mk_formula(y, x)
```

Now we'll build the logistic regression model, using the training dataset.

Listing 7.9   Fitting the logistic regression model

```
print(fmla)

## atRisk ~ PWGT + UPREVIS + CIG_REC + GESTREC3 + DPLURAL + ULD_MECO +
##      ULD_PRECIP + ULD_BREECH + URF_DIAB + URF_CHYPER + URF_PHYPER +
##      URF_ECLAM
## <environment: base>

model <- glm(fmla, data = train, family = binomial(link = "logit"))
```

This is similar to the linear regression call to `lm()`, with one additional argument: `family = binomial(link = "logit")`. The `family` function specifies the assumed distribution of the dependent variable y. In our case, we're modeling y as a binomial distribution, or as a coin whose probability of heads depends on x. The `link` function "links" the output to a linear model—it's as if you pass y through the link function, and then model the resulting value as a linear function of the x values. Different combinations of family functions and link functions lead to different kinds of generalized linear models (for example, Poisson, or probit). In this book, we'll only discuss logistic models, so we'll only need to use the binomial family with the logit link.[1]

DON'T FORGET THE FAMILY ARGUMENT! Without an explicit family argument, glm() defaults to standard linear regression (like lm).

The family argument can be used to select many different behaviors of the glm() function. For example, choosing family = quasipoisson chooses a "log" link, which models the logarithm of the prediction as linear in the inputs.

This would be another approach to try for the income prediction problem of section 7.1. However, it is a subtle point to determine whether a log transformation and linear model or a log-link and a generalized linear model is a better choice for a given problem. The log-link will be better at predicting total incomes (scoring an error of $50,000 for small and large incomes alike). The log-transform method will be better at predicting relative incomes (a scoring error of $50,000 being less dire for large incomes than for small incomes).

As before, we've stored the results in the object model.

7.2.3 *Making predictions*

Making predictions with a logistic model is similar to making predictions with a linear model—use the predict() function. The following code stores the predictions for the training and test sets as the column pred in the respective data frames.

Listing 7.10 Applying the logistic regression model

```
train$pred <- predict(model, newdata=train, type = "response")
test$pred <- predict(model, newdata=test, type="response")
```

Note the additional parameter type = "response". This tells the predict() function to return the predicted probabilities y. If you don't specify type = "response", then by default predict() will return the output of the link function, logit(y).

One strength of logistic regression is that it preserves the marginal probabilities of the training data. That means that if you sum the predicted probability scores for the entire training set, that quantity will be equal to the number of positive outcomes (atRisk == TRUE) in the training set. This is also true for subsets of the data determined by variables included in the model. For example, in the subset of the training data that has train$GESTREC == "<37 weeks" (the baby was premature), the sum of the predicted probabilities equals the number of positive training examples (see, for example http://mng.bz/j338).

---

[1] The logit link is the default link for the binomial family, so the call glm(fmla, data = train, family = binomial) works just fine. We explicitly specified the link in our example for the sake of discussion.

Listing 7.11   Preserving marginal probabilities with logistic regression
---

```
sum(train$atRisk == TRUE)        ⟵──────────── Counts the number of at-risk
  ## [1] 273                                    infants in the training set.

sum(train$pred)                  ⟵──────────────────────── Sums all the predicted
  ## [1] 273                                               probabilities over the
                                                           training set. Notice that
premature <- subset(train, GESTREC3 == "< 37 weeks") ⟵─── it adds to the number
sum(premature$atRisk == TRUE)                             of at-risk infants.
  ## [1] 112                             Counts the number of
                                         at-risk premature
sum(premature$pred)    ⟵────────         infants in the training set
  ## [1] 112

                       Sums all the predicted probabilities
                       for premature infants in the training
                       set. Note that it adds to the number
                       of at-risk premature infants.
```

Because logistic regression preserves marginal probabilities, you know that the model is in some sense consistent with the training data. When the model is applied to future data with distributions similar to the training data, it should then return results consistent with that data: about the correct probability mass of expected at-risk infants, distributed correctly with respect to the infants' characteristics. However, if the model is applied to future data with very different distributions (for example, a much higher rate of at-risk infants), the model may not predict as well.

CHARACTERIZING PREDICTION QUALITY

If your goal is to use the model to classify new instances into one of two categories (in this case, at-risk or not-at-risk), then you want the model to give high scores to positive instances and low scores otherwise. As we discussed in section 6.2.5, you can check if this is so by plotting the distribution of scores for both the positive and negative instances. Let's do this on the training set (you should also plot the test set, to make sure the performance is of similar quality).

Listing 7.12   Plotting distribution of prediction score grouped by known outcome
---

```
library(WVPlots)
DoubleDensityPlot(train, "pred", "atRisk",
                  title = "Distribution of natality risk scores")
```

The result is shown in figure 7.14. Ideally, we'd like the distribution of scores to be separated, with the scores of the negative instances (FALSE) to be concentrated on the left, and the distribution for the positive instances to be concentrated on the right. Earlier in figure 6.15 (reproduced here as figure 7.15), we showed an example of a classifier (the spam filter) that separates the positives and the negatives quite well. With the natality risk model, both distributions are concentrated on the left, meaning that both positive and negative instances score low. This isn't surprising, since the positive instances (the ones with the baby at risk) are rare (about 1.8% of all births in the dataset). The distribution of scores for the negative instances dies off sooner than the distribution for positive instances. This means that the model did identify subpopulations in the data where the rate of at-risk newborns is higher than the average, as is pointed out in figure 7.14.

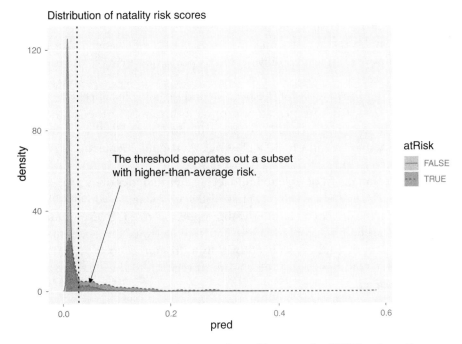

Figure 7.14   Distribution of score broken up by positive examples (TRUE) and negative examples (FALSE)

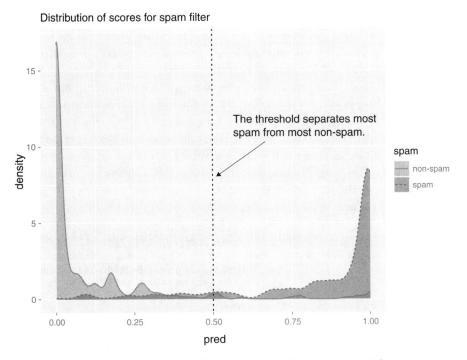

Figure 7.15   Reproduction of the spam filter score distributions from chapter 6

In order to use the model as a classifier, you must pick a threshold; scores above the threshold will be classified as positive, those below as negative. When you pick a threshold, you're trying to balance the *precision* of the classifier (what fraction of the predicted positives are true positives) and its *recall* (how many of the true positives the classifier finds).

If the score distributions of the positive and negative instances are well separated, as in figure 7.15, you can pick an appropriate threshold in the "valley" between the two peaks. In the current case, the two distributions aren't well separated, which indicates that the model can't build a classifier that simultaneously achieves good recall and good precision.

However, you might be able to build a classifier that identifies a subset of situations with a higher-than-average rate of at-risk births: for example, you may be able to find a threshold that produces a classifier with a precision of 3.6%. Even though this precision is low, it represents a subset of the data that has twice the risk as the overall population (3.6% versus 1.8%), so preprovisioning resources to those situations may be advised. We'll call the ratio of the classifier precision to the average rate of positives the *enrichment rate*.

The higher you set the threshold, the more precise the classifier will be (you'll identify a set of situations with a much higher-than-average rate of at-risk births); but you'll also miss a higher percentage of at-risk situations, as well. When picking the threshold, you should use the training set, since picking the threshold is part of classifier-building. You can then use the test set to evaluate classifier performance.

To help pick the threshold, you can use a plot like figure 7.16, which shows both enrichment and recall as functions of the threshold.

Looking at figure 7.16, you see that higher thresholds result in more-precise classifications (precision is proportional to enrichment), at the cost of missing more cases; a lower threshold will identify more cases, at the cost of many more false positives (lower precision). The best trade-off between precision/enrichment and recall is a function of how many resources the hospital has available to allocate, and how many they can keep in reserve (or redeploy) for situations that the classifier missed. A threshold of 0.02 (marked in figure 7.16 by the dashed line) might be a good trade-off. The resulting classifier will identify a subset of the population where the rate of risky births is 2.5 times higher than in the overall population, and which contains about half of all the true at-risk situations.

You can produce figure 7.16 using the PRTPlot() function in WVPlots.

Listing 7.13 Exploring modeling trade-offs

Calls PRTPlot() where pred is the column of predictions, atRisk is the true outcome column, and TRUE is the class of interest

```
library("WVPlots")
library("ggplot2")
plt <- PRTPlot(train, "pred", "atRisk", TRUE,        ◁
         plotvars = c("enrichment", "recall"),
         thresholdrange = c(0,0.05),
         title = "Enrichment/recall vs. threshold for natality model")
plt + geom_vline(xintercept = 0.02, color="red", linetype = 2)
```

Adds a line to mark threshold = 0.02.

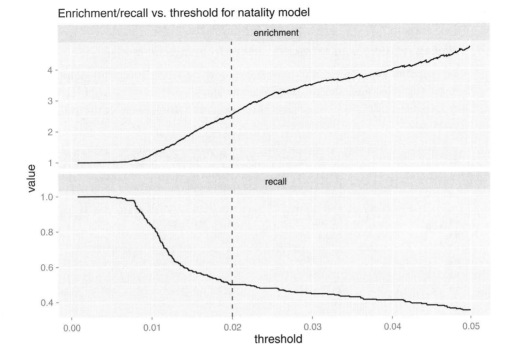

Figure 7.16 Enrichment (top) and recall (bottom) plotted as functions of threshold for the training set

Once you've picked an appropriate threshold, you can evaluate the resulting classifier by looking at the confusion matrix, as we discussed in section 6.2.3. Let's use the test set to evaluate the classifier with a threshold of 0.02.

Listing 7.14 Evaluating the chosen model

```
( ctab.test <- table(pred = test$pred > 0.02, atRisk = test$atRisk)  )

##          atRisk
## pred     FALSE TRUE
##    FALSE  9487   93
##    TRUE   2405  116

( precision <- ctab.test[2,2] / sum(ctab.test[2,]) )
## [1] 0.04601349

( recall <- ctab.test[2,2] / sum(ctab.test[,2]) )
## [1] 0.5550239

( enrichment <- precision / mean(as.numeric(test$atRisk))  )
## [1] 2.664159
```

Builds the confusion matrix. The rows contain predicted negatives and positives; columns contain actual negatives and positives.

The resulting classifier is low-precision, but identifies a set of potential at-risk cases that contains 55.5% of the true positive cases in the test set, at a rate 2.66 times higher than the overall average. This is consistent with the results on the training set.

In addition to making predictions, a logistic regression model also helps you extract useful information and advice. We'll show this in the next section.

7.2.4 Finding relations and extracting advice from logistic models

The coefficients of a logistic regression model encode the relationships between the input variables and the output in a way similar to how the coefficients of a linear regression model do. You can get the model's coefficients with the call `coefficients (model)`.

Listing 7.15 The model coefficients

```
coefficients(model)
##              (Intercept)                      PWGT
##              -4.41218940                0.00376166
##                   UPREVIS               CIG_RECTRUE
##              -0.06328943                0.31316930
##      GESTREC3< 37 weeks DPLURALtriplet or higher
##               1.54518311                1.39419294
##              DPLURALtwin               ULD_MECOTRUE
##               0.31231871                0.81842627
##           ULD_PRECIPTRUE            ULD_BREECHTRUE
##               0.19172008                0.74923672
##             URF_DIABTRUE            URF_CHYPERTRUE
##              -0.34646672                0.56002503
##           URF_PHYPERTRUE             URF_ECLAMTRUE
##               0.16159872                0.49806435
```

Negative coefficients that are statistically significant[1] correspond to variables that are negatively correlated to the odds (and hence to the probability) of a positive outcome (the baby being at risk). Positive coefficients that are statistically significant are positively correlated to the odds of the baby being at risk.

As with linear regression, every categorical variable is expanded to a set of indicator variables. If the original variable has n levels, there will be `n-1` indicator variables; the remaining level is the reference level.

For example, the variable DPLURAL has three levels corresponding to single births, twins, and triplets or higher. The logistic regression model has two corresponding coefficients: `DPLURALtwin` and `DPLURALtriplet or higher`. The reference level is single births. Both of the DPLURAL coefficients are positive, indicating that multiple births have higher odds of being at risk than single births do, all other variables being equal.

LOGISTIC REGRESSION ALSO DISLIKES A VERY LARGE VARIABLE COUNT   And as with linear regression, you should avoid categorical variables with too many levels.

---

[1] We'll show how to check for statistical significance in the next section.

INTERPRETING THE COEFFICIENTS

Interpreting coefficient values is a little more complicated with logistic than with linear regression. If the coefficient for the variable x[,k] is b[k], then the odds of a positive outcome are multiplied by a factor of exp(b[k]) for every unit change in x[,k].

> **Example** *Suppose a full-term baby with certain characteristics has a 1% probability of being at risk. Then the risk odds for that baby are p/(1-p), or 0.01/0.99 = 0.0101. What are the risk odds (and the risk probability) for a baby with the same characteristics, but born prematurely?*

The coefficient for GESTREC3< 37 weeks (for a premature baby) is 1.545183. So for a premature baby, the odds of being at risk are exp(1.545183)= 4.68883 times higher compared to a baby that's born full-term, with all other input variables unchanged. The risk odds for a premature baby with the same characteristics as our hypothetical full-term baby are 0.0101 * 4.68883 = 0.047.

You can invert the formula odds = p / (1 - p) to solve for p as a function of odds:

```
p = odds * (1 - p) = odds - p * odds
p * (1 + odds) = odds
p = odds/(1 + odds)
```

The probability of this premature baby being at risk is 0.047/1.047, or about 4.5%—quite a bit higher than the equivalent full-term baby

Similarly, the coefficient for UPREVIS (number of prenatal medical visits) is about −0.06. This means every prenatal visit lowers the odds of an at-risk baby by a factor of exp(-0.06), or about 0.94. Suppose the mother of a premature baby had made no prenatal visits; a baby in the same situation whose mother had made three prenatal visits would have odds of being at risk of about 0.047 * 0.94 * 0.94 * 0.94 = 0.039. This corresponds to a probability of being at risk of 3.75%.

The general advice in this case might be to keep a special eye on premature births (and multiple births), and encourage expectant mothers to make regular prenatal visits.

7.2.5 *Reading the model summary and characterizing coefficients*

As we mentioned earlier, conclusions about the coefficient values are only to be trusted if the coefficient values are statistically significant. We also want to make sure that the model is actually explaining something. The diagnostics in the model summary will help us determine some facts about model quality. The call, as before, is summary(model).

Listing 7.16 The model summary

```
summary(model)

## Call:
## glm(formula = fmla, family = binomial(link = "logit"), data = train)
##
## Deviance Residuals:
##     Min      1Q   Median      3Q      Max
```

```
## -0.9732  -0.1818  -0.1511  -0.1358   3.2641
##
## Coefficients:
##                            Estimate Std. Error z value Pr(>|z|)
## (Intercept)               -4.412189   0.289352 -15.249  < 2e-16 ***
## PWGT                       0.003762   0.001487   2.530 0.011417 *
## UPREVIS                   -0.063289   0.015252  -4.150 3.33e-05 ***
## CIG_RECTRUE                0.313169   0.187230   1.673 0.094398 .
## GESTREC3< 37 weeks         1.545183   0.140795  10.975  < 2e-16 ***
## DPLURALtriplet or higher   1.394193   0.498866   2.795 0.005194 **
## DPLURALtwin                0.312319   0.241088   1.295 0.195163
## ULD_MECOTRUE               0.818426   0.235798   3.471 0.000519 ***
## ULD_PRECIPTRUE             0.191720   0.357680   0.536 0.591951
## ULD_BREECHTRUE             0.749237   0.178129   4.206 2.60e-05 ***
## URF_DIABTRUE              -0.346467   0.287514  -1.205 0.228187
## URF_CHYPERTRUE             0.560025   0.389678   1.437 0.150676
## URF_PHYPERTRUE             0.161599   0.250003   0.646 0.518029
## URF_ECLAMTRUE              0.498064   0.776948   0.641 0.521489
## ---
## Signif. codes:  0 '***' 0.001 '**' 0.01 '*' 0.05 '.' 0.1 ' ' 1
##
## (Dispersion parameter for binomial family taken to be 1)
##
##     Null deviance: 2698.7  on 14211   degrees of freedom
## Residual deviance: 2463.0  on 14198   degrees of freedom
## AIC: 2491
##
## Number of Fisher Scoring iterations: 7
```

Again, you're likely to be asked about elements of the model summary when presenting results, so we'll discuss what the fields mean, and how to use them to interpret your model.

THE ORIGINAL MODEL CALL

The first line of the summary is the call to `glm()`:

```
Call:
glm(formula = fmla, family = binomial(link = "logit"), data = train)
```

Here is where we check that we've used the correct training set and the correct formula (although in our case, the formula itself is in another variable). We can also verify that we used the correct family and link function to produce a logistic model.

THE DEVIANCE RESIDUALS SUMMARY

The deviance residuals are the analog to the residuals of a linear regression model:

```
Deviance Residuals:
    Min       1Q   Median       3Q      Max
-0.9732  -0.1818  -0.1511  -0.1358   3.2641
```

Linear regression models are found by minimizing the sum of the squared residuals; logistic regression models are found by minimizing the sum of the residual deviances, which is equivalent to maximizing the log likelihood of the data, given the model (we'll talk about log likelihood later in this chapter).

Logistic models can also be used to explicitly compute rates: given several groups of identical data points (identical except the outcome), predict the rate of positive outcomes in each group. This kind of data is called *grouped data*. In the case of grouped data, the deviance residuals can be used as a diagnostic for model fit. This is why the deviance residuals are included in the summary. We're using *ungrouped data*—every data point in the training set is potentially unique. In the case of ungrouped data, the model fit diagnostics that use the deviance residuals are no longer valid, so we won't discuss them here.[1]

THE SUMMARY COEFFICIENTS TABLE

The summary coefficients table for logistic regression has the same format as the coefficients table for linear regression:

```
Coefficients:
                           Estimate Std. Error z value Pr(>|z|)
(Intercept)               -4.412189   0.289352 -15.249  < 2e-16  ***
PWGT                       0.003762   0.001487   2.530 0.011417  *
UPREVIS                   -0.063289   0.015252  -4.150 3.33e-05  ***
CIG_RECTRUE                0.313169   0.187230   1.673 0.094398  .
GESTREC3< 37 weeks         1.545183   0.140795  10.975  < 2e-16  ***
DPLURALtriplet or higher   1.394193   0.498866   2.795 0.005194  **
DPLURALtwin                0.312319   0.241088   1.295 0.195163
ULD_MECOTRUE               0.818426   0.235798   3.471 0.000519  ***
ULD_PRECIPTRUE             0.191720   0.357680   0.536 0.591951
ULD_BREECHTRUE             0.749237   0.178129   4.206 2.60e-05  ***
URF_DIABTRUE              -0.346467   0.287514  -1.205 0.228187
URF_CHYPERTRUE             0.560025   0.389678   1.437 0.150676
URF_PHYPERTRUE             0.161599   0.250003   0.646 0.518029
URF_ECLAMTRUE              0.498064   0.776948   0.641 0.521489
---
Signif. codes:  0 '***' 0.001 '**' 0.01 '*' 0.05 '.' 0.1 ' ' 1
```

The columns of the table represent

- A coefficient
- Its estimated value
- The error around that estimate
- The signed distance of the estimated coefficient value from 0 (using the standard error as the unit of distance)
- The probability of seeing a coefficient value at least as large as we observed, under the null hypothesis that the coefficient value is really zero

This last value, called the *p-value* or *significance*, tells us whether we should trust the estimated coefficient value. The common practice is to assume that coefficients with p-values less than 0.05 are reliable, although some researchers prefer stricter thresholds.

For the birth data, we can see from the coefficient summary that premature birth and triplet birth are strong predictors of the newborn needing extra medical

---

[1] See Daniel Powers and Yu Xie, *Statistical Methods for Categorical Data Analysis*, 2nd ed, Emerald Group Publishing Ltd., 2008.

attention: the coefficient magnitudes are non-negligible and the p-values indicate significance. Other variables that affect the outcome are

- *PWGT*—The mother's prepregnancy weight (heavier mothers indicate higher risk—slightly surprising)
- *UPREVIS*—The number of prenatal medical visits (the more visits, the lower the risk)
- *ULD_MECOTRUE*—Meconium staining in the amniotic fluid
- ULD_BREECHTRUE—Breech position at birth

There might be a positive correlation between a mother's smoking and an at-risk birth, but the data doesn't indicate it definitively. None of the other variables show a strong relationship to an at-risk birth.

Lack of significance could mean collinear inputs

As with linear regression, logistic regression can predict well with collinear (or correlated) inputs, but the correlations can mask good advice.

To see this for yourself, we left data about the babies' birth weight in grams in the dataset sdata. It's present in both the test and training data as the column DBWT. Try adding DBWT to the logistic regression model in addition to all the other variables; you'll see that the coefficient for baby's birth weight will be significant, non-negligible (has a substantial impact on prediction), and negatively correlated with risk. The coefficient for DPLURALtriplet or higher will appear insignificant, and the coefficient for GESTREC3< 37 weeks has a much smaller magnitude. This is because low birth weight is correlated to both prematurity and multiple birth. Of the three related variables, birth weight is the best single predictor of the outcome: knowing that the baby is a triplet adds no additional useful information, and knowing the baby is premature adds only a little information.

In the context of the modeling goal—to proactively allocate emergency resources where they're more likely to be needed—birth weight isn't very useful a variable, because we don't know the baby's weight until it's born. We do know ahead of time if it's being born prematurely, or if it's one of multiple babies. So it's better to use GESTREC3 and DPLURAL as input variables, instead of DBWT.

Other signs of possibly collinear inputs are coefficients with the wrong sign and unusually large coefficient magnitudes with giant standard errors.

OVERALL MODEL QUALITY SUMMARIES

The next section of the summary contains the model quality statistics:

```
Null deviance: 2698.7  on 14211  degrees of freedom
Residual deviance: 2463.0  on 14198  degrees of freedom
AIC: 2491
```

Null and residual deviances

Deviance is a measure of how well the model fits the data. It is two times the negative *log likelihood* of the dataset, given the model. As we discussed previously in section 6.2.5, the idea behind log likelihood is that positive instances y should have high probability py of occurring under the model; negative instances should have low probability of occurring (or putting it another way, (1 - py) should be large). The log likelihood function rewards matches between the outcome y and the predicted probability py, and penalizes mismatches (high py for negative instances, and vice versa).

If you think of deviance as analogous to variance, then the *null deviance* is similar to the variance of the data around the average rate of positive examples. The *residual deviance* is similar to the variance of the data around the model. As with variance, you want the residual deviance to be small, compared to the null deviance. The model summary reports the deviance and null deviance of the model on the training data; you can (and should) also calculate them for test data. In the following listing we calculate the deviances for both the training and test sets.

Listing 7.17 Computing deviance

**Function to calculate the log likelihood of a dataset.
Variable y is the outcome in numeric form (1 for positive
examples, 0 for negative). Variable py is the predicted
probability that y==1.**

```
loglikelihood <- function(y, py) {
    sum(y * log(py) + (1-y)*log(1 - py))
}

(pnull <- mean(as.numeric(train$atRisk))  )       ◁── Calculates the rate of positive
## [1] 0.01920912                                      examples in the dataset

(null.dev <- -2  *loglikelihood(as.numeric(train$atRisk), pnull) )  ◁── Calculates the
## [1] 2698.716                                                          null deviance

model$null.deviance       ◁──  For training data, the null deviance is
## [1] 2698.716                 stored in the slot model$null.deviance.

pred <- predict(model, newdata = train, type = "response")   ◁── Predicts probabilities
(resid.dev <- -2 * loglikelihood(as.numeric(train$atRisk), pred) )  ◁──  for the training data
## [1] 2462.992            For training data, model deviance is          Calculates deviance
                          stored in the slot model$deviance.            of the model for
model$deviance        ◁──                                               training data
## [1] 2462.992

testy <- as.numeric(test$atRisk)    ◁── Calculates the null
testpred <- predict(model, newdata = test,    deviance and
                    type = "response")         residual deviance
( pnull.test <- mean(testy) )                  for the test data
## [1] 0.0172713

( null.dev.test <- -2 * loglikelihood(testy, pnull.test) )
## [1] 2110.91

( resid.dev.test <- -2 * loglikelihood(testy, testpred) )
## [1] 1947.094
```

The pseudo R-squared

A useful goodness-of-fit measure based on the deviances is the pseudo R-squared: 1 - (dev.model/dev.null). The pseudo R-squared is the analog to the R-squared measure for linear regression. It's a measure of how much of the deviance is "explained" by the model. Ideally, you want the pseudo R-squared to be close to 1. Let's calculate the pseudo R-squared for both the test and training data.

Listing 7.18   Calculating the pseudo R-squared

```
pr2 <- 1 - (resid.dev / null.dev)

print(pr2)
## [1] 0.08734674
pr2.test <- 1 - (resid.dev.test / null.dev.test)
print(pr2.test)
## [1] 0.07760427
```

The model only explains about 7.7–8.7% of the deviance; it's not a highly predictive model (you should have suspected that already from figure 7.14). This tells us that we haven't yet identified all the factors that actually predict at-risk births.

Model significance

The other thing you can do with the null and residual deviances is check whether the model's probability predictions are better than just guessing the average rate of positives, statistically speaking. In other words, is the reduction in deviance from the model meaningful, or just something that was observed by chance? This is similar to calculating the F-test statistic and associated p-value that are reported for linear regression. In the case of logistic regression, the test you'll run is the *chi-squared test*. To do that, you need to know the degrees of freedom for the null model and the actual model (which are reported in the summary). The degrees of freedom of the null model is the number of data points minus 1:

```
df.null =  dim(train)[[1]] - 1
```

The degrees of freedom of the model that you fit is the number of data points minus the number of coefficients in the model:

```
df.model = dim(train)[[1]] - length(model$coefficients)
```

If the number of data points in the training set is large, and df.null - df.model is small, then the probability of the difference in deviances null.dev - resid.dev being as large as we observed is approximately distributed as a chi-squared distribution with df.null - df.model degrees of freedom.

Listing 7.19   Calculating the significance of the observed fit

```
( df.null <- dim(train)[[1]] - 1  )
  ## [1] 14211
```
⟵ **The null model has (number of data points - 1) degrees of freedom.**

```
( df.model <- dim(train)[[1]] - length(model$coefficients) )
  ## [1] 14198
```
⟵ **The fitted model has (number of data points - number of coefficients) degrees of freedom.**

```
( delDev <- null.dev - resid.dev )
 ## [1] 235.724
( deldf <- df.null - df.model )
 ## [1] 13
( p <- pchisq(delDev, deldf, lower.tail = FALSE) )
 ## [1] 5.84896e-43
```

Computes the difference in deviances and difference in degrees of freedom

Estimates the probability of seeing the observed difference in deviances under the null model (the p-value) using chi-squared distribution

The p-value is very small; it's extremely unlikely that we could've seen this much reduction in deviance by chance. This means it is plausible (but unfortunately not definitive) that this model has found informative patterns in the data.

Goodness of fit vs. significance

It's worth noting that the model we found is a significant model, just not a powerful one. The good p-value tells us that the model is significant: it predicts at-risk birth in the training data at a quality that is unlikely to be pure chance. The poor pseudo R-squared means that the model isn't giving us enough information to effectively distinguish between low-risk and high-risk births.

It's also possible to have good pseudo R-squared (on the training data) with a bad p-value. This is an indication of overfit. That's why it's a good idea to check both, or better yet, check the pseudo R-squared of the model on both training and test data.

The AIC

The last metric given in the section of the summary is the AIC, or the *Akaike information criterion*. The AIC is the log likelihood adjusted for the number of coefficients. Just as the R-squared of a linear regression is generally higher when the number of variables is higher, the log likelihood also increases with the number of variables.

Listing 7.20 Calculating the Akaike information criterion

```
aic <- 2 * (length(model$coefficients) -
        loglikelihood(as.numeric(train$atRisk), pred))
aic
## [1] 2490.992
```

The AIC is generally used to decide which and how many input variables to use in the model. If you train many different models with different sets of variables on the same training set, you can consider the model with the lowest AIC to be the best fit.

FISHER SCORING ITERATIONS

The last line of the model summary is the number of Fisher scoring iterations:

```
Number of Fisher Scoring iterations: 7
```

The Fisher scoring method is an iterative optimization method, similar to Newton's method, that glm() uses to find the best coefficients for the logistic regression model.

You should expect it to converge in about six to eight iterations. If there are many more iterations than that, then the algorithm may not have converged, and the model may not be valid.

Separation and quasi-separation

The probable reason for non-convergence is separation or quasi-separation: one of the model variables or some combination of the model variables predicts the outcome perfectly for at least a subset of the training data. You'd think this would be a good thing; but, ironically, logistic regression fails when the variables are too powerful. Ideally, `glm()` will issue a warning when it detects separation or quasi-separation:

```
Warning message:
glm.fit: fitted probabilities numerically 0 or 1 occurred
```

Unfortunately, there are situations when it seems that no warning is issued, but there are other warning signs:

- An unusually high number of Fisher iterations
- Very large coefficients, usually with extremely large standard errors
- Residual deviances larger than the null deviances

If you see any of these signs, the model is suspect. The last section of this chapter covers one way to address the problem: regularization.

7.2.6 Logistic regression takeaways

Logistic regression is the go-to statistical modeling method for binary classification. As with linear regression, the coefficients of a logistic regression model can often function as advice. Here are some points to remember about logistic regression:

- Logistic regression is well calibrated: it reproduces the marginal probabilities of the data.
- Pseudo R-squared is a useful goodness-of-fit heuristic.
- Logistic regression will have trouble with problems with a very large number of variables, or categorical variables with a very large number of levels.
- Logistic regression can predict well even in the presence of correlated variables, but correlated variables lower the quality of the advice.
- Overly large coefficient magnitudes, overly large standard errors on the coefficient estimates, and the wrong sign on a coefficient could be indications of correlated inputs.
- Too many Fisher iterations, or overly large coefficients with very large standard errors, could be signs that your logistic regression model has not converged, and may not be valid.
- `glm()` provides good diagnostics, but rechecking your model on test data is still your most effective diagnostic.

7.3   *Regularization*

As mentioned earlier, overly large coefficient magnitudes and overly large standard errors can indicate some issues in your model: nearly collinear variables in either a linear or logistic regression, or separation or quasi-separation in a logistic regression system.

Nearly collinear variables can cause the regression solver to needlessly introduce large coefficients that often nearly cancel each other out, and that have large standard errors. Separation/quasi-separation can cause a logistic regression to not converge to the intended solution; this is a separate source of large coefficients and large standard errors.

Overly large coefficient magnitudes are less trustworthy and can be hazardous when the model is applied to new data. Each of the coefficient estimates has some measurement noise, and with large coefficients this noise in estimates can drive large variations (and errors) in prediction. Intuitively speaking, large coefficients fit to nearly collinear variables must cancel each other out in the training data to express the observed effect of the variables on the outcome. This set of cancellations is an overfit of the training data, if the same variables don't balance out in exactly the same way in future data.

Example   *Suppose that* age *and* years_in_workforce *are strongly correlated, and being one year older/one year longer in the workforce increases log income by one unit in the training data. If only* years_in_workforce *is in the model, it would get a coefficient of about 1. What happens if the model includes* age *as well?*

In some circumstances, if both age and years_in_workforce are in the model, linear regression might give years_in_workforce and age large counterbalancing coefficients of opposite sign; for instance a coefficient of 99 for years_in_workforce and age a coefficient of –98. These large coefficients would "cancel each other out" to the appropriate effect.

A similar effect can arise in a logistic model due to quasi-separation, even when there are no collinear variables. To demonstrate this, we'll introduce the bigger scenario that we will work with in this section.

7.3.1   *An example of quasi-separation*

Example   *Suppose a car review site rates cars on several characteristics, including affordability and safety rating. Car ratings can be "very good," "good," "acceptable," or "unacceptable." Your goal is to predict whether a car will fail the review: that is, get an unacceptable rating.*

For this example, you will use again use the car data from the UCI Machine Learning Repository that you used in chapter 2. This dataset has information on 1728 makes of auto, with the following variables:

- *car_price*—(vhigh, high, med, low)
- *maint_price*—(vhigh, high, med, low)
- *doors*—(2, 3, 4, 5, more)
- *persons*—(2, 4, more)
- *lug_boot*—(small, med, big)
- *safety*—(low, med, high)

The outcome variable is rating (vgood, good, acc, unacc).

First, let's read in the data and split it into training and test. If you have not done so already, download car.data.csv from https://github.com/WinVector/PDSwR2/ blob/master/UCICar/car.data.csv and make sure the file is in your working directory.

Listing 7.21   Preparing the cars data

```
cars <- read.table(
  'car.data.csv',
  sep = ',',
  header = TRUE,
  stringsAsFactor = TRUE
)

vars <- setdiff(colnames(cars), "rating")    ⟵──┐  Gets the input variables

cars$fail <- cars$rating == "unacc"              You want to predict whether the
outcome <- "fail"    ⟵────────                   car gets an unacceptable rating

set.seed(24351)
gp <- runif(nrow(cars))    ⟵────────┐  Creates the grouping variable for the
                                        test/train split (70% for training, 30% for test)
library("zeallot")
c(cars_test, cars_train) %<-% split(cars, gp < 0.7)    ⟵──┐

nrow(cars_test)            The split() function returns a list of two groups
## [1] 499                 with the group gp < 0.7 == FALSE first. The
nrow(cars_train)           zeallot package's %<-% multiassignment takes
## [1] 1229                this list of values and unpacks them into the
                           variables named cars_test and cars_train.
```

The first thing you might do to solve this problem is try a simple logistic regression.

Listing 7.22   Fitting a logistic regression model

```
library(wrapr)
(fmla <- mk_formula(outcome, vars) )

## fail ~ car_price + maint_price + doors + persons + lug_boot +
##      safety
## <environment: base>

model_glm <- glm(fmla,
            data = cars_train,
            family = binomial)
```

You will see that `glm()` returns a warning:

```
## Warning: glm.fit: fitted probabilities numerically 0 or 1 occurred
```

This warning indicates that the problem is quasi-separable: some set of variables perfectly predicts a subset of the data. In fact, this problem is simple enough that you can easily determine that a safety rating of low perfectly predicts that a car will fail the review (we leave that as an exercise for the reader). However, even cars with higher safety ratings can get ratings of unacceptable, so the safety variable only predicts a subset of the data.

You can also see the problem if you look at the summary of the model.

Listing 7.23 Looking at the model summary

```
summary(model_glm)

##
## Call:
## glm(formula = fmla, family = binomial, data = cars_train)
##
## Deviance Residuals:
##      Min        1Q    Median        3Q       Max
## -2.35684  -0.02593   0.00000   0.00001   3.11185
##
## Coefficients:
##                   Estimate Std. Error z value Pr(>|z|)
## (Intercept)        28.0132  1506.0310   0.019 0.985160
## car_pricelow       -4.6616     0.6520  -7.150 8.67e-13 ***
## car_pricemed       -3.8689     0.5945  -6.508 7.63e-11 ***
## car_pricehigh       1.9139     0.4318   4.433 9.30e-06 ***
## maint_pricelow     -3.2542     0.5423  -6.001 1.96e-09 ***
## maint_pricemed     -3.2458     0.5503  -5.899 3.66e-09 ***
## maint_pricevhigh    2.8556     0.4865   5.869 4.38e-09 ***
## doors3             -1.4281     0.4638  -3.079 0.002077 **
## doors4             -2.3733     0.4973  -4.773 1.82e-06 ***
## doors5more         -2.2652     0.5090  -4.450 8.58e-06 ***
## persons4          -29.8240  1506.0310  -0.020 0.984201    <──┐
## personsmore       -29.4551  1506.0310  -0.020 0.984396
## lug_bootmed         1.5608     0.4529   3.446 0.000568 ***
## lug_bootsmall       4.5238     0.5721   7.908 2.62e-15 ***
## safetylow          29.9415  1569.3789   0.019 0.984778    <──┐
## safetymed           2.7884     0.4134   6.745 1.53e-11 ***
## ---
## Signif. codes:  0 '***' 0.001 '**' 0.01 '*' 0.05 '.' 0.1 ' ' 1
##
## (Dispersion parameter for binomial family taken to be 1)
##
##     Null deviance: 1484.7  on 1228  degrees of freedom
## Residual deviance:  245.5  on 1213  degrees of freedom
## AIC: 277.5
##
## Number of Fisher Scoring iterations: 21)    <──
```

The variables persons4 and personsmore have notably large negative magnitudes, and a giant standard error.

The variable safetylow has a notably large positive magnitude, and a giant standard error.

The algorithm ran for an unusually large number of Fisher scoring iterations.

The variables `safetylow`, `persons4`, and `personsmore` all have unusually high magnitudes and very high standard errors. As mentioned earlier, `safetylow` always corresponds to an unacceptable rating, so `safetylow` is a strong indicator of failing the review. However, larger cars (cars that hold more people) are not always going to pass the review. It's possible that the algorithm has observed that larger cars tend to be safer (get a safety rating better than `safetylow`), and so it is using the `persons4` and `personsmore` variables to cancel out the overly high coefficient from `safetylow`.

In addition, you can see that the number of Fisher scoring iterations is unusually high; the algorithm did not converge.

This problem is fairly simple, so the model may predict acceptably well on the test set; however, in general, when you see evidence that `glm()` did not converge, you should not trust the model.

For comparison with the regularized algorithms, let's plot the coefficients of the logistic regression model (figure 7.17).

Listing 7.24   Looking at the logistic model's coefficients

```
coefs <- coef(model_glm)[-1]              ⊲──┐  Gets the coefficients
coef_frame <- data.frame(coef = names(coefs),    (except the intercept)
                         value = coefs)

library(ggplot2)
ggplot(coef_frame, aes(x = coef, y = value)) +
  geom_pointrange(aes(ymin = 0, ymax = value)) +
  ggtitle("Coefficients of logistic regression model") +
  coord_flip()
```

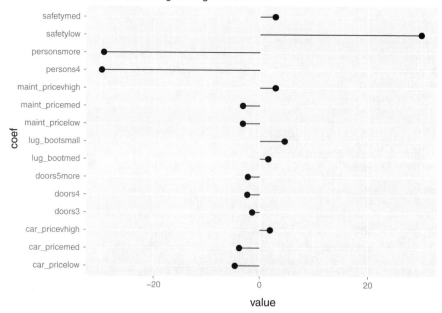

Figure 7.17   Coefficients of the logistic regression model

In the plot, coefficients that point to the right are positively correlated with failing the review, and coefficients that point to the left are negatively correlated with failure.

You can also look at the model's performance on the test data.

> **Listing 7.25 The logistic model's test performance**

Gets the model's predictions on the test set

Attaches the sigr package for deviance calculation (sigr includes a number of goodness-of-fit summaries and tests)

```
cars_test$pred_glm <- predict(model_glm,
                              newdata=cars_test,
                              type = "response")

library(sigr)
```

Convenience function to print confusion matrix, accuracy, and deviance

```
confmat <- function(dframe, predvar) {
  cmat <- table(truth = ifelse(dframe$fail, "unacceptable", "passed"),
                prediction = ifelse(dframe[[predvar]] > 0.5,
                                    "unacceptable", "passed"))
  accuracy <- sum(diag(cmat)) / sum(cmat)
  deviance <- calcDeviance(dframe[[predvar]], dframe$fail)

  list(confusion_matrix = cmat,
       accuracy = accuracy,
       deviance = deviance)

}

confmat(cars_test, "pred_glm")
## $confusion_matrix
##               prediction
## truth          passed unacceptable
##    passed         150            9
##    unacceptable    17          323
##
## $accuracy
## [1] 0.9478958
##
## $deviance
## [1] 97.14902
```

In this case, the model seems to be good. However, you cannot always trust non-converged models, or models with needlessly large coefficients.

In situations where you see suspiciously large coefficients with extremely large standard errors, whether due to collinearity or quasi-separation, we recommend regularization.[1] Regularization adds a penalty to the formulation that biases the model's coefficients towards zero. This makes it harder for the solver to drive the coefficients to unnecessarily large values.

---

[1] Some people suggest using principal components regression (PCR) to deal with collinear variables: PCR uses the existing variables to create synthetic variables that are mutually orthogonal, eliminating the collinearities. This won't help with quasi-separation. We generally prefer regularization.

Regarding overfitting

The modeling goal is to predict well on future application data. Improving your measured performance on training data does not always do this. This is what we've been discussing as overfit. Regularization degrades the quality of the training data fit, in the hope of improving future model performance.

7.3.2   *The types of regularized regression*

There are multiple types of regularized regression, each defined by the penalty that is put on the model's coefficients. Here we cover the different regularization approaches.

RIDGE REGRESSION

Ridge regression (or L2-regularized regression) tries to minimize the training prediction error, subject to also minimizing the sum of the squared magnitudes of the coefficients.[1] Let's look at ridge regularized linear regression. Remember that linear regression tries to find the coefficients b such that

```
f(x[i,]) = b[0] + b[1] x[i,1] + ... b[n] x[i,n]
```

is as close as possible to `y[i]` for all the training data. It does this by minimizing `(y - f(x))^2`, the sum of the squared error between `y` and `f(x)`. Ridge regression tries to find the b that minimizes

```
(y - f(x))^2 + lambda * (b[1]^2 + ...  + b[n]^2)
```

where `lambda >= 0`. When `lambda = 0`, this reduces to regular linear regression; the larger `lambda` is, the harder the algorithm will penalize large coefficients. The expression for regularized logistic regression is similar.

How ridge regression affects coefficients

When variables are nearly collinear, ridge regression tends to average the collinear variables together. You can think of this as "ridge regression shares the credit."

For instance, let's go back to the example of fitting a linear regression for log income using both age and years in workforce (which are nearly collinear). Recall that being one year older/one year longer in the workforce increases log income by one unit in the training data.

In this situation, ridge regression might assign both variables age and years_in_workforce a coefficient of 0.5, which adds up to the appropriate effect.

---

[1] This is called "the L2 norm of the vector of coefficients," hence the name.

LASSO REGRESSION

Lasso regression (or L1-regularized regression) tries to minimize the training prediction error, subject to also minimizing the sum of the absolute value of the coefficients.[1] For linear regression, this looks like minimizing

```
(y - f(x))^2 + lambda * ( abs(b[1]) + abs(b[2]) + .... abs(b[n]) )
```

> ### How lasso regression affects coefficients
>
> When variables are nearly collinear, lasso regression tends to drive one or more of them to zero. So in the income scenario, lasso regression might assign `years_in_workforce` a coefficient of 1 and `age` a coefficient of 0.[a] For this reason, lasso regression is often used as a form of variable selection. A larger lambda will tend to drive more coefficients to zero.
>
> ---
>
> [a] As Hastie et al. point out in *The Elements of Statistical Learning*, 2nd ed (Springer, 2009), which of the correlated variables get zeroed out is somewhat arbitrary.

ELASTIC NET

In some situations, like quasi-separability, the ridge solution may be preferred. In other situations, such as when you have a very large number of variables, many of which are correlated to each other, the lasso may be preferred. You may not be sure which is the best approach, so one compromise is to combine the two. This is called *elastic net*. The penalty of using elastic net is a combination of the ridge and the lasso penalties:

```
(1 - alpha) * (b[1]^2 + ...  + b[n]^2) +
    alpha * ( abs(b[1]) + abs(b[2]) + .... abs(b[n]) )
```

When `alpha = 0`, this reduces to ridge regression; when `alpha = 1`, it reduces to lasso. Different values of `alpha` between 0 and 1 give different trade-offs between sharing the credit among correlated variables, and only keeping a subset of them.

7.3.3 *Regularized regression with glmnet*

All the types of regularized regression that we've discussed are implemented in R by the package `glmnet`. Unfortunately, the `glmnet` package uses a calling interface that is not very R-like; in particular, it expects that the input data is a numeric matrix rather than a data frame. So we'll use the `glmnetUtils` package to provide a more R-like interface to the functions.

---

[1] Or the "L1 norm of the vector of coefficients."

> ## Calling interfaces
>
> It would be best if all modeling procedures had the same calling interface. The `lm()` and `glm()` packages nearly do, and `glmnetUtils` helps make `glmnet` more compatible with R's calling interface conventions.
>
> However, to use a given method correctly, you must know some things about its particular constraints and consequences. This means that even if all modeling methods had the same calling interface, you still must study the documentation to understand how to use it properly.

Let's compare the different regularization approaches on the car-ratings prediction problem.

THE RIDGE REGRESSION SOLUTION

When reducing the number of variables is not an issue, we generally try ridge regression first, because it's a smoother regularization that we feel retains the most interpretability for the coefficients (but see the warning later in this section). The parameter `alpha` specifies the mixture of ridge and lasso penalties (0=ridge, 1=lasso); so for ridge regression, set `alpha = 0`. The parameter `lambda` is the regularization penalty.

Since you generally don't know the best `lambda`, the original function `glmnet::glmnet()` tries several values of `lambda` (100 by default) and returns the models corresponding to each value. The function `glmnet::cv.glmnet()` in addition does the cross-validation needed to pick the `lambda` that gives the minimum cross-validation error for a fixed `alpha`, and returns it as the field `lambda.min`. It also returns a value `lambda.1se`, the largest value of `lambda` such that the error is within 1 standard error of the minimum. This is shown in figure 7.18.

The function `glmnetUtils::cv.glmnet()` lets you call the cross-validated version in an R-friendlier way.

When using regularized regression, it's a good idea to standardize, or center and scale the data (see section 4.2.2). Fortunately, `cv.glmnet()` does this by default. If for some reason you want to turn this off (perhaps you have already standardized the data), use the parameter `standardize = FALSE`.[1]

Listing 7.26 Fitting the ridge regression model

```
library(glmnet)
library(glmnetUtils)

(model_ridge <- cv.glmnet(fmla,
                    cars_train,
                    alpha = 0,
                    family = "binomial"))
```

For logistic regression-style models, use family = "binomial".
For linear regression-style models, use family = "gaussian".

---

[1] For help/documentation on `glmnetUtils::cv.glmnet()`, see `help(cv.glmnet, package = "glmnetUtils")`, `help(cv.glmnet, package = "glmnet")`, and `help(glmnet, package = "glmnet")`.

```
## Call:
## cv.glmnet.formula(formula = fmla, data = cars_train, alpha = 0,
##      family = "binomial")
##
## Model fitting options:
##      Sparse model matrix: FALSE
##      Use model.frame: FALSE
##      Number of crossvalidation folds: 10
##      Alpha: 0
##      Deviance-minimizing lambda: 0.02272432   (+1 SE): 0.02493991
```

Printing out `model_ridge` tells you the lambda that corresponds to the minimum cross-validation error (the deviance)—that is, `model_ridge$lambda.min`. It also reports the value of `model_ridge$lambda.1se`.

Remember that `cv.glmnet()` returns 100 (by default) models; of course, you really only want one—the "best" one. As shown in figure 7.18, when you call a function like `predict()` or `coef()`, the `cv.glmnet` object by default uses the model

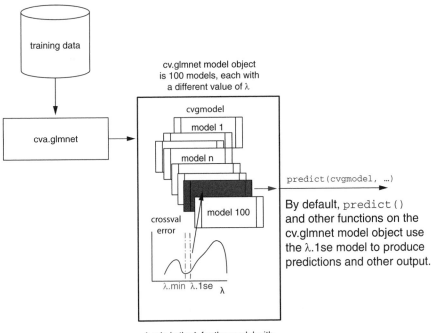

Figure 7.18   Schematic of `cv.glmnet()`

corresponding to `lambda.1se`, as some people consider `lambda.1se` less likely to be overfit than `lambda.min`.

The following listing examines the coefficients of the `lambda.1se` model. If you want to see the model corresponding to `lambda.min`, replace the first line of the listing with (`coefs <- coef(model_ridge, s = model_ridge$lambda.min)`).

Listing 7.27 Looking at the ridge model's coefficients

```
(coefs <- coef(model_ridge))

## 22 x 1 sparse Matrix of class "dgCMatrix"
##                              1
## (Intercept)         2.01098708
## car_pricehigh       0.34564041
## car_pricelow       -0.76418240
## car_pricemed       -0.62791346
## car_pricevhigh      1.05949870
## maint_pricehigh     0.18896383
## maint_pricelow     -0.72148497
## maint_pricemed     -0.60000546
## maint_pricevhigh    1.14059599
## doors2              0.37594292
## doors3              0.01067978
## doors4             -0.21546650
## doors5more         -0.17649206
## persons2            2.61102897          Note that all the levels of the
## persons4           -1.35476871          categorical variable persons are
## personsmore        -1.26074907          present (no reference level).
## lug_bootbig        -0.52193562
## lug_bootmed        -0.18681644
## lug_bootsmall       0.68419343
## safetyhigh         -1.70022006
## safetylow           2.54353980
## safetymed          -0.83688361

coef_frame <- data.frame(coef = rownames(coefs)[-1],
                         value = coefs[-1,1])

ggplot(coef_frame, aes(x = coef, y = value)) +
  geom_pointrange(aes(ymin = 0, ymax = value)) +
  ggtitle("Coefficients of ridge model") +
  coord_flip()
```

Notice that `cv.glmnet()` does not use reference levels for categorical variables: for instance, the `coefs` vector includes the variables `persons2`, `persons4`, and `personsmore`, corresponding to the levels 2, 4, and "more" for the `persons` variable. The logistic regression model in section 7.3.1 used the variables `persons4` and `personsmore`, and used the level value 2 as the reference level. Using all the variable levels when regularizing has the advantage that the coefficient magnitudes are regularized toward zero, rather than toward a (possibly arbitrary) reference level.

You can see in figure 7.19 that this model no longer has the unusually large magnitudes. The directions of the coefficients suggest that low safety ratings, small cars, and

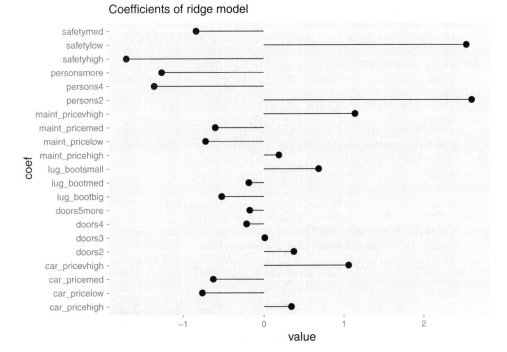

Figure 7.19   Coefficients of the ridge regression model

very high purchase or maintenance price all positively predict rating of unacceptable. One might suspect that small cars correlate with low safety ratings, so `safetylow` and `persons2` are probably sharing the credit.

REGULARIZATION AFFECTS INTERPRETABILITY   Because regularization adds an additional term to the algorithm's optimization function, you can't quite interpret the coefficients the same way you did in sections 7.1.4 and 7.2.4. For instance, no coefficient significances are reported. However, you can at least use the signs of the coefficients as indications of which variables are positively or negatively correlated with the outcome in the joint model.

You can also evaluate the performance of `model_ridge` on the test data.

Listing 7.28   Looking at the ridge model's test performance

```
prediction <- predict(model_ridge,
                  newdata = cars_test,
                  type = "response")

cars_test$pred_ridge <- as.numeric(prediction)      ◁──┐ The prediction variable is a
                                                          1-d matrix; convert it to a
confmat(cars_test, "pred_ridge")                          vector before adding it to
## $confusion_matrix                                      the cars_test data frame.
##              prediction
```

```
## truth           passed unacceptable
##   passed           147           12
##   unacceptable      16          324
##
## $accuracy
## [1] 0.9438878
##
## $deviance
## [1] 191.9248
```

To look at the predictions for the model corresponding to `lambda.min`, replace the first command of the preceding listing with this:

```
prediction <- predict(model_ridge,
                      newdata = cars_test,
                      type="response",
                      s = model_ridge$lambda.min)
```

THE LASSO REGRESSION SOLUTION

You can run the same steps as in the previous section with `alpha = 1` (the default) to fit a lasso regression model. We leave fitting the model as an exercise for the reader; here are the results.

Listing 7.29   The lasso model's coefficients

```
## 22 x 1 sparse Matrix of class "dgCMatrix"
##                                 1
## (Intercept)        -3.572506339
## car_pricehigh       2.199963497
## car_pricelow       -0.511577936
## car_pricemed       -0.075364079
## car_pricevhigh      3.558630135
## maint_pricehigh     1.854942910
## maint_pricelow     -0.101916375
## maint_pricemed     -0.009065081
## maint_pricevhigh    3.778594043
## doors2              0.919895270
## doors3              .
## doors4             -0.374230464
## doors5more         -0.300181160
## persons2            9.299272641
## persons4           -0.180985786
## personsmore         .
## lug_bootbig        -0.842393694
## lug_bootmed         .
## lug_bootsmall       1.886157531
## safetyhigh         -1.757625171
## safetylow           7.942050790
## safetymed           .
```

As you see in figure 7.20, `cv.glmnet()` did not reduce the magnitudes of the largest coefficients as much, although it did zero out a few variables (doors3, personsmore, lug_boot_med, safety_med), and it selected a similar set of variables as strongly predictive of an unacceptable rating.

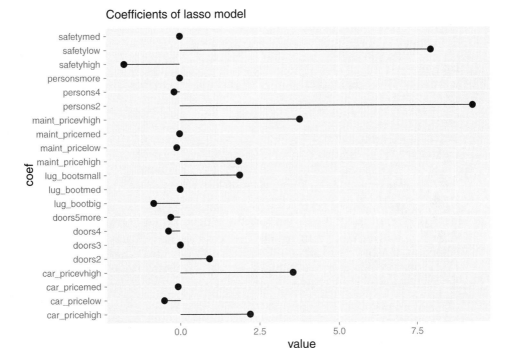

Figure 7.20 Coefficients of the lasso regression model

The lasso model's accuracy on the test data is similar to the ridge model's, but the deviance is much lower, indicating better model performance on the test data.

Listing 7.30 The lasso model's test performance

```
### $confusion_matrix
##                 prediction
## truth         passed unacceptable
##    passed        150            9
##    unacceptable   17          323
##
## $accuracy
## [1] 0.9478958
##
## $deviance
## [1] 112.7308
```

THE ELASTIC NET SOLUTION: PICKING ALPHA

The cv.glmnet() function only optimizes over lambda; it assumes that alpha, the variable that specifies the mix of the ridge and lasso penalties, is fixed. The glmnetUtils package provides a function called cva.glmnet() that will simultaneously cross-validate for both alpha and lambda.

Listing 7.31   Cross-validating for both `alpha` and `lambda`

```
(elastic_net <- cva.glmnet(fmla,
                           cars_train,
                           family = "binomial"))
## Call:
## cva.glmnet.formula(formula = fmla, data = cars_train, family = "binomial")
##
## Model fitting options:
##     Sparse model matrix: FALSE
##     Use model.frame: FALSE
##     Alpha values: 0 0.001 0.008 0.027 0.064 0.125 0.216 0.343 0.512 0.729 1
##     Number of crossvalidation folds for lambda: 10
```

The process of extracting the best model is a bit involved. Unlike `cv.glmnet`, `cva.glmnet` doesn't return an `alpha.min` or an `alpha.1se`. Instead, the field `elastic_net$alpha` returns all the alphas that the function tried (11 of them, by default), and `elastic_net$modlist` returns all the corresponding `glmnet::cv.glmnet` model objects (see figure 7.21). Each one of these model objects is really 100 models, so for a given `alpha`, we'll choose the `lambda.1se` model as "the best model."

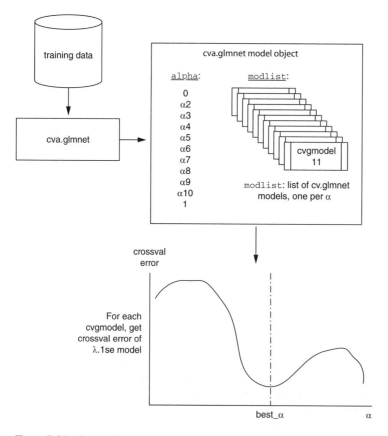

Figure 7.21   Schematic of using `cva.glmnet` to pick `alpha`

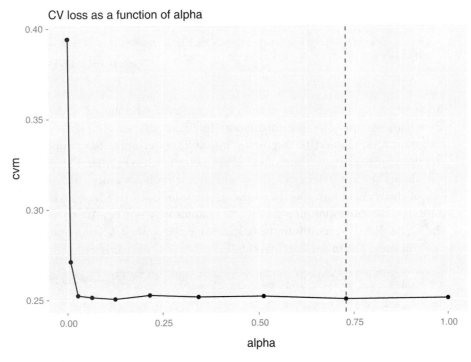

CV loss as a function of alpha

Figure 7.22   Cross-validation error as a function of `alpha`

The following listing implements the process sketched in figure 7.21 to get the mean cross-validation error for each "best model," and plot the errors as a function of `alpha` (figure 7.22). You can create a similar plot using the function `minlossplot(elastic_net)`, but the following listing also returns the value of the best tested `alpha`.

Listing 7.32   Finding the minimum error `alpha`

A function to get the mean cross-validation error of a cv.glmnet lambda.lse model

Gets the alphas that the algorithm tried

```
get_cvm <- function(model) {
    index <- match(model$lambda.1se, model$lambda)
    model$cvm[index]
}

enet_performance <- data.frame(alpha = elastic_net$alpha)
models <- elastic_net$modlist
enet_performance$cvm <- vapply(models, get_cvm, numeric(1))

minix <- which.min(enet_performance$cvm)
(best_alpha <- elastic_net$alpha[minix])
## [1] 0.729
```

Gets the model objects produced

Gets the errors of each best model

Finds the minimum cross-validation error

Gets the corresponding alpha

```
ggplot(enet_performance, aes(x = alpha, y = cvm)) +
  geom_point() +
  geom_line() +
  geom_vline(xintercept = best_alpha, color = "red", linetype = 2) +
  ggtitle("CV loss as a function of alpha")
```

Plots the model performances as a function of alpha

Remember that both `cv.glmnet` and `cva.glmnet` are randomized, so the results can vary from run to run. The documentation for `glmnetUtils` (https://cran.r-project.org/web/packages/glmnetUtils/vignettes/intro.html) recommends running `cva.glmnet` multiple times to reduce the noise. If you want to cross-validate for `alpha`, we suggest calculating the equivalent of `enet_performance` multiple times, and averaging the values of the `cvm` column together—the `alpha` values will be identical from run to run, although the corresponding `lambda.1se` values may not be. After you've determined the `alpha` that corresponds to the best average `cvm`, call `cv.glmnet` one more time with the chosen `alpha` to get the final model.

Listing 7.33 Fitting and evaluating the elastic net model

```
(model_enet <- cv.glmnet(fmla,
                    cars_train,
                    alpha = best_alpha,
                    family = "binomial"))
## Call:
## cv.glmnet.formula(formula = fmla, data = cars_train, alpha = best_alpha,
##     family = "binomial")
##
## Model fitting options:
##     Sparse model matrix: FALSE
##     Use model.frame: FALSE
##     Number of crossvalidation folds: 10
##     Alpha: 0.729
##     Deviance-minimizing lambda: 0.0002907102   (+1 SE): 0.002975509

prediction <- predict(model_enet,
                    newdata = cars_test,
                    type = "response")

cars_test$pred_enet <- as.numeric(prediction)

confmat(cars_test, "pred_enet")

## $confusion_matrix
##                 prediction
## truth          passed unacceptable
##    passed          150            9
##    unacceptable     17          323
##
## $accuracy
## [1] 0.9478958
##
## $deviance
## [1] 117.7701
```

It's also worth noting that in this case, the cross-validated loss falls off quite quickly after `alpha=0`, so in practice, almost any non-zero `alpha` will give models of similar quality.

Summary

Both linear and logistic regression assume that the outcome is a function of a linear combination of the inputs. This seems restrictive, but in practice linear and logistic regression models can perform well even when the theoretical assumptions aren't exactly met. We'll show how to further work around these limits in chapter 10.

Linear and logistic regression can also provide *advice* by quantifying the relationships between the outcomes and the model's inputs. Since the models are expressed completely by their coefficients, they're small, portable, and efficient—all valuable qualities when putting a model into production. If the model's errors are uncorrelated with *y*, the model might be trusted to extrapolate predictions outside the training range. Extrapolation is never completely safe, but it's sometimes necessary.

In situations where variables are correlated or the prediction problem is quasiseparable, linear methods may not perform as well. In these cases, regularization methods can produce models that are safer to apply to new data, although the coefficients of these models are not as useful for advice about the relationships between variables and the outcome.

While learning about linear models in this chapter, we have assumed that the data is well behaved: the data has no missing values, the number of possible levels for categorical variables is low, and all possible levels are present in the training data. In real-world data, these assumptions are not always true. In the next chapter, you will learn about advanced methods to prepare ill-behaved data for modeling.

In this chapter you have learned

- How to predict numerical quantities with linear regression models
- How to predict probabilities or classify using logistic regression models
- How to interpret the diagnostics from `lm()` and `glm()` models
- How to interpret the coefficients of linear models
- How to diagnose when a linear model may not be "safe" or not as reliable (collinearity, quasi-separation)
- How to use `glmnet` to fit regularized linear and logistic regression models

Advanced
data preparation

This chapter covers

- Using the `vtreat` package for advanced data preparation
- Cross-validated data preparation

In our last chapter, we built substantial models on nice or well-behaved data. In this chapter, we will learn how to prepare or treat messy real-world data for modeling. We will use the principles of chapter 4 and the advanced data preparation package: vtreat. We will revisit the issues that arise with missing values, categorical variables, recoding variables, redundant variables, and having too many variables. We will spend some time on variable selection, which is an important step even with current machine learning methods. The mental model summary (figure 8.1) of this chapter emphasizes that this chapter is about working with data and preparing for machine learning modeling. We will first introduce the vtreat package, then work a detailed real-world problem, and then go into more detail about using the vtreat package.

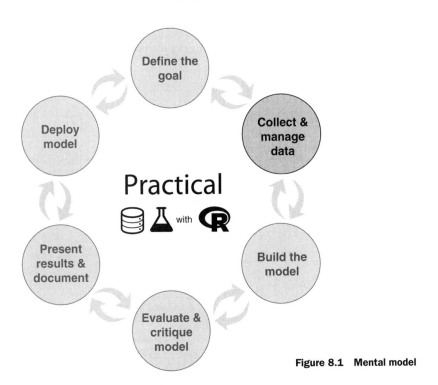

Figure 8.1 Mental model

8.1   *The purpose of the vtreat package*

vtreat is an R package designed to prepare real-world data for supervised learning or predictive modeling. It is designed to deal with a lot of common issues, so the data scientist doesn't have to. This leaves them much more time to find and work on unique domain-dependent issues. vtreat is an excellent realization of the concepts discussed in chapter 4 as well as many other concepts. One of the goals of chapter 4 was to give you an understanding of some of the issues we can run into working with data, and principled steps to take in dealing with such data. vtreat automates these steps into a high-performance production-capable package, and is a formally citable methodology you can incorporate into your own work. We can't succinctly explain everything vtreat does with data, as it does a lot; for details please see the long-form documentation here: https://arxiv.org/abs/1611.09477. In addition, vtreat has many explanatory vignettes and worked examples here: https://CRAN.R-project.org/package=vtreat.

We will work through vtreat's capabilities in this chapter using an example of predicting account cancellation (called *customer churn*) using the KDD Cup 2009 dataset. In this example scenario, we will use vtreat to prepare the data for use in later modeling steps. Some of the issues vtreat helps with include the following:

- Missing values in numeric variables
- Extreme or out-of-range values in numeric variables
- Missing values in categorical variables

- Rare values in categorical data
- Novel values (values seen during testing or application, but not during training) in categorical data
- Categorical data with very many possible values
- Overfit due to a large number of variables
- Overfit due to "nested model bias"

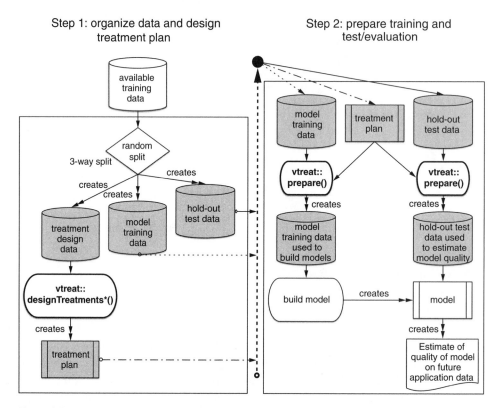

Figure 8.2   vtreat three-way split strategy

The basic vtreat workflow (shown in figure 8.2) is to use some of the training data to create a *treatment plan* that records key characteristics of the data such as relationships between individual variables and the outcome. This treatment plan is then used to *prepare* data that will be used to fit the model, as well as to prepare data that the model will be applied to. The idea is that this prepared or treated data will be "safe," with no missing or unexpected values, and will possibly have new synthetic variables that will improve the model fitting. In this sense, vtreat itself looks a lot like a model.

We saw a simple use of vtreat in chapter 4 to treat missing values. In this chapter, we will use vtreat's full coding power on our customer churn example. For motivation, we will solve the KDD Cup 2009 problem, and then we will discuss how to use vtreat in general.

The KDD Cup 2009 provided a dataset about customer relationship management. This contest data supplied 230 facts about 50,000 credit card accounts. From these features, one of the contest goals was to predict account cancellation (called *churn*).

The basic way to use `vtreat` is with a three-way data split: one set for learning the data treatment, one for modeling, and a third for estimating the model quality on new data. Figure 8.2 shows the concept, which will serve as a good mnemonic once we have worked an example. As the diagram shows, to use `vtreat` in this manner, we split the data three ways and use one subset to prepare the treatment plan. Then we use the treatment plan to prepare the other two subsets: one subset to fit the desired model, and the other subset to evaluate the fitted model. The process may seem complicated, but from the user's point of view it is very simple.

Let's start with a look at an example scenario using `vtreat` with the KDD Cup 2009 account cancellation prediction problem.

8.2   KDD and KDD Cup 2009

Example   *We are given the task of predicting which credit card accounts will cancel in a given time period. This sort of cancellation is called churn. To build our model, we have supervised training data available. For each account in the training data, we have hundreds of measured features and we know whether the account later cancelled. We want to build a model that identifies "at risk of canceling" accounts in this data, as well as for future application.*

To simulate this scenario, we will use the KDD Cup 2009 contest dataset.[1]

Shortcomings of the data

As with many score-based competitions, this contest concentrated on machine learning and deliberately abstracted out or skipped over a number of important data science issues, such as cooperatively defining goals, requesting new measurements, collecting data, and quantifying classifier performance in terms of business goals. For this contest data, we don't have names or definitions for any of the independent (or input) variables[a] and no real definition of the dependent (or outcome) variables. We have the advantage that the data comes in a ready-to-model format (all input variables and the results arranged in single rows). But we don't know the meaning of any variable (so we unfortunately can't join in outside data sources), and we can't use any method that treats time and repetition of events carefully (such as time series methods or survival analysis).

---

[a]   We'll call variables or columns used to build the model variously *variables*, *independent variables*, *input variables*, and so on to try and distinguish them from the value to be predicted (which we'll call *the outcome* or *dependent variable*).

---

[1]   We share the data and steps to prepare this data for modeling in R here: https://github.com/WinVector/PDSwR2/tree/master/KDD2009.

To simulate the data science processes, we'll assume that we can use any column we're given to make predictions (that all of these columns are known prior to needing a prediction).[2] We will assume the contest metric (*AUC*, or *area under the curve* as discussed in section 6.2.5) is the correct one, and the AUC of the top contestant is a good upper bound (telling us when to stop tuning).[3]

8.2.1 Getting started with KDD Cup 2009 data

For our example, we'll try to predict churn in the KDD dataset. The KDD contest was judged in terms of AUC (*area under the curve*, a measure of prediction quality discussed in section 6.2.5), so we'll also use AUC as our measure of performance.[4] The winning team achieved an AUC of 0.76 on churn, so we'll treat that as our upper bound on possible performance. Our lower bound on performance is an AUC of 0.5, as an AUC below 0.5 is worse than random predictions.

This problem has a large number of variables, many of which are categorical variables that have a large number of possible levels. As we will see, such variables are especially liable to overfit, even during the process of creating the treatment plan. Because of this concern, we'll split our data into three sets: training, calibration, and test. In the following example, we'll use the training set to design the treatment plan, and the calibration set to check for overfit in the treatment plan. The test set is reserved for a final estimate of model performance. This three-way split procedure is recommended by many researchers.[5]

Let's start work as shown in the following listing, where we prepare the data for analysis and modeling.[6]

Listing 8.1   Preparing the KDD data for analysis

Reads the file of independent variables. All the data is from
https://github.com/WinVector/PDSwR2/tree/master/KDD2009.

```
d <- read.table('orange_small_train.data.gz',
    header = TRUE,
    sep = '\t',                        Treats both NA and the empty
    na.strings = c('NA', ''))          string as missing data
```

---

[2] Checking if a column is actually going to be available during prediction (and not some later function of the unknown output) is a critical step in data science projects.

[3] AUC is a good initial screening metric, as it measures if any monotone transformation of your score is a good score. For fine tuning, we will use R-squared and pseudo R-squared (also defined in chapter 6) as they are stricter, measuring if the exact values at hand are good scores.

[4] Also, as is common for example problems, we have no project sponsor to discuss metrics with, so our choice of evaluation is a bit arbitrary.

[5] Normally, we would use the calibration set to design the treatment plan, the training set to train the model, and the test set to evaluate the model. Since the focus of this chapter is on the data treatment process, we'll use the largest set (dTrain) to design the treatment plan, and the other sets to evaluate it.

[6] Please either work in the KDD2009 subdirectory of the PDSwR2 support materials, or copy the relevant files to where you are working. The PDSwR2 support materials are available from https://github.com/WinVector/PDSwR2, and instructions for getting started can be found in appendix A.

Reads the known churn outcomes

Adds churn as a new column

By setting the seed to the pseudo-random number generator, we make our work reproducible: someone redoing it will see the exact same results.

```
churn <- read.table('orange_small_train_churn.labels.txt',
   header = FALSE, sep = '\t')
d$churn <- churn$V1

set.seed(729375)
rgroup <- base::sample(c('train', 'calibrate', 'test'),
   nrow(d),
   prob = c(0.8, 0.1, 0.1),
   replace = TRUE)
dTrain <- d[rgroup == 'train', , drop = FALSE]
dCal <- d[rgroup == 'calibrate', , drop = FALSE]
dTrainAll <- d[rgroup %in% c('train', 'calibrate'), , drop = FALSE]
dTest <- d[rgroup == 'test', , drop = FALSE]

outcome <- 'churn'
vars <- setdiff(colnames(dTrainAll), outcome)

rm(list=c('d', 'churn', 'rgroup'))
```

Splits data into train, calibration, and test sets. Explicitly specifies the base::sample() function to avoid name collision with dplyr::sample(), if the dplyr package is loaded.

Removes unneeded objects from the workspace

We have also saved an R workspace with most of the data, functions, and results of this chapter in the GitHub repository, which you can load with the command `load('KDD2009.Rdata')`. We're now ready to build some models.

We want to remind the reader: always look at your data. Looking at your data is the quickest way to find surprises. Two functions are particularly helpful for taking an initial look at your data: `str()` (which shows the structure of the first few rows in transposed form) and `summary()`.

Exercise: Using str() and summary()

Before moving on, please run all of the steps in listing 8.1, and then try running `str(dTrain)` *and* `summary(dTrain)` *yourself. We try to avoid overfit by not making modeling decisions based on looking at our holdout data.*

Subsample to prototype quickly

Often the data scientist will be so engrossed with the business problem, math, and data that they forget how much trial and error is needed. It's often an excellent idea to first work on a small subset of your training data, so that it takes seconds to debug your code instead of minutes. Don't work with large and slow data sizes until you have to.

CHARACTERIZING THE OUTCOME

Before starting on modeling, we should look at the distribution of the outcome. This tells how much variation there is to even attempt to predict. We can do this as follows:

```
outcome_summary <- table(
   churn = dTrain[, outcome],
   useNA = 'ifany')
knitr::kable(outcome_summary)
```

Tabulates levels of churn outcome

Includes NA values in the tabulation

```
outcome_summary["1"] / sum(outcome_summary)     ◁────────   Estimates the observed
#             1                                              churn rate or prevalence
# 0.07347764
```

The table in figure 8.3 indicates that churn takes on two values: −1 and 1. The value 1 (indicating a churn, or cancellation of account, has happened) is seen about 7% of the time. So we could trivially be 93% accurate by predicting that no account ever cancels, though obviously this is not a useful model![7]

churn	Freq
-1	37110
1	2943

Figure 8.3   KDD2009 churn rate

8.2.2   *The bull-in-the-china-shop approach*

Let's deliberately ignore our advice to look at the data, to look at the columns, and to characterize the relations between the proposed explanatory variables and the quantity to be predicted. For this first attempt, we aren't building a treatment plan, so we'll use both the dTrain and dCal data together to fit the model (as the set dTrainAll). Let's see what happens if we jump in and immediately try to build a model for churn == 1, given the explanatory variables (hint: it won't be pretty).

Listing 8.2   Attempting to model without preparation

```
library("wrapr")     ◁────────────────────────   Attaches the wrapr package for
                                                  convenience functions, such as
outcome <- 'churn'                                mk_formula()
vars <- setdiff(colnames(dTrainAll), outcome)

formula1 <- mk_formula("churn", vars, outcome_target = 1)
model1 <- glm(formula1, data = dTrainAll, family = binomial)   ◁────────

# Error in `contrasts ...   ◁─────┐  The attempt failed     Asks the glm() function
                                     with an error.          to build a logistic
Builds a model formula specification, asking                 regression model
churn == 1 to be predicted as a function of
our explanatory variables
```

As we can see, this first attempt failed. Some research will show us that some of the columns we are attempting to use as explanatory variables do not vary and have the exact same value for every row or example. We could attempt to filter these bad columns out by hand, but fixing common data issues in an ad hoc manner is tedious. For example, listing 8.3 shows what happens if we try to use just the first explanatory variable Var1 to build a model.

---

[7] See http://www.win-vector.com/blog/2009/11/i-dont-think-that-means-what-you-think-it-means-statistics-to-english-translation-part-1-accuracy-measures/.

Explanatory variables

Explanatory variables are columns or variables we are trying to use as inputs for our model. In this case, the variables came to us without informative names, so they go by the names `Var#` where `#` is a number. In a real project, this would be a possible sign of uncommitted data-managing partners, and something to work on fixing before attempting modeling.

Listing 8.3 Trying just one variable

```
model2 <- glm((churn == 1) ~ Var1, data = dTrainAll, family = binomial)
summary(model2)
#
# Call:
# glm(formula = (churn == 1) ~ Var1, family = binomial, data = dTrainAll)
#
# Deviance Residuals:
#     Min       1Q   Median       3Q      Max
# -0.3997  -0.3694  -0.3691  -0.3691   2.3326
#
# Coefficients:
#               Estimate Std. Error z value Pr(>|z|)
# (Intercept) -2.6523837  0.1674387 -15.841   <2e-16 ***
# Var1         0.0002429  0.0035759   0.068    0.946
# ---
# Signif. codes:  0 '***' 0.001 '**' 0.01 '*' 0.05 '.' 0.1 ' ' 1
#
# (Dispersion parameter for binomial family taken to be 1)
#
#     Null deviance: 302.09  on 620  degrees of freedom
# Residual deviance: 302.08  on 619  degrees of freedom
#   (44407 observations deleted due to missingness)
# AIC: 306.08
#
# Number of Fisher Scoring iterations: 5

dim(dTrainAll)
# [1] 45028    234
```

This means the modeling procedure threw out this much (almost all) of our training data.

We saw how to read the model summary in detail in section 7.2. What jumps out here is the line "44407 observations deleted due to missingness." This means the modeling procedures threw out 44407 of our 45028 training rows, building a model on the remaining 621 rows of data. So in addition to columns that do not vary, we have columns that have damaging amounts of missing values.

The data problems do not end there. Take a look at another variable, this time the one named `Var200`:

```
head(dTrainAll$Var200)
# [1] <NA>      <NA>      vynJTq9   <NA>      0v21jmy   <NA>
# 15415 Levels: _84etK_ _9bTOWp _A3VKFm _bq4Nkb _ct4nkXBMp ... zzQ9udm

length(unique(dTrainAll$Var200))
# [1] 14391
```

The head() command shows us the first few values of Var200, telling us this column has string values encoded as factors. Factors are R's representation for strings taken from a known set. And this is where an additional problem lies. Notice the listing says the factor has 15415 possible levels. A factor or string variable with this many distinct levels is going to be a big problem in terms of overfitting and also difficult for the glm() code to work with. In addition, the length(unique(dTrainAll$Var200)) summary tells us that Var200 takes on only 14391 distinct values in our training sample. This tells us our training data sample did not see all known values for this variable. Our held-out test set contains, in addition to values seen during training, new values not in the training set. This is quite common for string-valued or categorical variables with a large number of levels, and causes most R modeling code to error-out when trying to make predictions on new data.

We could go on. We have not yet exhausted the section 8.1 list of things that can commonly go wrong. At this point, we hope the reader will agree: a sound systematic way of identifying, characterizing, and mitigating common data quality issues would be a great help. Having a good way to work though common data quality issues in a domain-independent way leaves us more time to work with the data and work through any domain-specific issues. The vtreat package is a great tool for this task. For the rest of this chapter, we will work a bit with the KDD Cup 2009 data, and then master using vtreat in general.

8.3   *Basic data preparation for classification*

vtreat prepares data for use by both cleaning up existing columns or variables and by introducing new columns or variables. For our order cancellation scenario, vtreat will address the missing values, the categorical variables with very many levels, and other issues. Let's master the vtreat process here.

First, we'll use a portion of our data (the dTrain set) to design our variable treatments.

> **Listing 8.4   Basic data preparation for classification**

```
library("vtreat")

(parallel_cluster <- parallel::makeCluster(parallel::detectCores()))

treatment_plan <- vtreat::designTreatmentsC(
    dTrain,
    varlist = vars,
    outcomename = "churn",
    outcometarget = 1,
    verbose = FALSE,
    parallelCluster = parallel_cluster)
```

Attaches the vtreat package for functions such as designTreatmentsC()

Starts up a parallel cluster to speed up calculation. If you don't want a parallel cluster, just set parallel_ cluster to NULL.

Uses designTreatmentsC() to learn the treatment plan from the training data. For a dataset the size and complexity of KDD2009, this can take a few minutes.

Then, we'll use the treatment plan to prepare cleaned and treated data. The `prepare()` method builds a new data frame with the same row order as the original data frame, and columns from the treatment plan (plus copying over the dependent variable column if it is present). The idea is illustrated in figure 8.4. In listing 8.5, we apply the treatment plan to the `dTrain` data, so we can compare the treated data to the original data.

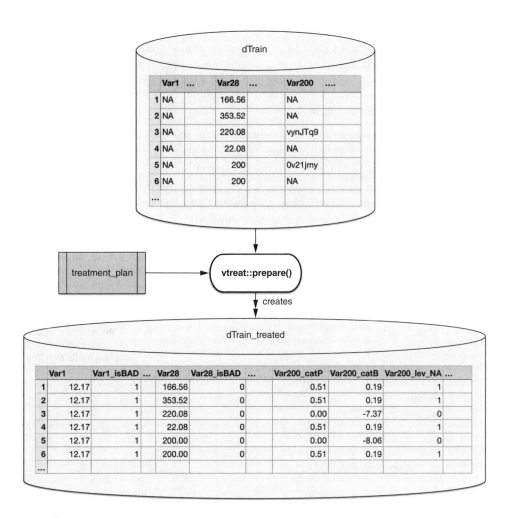

Figure 8.4 `vtreat` **variable preparation**

Listing 8.5   Preparing data with `vtreat`

```
dTrain_treated <- prepare(treatment_plan,
                          dTrain,
                          parallelCluster = parallel_cluster)

head(colnames(dTrain))
## [1] "Var1" "Var2" "Var3" "Var4" "Var5" "Var6"
head(colnames(dTrain_treated))
## [1] "Var1"       "Var1_isBAD" "Var2"       "Var2_isBAD" "Var3"
## [6] "Var3_isBAD"
```

> Compares the columns of the original dTrain data to its treated counterpart

Note that the treated data both converts existing columns and introduces new columns or derived variables. In the next section, we will work through what those new variables are and how to use them.

8.3.1   *The variable score frame*

The `vtreat` process we have worked with up to now centers around `design-TreatmentsC()`, which returns the treatment plan. The treatment plan is an R object with two purposes: to be used in data preparation by the `prepare()` statement, and to deliver a simple summary and initial critique of the proposed variables. This simple summary is encapsulated in the *score frame*. The score frame lists the variables that will be created by the `prepare()` method, along with some information about them. The score frame is our guide to the new variables `vtreat` introduces to make our modeling work easier. Let's take a look at the score frame:

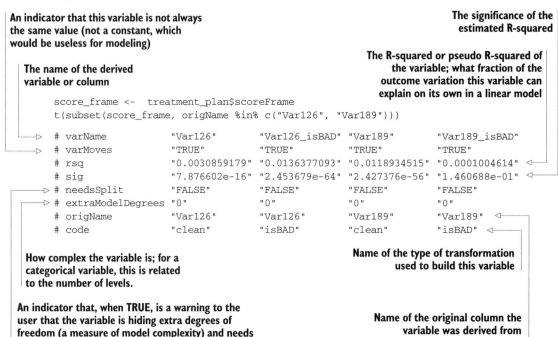

An indicator that this variable is not always the same value (not a constant, which would be useless for modeling)

The name of the derived variable or column

The significance of the estimated R-squared

The R-squared or pseudo R-squared of the variable; what fraction of the outcome variation this variable can explain on its own in a linear model

```
score_frame <-  treatment_plan$scoreFrame
t(subset(score_frame, origName %in% c("Var126", "Var189")))
# varName            "Var126"          "Var126_isBAD" "Var189"          "Var189_isBAD"
# varMoves           "TRUE"            "TRUE"         "TRUE"            "TRUE"
# rsq                "0.0030859179"    "0.0136377093" "0.0118934515"    "0.0001004614"
# sig                "7.876602e-16"    "2.453679e-64" "2.427376e-56"    "1.460688e-01"
# needsSplit         "FALSE"           "FALSE"        "FALSE"           "FALSE"
# extraModelDegrees  "0"               "0"            "0"               "0"
# origName           "Var126"          "Var126"       "Var189"          "Var189"
# code               "clean"           "isBAD"        "clean"           "isBAD"
```

How complex the variable is; for a categorical variable, this is related to the number of levels.

An indicator that, when TRUE, is a warning to the user that the variable is hiding extra degrees of freedom (a measure of model complexity) and needs to be evaluated using cross-validation techniques

Name of the type of transformation used to build this variable

Name of the original column the variable was derived from

The score frame is a data.frame with one row per derived explanatory variable. Each row shows which original variable the derived variable will be produced from (orig-Name), what type of transform will be used to produce the derived variable (code), and some quality summaries about the variable.

In our example, Var126 produces two new or derived variables: Var126 (a cleaned-up version of the original Var126 that has no NA/missing values), and Var116_isBAD (an indicator variable that indicates which rows of Var126 originally held missing or bad values).

The rsq column records the pseudo R-squared of the given variable, which is an indication of how informative the variable would be if treated as a single-variable model for the outcome. The sig column is an estimate of the significance of this pseudo R-squared. Notice that var126_isBAD is more informative than the cleaned up original variable var126. This indicates we should consider including var126_isBAD in our model, even if we decide not to include the cleaned-up version of var126 itself!

Informative missing values

In production systems, missingness is often very informative. Missingness usually indicates the data in question was subject to some condition (temperature out of range, test not run, or something else) and gives a lot of context in an encoded form. We have seen many situations where the information that a variable is missing is more informative than the cleaned-up values of the variable itself.

Let's look at a categorical variable. The original Var218 has two possible levels: cJvF and UYBR.

```
t(subset(score_frame, origName == "Var218"))
```

# varName	"Var218_catP"	"Var218_catB"	"Var218_lev_x_cJvF"	"Var218_lev_x_UYBR"
# varMoves	"TRUE"	"TRUE"	"TRUE"	"TRUE"
# rsq	"0.011014574"	"0.012245152"	"0.005295590"	"0.001970131"
# sig	"2.602574e-52"	"5.924945e-58"	"4.902238e-26"	"1.218959e-10"
# needsSplit	" TRUE"	" TRUE"	"FALSE"	"FALSE"
# extraModelDegrees	"2"	"2"	"0"	"0"
# origName	"Var218"	"Var218"	"Var218"	"Var218"
# code	"catP"	"catB"	"lev"	"lev"

The original variable Var218 produced four derived variables. In particular, notice that the levels cJvF and UYBR each gave us new derived columns or variables.

Level variables (lev)

Var218_lev_x_cJvF and Var218_lev_x_UYBR are indicator variables that have the value 1 when the original Var218 had the values cJvF and UYBR respectively;[8] we will

---

[8] In a real modeling project, we would insist on meaningful level names and a *data dictionary* describing the meanings of the various levels. The KDD2009 contest data did not supply such information, which is a limitation of the contest data and prevents powerful methods such as using variables to join in additional information from external data sources.

discuss the other two variables in a bit. Recall from chapter 7 that most modeling methods work with a categorical variable with *n* possible levels by converting it to *n* (or *n-1*) binary variables, or indicator variables (sometimes referred to as *one-hot encoding* or *dummies*). Many modeling functions in R, such as `lm` or `glm`, do this conversion automatically; others, such as `xgboost`, don't. `vtreat` tries to explicitly one-hot encode categoricals when it is feasible. In this way, the data can be used either by modeling functions like `glm`, or by functions like `xgboost`.

By default, `vtreat` only creates indicator variables for "non-rare" levels: levels that appear more than 2% of the time. As we will see, `Var218` also has some missing values, but the missingness only occurs 1.4% of the time. If missingness had been more informative, then `vtreat` would have also created a `Var218_lev_x_NA` indicator, as well.

Impact variables (catB)

One-hot encoding creates a new variable for every non-rare level of a categorical variable. The `catB` encoding returns a single new variable, with a numerical value for every possible level of the original categorical variable. This value represents how informative a given level is: values with large magnitudes correspond to more-informative levels. We call this the *impact* of the level on the outcome; hence, the term "impact variable." To understand impact variables, let's compare the original `Var218` to `Var218_catB`:

```
comparison <- data.frame(original218 = dTrain$Var218,
                         impact218 = dTrain_treated$Var218_catB)

head(comparison)
  ##    original218  impact218
  ## 1         cJvF -0.2180735
  ## 2         <NA>  1.5155125
  ## 3         UYBR  0.1221393
  ## 4         UYBR  0.1221393
  ## 5         UYBR  0.1221393
  ## 6         UYBR  0.1221393
```

For classification problems, the values of impact encoding are related to the predictions of a logistic regression model that predicts churn from `Var218`. To see this, we'll use the simple missingness treatment that we used in section 4.1.3 to explicitly convert the `NA` values in `Var218` to a new level. We will also use the `logit`, or log-odds function that we saw in chapter 7.

Simple treatment to turn NA into a safe string   **Creates the treated data**

```
treatment_plan_2 <- design_missingness_treatment(dTrain, varlist = vars)
dtrain_2 <- prepare(treatment_plan_2, dTrain)
head(dtrain_2$Var218)

  ## [1] "cJvF"      "_invalid_" "UYBR"      "UYBR"      "UYBR"      "UYBR"

model <- glm(churn ==1  ~ Var218,      ◁─┐ Fits the one-variable logistic
             data = dtrain_2,             │ regression model
             family = "binomial")
```

```
pred <- predict(model,                      Makes predictions
                newdata = dtrain_2,         on the data
                type = "response")

(prevalence <- mean(dTrain$churn == 1) )    Calculates the global
 ## [1] 0.07347764                          probability of churn.

logit <- function(p) {        A function to calculate the logit,
   log ( p / (1-p) )          or log-odds of a probability
}

comparison$glm218 <- logit(pred) - logit(prevalence)    Calculates the catB
 head(comparison)                                        values by hand

##   original218  impact218     glm218
## 1        cJvF -0.2180735 -0.2180735     Notice that the impact codes from
## 2        <NA>  1.5155125  1.5155121     vtreat match the "delta logit"
## 3        UYBR  0.1221393  0.1221392     encoded predictions from the
## 4        UYBR  0.1221393  0.1221392     standard glm model. This helps
## 5        UYBR  0.1221393  0.1221392     illustrate how vtreat is implemented.
## 6        UYBR  0.1221393  0.1221392
```

In our KDD2009 example, we see the catB impact encoding is replacing a categorical variable with the predictions of the corresponding one-variable logistic regression model. For technical reasons, the predictions are in "link space," or logit space, rather than in probability space, and are expressed as a difference from the null model of always predicting the global probability of the outcome. In all cases this data preparation takes a potentially complex categorical variable (that may imply many degrees of freedom, or dummy variable columns) and derives a single numeric column that picks up most of the variable's modeling utility.

When the modeling problem is a regression rather than a classification (the outcome is numeric), the impact encoding is related to the predictions of a one-variable linear regression. We'll see an example of this later in the chapter.

The prevalence variables (catP)

The idea is this: for some variables, knowing how often a level occurs is very informative. For example, for United States ZIP codes, rare ZIP codes may all be from low-population rural areas. The prevalence variable simply encodes what fraction of the time the original variable takes the given level, making these whole-dataset statistics available to the modeling process in a convenient per-example format.

Let's look at what happened to another variable that was giving us trouble: Var200. Recall that this variable has 15415 possible values, of which only 13324 appear in the training data.

Variable ethics

Note: For some applications, certain variables and inference may be either unethical or illegal to use. For example, ZIP code and race are both prohibited in the United States for credit approval decisions, due to historic "red lining" discrimination practices.

Having a sensitivity to ethical issues and becoming familiar with data and modeling law are critical in real-world applications.

```
score_frame[score_frame$origName == "Var200", , drop = FALSE]

#             varName varMoves             rsq             sig needsSplit
            extraModelDegrees origName code
# 361    Var200_catP     TRUE 0.005729835 4.902546e-28
                         TRUE             13323    Var200 catP
# 362    Var200_catB     TRUE 0.001476298 2.516703e-08
                         TRUE             13323    Var200 catB
# 428 Var200_lev_NA     TRUE 0.005729838 4.902365e-28
                        FALSE                 0    Var200  lev
```

Note that `vtreat` only returned one indicator variable, indicating missing values. All the other possible values of Var200 were rare: they occurred less than 2% of the time. For a variable like Var200 with a very large number of levels, it isn't practical to encode all the levels as indicator variables when modeling; it's more computationally efficient to represent the variable as a single numeric variable, like the `catB` variable.

In our example, the `designTreatmentsC()` method recoded the original 230 explanatory variables into 546 new all-numeric explanatory variables that have no missing values. The idea is that these 546 variables are easier to work with and have a good shot of representing most of the original predictive signal in the data. A full description of what sorts of new variables `vtreat` can introduce can be found in the vtreat package documentation.[9]

8.3.2   *Properly using the treatment plan*

The primary purpose of the treatment plan object is to allow `prepare()` to convert new data into a safe, clean form before fitting and applying models. Let's see how that is done. Here, we apply the treatment plan that we learned from the dTrain set to the calibration set, dCal, as shown in figure 8.5.

```
dCal_treated <- prepare(treatment_plan,
                        dCal,
                        parallelCluster = parallel_cluster)
```

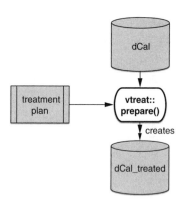

Figure 8.5   Preparing held-out data

---

[9]   See https://winvector.github.io/vtreat/articles/vtreatVariableTypes.html.

Normally, we could now use dCal_treated to fit a model for churn. In this case, we'll use it to illustrate the risk of overfit on transformed variables that have needsSplit == TRUE in the score frame.

As we mentioned earlier, you can think of the Var200_catB variable as a single-variable logistic regression model for churn. This model was fit using dTrain when we called designTreatmentsC(); it was then applied to the dCal data when we called prepare(). Let's look at the AUC of this model on the training and calibration sets:

```
library("sigr")

calcAUC(dTrain_treated$Var200_catB, dTrain_treated$churn)

# [1] 0.8279249

calcAUC(dCal_treated$Var200_catB, dCal_treated$churn)

# [1] 0.5505401
```

Notice the AUC estimated in the training data is 0.83, which seems very good. However, this AUC is not confirmed when we look at the calibration data that was not used to design the variable treatment. Var200_catB is overfit with respect to dTrain_treated. Var200_catB is a useful variable, just not as good as it appears to be on the training data.

> **DO NOT DIRECTLY REUSE THE SAME DATA FOR FITTING THE TREATMENT PLAN AND THE MODEL!** To avoid overfit, the general rule is that whenever a premodeling data processing step uses knowledge of the outcome, you should not use the same data for the premodeling step and the modeling.
>
> The AUC calculations in this section show that Var200_catB looks "too good" on the training data. Any model-fitting algorithm using dTrain_treated to fit a churn model will likely overuse this variable based on its apparent value. The resulting model then fails to realize that value on new data, and it will not predict as well as expected.

The correct procedure is to not reuse dTrain after designing the data treatment plan, but instead use dCal_treated for model training (although in this case, we should use a larger fraction of the available data than we originally allocated). With enough data and the right data split (say, 40% data treatment design, 50% model training, and 10% model testing/evaluation), this is an effective strategy.

In some cases, we may not have enough data for a good three-way split. The built-in vtreat cross-validation procedures allow us to use the same training data both for designing the data treatment plan and to correctly build models. This is what we will master next.

8.4   *Advanced data preparation for classification*

Now that we have seen how to prepare messy data for classification, let's work through how to do this in a more statistically efficient manner. That is, let's master techniques that let us safely reuse the same data for both designing the treatment plan and model training.

8.4.1   *Using mkCrossFrameCExperiment()*

Safely using the same data for data treatment design and for model construction is easy using vtreat. All we do is use the method mkCrossFrameCExperiment() instead of designTreatmentsC(). The designTreatmentsC() method uses cross-validation techniques to produce a special *cross-frame* for training instead of using prepare() on the training data, which we review in figure 8.6.

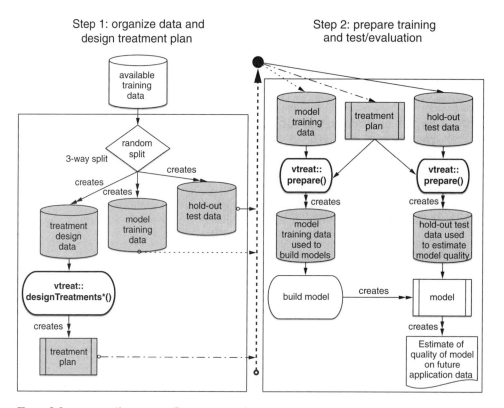

Figure 8.6   vtreat **three-way split strategy again**

The cross-frame is special surrogate training data that behaves as if it hadn't been used to build its own treatment plan. The process is shown in figure 8.7, which we can contrast with figure 8.6.

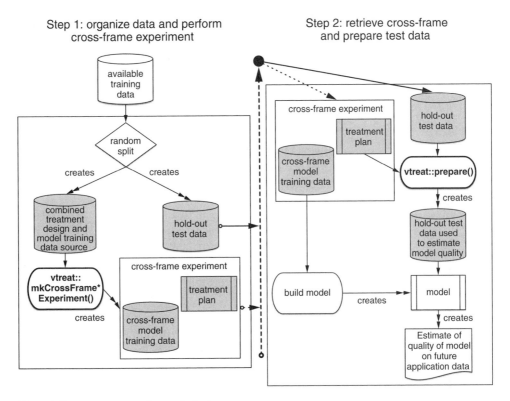

Figure 8.7 `vtreat` **cross-frame strategy**

The user-visible parts of the procedures are small and simple. Figure 8.7 only looks complex because `vtreat` is supplying a very sophisticated service: the proper cross-validated organization that allows us to safely reuse data for both treatment design and model training.

The treatment plan and cross-frame can be built as follows. Here, we use all the data that we originally allocated for training and calibration as a single training set, `dTrainAll`. Then we will evaluate the data on the test set.

Listing 8.6 Advanced data preparation for classification

```
library("vtreat")

parallel_cluster <- parallel::makeCluster(parallel::detectCores())

cross_frame_experiment <- vtreat::mkCrossFrameCExperiment(
  dTrainAll,
  varlist = vars,
  outcomename = "churn",
  outcometarget = 1,
  verbose = FALSE,
  parallelCluster = parallel_cluster)
```

Prepares
the test set
so we can
call the
model on it

```
dTrainAll_treated <- cross_frame_experiment$crossFrame
treatment_plan <- cross_frame_experiment$treatments
score_frame <- treatment_plan$scoreFrame

dTest_treated <- prepare(treatment_plan,
                         dTest,
                         parallelCluster = parallel_cluster)
```

**We will use the
cross-frame to train
the logistic
regression model.**

The steps in listing 8.6 are intentionally very similar to those of listing 8.4. Notice that
dTrainAll_treated is a value returned as part of the experiment, not something we
use prepare() to produce. This overall data treatment strategy implements the ideas
of figure 8.7.

Let's recheck the estimated prediction quality of Var200 on both the training and
test sets:

```
library("sigr")

calcAUC(dTrainAll_treated$Var200_catB, dTrainAll_treated$churn)

# [1] 0.5450466

calcAUC(dTest_treated$Var200_catB, dTest_treated$churn)

# [1] 0.5290295
```

Notice that the estimated utility of Var200 on the training data is now much closer to
its future performance on the test data.[10] This means decisions made on the training
data have a good chance of being correct when later retested on held-out test data or
future application data.

8.4.2   *Building a model*

Now that we have treated our variables, let's try again to build a model.

VARIABLE SELECTION

A key part of building many variable models is selecting what variables to use. Each
variable we use represents a chance of explaining more of the outcome variation (a
chance of building a better model), but also represents a possible source of noise and
overfitting. To control this effect, we often preselect which subset of variables we'll use
to fit. Variable selection can be an important defensive modeling step, even for types
of models that "don't need it." The large number of columns typically seen in modern
data warehouses can overwhelm even state-of-the-art machine learning algorithms.[11]

vtreat supplies two ways to filter variables: the summary statistics in the score
frame and also a method called value_variables_C(). The summaries in the score
frame are the qualities of the linear fits of each variable, so they may undervalue
complex non-linear numeric relationships. In general, you might want to try value_

---

[10] Remember we are estimating performance from data subject to sampling, so all quality estimates are noisy,
and we should not consider this observed difference to be an issue.

[11] See http://www.win-vector.com/blog/2014/02/bad-bayes-an-example-of-why-you-need-hold-out-testing/.

`variables_C()` to properly score non-linear relationships. For our example, we'll fit a linear model, so using the simpler score frame method is appropriate.[12]

We are going to filter the variables on significances, but be aware that significance estimates are themselves very noisy, and variable selection itself can be a source of errors and biases if done improperly.[13] The idea we'll use is this: assume some columns are in fact irrelevant, and use the loosest criterion that would only allow a moderate number of irrelevant columns to pass through. We use the loosest condition to try to minimize the number of actual useful columns or variables that we may accidentally filter out. Note that, while relevant columns should have a significance value close to zero, irrelevant columns should have a significance that is uniformly distributed in the interval zero through one (this is very closely related to the definition of significance). So a good selection filter would be to retain all variables that have a significance of no more than `k/nrow(score_frame)`; we would expect only about `k` irrelevant variables to pass through such a filter.

This variable selection can be performed as follows:

```
k <- 1                          ⟵──────────────────────┐  Uses our filter significances at k / nrow
  (significance_cutoff <- k / nrow(score_frame))        │  (score_frame) heuristic with k = 1
# [1] 0.001831502
score_frame$selected <- score_frame$sig < significance_cutoff

suppressPackageStartupMessages(library("dplyr"))   ⟵──┐  Brings in the dplyr package to
                                                      │  help summarize the selections
score_frame %>%
  group_by(., code, selected) %>%
  summarize(.,
            count = n()) %>%
  ungroup(.) %>%
  cdata::pivot_to_rowrecs(.,
                          columnToTakeKeysFrom = 'selected',
                          columnToTakeValuesFrom = 'count',
                          rowKeyColumns = 'code',
                          sep = '=')

# # A tibble: 5 x 3
#   code  `selected=FALSE` `selected=TRUE`
#   <chr>            <int>           <int>
# 1 catB                12              21
# 2 catP                 7              26
# 3 clean              158              15
# 4 isBAD               60             111
# 5 lev                 74              62
```

The table shows for each converted variable type how many variables were selected or rejected. In particular, notice that almost all the variables of type `clean` (which is the

---

[12] We share a worked `xgboost` solution at https://github.com/WinVector/PDSwR2/blob/master/KDD2009/ KDD2009vtreat.md, which achieves similar performance (as measured by AUC) as the linear model. Things can be improved, but we appear to be getting into a region of diminishing returns.

[13] A good article on this effect is Freedman, "A note on screening regression equations," *The American Statistician*, volume 37, pp. 152-155, 1983.

code for cleaned up numeric variables) are discarded as being unusable. This is possible evidence that linear methods may not be sufficient for this problem, and that we should consider non-linear models instead. In this case, you might use `value_variables_C()` (which returns a structure similar to the score frame) to select variables, and also use the advanced non-linear machine learning methods of chapter 10. In this chapter, we are focusing on the variable preparation steps, so we will only build a linear model, and leave trying different modeling techniques as an important exercise for the reader.[14]

BUILDING A MULTIVARIABLE MODEL

Once we have our variables ready to go, building the model seems relatively straightforward. For this example, we will use a logistic regression (the topic of section 7.2). The code to fit the multivariable model is given in the next listing.

Listing 8.7   Basic variable recoding and selection

```
library("wrapr")

newvars <- score_frame$varName[score_frame$selected]

f <- mk_formula("churn", newvars, outcome_target = 1)
model <- glm(f, data = dTrainAll_treated, family = binomial)
# Warning message:
# glm.fit: fitted probabilities numerically 0 or 1 occurred
```

Builds a formula specifying modeling churn == 1 as a function of all variables

Uses the modeling formula with R's glm() function

Take heed of this warning: it is hinting we should move on to a regularized method such as glmnet.

EVALUATING THE MODEL

Now that we have a model, let's evaluate it on our test data:

Adds the model prediction to the evaluation data as a new column

Again, take heed of this warning: it is hinting we should move on to a regularized method such as glmnet.

```
library("sigr")

dTest_treated$glm_pred <- predict(model,
                            newdata = dTest_treated,
                            type = 'response')
# Warning message:
# In predict.lm(object, newdata, se.fit, scale = 1, type = ifelse(type ==  :
#   prediction from a rank-deficient fit may be misleading

calcAUC(dTest_treated$glm_pred, dTest_treated$churn == 1)
## [1] 0.7232192
```

Calculates the AUC of the model on holdout data

---

[14] Though we do share a worked `xgboost` solution here: https://github.com/WinVector/PDSwR2/blob/master/KDD2009/KDD2009vtreat.md.

```
permTestAUC(dTest_treated, "glm_pred", "churn", yTarget = 1)
  ## [1] "AUC test alt. hyp. AUC>AUC(permuted): (AUC=0.7232, s.d.=0.01535, p<1
     e-05)."

var_aucs <- vapply(newvars,
       function(vi) {
         calcAUC(dTrainAll_treated[[vi]], dTrainAll_treated$churn == 1)
       }, numeric(1))
(best_train_aucs <- var_aucs[var_aucs >= max(var_aucs)])
## Var216_catB
##   0.5873512
```

Calculates the AUC a second time, using an alternative method that also estimates a standard deviation or error bar

Here we calculate the best single variable model AUC for comparison.

The model's AUC is 0.72. This is not as good as the winning entry's 0.76 (on different test data), but much better than the quality of the best input variable treated as a single variable model (which showed an AUC of 0.59). Keep in mind that the perm-TestAUC() calculation indicated a standard deviation of the AUC estimate of 0.015 for a test set of this size. This means a difference of plus or minus 0.015 in AUC is not statistically significant.

Turning the logistic regression model into a classifier

As we can see from the double density plot of the model's scores (figure 8.8), this model only does a moderate job of separating accounts that churn from those that don't. If we made the mistake of using this model as a hard classifier where all individuals with a predicted churn propensity above 50% are considered at risk, we would see the following awful performance:

```
table(prediction = dTest_treated$glm_pred >= 0.5,
      truth = dTest$churn)
#            truth
# prediction   -1    1
#      FALSE 4591  375
#      TRUE     8    1
```

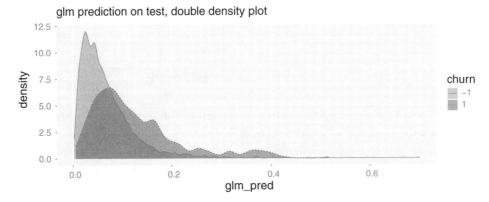

Figure 8.8 Distribution of the glm model's scores on test data

The model only identifies nine individuals with such a high probability, and only one of those churn. Remember this was an unbalanced classification problem; only 7.6% of the test examples do in fact churn. What the model can identify is individuals at an elevated risk of churning, not those that will certainly churn. For example, what if we ask the model for the individuals that are predicted to have double the expected churn risk:

```
table(prediction = dTest_treated$glm_pred>0.15,
      truth = dTest$churn)
#            truth
# prediction   -1    1
#      FALSE 4243  266
#      TRUE   356  110
```

Notice that in this case, using 0.15 as our scoring threshold, the model identified 466 potentially at-risk accounts, of which 101 did in fact churn. This subset therefore has a churn rate of 24%, or about 3 times the overall churn rate. And this model identified 110 of the 376 churners, or 29% of them. From a business point of view, this model is identifying a 10% subgroup of the population that is responsible for 29% of the churning. This can be useful.

In section 7.2.3, we saw how to present the family of trade-offs between recall (what fraction of the churners are detected) and enrichment or lift (how much more common churning is in the selected set) as a graph. Figure 8.9 shows the plot of recall and enrichment as a function of threshold for the churn model.

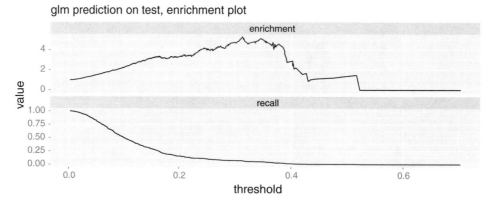

Figure 8.9   `glm` recall and enrichment as a function of threshold

One way to use figure 8.9 is to draw a vertical line at a chosen x-axis threshold, say 0.2. Then the height at which this vertical line crosses each curve tells us the simultaneous enrichment and recall we would see if we classify scores above our threshold as positive. In this case, we would have a recall of around 0.12 (meaning we identify about 12% of the at-risk accounts), and an enrichment of around 3 (meaning the population we warn about has an account cancellation rate of 3 times the general population, indicating this is indeed an enhanced-risk population).

The code to produce these charts looks like this:

```
WVPlots::DoubleDensityPlot(dTest_treated, "glm_pred", "churn",
                          "glm prediction on test, double density plot")

WVPlots::PRTPlot(dTest_treated, "glm_pred", "churn",
                "glm prediction on test, enrichment plot",
                truthTarget = 1,
                plotvars = c("enrichment", "recall"),
                thresholdrange = c(0, 1.0))
```

And now we have worked a substantial classification problem using vtreat.

8.5 *Preparing data for regression modeling*

Preparing data for regression is very similar to preparing data for classification. Instead of calling designTreatmentsC() or mkCrossFrameCExperiment(), we call designTreatmentsN() or mkCrossFrameNExperiment().

> **Example**   *You wish to predict automobile fuel economy stated in miles per gallon from other facts about cars, such as weight and horsepower.*

To simulate this scenario, we will use the Auto MPG Data Set from the UCI Machine Learning Repository. We can load this data from the file auto_mpg.RDS in the directory auto_mpg/ of https://github.com/WinVector/PDSwR2/ (after downloading this repository).

```
auto_mpg <- readRDS('auto_mpg.RDS')        ⎤  Take a quick look
                                           ⎦  at the data.
knitr::kable(head(auto_mpg))        ⟵
```

mpg	cylinders	displacement	horsepower	weight	acceleration	model_year	origin	car_name
18	8	307	130	3504	12.0	70	1	"chevrolet chevelle malibu"
15	8	350	165	3693	11.5	70	1	"buick skylark 320"
18	8	318	150	3436	11.0	70	1	"plymouth satellite"
16	8	304	150	3433	12.0	70	1	"amc rebel sst"
17	8	302	140	3449	10.5	70	1	"ford torino"
15	8	429	198	4341	10.0	70	1	"ford galaxie 500"

Figure 8.10   The first few rows of the `auto_mpg` data

Having glanced at the data in figure 8.10, let's take the "bull in the china shop" approach to modeling, and directly call lm() without examining or treating the data:

```
library("wrapr")

vars <- c("cylinders", "displacement",        Jump into modeling without
          "horsepower", "weight", "acceleration",   bothering to treat the data.
          "model_year", "origin")
f <- mk_formula("mpg", vars)
model <- lm(f, data = auto_mpg)              Adds the model
                                             predictions as a
auto_mpg$prediction <- predict(model, newdata = auto_mpg)   new column

str(auto_mpg[!complete.cases(auto_mpg), , drop = FALSE])

# 'data.frame':     6 obs. of  10 variables:
# $ mpg          : num   25 21 40.9 23.6 34.5 23
# $ cylinders    : num   4 6 4 4 4 4              Notice that these cars
# $ displacement : num   98 200 85 140 100 151    do not have a recorded
# $ horsepower   : num   NA NA NA NA NA NA         horsepower.
# $ weight       : num   2046 2875 1835 2905 2320 ...
# $ acceleration : num   19 17 17.3 14.3 15.8 20.5
# $ model_year   : num   71 74 80 80 81 82
# $ origin       : Factor w/ 3 levels "1","2","3": 1 1 2 1 2 1
# $ car_name     : chr   "\"ford pinto\"" "\"ford maverick\"" "\"renault lecar
      deluxe\"" ...
# $ prediction   : num   NA NA NA NA NA NA         So these cars do not
                                                   get a prediction.
```

Because the dataset had missing values, the model could not return a prediction for every row. Now, we'll try again, using vtreat to treat the data first:

```
library("vtreat")

cfe <- mkCrossFrameNExperiment(auto_mpg, vars, "mpg",    Try it again with vtreat
                               verbose = FALSE)          data preparation.
treatment_plan <- cfe$treatments
auto_mpg_treated <- cfe$crossFrame
score_frame <- treatment_plan$scoreFrame
new_vars <- score_frame$varName

newf <- mk_formula("mpg", new_vars)
new_model <- lm(newf, data = auto_mpg_treated)

auto_mpg$prediction <- predict(new_model, newdata = auto_mpg_treated)
# Warning in predict.lm(new_model, newdata = auto_mpg_treated): prediction
# from a rank-deficient fit may be misleading
str(auto_mpg[!complete.cases(auto_mpg), , drop = FALSE])
# 'data.frame':     6 obs. of  10 variables:
# $ mpg          : num   25 21 40.9 23.6 34.5 23
# $ cylinders    : num   4 6 4 4 4 4
# $ displacement : num   98 200 85 140 100 151
# $ horsepower   : num   NA NA NA NA NA NA
# $ weight       : num   2046 2875 1835 2905 2320 ...
# $ acceleration : num   19 17 17.3 14.3 15.8 20.5
# $ model_year   : num   71 74 80 80 81 82
# $ origin       : Factor w/ 3 levels "1","2","3": 1 1 2 1 2 1
```

```
#  $ car_name    : chr  "\"ford pinto\"" "\"ford maverick\"" "\"renault lecar
      deluxe\"" ...
#  $ prediction  : num  24.6 22.4 34.2 26.1 33.3 ... ◁─┐
```

> **Now we can make predictions, even
> for items that have missing data.**

Now, the model returns a prediction for every row, including those with missing data.

8.6 *Mastering the vtreat package*

Now that we have seen how to use the vtreat package, we will take some time to review what the package is doing for us. This is easiest to see with toy-sized examples.

vtreat is designed to prepare data for supervised machine learning or predictive modeling. The package is designed to help with the task of relating a bunch of input or explanatory variables to a single output to be predicted or to a dependent variable.

8.6.1 *The vtreat phases*

As illustrated in figure 8.11, vtreat works in two phases: a design phase and an application/prepare phase. In the design phase, vtreat learns details of your data. For each explanatory variable, it estimates the variable's relationship to the outcome, so both the explanatory variables and the dependent variable must be available. In the application phase, vtreat introduces new variables that are derived from the explanatory variables, but are better suited for simple predictive modeling. The transformed

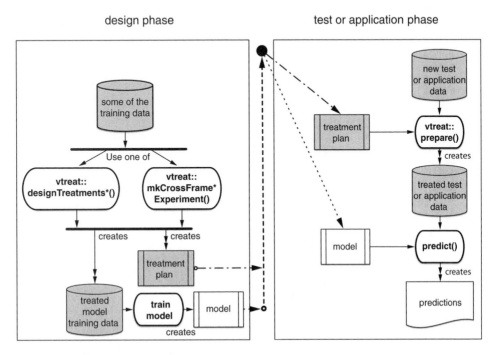

Figure 8.11 The two vtreat phases

data is all numeric and has no missing values.[15] R itself has methods for dealing with missing values, including many missing value imputation packages.[16] R also has a canonical method to convert arbitrary `data.frames` to numeric data: `model.matrix()`, which many models use to accept arbitrary data. `vtreat` is a specialized tool for these tasks that is designed to work very well for supervised machine learning or predictive modeling tasks.

For the treatment-design phase, call one of the following functions:

- *designTreatmentsC()*—Designs a variable treatment plan for a binary classification task. A binary classification task is where we want to predict if an example is in a given category, or predict the probability that an example is in the given category.

- *designTreatmentsN()*—Designs a variable treatment plan for a regression task. A regression task predicts a numeric outcome, given example numeric outcomes.

- *designTreatmentsZ()*—Designs a simple variable treatment plan that does not look at the training data outcomes. This plan deals with missing values and recodes strings as indicator variables (one-hot encoding), but it does not produce impact variables (which require knowledge of the training data outcomes).

- *design_missingness_treatment()*—Designs a very simple treatment that only deals with missing values, but does not one-hot encode categorical variables. Instead, it replaces NA with the token `"_invalid_"`.

- *mkCrossFrameCExperiment()*—Prepares data for classification, using a cross-validation technique so the data used to design the variable treatment can be safely reused to train the model.

- *mkCrossFrameNExperiment()*—Prepares data for regression, using a cross-validation technique so the data used to design the variable treatment can be safely reused to train the model.

For the application or data preparation phase, we always call the `prepare()` method.

The `vtreat` package comes with a large amount of documentation and examples that can be found at https://winvector.github.io/vtreat/. However, in addition to knowing how to operate the package, it is critical that data scientists know what the packages they use are doing for them. So we will discuss what `vtreat` actually does here.

The concepts we need to review include these:

- Missing values
- Indicator variables

---

[15] Remember: missing values are not the only thing that can go wrong with the data, and not the only point `vtreat` addresses.

[16] See https://cran.r-project.org/web/views/MissingData.html.

- Impact coding
- The treatment plan
- The variable score frame
- The cross-frame

These are a lot of concepts, but they are key to data repair and preparation. We will keep this concrete by working specific, but tiny, examples. Larger examples showing the performance of these can be found at https://arxiv.org/abs/1611.09477.

8.6.2   Missing values

As we have discussed before, R has a special code for values that are missing, not known, or not available: NA. Many modeling procedures will not accept data with missing values, so if they occur, we must do something about them. The common strategies include these:

- *Restricting down to "complete cases"*—Using only the data rows where no columns have missing values. This can be problematic for model training, as the complete cases may not be distributed the same or representative of the actual dataset. Also, this strategy does not give a good idea of how to score new data that has missing values. There are some theories about how to reweight data to make it more representative, but we do not encourage these methods.
- *Missing-value imputation*—These are methods that use the non-missing values to infer or impute values (or distributions of values) for the missing values. An R task view dedicated to these methods can be found at https://cran.r-project .org/web/views/MissingData.html.
- *Using models that tolerate missing values*—Some implementations of decision trees or random forests can tolerate missing values.
- *Treating missingness as observable information*—Replacing missing values with stand-in information.

vtreat supplies an implementation of the last idea (treating missingness as observable information), as this is easy to do and very suitable for supervised machine learning or predictive modeling. The idea is simple: the missing values are replaced with some stand-in value (it can be zero, or it can be the average of the non-missing values), and an extra column is added to indicate this replacement has taken place. This extra column gives any modeling step an extra degree of freedom, or the ability to treat the imputed values separately from not-imputed values.

The following is a simple example showing the addition of the transformation:

```
library("wrapr")                                        Brings in the wrapr package
                                                        for build_frame and the
d <- build_frame(                                       wrapr "dot pipe"
   "x1"     , "x2"         , "x3", "y" |
   1        , "a"          , 6   , 10  |
   NA_real_, "b"           , 7   , 20  |
   3        , NA_character_, 8   , 30  )
```

```
knitr::kable(d)

plan1 <- vtreat::design_missingness_treatment(d)
vtreat::prepare(plan1, d) %.>%    ◁──────
    knitr::kable(.)
```

> Using wrapr's dot pipe instead of magrittr's forward pipe. The dot pipe requires the explicit dot argument notation discussed in chapter 5.

Notice that in figure 8.12 the x1 column has the missing value, and that value is replaced in figure 8.13 by a stand-in value, the average of the known values. The treated or prepared data (see figure 8.13) also has a new column, x1_isBAD, indicating where x1 was replaced. Finally, notice that for the string-valued column x2, the NA value is replaced with a special level code.

x1	x2	x3	y
1	a	6	10
NA	b	7	20
3	NA	8	30

Figure 8.12   Our simple example data: raw

x1	x1_isBAD	x2	x3	y
1	0	a	6	10
2	1	b	7	20
3	0	*invalid*	8	30

Figure 8.13   Our simple example data: treated

8.6.3 Indicator variables

Many statistical and machine learning procedures expect all variables to be numeric. Some R users may not be aware of this, as many R model implementations call model.matrix() under the covers to convert arbitrary data to numeric data. For real-world projects, we advise using a more controllable explicit transformation such as vtreat.[17]

This transformation goes by a number of names, including indicator variables, dummy variables, and one-hot encoding. The idea is this: for each possible value of a string-valued variable, we create a new data column. We set each of these new columns to 1 when the string-valued variable has a value matching the column label, and zero otherwise. This is easy to see in the following example:

```
d <- build_frame(
    "x1"     , "x2"          , "x3", "y" |
    1        , "a"           , 6  , 10  |
    NA_real_, "b"           , 7  , 20  |
    3        , NA_character_, 8  , 30  )
```

---

[17] However, in this book, for didactic purposes, we will try to minimize the number of preparation steps in each example when these steps are not the subject being discussed.

```
print(d)
#     x1    x2 x3  y
# 1  1      a  6 10          The second value
# 2 NA      b  7 20       ◁── of x2 is b.
# 3  3   <NA>  8 30
plan2 <- vtreat::designTreatmentsZ(d,
                                   varlist = c("x1", "x2", "x3"),
                                   verbose = FALSE)
vtreat::prepare(plan2, d)
#    x1 x1_isBAD x3 x2_lev_NA x2_lev_x_a x2_lev_x_b     In the second row of
# 1  1        0  6         0          1          0      the treated data,
# 2  2        1  7         0          0          1  ◁── x2_lev_x_b = 1.
# 3  3        0  8         1          0          0
```

Notice that x2_lev_x_b is 1 in the second prepared data row. This is how the transformed data retains the information that the x2 variable originally had the value of b in this row.

As we saw in the discussions of lm() and glm() in chapter 7, it is traditional statistical practice to not actually reserve a new column for one possible level of the string-valued variable. This level is called the *reference level*. We can identify rows where the string-valued variable was equal to the reference level, as all the other level columns are zero in such rows (other rows have exactly one 1 in the level columns). For supervised learning in general, and especially for advanced techniques such as regularized regression, we recommend encoding all levels, as seen here.

8.6.4 *Impact coding*

Impact coding is a good idea that gets rediscovered often under different names (*effects* coding, *impact* coding, and more recently *target* encoding).[18]

When a string-valued variable has thousands of possible values or levels, producing a new indicator column for each possible level causes extreme data expansion and overfitting (if the model fitter can even converge in such situations). So instead we use an *impact code*: replacing the level code with its effect as a single-variable model. This is what produced derived variables of type catB in our KDD2009 credit account cancellation example, and produced catN-style variables in the case of regression.

Let's see the effect of a simple numeric prediction or regression example:

```
d <- build_frame(
   "x1"      , "x2"          , "x3", "y" |
   1         , "a"           , 6   , 10  |
   NA_real_, "b"             , 7   , 20  |
   3         , NA_character_, 8    , 30  )

print(d)
#     x1 x2 x3  y
```

---

[18] The earliest discussion we can find on effects coding is Robert E. Sweeney and Edwin F. Ulveling, "A Transformation for Simplifying the Interpretation of Coefficients of Binary Variables in Regression Analysis." *The American Statistician*, 26(5), 30–32, 1972. We, the authors, have produced research and popularized the methodology among R and Kaggle users, adding key cross-validation methods similar to a method called "stacking" https://arxiv.org/abs/1611.09477.

```
# 1  1     a  6 10
# 2 NA     b  7 20
# 3  3 <NA>  8 30
plan3 <- vtreat::designTreatmentsN(d,
                                   varlist = c("x1", "x2", "x3"),
                                   outcomename = "y",
                                   codeRestriction = "catN",
                                   verbose = FALSE)
vtreat::prepare(plan3, d)
#   x2_catN  y
# 1    -10 10
# 2      0 20
# 3     10 30
```

The impact-coded variable is in the new column named x2_catN. Notice that in the first row it is -10, as the y-value is 10, which is 10 below the average value of y. This encoding of "conditional delta from mean" is where names like "impact code" or "effect code" come from.

The impact coding for categorical variables is similar, except they are in logarithmic units, just like the logistic regression in section 8.3.1. In this case, for data this small, the naive value of x2_catB would be minus infinity in rows 1 and 3, and plus infinity in row 2 (as the x2 level values perfectly predict or separate cases whether y == 20 or not). The fact that we see values near plus or minus 10 is due to an important adjustment called *smoothing* which says when computing conditional probabilities, add a little bias towards "no effect" for safer calculations.[19] An example of using vtreat to prepare data for a possible classification task is given next:

```
plan4 <- vtreat::designTreatmentsC(d,
                                   varlist = c("x1", "x2", "x3"),
                                   outcomename = "y",
                                   outcometarget = 20,
                                   codeRestriction = "catB",
                                   verbose = FALSE)
vtreat::prepare(plan4, d)
#      x2_catB  y
# 1 -8.517343 10
# 2  9.903538 20
# 3 -8.517343 30
```

Smoothing

Smoothing is a method to prevent some degree of overfit and nonsense answers on small data. The idea of smoothing is an attempt to obey *Cromwell's rule* that no probability estimate of zero should ever be used in empirical probabilistic reasoning. This is because if you're combining probabilities by multiplication (the most common method of combining probability estimates), then once some term is 0, the entire

---

[19] A reference on smoothing can be found here: https://en.wikipedia.org/wiki/Additive_smoothing.

estimate will be 0 *no matter what the values of the other terms are*. The most common form of smoothing is called *Laplace smoothing*, which counts k successes out of n trials as a success ratio of (k+1)/(n+1) and not as a ratio of k/n (defending against the k=0 case). Frequentist statisticians think of smoothing as a form of regularization, and Bayesian statisticians think of smoothing in terms of priors.

8.6.5 *The treatment plan*

The treatment plan specifies how training data will be processed before using it to fit a model, and how new data will be processed before applying the model. It is returned directly by the design*() methods. For the mkExperiment*() methods, the treatment plan is the item with the key treatments on the returned result. The following code shows the structure of a treatment plan:

```
class(plan4)
# [1] "treatmentplan"

names(plan4)

# [1] "treatments"   "scoreFrame"  "outcomename" "vtreatVersion" "outcomeType"

# [6] "outcomeTarget" "meanY"              "splitmethod"
```

THE VARIABLE SCORE FRAME

An important item included in all treatment plans is the score frame. It can be pulled out of a treatment plan as follows (continuing our earlier example):

```
plan4$scoreFrame

#    varName varMoves rsq    sig needsSplit extraModelDegrees origName code
# 1 x2_catB    TRUE   0.0506719 TRUE    2        x2 catB
```

The score frame is a data.frame with one row per derived explanatory variable. Each row shows which original variable the derived variable was produced from (orig-Name), what type of transform was used to produce the derived variable (code), and some quality summaries about the variable. For instance, needsSplit is an indicator that, when TRUE, indicates the variable is complex and requires cross-validated scoring, which is in fact how vtreat produces the variable quality estimates.

8.6.6 *The cross-frame*

A critical innovation of vtreat is the *cross-frame*. The cross-frame is an item found in the list of objects returned by the mkCrossFrame*Experiment() methods. It is an innovation that allows the safe use of the same data both for the design of the variable treatments and for training a model. Without this cross-validation method, you must reserve some of the training data to build the variable treatment plan and a disjoint set of training data to fit treated data. Otherwise, the composite system (data preparation plus model application) may suffer from severe nested model bias: producing a model that appears good on training data, but later fails on test or application data.

THE DANGERS OF NAIVELY REUSING DATA

Here is an example of the problem. Suppose we start with some example data where there is in fact no relation between x and y. In this case, we know that any relation we think we find between them is just an artifact of our procedures, and not really there.

Listing 8.8   An information-free dataset

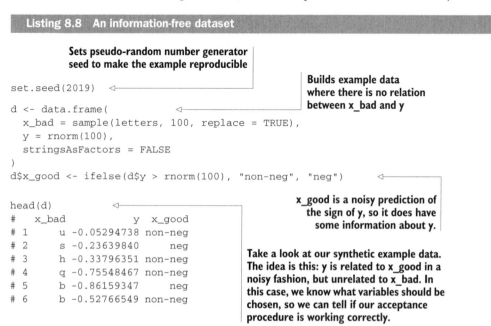

Sets pseudo-random number generator
seed to make the example reproducible

```
set.seed(2019)
```

Builds example data
where there is no relation
between x_bad and y

```
d <- data.frame(
  x_bad = sample(letters, 100, replace = TRUE),
  y = rnorm(100),
  stringsAsFactors = FALSE
)
d$x_good <- ifelse(d$y > rnorm(100), "non-neg", "neg")
```

x_good is a noisy prediction of
the sign of y, so it does have
some information about y.

```
head(d)
#   x_bad            y x_good
# 1     u -0.05294738 non-neg
# 2     s -0.23639840     neg
# 3     h -0.33796351 non-neg
# 4     q -0.75548467 non-neg
# 5     b -0.86159347     neg
# 6     b -0.52766549 non-neg
```

Take a look at our synthetic example data.
The idea is this: y is related to x_good in a
noisy fashion, but unrelated to x_bad. In
this case, we know what variables should be
chosen, so we can tell if our acceptance
procedure is working correctly.

We naively use the training data to create the treatment plan, and then prepare the same data prior to fitting the model.

Listing 8.9   The dangers of reusing data

Designs a variable treatment plan
using x_bad and x_good to predict y

```
plan5 <- vtreat::designTreatmentsN(d,
                                   varlist = c("x_bad", "x_good"),
                                   outcomename = "y",
                                   codeRestriction = "catN",
                                   minFraction = 2,
                                   verbose = FALSE)

class(plan5)
# [1] "treatmentplan"
```

```
  print(plan5)
  #   origName    varName code        rsq           sig extraModelDegrees

  # 1   x_bad   x_bad_catN catN 4.906903e-05 9.448548e-01                 24
  # 2   x_good x_good_catN catN 2.602702e-01 5.895285e-08                  1

  training_data1 <- vtreat::prepare(plan5, d)

  res1 <- vtreat::patch_columns_into_frame(d, training_data1)
   head(res1)
  #   x_bad  x_good x_bad_catN x_good_catN              y
  # 1     u non-neg  0.4070979   0.4305195 -0.05294738
  # 2     s     neg -0.1133011  -0.5706886 -0.23639840
  # 3     h non-neg -0.3202346   0.4305195 -0.33796351
  # 4     q non-neg -0.5447443   0.4305195 -0.75548467
  # 5     b     neg -0.3890076  -0.5706886 -0.86159347
  # 6     b non-neg -0.3890076   0.4305195 -0.52766549

  sigr::wrapFTest(res1, "x_good_catN", "y")
  # [1] "F Test summary: (R2=0.2717, F(1,98)=36.56, p<1e-05)."

  sigr::wrapFTest(res1, "x_bad_catN", "y")
  # [1] "F Test summary: (R2=0.2342, F(1,98)=29.97, p<1e-05)."
```

Combines the data frames d and training_data1, using training_data1 when there are columns with duplicate names

Calls prepare() on the same data used to design the treatment plan—this is not always safe, as we shall see.

x_bad_catN's F-test is inflated and falsely looks significant. This is due to failure to use cross-validated methods.

Uses a statistical F-test to check the predictive power of x_good_catN

Notice that the derived variable x_good_catN comes out as having a significant signal, and x_bad_catN does not. This is due to the proper use of cross-validation in the vtreat quality estimates.

In this example, notice the sigr F-test reports an R-squared of 0.23 between x_bad_catN and the outcome variable y. This is the technical term for checking if the fraction of variation explained (itself called the R-squared) is statistically insignificant (a common occurrence under pure chance). So we *want* the true R-squared to be high (near 1) and true F-test significance low (near zero) for the good variable. We also expect the true R-squared to be low (near 0), and the true F-test significance to be non-vanishing (not near zero) for the bad variable.

However, notice both the good and bad variables received favorable evaluations! This is an error, and happened because the variables we are testing, x_good_catN and x_bad_catN, are both impact codes of high-cardinality string-valued variables. When we test these variables on the same data they were constructed on, we suffer from overfitting, which erroneously inflates our variable quality estimate. In this case, a lot of the *apparent* quality of fit is actually just a measure of a variable's complexity (or ability to overfit).

Also notice that the R-squared and significance reported in the score frame correctly indicate that x_bad_catN is not a high-quality variable (R-squared near zero, and significance not near zero). This is because the score frame uses cross-validation to estimate variable significance. This matters because a modeling process involving multiple variables might pick the variable x_bad_catN over other actual useful variables due to x_bad_catN's overfit inflated quality score.

As mentioned in previous sections, the way to fix the overfitting is to use one portion of our training data for the designTreatments*() step and a disjoint portion of our training data for the variable use or evaluation (such as the sigr::wrapFTest() step).

THE CROSS-FRAME TO SAFELY REUSE DATA

Another way to do this, which lets us use all of the training data both for the design of the variable treatment plan and for model fitting, is called the *cross-frame* method. This is a special cross-validation method built into vtreat's mkCrossFrame*Experiment() methods. All we do in this case is call mkCrossFrameNExperiment() instead of design-TreatmentsN and get the prepared training data from the crossFrame element of the returned list object (instead of calling prepare()). For future test or application data, we do call prepare() from the treatment plan (which is returned as the treatments item on the returned list object), but for training we do not call prepare().

The code is as follows.

Listing 8.10   Using `mkCrossFrameNExperiment()`

```
cfe <- vtreat::mkCrossFrameNExperiment(d,
                                   varlist = c("x_bad", "x_good"),
                                   outcomename = "y",
                                   codeRestriction = "catN",
                                   minFraction = 2,
                                   verbose = FALSE)
plan6 <- cfe$treatments

training_data2 <- cfe$crossFrame
res2 <- vtreat::patch_columns_into_frame(d, training_data2)

head(res2)
#    x_bad  x_good x_bad_catN x_good_catN          y
# 1      u non-neg  0.2834739   0.4193180 -0.05294738
# 2      s     neg -0.1085887  -0.6212118 -0.23639840
# 3      h non-neg  0.0000000   0.5095586 -0.33796351
# 4      q non-neg -0.5142570   0.5095586 -0.75548467
# 5      b     neg -0.3540889  -0.6212118 -0.86159347
# 6      b non-neg -0.3540889   0.4193180 -0.52766549

sigr::wrapFTest(res2, "x_bad_catN", "y")
# [1] "F Test summary: (R2=-0.1389, F(1,98)=-11.95, p=n.s.)."

sigr::wrapFTest(res2, "x_good_catN", "y")
# [1] "F Test summary: (R2=0.2532, F(1,98)=33.22, p<1e-05)."
```

```
plan6$scoreFrame                            ◁
  #      varName varMoves        rsq            sig needsSplit
  # 1  x_bad_catN     TRUE 0.01436145 2.349865e-01       TRUE
  # 2 x_good_catN     TRUE 0.26478467 4.332649e-08       TRUE
  #   extraModelDegrees origName code
  # 1                24    x_bad catN
  # 2                 1   x_good catN
```

The F-tests on the data and the scoreFrame statistics now largely agree.

Notice now that sigr::wrapFTest() correctly considers x_bad_catN to be a low-value variable. This scheme also scores good variables correctly, meaning we can tell good from bad. We can use the cross-frame training_data2 for fitting models, with good protection against overfit from the variable treatment.

Nested model bias

Overfit due to using the result of one model as an input to another is called *nested-model bias*. With vtreat, this could be an issue with the impact codes, which are themselves models. For data treatments that do not look at the outcome, like design_missingness_treatment() and designTreatmentsZ(), it is safe to use the same data to design the treatment plan and fit the model. However, when the data treatment uses the outcome, we suggest either an additional data split or using the mkCross-Frame*Experiment()/$crossFrame pattern from section 8.4.1.

vtreat uses cross-validation procedures to create the cross-frame. For details, see https://winvector.github.io/vtreat/articles/vtreatCrossFrames.html.

> **DESIGNTREATMENTS*() VS. MKCROSSFRAME*EXPERIMENT()** For larger datasets, it's easier to use a three-way split of the training data and the design-Treatments*()/prepare() pattern to design the treatment plan, fit the model, and evaluate it. For datasets that seem too small to split three ways (especially datasets with a very large number of variables), you may get better models by using the mkCrossFrame*Experiment()/prepare() pattern.

Summary

Real-world data is often messy. Raw uninspected and untreated data may crash your modeling or predicting step, or may give bad results. "Fixing" data does not compete with having better data. But being able to work with the data you have (instead of the data you want) is an advantage.

In addition to many domain-specific or problem-specific problems, you may find that in your data, there are a number of common problems that should be anticipated and dealt with systematically. vtreat is a package specialized for preparing data for supervised machine learning or predictive modeling tasks. It can also reduce your project documentation requirements through its citable documentation.[20] However, remember that tools are not an excuse to avoid looking at your data.

---

[20] See https://arxiv.org/abs/1611.09477.

In this chapter you have learned

- How to use the `vtreat` package's `designTreatments*()`/`prepare()` pattern with a three-way split of your training data to prepare messy data for model fitting and model application
- How to use the `vtreat` package's `mkCrossFrame*Experiment()`/`prepare()` pattern with a two-way split of your training data to prepare messy data for model fitting and model application, when statistical efficiency is important

Unsupervised methods

This chapter covers

- Using R's clustering functions to explore data and look for similarities
- Choosing the right number of clusters
- Evaluating a cluster
- Using R's association rules functions to find patterns of co-occurrence in data
- Evaluating a set of association rules

In the previous chapter, we covered using the `vtreat` package to prepare messy real-world data for modeling. In this chapter, we'll look at methods to discover unknown relationships in data. These methods are called *unsupervised methods*. With unsupervised methods, there's no outcome that you're trying to predict; instead, you want to discover patterns in the data that perhaps you hadn't previously suspected. For example, you may want to find groups of customers with similar purchase patterns, or correlations between population movement and socioeconomic factors. We will still consider this pattern discovery to be "modeling," and as such, the outcomes of the algorithms can still be evaluated, as shown in the mental model for this chapter (figure 9.1).

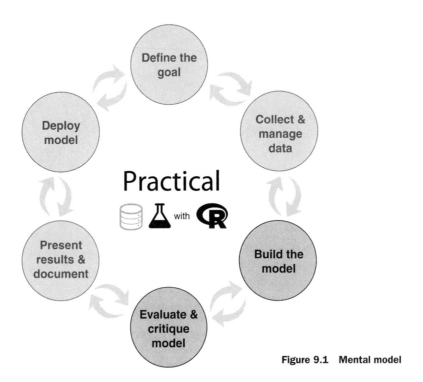

Figure 9.1   Mental model

Unsupervised analyses are often not ends in themselves; rather, they're ways of finding relationships and patterns that can be used to build predictive models. In fact, we encourage you to think of unsupervised methods as exploratory—procedures that help you get your hands in the data—rather than as black-box approaches that mysteriously and automatically give you "the right answer."

In this chapter, we'll look at two classes of unsupervised methods:

- *Cluster analysis* finds groups with similar characteristics.
- *Association rule mining* finds elements or properties in the data that tend to occur together.

9.1   *Cluster analysis*

In cluster analysis, the goal is to group the observations in your data into *clusters* such that every datum in a cluster is more similar to other datums in the same cluster than it is to datums in other clusters. For example, a company that offers guided tours might want to cluster its clients by behavior and tastes: which countries they like to visit; whether they prefer adventure tours, luxury tours, or educational tours; what kinds of activities they participate in; and what sorts of sites they like to visit. Such information can help the company design attractive travel packages and target the appropriate segments of their client base with them.

Cluster analysis is a topic worthy of a book in itself; in this chapter, we'll discuss two approaches. *Hierarchical clustering* finds nested groups of clusters. An example of hierarchical clustering might be the standard plant taxonomy, which classifies plants by family, then genus, then species, and so on. The second approach we'll cover is *k-means*, which is a quick and popular way of finding clusters in quantitative data.

> ### Clustering and density estimation
> Historically, cluster analysis is related to the problem of *density estimation*: if you think of your data as living in a large dimensional space, then you want to find the regions of the space where the data is densest. If those regions are distinct, or nearly so, then you have clusters.

9.1.1 Distances

In order to cluster, you need the notions of *similarity* and *dissimilarity*. Dissimilarity can be thought of as distance, so that the points in a cluster are closer to each other than they are to the points in other clusters. This is shown in figure 9.2.

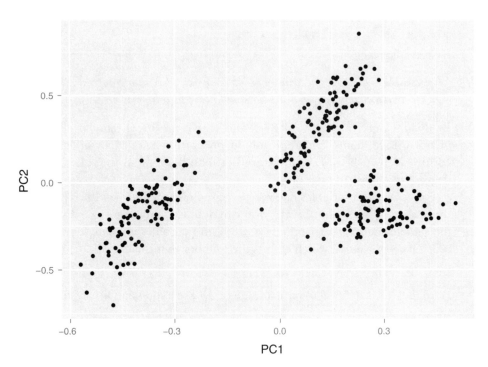

Figure 9.2   An example of data in three clusters

Different application areas will have different notions of distance and dissimilarity. In this section, we'll cover a few of the most common ones:

- Euclidean distance
- Hamming distance
- Manhattan (city block) distance
- Cosine similarity

EUCLIDEAN DISTANCE

> **Example**   *Suppose you have measurements on how many minutes per day subjects spend on different activities, and you want to group the subjects by their activity patterns.*

Since your measurements are numerical and continuous, *Euclidean distance* is a good distance to use for clustering. Euclidean distance is the measure people tend to think of when they think of "distance." Optimizing squared Euclidean distance is the basis of k-means. Of course, Euclidean distance only makes sense when all the data is real-valued (quantitative). If the data is categorical (in particular, binary), then other distances should be used.

The Euclidean distance between two vectors x and y is defined as

```
edist(x, y) <- sqrt((x[1] - y[1])^2 + (x[2] - y[2])^2 + ...)
```

HAMMING DISTANCE

> **Example**   *Suppose you want to group your recipe box into groups of similar recipes. One way to do that is to measure the similarity of their ingredients lists.*

By this measure, pancakes, waffles, and crepes are highly similar (they have almost identical ingredients, and vary only in proportions); they all differ somewhat from cornbread (which uses cornmeal, rather than flour); and they all differ to a greater degree from mashed potatoes.

For categorical variables like recipe ingredients, gender (male/female), or qualitative size (small/medium/large), you can define the distance as 0 if two points are in the same category, and 1 otherwise. If all the variables are categorical, then you can use *Hamming distance*, which counts the number of mismatches:

```
hdist(x, y) <- sum((x[1] != y[1]) + (x[2] != y[2]) + ...)
```

Here, a != b is defined to have a value of 1 if the expression is true, and a value of 0 if the expression is false.

You can also expand categorical variables to indicator variables (as we discussed in section 7.1.4), one for each level of the variable.

If the categories are ordered (like small/medium/large) so that some categories are "closer" to each other than others, then you can convert them to a numerical sequence. For example, (small/medium/large) might map to (1/2/3). Then you can use Euclidean distance or other distances for quantitative data.

Manhattan (city block) distance

Example *Suppose you run a delivery service that caters to downtown businesses. You want to cluster your clients so that you can place pickup/drop-off boxes that are centrally located in each cluster.*

Manhattan distance measures distance in the number of horizontal and vertical units it takes to get from one (real-valued) point to the other (no diagonal moves). This is also known as *L1 distance* (and squared Euclidean distance is *L2 distance*).

In this example, Manhattan distance is more appropriate because you want to measure distance by how far people will walk along the streets, not diagonally point-to-point (Euclidean distance). For example, in figure 9.3, client A is 2 blocks north of the site and 2 blocks west, while client B is 3 blocks south of the site and 1 block east. They are equidistant from the site (4 blocks) by Manhattan distance. But client B is further by Euclidean distance: the diagonal of a 3-by-1 rectangle is longer than the diagonal of a 2-by-2 square.

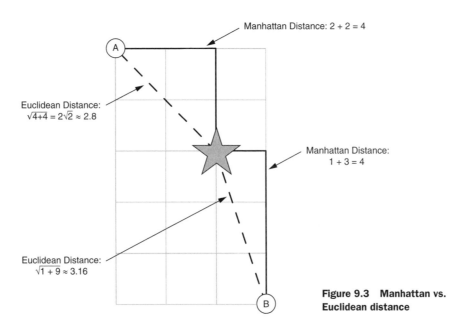

Figure 9.3   Manhattan vs. Euclidean distance

The Manhattan distance between two vectors x and y is defined as

```
mdist(x, y) <- sum(abs(x[1] - y[1]) + abs(x[2] - y[2]) + ...)
```

Cosine similarity

Example *Suppose you represent a document as rows of a document-text matrix, as we did in section 6.3.3, where each element i of the row vector gives the number of times that word i appeared in the document. Then the cosine similarity between two row vectors is a measure of the similarity of the corresponding documents.*

Cosine similarity is a common similarity metric in text analysis. It measures the smallest angle between two vectors. In our text example, we assume non-negative vectors, so the angle theta between two vectors is between 0 and 90 degrees. Cosine similarity is shown in figure 9.4.

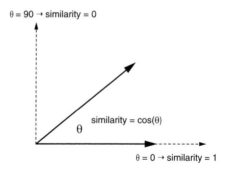

Two perpendicular vectors (theta = 90 degrees) are the most dissimilar; the cosine of 90 degrees is 0. Two parallel vectors are the most similar (identical, if you assume they're both based at the origin); the cosine of 0 degrees is 1.

Figure 9.4   Cosine similarity

From elementary geometry, you can derive that the cosine of the angle between two vectors is given by the normalized dot product between the two vectors:

```
dot(x, y) <- sum(x[1] * y[1] + x[2] * y[2] + ...)
cossim(x, y) <- dot(x, y) / (sqrt(dot(x,x) * dot(y, y)))
```

You can turn the cosine similarity into a pseudo distance by subtracting it from 1.0 (though to get an actual metric, you should use `1 - 2 * acos(cossim(x, y)) / pi`).

Different distance metrics will give you different clusters, as will different clustering algorithms. The application domain may give you a hint as to the most appropriate distance, or you can try several distance metrics. In this chapter, we'll use (squared) Euclidean distance, as it's the most natural distance for quantitative data.

9.1.2   Preparing the data

To demonstrate clustering, we'll use a small dataset from 1973 on protein consumption from nine different food groups in 25 countries in Europe.[1] The goal is to group the countries based on patterns in their protein consumption. The dataset is loaded into R as a data frame called protein, as shown in the next listing.

Listing 9.1   Reading the protein data

```
protein <- read.table("protein.txt", sep = "\t", header=TRUE)
summary(protein)
##           Country        RedMeat          WhiteMeat           Eggs
##   Albania       : 1   Min.   : 4.400   Min.   : 1.400   Min.   :0.500
##   Austria       : 1   1st Qu.: 7.800   1st Qu.: 4.900   1st Qu.:2.700
##   Belgium       : 1   Median : 9.500   Median : 7.800   Median :2.900
##   Bulgaria      : 1   Mean   : 9.828   Mean   : 7.896   Mean   :2.936
##   Czechoslovakia: 1   3rd Qu.:10.600   3rd Qu.:10.800   3rd Qu.:3.700
```

---

[1] The original dataset was from the Data and Story Library, previously hosted at CMU. It is no longer online there. A tab-separated text file with the data can be found at https://github.com/WinVector/ PDSwR2/tree/master/Protein/. The data file is called protein.txt; additional information can be found in the file protein_README.txt.

```
##    Denmark        : 1    Max.   :18.000    Max.    :14.000    Max.    :4.700
##    (Other)       :19
##        Milk              Fish            Cereals            Starch
##    Min.   : 4.90   Min.   : 0.200   Min.   :18.60   Min.   :0.600
##    1st Qu.:11.10   1st Qu.: 2.100   1st Qu.:24.30   1st Qu.:3.100
##    Median :17.60   Median : 3.400   Median :28.00   Median :4.700
##    Mean   :17.11   Mean   : 4.284   Mean   :32.25   Mean   :4.276
##    3rd Qu.:23.30   3rd Qu.: 5.800   3rd Qu.:40.10   3rd Qu.:5.700
##    Max.   :33.70   Max.   :14.200   Max.   :56.70   Max.   :6.500
##
##        Nuts            Fr.Veg
##    Min.   :0.700   Min.   :1.400
##    1st Qu.:1.500   1st Qu.:2.900
##    Median :2.400   Median :3.800
##    Mean   :3.072   Mean   :4.136
##    3rd Qu.:4.700   3rd Qu.:4.900
##    Max.   :7.800   Max.   :7.900
```

UNITS AND SCALING

The documentation for this dataset doesn't mention what the units of measurement are; we will assume all the columns are measured in the same units. This is important: units (or, more precisely, *disparity* in units) affect what clusterings an algorithm will discover. If you measure vital statistics of your subjects as age in years, height in feet, and weight in pounds, you'll get different distances—and possibly different clusters—than if you measure age in years, height in meters, and weight in kilograms.

Ideally, you want a unit of change in each coordinate to represent the same degree of difference. In the protein dataset, we assume that the measurements are all in the same units, so it might seem that we're okay. This may well be a correct assumption, but different food groups provide different amounts of protein. Animal-based food sources in general have more grams of protein per serving than plant-based food sources, so one could argue that a change in consumption of five grams is a bigger difference in terms of vegetable consumption than it is in terms of red meat consumption.

One way to try to make the units of each variable more compatible is to transform all the columns to have a mean value of 0 and a standard deviation of 1. This makes the standard deviation the unit of measurement in each coordinate. Assuming that your training data has a distribution that accurately represents the population at large, then a standard deviation represents approximately the same degree of difference in every coordinate.

You can scale numeric data in R using the function scale(). The output of scale() is a matrix. For the purposes of this chapter, you can mostly think of a matrix as a data frame with all numeric columns (this isn't strictly true, but it's close enough).

The scale() function annotates its output with two attributes—scaled:center returns the mean values of all the columns, and scaled:scale returns the standard deviations. You'll store these away so you can "unscale" the data later.

Listing 9.2   Rescaling the dataset

```
vars_to_use <- colnames(protein)[-1]        ⊲─────────┐   Uses all the columns except
  pmatrix <- scale(protein[, vars_to_use])            │   the first (Country)
pcenter <- attr(pmatrix, "scaled:center")   ⊲────┐
  pscale <- attr(pmatrix, "scaled:scale")        │       Stores the scaling attributes

rm_scales <- function(scaled_matrix) {      ⊲────┐
  attr(scaled_matrix, "scaled:center") <- NULL       Convenience function to
  attr(scaled_matrix, "scaled:scale") <- NULL        remove scale attributes
  scaled_matrix                                      from a scaled matrix.
}

pmatrix <- rm_scales(pmatrix)  ⊲───────  Nulls out the scale attributes for safety
```

Figure 9.5 shows the effect of scaling on two variables, Fr.Veg and RedMeat. The raw (unscaled) variables have different ranges, reflecting the fact that the amount of protein supplied via red meat tends to be higher than the amount of protein supplied via fruits and vegetables. The scaled variables now have similar ranges, which makes comparing relative variation in each variable easier.

Now you are ready to cluster the protein data. We'll start with hierarchical clustering.

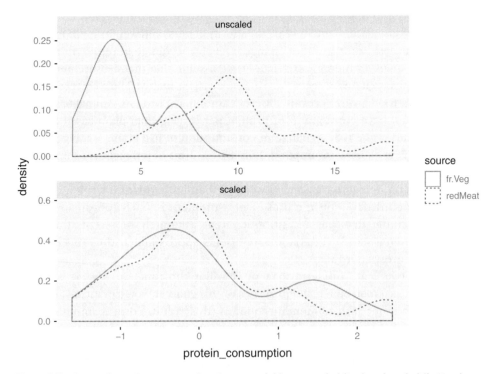

Figure 9.5   Comparison of Fr.Veg and RedMeat variables, unscaled (top) and scaled (bottom)

9.1.3 *Hierarchical clustering with hclust*

The `hclust()` function takes as input a distance matrix (as an object of class `dist`), which records the distances between all pairs of points in the data (using any one of a variety of metrics). You can compute the distance matrix using the function `dist()`.

`dist()` will calculate distance functions using the (squared) Euclidean distance (`method = "euclidean"`), the Manhattan distance (`method = "manhattan"`), and something like the Hamming distance, when categorical variables are expanded to indicators (`method = "binary"`). If you want to use another distance metric, you'll have to compute the appropriate distance matrix and convert it to a `dist` object using the `as.dist()` call (see `help(dist)` for further details).

`hclust()` also uses one of a variety of clustering methods to produce a tree that records the nested cluster structure. We'll use Ward's method, which starts out with each data point as an individual cluster and merges clusters iteratively so as to minimize the total *within sum of squares* (WSS) of the clustering (we'll explain more about WSS later in the chapter).

Let's cluster the protein data.

Listing 9.3 Hierarchical clustering

```
distmat <- dist(pmatrix, method = "euclidean")  ◁──── Creates the distance matrix
pfit <- hclust(distmat, method = "ward.D")  ◁──── Does the clustering
plot(pfit, labels = protein$Country)  ◁──── Plots the dendrogram
```

`hclust()` returns a *dendrogram*: a tree that represents the nested clusters. The dendrogram for the protein data is shown in figure 9.6. The leaves of the tree are in the same cluster if there is a path between them. By cutting the tree at a certain depth, you disconnect some of the paths, and so create more, smaller clusters.

This dendrogram suggests five clusters might be an appropriate number, as shown in figure 9.6. You can draw the rectangles on the dendrogram using the function `rect.hclust()`:

```
rect.hclust(pfit, k=5)
```

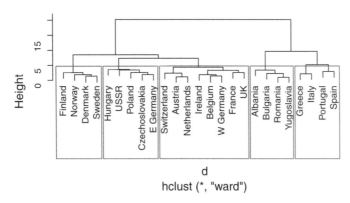

Figure 9.6 Dendrogram of countries clustered by protein consumption

To extract the members of each cluster from the hclust object, use cutree().

Listing 9.4   **Extracting the clusters found by hclust()**

```
groups <- cutree(pfit, k = 5)

print_clusters <- function(data, groups, columns) { ◁─────────────┐
   groupedD <- split(data, groups)
   lapply(groupedD,
          function(df) df[, columns])
}

cols_to_print <- wrapr::qc(Country, RedMeat, Fish, Fr.Veg)
print_clusters(protein, groups, cols_to_print)
```

> A convenience function for printing out the countries in each cluster, along with the values for red meat, fish, and fruit/vegetable consumption. We'll use this function throughout this section. Note that the function assumes the data is in a data.frame (not a matrix).

```
## $`1`
##          Country RedMeat Fish Fr.Veg
## 1        Albania    10.1  0.2    1.7
## 4       Bulgaria     7.8  1.2    4.2
## 18       Romania     6.2  1.0    2.8
## 25   Yugoslavia     4.4  0.6    3.2
##
## $`2`
##          Country RedMeat Fish Fr.Veg
## 2        Austria     8.9  2.1    4.3
## 3        Belgium    13.5  4.5    4.0
## 9         France    18.0  5.7    6.5
## 12       Ireland    13.9  2.2    2.9
## 14   Netherlands     9.5  2.5    3.7
## 21   Switzerland    13.1  2.3    4.9
## 22            UK    17.4  4.3    3.3
## 24     W Germany    11.4  3.4    3.8
##
## $`3`
##              Country RedMeat Fish Fr.Veg
## 5     Czechoslovakia     9.7  2.0    4.0
## 7          E Germany     8.4  5.4    3.6
## 11           Hungary     5.3  0.3    4.2
## 16            Poland     6.9  3.0    6.6
## 23              USSR     9.3  3.0    2.9
##
## $`4`
##      Country RedMeat Fish Fr.Veg
## 6    Denmark    10.6  9.9    2.4
## 8    Finland     9.5  5.8    1.4
## 15    Norway     9.4  9.7    2.7
## 20    Sweden     9.9  7.5    2.0
##
## $`5`
##      Country RedMeat Fish Fr.Veg
## 10    Greece    10.2  5.9    6.5
## 13     Italy     9.0  3.4    6.7
## 17  Portugal     6.2 14.2    7.9
## 19     Spain     7.1  7.0    7.2
```

There's a certain logic to these clusters: the countries in each cluster tend to be in the same geographical region. It makes sense that countries in the same region would have similar dietary habits. You can also see that

- Cluster 2 is made of countries with higher-than-average red meat consumption.
- Cluster 4 contains countries with higher-than-average fish consumption, but low produce consumption.
- Cluster 5 contains countries with high fish and produce consumption.

This dataset has only 25 points; it's harder to "eyeball" the clusters and the cluster members when there are very many data points. In the next few sections, we'll look at some ways to examine clusters more holistically.

VISUALIZING CLUSTERS USING PRINCIPAL COMPONENTS ANALYSIS

As we mentioned in chapter 3, visualization is an effective way to get an overall view of the data, or in this case, the clusterings. The protein data is nine-dimensional, so it's hard to visualize with a scatter plot.

We can try to visualize the clustering by projecting the data onto the first two *principal components* of the data.[1] If N is the number of variables that describe the data, then the principal components describe the hyperellipsoid in N-space that roughly bounds the data. Each principal component is an N-dimensional vector that describes an axis of that hyperellipsoid. Figure 9.7 shows this for $N = 3$.

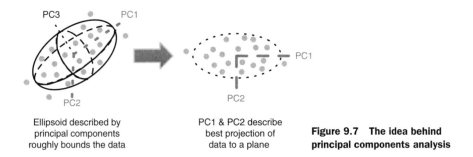

Ellipsoid described by principal components roughly bounds the data

PC1 & PC2 describe best projection of data to a plane

Figure 9.7   The idea behind principal components analysis

If you order the principal components by the length of the hyperellipsoid's corresponding axes (longest first), then the first two principal components describe a plane in N-space that captures as much of the variation of the data as can be captured in two dimensions. In other words, it describes the best 2-D projection of the data. We'll use the `prcomp()` call to do the principal components decomposition.

---

[1] We can project the data onto any two of the principal components, but the first two are the most likely to show useful information.

Listing 9.5   Projecting the clusters on the first two principal components

```
library(ggplot2)
princ <- prcomp(pmatrix)              Calculates the principal
nComp <- 2                            components of the data
project <- predict(princ, pmatrix)[, 1:nComp]
project_plus <- cbind(as.data.frame(project),
                      cluster = as.factor(groups),
                      country = protein$Country)

ggplot(project_plus, aes(x = PC1, y = PC2)) +
  geom_point(data = as.data.frame(project), color = "darkgrey") +
  geom_point() +
  geom_text(aes(label = country),
            hjust = 0, vjust = 1) +
  facet_wrap(~ cluster, ncol = 3, labeller = label_both)
```

The predict() function will rotate the data into the coordinates described by the principal components. The first two columns of the rotated data are the projection of the data on the first two principal components.

Plot it. Put each cluster in a separate facet for legibility.

Creates a data frame with the transformed data, along with the cluster label and country label of each point

You can see in figure 9.8 that cluster 1 (Romania/Yugoslavia/Bulgaria/Albania) and the Mediterranean cluster (cluster 5) are separated from the others. The other three clusters comingle in this projection, though they're probably more separated in other projections.

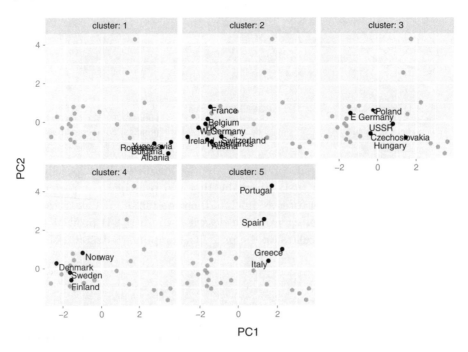

Figure 9.8   Plot of countries clustered by protein consumption, projected onto the first two principal components

BOOTSTRAP EVALUATION OF CLUSTERS

An important question when evaluating clusters is whether a given cluster is "real"—does the cluster represent actual structure in the data, or is it an artifact of the clustering algorithm? As you'll see, this is especially important with clustering algorithms like k-means, where the user has to specify the number of clusters beforehand. It's been our experience that clustering algorithms will often produce several clusters that represent actual structure or relationships in the data, and then one or two clusters that are buckets that represent "other" or "miscellaneous." Clusters of "other" tend to be made up of data points that have no real relationship to each other; they just don't fit anywhere else.

One way to assess whether a cluster represents true structure is to see if the cluster holds up under plausible variations in the dataset. The `fpc` package has a function called `clusterboot()` that uses bootstrap resampling to evaluate how stable a given cluster is.[1] `clusterboot()` is an integrated function that both performs the clustering and evaluates the final produced clusters. It has interfaces to a number of R clustering algorithms, including both `hclust` and `kmeans`.

`clusterboot`'s algorithm uses the *Jaccard coefficient*, a similarity measure between sets. The Jaccard similarity between two sets A and B is the ratio of the number of elements in the intersection of A and B over the number of elements in the union of A and B. This is shown in figure 9.9.

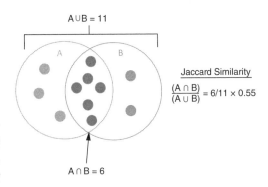

Figure 9.9   Jaccard similarity

The basic general strategy is as follows:

1 Cluster the data as usual.

2 Draw a new dataset (of the same size as the original) by resampling the original dataset with replacement (meaning that some of the data points may show up more than once, and others not at all). Cluster the new dataset.

3 For every cluster in the original clustering, find the most similar cluster in the new clustering (the one that gives the maximum Jaccard coefficient) and record that value. If this maximum Jaccard coefficient is less than 0.5, the original cluster is considered to be *dissolved*—it didn't show up in the new clustering. A cluster that's dissolved too often is probably not a "real" cluster.

4 Repeat steps 2–3 several times.

---

[1] For a full description of the algorithm, see Christian Henning, "Cluster-wise assessment of cluster stability," Research Report 271, Dept. of Statistical Science, University College London, December 2006.

The *cluster stability* of each cluster in the original clustering is the mean value of its Jaccard coefficient over all the bootstrap iterations. As a rule of thumb, clusters with a stability value less than 0.6 should be considered unstable. Values between 0.6 and 0.75 indicate that the cluster is measuring a pattern in the data, but there isn't high certainty about which points should be clustered together. Clusters with stability values above about 0.85 can be considered highly stable (they're likely to be real clusters).

Different clustering algorithms can give different stability values, even when the algorithms produce highly similar clusterings, so clusterboot() is also measuring how stable the clustering algorithm is.

Let's run clusterboot() on the protein data, using hierarchical clustering with five clusters. Note that clusterboot() is randomized, so you may not get identical results.

Listing 9.6 Running `clusterboot()` on the protein data

```
library(fpc)                                         Loads the fpc package. You
kbest_p <- 5                                         may have to install it first.
cboot_hclust <- clusterboot(pmatrix,
                    clustermethod = hclustCBI,
                                                     Runs clusterboot() with
                    method = "ward.D",               hclust (clustermethod =
                    k = kbest_p)                     hclustCBI) using Ward's
                                                     method (method =
summary(cboot_hclust$result)                         "ward.D") and kbest_p
                                                     clusters (k = kbest_p).
##                  Length Class  Mode               Returns the results in an
## result           7      hclust list               object called cboot_hclust.
## noise            1      -none- logical
## nc               1      -none- numeric            The results of the
## clusterlist      5      -none- list               clustering are in
## partition        25     -none- numeric            cboot_hclust$result.
## clustermethod    1      -none- character
## nccl             1      -none- numeric

groups <- cboot_hclust$result$partition
print_clusters(protein, groups, cols_to_print)

## $`1`
##          Country RedMeat Fish Fr.Veg
## 1        Albania    10.1  0.2    1.7
## 4        Bulgaria    7.8  1.2    4.2
## 18        Romania    6.2  1.0    2.8
## 25 Yugoslavia       4.4  0.6    3.2
##
## $`2`
##          Country RedMeat Fish Fr.Veg
## 2        Austria     8.9  2.1    4.3
## 3        Belgium    13.5  4.5    4.0
## 9         France    18.0  5.7    6.5
## 12       Ireland    13.9  2.2    2.9
## 14 Netherlands      9.5  2.5    3.7
## 21 Switzerland     13.1  2.3    4.9
## 22            UK    17.4  4.3    3.3
```

Sets the desired number of clusters *(annotation for `kbest_p <- 5`)*

cboot_hclust$result$partition returns a vector of cluster labels.

The clusters are the same as those produced by a direct call to hclust().

```
## 24    W Germany    11.4  3.4    3.8
##
## $`3`
##              Country RedMeat Fish Fr.Veg
## 5  Czechoslovakia    9.7  2.0    4.0
## 7         E Germany  8.4  5.4    3.6
## 11          Hungary  5.3  0.3    4.2
## 16           Poland  6.9  3.0    6.6
## 23             USSR  9.3  3.0    2.9
##
## $`4`
##     Country RedMeat Fish Fr.Veg
## 6   Denmark    10.6  9.9    2.4
## 8   Finland     9.5  5.8    1.4
## 15  Norway      9.4  9.7    2.7
## 20  Sweden      9.9  7.5    2.0
##
## $`5`
##      Country RedMeat Fish Fr.Veg
## 10    Greece    10.2  5.9    6.5
## 13     Italy     9.0  3.4    6.7
## 17  Portugal     6.2 14.2    7.9
## 19     Spain      7.1  7.0    7.2

cboot_hclust$bootmean  ◁────────────────────
## [1] 0.8090000 0.7939643 0.6247976 0.9366667 0.7815000

cboot_hclust$bootbrd  ◁
## [1] 19 14 45  9 30
```

The vector of cluster stabilities

The count of how many times each cluster was dissolved. By default, clusterboot() runs 100 bootstrap iterations.

The clusterboot() results show that the cluster of countries with high fish consumption (cluster 4) is highly stable: the cluster stability is high, and the cluster was dissolved relatively few times. Clusters 1 and 2 are also quite stable; cluster 5 less so (you can see in figure 9.8 that the members of cluster 5 are separated from the other countries, but also fairly separated from each other). Cluster 3 has the characteristics of what we've been calling the "other" cluster.

clusterboot() assumes that you know the number of clusters, k. We eyeballed the appropriate k from the dendrogram, but this isn't always feasible with a large dataset. Can we pick a plausible k in a more automated fashion? We'll look at this question in the next section.

PICKING THE NUMBER OF CLUSTERS

There are a number of heuristics and rules of thumb for picking clusters; a given heuristic will work better on some datasets than others. It's best to take advantage of domain knowledge to help set the number of clusters, if that's possible. Otherwise, try a variety of heuristics, and perhaps a few different values of k.

Total within sum of squares

One simple heuristic is to compute the total within sum of squares (WSS) for different values of k and look for an "elbow" in the curve. We'll walk through the definition of WSS in this section.

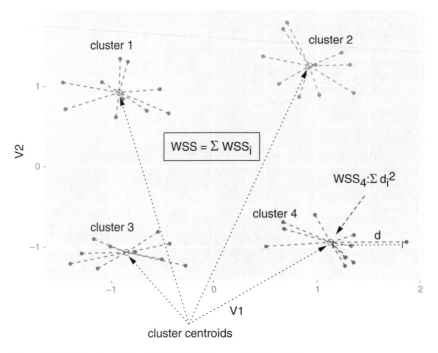

Figure 9.10   Cluster WSS and total WSS for a set of four clusters

Figure 9.10 shows data with four clusters. Define the *centroid* of each cluster as the point that is the mean value of all the points in the cluster. The centroid will be in the center of the cluster, as shown in the figure. The within sum of squares (or `WSS_i`) for a single cluster is the summed squared distance of each point in the cluster from the cluster's centroid. This is shown in the figure for cluster 4.

The total within sum of squares is the sum of the `WSS_i` of all the clusters. We show the calculation in the following listing.

Listing 9.7   Calculating total within sum of squares

Function to calculate squared distance between two vectors

Function to calculate the WSS for a single cluster, which is represented as a matrix (one row for every point)

Calculates the centroid of the cluster (the mean of all the points)

Calculates the squared difference of every point in the cluster from the centroid, and sums all the distances

```
sqr_edist <- function(x, y) {
    sum((x - y)^2)
}

wss_cluster <- function(clustermat) {
    c0 <- colMeans(clustermat)
    sum(apply(clustermat, 1, FUN = function(row) { sqr_edist(row, c0) }))
}
```

```
wss_total <- function(dmatrix, labels) {   ◁──── Function to compute the total WSS from
  wsstot <- 0                                      a set of data points and cluster labels
  k <- length(unique(labels))
  for(i in 1:k)
    wsstot <- wsstot + wss_cluster(subset(dmatrix, labels == i))   ◁────
  wsstot                                                    Extracts each cluster,
}                                                         calculates the cluster's
                                                         WSS, and sums all the values
wss_total(pmatrix, groups)   ◁────
                                       Calculates the total WSS for
## [1] 71.94342                        the current protein clustering
```

The total WSS will decrease as the number of clusters increases, because each cluster will be smaller and tighter. The hope is that the rate at which the WSS decreases will slow down for *k* beyond the optimal number of clusters. In other words, the graph of WSS versus *k* should flatten out beyond the optimal *k*, so the optimal *k* will be at the "elbow" of the graph. Let's try calculating WSS for up to 10 clusters.

Listing 9.8   Plotting WSS for a range of k

```
get_wss <- function(dmatrix, max_clusters) {   ◁────   A function to get the total
  wss = numeric(max_clusters)                             WSS for a range of clusters
                                                          from 1 to max

  wss[1] <- wss_cluster(dmatrix)   ◁────   wss[1] is just the
                                             WSS of all the data.
  d <- dist(dmatrix, method = "euclidean")
  pfit <- hclust(d, method = "ward.D")    ◁── Clusters the data

  for(k in 2:max_clusters) {   ◁────   For each k, calculates the cluster
                                        labels and the cluster WSS
    labels <- cutree(pfit, k = k)
    wss[k] <- wss_total(dmatrix, labels)
  }

  wss
}

kmax <- 10
cluster_meas <- data.frame(nclusters = 1:kmax,
                    wss = get_wss(pmatrix, kmax))

breaks <- 1:kmax
ggplot(cluster_meas, aes(x=nclusters, y = wss)) +   ◁── Plots WSS as a function of k
  geom_point() + geom_line() +
  scale_x_continuous(breaks = breaks)
```

Figure 9.11 shows the plot of WSS as a function of *k*. Unfortunately, in this case the elbow of the graph is hard to see, although if you squint your eyes you might be able to convince yourself that there is an elbow at k = 2, and another one at k = 5 or 6. This means the best clusterings might be 2 clusters, 5 clusters, or 6 clusters.

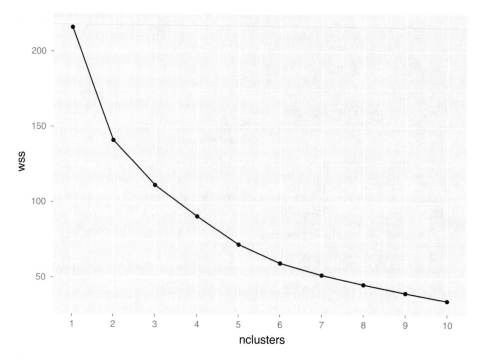

Figure 9.11   WSS as a function of k for the protein data

Calinski-Harabasz index

The *Calinski-Harabasz index* is another commonly used measure of cluster goodness. It tries to find the point where all the clusters are tight, and also far apart from each other. To motivate (and calculate) the Calinski-Harabasz index (CH index, for short), we first need to define a few more terms.

As shown in figure 9.12, the *total sum of squares* (TSS) of a set of points is the sum of the squared distances of all the points from the centroid of the data. In the function get_wss() of listing 9.8, the value wss[1] is the TSS, and it is independent of the clustering. For a given clustering with total within sum of squares, we can also define the *between sum of squares* (BSS):

```
BSS = TSS - WSS
```

BSS measures how far apart the clusters are from each other. A good clustering has a small WSS (all the clusters are tight around their centers) and a large BSS. We can compare how BSS and WSS vary as we vary the number of clusters.

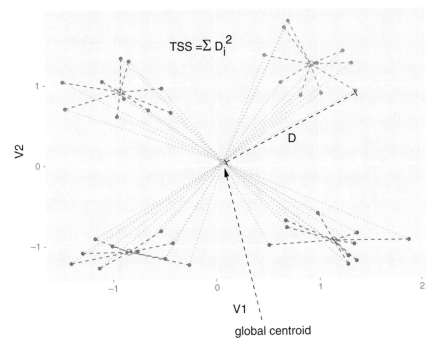

Figure 9.12 Total sum of squares for a set of four clusters

Listing 9.9 Plotting BSS and WSS as a function of *k*

```
total_ss <- function(dmatrix) {
  grandmean <- colMeans(dmatrix)
  sum(apply(dmatrix, 1, FUN = function(row) { sqr_edist(row, grandmean) }))
}

tss <- total_ss(pmatrix)
cluster_meas$bss <- with(cluster_meas, tss - wss)

library(cdata)
cmlong <- unpivot_to_blocks(cluster_meas,
                    nameForNewKeyColumn = "measure",
                    nameForNewValueColumn = "value",
                    columnsToTakeFrom = c("wss", "bss"))

ggplot(cmlong, aes(x = nclusters, y = value)) +
  geom_point() + geom_line() +
  facet_wrap(~measure, ncol = 1, scale = "free_y") +
  scale_x_continuous(breaks = 1:10)
```

Calculates the total sum of squares: TSS

Reshapes cluster_meas so that the WSS and the BSS are in the same column

Loads the cdata package to reshape the data

Figure 9.13 shows that as *k* increases, BSS increases, while WSS decreases. We want a clustering with a good balance of BSS and WSS. To find such a clustering, we have to look at a couple of measures related to the BSS and the WSS.

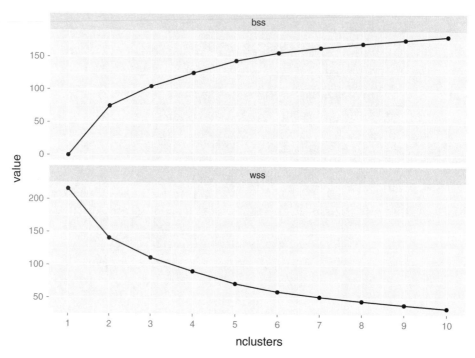

Figure 9.13   BSS and WSS as a function of *k*

The *within cluster variance W* is given by

```
W = WSS / (n - k)
```

Here, *n* is the number of data points and *k* is the number of clusters. You can think of *W* as the "average" WSS.

The *between cluster variance B* is given by

```
B = BSS / (k - 1)
```

Again, you can think of *B* as the average contribution to the BSS from each cluster.

A good clustering should have a small average WSS and a large average BSS, so we might try to maximize the ratio of *B* to *W*. This is the Calinski-Harabasz (CH) index. Let's calculate the CH index and plot it for up to 10 clusters.

Listing 9.10   The Calinski-Harabasz index

```
cluster_meas$B <- with(cluster_meas,  bss / (nclusters - 1))   ⤶

n = nrow(pmatrix)
cluster_meas$W <- with(cluster_meas,  wss / (n - nclusters))   ⤶

cluster_meas$ch_crit <- with(cluster_meas, B / W)
ggplot(cluster_meas, aes(x = nclusters, y = ch_crit)) +
  geom_point() + geom_line() +
  scale_x_continuous(breaks = 1:kmax)
```

Calculates the CH index ⤑

Calculates the within cluster variance W

Calculates the between cluster variance B

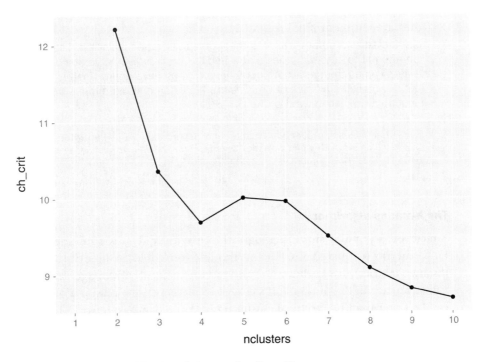

Figure 9.14   The Calinski-Harabasz index as a function of *k*

Looking at figure 9.14, you see that the CH criterion is maximized at k = 2, with another local maximum at k = 5. The k = 2 clustering corresponds to the first split of the protein data dendrogram, as shown in figure 9.15; if you use clusterboot() to do the clustering, you'll see that the clusters are highly stable, though perhaps not very informative.

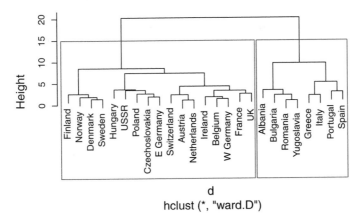

Figure 9.15   The protein data dendrogram with two clusters

Other measures of cluster quality

There are several other measures that you can try when picking k. The *gap statistic*[a] is an attempt to automate the "elbow finding" on the WSS curve. It works best when the data comes from a mix of populations that all have approximately Gaussian distributions (called a *mixture of Gaussians*). We'll see one more measure, the *average silhouette width*, when we discuss kmeans().

---

[a] See Robert Tibshirani, Guenther Walther, and Trevor Hastie, "Estimating the number of clusters in a data set via the gap statistic," *Journal of the Royal Statistical Society B*, 2001. 63(2), pp. 411-423; www.stanford.edu/~hastie/Papers/gap.pdf.

9.1.4   *The k-means algorithm*

K-means is a popular clustering algorithm when the data is all numeric and the distance metric is squared Euclidean (though you could in theory run it with other distance metrics). It's fairly ad hoc and has the major disadvantage that you must pick *k* in advance. On the plus side, it's easy to implement (one reason it's so popular) and can be faster than hierarchical clustering on large datasets. It works best on data that looks like a mixture of Gaussians, which the protein data unfortunately doesn't appear to be.

THE KMEANS() FUNCTION

The function to run k-means in R is kmeans(). The output of kmeans() includes the cluster labels, the centers (centroids) of the clusters, the total sum of squares, total WSS, total BSS, and the WSS of each cluster.

The k-means algorithm is illustrated in figure 9.16, with *k* = 2. This algorithm isn't guaranteed to have a unique stopping point. K-means can be fairly unstable, in that the final clusters depend on the initial cluster centers. It's good practice to run k-means several times with different random starts, and then select the clustering with the lowest total WSS. The kmeans() function can do this automatically, though it defaults to using only one random start.

Let's run kmeans() on the protein data (scaled to 0 mean and unit standard deviation, as before). We'll use k = 5, as shown in listing 9.11. Note that kmeans() is randomized code, so you may not get exactly the results shown.

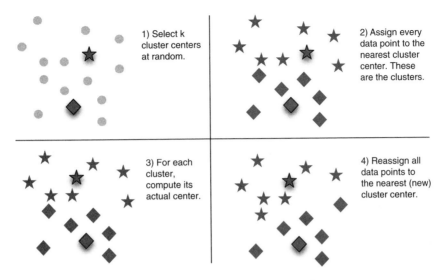

Figure 9.16   The k-means procedure. The two cluster centers are represented by the outlined star and diamond.

Listing 9.11   Running k-means with k = 5

```
kbest_p <- 5

pclusters <- kmeans(pmatrix, kbest_p, nstart = 100, iter.max = 100)     <──┐
summary(pclusters)     <────                                              │
##              Length Class  Mode                  Runs kmeans() with five
## cluster        25    -none- numeric              clusters (kbest_p = 5), 100
## centers        45    -none- numeric              random starts, and 100
## totss           1    -none- numeric              maximum iterations per run
## withinss        5    -none- numeric
## tot.withinss    1    -none- numeric       kmeans() returns all the
## betweenss       1    -none- numeric       sum-of-squares measures.
## size            5    -none- numeric
## iter            1    -none- numeric       pclusters$centers is a matrix whose rows are
## ifault          1    -none- numeric       the centroids of the clusters. Note that
                                             pclusters$centers is in the scaled coordinates,
pclusters$centers     <────                  not the original protein coordinates.

##       RedMeat  WhiteMeat        Eggs       Milk       Fish    Cereals
## 1 -0.570049402  0.5803879 -0.08589708 -0.4604938 -0.4537795  0.3181839
## 2 -0.508801956 -1.1088009 -0.41248496 -0.8320414  0.9819154  0.1300253
## 3 -0.807569986 -0.8719354 -1.55330561 -1.0783324 -1.0386379  1.7200335
## 4  0.006572897 -0.2290150  0.19147892  1.3458748  1.1582546 -0.8722721
## 5  1.011180399  0.7421332  0.94084150  0.5700581 -0.2671539 -0.6877583
##       Starch       Nuts      Fr.Veg
```

```
## 1   0.7857609 -0.2679180  0.06873983
## 2  -0.1842010  1.3108846  1.62924487
## 3  -1.4234267  0.9961313 -0.64360439
## 4   0.1676780 -0.9553392 -1.11480485
## 5   0.2288743 -0.5083895  0.02161979
```

pclusters$size returns the number of points in each cluster. Generally (though not always), a good clustering will be fairly well balanced: no extremely small clusters and no extremely large ones.

```
pclusters$size
 ## [1] 5 4 4 4 8
```

```
groups <- pclusters$cluster
```

pclusters$cluster is a vector of cluster labels.

```
cols_to_print = wrapr::qc(Country, RedMeat, Fish, Fr.Veg)
print_clusters(protein, groups, cols_to_print)
```

In this case, kmeans() and hclust () return the same clustering. This won't always be true.

```
## $`1`
##               Country RedMeat Fish Fr.Veg
## 5  Czechoslovakia     9.7   2.0    4.0
## 7       E Germany     8.4   5.4    3.6
## 11        Hungary     5.3   0.3    4.2
## 16         Poland     6.9   3.0    6.6
## 23           USSR     9.3   3.0    2.9
##
## $`2`
##       Country RedMeat Fish Fr.Veg
## 10     Greece   10.2  5.9    6.5
## 13      Italy    9.0  3.4    6.7
## 17   Portugal    6.2 14.2    7.9
## 19      Spain    7.1  7.0    7.2
##
## $`3`
##          Country RedMeat Fish Fr.Veg
## 1        Albania    10.1  0.2    1.7
## 4       Bulgaria     7.8  1.2    4.2
## 18       Romania     6.2  1.0    2.8
## 25    Yugoslavia     4.4  0.6    3.2
##
## $`4`
##       Country RedMeat Fish Fr.Veg
## 6     Denmark    10.6  9.9    2.4
## 8     Finland     9.5  5.8    1.4
## 15     Norway     9.4  9.7    2.7
## 20     Sweden     9.9  7.5    2.0
##
## $`5`
##          Country RedMeat Fish Fr.Veg
## 2        Austria     8.9  2.1    4.3
## 3        Belgium    13.5  4.5    4.0
## 9         France    18.0  5.7    6.5
## 12       Ireland    13.9  2.2    2.9
## 14   Netherlands     9.5  2.5    3.7
## 21   Switzerland    13.1  2.3    4.9
## 22            UK    17.4  4.3    3.3
## 24     W Germany    11.4  3.4    3.8
```

THE KMEANSRUNS() FUNCTION FOR PICKING K

To run kmeans(), you must know *k*. The fpc package (the same package that has clusterboot()) has a function called kmeansruns() that calls kmeans() over a range of *k* and estimates the best *k*. It then returns its pick for the best value of *k*, the output of kmeans() for that value, and a vector of criterion values as a function of *k*. Currently, kmeansruns() has two criteria: the Calinski-Harabasz index ("ch") and the *average silhouette width* ("asw"). For either criterion, the maximum value indicates the optimal number of clusters (for more about silhouette clustering, see http://mng.bz/Qe15). It's a good idea to examine the criterion values over the entire range of *k*, since you may see evidence for a *k* that the algorithm didn't automatically pick. The following listing illustrates this point.

> **Listing 9.12 Plotting cluster criteria**

The ch criterion picks two clusters.

Runs kmeansruns() from 1–10 clusters, and the ch criterion. By default, kmeansruns() uses 100 random starts and I00 maximum iterations per run.

Runs kmeansruns() from 1–10 clusters, and the average silhouette width criterion. The average silhouette width picks 3 clusters.

```
clustering_ch <- kmeansruns(pmatrix, krange = 1:10, criterion = "ch")
clustering_ch$bestk
## [1] 2

clustering_asw <- kmeansruns(pmatrix, krange = 1:10, criterion = "asw")
clustering_asw$bestk
## [1] 3
```

Looks at the values of the asw criterion as a function of k

```
clustering_asw$crit
## [1] 0.0000000 0.3271084 0.3351694 0.2617868 0.2639450 0.2734815 0.2471165
## [8] 0.2429985 0.2412922 0.2388293
```

Looks at the values of the ch criterion as a function of k

```
clustering_ch$crit
##  [1]  0.000000 14.094814 11.417985 10.418801 10.011797  9.964967  9.861682
##  [8]  9.412089  9.166676  9.075569

cluster_meas$ch_crit
##  [1]       NaN 12.215107 10.359587  9.690891 10.011797  9.964967  9.506978
##  [8]  9.092065  8.822406  8.695065
```

Compares these to the ch values for the hclust() clustering. They're not quite the same, because the two algorithms didn't pick the same clusters.

kmeansruns() also returns the output of kmeans for k = bestk.

```
summary(clustering_ch)
##                 Length Class  Mode
## cluster         25     -none- numeric
## centers         18     -none- numeric
## totss            1     -none- numeric
## withinss         2     -none- numeric
## tot.withinss     1     -none- numeric
## betweenss        1     -none- numeric
## size             2     -none- numeric
## iter             1     -none- numeric
```

```
## ifault         1      -none- numeric
## crit          10      -none- numeric
## bestk          1      -none- numeric
```

The top graph of figure 9.17 compares the results of the two clustering criteria provided by `kmeansruns`. Both criteria have been scaled to be in compatible units. They suggest two to three clusters as the best choice. However, if you compare the values of the (unscaled) CH criterion for the `kmeans` and `hclust` clusterings, as shown in the bottom graph of figure 9.17, you'll see that the CH criterion produces different curves for `kmeans()` and `hclust()` clusterings, but it did pick the same value (which probably means it picked the same clusters) for k = 5 and k = 6, which might be taken as evidence that either 5 or 6 is the optimal choice for *k*.

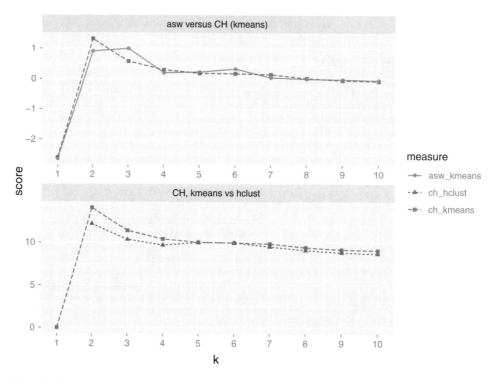

Figure 9.17   Top: Comparison of the (scaled) CH and average silhouette width indices for `kmeans` clusterings. Bottom: Comparison of CH indices for `kmeans` and `hclust` clusterings.

CLUSTERBOOT() REVISITED

We can run `clusterboot()` using the k-means algorithm, as well.

Listing 9.13   Running `clusterboot()` with k-means

```
kbest_p <- 5
cboot <- clusterboot(pmatrix, clustermethod = kmeansCBI,
          runs = 100,iter.max = 100,
```

```
                 krange = kbest_p, seed = 15555)   ◁─┐ We've set the seed for the
groups <- cboot$result$partition                     │ random generator so the
print_clusters(protein, groups, cols_to_print)       │ results are reproducible.
## $`1`
##         Country RedMeat Fish Fr.Veg
## 1       Albania    10.1  0.2    1.7
## 4      Bulgaria     7.8  1.2    4.2
## 18      Romania     6.2  1.0    2.8
## 25 Yugoslavia      4.4  0.6    3.2
##
## $`2`
##     Country RedMeat Fish Fr.Veg
## 6   Denmark    10.6  9.9    2.4
## 8   Finland     9.5  5.8    1.4
## 15   Norway     9.4  9.7    2.7
## 20   Sweden     9.9  7.5    2.0
##
## $`3`
##           Country RedMeat Fish Fr.Veg
## 5  Czechoslovakia     9.7  2.0    4.0
## 7       E Germany     8.4  5.4    3.6
## 11        Hungary     5.3  0.3    4.2
## 16         Poland     6.9  3.0    6.6
## 23           USSR     9.3  3.0    2.9
##
## $`4`
##          Country RedMeat Fish Fr.Veg
## 2        Austria     8.9  2.1    4.3
## 3        Belgium    13.5  4.5    4.0
## 9         France    18.0  5.7    6.5
## 12       Ireland    13.9  2.2    2.9
## 14   Netherlands     9.5  2.5    3.7
## 21   Switzerland    13.1  2.3    4.9
## 22            UK    17.4  4.3    3.3
## 24     W Germany    11.4  3.4    3.8
##
## $`5`
##      Country RedMeat Fish Fr.Veg
## 10    Greece    10.2  5.9    6.5
## 13     Italy     9.0  3.4    6.7
## 17  Portugal     6.2 14.2    7.9
## 19     Spain     7.1  7.0    7.2

cboot$bootmean
## [1] 0.8670000 0.8420714 0.6147024 0.7647341 0.7508333

cboot$bootbrd
## [1] 15 20 49 17 32
```

Note that the stability numbers as given by cboot$bootmean (and the number of times that the clusters were "dissolved" as given by cboot$bootbrd) are different for the hierarchical clustering and k-means, even though the discovered clusters are the same. This shows that the stability of a clustering is partly a function of the clustering algorithm, not just the data. Again, the fact that both clustering algorithms discovered the same clusters might be taken as an indication that 5 is the optimal number of clusters.

9.1.5   *Assigning new points to clusters*

Clustering is often used as part of data exploration, or as a precursor to other supervised learning methods. But you may want to use the clusters that you discovered to categorize new data, as well. One common way to do so is to treat the centroid of each cluster as the representative of the cluster as a whole, and then assign new points to the cluster with the nearest centroid. Note that if you scaled the original data before clustering, then you should also scale the new data point the same way before assigning it to a cluster.

Listing 9.14 shows an example of a function that assigns a new data point, newpt (represented as a vector), to a clustering, centers, which is represented as a matrix where each row is a cluster centroid. This is the representation of cluster centroids that kmeans() returns. If the data was scaled using scale() before clustering, then xcenter and xscale are the scaled:center and scaled:scale attributes, respectively.

Listing 9.14 A function to assign points to a cluster

```
assign_cluster <- function(newpt, centers, xcenter = 0, xscale = 1) {
    xpt <- (newpt - xcenter) / xscale
    dists <- apply(centers, 1, FUN = function(c0) { sqr_edist(c0, xpt) })
    which.min(dists)
}
```

Centers and scales the new data point

Returns the cluster number of the closest centroid

Calculates how far the new data point is from each of the cluster centers

Note that the function sqr_edist() (the squared Euclidean distance) was defined previously, in section 9.1.1.

Let's look at an example of assigning points to clusters, using synthetic data. First, we'll generate the data.

Listing 9.15 Generating and clustering synthetic data

```
mean1 <- c(1, 1, 1)
sd1 <- c(1, 2, 1)

mean2 <- c(10, -3, 5)
sd2 <- c(2, 1, 2)

mean3 <- c(-5, -5, -5)
sd3 <- c(1.5, 2, 1)

library(MASS)
clust1 <- mvrnorm(100, mu = mean1, Sigma = diag(sd1))
clust2 <- mvrnorm(100, mu = mean2, Sigma = diag(sd2))
clust3 <- mvrnorm(100, mu = mean3, Sigma = diag(sd3))
toydata <- rbind(clust3, rbind(clust1, clust2))

tmatrix <- scale(toydata)

tcenter <- attr(tmatrix, "scaled:center")
tscale <-attr(tmatrix, "scaled:scale")
tmatrix <- rm_scales(tmatrix)
```

Sets the parameters for three 3D Gaussian clusters

Uses the mvrnorm() function from the MASS package to generate 3D axis-aligned Gaussian clusters

Scales the synthetic data

Gets the scaling attributes, then removes them from the matrix

```
kbest_t <- 3
tclusters <- kmeans(tmatrix, kbest_t, nstart = 100, iter.max = 100)    <──┐
                                                                          │
tclusters$size    <──┐  The generated clusters are    Clusters the synthetic data
                     │  consistent in size with the    into three clusters
## [1] 101 100  99   │  true clusters.                                     │
```

Let's compare the centers of the found k-means clusters to the true cluster centers. To do that, we need to unscale `tclusters$centers`. The `scale()` function works by subtracting the center vector, then dividing by the scale vector. So to reverse the process, first "unscale" the scaled matrix, then "uncenter" it.

Listing 9.16 Unscaling the centers

```
unscaled = scale(tclusters$centers, center = FALSE, scale = 1 / tscale)
rm_scales(scale(unscaled, center = -tcenter, scale = FALSE))

##         [,1]       [,2]        [,3]
## 1  9.8234797 -3.005977   4.7662651
## 2 -4.9749654 -4.862436  -5.0577002
## 3  0.8926698  1.185734   0.8336977
```

Comparing the unscaled centers to mean1, mean2, and mean3 in listing 9.15, we see that

- The first discovered center corresponds to mean2: (10, –3, 5).
- The second discovered center corresponds to mean3: (–5, –5, –5).
- The third discovered center corresponds to mean1: (1, 1, 1).

So it appears that the discovered clusters are consistent with the true clusters.

Now we can demonstrate assigning new points to the clusters. Let's generate a point from each of the true clusters, and see which k-means cluster it is assigned to.

Listing 9.17 An example of assigning points to clusters

```
assign_cluster(mvrnorm(1, mean1, diag(sd1))    <──┐  This should be
               tclusters$centers,                  │  assigned to cluster 3.
               tcenter, tscale)

## 3
## 3

assign_cluster(mvrnorm(1, mean2, diag(sd2))    <──┐  This should be
               tclusters$centers,                  │  assigned to cluster 1.
               tcenter, tscale)

## 1
## 1

assign_cluster(mvrnorm(1, mean3, diag(sd3))    <──┐  This should be
               tclusters$centers,                  │  assigned to cluster 2.
               tcenter, tscale)

## 2
## 2
```

The `assign_cluster()` function has correctly assigned each point to the appropriate cluster.

9.1.6   Clustering takeaways

At this stage, you have learned how to estimate the appropriate number of clusters for a dataset, how to cluster a dataset using both hierarchical clustering and k-means, and how to evaluate the resulting clusters. Here's what you should remember about clustering:

- The goal of clustering is to discover or draw out similarities among subsets of your data.
- In a good clustering, points in the same cluster should be more similar (nearer) to each other than they are to points in other clusters.
- When clustering, the units that each variable is measured in matter. Different units cause different distances and potentially different clusterings.
- Ideally, you want a unit change in each coordinate to represent the same degree of change. One way to approximate this is to transform all the columns to have a mean value of 0 and a standard deviation of 1.0, for example, by using the function `scale()`.
- Clustering is often used for data exploration or as a precursor to supervised learning methods.
- Like visualization, clustering is more iterative and interactive, and less automated, than supervised methods.
- Different clustering algorithms will give different results. You should consider different approaches, with different numbers of clusters.
- There are many heuristics for estimating the best number of clusters. Again, you should consider the results from different heuristics and explore various numbers of clusters.

Sometimes, rather than looking for subsets of data points that are highly similar to each other, you'd like to know what kinds of data (or which data attributes) tend to occur together. In the next section, we'll look at one approach to this problem.

9.2   Association rules

Association rule mining is used to find objects or attributes that frequently occur together—for example, products that are often bought together during a shopping session, or queries that tend to occur together during a session on a website's search engine. Such information can be used to recommend products to shoppers, to place frequently bundled items together on store shelves, or to redesign websites for easier navigation.

9.2.1   Overview of association rules

> **Example**   *Suppose you work in a library. You want to know which books tend to be checked out together, to help you make predictions about book availability.*

The unit of "togetherness" when mining association rules is called a *transaction*. Depending on the problem, a transaction could be a single shopping basket, a single user session on a website, or even a single customer. The objects that comprise a transaction are referred to as *items* in an *itemset*: the products in the shopping basket, the pages visited during a website session, the actions of a customer. Sometimes transactions are referred to as *baskets*, from the shopping basket analogy.

When a library patron checks out a set of books, that's a transaction; the books that the patron checks out are the itemset that comprise the transaction. Table 9.1 represents a database of transactions (you run a library where fantasy is quite popular).

Table 9.1 A database of library transactions

Transaction ID	Books checked out
1	*The Hobbit, The Princess Bride*
2	*The Princess Bride, The Last Unicorn*
3	*The Hobbit*
4	*The Neverending Story*
5	*The Last Unicorn*
6	*The Hobbit, The Princess Bride, The Fellowship of the Ring*
7	*The Hobbit, The Fellowship of the Ring, The Two Towers, The Return of the King*
8	*The Fellowship of the Ring, The Two Towers, The Return of the King*
9	*The Hobbit, The Princess Bride, The Last Unicorn*
10	*The Last Unicorn, The Neverending Story*

Mining for association rules occurs in two steps:

1. Look for all the itemsets (subsets of transactions) that occur more often than in a minimum fraction of the transactions.
2. Turn those itemsets into rules.

Let's look at the transactions that involve the items *The Hobbit* (H for short) and *The Princess Bride* (PB for short). The columns of table 9.2 represent transactions; the rows mark the transactions where a given itemset appears.

Table 9.2 Looking for The Hobbit and The Princess Bride

	1	2	3	4	5	6	7	8	9	10	Total
H	X		X			X	X		X		5
PB	X	X				X			X		4
{H, PB}	X					X			X		3

Looking over all the transactions in table 9.2, you find that

- *The Hobbit* is in 5/10, or 50% of all transactions.
- *The Princess Bride* is in 4/10, or 40% of all transactions.
- Both books are checked out together in 3/10, or 30% of all transactions.

We'd say the *support* of the itemset {*The Hobbit, The Princess Bride*} is 30%.

- Of the five transactions that include *The Hobbit*, three (3/5 = 60%) also include *The Princess Bride.*

So you can make a rule: "People who check out *The Hobbit* also check out *The Princess Bride.*" This rule should be correct (according to your data) 60% of the time. We'd say that the *confidence* of the rule is 60%.

- Conversely, of the four times *The Princess Bride* is checked out, *The Hobbit* appears three times, or 3/4 = 75% of the time.

So the rule "People who check out *The Princess Bride* also check out *The Hobbit*" has 75% confidence.

Let's formally define rules, support, and confidence.

RULES

The rule "if X, then Y" means that every time you see the itemset X in a transaction, you expect to also see Y (with a given confidence). For the apriori algorithm (which we'll look at in this section), Y is always an itemset with one item.

SUPPORT

Suppose that your database of transactions is called T, and X is an itemset. Then support(X) is the number of transactions that contain X divided by the total number of transactions in T.

CONFIDENCE

The confidence of the rule "if X, then Y" gives the fraction or percentage of the time that a rule is true, relative to how often you see X. In other words, if support(X) is how often the itemset X occurs in a transaction, and support({X, Y}) is how often both itemsets X and Y occur in a transaction, then the confidence of the rule "if X, then Y" is support({X, Y})/support(X).

The goal in association rule mining is to find all the interesting rules in the database with at least a given minimum support (say, 10%) and a minimum given confidence (say, 60%).

9.2.2   *The example problem*

Example   *Suppose you work for a bookstore, and you want to recommend books that a customer might be interested in, based on all of their previous purchases and book interests. You want to use historical book interest information to develop some recommendation rules.*

You can get information about customers' book interests two ways: either they've purchased a book from you, or they've rated a book on your website (even if they bought the book somewhere else). In this case, a transaction is a customer, and an itemset is all the books that they've expressed an interest in, either by purchase or by rating.

The data that you'll use is based on data collected in 2004 from the book community Book-Crossing[1] for research conducted at the Institut für Informatik, University of Freiburg.[2] The information is condensed into a single tab-separated text file called bookdata.tsv. Each row of the file consists of a user ID, a book title (which has been designed as a unique ID for each book), and the rating (which you won't actually use in this example):

```
|token                 | userid| rating|title                 |
|:---------------------|------:|------:|:---------------------|
|always have popsicles | 172742|      0|Always Have Popsicles |
```

The token column contains lowercase column strings; the tokens were used to identify books with different ISBNs (the original book IDs) that had the same title except for casing. The title column holds properly capitalized title strings; these are unique per book, so for this example you will use them as book IDs.

In this format, the transaction (customer) information is diffused through the data, rather than being all in one row; this reflects the way the data would naturally be stored in a database, since the customer's activity would be diffused throughout time. Books generally come in different editions or from different publishers. For this example, we've condensed all different versions into a single item; hence, different copies or printings of *Little Women* will all map to the same item ID in our data (namely, the title "Little Women").

The original data includes approximately a million ratings of 271,379 books from 278,858 readers. Our data will have fewer books due to the mapping that we discussed earlier.

Now you're ready to mine.

9.2.3 *Mining association rules with the arules package*

You'll use the package arules for association rule mining. arules includes an implementation of the popular association rule algorithm *apriori*, as well as implementations to read in and examine transaction data.[3] The package uses special data types to hold and manipulate the data; you'll explore these data types as you work the example.

---

[1] The original data repository can be found at http://mng.bz/2052. Since some artifacts in the original files caused errors when reading into R, we're providing copies of the data as a prepared RData object: https://github.com/WinVector/PDSwR2/blob/master/Bookdata/bxBooks.RData. The prepared version of the data that we'll use in this section is at https://github.com/WinVector/PDSwR2/blob/master/Bookdata/bookdata.tsv.gz. Further information and scripts for preparing the data can be found at https://github.com/WinVector/PDSwR2/tree/master/Bookdata.

[2] The researchers' original paper is "Improving Recommendation Lists Through Topic Diversification," Cai-Nicolas Ziegler, Sean M. McNee, Joseph A. Konstan, Georg Lausen; Proceedings of the 14th International World Wide Web Conference (WWW '05), May 10-14, 2005, Chiba, Japan. It can be found online at http://mng.bz/7trR.

[3] For a more comprehensive introduction to arules than we can give in this chapter, please see Hahsler, Grin, Hornik, and Buchta, "Introduction to arules—A computational environment for mining association rules and frequent item sets," online at cran.r-project.org/web/packages/arules/vignettes/arules.pdf.

READING IN THE DATA

You can read the data directly from the bookdata.tsv.gz file into the object book-baskets using the function read.transactions().

Listing 9.18   Reading in the book data

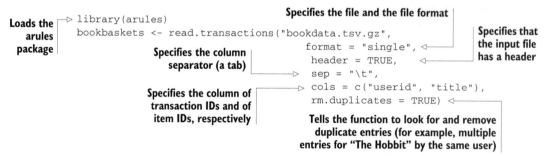

Loads the arules package
→ `library(arules)`

Specifies the file and the file format

`bookbaskets <- read.transactions("bookdata.tsv.gz",`

Specifies the column separator (a tab)

`    format = "single",` ← Specifies that the input file has a header

`    header = TRUE,` ←

`    sep = "\t",`

Specifies the column of transaction IDs and of item IDs, respectively

`    cols = c("userid", "title"),`

`    rm.duplicates = TRUE)` ←

Tells the function to look for and remove duplicate entries (for example, multiple entries for "The Hobbit" by the same user)

The read.transactions() function reads data in two formats: the format where every row corresponds to a single item (like bookdata.tsv.gz), and a format where each row corresponds to a single transaction, possibly with a transaction ID, like table 9.1. To read data in the first format, use the argument format = "single"; to read data in the second format, use the argument format = "basket".

It sometimes happens that a reader will buy one edition of a book and then later add a rating for that book under a different edition. Because of the way we're representing books for this example, these two actions will result in duplicate entries. The rm.duplicates = TRUE argument will eliminate them. It will also output some (not too useful) diagnostics about the duplicates.

Once you've read in the data, you can inspect the resulting object.

EXAMINING THE DATA

Transactions are represented as a special object called transactions. You can think of a transactions object as a 0/1 matrix, with one row for every transaction (in this example, a customer) and one column for every possible item (in this example, a book). The matrix entry (i, j) is 1 if the ith transaction contains item j, or if customer i has expressed an interest in book j. There are a number of calls you can use to examine the transaction data, as the next listing shows.

Listing 9.19   Examining the transaction data

```
class(bookbaskets)       ←   The object is of class
## [1] "transactions"        transactions.
## attr(,"package")
## [1] "arules"
bookbaskets              ←
## transactions in sparse format with    Printing the object tells
## 92108 transactions (rows) and          you its dimensions.
## 220447 items (columns)
dim(bookbaskets)         ←
## [1]  92108 220447         You can also use dim() to see
                            the dimensions of the matrix.
```

```
colnames(bookbaskets)[1:5]
## [1] " A Light in the Storm:[...]"
## [2] " Always Have Popsicles"
## [3] " Apple Magic"
## [4] " Ask Lily"
## [5] " Beyond IBM: Leadership Marketing and Finance for the 1990s"
rownames(bookbaskets)[1:5]
## [1] "10"      "1000"   "100001" "100002" "100004"
```

← **The columns are labeled by book title.**

← **The rows are labeled by customer.**

You can examine the distribution of transaction sizes (or basket sizes) with the function `size()`:

```
basketSizes <- size(bookbaskets)
summary(basketSizes)
##    Min. 1st Qu.  Median   Mean 3rd Qu.     Max.
##     1.0     1.0     1.0    11.1     4.0  10250.0
```

Most customers (at least half of them, in fact) only expressed interest in one book. But someone has expressed interest in more than 10,000! You probably want to look more closely at the size distribution to see what's going on.

Listing 9.20 Examining the size distribution

```
quantile(basketSizes, probs = seq(0, 1, 0.1))
##    0%   10%   20%   30%   40%   50%   60%   70%   80%   90%  100%
##     1     1     1     1     1     1     2     3     5    13 10253
library(ggplot2)
ggplot(data.frame(count = basketSizes)) +
  geom_density(aes(x = count)) +
  scale_x_log10()
```

→ (pointing to quantile line) **Looks at the basket size distribution, in 10% increments**

← (pointing to library line) **Plots the distribution to get a better look**

Figure 9.18 shows the distribution of basket sizes. 90% of customers expressed interest in fewer than 15 books; most of the remaining customers expressed interest in up to about 100 books or so; the call `quantile(basketSizes, probs = c(0.99, 1))` will show you that 99% of customers expressed interest in 179 books or fewer. Still, a few people have expressed interest in several hundred, or even several thousand books.

Which books are they reading? The function `itemFrequency()` can tell you how often each book shows up in the transaction data.

Listing 9.21 Counting how often each book occurs

```
bookCount <- itemFrequency(bookbaskets, "absolute")
summary(bookCount)

##    Min. 1st Qu.  Median   Mean 3rd Qu.     Max.
##   1.000   1.000   1.000   4.638   3.000 2502.000
```

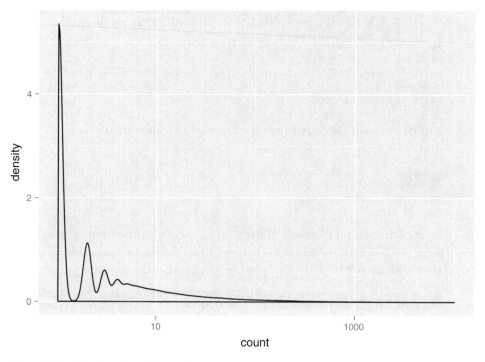

Figure 9.18   A density plot of basket sizes

You can also find the 10 most frequently occurring books.

Listing 9.22   Finding the 10 most frequently occurring books

```
orderedBooks <- sort(bookCount, decreasing = TRUE)      ◁──── Sorts the counts in
knitr::kable(orderedBooks[1:10])      ◁─────────────────────  decreasing order

                                                             Displays the top 10
# |                                                | x|      books in a nice format
# |:-----------------------------------------------|----:|
# |Wild Animus                                     | 2502|
# |The Lovely Bones: A Novel                       | 1295|
# |She's Come Undone                               |  934|
# |The Da Vinci Code                               |  905|
# |Harry Potter and the Sorcerer's Stone           |  832|
# |The Nanny Diaries: A Novel                      |  821|
# |A Painted House                                 |  819|
# |Bridget Jones's Diary                           |  772|
# |The Secret Life of Bees                         |  762|
# |Divine Secrets of the Ya-Ya Sisterhood: A Novel |  737|

orderedBooks[1] / nrow(bookbaskets)      ◁──── The most popular book
                                               in the dataset occurred
## Wild Animus                                 in fewer than 3% of the
##   0.02716376                                baskets.
```

The last observation in the preceding listing highlights one of the issues with mining high-dimensional data: when you have thousands of variables, or thousands of items, almost every event is rare. Keep this point in mind when deciding on support thresholds for rule mining; your thresholds will often need to be quite low.

Before we get to the rule mining, let's refine the data a bit more. As you observed earlier, half of the customers in the data only expressed interest in a single book. Since you want to find books that occur together in people's interest lists, you can't make any direct use of people who haven't yet shown interest in multiple books. You can restrict the dataset to customers who have expressed interest in at least two books:

```
bookbaskets_use <- bookbaskets[basketSizes > 1]
dim(bookbaskets_use)
## [1]  40822 220447
```

Now you're ready to look for association rules.

THE APRIORI() FUNCTION

In order to mine rules, you need to decide on a minimum support level and a minimum threshold level. For this example, let's try restricting the itemsets that we'll consider to those with a minimum support of 0.2%, or 0.002. This corresponds to itemsets that appear at least `0.002 * nrow(bookbaskets_use)` times, which is about 82 transactions. We'll use a confidence threshold of 75%.

Listing 9.23   Finding the association rules

```
rules <- apriori(bookbaskets_use,                    ⟵──────────────────┐   Calls apriori() with a minimum
                 parameter = list(support = 0.002, confidence = 0.75))      support of 0.002 and a
                                                                            minimum confidence of 0.75
summary(rules)
## set of 191 rules   ⟵── The number of rules found
##
## rule length distribution (lhs + rhs):sizes   ⟵────┐   The distribution of rule lengths
##  2   3   4   5                                      (in this example, most rules
## 11 100  66  14                                      contain 3 items—2 on the left
##                                                     side, X (lhs), and one on the
##    Min. 1st Qu.  Median    Mean 3rd Qu.    Max.     right side, Y (rhs))
##   2.000   3.000   3.000   3.435   4.000   5.000
##
## summary of quality measures:
##     support          confidence           lift              count
##  Min.   :0.002009   Min.   :0.7500   Min.   : 40.89   Min.   : 82.0
##  1st Qu.:0.002131   1st Qu.:0.8113   1st Qu.: 86.44   1st Qu.: 87.0
##  Median :0.002278   Median :0.8468   Median :131.36   Median : 93.0
##  Mean   :0.002593   Mean   :0.8569   Mean   :129.68   Mean   :105.8
##  3rd Qu.:0.002695   3rd Qu.:0.9065   3rd Qu.:158.77   3rd Qu.:110.0
##  Max.   :0.005830   Max.   :0.9882   Max.   :321.89   Max.   :238.0
##
## mining info:              ⟵────────────────────┐
##           data ntransactions support confidence
##  bookbaskets_use       40822   0.002       0.75
```

A summary of rule quality measures,
including support and confidence

Some information on
how apriori() was called

The quality measures on the rules include a rule's support and confidence, the support count (how many transactions the rule applied to), and a quantity called *lift*. Lift compares the frequency of an observed pattern with how often you'd expect to see that pattern just by chance. The lift of a rule "if X, then Y" is given by support({X, Y}) / (support(X) * support(Y)). If the lift is near 1, then there's a good chance that the pattern you observed is occurring just by chance. The larger the lift, the more likely that the pattern is "real." In this case, all the discovered rules have a lift of at least 40, so they're likely to be real patterns in customer behavior.

INSPECTING AND EVALUATING RULES

There are also other metrics and interest measures you can use to evaluate the rules by using the function interestMeasure(). We'll look at two of these measures: coverage and fishersExactTest. *Coverage* is the support of the left side of the rule (X); it tells you how often the rule would be applied in the dataset. *Fisher's exact test* is a significance test for whether an observed pattern is real or chance (the same thing lift measures; Fisher's test is more formal). Fisher's exact test returns the p-value, or the probability that you would see the observed pattern by chance; you want the p-value to be small.

Listing 9.24   Scoring rules

The first argument to interestMeasure() is the discovered rules.

The second argument is a list of interest measures to apply.

```
measures <- interestMeasure(rules,
                measure=c("coverage", "fishersExactTest"),
                transactions = bookbaskets_use)
summary(measures)
##      coverage          fishersExactTest
## Min.   :0.002082    Min.   : 0.000e+00
## 1st Qu.:0.002511    1st Qu.: 0.000e+00
## Median :0.002719    Median : 0.000e+00
## Mean   :0.003039    Mean   :5.080e-138
## 3rd Qu.:0.003160    3rd Qu.: 0.000e+00
## Max.   :0.006982    Max.   :9.702e-136
```

The last argument is a dataset to evaluate the interest measures over. This is usually the same set used to mine the rules, but it needn't be. For instance, you can evaluate the rules over the full dataset, bookbaskets, to get coverage estimates that reflect all the customers, not just the ones who showed interest in more than one book.

The coverage of the discovered rules ranges from 0.002–0.007, equivalent to a range of about 82–286 people. All the p-values from Fisher's test are small, so it's likely that the rules reflect actual customer behavior patterns.

You can also call interestMeasure() with the methods support, confidence, and lift, among others. This would be useful in our example if you wanted to get support, confidence, and lift estimates for the full dataset bookbaskets, rather than the filtered dataset bookbaskets_use—or for a subset of the data, for instance, only customers from the United States.

The function inspect() pretty-prints the rules. The function sort() allows you to sort the rules by a quality or interest measure, like confidence. To print the five most confident rules in the dataset, you could use the following statement, which we will expand out using pipe notation.

Listing 9.25 Getting the five most confident rules

```
library(magrittr)   <— Attaches magrittr to get pipe notation

rules %>%
  sort(., by = "confidence") %>%   <— Sorts rules by confidence

  head(., n = 5) %>%   <— Gets the first five rules

  inspect(.)   <— Calls inspect() to pretty-print the rules
```

For legibility, we show the output of this command in table 9.3.

Table 9.3 The five most confident rules discovered in the data

Left side	Right side	Support	Confidence	Lift	Count
Four to Score *High Five* *Seven Up* *Two for the Dough*	*Three to Get Deadly*	0.002	0.988	165	84
Harry Potter and the Order of the Phoenix *Harry Potter and the Prisoner of Azkaban* *Harry Potter and the Sorcerer's Stone*	*Harry Potter and the Chamber of Secrets*	0.003	0.966	73	117
Four to Score *High Five* *One for the Money* *Two for the Dough*	*Three to Get Deadly*	0.002	0.966	162	85
Four to Score *Seven Up* *Three to Get Deadly* *Two for the Dough*	*High Five*	0.002	0.966	181	84
High Five *Seven Up* *Three to Get Deadly* *Two for the Dough*	*Four to Score*	0.002	0.966	168	84

There are two things to notice in table 9.3. First, the rules concern books that come in series: the numbered series of novels about bounty hunter Stephanie Plum, and the Harry Potter series. So these rules essentially say that if a reader has read four Stephanie Plum or three Harry Potter books, they're almost sure to buy another one.

The second thing to notice is that rules 1, 4, and 5 are permutations of the same itemset. This is likely to happen when the rules get long.

RESTRICTING WHICH ITEMS TO MINE

You can restrict which items appear in the left side or right side of a rule. Suppose you're interested specifically in books that tend to co-occur with the novel *The Lovely*

Bones. You can do this by restricting which books appear on the right side of the rule, using the appearance parameter.

Listing 9.26   Finding rules with restrictions

```
brules <- apriori(bookbaskets_use,
                  parameter = list(support = 0.001,
                                   confidence = 0.6),
                  appearance = list(rhs = c("The Lovely Bones: A Novel"),
                                    default = "lhs"))
 summary(brules)
## set of 46 rules
##
## rule length distribution (lhs + rhs):sizes
## 3  4
## 44  2
##
##    Min. 1st Qu.  Median    Mean 3rd Qu.    Max.
##   3.000   3.000   3.000   3.043   3.000   4.000
##
## summary of quality measures:
##     support            confidence          lift              count
##   Min.   :0.001004   Min.   :0.6000   Min.   :21.81   Min.   :41.00
##   1st Qu.:0.001029   1st Qu.:0.6118   1st Qu.:22.24   1st Qu.:42.00
##   Median :0.001102   Median :0.6258   Median :22.75   Median :45.00
##   Mean   :0.001132   Mean   :0.6365   Mean   :23.14   Mean   :46.22
##   3rd Qu.:0.001219   3rd Qu.:0.6457   3rd Qu.:23.47   3rd Qu.:49.75
##   Max.   :0.001396   Max.   :0.7455   Max.   :27.10   Max.   :57.00
##
## mining info:
##             data ntransactions support confidence
##   bookbaskets_use         40822   0.001         0.6
```

> **Relaxes the minimum support to 0.001 and the minimum confidence to 0.6**

> **Only "The Lovely Bones" is allowed to appear on the right side of the rules.**

> **By default, all the books can go into the left side of the rules.**

The supports, confidences, counts, and lifts are lower than they were in our previous example, but the lifts are still much greater than one, so it's likely that the rules reflect real customer behavior patterns.

Let's inspect the rules, sorted by confidence. Since they'll all have the same right side, you can use the lhs() function to only look at the left sides.

Listing 9.27   Inspecting rules

```
brules %>%
  sort(., by = "confidence") %>%
  lhs(.) %>%
  head(., n = 5) %>%
  inspect(.)
##    items
## 1 {Divine Secrets of the Ya-Ya Sisterhood: A Novel,
##    Lucky : A Memoir}
## 2 {Lucky : A Memoir,
##    The Notebook}
```

> **Gets the left-hand side of the sorted rules**

```
## 3 {Lucky : A Memoir,
##    Wild Animus}
## 4 {Midwives: A Novel,
##    Wicked: The Life and Times of the Wicked Witch of the West}
## 5 {Lucky : A Memoir,
##    Summer Sisters}
```

Note that four of the five most confident rules include *Lucky: A Memoir* in the left side, which perhaps isn't surprising, since *Lucky* was written by the author of *The Lovely Bones*. Suppose you want to find out about works by other authors that are interesting to people who showed interest in *The Lovely Bones*; you can use subset() to filter down to only rules that don't include *Lucky*.

Listing 9.28 Inspecting rules with restrictions

```
brulesSub <- subset(brules, subset = !(lhs %in% "Lucky : A Memoir"))   ◁——┐
 brulesSub %>%
   sort(., by = "confidence") %>%                Restricts to the subset
   lhs(.) %>%                                    of rules where Lucky is
   head(., n = 5) %>%                            not in the left side
   inspect(.)

brulesConf <- sort(brulesSub, by="confidence")

inspect(head(lhs(brulesConf), n = 5))
##    items
## 1 {Midwives: A Novel,
##    Wicked: The Life and Times of the Wicked Witch of the West}
## 2 {She's Come Undone,
##    The Secret Life of Bees,
##    Wild Animus}
## 3 {A Walk to Remember,
##    The Nanny Diaries: A Novel}
## 4 {Beloved,
##    The Red Tent}
## 5 {The Da Vinci Code,
##    The Reader}
```

These examples show that association rule mining is often highly interactive. To get interesting rules, you must often set the support and confidence levels fairly low; as a result, you can get many, many rules. Some rules will be more interesting or surprising to you than others; to find them requires sorting the rules by different interest measures, or perhaps restricting yourself to specific subsets of rules.

9.2.4 *Association rule takeaways*

You've now walked through an example of using association rules to explore common patterns in purchase data. Here's what you should remember about association rules:

- The goal of association rule mining is to find relationships in the data: items or attributes that tend to occur together.
- A good rule "if X then Y" should occur more often than you'd expect to observe by chance. You can use lift or Fisher's exact test to check if this is true.

- When it's possible for a large number of different items to be in a basket (in our example, thousands of different books), most events will be rare (have low support).

- Association rule mining is often interactive, as there can be many rules to sort and sift through.

Summary

In this chapter, you've learned how to find similarities in data using two different clustering methods in R, and how to find items that tend to occur together in data using association rules. You've also learned how to evaluate your discovered clusters and your discovered rules.

Unsupervised methods like the ones we've covered in this chapter are really more exploratory in nature. Unlike with supervised methods, there's no "ground truth" to evaluate your findings against. But the findings from unsupervised methods can be the starting point for more-focused experiments and modeling.

In the last few chapters, we've covered the most basic modeling and data analysis techniques; they're all good first approaches to consider when you're starting a new project. In the next chapter, we'll touch on a few more-advanced methods.

In this chapter you have learned

- How to cluster unlabeled data, using both hierarchical methods and k-means
- How to estimate what the appropriate number of clusters should be
- How to evaluate an existing clustering for cluster stability
- How to find patterns (association rules) in transaction data using apriori
- How to evaluate and sort through discovered association rules

10

Exploring advanced methods

This chapter covers

- Decision tree–based models
- Generalized additive models
- Support vector machines

In chapter 7, you learned about linear methods for fitting predictive models. These models are the bread-and-butter methods of machine learning; they are easy to fit; they are small, portable, and efficient; they sometimes provide useful advice; and they can work well in a wide variety of situations. However, they also make strong assumptions about the world: namely, that the outcome is linearly related to all the inputs, and all the inputs contribute additively to the outcome. In this chapter, you will learn about methods that relax these assumptions.

Figure 10.1 represents our mental model for what we'll do in this chapter: use R to master the science of building supervised machine learning models.

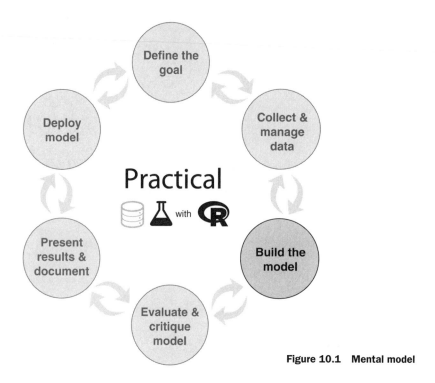

Figure 10.1   Mental model

Example   *Suppose you want to study the relationship between mortality rates and measures of a person's health or fitness, including BMI (body mass index).*

Figure 10.2 shows the relationship between BMI and mortality hazard ratio for a population of older Thais over a four-year period.[1] It shows that both high and low BMI are associated with higher mortality rates: the relationship between BMI and mortality is not linear. So a straightforward linear model to predict mortality rates based (partly) on BMI may not perform well.

In addition, there may be *interactions* between BMI and other factors, like how active a person is. For example, for people who are highly active, BMI may affect mortality rates much less than for people who are sedentary. Some interactions, such as "if-then" relationships among variables, or multiplicative effects between variables, may not always be expressible in linear models.[2]

The machine learning techniques in this chapter use a variety of methods to address non-linearity, interactions, and other issues in modeling.

---

[1] Data from Vapattanawong, et.al. "Obesity and mortality among older Thais: a four year follow up study," *BMC Public Health*, 2010. https://doi.org/10.1186/1471-2458-10-604.

[2] One can model interactions in linear models, but it must be done explicitly by the data scientist. Instead, we'll focus on machine learning techniques, such as tree-based methods, that can learn at least certain types of interactions directly.

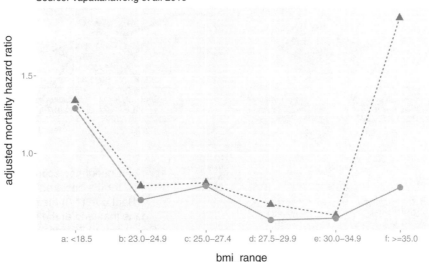

Figure 10.2 **Mortality rates of men and women as a function of body mass index**

10.1 *Tree-based methods*

You saw an example of a basic decision tree model in chapter 1 (reproduced in figure 10.3). Decision trees are useful for both classification and regression, and they are an attractive method for a number of reasons:

- They take any type of datums, numerical or categorical, without any distributional assumptions and without preprocessing.
- Most implementations (in particular, R) handle missing data; the method is also robust to redundant and non-linear data.
- The algorithm is easy to use, and the output (the tree) is relatively easy to understand.
- They naturally express certain kinds of interactions among the input variables: those of the form "IF x is true AND y is true, THEN...."
- Once the model is fit, scoring is fast.

On the other hand, decision trees do have some drawbacks:

- They have a tendency to overfit, especially without pruning.
- They have high training variance: samples drawn from the same population can produce trees with different structures and different prediction accuracy.
- Simple decision trees are not as reliable as the other tree-based ensemble methods we'll discuss in this chapter.[3]

---

[3] See Lim, Loh, and Shih, "A Comparison of Prediction Accuracy, Complexity, and Training Time of Thirty-three Old and New Classification Algorithms," *Machine Learning*, 2000. 40, 203–229; online at http://mng .bz/qX06.

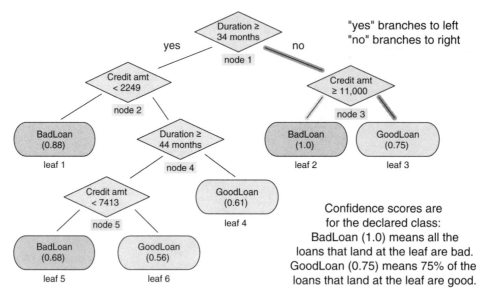

Figure 10.3   Example decision tree (from chapter 1)

For these reasons, we don't emphasize the use of basic decision trees in this book. However, there are a number of techniques to fix these weaknesses that lead to state-of-the-art, useful, and performant modeling algorithms. We'll discuss some of these techniques in this section.

10.1.1 A basic decision tree

To motivate the discussion of tree-based methods, we'll return to an example that we used in chapter 6 and build a basic decision tree.

> **Example** *Suppose you want to classify email into spam (email you do not want) and non-spam (email you want).*

For this example, you'll again use the Spambase dataset. The dataset consists of about 4,600 documents and 57 features that describe the frequency of certain keywords and characters. Here's the process:

- First, you'll train a decision tree to estimate the probability that a given document is spam.
- Next, you'll evaluate the tree's performance according to several performance measures, including accuracy, F1, and deviance (all discussed in chapter 7).

Recall from discussions in chapters 6 and 7 that we want accuracy and F1 to be high, and deviance (which is similar to variance) to be low.

First, let's load the data. As you did in section 6.2, download a copy of spamD.tsv from https://github.com/WinVector/PDSwR2/raw/master/Spambase/spamD.tsv. Then, write a few convenience functions and train a decision tree, as in the following listing.

Listing 10.1 Preparing Spambase data and evaluating a decision tree model

A function to calculate log likelihood (for calculating deviance)

Loads the data and splits into training (90% of data) and test (10% of data) sets

Uses all the features and does binary classification, where TRUE corresponds to spam documents

```
spamD <- read.table('spamD.tsv', header = TRUE, sep = '\t')
spamD$isSpam <- spamD$spam == 'spam'
spamTrain <- subset(spamD, spamD$rgroup >= 10)
spamTest <- subset(spamD, spamD$rgroup < 10)

spamVars <- setdiff(colnames(spamD), list('rgroup', 'spam', 'isSpam'))
library(wrapr)
spamFormula <- mk_formula("isSpam", spamVars)

loglikelihood <- function(y, py) {
   pysmooth <- ifelse(py == 0, 1e-12,
                    ifelse(py == 1, 1 - 1e-12, py))

  sum(y * log(pysmooth) + (1 - y) * log(1 - pysmooth))
}

accuracyMeasures <- function(pred, truth, name = "model") {
   dev.norm <- -2 * loglikelihood(as.numeric(truth), pred) / length(pred)
   ctable <- table(truth = truth,
                 pred = (pred > 0.5))
   accuracy <- sum(diag(ctable)) / sum(ctable)
   precision <- ctable[2, 2] / sum(ctable[, 2])
   recall <- ctable[2, 2] / sum(ctable[2, ])
   f1 <- 2 * precision * recall / (precision + recall)
   data.frame(model = name, accuracy = accuracy, f1 = f1, dev.norm)
}

library(rpart)
treemodel <- rpart(spamFormula, spamTrain, method = "class")

library(rpart.plot)
rpart.plot(treemodel, type = 5, extra = 6)

predTrain <- predict(treemodel, newdata = spamTrain)[, 2]

trainperf_tree <- accuracyMeasures(predTrain,

                 spamTrain$spam == "spam",
                 name = "tree, training")

predTest <- predict(treemodel, newdata = spamTest)[, 2]
testperf_tree <- accuracyMeasures(predTest,
                 spamTest$spam == "spam",
```

A function to calculate and return various measures on the model: normalized deviance, prediction accuracy, and f1

Normalizes the deviance by the number of data points so we can compare the deviance across training and test sets

For plotting the tree

Evaluates the decision tree model against the training and test sets

Gets the predicted probabilities of the class "spam"

Loads the rpart library and fits a decision tree model

Converts the class probability estimator into a classifier by labeling documents that score greater than 0.5 as spam

The resulting decision tree model is shown in figure 10.4. The output of the two calls to accuracyMeasures() looks like the following:

```
library(pander)                                          A package to make nicely
                                                         formatted ASCII tables

panderOptions("plain.ascii", TRUE)
panderOptions("keep.trailing.zeros", TRUE)               Sets some options globally
panderOptions("table.style", "simple")                   so we don't have to keep
perf_justify <- "lrrr"                                   setting them in every call

perftable <- rbind(trainperf_tree, testperf_tree)
pandoc.table(perftable, justify = perf_justify)

##
##
## model              accuracy        f1    dev.norm
## ---------------   ----------   --------   ----------
## tree, training      0.8996      0.8691      0.6304
## tree, test          0.8712      0.8280      0.7531
```

As expected, the accuracy and F1 scores both degrade on the test set, and the deviance increases.

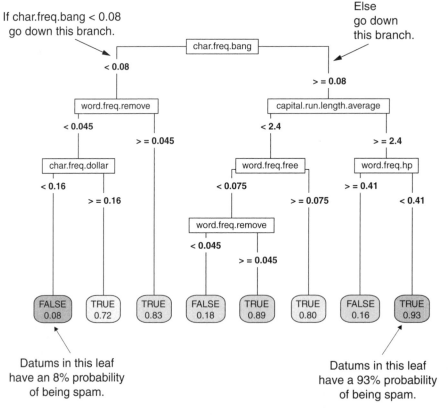

Figure 10.4   Decision tree model for spam filtering

10.1.2 *Using bagging to improve prediction*

One way to mitigate the shortcomings of decision tree models is by bootstrap aggregation, or *bagging*. In bagging, you draw bootstrap samples (random samples with replacement) from your data. From each sample, you build a decision tree model. The final model is the average of all the individual decision trees. This is shown in figure 10.5[4]

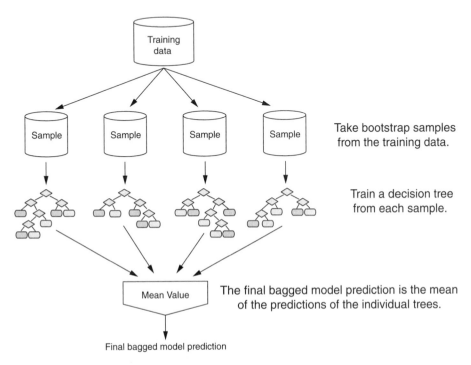

Figure 10.5 Bagging decision trees

To make this concrete, suppose that x is an input datum, $y\_i(x)$ is the output of the ith tree, $c(y\_1(x), y\_2(x), \ldots y\_n(x))$ is the vector of individual outputs, and y is the output of the final model:

- For regression, or for estimating class probabilities, $y(x)$ is the average of the scores returned by the individual trees: $y(x) = \mathrm{mean}(c(y\_1(x), \ldots y\_n(x)))$.
- For classification, the final model assigns the class that got the most votes from the individual trees.

---

[4] Bagging, random forests, and gradient-boosted trees are variations of a general technique called *ensemble learning*. An ensemble model is composed of the combination of several smaller simple models (often small decision trees). Giovanni Seni and John Elder's *Ensemble Methods in Data Mining* (Morgan & Claypool, 2010) is an excellent introduction to the general theory of ensemble learning.

Bagging decision trees stabilizes the final model by lowering the variance; this improves the accuracy. A bagged ensemble of trees is also less likely to overfit the data.

Try bagging some tree models for the spam example.

Listing 10.2   Bagging decision trees

> **Uses bootstrap samples the same size as the training set, with 100 trees**

```
ntrain <- dim(spamTrain)[1]
n <- ntrain          ◁
ntree <- 100
samples <- sapply(1:ntree,    ◁
```

> **Builds the bootstrap samples by sampling the row indices of spamTrain with replacement. Each column of the matrix samples represents the row indices into spamTrain that comprise the bootstrap sample.**

```
                FUN = function(iter)
                    { sample(1:ntrain, size = n, replace = TRUE) })
▷ treelist <-lapply(1:ntree,
```

Trains the individual decision trees and returns them in a list. Note: This step can take a few minutes.

```
                    FUN = function(iter) {
                        samp <- samples[, iter];
                        rpart(spamFormula, spamTrain[samp, ], method = "class") }
            )
predict.bag <- function(treelist, newdata) {    ◁

    preds <- sapply(1:length(treelist),
                FUN = function(iter) {
                        predict(treelist[[iter]], newdata = newdata)[, 2] })
    predsums <- rowSums(preds)
    predsums / length(treelist)
}
pred <- predict.bag(treelist, newdata = spamTrain)
trainperf_bag <- accuracyMeasures(pred,          ◁
                spamTrain$spam == "spam",
                name = "bagging, training")
pred <- predict.bag(treelist, newdata = spamTest)
testperf_bag <- accuracyMeasures(pred,
                spamTest$spam == "spam",
                name = "bagging, test")

perftable <- rbind(trainperf_bag, testperf_bag)
pandoc.table(perftable, justify = perf_justify)
##
##
## model               accuracy      f1    dev.norm
## ------------------- ---------- -------- ----------
## bagging, training      0.9167   0.8917     0.5080
## bagging, test          0.9127   0.8824     0.5793
```

> **predict.bag assumes the underlying classifier returns decision probabilities, not decisions. predict.bag takes the mean of the predictions of all the individual trees**

> **Evaluates the bagged decision trees against the training and test sets**

As you see, bagging improves accuracy and F1, and reduces deviance over both the training and test sets when compared to the single decision tree (you'll see a direct comparison of the scores a little later on). There is also less degradation in the bagged model's performance going from training to test than there is with the decision tree.

You can further improve prediction performance by going from bagging to random forests.

> ### Bagging classifiers
>
> The proofs that bagging reduces variance are only valid for regression and for estimating class probabilities, not for classifiers (a model that only returns class membership, not class probabilities). Bagging a bad classifier can make it worse. So you definitely want to work over estimated class probabilities, if they're at all available. But it can be shown that for CART trees (which is the decision tree implementation in R) under mild assumptions, bagging tends to increase classifier accuracy. See Clifton D. Sutton, "Classification and Regression Trees, Bagging, and Boosting," *Handbook of Statistics, Vol. 24* (Elsevier, 2005) for more details.

10.1.3 *Using random forests to further improve prediction*

In bagging, the trees are built using randomized datasets, but each tree is built by considering the exact same set of features. This means that all the individual trees are likely to use very similar sets of features (perhaps in a different order or with different split values). Hence, the individual trees will tend to be overly correlated with each other. If there are regions in feature space where one tree tends to make mistakes, then all the trees are likely to make mistakes there, too, diminishing our opportunity for correction. The random forest approach tries to decorrelate the trees by randomizing the set of variables that each tree is allowed to use.

The process is shown in figure 10.6. For each individual tree in the ensemble, the random forest method does the following:

1. Draws a bootstrapped sample from the training data
2. For each sample, grows a decision tree, and at each node of the tree
    a. Randomly draws a subset of `mtry` variables from the `p` total features that are available
    b. Picks the best variable and the best split from that set of `mtry` variables
    c. Continues until the tree is fully grown

The final ensemble of trees is then bagged to make the random forest predictions. This is quite involved, but fortunately all done by a single-line random forest call.

By default, the `randomForest()` function in R draws `mtry = p/3` variables at each node for regression trees, and `m = sqrt(p)` variables for classification trees. In theory, random forests aren't terribly sensitive to the value of `mtry`. Smaller values will grow the trees faster; but if you have a very large number of variables to choose from, of which only a small fraction are actually useful, then using a larger `mtry` is better, since with a larger `mtry` you're more likely to draw some useful variables at every step of the tree-growing procedure.

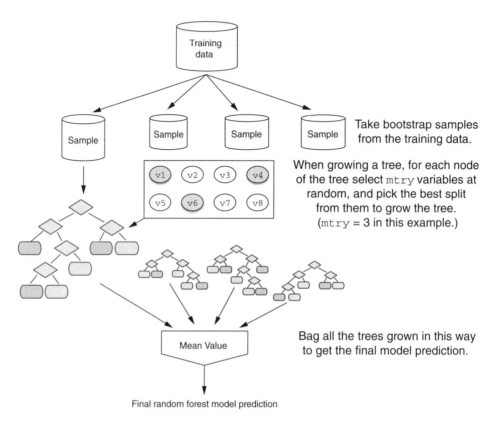

Take bootstrap samples from the training data.

When growing a tree, for each node of the tree select mtry variables at random, and pick the best split from them to grow the tree. (mtry = 3 in this example.)

Bag all the trees grown in this way to get the final model prediction.

Final random forest model prediction

Figure 10.6   Growing a random forest

Continuing from the data in section 10.1, try building a spam model using random forests.

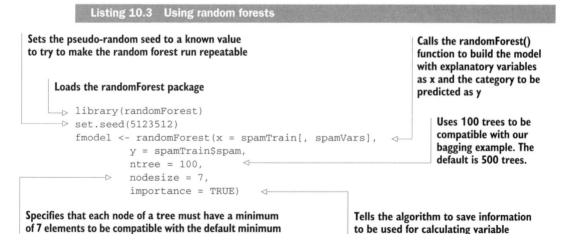

Listing 10.3   Using random forests

Sets the pseudo-random seed to a known value to try to make the random forest run repeatable

Calls the randomForest() function to build the model with explanatory variables as x and the category to be predicted as y

Loads the randomForest package

```
library(randomForest)
set.seed(5123512)
fmodel <- randomForest(x = spamTrain[, spamVars],
        y = spamTrain$spam,
        ntree = 100,
        nodesize = 7,
        importance = TRUE)
```

Uses 100 trees to be compatible with our bagging example. The default is 500 trees.

Specifies that each node of a tree must have a minimum of 7 elements to be compatible with the default minimum node size that rpart() uses on this training set

Tells the algorithm to save information to be used for calculating variable importance (we'll see this later)

```
pred <- predict(fmodel,
              spamTrain[, spamVars],
              type = 'prob')[, 'spam']
trainperf_rf <- accuracyMeasures(predict(fmodel,
    newdata = spamTrain[, spamVars], type = 'prob')[, 'spam'],
    spamTrain$spam == "spam", name = "random forest, train")

testperf_rf <- accuracyMeasures(predict(fmodel,
    newdata = spamTest[, spamVars], type = 'prob')[, 'spam'],
    spamTest$spam == "spam", name = "random forest, test")

perftable <- rbind(trainperf_rf, testperf_rf)
pandoc.table(perftable, justify = perf_justify)
##
##
## model                  accuracy      f1  dev.norm
## --------------------- ---------- -------- ----------
## random forest, train    0.9884   0.9852    0.1440
## random forest, test     0.9498   0.9341    0.3011
```

Reports the
model quality

You can summarize the results for all three of the models you've looked at. First, on training:

```
trainf <- rbind(trainperf_tree, trainperf_bag, trainperf_rf)
pandoc.table(trainf, justify = perf_justify)
##
##
## model                  accuracy      f1  dev.norm
## --------------------- ---------- -------- ----------
## tree, training          0.8996   0.8691    0.6304
## bagging, training       0.9160   0.8906    0.5106
## random forest, train    0.9884   0.9852    0.1440
```

Then, on test:

```
testf <- rbind(testperf_tree, testperf_bag, testperf_rf)
pandoc.table(testf, justify = perf_justify)
##
##
## model                  accuracy      f1  dev.norm
## --------------------- ---------- -------- ----------
## tree, test              0.8712   0.8280    0.7531
## bagging, test           0.9105   0.8791    0.5834
## random forest, test     0.9498   0.9341    0.3011
```

The random forest model performed dramatically better than the other two models on both training and test.

You can also look at performance change: the decrease in accuracy and F1 when going from training to test, and the corresponding increase in deviance.

```
difff <- data.frame(model = c("tree", "bagging", "random forest"),
                accuracy = trainf$accuracy - testf$accuracy,
                f1 = trainf$f1 - testf$f1,
                dev.norm = trainf$dev.norm - testf$dev.norm)

pandoc.table(difff, justify=perf_justify)
```

```
##
##
## model            accuracy          f1   dev.norm
## --------------- ---------- --------- ----------
## tree              0.028411   0.04111   -0.12275
## bagging           0.005523   0.01158   -0.07284
## random forest     0.038633   0.05110   -0.15711
```

The random forest's model degraded about as much as a single decision tree when going from training to test data, and much more than the bagged model did. This is one of the drawbacks of random forest models: the tendency to overfit the training data. However, in this case, the random forest model was still the best performing.

> **Random forests can overfit!**
>
> It's lore among random forest proponents that "random forests don't overfit." In fact, they can. Hastie et al. back up this observation in their chapter on random forests in *The Elements of Statistical Learning* (Springer, 2011). Seeing virtually perfect prediction on training data and less-than-perfect performance on holdout data is characteristic of random forest models. So when using random forest, it's extremely important to validate model performance on holdout data.

EXAMINING VARIABLE IMPORTANCE

A useful feature of the `randomForest()` function is its variable importance calculation. Since the algorithm uses a large number of bootstrap samples, each data point x has a corresponding set of *out-of-bag samples*: those samples that don't contain the point x. This is shown in figure 10.7 for the data point x1. The out-of-bag samples can be used in a way similar to *N*-fold cross-validation, to estimate the accuracy of each tree in the ensemble.

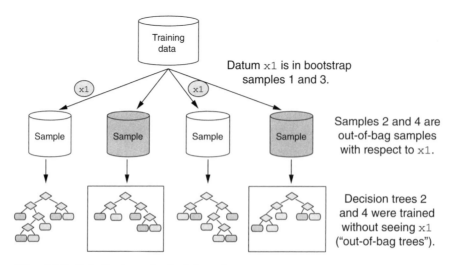

Figure 10.7 Out-of-bag samples for datum x1

To evaluate variable `v1`,
permute the values of `v1` in the training data.

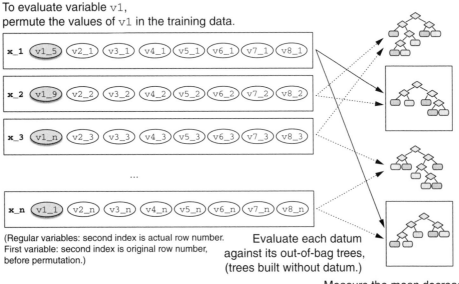

(Regular variables: second index is actual row number.
First variable: second index is original row number,
before permutation.)

Evaluate each datum
against its out-of-bag trees,
(trees built without datum.)

Measure the mean decrease
in accuracy of each tree to
get importance of variable `v1`.

Figure 10.8   Calculating variable importance of variable `v1`

To estimate the "importance" of a variable `v1`, the variable's values are randomly permuted. Each tree is then evaluated against its out-of-bag samples, and the corresponding decrease in each tree's accuracy is estimated. This is shown in figure 10.8.

If the average decrease over all the trees is large, then the variable is considered important—its value makes a big difference in predicting the outcome. If the average decrease is small, then the variable doesn't make much difference to the outcome. The algorithm also measures the decrease in node purity that occurs from splitting on a permuted variable (how this variable affects the quality of the tree).

You can calculate the variable importance by setting `importance = TRUE` in the `randomForest()` call (as you did in listing 10.3), and then calling the functions `importance()` and `varImpPlot()`.

Listing 10.4   `randomForest` variable importances

```
varImp <- importance(fmodel)        Calls importance() on the spam model

varImp[1:10, ]                                                          The importance()
##                       non-spam        spam MeanDecreaseAccuracy     function returns a
## word.freq.make        1.656795    3.432962             3.067899     matrix of
## word.freq.address     2.631231    3.800668             3.632077     importance
## word.freq.all         3.279517    6.235651             6.137927     measures (larger
## word.freq.3d          3.900232    1.286917             3.753238     values = more
## word.freq.our         9.966034   10.160010            12.039651     important).
## word.freq.over        4.657285    4.183888             4.894526
```

```
## word.freq.remove     19.172764 14.020182            20.229958
## word.freq.internet    7.595305  5.246213             8.036892
## word.freq.order       3.167008  2.505777             3.065529
## word.freq.mail        3.820764  2.786041             4.869502

varImpPlot(fmodel, type = 1)
```

Plots the variable importance as measured by accuracy change

The result of the `varImpPlot()` call is shown in figure 10.9. According to the plot, the most important variable for determining if an email is spam is `char.freq.bang`, or the number of times an exclamation point appears in an email, which makes some intuitive sense. The next most important variable is `word.freq.remove`, or the number of times the word "remove" appears in the email.

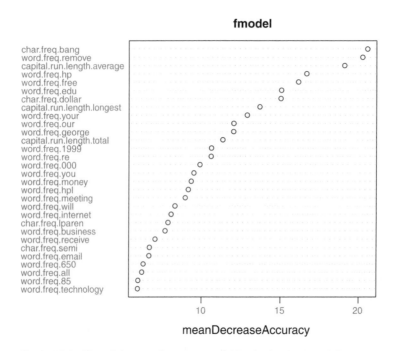

fmodel

Figure 10.9   Plot of the most important variables in the spam model, as measured by accuracy

Knowing which variables are most important (or at least, which variables contribute the most to the structure of the underlying decision trees) can help you with variable reduction. This is useful not only for building smaller, faster trees, but also for choosing variables to be used by another modeling algorithm, if that's desired. We can reduce the number of variables in this spam example from 57 to 30 without affecting the quality of the final model.

Variable screening as an initial screening

Data scientist Jeremy Howard (of Kaggle and fast.ai fame) is a big proponent of using an initial variable importance screen early in a data science project to eliminate variables that are not of interest and identify variables to discuss with business partners.

Listing 10.5 Fitting with fewer variables

```
sorted <- sort(varImp[, "MeanDecreaseAccuracy"],       ⊲ Sorts the variables by their
               decreasing = TRUE)                          importance, as measured by
                                                           accuracy change
selVars <- names(sorted)[1:30]
fsel <- randomForest(x = spamTrain[, selVars],         ⊲ Builds a random forest
                     y = spamTrain$spam,                   model using only the 30
                     ntree = 100,                          most important variables
                     nodesize = 7,
                     importance = TRUE)

trainperf_rf2 <- accuracyMeasures(predict(fsel,
   newdata = spamTrain[, selVars], type = 'prob')[, 'spam'],
   spamTrain$spam == "spam", name = "RF small, train")

testperf_rf2 <- accuracyMeasures(predict(fsel,
   newdata=spamTest[, selVars], type = 'prob')[, 'spam'],
   spamTest$spam == "spam", name = "RF small, test")

perftable <- rbind(testperf_rf, testperf_rf2)          ⊲ Compares the two
pandoc.table(perftable, justify = perf_justify)            random forest models
##                                                          on the test set
##
## model                 accuracy       f1  dev.norm
## --------------------- ---------- -------- ----------
## random forest, test      0.9498   0.9341     0.3011
## RF small, test           0.9520   0.9368     0.4000
```

The smaller model performs just as well as the random forest model built using all 57 variables.

Random forest variable importance versus LIME

Random forest variable importance measures how important individual variables are to the model's *overall* prediction performance. They tell you which variables generally affect the model's predictions the most, or which variables the model depends on the most.

LIME variable importances (discussed in section 6.3) measure how much different variables affect the model's prediction *on a specific example*. LIME explanations can help you determine if the model is using its variables appropriately, by explaining specific decisions.

10.1.4 *Gradient-boosted trees*

Gradient boosting is another ensemble method that improves the performance of decision trees. Rather than averaging the predictions of several trees together, as bagging and random forests do, gradient boosting tries to improve prediction performance by incrementally adding trees to an existing ensemble. The steps are as follows:

1. Use the current ensemble TE to make predictions on the training data.
2. Measure the residuals between the true outcomes and the predictions on the training data.
3. Fit a new tree T_i to the residuals. Add T_i to the ensemble TE.
4. Continue until the residuals have vanished, or another stopping criterion is achieved.

The procedure is sketched out in figure 10.10.

Gradient-boosted trees can also overfit, because at some point the residuals are just random noise. To mitigate overfitting, most implementations of gradient boosting provide cross-validation methods to help determine when to stop adding trees to the ensemble.

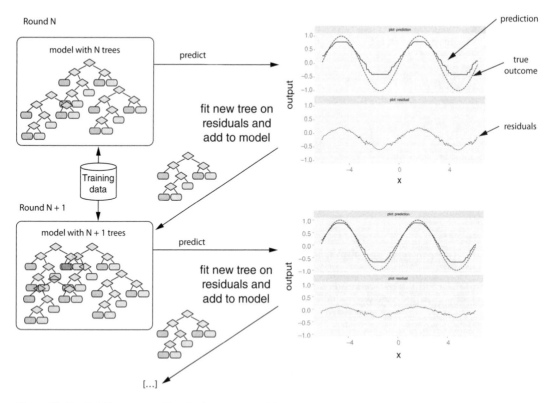

Figure 10.10   Building up a gradient-boosted tree model

You saw examples of gradient boosting when we discussed LIME in section 6.3, where you fit the gradient-boosted tree models using the xgboost package. In this section, we'll go over the modeling code that you used in section 6.3 in more detail.

THE IRIS EXAMPLE

Let's start with a small example.

> **Example**   *Suppose you have a dataset of petal and sepal measurements for three varieties of iris. The object is to predict whether a given iris is a setosa based on its petal and sepal dimensions.*

Listing 10.6   Loading the iris data

```
iris <- iris
iris$class <- as.numeric(iris$Species == "setosa")   ⟵  setosa is the
                                                         positive class.
set.seed(2345)
intrain <- runif(nrow(iris)) < 0.75   ⟵
train <- iris[intrain, ]                  Splits the data into
test <- iris[!intrain, ]                  training and test
head(train)                               (75%/25%)

##   Sepal.Length Sepal.Width Petal.Length Petal.Width Species class
## 1          5.1         3.5          1.4         0.2  setosa     1
## 2          4.9         3.0          1.4         0.2  setosa     1
## 3          4.7         3.2          1.3         0.2  setosa     1
## 4          4.6         3.1          1.5         0.2  setosa     1
## 5          5.0         3.6          1.4         0.2  setosa     1
## 6          5.4         3.9          1.7         0.4  setosa     1

input <- as.matrix(train[, 1:4])   ⟵  Creates the input matrix
```

Note that xgboost requires its input to be a numeric (no categorical variables) matrix, so in listing 10.6, you take the input data from the training data frame and create an input matrix.

In section 6.3, you fit the iris model by using the preprovided convenience function fit_iris_example(); here we'll explain the code from that function in detail. The first step is to run the cross-validation function xgb.cv() to determine the appropriate number of trees to use.

Listing 10.7   Cross-validating to determine model size

```
library(xgboost)                             The class labels, which must also
                                             be numeric (1 for setosa, 0 for
cv <- xgb.cv(input,   ⟵  The input matrix    not setosa)
          label = train$class,   ⟵
Uses 5-fold     params = list(
cross-validation     objective = "binary:logistic"   ⟵  Uses the objective "binary:logistic"
                 ),                                       for binary classification,
             nfold = 5,                                   "reg:linear" for regression
Builds an ensemble  nrounds = 100,
of 100 trees     print_every_n = 10,   ⟵  Prints a message every 10th iteration
                                          (use verbose = FALSE for no messages)
```

```
                   ▷ metrics = "logloss")

  evalframe <- as.data.frame(cv$evaluation_log)  ◁——— Gets the performance log

  head(evalframe)    ◁

  ##   iter train_logloss_mean train_logloss_std test_logloss_mean
  ## 1    1          0.4547800      7.758350e-05         0.4550578
  ## 2    2          0.3175798      9.268527e-05         0.3179284
  ## 3    3          0.2294212      9.542411e-05         0.2297848
  ## 4    4          0.1696242      9.452492e-05         0.1699816
  ## 5    5          0.1277388      9.207258e-05         0.1280816
  ## 6    6          0.0977648      8.913899e-05         0.0980894
  ##   test_logloss_std
  ## 1      0.001638487
  ## 2      0.002056267               evalframe records the training
  ## 3      0.002142687               and cross-validated logloss as a
  ## 4      0.002107535               function of the number of trees.
  ## 5      0.002020668
  ## 6      0.001911152

  (NROUNDS <- which.min(evalframe$test_logloss_mean))  ◁
  ## [1] 18

  library(ggplot2)
  ggplot(evalframe, aes(x = iter, y = test_logloss_mean)) +
    geom_line() +
    geom_vline(xintercept = NROUNDS, color = "darkred", linetype = 2) +
    ggtitle("Cross-validated log loss as a function of ensemble size")
```

Uses minimum cross-validated logloss (related to deviance) to pick the optimum number of trees. For regression, uses metrics = "rmse".

Finds the number of trees that gave the minimum cross-validated logloss

Figure 10.11 shows the cross-validated log loss as a function of the number of trees. In this case, xgb.cv() estimated that 18 trees gave the best model. Once you know the number of trees to use, you can call xgboost() to fit the appropriate model.

Listing 10.8   Fitting an xgboost model

```
model <- xgboost(data = input,
                 label = train$class,
                 params = list(
                    objective = "binary:logistic"
                 ),
                 nrounds = NROUNDS,
                 verbose = FALSE)

test_input <- as.matrix(test[, 1:4])  ◁       Creates the input
pred <- predict(model, test_input)  ◁         matrix for the test data

accuracyMeasures(pred, test$class)            Makes predictions

##   model accuracy f1  dev.norm
## 1 model        1  1 0.03458392
```

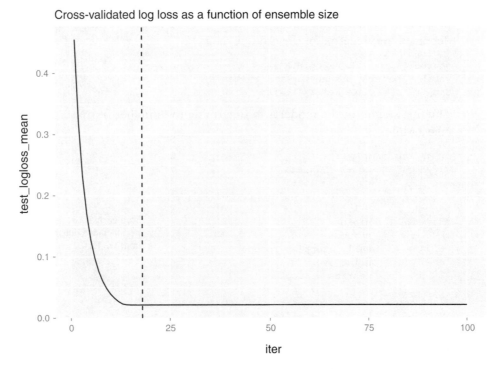
Cross-validated log loss as a function of ensemble size

Figure 10.11   Cross-validated log loss as a function of ensemble size

The model predicts perfectly on the holdout data, because this is an easy problem. Now that you are familiar with the steps, you can try xgboost on a harder problem: the movie review classification problem from section 6.3.3.

GRADIENT BOOSTING FOR TEXT CLASSIFICATION

> **Example**   *For this example, you will classify movie reviews from the Internet Movie Database (IMDB). The task is to identify positive reviews.*

As you did in section 6.3.3, you'll use the training and test data, IMDBtrain.RDS and IMDBtest.RDS, found at https://github.com/WinVector/PDSwR2/tree/master/IMDB. Each RDS object is a list with two elements: a character vector representing 25,000 reviews, and a vector of numeric labels where 1 means a positive review and 0 a negative review.

First, load the training data:

```
library(zeallot)
c(texts, labels) %<-% readRDS("IMDBtrain.RDS")
```

You have to convert the textual input data to a numeric representation. As in section 6.3.3, you'll convert the training data into a document-term matrix, implemented as a sparse matrix of class dgCMatrix. The convenience functions to do this conversion are in https://github.com/WinVector/PDSwR2/tree/master/IMDB/lime_imdb_ exam-ple.R. Next, you'll create the vocabulary of terms in the corpus, and then make the document-term matrix for the training data:

```
source("lime_imdb_example.R")
vocab <- create_pruned_vocabulary(texts)
dtm_train <- make_matrix(texts, vocab)
```

The first step to fit the model is to determine the number of trees to use. This may take a while.

```
cv <- xgb.cv(dtm_train,
             label = labels,
             params = list(
               objective = "binary:logistic"
               ),
             nfold = 5,                              Stop early if
             nrounds = 500,                          performance doesn't
             early_stopping_rounds = 20,    ⟵─────── improve for 20 rounds.
             print_every_n = 10,
             metrics = "logloss")

evalframe <- as.data.frame(cv$evaluation_log)
(NROUNDS <- which.min(evalframe$test_logloss_mean))
## [1] 319
```

Then fit the model and evaluate it:

```
model <- xgboost(data = dtm_train, label = labels,
                 params = list(
                   objective = "binary:logistic"
                 ),
                 nrounds = NROUNDS,
                 verbose = FALSE)

pred = predict(model, dtm_train)
trainperf_xgb =  accuracyMeasures(pred, labels, "training")

c(test_texts, test_labels) %<-% readRDS("IMDBtest.RDS")    ⟵  Loads the test data
dtm_test = make_matrix(test_texts, vocab)                      and converts it to a
                                                               document-term matrix
pred = predict(model, dtm_test)
testperf_xgb = accuracyMeasures(pred, test_labels, "test")

perftable <- rbind(trainperf_xgb, testperf_xgb)
pandoc.table(perftable, justify = perf_justify)
##
##
## model          accuracy        f1    dev.norm
## ----------    ----------    --------    ----------
## training        0.9891      0.9891      0.1723
## test            0.8725      0.8735      0.5955
```

As with random forests, this gradient-boosted model gives near-perfect performance on training data, and less-than-perfect, but still decent performance on holdout data. Even though the cross-validation step suggested 319 trees, you may want to examine evalframe (as you did in the iris example), and experiment with different numbers of trees, to see if that reduces the overfitting.

> ### Gradient boosting models vs. random forests
>
> In our own work, we've found that gradient boosting models tend to outperform random forests on most problems where we've tried both. However, there are occasionally situations where gradient boosting models perform poorly, while random forest models give acceptable performance. Your experiences may be different. In any case, it's a good idea to keep both methods in your arsenal.

USING XGBOOST WITH CATEGORICAL VARIABLES

In the iris example, all the input variables were numeric; in the movie review example, you converted the unstructured text input into a structured, numeric matrix representation. In many situations, you will have structured input data with categorical levels, as in the following example.

Example *Suppose you want to predict a newborn's birth weight as a function of several variables, both numeric and categorical, using* xgboost.

The data for this example is from the 2010 CDC natality dataset; it is similar to the data that you used in chapter 7 for predicting at-risk births.[5]

Listing 10.9 Loading the natality data

Splits the data into training and test sets

Uses all the variables in the model. DBWT (baby's birth weight) is the value to be predicted, and **ORIGRANDGROUP** is the grouping variable.

```
load("NatalBirthData.rData")
train <- sdata[sdata$ORIGRANDGROUP <= 5, ]

test <- sdata[sdata$ORIGRANDGROUP >5 , ]

input_vars <- setdiff(colnames(train), c("DBWT", "ORIGRANDGROUP"))

str(train[, input_vars])

## 'data.frame':	14386 obs. of  11 variables:
## $ PWGT    : int  155 140 151 160 135 180 200 135 112 98 ...
## $ WTGAIN  : int  42 40 1 47 25 20 24 51 36 22 ...
## $ MAGER   : int  30 32 34 32 24 25 26 26 20 22 ...
## $ UPREVIS : int  14 13 15 1 4 10 14 15 14 10 ...
## $ CIG_REC : logi  FALSE FALSE FALSE TRUE FALSE FALSE ...
## $ GESTREC3: Factor w/ 2 levels ">= 37 weeks",..: 1 1 1 2 1 1 1 1 1 1 ...
## $ DPLURAL : Factor w/ 3 levels "single","triplet or higher",..: 1 1 1 1
##    1 1 1 1 1 ...
## $ URF_DIAB  : logi  FALSE FALSE FALSE FALSE FALSE FALSE ...
## $ URF_CHYPER: logi  FALSE FALSE FALSE FALSE FALSE FALSE ...
## $ URF_PHYPER: logi  FALSE FALSE FALSE FALSE FALSE FALSE ...
## $ URF_ECLAM : logi  FALSE FALSE FALSE FALSE FALSE FALSE ...
```

---

[5] The dataset can be found at https://github.com/WinVector/PDSwR2/blob/master/CDC/NatalBirthData .rData.

As you can see, the input data has numerical variables, logical variables, and categorical (factor) variables. If you want to use xgboost() to fit a gradient-boosted model for a baby's birth weight using all of these variables, you must convert the input to all-numerical data. There are several ways to do this, including the base R model .matrix() function. We recommend using vtreat, as you did in chapter 8.

For this scenario, there are three ways you can use vtreat:

- Split the data into three sets: calibration/train/test. Use the calibration set with designTreatmentsN() to create the treatment plan; prepare() the training set to fit the xgboost model; and then prepare() the test set to validate the model.

  This is a good option when you have a large training set with either complex variables (categorical variables that take on a large number of possible levels), or a large number of categorical variables. It is also a good option if you want to prune some of the variables before fitting the model (using significance pruning—see section 8.4.2).

- Split the data into train/test (as we did here). Use mkCrossFrameNExperiment() to create the treatment plan and a cross-frame for training the xgboost model; prepare() the test set to validate the model.

  This is a good option when you don't have enough training data to split into three groups, but you have complex variables or a large number of categorical variables, and/or you want to prune some of the variables before fitting the model.

- Split the data into train/test. Use designTreatmentsZ() to create a treatment plan that manages missing values and converts categorical variables to indicator variables. prepare() both the training and test sets to create purely numeric input.

  This solution is quite similar to calling model.matrix(), with the added advantage that it manages missing values, and also gracefully handles situations where some categorical levels show up in either training or test, but not both. It's a good solution when you only have a few categorical variables, and none of the variables are too complex.

Since in this scenario there are only two categorical variables, and none of them are too complex (GESTREC3 takes on two values, and DPLURAL takes on three), you can use the third option.

Listing 10.10   Using `vtreat` to prepare data for `xgboost`

```
library(vtreat)

treatplan <- designTreatmentsZ(train,     ◁──────  Creates the treatment plan
                               input_vars,
                               codeRestriction = c("clean", "isBAD", "lev" ),
                               verbose = FALSE)
```

Creates clean numeric variables ("clean"), missingness indicators ("isBad"), indicator variables ("lev"), but not catP (prevalence) variables

```
train_treated <- prepare(treatplan, train)
str(train_treated)
```
Prepares the training data

```
## 'data.frame':    14386 obs. of  14 variables:
##  $ PWGT                          : num  155 140 151 160 135 180 200 135 1
       12 98 ...
##  $ WTGAIN                        : num  42 40 1 47 25 20 24 51 36 22 ...
##  $ MAGER                         : num  30 32 34 32 24 25 26 26 20 22 ...
##  $ UPREVIS                       : num  14 13 15 1 4 10 14 15 14 10 ...
##  $ CIG_REC                       : num  0 0 0 1 0 0 0 0 0 0 ...
##  $ URF_DIAB                      : num  0 0 0 0 0 0 0 0 0 0 ...
##  $ URF_CHYPER                    : num  0 0 0 0 0 0 0 0 0 0 ...
##  $ URF_PHYPER                    : num  0 0 0 0 0 0 0 0 0 0 ...
##  $ URF_ECLAM                     : num  0 0 0 0 0 0 0 0 0 0 ...
##  $ GESTREC3_lev_x_37_weeks       : num  0 0 0 1 0 0 0 0 0 0 ...
##  $ GESTREC3_lev_x_37_weeks_1     : num  1 1 1 0 1 1 1 1 1 1 ...
##  $ DPLURAL_lev_x_single          : num  1 1 1 1 1 1 1 1 1 1 ...
##  $ DPLURAL_lev_x_triplet_or_higher: num  0 0 0 0 0 0 0 0 0 0 ...
##  $ DPLURAL_lev_x_twin            : num  0 0 0 0 0 0 0 0 0 0 ...
```

Note that train_treated is purely numerical, with no missing values, and it doesn't contain the outcome column, so it's safe to use with xgboost (though you must convert it to a matrix first). To demonstrate this, the following listing directly fits a gradient-boosted model with 50 trees to the prepared training data (no cross-validation to pick the best size), and then applies the model to the prepared test data. This is just for demonstration purposes; normally you would want to call xgb.cv() to pick an appropriate number of trees first.

Listing 10.11 Fitting and applying an xgboost model for birth weight

```
birthwt_model <- xgboost(as.matrix(train_treated),
                    train$DBWT,
                    params = list(
                      objective = "reg:linear",
                      base_score = mean(train$DBWT)
                    ),
                    nrounds = 50,
                    verbose = FALSE)

test_treated <- prepare(treatplan, test)
pred <- predict(birthwt_model, as.matrix(test_treated))
```

Exercise: Try to use xgboost to solve the birth weight problem.
Try xgboost to predict DBWT, that is, set up the data and run the preceding code.

Bagging, random forests, and gradient boosting are after-the-fact improvements you can try in order to improve decision tree models. In the next section, you'll work with generalized additive models, which use a different method to represent non-linear relationships between inputs and outputs.

10.1.5 *Tree-based model takeaways*

Here's what you should remember about tree-based models:

- Trees are useful for modeling data with non-linear relationships between the input and the output, and potential interactions among variables.
- Tree-based ensembles generally have better performance than basic decision tree models.
- Bagging stabilizes decision trees and improves accuracy by reducing variance.
- Both random forests and gradient-boosted trees may have a tendency to overfit on training data. Be sure to evaluate the models on holdout data to get a better estimate of model performance.

10.2 *Using generalized additive models (GAMs) to learn non-monotone relationships*

In chapter 7, you used linear regression to model and predict quantitative output, and logistic regression to predict class probabilities. Linear and logistic regression models are powerful tools, especially when you want to understand the relationship between the input variables and the output. They're robust to correlated variables (when regularized), and logistic regression preserves the marginal probabilities of the data. The primary shortcoming of both these models is that they assume that the relationship between the inputs and the output is monotone. That is, if more is good, than much more is always better.

But what if the actual relationship is non-monotone? Consider the BMI example that you saw at the beginning of the chapter. For underweight adults, increasing BMI can lower mortality. But there's a limit: at some point a higher BMI is bad, and mortality will increase as BMI increases. Linear and logistic regression miss this distinction. For the data that we are working with, as figure 10.12 shows, a linear model would predict that mortality always decreases as BMI increases.

Generalized additive models (GAMs) are a way to model non-monotone responses within the framework of a linear or logistic model (or any other generalized linear model). In the mortality example, GAM would try to find a good "u-shaped" function of BMI, s(BMI), that describes the relationship between BMI and mortality, as shown in figure 10.12. GAM would then fit a function to predict mortality in terms of s(BMI).

10.2.1 *Understanding GAMs*

Recall that if y[i] is the numeric quantity you want to predict, and x[i,] is a row of inputs that corresponds to output y[i], then linear regression finds a function f(x) such that

```
f(x[i, ]) = b0 + b[1] * x[i, 1] + b[2] * x[i, 2] + ... b[n] * x[i, n]
```

And f(x[i,]) is as close to y[i] as possible.

In its simplest form, a GAM model relaxes the linearity constraint and finds a set of functions s_i() (and a constant term a0) such that

```
f(x[i,]) = a0 + s_1(x[i, 1]) + s_2(x[i, 2]) + ... s_n(x[i, n])
```

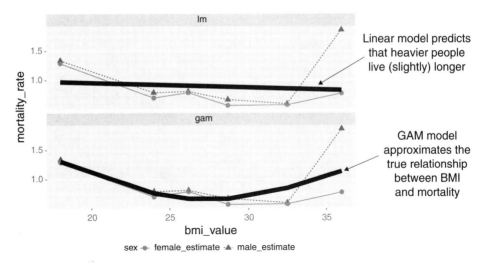

Figure 10.12   The effect of BMI on mortality: linear model vs. GAM

We also want f(x[i,]) to be as close to y[i] as possible. The functions s_i() are smooth curve fits that are built up from polynomials. The curves are called *splines* and are designed to pass as closely as possible through the data without being too "wiggly" (without overfitting). An example of a spline fit is shown in figure 10.13.

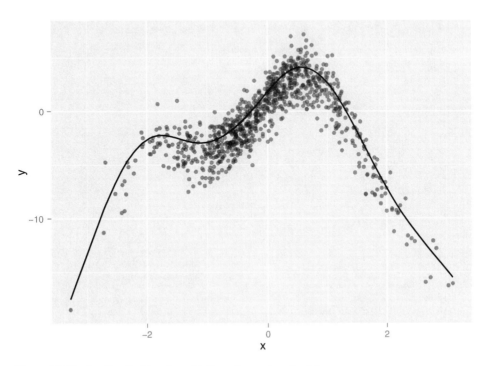

Figure 10.13   A spline that has been fit through a series of points

Let's work on a concrete example.

10.2.2 *A one-dimensional regression example*

First, consider this toy example.

> **Example**   *Suppose you want to fit a model to data where the response* y *is a noisy non-linear function of the input variable* x *(in fact, it's the function shown in figure 10.13).*

As usual, we'll split the data into training and test sets.

Listing 10.12   Preparing an artificial problem

```
set.seed(602957)

x <- rnorm(1000)
noise <- rnorm(1000, sd = 1.5)

y <- 3 * sin(2 * x) + cos(0.75 * x) - 1.5 * (x^2) + noise

select <- runif(1000)
frame <- data.frame(y = y, x = x)

train <- frame[select > 0.1, ]
test <-frame[select <= 0.1, ]
```

Given that the data is from the non-linear functions sin() and cos(), there shouldn't be a good linear fit from x to y. We'll start by building a (poor) linear regression.

Listing 10.13   Applying linear regression to the artificial example

```
lin_model <- lm(y ~ x, data = train)
summary(lin_model)

##
## Call:
## lm(formula = y ~ x, data = train)
##
## Residuals:
##      Min      1Q  Median      3Q     Max
## -17.698  -1.774   0.193   2.499   7.529
##
## Coefficients:
##              Estimate Std. Error t value Pr(>|t|)
## (Intercept)   -0.8330     0.1161  -7.175 1.51e-12 ***
## x              0.7395     0.1197   6.180 9.74e-10 ***
## ---
## Signif. codes:  0 '***' 0.001 '**' 0.01 '*' 0.05 '.' 0.1 ' ' 1
##
## Residual standard error: 3.485 on 899 degrees of freedom
## Multiple R-squared:  0.04075,    Adjusted R-squared:  0.03968
## F-statistic: 38.19 on 1 and 899 DF,  p-value: 9.737e-10

rmse <- function(residuals) {          ◁          A convenience function for calculating
    sqrt(mean(residuals^2))                        root mean squared error (RMSE )
}                                                   from a vector of residuals
```

```
train$pred_lin <- predict(lin_model, train)          Calculates the RMSE
resid_lin <- with(train, y - pred_lin)               of this model on the
rmse(resid_lin)                                       training data
## [1] 3.481091

library(ggplot2)                          Plots y versus prediction

ggplot(train, aes(x = pred_lin, y = y)) +
  geom_point(alpha = 0.3) +
  geom_abline()
```

The resulting model's predictions are plotted versus true response in figure 10.14. As expected, it's a very poor fit, with an R-squared of about 0.04. In particular, the errors are *not homoscedastic*: there are regions where the model systematically underpredicts and regions where it systematically overpredicts. If the relationship between x and y were truly linear (with independent noise), then the errors would be *homoscedastic*: the errors would be evenly distributed (mean 0) around the predicted value everywhere.

Now try finding a non-linear model that maps x to y. We'll use the function gam() in the package mgcv.[6] When using gam(), you can model variables as either linear or

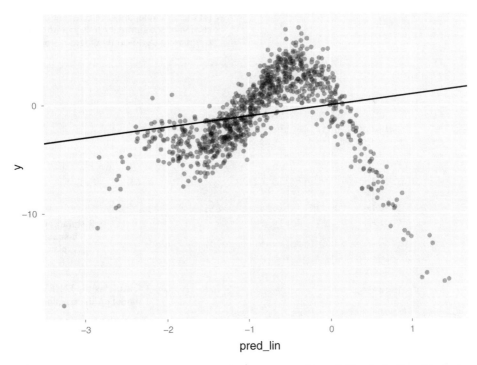

Figure 10.14   Linear model's predictions vs. actual response. The solid line is the line of perfect prediction (prediction == actual).

---

[6]   There's an older package called gam, written by Hastie and Tibshirani, the inventors of GAMs. The gam package works fine. But it's incompatible with the mgcv package, which ggplot already loads. Since we're using ggplot for plotting, we'll use mgcv for our examples.

non-linear. You model a variable x as non-linear by wrapping it in the s() notation. In this example, rather than using the formula y ~ x to describe the model, you'd use the formula y ~ s(x). Then gam() will search for the spline s() that best describes the relationship between x and y, as shown in listing 10.14. Only terms surrounded by s() get the GAM/spline treatment.

Listing 10.14   Applying GAM to the artificial example

Loads the mgcv package

Builds the model, specifying that x should be treated as a non-linear variable

The converged parameter tells you if the algorithm converged. You should only trust the output if this is TRUE.

```
library(mgcv)
gam_model <- gam(y ~ s(x), data = train)
gam_model$converged
## [1] TRUE

summary(gam_model)
```

Setting family = gaussian and link = identity tells you that the model was treated with the same distribution assumptions as a standard linear regression.

```
## Family: gaussian
## Link function: identity
##
## Formula:
## y ~ s(x)
##
```

The parametric coefficients are the linear terms (in this example, only the constant term). This section of the summary tells you which linear terms were significantly different from 0.

```
## Parametric coefficients:
##             Estimate Std. Error t value Pr(>|t|)
## (Intercept) -0.83467    0.04852   -17.2   <2e-16 ***
## ---
## Signif. codes:  0 '***' 0.001 '**' 0.01 '*' 0.05 '.' 0.1 ' ' 1
##
## Approximate significance of smooth terms:
##        edf Ref.df     F p-value
## s(x) 8.685  8.972 497.8  <2e-16 ***
## ---
## Signif. codes:  0 '***' 0.001 '**' 0.01 '*' 0.05 '.' 0.1 ' ' 1
##
## R-sq.(adj) =  0.832   Deviance explained = 83.4%
## GCV score =  2.144  Scale est. = 2.121      n = 901
```

R-sq.(adj) is the adjusted R-squared. "Deviance explained" is the raw R-squared (0.834).

```
train$pred <- predict(gam_model, train)
resid_gam <- with(train, y - pred)
rmse(resid_gam)

## [1] 1.448514
```

Calculates the RMSE of this model on the training data

```
ggplot(train, aes(x = pred, y = y)) +
  geom_point(alpha = 0.3) +
  geom_abline()
```

Plots y versus prediction

The smooth terms are the non-linear terms. This section of the summary tells you which non-linear terms were significantly different from 0. It also tells you the effective degrees of freedom (edf) used to build each smooth term. An edf near 1 indicates that the variable has an approximately linear relationship to the output.

The resulting model's predictions are plotted versus true response in figure 10.15. This fit is much better: the model explains over 80% of the variance (R-squared of 0.83), and the root mean squared error (RMSE) over the training data is less than half the RMSE of the linear model. Note that the points in figure 10.15 are distributed more or less evenly around the line of perfect prediction. The GAM has been fit to be homoscedastic, and any given prediction is as likely to be an overprediction as an underprediction.

Modeling linear relationships using gam()

By default, `gam()` will perform standard linear regression. If you were to call `gam()` with the formula `y ~ x`, you'd get the same model that you got using `lm()`. More generally, the call `gam(y ~ x1 + s(x2), data=...)` would model the variable `x1` as having a linear relationship with `y`, and try to fit the best possible smooth curve to model the relationship between `x2` and `y`. Of course, the best smooth curve could be a straight line, so if you're not sure whether the relationship between `x` and `y` is linear, you can use `s(x)`. If you see that the coefficient has an `edf` (effective degrees of freedom—see the model summary in listing 10.14) of about 1, then you can try refitting the variable as a linear term.

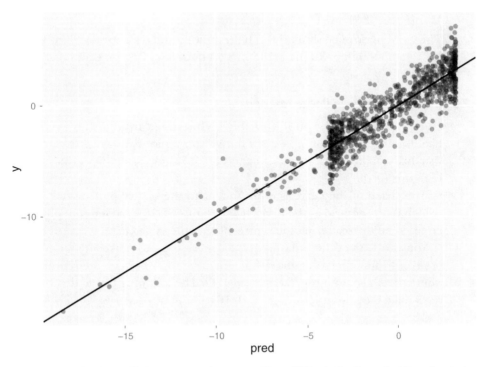

Figure 10.15 GAM's predictions vs. actual response. The solid line is the theoretical line of perfect prediction (`prediction == actual`).

The use of splines gives GAMs a richer model space to choose from; this increased flexibility brings a higher risk of overfitting. You should also check the models' performances on the test data.

Listing 10.15   Comparing linear regression and GAM performance

```
test <- transform(test,                                    ◁─────┐ Gets predictions from both
                  pred_lin = predict(lin_model, test),            models on the test data.
                  pred_gam = predict(gam_model, test) )           The function transform() is
                                                                  a base R version of
                                                                  dplyr::mutate().
test <- transform(test,
                  resid_lin = y - pred_lin,
                  resid_gam = y - pred_gam)
```

Calculates the residuals ─────▷ *(points to second transform block)*

```
rmse(test$resid_lin)                    ◁──────┐ Compares the RMSE of both
## [1] 2.792653                                  models on the test data

rmse(test$resid_gam)
## [1] 1.401399


library(sigr)                           ◁──────┐ Compares the R-squared of
 wrapFTest(test, "pred_lin", "y")$R2             both models on the test
## [1] 0.115395                                  data, using the sigr package

wrapFTest(test, "pred_gam", "y")$R2
## [1] 0.777239
```

The GAM performed similarly on both training and test sets: RMSE of 1.40 on test versus 1.45 on training; R-squared of 0.78 on test versus 0.83 on training. So there's likely no overfit.

10.2.3 *Extracting the non-linear relationships*

Once you fit a GAM, you'll probably be interested in what the s() functions look like. Calling plot() on a GAM will give you a plot for each s() curve, so you can visualize non-linearities. In our example, plot(gam_model) produces the top curve in figure 10.16.

The shape of the curve is quite similar to the scatter plot we saw in figure 10.13 (which is reproduced as the lower half of figure 10.16). In fact, the spline that's superimposed on the scatter plot in figure 10.13 is the same curve.

You can extract the data points that were used to make this graph by using the predict() function with the argument type = "terms". This produces a matrix where the ith column represents s(x[,i]). The following listing demonstrates how to reproduce the lower plot in figure 10.16.

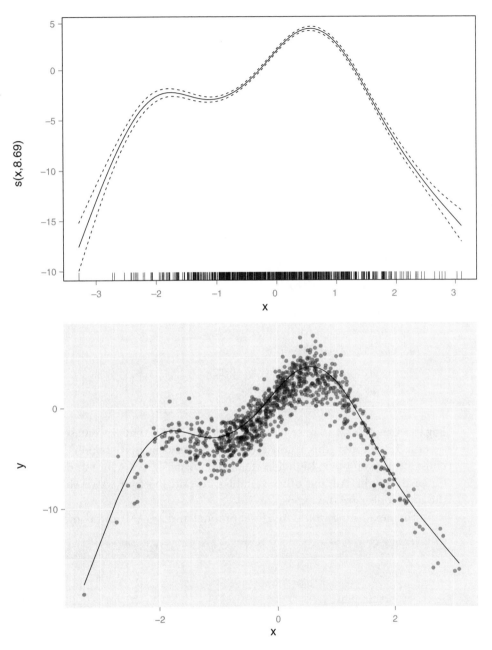

Figure 10.16   Top: The non-linear function `s(PWGT)` discovered by `gam()`, as output by `plot(gam_model)`. Bottom: The same spline superimposed over the training data.

Listing 10.16   Extracting a learned spline from a GAM

```
sx <- predict(gam_model, type = "terms")
summary(sx)
##         s(x)
##  Min.   :-17.527035
##  1st Qu.: -2.378636
##  Median :  0.009427
##  Mean   :  0.000000
##  3rd Qu.:  2.869166
##  Max.   :  4.084999

xframe <- cbind(train, sx = sx[,1])

ggplot(xframe, aes(x = x)) +
    geom_point(aes(y = y), alpha = 0.4) +
    geom_line(aes(y = sx))
```

Now that you've worked through a simple example, you are ready to try a more realistic example with more variables.

10.2.4 *Using GAM on actual data*

> **Example** *Suppose you want to predict a newborn baby's weight (DBWT) from a number of variables:*
>
> - *Mother's weight (PWGT)*
> - *Mother's pregnancy weight gain (WTGAIN)*
> - *Mother's age (MAGER)*
> - *The number of prenatal medical visits (UPREVIS)*

For this example, you'll use data from the 2010 CDC natality dataset that you used in section 7.2 (though this is not the risk data used in that chapter).[7] Note that we've chosen this example to highlight the mechanisms of gam(), not to find the best model for birth weight. Adding other variables beyond the four we've chosen will improve the fit, but obscure the exposition.

In the next listing, you'll fit a linear model and a GAM, and compare.

Listing 10.17   Applying linear regression (with and without GAM) to health data

```
library(mgcv)
library(ggplot2)
load("NatalBirthData.rData")
train <- sdata[sdata$ORIGRANDGROUP <= 5, ]
test <- sdata[sdata$ORIGRANDGROUP > 5, ]

form_lin <- as.formula("DBWT ~ PWGT + WTGAIN + MAGER + UPREVIS")
linmodel <- lm(form_lin, data = train)     ◁┐  Builds a linear model
                                             │  with four variables
summary(linmodel)

## Call:
```

---

[7] The dataset can be found at https://github.com/WinVector/PDSwR2/blob/master/CDC/NatalBirthData .rData. A script for preparing the dataset from the original CDC extract can be found at https://github.com/WinVector/PDSwR2/blob/master/CDC/prepBirthWeightData.R.

```
## lm(formula = form_lin, data = train)
##
## Residuals:
##      Min       1Q   Median       3Q      Max
## -3155.43  -272.09    45.04   349.81  2870.55
##
## Coefficients:
##              Estimate Std. Error t value Pr(>|t|)
## (Intercept) 2419.7090    31.9291  75.784  < 2e-16 ***
## PWGT           2.1713     0.1241  17.494  < 2e-16 ***
## WTGAIN         7.5773     0.3178  23.840  < 2e-16 ***
## MAGER          5.3213     0.7787   6.834  8.6e-12 ***
## UPREVIS       12.8753     1.1786  10.924  < 2e-16 ***
## ---
## Signif. codes:  0 '***' 0.001 '**' 0.01 '*' 0.05 '.' 0.1 ' ' 1
##
## Residual standard error: 562.7 on 14381 degrees of freedom
## Multiple R-squared:  0.06596,    Adjusted R-
      squared:  0.0657
## F-statistic: 253.9 on 4 and 14381 DF,  p-value: < 2.2e-16
```

⟵ **The model explains about 6.6% of the variance; all coefficients are significantly different from 0.**

```
form_gam <- as.formula("DBWT ~ s(PWGT) + s(WTGAIN) +
                        s(MAGER) + s(UPREVIS)")
gammodel <- gam(form_gam, data = train)
gammodel$converged
## [1] TRUE

summary(gammodel)
```

⟵ **Builds a GAM with the same variables**

⟵ **Verifies that the model has converged**

```
##
## Family: gaussian
## Link function: identity
##
## Formula:
## DBWT ~ s(PWGT) + s(WTGAIN) + s(MAGER) + s(UPREVIS)
##
## Parametric coefficients:
##             Estimate Std. Error t value Pr(>|t|)
## (Intercept) 3276.948      4.623   708.8   <2e-16 ***
## ---
## Signif. codes:  0 '***' 0.001 '**' 0.01 '*' 0.05 '.' 0.1 ' ' 1
##
## Approximate significance of smooth terms:
##                edf Ref.df       F  p-value
## s(PWGT)      5.374  6.443  69.010  < 2e-16 ***
## s(WTGAIN)    4.719  5.743 102.313  < 2e-16 ***
## s(MAGER)     7.742  8.428   7.145 1.37e-09 ***
## s(UPREVIS)   5.491  6.425  48.423  < 2e-16 ***
## ---
## Signif. codes:  0 '***' 0.001 '**' 0.01 '*' 0.05 '.' 0.1 ' ' 1
##
## R-sq.(adj) =  0.0927   Deviance explained = 9.42% ⟵
## GCV = 3.0804e+05  Scale est. = 3.0752e+05  n = 14386
```

The model explains a little over 9% of the variance; all variables have a non-linear effect significantly different from 0.

The GAM has improved the fit, and all four variables seem to have a non-linear relationship with birth weight, as evidenced by edfs all greater than 1. You could use plot(gammodel) to examine the shape of the s() functions; instead, let's compare them with a direct smoothing curve of each variable against mother's weight.

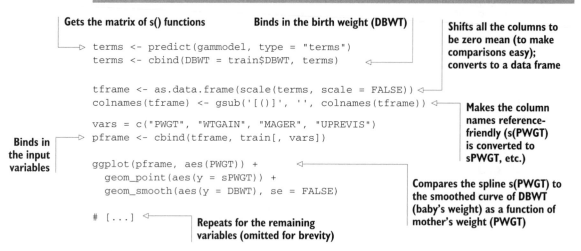

Figure 10.17 shows the s() splines learned by gam() as the dotted curves. These splines are gam()'s estimate of the (joint) relationship between each variable and the outcome, DBWT. The sum of the splines (plus an offset) is the model's best estimate of DBWT as a function of the input variables.

The figure also shows the smoothing curves that directly relate each variable to DBWT. The smooth curves in each case are similar to the corresponding s() in shape, and non-linear for all the variables. The differences in shape are because the splines are fit jointly (which is more useful for modeling), and the smoothing curves are merely calculated one at a time.

As usual, you should check for overfit with holdout data.

> **Listing 10.19   Checking GAM model performance on holdout data**

```
test <- transform(test,                          Gets predictions from
                  pred_lin = predict(linmodel, test),     both models on test data
                  pred_gam = predict(gammodel, test) )


test <- transform(test,                          Gets the residuals
                  resid_lin = DBWT - pred_lin,
                  resid_gam = DBWT - pred_gam)

rmse(test$resid_lin)          Compares the RMSE of both
## [1] 566.4719               models on the test data

rmse(test$resid_gam)
## [1] 558.2978

wrapFTest(test, "pred_lin", "DBWT")$R2       Compares the R-squared of
## [1] 0.06143168                             both models on the test
                                              data, using sigr
wrapFTest(test, "pred_gam", "DBWT")$R2
## [1] 0.08832297
```

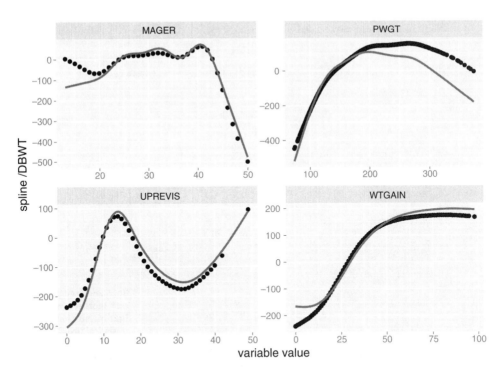

Figure 10.17 Smoothing curves of each of the four input variables plotted against birth weight, compared with the splines discovered by `gam()`. All curves have been shifted to be zero mean for comparison of shape.

The performance of the linear model and the GAM were similar on the test set, as they were on the training set, so in this example, there's no substantial overfit.

10.2.5 Using GAM for logistic regression

The `gam()` function can be used for logistic regression as well.

> **Example**   *Suppose you want to predict when a baby will be born underweight (defined as* `DBWT` $<$ 2000*), using the same input variables as the previous scenario.*

The logistic regression call to do this is shown in the following listing.

Listing 10.20 GLM logistic regression

```
form <- as.formula("DBWT < 2000 ~ PWGT + WTGAIN + MAGER + UPREVIS")
logmod <- glm(form, data = train, family = binomial(link = "logit"))
```

The corresponding call to `gam()` also specifies the binomial family with the `logit` link.

Listing 10.21   GAM logistic regression

```
form2 <- as.formula("DBWT < 2000 ~ s(PWGT) + s(WTGAIN) +
                                        s(MAGER) + s(UPREVIS)")
glogmod <- gam(form2, data = train, family = binomial(link = "logit"))

glogmod$converged
## [1] TRUE

summary(glogmod)
## Family: binomial
## Link function: logit
##
## Formula:
## DBWT < 2000 ~ s(PWGT) + s(WTGAIN) + s(MAGER) + s(UPREVIS)
##
## Parametric coefficients:
##              Estimate Std. Error z value Pr(>|z|)
## (Intercept) -3.94085    0.06794     -58   <2e-16 ***
## ---
## Signif. codes:  0 '***' 0.001 '**' 0.01 '*' 0.05 '.' 0.1 ' ' 1
##
## Approximate significance of smooth terms:
##             edf Ref.df  Chi.sq  p-value
## s(PWGT)   1.905  2.420   2.463  0.36412
## s(WTGAIN) 3.674  4.543  64.426 1.72e-12 ***
## s(MAGER)  1.003  1.005   8.335  0.00394 **
## s(UPREVIS) 6.802 7.216 217.631  < 2e-16 ***
## ---
## Signif. codes:  0 '***' 0.001 '**' 0.01 '*' 0.05 '.' 0.1 ' ' 1
##
## R-sq.(adj) =  0.0331   Deviance explained = 9.14%
## UBRE score = -0.76987  Scale est. = 1         n = 14386
```

> **Note the large p-value associated with mother's weight (PGWT). That means that there's no statistical proof that the mother's weight (PWGT) has a significant effect on the outcome.**

> **"Deviance explained" is the pseudo R-squared: 1 - (deviance/null.deviance).**

As with the standard logistic regression call, we recover the class probabilities with the call `predict(glogmodel, newdata = train, type = "response")`. Again, these models are coming out with low quality, and in practice we would look for more explanatory variables to build better screening models.

10.2.6   *GAM takeaways*

Here's what you should remember about GAMs:

- GAMs let you represent non-linear and non-monotonic relationships between variables and outcome in a linear or logistic regression framework.
- In the `mgcv` package, you can extract the discovered relationship from the GAM model using the `predict()` function with the `type = "terms"` parameter.
- You can evaluate the GAM with the same measures you'd use for standard linear or logistic regression: residuals, deviance, R-squared, and pseudo R-squared.

The gam() summary also gives you an indication of which variables have a significant effect on the model.

- Because GAMs have increased complexity compared to standard linear or logistic regression models, there's more risk of overfit.

GAMs extend linear methods (and generalized linear methods) by allowing variables to have non-linear (or even non-monotone) effects on outcome. Another approach is to form new variables from non-linear *combinations* of existing variables. The data scientist can do this by hand, by adding interactions or new synthetic variables, or it can be done mechanically, by support vector machines (SVMs), as shown in the next section. The hope is that with access to enough of these new variables, your modeling problem becomes easier.

In the next section, we'll work with two of the most popular ways to add and manage new variables: *kernel methods* and *support vector machines.*

10.3 Solving "inseparable" problems using support vector machines

Some classification problems are called *inseparable*: instances of one class, A, are inside regions bounded by another class, B, so that class A can't be separated from class B by a flat boundary. For example, in figure 10.18, we see a number of o's inside a triangle

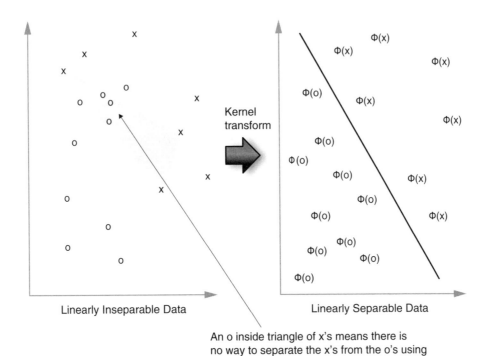

Figure 10.18 **Notional illustration of a kernel transform (based on Cristianini and Shawe-Taylor, 2000)**

defined by x's (and we also see the data converted to a nice separable arrangement by a so-called kernel function phi()). The original arrangement on the left side is *linearly inseparable*: there is no hyperplane that separates the x's from the o's. Hence, it would be impossible for linear methods to completely separate the two classes. We could use the tree-based methods demonstrated in section 10.1 to fit a classifier, or we could use a technique called *kernel methods*. In this section, we will use SVMs and kernel methods to build good classifiers on linearly inseparable data.

> **Having more than one way to do things**
>
> At this point, we have seen a number of advanced methods that give us more than one way to handle complex problems. For example: random forests, boosting, and SVMs can all introduce variable interactions to solve problems. It would be nice if there were always one obvious best method. However, each of these methodologies can dominate for different problems. So there is no one best method.
>
> Our advice is try simple methods such as linear and logistic regression first. Then bring in and try advanced methods such as GAMs (which can handle single-variable reshaping), tree-based methods (which can handle many-variable interactions), and SVMs (which can handle many-variable reshapings) to address modeling issues.

10.3.1 *Using an SVM to solve a problem*

Let's start with an example adapted from R's kernlab library documentation. Learning to separate two spirals is a famous "impossible" problem that cannot be solved by linear methods (though it is solvable by spectral clustering, kernel methods, SVMs, and deep learning or deep neural nets).

> **Example**   *Figure 10.19 shows two spirals, one within the other. Your task is to build a decision procedure that cuts up the plane such that the 1-labeled examples are in one region and the 2-labeled examples are in the complimentary region.*[8]

Support vector machines excel at learning concepts of the form "examples that are near each other should be given the same classification." To use the SVM technique, the user must choose a kernel (to control what is considered "near" or "far"), and pick a value for a hyperparameter called C or nu (to try to control model complexity).

SPIRAL EXAMPLE

Listing 10.22 shows the recovery and labeling of the two spirals shown in figure 10.19. You will use the labeled data for the example task: given the labeled data, recover the 1 versus 2 regions by supervised machine learning.

---

[8]   See K. J. Lang and M. J. Witbrock, "Learning to tell two spirals apart" in Proceedings of the 1988 Connectionist Models Summer School, D. Touretzky, G. Hinton, and T. Sejnowski (eds), Morgan Kaufmann, 1988 (pp. 52–59).

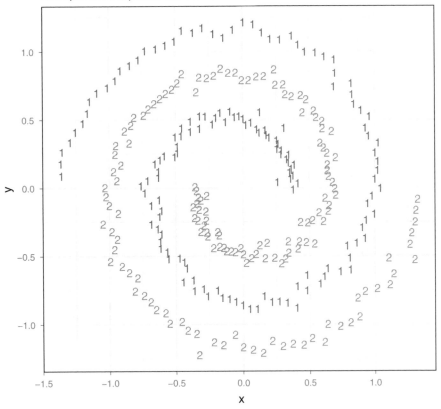

example task: separate the 1's from the 2's

Figure 10.19   The spiral counterexample

Listing 10.22   Setting up the spirals data as a classification problem

```
library('kernlab')
data(spirals)
 sc <- specc(spirals, centers = 2)
 s <- data.frame(x = spirals[, 1], y = spirals[, 2],
    class = as.factor(sc))

library('ggplot2')
ggplot(data = s) +
             geom_text(aes(x = x, y = y,
             label = class, color = class)) +
    scale_color_manual(values = c("#d95f02", "#1b9e77")) +
    coord_fixed() +
    theme_bw() +
    theme(legend.position  = 'none') +
    ggtitle("example task: separate the 1s from the 2s")
```

Loads the kernlab kernel and SVM package and then asks that the included example spirals be made available

Uses kernlab's spectral clustering routine to identify the two different spirals in the example dataset

Plots the spirals with class labels

Combines the spiral coordinates and the spiral label into a data frame

Figure 10.19 shows the labeled spiral dataset. Two classes (represented by digits) of data are arranged in two interwoven spirals. This dataset is difficult for methods that don't have a rich enough concept space (perceptrons, shallow neural nets) and easy for more-sophisticated learners that can introduce the right new features. Support vector machines, with the right kernel, are a way to introduce new composite features in order to solve the problem.

SUPPORT VECTOR MACHINES WITH AN OVERSIMPLE KERNEL

Support vector machines are powerful, but without the correct kernel, they have difficulty with some concepts (such as the spiral example). Listing 10.23 shows a failed attempt to learn the spiral concept with an SVM using the identity or dot-product (linear) kernel. The linear kernel does no transformations on the data; it can work for some applications, but in this case it does not give us the data-separating properties we want.

> **Listing 10.23   SVM with a poor choice of kernel**

Prepares to try to learn spiral class label from coordinates using an SVM

```
set.seed(2335246L)
s$group <- sample.int(100, size = dim(s)[[1]], replace = TRUE)
sTrain <- subset(s, group > 10)
sTest <- subset(s,group <= 10)
```
Builds the support vector model using a vanilladot kernel (not a very good kernel)

```
library('e1071')
mSVMV <- svm(class ~ x + y, data = sTrain, kernel = 'linear', type =
    'nu-classification')
sTest$predSVMV <- predict(mSVMV, newdata = sTest, type = 'response')
```

```
shading <- expand.grid(
    x = seq(-1.5, 1.5, by = 0.01),
    y = seq(-1.5, 1.5, by = 0.01))
shading$predSVMV <- predict(mSVMV, newdata = shading, type = 'response')
```
Uses the model to predict class on held-out data

```
ggplot(mapping = aes(x = x, y = y)) +
  geom_tile(data = shading, aes(fill = predSVMV),
          show.legend = FALSE, alpha = 0.5) +
  scale_color_manual(values = c("#d95f02", "#1b9e77")) +
  scale_fill_manual(values = c("white", "#1b9e77")) +
  geom_text(data = sTest, aes(label = predSVMV),
          size = 12) +
  geom_text(data = s, aes(label = class, color = class),
          alpha = 0.7) +
  coord_fixed() +
  theme_bw() +
  theme(legend.position = 'none') +
  ggtitle("linear kernel")
```
Plots the predictions on top of a grey copy of all the data so we can see if predictions agree with the original markings

Calls the model on a grid of points to generate background shading indicating the learned concept

This attempt results in figure 10.20. The figure shows the total dataset in a small font and the SVM classifications of the test dataset in large text. It also indicates the learned concept by shading. The SVM didn't produce a good model with the identity kernel, as it was forced to pick a linear separator. In the next section, you'll repeat the process with the Gaussian radial kernel and get a much better result.

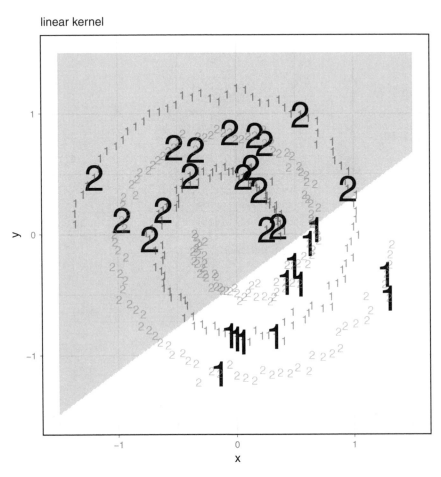

Figure 10.20   Identity kernel failing to learn the spiral concept

SUPPORT VECTOR MACHINES WITH A GOOD KERNEL

In listing 10.24, you'll repeat the SVM fitting process, but this time specifying the Gaussian or radial kernel. Figure 10.21 again plots the SVM test classifications in black (with the entire dataset in a smaller font). Note that this time the algorithm correctly learned the actual spiral concept, as indicated by the shading.

radial/Gaussian kernel

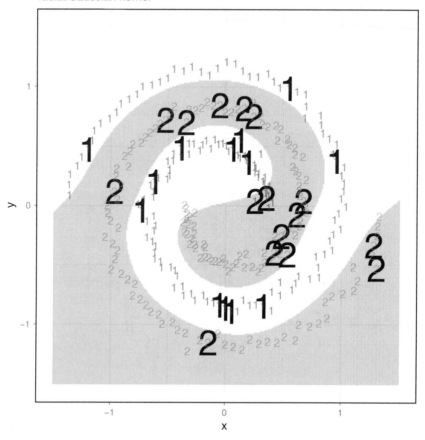

Figure 10.21   Radial kernel successfully learning the spiral concept

---

Listing 10.24   SVM with a good choice of kernel

```
mSVMG <- svm(class ~ x + y, data = sTrain, kernel = 'radial', type =
     'nu-classification')                    <─
sTest$predSVMG <- predict(mSVMG, newdata = sTest, type = 'response')

shading <- expand.grid(
  x = seq(-1.5, 1.5, by = 0.01),
  y = seq(-1.5, 1.5, by = 0.01))
shading$predSVMG <- predict(mSVMG, newdata = shading, type = 'response')

ggplot(mapping = aes(x = x, y = y)) +
  geom_tile(data = shading, aes(fill = predSVMG),
            show.legend = FALSE, alpha = 0.5) +
  scale_color_manual(values = c("#d95f02", "#1b9e77")) +
  scale_fill_manual(values = c("white", "#1b9e77")) +
  geom_text(data = sTest, aes(label = predSVMG),
            size = 12) +
```

This time uses the "radial" or Gaussian kernel, which is a nice geometric distance measure

```
geom_text(data = s,aes(label = class, color = class),
          alpha = 0.7) +
coord_fixed() +
theme_bw() +
theme(legend.position = 'none') +
ggtitle("radial/Gaussian kernel")
```

Exercise: Try to use xgboost to solve the spirals problem.

As we stated, some methods work better on some problems than others. Try to use the xgboost *package to solve the spirals problem. Do you find the* xgboost *results to be better or worse than the SVM results? (A worked version of this example can be found here: https://github.com/WinVector/PDSwR2/tree/master/Spirals.)*

10.3.2 *Understanding support vector machines*

An SVM is often portrayed as a magic machine that makes classification easier.[9] To dispel the awe and be able to use support vector methods with confidence, we need to take some time to learn their principles and how they work. The intuition is this: *SVMs with the radial kernel are very good nearest-neighbor-style classifiers.*

In figure 10.22, in the "real space" (on the left), the data is separated by a non-linear boundary. When the data is lifted into the higher-dimensional kernel space (on the right), the lifted points are separated by a hyperplane. Let's call the normal to that hyperplane w and the offset from the origin b (not shown).

An SVM finds a linear decision function (determined by parameters w and b), where for a given example x the machine decides x is in the class if

```
w %*% phi(x) + b >= 0
```

for some w and b, and not in the class otherwise. The model is completely determined by the function phi(), the vector w, and the scalar offset b. The idea is that phi() lifts or reshapes the data into a nicer space (where things are linearly separable), and then the SVM finds a linear boundary separating the two data classes in this new space (represented by w and b). This linear boundary in the lifted space can be pulled back as a general curved boundary in the original space. The principle is sketched out in figure 10.22.

The support vector training operation finds w and b. There are variations on the SVM that make decisions between more than two classes, perform scoring/regression, and detect novelty. But we'll discuss only the SVMs for simple classification.

As a user of SVMs, you don't immediately need to know how the training procedure works; that's what the software does for you. But you do need to have some notion of what it's trying to do. The model w, b is ideally picked so that

```
w %*% phi(x) + b >= u
```

for all training xs that were in the class, and

```
w %*% phi(x) + b <= v
```

for all training examples not in the class.

---

[9] Support vector machines can also be used for regression, but we will not cover that here.

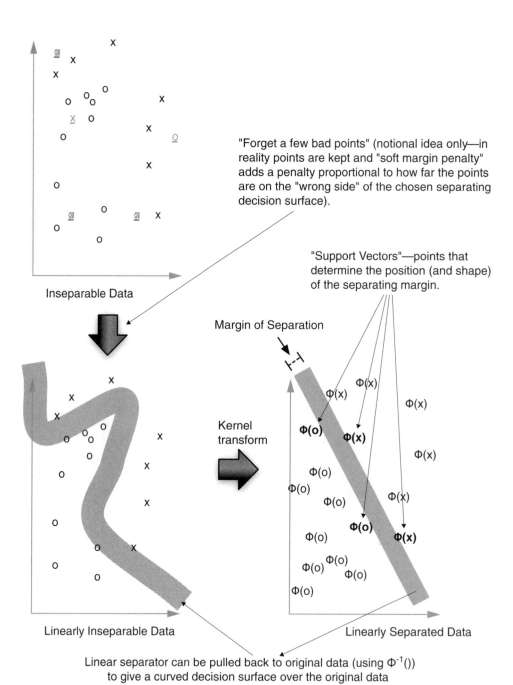

"Forget a few bad points" (notional idea only—in reality points are kept and "soft margin penalty" adds a penalty proportional to how far the points are on the "wrong side" of the chosen separating decision surface).

"Support Vectors"—points that determine the position (and shape) of the separating margin.

Inseparable Data

Margin of Separation

Kernel transform

Linearly Inseparable Data

Linearly Separated Data

Linear separator can be pulled back to original data (using $\Phi^{-1}()$) to give a curved decision surface over the original data

Figure 10.22   Notional illustration of SVM

The data is called *separable* if u > v. The size of the separation is (u - v) / sqrt(w %*% w), and is called the *margin*. The goal of the SVM optimizer is to maximize the margin. A large margin can actually ensure good behavior on future data (good generalization performance). In practice, real data isn't always separable even in the presence of a kernel. To work around this, most SVM implementations implement the so-called *soft margin* optimization goal.

A soft margin optimizer adds additional error terms that are used to allow a limited fraction of the training examples to be on the wrong side of the decision surface.[10] The model doesn't actually perform well on the altered training examples, but trades the error on these examples against increased margin on the remaining training examples. For most implementations, the model hyperparameter C or nu determines the trade-off between margin width for the remaining data and how much data is pushed around to achieve the margin. We will use the nu hyperparameter. nu takes settings between zero and one; lower values allow fewer training misclassifications, favoring more-complex models (more support vectors).[11] For our example, we will just use the function default value: 0.5.

10.3.3 *Understanding kernel functions*

The SVM picks which data is unimportant (left out) and which is very important (used as support vectors). But the reshaping of the problem to make the data separable is actually performed by what are called *kernel methods* or *kernel functions*.

Figure 10.22 illustrates[12] what we hope for from a good kernel: our data being pushed around so it's easier to sort or classify. By using a kernel transformation, we move to a situation where the distinction we're trying to learn is representable by a linear separator of our transformed data.

To begin to understand SVMs, we need to take a quick look at the common math and terminology that a user of SVMs and kernel methods should be conversant with. First is the notion of a kernel function, which is used to implement the phi() we saw reshaping space.

FORMAL DEFINITION OF A KERNEL FUNCTION

In our application, a kernel is a function with a very specific definition. Let u and v be any pair of variables. u and v are typically vectors of input or independent variables (possibly taken from two rows of a dataset). A function k(,) that maps pairs (u,v) to numbers is called a *kernel function* if and only if there is some function phi() mapping (u,v)s to a vector space such that k(u,v) = phi(u) %*% phi(v) for all u,v.[13] We'll informally

---

[10] A common type of dataset that is inseparable under any kernel is a dataset where there are at least two examples belonging to different outcome classes with the exact same values for all input or x variables. The original "hard margin" SVM couldn't deal with this sort of data and was for that reason not considered to be practical.

[11] For more details on SVMs, we recommend Cristianini and Shawe-Taylor's *An Introduction to Support Vector Machines and Other Kernel-based Learning Methods*, Cambridge University Press, 2000.

[12] Cristianini and Shawe-Taylor, *An Introduction to Support Vector Machines and Other Kernel-based Learning Methods*.

[13] %*% is R's notation for dot product or inner product; see help('%*%') for details. Note that phi() is allowed to map to very large (and even infinite) vector spaces.

call the expression k(u,v) = phi(u) %*% phi(v) the *Mercer expansion of the kernel* (in reference to Mercer's theorem; see http://mng.bz/xFD2) and consider phi() the certificate that tells us k(,) is a good kernel. This is much easier to understand from a concrete example. In the following listing, we show an equivalent phi() / k(,) pair.

> ### Listing 10.25   An artificial kernel example

```
u <- c(1, 2)
v <- c(3, 4)
k <- function(u, v) {                      ⊲─────┐  Defines a function of two
    u[1] * v[1] +                                │  vector variables (both two
       u[2] * v[2] +                             │  dimensional) as the sum of
       u[1] * u[1] * v[1] * v[1] +               │  various products of terms
       u[2] * u[2] * v[2] * v[2] +
       u[1] * u[2] * v[1] * v[2]
}
phi <- function(x) {                       ⊲─────┐  Defines a function of a single vector variable
    x <- as.numeric(x)                           │  that returns a vector containing the original
    c(x, x*x, combn(x, 2, FUN = prod))           │  entries plus all products of entries
}
print(k(u, v))      ⊲────────── Example evaluation of k (,)
 ## [1] 108
print(phi(u))
## [1] 1 2 1 4 2                                     ┐  Confirms phi() agrees with
print(phi(v))                                        │  k(,). phi() is the certificate
## [1]  3   4   9 16 12                               │  that shows k(,) is in fact a
print(as.numeric(phi(u) %*% phi(v)))  ⊲──────┘  kernel.
 ## [1] 108
```

Most kernel methods use the function k(,) directly and only use properties of k(,) guaranteed by the matching phi() to ensure method correctness. The k(,) function is usually quicker to compute than the notional function phi(). A simple example of this is what we'll call the *dot-product similarity* of documents. The dot-product document similarity is defined as the dot product of two vectors where each vector is derived from a document by building a huge vector of indicators, one for each possible feature. For instance, if the features you're considering are word pairs, then for every pair of words in a given dictionary, the document gets a feature of 1 if the pair occurs as a consecutive utterance in the document and 0 if not. This method is the phi(), but in practice we never use the phi() procedure. Instead, when comparing two documents, each consecutive pair of words in one document is generated and a bit of score is added if this pair is both in the dictionary and found consecutively in the other document. For moderate-sized documents and large dictionaries, this direct k(,) implementation is vastly more efficient than the phi() implementation.

THE SUPPORT VECTORS

The support vector machine gets its name from how the vector w is usually represented: as a linear combination of training examples—the support vectors. Recall we said in section 10.3.3 that the function phi() is allowed, in principle, to map into a very large or even infinite vector space. This means it may not be possible to directly write down w.

Support vector machines work around the "can't write down w" issue by restricting to ws that are in principle a sum of phi() terms as shown here:

```
w = sum(a1 * phi(s1), ... , am * phi(sm))
```

The vectors s1, ..., sm are actually m training examples and are called the support vectors. The preceding formulation helps because such sums are (with some math) equivalent to sums of k(,x) kernel terms of the form we show next:

```
w %*% phi(x) + b = sum(a1 * k(s1, x),... , am * k(sm, x)) + b
```

The right side is a quantity we can compute.

The work of the support vector training algorithm is to pick the vectors s1, ..., sm, the scalars a1, ..., am, and the offset b. All of this is called "the kernel trick."

WHAT TO REMEMBER ABOUT A SUPPORT VECTOR MODEL A support vector model consists of these things:

- A *kernel* phi() that reshapes space (chosen by the user)
- A subset of training data examples, called the *support vectors* (chosen by the SVM algorithm)
- A set of scalars a1, ..., am that specify what linear combination of the support vectors define the separating surface (chosen by the SVM algorithm)
- A scalar threshold b we compare to (chosen by the SVM algorithm)

The reason why the data scientist must be aware of the support vectors is that they're stored in the support vector model. For example, with too complex a model, there can be a very large number of support vectors, causing the model to be large and expensive to evaluate. In the worst case, the number of support vectors in the model can be almost as large as the number of training examples, making support vector model evaluation potentially as expensive as nearest-neighbor evaluation, and increasing the risk of overfit. The user picks a good number of support vectors by picking a good value of C or nu through cross-validation.

Exercise: Try different values of nu on the spirals problem.
nu is the important hyperparameter for SVMs. Ideally, we should cross-validate for a good value of nu. Instead of full cross-validation, just try a few values of nu to get the landscape. (We have a worked solution here: https://github.com/WinVector/PDSwR2/tree/master/Spirals.)

10.3.4 *Support vector machine and kernel methods takeaways*

Here's what you should remember from this section:

- Support vector machines are a kernel-based classification approach where a complex separating surface is parameterized in terms of a (possibly very large) subset of the training examples (called the support vectors).
- The goal of "the kernel trick" is to lift the data into a space where the data is separable, or where linear methods can be used directly. Support vector

machines and kernel methods work best when the problem has a moderate number of variables and the data scientist suspects that the relation to be modeled is a non-linear combination of variable effects.

Summary

In this chapter, we demonstrated some advanced methods to fix specific issues with basic modeling approaches: modeling variance, modeling bias, issues with non-linearity, and issues with variable interactions. An important additional family of methods we wish we had time to touch on is *deep learning*, the improved modern treatment of neural nets. Fortunately there is already a good book we can recommend on this topic: *Deep Learning with R*, by François Chollet with J. J. Allaire, Manning, 2018.

You should understand that you bring in advanced methods and techniques to fix specific modeling problems, not because they have exotic names or exciting histories. We also feel you should at least try to find an existing technique to fix a problem you suspect is hiding in your data *before* building your own custom technique; often the existing technique already incorporates a lot of tuning and wisdom. Which method is best depends on the data, and there are many advanced methods to try. Advanced methods can help fix overfit, variable interactions, non-additive relations, and unbalanced distributions, but not lack of features or data.

Finally, the goal of learning the theory of advanced techniques is not to be able to recite the steps of the common implementations, but to know when the techniques apply and what trade-offs they represent. The data scientist needs to supply thought and judgment and realize that the platform can supply implementations.

In this chapter you have learned

- How to bag decision trees to stabilize their models and improve prediction performance
- How to further improve decision-tree-based models by using random forests or gradient boosting
- How to use random forest variable importances to help with variable selection
- How to use generalized additive models to better model non-linear relationships between inputs and outputs in the context of linear and logistic regression
- How to use support vector machines with the Gaussian kernel to model classification tasks with complex decision surfaces, especially nearest-neighbor-style tasks.

The actual point of a modeling project is to deliver results for production deployment and to present useful documentation and evaluations to your partners. The next part of this book will address best practices for delivering your results.

Part 3

Working in the real world

In part 2, we covered how to build a model that addresses the problem that you want to solve. The next steps are to implement your solution and communicate your results to other interested parties. In part 3, we conclude with the important steps of deploying work into production, documenting work, and building effective presentations.

Chapter 11 covers the documentation necessary for sharing or transferring your work to others, in particular those who will be deploying your model in an operational environment. This includes effective code commenting practices, as well as proper version management and collaboration with the version control software, Git. We also discuss the practice of reproducible research using `knitr`. Chapter 11 also covers how to export models you've built from R, or deploy them as HTTP services.

Chapter 12 discusses how to present the results of your projects to different audiences. Project sponsors, project consumers (people in the organization who'll be using or interpreting the results of your model), and fellow data scientists will all have different perspectives and interests. We also give examples of how to tailor your presentations to the needs and interests of a specific audience.

On completing part 3, you'll understand how to document and transfer the results of your project and how to effectively communicate your findings to other interested parties.

Documentation and deployment

11

This chapter covers

- Producing effective milestone documentation
- Managing project history using source control
- Deploying results and making demonstrations

In this chapter, we'll survey techniques for documenting and deploying your work. We will work specific scenarios, and point to resources for further study if you want to master the techniques being discussed. The theme is this: now that you can build machine learning models, you should explore tools and procedures to become proficient at saving, sharing, and repeating successes. Our mental model (figure 11.1) for this chapter emphasizes that this chapter is all about sharing what you model. Let's use table 11.1 to get some more-specific goals in this direction.

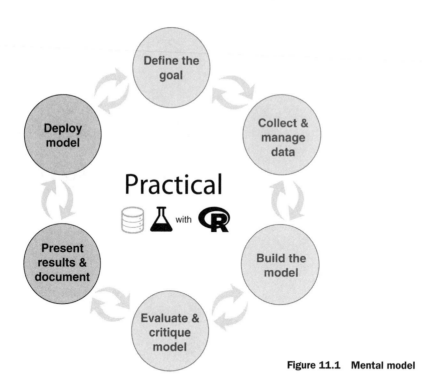

Figure 11.1   Mental model

Table 11.1   Chapter goals

Goal	Description
Produce effective milestone documentation	A readable summary of project goals, data provenance, steps taken, and technical results (numbers and graphs). Milestone documentation is usually read by collaborators and peers, so it can be concise and can often include actual code. We'll demonstrate a great tool for producing excellent milestone documentation: the R *knitr* and *rmarkdown* packages, which we will refer to generically as *R markdown*. R markdown is a product of the "reproducible research" movement (see Christopher Gandrud's *Reproducible Research with R and RStudio,* Second Edition, Chapman and Hall, 2015) and is an excellent way to produce a reliable snapshot that not only shows the state of a project, but allows others to confirm the project works.
Manage a complete project history	It makes little sense to have exquisite milestone or checkpoint documentation of how your project worked last February if you can't get a copy of February's code and data. This is why you need good version control discipline to protect code, and good data discipline to preserve data.
Deploy demonstrations	True production deployments are best done by experienced engineers. These engineers know the tools and environment they will be deploying to. A good way to jump-start production deployment is to have a reference application. This allows engineers to experiment with your work, test corner cases, and build acceptance tests.

This chapter explains how to share your work—even sharing it with your future self. We'll discuss how to use R markdown to create substantial project milestone documentation and automate reproduction of graphs and other results. You'll learn about using effective comments in code, and using Git for version management and for collaboration. We'll also discuss deploying models as HTTP services and applications.

For some of the examples, we will use RStudio, which is an integrated development environment (IDE) that is a product of RStudio, Inc. (and not part of R/CRAN itself). Everything we show can be done without RStudio, but RStudio supplies a basic editor and some single-button-press alternatives to some scripting tasks.

11.1 *Predicting buzz*

> **Example** *For our example scenario, we want to use metrics collected about the first few days of article views to predict the long-term popularity of an article. This can be important for selling advertising and predicting and managing revenue. To be specific: we will use measurements taken during the first eight days of an article's publication to predict if the article will remain popular in the long term.*
>
> *Our tasks for this chapter are to save and share our Buzz model, document the model, test the model, and deploy the model into production.*

To simulate our example scenario of predicting long term article popularity or buzz we will use the *Buzz dataset* from http://ama.liglab.fr/datasets/buzz/. We'll work with the data found in the file TomsHardware-Relative-Sigma-500.data.txt.[1] The original supplied documentation (TomsHardware-Relative-Sigma-500.names.txt and Buzz-DataSetDoc.pdf) tells us the Buzz data is structured as shown in table 11.2.

Table 11.2 Buzz data description

Attribute	Description
Rows	Each row represents many different measurements of the popularity of a technical personal computer discussion topic.
Topics	Topics include technical issues about personal computers such as brand names, memory, overclocking, and so on.
Measurement types	For each topic, measurement types are quantities such as the number of discussions started, number of posts, number of authors, number of readers, and so on. Each measurement is taken at eight different times.
Times	The eight relative times are named 0 through 7 and are likely days (the original variable documentation is not completely clear and the matching paper has not yet been released). For each measurement type, all eight relative times are stored in different columns in the same data row.

---

[1] All files mentioned in this chapter are available from https://github.com/WinVector/PDSwR2/tree/master/Buzz.

Table 11.2   Buzz data description *(continued)*

Attribute	Description
Buzz	The quantity to be predicted is called *buzz* and is defined as being `true` or 1 if the ongoing rate of additional discussion activity is at least 500 events per day averaged over a number of days after the observed days. Likely buzz is a future average of the seven variables labeled *NAC* (the original documentation is unclear on this).

In *our* initial Buzz documentation, we list what we know (and, importantly, admit what we're not sure about). We don't intend any disrespect in calling out issues in the supplied Buzz documentation. That documentation is about as good as you see at the beginning of a project. In an actual project, you'd clarify and improve unclear points through discussions and work cycles. This is one reason why having access to active project sponsors and partners is critical in real-world projects.

In this chapter, we'll use the Buzz model and dataset as is and concentrate on demonstrating the tools and techniques used in producing documentation, deployments, and presentations. In actual projects, we advise you to start by producing notes like those in table 11.2. You'd also incorporate meeting notes to document your actual project goals. As this is only a demonstration, we'll emphasize technical documentation: data provenance and an initial trivial analysis to demonstrate we have control of the data. Our example initial Buzz analysis is found here: https://github.com/WinVector/PDSwR2/blob/master/Buzz/buzzm.md. We suggest you skim it before we work through the tools and steps used to produce the documents in our next section.

11.2   *Using R markdown to produce milestone documentation*

The first audience you'll have to prepare documentation for is yourself and your peers. You may need to return to previous work months later, and it may be in an urgent situation like an important bug fix, presentation, or feature improvement. For self/peer documentation, you want to concentrate on facts: what the stated goals were, where the data came from, and what techniques were tried. You assume that as long as you use standard terminology or references, the reader can figure out anything else they need to know. You want to emphasize any surprises or exceptional issues, as they're exactly what's expensive to relearn. You can't expect to share this sort of documentation with clients, but you can later use it as a basis for building wider documentation and presentations.

The first sort of documentation we recommend is project milestone or checkpoint documentation. At major steps of the project, you should take some time out to repeat your work in a clean environment (proving you know what's in intermediate files and you can in fact recreate them). An important, and often neglected, milestone is the start of a project. In this section, we'll use the knitr and rmarkdown R packages to document starting work with the Buzz data.

Documentation scenario: Share the ROC curve for the Buzz model

Our first task is to build a document that contains the ROC curve for the example model. We want to be able to rebuild this document automatically if we change model or evaluation data, so we will use R markdown to produce the document.

11.2.1 What is R markdown?

R markdown is a variation of the Markdown document specification[2] that allows the inclusion of R code and results inside documents. The concept of processing a combination of code and text should be credited to the R Sweave package[3] and from Knuth's formative ideas of literate programming.[4] In practice, you maintain a master file that contains both user-readable documentation and chunks of program source code. The document types supported by R markdown include Markdown, HTML, LaTeX, and Word. LaTeX format is a good choice for detailed, typeset, technical documents. Markdown format is a good choice for online documentation and wikis.

The engine that performs the document creation task is called knitr. knitr's main operation is called a *knit*: knitr extracts and executes all of the R code and then builds a new result document that assembles the contents of the original document plus pretty-printed code and results. Figure 11.2 shows how knitr treats documents as pieces (called *chunks*) and transforms chunks into sharable results.

The process is best demonstrated by a few examples.

A SIMPLE R MARKDOWN EXAMPLE

Markdown (http://daringfireball.net/projects/markdown/) is a simple web-ready format that's used in many wikis. The following listing shows a simple Markdown document with R markdown annotation blocks denoted with ``` ``` ```.

Listing 11.1 R-annotated Markdown

YAML (yet another markup language) header specifying some metadata: title and default output format

An R markdown "start code chunk" annotation. The "include = FALSE" directive says the block is not shown in the rendering.

End of the R markdown block; all content between the start and end marks is treated as R code and executed.

```
---
title: "Buzz scoring example"
output: github_document
---

```{r, include = FALSE}
# process document with knitr or rmarkdown.
# knitr::knit("Buzz_score_example.Rmd") # creates Buzz_score_example.md
# rmarkdown::render("Buzz_score_example.Rmd",
#                   rmarkdown::html_document()) # creates Buzz_score_example.html
```

Example scoring (making predictions with) the Buzz data set.
```

Free Markdown text

---

[2] Markdown itself is a popular document-formatting system based on the idea of imitating how people hand-annotate emails: https://en.wikipedia.org/wiki/Markdown.

[3] See http://leisch.userweb.mwn.de/Sweave/.

[4] See http://www.literateprogramming.com/knuthweb.pdf.

First attach the `randomForest` package and load the model and test data.

```{r}
suppressPackageStartupMessages(library("randomForest"))

lst <- readRDS("thRS500.RDS")
varslist <- lst$varslist
fmodel <- lst$fmodel
buzztest <- lst$buzztest
rm(list = "lst")
```

> **Another R code block. In this case, we are loading an already produced random Forest model and test data.**

Now show the quality of our model on held-out test data. ⟵— **More free test**

```{r}``` ⟵— **Another R code chunk**
```
buzztest$prediction <-
    predict(fmodel, newdata = buzztest, type = "prob")[, 2, drop = TRUE]

WVPlots::ROCPlot(buzztest, "prediction",
                "buzz", 1,
                "ROC curve estimating quality of model predictions on held-
    out data")
```

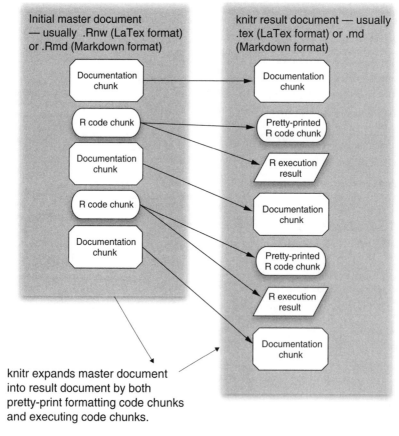

knitr expands master document into result document by both pretty-print formatting code chunks and executing code chunks.

Figure 11.2   R markdown process schematic
```

The contents of listing 11.1 are available in the file https://github.com/WinVector/ PDSwR2/blob/master/Buzz/Buzz_score_example.Rmd. In R we'd process it like this:

```
rmarkdown::render("Buzz_score_example.Rmd", rmarkdown::html_document())
```

This produces the new file Buzz_score_example.html, which is a finished report in HTML format. Adding this sort of ability to your workflow (either using Sweave or knitr/rmarkdown) is game changing.

THE PURPOSE OF R MARKDOWN

The purpose of R markdown is to produce reproducible work. The same data and techniques should be rerunnable to get equivalent results, without requiring error-prone direct human intervention such as selecting spreadsheet ranges or copying and pasting. When you distribute your work in R markdown format (as we do in section 11.2.3), anyone can download your work and, without great effort, rerun it to confirm they get the same results you did. This is the ideal standard of scientific research, but is rarely met, as scientists usually are deficient in sharing all of their code, data, and actual procedures. knitr collects and automates all the steps, so it becomes obvious if something is missing or doesn't actually work as claimed. knitr automation may seem like a mere convenience, but it makes the essential work listed in table 11.3 much easier (and therefore more likely to actually be done).

Table 11.3 Maintenance tasks made easier by R markdown

Task	Discussion
Keeping code in sync with documentation	With only one copy of the code (already in the document), it's not so easy to get out of sync.
Keeping results in sync with data	Eliminating all by-hand steps (such as cutting and pasting results, picking filenames, and including figures) makes it much more likely you'll correctly rerun and recheck your work.
Handing off correct work to others	If the steps are sequenced so a machine can run them, then it's much easier to rerun and confirm them. Also, having a container (the master document) to hold all your work makes managing dependencies much easier.

11.2.2 *knitr technical details*

To use knitr on a substantial project, you need to know more about how knitr code chunks work. In particular, you need to be clear how chunks are marked and what common chunk options you'll need to manipulate. Figure 11.3 shows the steps to prepare an R markdown document.

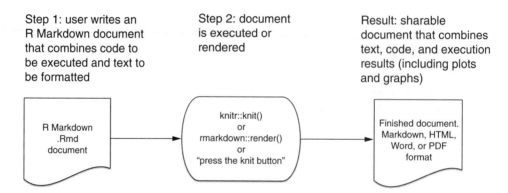

Step 1: user writes an R Markdown document that combines code to be executed and text to be formatted

Step 2: document is executed or rendered

Result: sharable document that combines text, code, and execution results (including plots and graphs)

Figure 11.3   The R markdown process

KNITR BLOCK DECLARATION FORMAT

In general, a knitr code block starts with the block declaration (``` in Markdown and << in LaTeX). The first string is the name of the block (must be unique across the entire project). After that, a number of comma-separated `option=value` chunk option assignments are allowed.

KNITR CHUNK OPTIONS

A sampling of useful option assignments is given in table 11.4.

Table 11.4   Some useful knitr options

Option name	Purpose
`cache`	Controls whether results are cached. With `cache = FALSE` (the default), the code chunk is always executed. With `cache = TRUE`, the code chunk isn't executed if valid cached results are available from previous runs. Cached chunks are essential when you are revising knitr documents, but you should always delete the cache directory (found as a subdirectory of where you're using knitr) and do a clean rerun to make sure your calculations are using current versions of the data and settings you've specified in your document.
`echo`	Controls whether source code is copied into the document. With `echo = TRUE` (the default), pretty-formatted code is added to the document. With `echo = FALSE`, code isn't echoed (useful when you only want to display results).
`eval`	Controls whether code is evaluated. With `eval = TRUE` (the default), code is executed. With `eval = FALSE`, it's not (useful for displaying instructions).
`message`	Set `message = FALSE` to direct R `message()` commands to the console running R instead of to the document. This is useful for issuing progress messages to the user, that you don't want in the final document.
`results`	Controls what's to be done with R output. Usually you don't set this option and output is intermingled (with ## comments) with the code. A useful option is `results='hide'`, which suppresses output.

Table 11.4　Some useful knitr options *(continued)*

Option name	Purpose
tidy	Controls whether source code is reformatted before being printed. We used to set tidy = FALSE, as one version of knitr misformatted R comments when tidying.

Most of these options are demonstrated in our Buzz example, which we'll work through in the next section.

11.2.3　Using knitr to document the Buzz data and produce the model

The model we were just evaluating itself was produced using an R markdown script: the file buzzm.Rmd found at https://github.com/WinVector/PDSwR2/tree/master/Buzz. Knitting this file produced the Markdown result buzzm.md and the saved model file thRS500.RDS that drives our examples. All steps we'll mention in this chapter are completely demonstrated in the Buzz example directory. We'll show excerpts from buzzm.Rmd.

> **BUZZ DATA NOTES**　For the Buzz data, the preparation notes can be found in the files buzzm.md and buzzm.html. We suggest viewing one of these files and table 11.2. The original description files from the Buzz project (Toms-Hardware-Relative-Sigma-500.names.txt and BuzzDataSetDoc.pdf) are also available at https://github.com/WinVector/PDSwR2/tree/master/Buzz.

CONFIRMING DATA PROVENANCE

Because knitr is automating steps, you can afford to take a couple of extra steps to confirm the data you're analyzing is in fact the data you thought you had. For example, we'll start our Buzz data analysis by confirming that the SHA cryptographic hash of the data we're starting from matches what we thought we had downloaded. This is done (assuming your system has the sha cryptographic hash installed) as shown in the following listing (note: always look to the first line of chunks for chunk options such as cache = TRUE).

Listing 11.2　Using the system() command to compute a file hash

```
```{r dataprep}
infile <- "TomsHardware-Relative-Sigma-500.data.txt"
paste('checked at', date())
system(paste('shasum', infile), intern = TRUE)    <─── Runs a system-installed cryptographic hash program (this program is outside of R's install image)
buzzdata <- read.table(infile, header = FALSE, sep = ",")
...
```

This code sequence depends on a program named *shasum* being on your execution path. You have to have a cryptographic hash installed, and you can supply a direct path to the program if necessary. Common locations for a cryptographic hash include /usr/bin/shasum, /sbin/md5, and fciv.exe, depending on your actual system configuration.
```

```
infile <- "TomsHardware-Relative-Sigma-500.data.txt"
paste('checked at' ,date())

##[1]"checkedatFriNov815:01:392013"

system(paste('shasum' ,infile), intern=T) #write down file hash

##[1]"c239182c786baf678b55f559b3d0223da91e869cTomsHardware-Relative-Sigma-500.data.txt"
```

Figure 11.4   knitr documentation of Buzz data load

This code produces the output shown in figure 11.4. In particular, we've documented that the data we loaded has the same cryptographic hash we recorded when we first downloaded the data. Having confidence you're still working with the exact same data you started with can speed up debugging when things go wrong. Note that we're using the cryptographic hash only to defend against accident (using the wrong version of a file or seeing a corrupted file) and not to defend against adversaries or external attacks. For documenting data that may be changing under external control, it is critical to use up-to-date cryptographic techniques.

Figure 11.5 is the same check, rerun in 2019, which gives us some confidence we are in fact dealing with the same data.

```
infile <- "TomsHardware-Relative-Sigma-500.data.txt"
paste('checked at' ,date())

##[1]"checked at Thu Apr 18 09:30:23 2019"

system(paste('shasum' ,infile), intern=T) #write down file hash

##[1]"c239182c786baf678b55f559b3d0223da91e869c  TomsHardware-
Relative-Sigma-500.data.txt"
```

Figure 11.5   knitr documentation of Buzz data load 2019: buzzm.md

RECORDING THE PERFORMANCE OF THE NAIVE ANALYSIS
The initial milestone is a good place to try to record the results of a naive "just apply a standard model to whatever variables are present" analysis. For the Buzz data analysis, we'll use a random forest modeling technique (not shown here, but in our knitr documentation) and apply the model to test data.

Save your data!
Always save a copy of your training data. Remote data (URLs, databases) has a habit of changing or disappearing. To reproduce your work, you must save your inputs.

Listing 11.3 Calculating model performance

```
``` {r}
rtest <- data.frame(truth = buzztest$buzz,
pred = predict(fmodel, newdata = buzztest, type = "prob")[, 2, drop = TRUE])
print(accuracyMeasures(rtest$pred, rtest$truth))
```
```

```
## [1] "precision= 0.832402234636871 ; recall= 0.84180790960452"
##       pred
## truth FALSE TRUE
##     0   584   30
##     1    28  149
##   model  accuracy        f1 dev.norm      AUC
## 1 model 0.9266751 0.8370787  0.42056 0.9702102
```

USING MILESTONES TO SAVE TIME

Now that we've gone to all the trouble to implement, write up, and run the Buzz data preparation steps, we'll end our knitr analysis by saving the R workspace. We can then start additional analyses (such as introducing better variables for the time-varying data) from the saved workspace. In the following listing, we'll show how to save a file, and how to again produce a cryptographic hash of the file (so we can confirm work that starts from a file with the same name is in fact starting from the same data).

Listing 11.4 Saving data

Save variable names, model, and test data.

```
``` {r}
fname <- 'thRS500.RDS'
items <- c("varslist", "fmodel", "buzztest")
saveRDS(object = list(varslist = varslist,
                      fmodel = fmodel,
                      buzztest = buzztest),
        file = fname)
message(paste('saved', fname))  # message to running R console
print(paste('saved', fname))    # print to document
```
```

```
## [1] "saved thRS500.RDS"
```

```
``` {r}
paste('finished at', date())
```
```

```
## [1] "finished at Thu Apr 18 09:33:05 2019"
```

```
``` {r}
system(paste('shasum', fname), intern = TRUE)  # write down file hash
```
```

```
## [1] "f2b3b80bc6c5a72079b39308a5758a282bcdd5bf  thRS500.RDS"
```

KNITR TAKEAWAY

In our knitr example, we worked through the steps we've done for every dataset in this book: load data, manage columns/variables, perform an initial analysis, present results, and save a workspace. The key point is that because we took the extra effort to do this work in knitr, we have the following:

- Nicely formatted documentation (buzzm.md)
- Shared executable code (buzzm.Rmd)

This makes debugging (which usually involves repeating and investigating earlier work), sharing, and documentation much easier and more reliable.

> **Project organization, further reading**
> To learn more about R markdown we recommend Yihui Xie, *Dynamic Documents with R and knitr* (CRC Press, 2013). Some good ideas on how to organize a data project in reproducible fashion can be found in *Reproducible Research with R and RStudio, Second Edition.*

11.3 *Using comments and version control for running documentation*

Another essential record of your work is what we call *running documentation*. Running documentation is less formal than milestone/checkpoint documentation and is easily maintained in the form of code comments and version control records. Undocumented, untracked code runs up a great deal of *technical debt* (see http://mng .bz/IaTd) that can cause problems down the road.

> **Example** *Suppose you want to work on formatting Buzz modeling results. You need to save this work to return to it later, document what steps you have taken, and share your work with others.*

In this section, we'll work through producing effective code comments and using Git for version control record keeping.

11.3.1 *Writing effective comments*

R's comment style is simple: everything following a # (that isn't itself quoted) until the end of a line is a comment and ignored by the R interpreter. The following listing is an example of a well-commented block of R code.

Listing 11.5 Example code comments

```
#' Return the pseudo logarithm, base 10.
#'
#' Return the pseudo logarithm (base 10) of x, which is close to
```

```
#' sign(x)*log10(abs(x)) for x such that abs(x) is large
#' and doesn't "blow up" near zero.  Useful
#' for transforming wide-range variables that may be negative
#' (like profit/loss).
#'
#' See: \url{http://www.win-vector.com/blog/2012/03/modeling-trick-the-
     signed-pseudo-logarithm/}
#'
#' NB: This transform has the undesirable property of making most
#' signed distributions appear bi-modal around the origin, no matter
#' what the underlying distribution really looks like.
#' The argument x is assumed be numeric and can be a vector.
#'
#' @param x numeric vector
#' @return pseudo logarithm, base 10 of x
#'
#' @examples
#'
#' pseudoLog10(c(-5, 0, 5))
#' # should be: [1] -0.7153834  0.0000000  0.7153834
#'
#' @export
#'
pseudoLog10 <- function(x) {
  asinh(x / 2) / log(10)
}
```

When such comments (with the #' marks and @ marks) is included in an R package, the documentation management engine can read the structured information and use it to produce additional documentation and even online help. For example, when we saved the preceding code in an R package at https://github.com/WinVector/PDSwR2/blob/master/PseudoLog10/R/pseudoLog10.R, we could use the roxygen2 R package to generate the online help shown in figure 11.6.

Good comments include what the function does, what types arguments are expected to be used, limits of domain, why you should care about the function, and where it's from. Of critical importance are any NB (*nota bene* or *note well*) or TODO notes. It's vastly more important to document any unexpected features or limitations in your code than to try to explain the obvious. Because R variables don't have types (only objects they're pointing to have types), you may want to document what types of arguments you're expecting. It's critical to state if a function works correctly on lists, data frame rows, vectors, and so on.

For more on packages and documentation, we recommend Hadley Wickham, *R Packages: Organize, Test, Document, and Share Your Code* (O'Reilly, 2015).

---

pseudoLog10 Return the pseudo logarithm, base 10.

Description

Return the pseudo logarithm (base 10) of x, which is close to sign(x)*log10(abs(x)) for x such that abs(x) is large and doesn't "blow up" near zero. Useful for transforming wide-range variables that may be negative (like profit/loss).

Usage

pseudoLog10(x)

Arguments

x numeric vector

Details

See: http://www.win-vector.com/blog/2012/03/modeling-trick-the-signed-pseudo-logarithm/

NB: This transform has the undesirable property of making most signed distributions appear bi- modal around the origin, no matter what the underlying distribution really looks like. The argument x is assumed be numeric and can be a vector.

Value

pseudo logarithm, base 10 of x

Examples

```
pseudoLog10(c(-5, 0, 5))
# should be: [1] -0.7153834  0.0000000  0.7153834
```

Figure 11.6 `roxygen@-generated` online help

11.3.2 *Using version control to record history*

Version control can both maintain critical snapshots of your work in earlier states and produce running documentation of what was done by whom and when in your project. Figure 11.7 shows a cartoon "version control saves the day" scenario that is in fact common.

In this section, we'll explain the basics of using Git (http://git-scm.com/) as a version control system. To really get familiar with Git, we recommend a good book such as Jon Loeliger and Matthew McCullough's *Version Control with Git,* Second Edition, (O'Reilly, 2012). Or, better yet, work with people who know Git. In this chapter, we assume you know how to run an interactive shell on your computer (on Linux and OS X you tend to use bash as your shell; on Windows you can install Cygwin—http://www.cygwin.com).

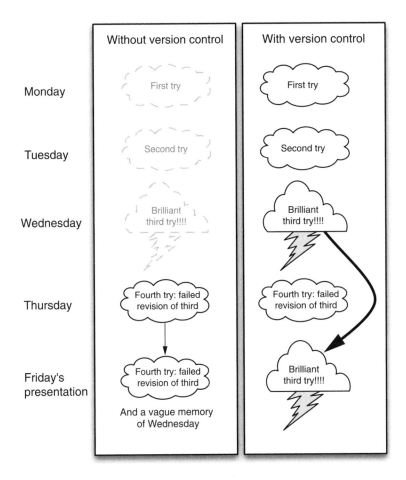

Figure 11.7 Version control saving the day

WORKING IN BRIGHT LIGHT   Sharing your Git repository means you're sharing a lot of information about your work habits and also sharing your mistakes. You're much more exposed than when you just share final work or status reports. Make this a virtue: know you're working in bright light. One of the most critical features in a good data scientist (perhaps even before analytic skill) is scientific honesty.

To get most of the benefit from Git, you need to become familiar with a few commands, which we will demonstrate in terms of specific tasks next.

CHOOSING A PROJECT DIRECTORY STRUCTURE

Before starting with source control, it's important to settle on and document a good project directory structure. *Reproducible Research with R and RStudio*, Second Edition, has good advice and instructions on how to do this. A pattern that's worked well for us is to start a new project with the directory structure described in table 11.5.

Table 11.5   A possible project directory structure

Directory	Description
Data	Where we save original downloaded data. This directory must usually be excluded from version control (using the .gitignore feature) due to file sizes, so you must ensure it's backed up. We tend to save each data refresh in a separate subdirectory named by date.
Scripts	Where we store all code related to analysis of the data.
Derived	Where we store intermediate results that are derived from data and scripts. This directory must be excluded from source control. You also should have a master script that can rebuild the contents of this directory in a single command (and test the script from time to time).
Results	Similar to derived, but this directory holds smaller, later results (often based on derived) and hand-written content. These include important saved models, graphs, and reports. This directory is under version control, so collaborators can see what was said when. Any report shared with partners should come from this directory.

STARTING A GIT PROJECT USING THE COMMAND LINE

When you've decided on your directory structure and want to start a version-controlled project, do the following:

1 Start the project in a new directory. Place any work either in this directory or in subdirectories.
2 Move your interactive shell into this directory and type `git init`. It's okay if you've already started working and there are already files present.
3 Exclude any subdirectories you don't want under source control with .gitignore control files.

You can check if you've already performed the init step by typing `git status`. If the init hasn't been done, you'll get a message similar to `fatal: Not a git repository (or any of the parent directories): .git`. If the init has been done, you'll get a status message telling you something like `on branch master` and listing facts about many files.

The init step sets up in your directory a single hidden file tree called .git and prepares you to keep extra copies of every file in your directory (including subdirectories). Keeping all of these extra copies is called *versioning* and what is meant by *version control.* You can now start working on your project: save everything related to your work in this directory or some subdirectory of this directory.

Again, you only need to init a project once. Don't worry about accidentally running `git init.` a second time; that's harmless.

USING ADD/COMMIT PAIRS TO CHECKPOINT WORK

GET NERVOUS ABOUT UNCOMMITTED STATE　Here's a good rule of thumb for Git: you should be as nervous about having uncommitted changes as you should be about not having clicked Save. You don't need to push/pull often, but you do need to make local commits often (even if you later squash them with a Git technique called *rebasing*).

As often as practical, enter the following two commands into an interactive shell in your project directory:

```
git add -A        ◁─────────────┐   Stages results to commit (specifies
git commit        ◁───────┐     │   what files should be committed)
                          │
                  Actually performs the commit
```

Checking in a file is split into two stages: add and commit. This has some advantages (such as allowing you to inspect before committing), but for now just consider the two commands as always going together. The `commit` command should bring up an editor where you enter a comment as to what you're up to. Until you're a Git expert, allow yourself easy comments like "update," "going to lunch," "just added a paragraph," or "corrected spelling." Run the add/commit pair of commands after every minor accomplishment on your project. Run these commands every time you leave your project (to go to lunch, to go home, or to work on another project). Don't fret if you forget to do this; just run the commands next time you remember.

> ### A "wimpy commit" is better than no commit
> We've been a little loose in our instructions to commit often and not worry too much about having a long commit message. Two things to keep in mind are that usually you want commits to be meaningful with the code working (so you tend not to commit in the middle of an edit with syntax errors), and good commit notes are to be preferred (just don't forgo a commit because you don't feel like writing a good commit note).

USING GIT LOG AND GIT STATUS TO VIEW PROGRESS

Any time you want to know about your work progress, type either `git status` to see if there are any edits you can put through the add/commit cycle, or `git log` to see the history of your work (from the viewpoint of the add/commit cycles).

The following listing shows the `git status` from our copy of this book's examples repository (https://github.com/WinVector/PDSwR2).

Listing 11.6　Checking your project status

```
$ git status
On branch master
Your branch is up to date with 'origin/master'.

nothing to commit, working tree clean
```

And the next listing shows a `git log` from the same project.

Listing 11.7   Checking your project history

```
$ git log
commit d22572281d40522bc6ab524bbdee497964ff4af0 (HEAD -
    > master, origin/master)
Author: John Mount <jmount@win-vector.com>
Date:   Tue Apr 16 16:24:23 2019 -0700

    technical edits ch7
```

The indented lines are the text we entered at the `git commit` step; the dates are tracked automatically.

USING GIT THROUGH RSTUDIO

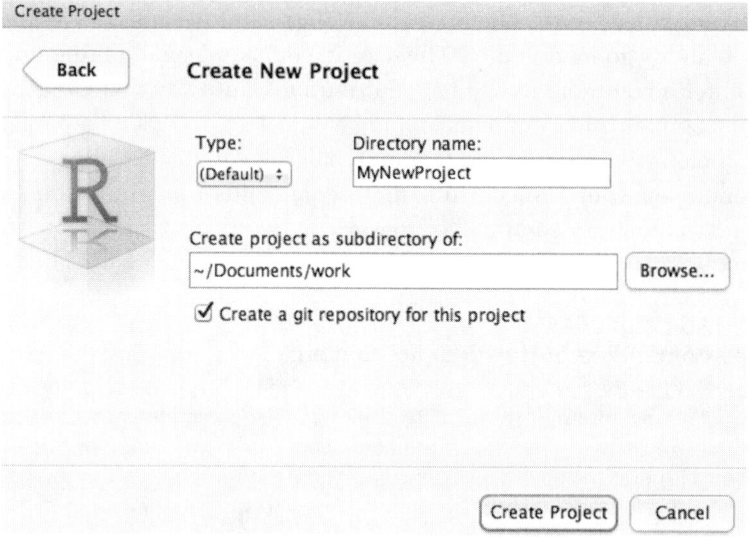

Figure 11.8   RStudio new project pane

The RStudio IDE supplies a graphical user interface to Git that you should try. The add/commit cycle can be performed as follows in RStudio:

- Start a new project. From the RStudio command menu, select Project > Create Project, and choose New Project. Then select the name of the project and what directory to create the new project directory in; leave the type as (Default), and make sure Create a Git Repository for this Project is checked. When the new project pane looks something like figure 11.8, click Create Project, and you have a new project.
- Do some work in your project. Create new files by selecting File > New > R Script. Type some R code (like 1/5) into the editor pane and then click the

save icon to save the file. When saving the file, be sure to choose your project directory or a subdirectory of your project.

- Commit your changes to version control. Figure 11.9 shows how to do this. Select the Git control pane in the top right of RStudio. This pane shows all changed files as line items. Check the Staged check box for any files you want to stage for this commit. Then click Commit, and you're done.

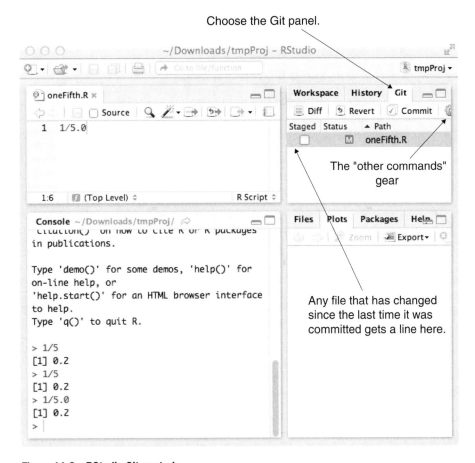

Figure 11.9   RStudio Git controls

You may not yet deeply understand or like Git, but you're able to safely check in all of your changes every time you remember to stage and commit. This means all of your work history is there; you can't clobber your committed work just by deleting your working file. Consider all of your working directory as "scratch work"—only checked-in work is safe from loss.

Your Git history can be seen by pulling down on the Other Commands gear (shown in the Git pane in figure 11.9) and selecting History (don't confuse this with the nearby History pane, which is command history, not Git history). In an emergency, you can find Git help and find your earlier files. If you've been checking in, then your older versions are there; it's just a matter of getting some help in accessing them. Also, if you're working with others, you can use the push/pull menu items to publish and receive updates. Here's all we want to say about version control at this point: *commit often, and if you're committing often, all problems can be solved with some further research.* Also, be aware that since your primary version control is on your own machine, you need to make sure you have an independent backup of your machine. If your machine fails and your work hasn't been backed up or shared, then you lose both your work and your version repository.

11.3.3 *Using version control to explore your project*

Up until now, our model of version control has been this: Git keeps a complete copy of all of our files each time we successfully enter the pair of add/commit lines. We'll now use these commits. If you add/commit often enough, Git is ready to help you with any of the following tasks:

- Tracking your work over time
- Recovering a deleted file
- Comparing two past versions of a file
- Finding when you added a specific bit of text
- Recovering a whole file or a bit of text from the past (undo an edit)
- Sharing files with collaborators
- Publicly sharing your project (à la GitHub at https://github.com/, Gitlab https://gitlab.com/, or Bitbucket at https://bitbucket.org)
- Maintaining different versions (branches) of your work

And that's why you want to add and commit often.

> **GETTING HELP ON GIT**   For any Git command, you can type `git help [command]` to get usage information. For example, to learn about `git log`, type `git help log`.

FINDING OUT WHO WROTE WHAT AND WHEN

In section 11.3.1, we implied that a good version control system can produce a lot of documentation on its own. One powerful example is the command `git blame`. Look what happens if we download the Git repository https://github.com/WinVector/PDSwR2 (with the command `git clone git@github.com:WinVector/PDSwR2.git`) and run the command `git blame Buzz/buzzapp/server.R` (to see who "wrote" each line in the file).

Listing 11.8   Finding out who committed what

```
git blame Buzz/buzzapp/server.R
4efb2b78 (John Mount 2019-04-24 16:22:43 -0700  1) #
```

```
4efb2b78 (John Mount 2019-04-24 16:22:43 -0700  2)
    # This is the server logic of a Shiny web application. You can run the
4efb2b78 (John Mount 2019-04-24 16:22:43 -0700  3)
    # application by clicking 'Run App' above.
4efb2b78 (John Mount 2019-04-24 16:22:43 -0700  4) #
```

The `git blame` information takes each line of the file and prints the following:

- The prefix of the line's Git commit hash. This is used to identify which commit the line we're viewing came from.
- Who committed the line.
- When they committed the line.
- The line number.
- And, finally, the contents of the line.

GIT BLAME DOESN'T TELL THE WHOLE STORY   It is important to understand that many of the updates that `git blame` reports may be mechanical (somebody using a tool to reformat files), or somebody acting on somebody else's behalf. You *must* look at the commits to see what happened. In this particular example, the commit message was "add Nina's Shiny example," so this was work done by Nina Zumel, who had delegated checking it in to John Mount.

A famous example of abusing similar lines of code metrics was the attempt to discredit Katie Bouman's leadership in creating the first image of a black hole. One of the (false) points raised was that collaborator Andrew Chael had contributed more lines of code to the public repository. Fortunately, Chael himself responded, defending Bouman's role and pointing out the line count attributed to him was machine-generated model files he had checked into the repository as part of his contribution, not authored lines of code.

USING GIT DIFF TO COMPARE FILES FROM DIFFERENT COMMITS

The `git diff` command allows you to compare any two committed versions of your project, or even to compare your current uncommitted work to any earlier version. In Git, commits are named using large hash keys, but you're allowed to use prefixes of the hashes as names of commits.[5] For example, the following listing demonstrates finding the differences in two versions of https://github.com/WinVector/PDSwR2 in a diff or patch format.

> **Listing 11.9   Finding line-based differences between two committed versions**

```
diff --git a/CDC/NatalBirthData.rData b/CDC/NatalBirthData.rData
...
+++ b/CDC/prepBirthWeightData.R
@@ -0,0 +1,83 @@
+data <- read.table("natal2010Sample.tsv.gz",
+                   sep="\t", header = TRUE, stringsAsFactors = FALSE)
+
+# make a boolean from Y/N data
```

---

[5] You can also create meaningful names for commits with the `git tag` command.

```
+makevarYN = function(col) {
+    ifelse(col %in% c("", "U"), NA, col=="Y")
+}
...
```

TRY TO NOT CONFUSE GIT COMMITS AND GIT BRANCHES   A Git commit represents the complete state of a directory tree at a given time. A Git branch represents a sequence of commits and changes as you move through time. Commits are immutable; branches record progress.

USING GIT LOG TO FIND THE LAST TIME A FILE WAS AROUND

> **Example**   *At some point there was a file named Buzz/buzz.pdf in our repository. Somebody asks us a question about this file. How do we use Git to find when this file was last in the repository, and what its contents had been?*

After working on a project for a while, we often wonder, when did we delete a certain file and what was in it at the time? Git makes answering this question easy. We'll demonstrate this in the repository https://github.com/WinVector/PDSwR2. We remember the Buzz directory having a file named buzz.pdf, but there is no such file now and we want to know what happened to it. To find out, we'll run the following:

```
git log --name-status -- Buzz/buzz.pdf
commit 96503d8ca35a61ed9765edff9800fc9302554a3b
Author: John Mount <jmount@win-vector.com>
Date:   Wed Apr 17 16:41:48 2019 -0700

    fix links and re-build Buzz example

D       Buzz/buzz.pdf
```

We see the file was deleted by John Mount. We can view the contents of this older file with the command `git checkout 96503d8^1 -- Buzz/buzz.pdf`. The `96503d8` is the prefix of the commit number (which was enough to specify the commit that deleted the file), and the `^1` means "the state of the file one commit before the named commit" (the last version before the file was deleted).

11.3.4   *Using version control to share work*

> **Example**   *We want to work with multiple people and share results. One way to use Git to accomplish this is by individually setting up our own repository and sharing with a central repository.*

In addition to producing work, you must often share it with peers. The common (and bad) way to do this is emailing zip files. Most of the bad sharing practices take excessive effort, are error prone, and rapidly cause confusion. We advise using version control to share work with peers. To do that effectively with Git, you need to start using additional commands such as `git pull`, `git rebase`, and `git push`. Things seem more confusing at this point (though you still don't need to worry about branching in its full generality), but are in fact far less confusing and less error-prone than ad hoc solutions. We almost always advise sharing work in *star workflow*, where each worker has their own repository, and a single common "naked" repository (a repository with only Git data structures and no ready-to-use files) is used to coordinate (thought of as a server or gold standard, often named *origin*). Figure 11.10 shows one arrangement of repositories that allows multiple authors to collaborate.

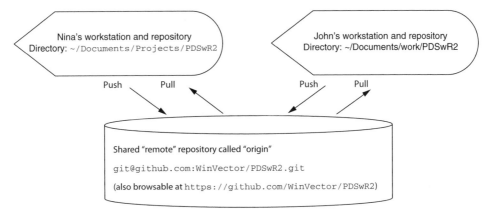

Figure 11.10   Multiple repositories working together

The usual shared workflow is like this:

- *Continuously*—Work, work, work.
- *Frequently*—Commit results to the local repository using a `git add`/`git commit` pair.
- *Every once in a while*—Pull a copy of the remote repository into our view with some variation of `git pull` and then use `git push` to push work upstream.

The main rule of Git is this: don't try anything clever (push/pull, and so on) unless you're in a "clean" state (everything committed, confirmed with `git status`).

SETTING UP REMOTE REPOSITORY RELATIONS

For two or more Git repositories to share work, the repositories need to know about each other through a relation called *remote*. A Git repository is able to share its work to a remote repository by the `push` command and pick up work from a remote repository by the `pull` command. The next listing shows the declared remotes for the authors' local copy of the https://github.com/WinVector/PDSwR2 repository.

Listing 11.10   `git remote`

```
$ git remote --verbose
origin  git@github.com:WinVector/PDSwR2.git (fetch)
origin  git@github.com:WinVector/PDSwR2.git (push)
```

The remote relation is set when you create a copy of a repository using the `git clone` command or can be set using the `git remote add` command. In listing 11.10, the remote repository is called `origin`—this is the traditional name for a remote repository that you're using as your master or gold standard. (Git tends not to use the name *master* for repositories because master is the name of the branch you're usually working on.)

USING PUSH AND PULL TO SYNCHRONIZE WORK WITH REMOTE REPOSITORIES

Once your local repository has declared some other repository as remote, you can push and pull between the repositories. When pushing or pulling, always make sure you're clean (have no uncommitted changes), and you usually want to pull before you push (as that's the quickest way to spot and fix any potential conflicts). For a description of what version control conflicts are and how to deal with them, see http://mng .bz/5pTv.

Usually, for simple tasks we don't use branches (a technical version control term), and we use the `rebase` option on pull so that it appears that every piece of work is recorded into a simple linear order, even though collaborators are actually working in parallel. This is what we call an *essential* difficulty of working with others: time and order become separate ideas and become hard to track (and this is *not* a needless complexity added by using Git—there *are* such needless complexities, but this is not one of them).

The new Git commands you need to learn are these:

- `git push` (usually used in the `git push -u origin master` variation)
- `git pull` (usually used in the `git fetch; git merge -m pull master origin/ master` or `git pull --rebase origin master` variations)

Typically, two authors may be working on different files in the same project at the same time. As you can see in figure 11.11, the second author to push their results to the shared repository must decide how to specify the parallel work that was performed. Either they can say the work was truly in parallel (represented by two branches being formed and then a merge record joining the work), or they can rebase their own work to claim their work was done "after" the other's work (preserving a linear edit history and avoiding the need for any merge records). Note: *before* and *after* are tracked in terms of arrows, not time.

Merging is what's really happening, but *rebase* is much simpler to read. The general rule is that you should only rebase work you haven't yet shared (in our example, Worker B should feel free to rebase their edits to appear to be after Worker A's edits, as Worker B hasn't yet successfully pushed their work anywhere). You should avoid rebasing records people have seen, as you're essentially hiding the edit steps they may be basing their work on (forcing them to merge or rebase in the future to catch up with your changed record keeping).

> **KEEP NOTES** Git commands are confusing; you'll want to keep notes. One idea is to write a 3×5 card for each command you're regularly using. Ideally, you can be at the top of your Git game with about seven cards.

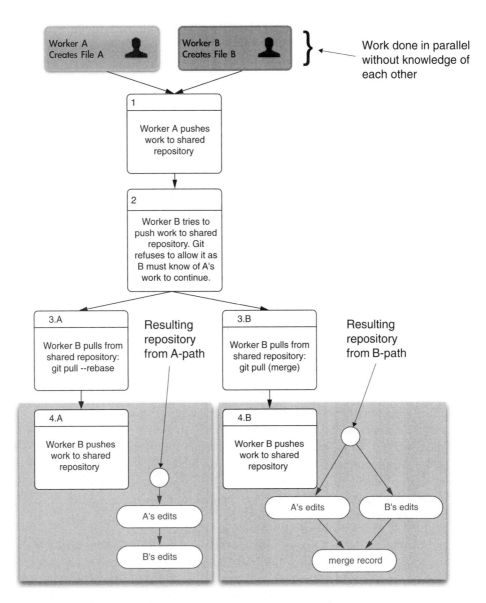

Figure 11.11 `git pull`: rebase versus merge

For most projects, we try to use a rebase-only strategy. For example, this book itself is maintained in a Git repository. We have only two authors who are in close proximity (so able to easily coordinate), and we're only trying to create one final copy of the book (we're not trying to maintain many branches for other uses). If we always rebase, the edit history will appear totally ordered (for each pair of edits, one is always recorded as having come before the other), and this makes talking about versions of the book much easier (again, *before* is determined by arrows in the edit history, not by time stamp).

DON'T CONFUSE VERSION CONTROL WITH BACKUP   Git keeps multiple copies and records of all of your work. But until you push to a remote destination, all of these copies are on your machine in the .git directory. So don't confuse basic version control with remote backups; they're complementary.

A BIT ON THE GIT PHILOSOPHY

Git is interesting in that it automatically detects and manages so much of what you'd have to specify with other version control systems (for example, Git finds which files have changed instead of you having to specify them, and Git also decides which files are related). Because of the large degree of automation, beginners usually severely underestimate how much Git tracks for them. This makes Git fairly quick except when Git insists you help decide how a possible global inconsistency should be recorded in history (either as a rebase or a branch followed by a merge record). The point is this: Git suspects possible inconsistency based on global state (even when the user may not think there is such) and then forces the committer to decide how to annotate the issue *at the time of commit* (a great service to any possible readers in the future). Git automates so much of the record keeping that it's always a shock when you have a conflict and have to express opinions on nuances you didn't know were being tracked. Git is also an "anything is possible, but nothing is obvious or convenient" system. This is hard on the user at first, but in the end is much better than an "everything is smooth, but little is possible" version control system (which can leave you stranded).

11.4   *Deploying models*

Good data science shares a rule with good writing: show, don't tell. And a successful data science project should include at least a demonstration deployment of any techniques and models developed. Good documentation and presentation are vital, but at some point, people have to see things working and be able to try their own tests. We strongly encourage partnering with a development group to produce the actual production-hardened version of your model, but a good demonstration helps recruit these collaborators.

> **Example**   *Suppose you are asked to make your model predictions available to other software so it can be reflected in reports and used to make decisions. This means you must somehow "deploy your model." This can vary from scoring all data in a known database, exporting the model for somebody else to deploy, or setting up your own web application or HTTP service.*

The statistician or analyst's job often ends when the model is created or a report is finished. For the data scientist, this is just the acceptance phase. The real goal is getting the model into production: scoring data that wasn't available when the model was built and driving decisions made by other software. This means that helping with deployment is part of the job. In this section, we will outline useful methods for achieving different styles of R model deployment.

We outline some deployment methods in table 11.6.

Table 11.6 Methods to deploy models

Method	Description
Batch	Data is brought into R, scored, and then written back out. This is essentially an extension of what you're already doing with test data.
Cross-language linkage	R supplies answers to queries from another language (C, C++, Python, Java, and so on). R is designed with efficient cross-language calling in mind (in particular the Rcpp package), but this is a specialized topic we won't cover here.
Services	R can be set up as an HTTP service to take new data as an HTTP query and respond with results.
Export	Often, model evaluation is simple compared to model construction. In this case, the data scientist can export the model and a specification for the code to evaluate the model, and the production engineers can implement (with tests) model evaluation in the language of their choice (SQL, Java, C++, and so on).
PMML	*PMML*, or *Predictive Model Markup Language*, is a shared XML format that many modeling packages can export to and import from. If the model you produce is covered by R's package `pmml`, you can export it without writing any additional code. Then any software stack that has an importer for the model in question can use your model.

Models in production

There are some basic defenses one should set up when placing a model in production. We mention these as we rarely see these valuable precautions taken:

- All models and all predictions from models should be annotated with the model version name and a link to the model documentation. This simple precaution has saved one of the authors when they were able to show a misclassification was not from the model they had just deployed, but from a human tagger.
- Machine learning model results should never be directly used as decisions. Instead, they should be an input to configurable business logic that makes decisions. This allows both patching the model to make it more reasonable (such as bounding probability predictions into a reasonable range such as 0.01 to 0.99) and turning it off (changing the business logic to not use the model prediction in certain cases).

You always want the last stage in any automated system to be directly controllable. So even a trivial business logic layer that starts by directly obeying a given model's determination is high value, as it gives a place where you can correct special cases.

We've already demonstrated batch operation of models each time we applied a model to a test set. We won't work through an R cross-language linkage example as it's very specialized and requires knowledge of the system you're trying to link to. We'll demonstrate service and export strategies.

11.4.1 *Deploying demonstrations using Shiny*

> **Example**   *Suppose we want to build an interactive dashboard or demo for our boss. Our boss wants to try different classification thresholds against our Buzz score to see what precision and recall are available at each threshold. We could do this as a graph, but we are asked do this as an interactive service (possibly part of a larger drill-down/exploration service).*

We will solve this scenario by using *Shiny*, a tool for building interactive web applications in R. Here we will use Shiny to let our boss pick the threshold that converts our Buzz score into a "will Buzz"/"won't Buzz" decision. The entire code for this demonstration is in the Buzz/buzzapp directory of https://github.com/WinVector/PDSwR2.

The easiest way to run the Shiny application is to open the file server.R from that directory in RStudio. Then, as shown in figure 11.12, there will be a button on the upper right of the RStudio editor pane called Run App. Clicking this button will run the application.

Figure 11.12   Launching the Shiny server from RStudio

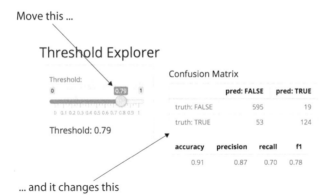

Move this ...

Threshold Explorer

Threshold: 0.79

... and it changes this

Figure 11.13 Interacting with the Shiny application

The running application will look like figure 11.13. The user can move the threshold control slider and get a new confusion matrix and model metrics (such as precision and recall) for each slider position.

Shiny's program principles are based on an idea called *reactive programming* where the user specifies what values may change due to user interventions. The Shiny software then handles rerunning and updating the display as the user uses the application. Shiny is a very large topic, but you can get started by copying an example application and editing it to fit your own needs.

FURTHER SHINY READING
We don't currently have a Shiny book recommendation. A good place to start on Shiny documentation, examples, and tutorials is https://shiny.rstudio.com.

11.4.2 Deploying models as HTTP services

> **Example**   *Our model looked good in testing, and our boss likes working with our interactive web application. So we now want to fully "put our model in production." In this case, the model is considered "in production" if other servers can send data to it and get scored results. That is, our model is to be partly deployed in production as part of a services oriented architecture (SOA).*

Our model can be used by other software either by linking to it or having the model exposed as a service. In this case, we will deploy our Buzz model as an HTTP service. Once we have done this, other services at our company can send data to our model for scoring. For example, a revenue management dashboard can send a set of articles it is managing to our model for "buzz scoring," meaning the buzz score can be incorporated into this dashboard. This is more flexible than having our Buzz model score all known articles in a database, as the dashboard can ask about any article for which it has the details.

One easy way to demonstrate an R model in operation is to expose it as an HTTP service. In the following listing, we show how to do this for our Buzz model (predicting discussion topic popularity). Listing 11.11 shows the first few lines of the file

PDSwR2/Buzz/plumber.R. This .R file can be used with the plumber R package to expose our model as an HTTP service, either for production use or testing.

Listing 11.11   Buzz model as an R-based HTTP service

```
library("randomForest")                              Attaches the randomForest
                                                      package, so we can run our
lst <- readRDS("thRS500.RDS")                         randomForest model
varslist <- lst$varslist
fmodel <- lst$fmodel
buzztest <- lst$buzztest
rm(list = "lst")

#* Score a data frame.
#* @param d data frame to score
#* @post /score_data
function(d) {
  predict(fmodel, newdata = d, type = "prob")
}
```

We would then start the server with the following code:

```
library("plumber")
r <- plumb("plumber.R")
r$run(port=8000)
```

The next listing is the contents of the file PDSwR2/Buzz/RCurl_client_example.Rmd, and shows how to call the HTTP service from R. However, this is just to demonstrate the capability—the whole point of setting up an HTTP service is that something other than R wants to use the service.

Listing 11.12   Calling the Buzz HTTP service

```
library("RCurl")
library("jsonlite")                                  Wraps the services
                                                      as a function
post_query <- function(method, args) {
   hdr <- c("Content-Type" = "application/x-www-form-urlencoded")
   resp <- postForm(
    paste0("http://localhost:8000/", method),
    .opts=list(httpheader = hdr,
               postfields = toJSON(args)))
   fromJSON(resp)
}

data <- read.csv("buzz_sample.csv",
                 stringsAsFactors = FALSE,
                 strip.white = TRUE)

scores <- post_query("score_data",
                     list(d = data))
knitr::kable(head(scores))

tab <- table(pred = scores[, 2]>0.5, truth = data$buzz)
knitr::kable(tab)
```

```
knitr::kable(head(scores))
```

0.998	0.002
0.350	0.650
1.000	0.000
1.000	0.000
0.748	0.252
0.008	0.992

```
tab <- table(pred = scores[, 2]>0.5, truth = data$buzz)
knitr::kable(tab)
```

	0	1
FALSE	77	3
TRUE	4	16

Figure 11.14   Top of HTML form that asks server for Buzz classification on submit

This produces the result PDSwR2/Buzz/RCurl_client_example.md, shown in figure 11.14 (also saved in our example GitHub repository).

For more on `plumber`, we suggest starting with the `plumber` package documentation: https://CRAN.R-project.org/package=plumber.

11.4.3 Deploying models by export

It often makes sense to export a copy of the finished model from R, instead of attempting to reproduce all the details of model construction in another system or to use R itself in production. When exporting a model, you're depending on development partners to handle the hard parts of hardening a model for production (versioning, dealing with exceptional conditions, and so on). Software engineers tend to be good at project management and risk control, so sharing projects with them is a good opportunity to learn.

The steps required depend a lot on the model and data treatment. For many models, you only need to save a few coefficients. For random forests, you need to export the trees. In all cases, you need to write code in your target system (be it SQL, Java, C, C++, Python, Ruby, or other) to evaluate the model.

One of the issues of exporting models is that you must repeat any data treatment. So part of exporting a model is producing a specification of the data treatment (so it can be reimplemented outside of R).

EXPORTING RANDOM FORESTS TO SQL WITH TIDYPREDICT

Exercise: Run our random forest model in SQL

Our goal is to export our random forest model as SQL code that can be then run in a database, without any further use of R.

The R package `tidypredict`[6] provides methods to export models such as our random forest Buzz model to SQL, which could then be run in a database. We will just show a bit of what this looks like. The random forest model consists of 500 trees that vote on the answer. The top of the first tree is shown in figure 11.15 (random forest trees tend not to be that legible). Remember that trees classify by making sequential decisions from the top-most node down.

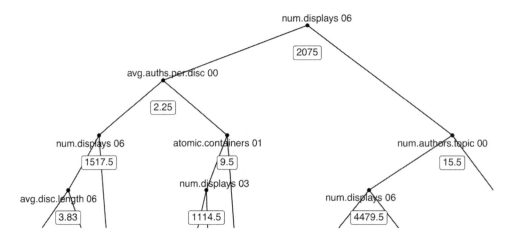

Figure 11.15   The top of the first tree (of 500) from the random forest model

Now let's look at the model that `tidypredict` converted to SQL. The conversion was performed in the R markdown file PDSwR2/Buzz/model_export.Rmd, which produces the rendered result PDSwR2/Buzz/model_export.md. We won't show the code here, but instead show the first few lines of the what the first random forest tree is translated into:

```
CASE
  WHEN (`num.displays_06` >= 1517.5 AND
        `avg.auths.per.disc_00` < 2.25 AND
        `num.displays_06` < 2075.0) THEN ('0')
  WHEN (`num.displays_03` >= 1114.5 AND
        `atomic.containers_01` < 9.5 AND
        `avg.auths.per.disc_00` >= 2.25 AND
        `num.displays_06` < 2075.0) THEN ('0')
  WHEN ...
```

---

6   See https://CRAN.R-project.org/package=tidypredict.

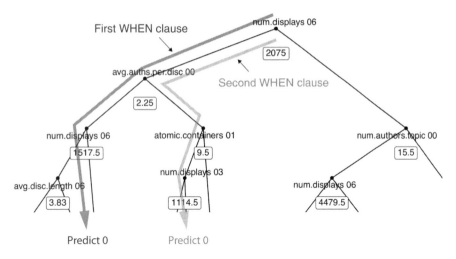

Figure 11.16 Annotating CASE/WHEN paths

The preceding code is enumerating each path from the root of the tree down. Remember that decision trees are just huge nested if/else blocks, and SQL writes if/else as CASE/WHEN. Each SQL WHEN clause is a path in the original decision tree. This is made clearer in figure 11.16.

In the SQL export, each tree is written as a series of WHEN cases over all of its paths, allowing the tree calculation to be performed in SQL. As a user, we would evaluate a tree by tracing down from the root node and moving down nodes, and left/right depending on the node conditions. The SQL code instead evaluates all paths from the roots to the leaves and keeps the result from the unique path for which all the conditions are met. It is an odd way to evaluate a tree, but it converts everything into an all-at-once formula that can be exported to SQL.

The overall idea is this: we have exported the random forest model into a format something else can read, SQL. Somebody else can own the finished model from that point on.

An important export system to consider using is *Predictive Model Markup Language* (PMML) which is an XML standard for sharing models across different systems.[7]

11.4.4 What to take away

You should now be comfortable demonstrating R models to others. Deployment and demonstration techniques include

- Setting up a model as an HTTP service that can be experimented with by others
- Setting up micro applications using Shiny
- Exporting models so a model application can be reimplemented in a production environment

[7] See, for example, the PMML package https://CRAN.R-project.org/package=pmml.

Summary

In this chapter, we worked on managing and sharing your work. In addition, we showed some techniques to set up demonstration HTTP services and export models for use by other software (so you don't add R as a dependency in production). At this point, you have been building machine learning models for some time, and you now have some techniques for working proficiently with models over time and with collaborators.

Here are some key takeaways:

- Use knitr to produce significant reproducible milestone/checkpoint documentation.
- Write effective comments.
- Use version control to save your work history.
- Use version control to collaborate with others.
- Make your models available to your partners for experimentation, testing, and production deployment.

In our next chapter, we will explore how to formally present and explain your work.

Producing effective presentations

In the previous chapter, you saw how to effectively document your day-to-day project work and how to deploy your model into production. This included the additional documentation needed to support operations teams. In this chapter, we'll look at how to present the results of your project to other interested parties. As we see in the mental model (figure 12.1), this chapter is all about documentation and presentation.

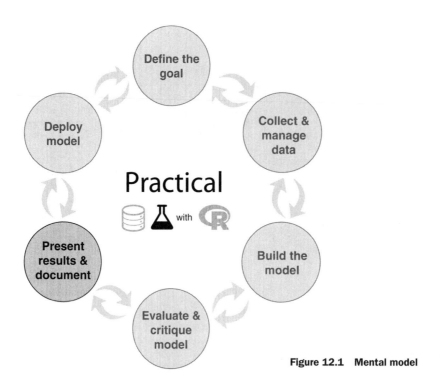

Figure 12.1   Mental model

We'll continue with the example from the last chapter.

Example   *Suppose your company (let's call it WVCorp) makes and sells home elec-*
tronic devices and associated software and apps. WVCorp wants to monitor topics on
the company's product forums and discussion board to identify "about-to-buzz" issues:
topics that are poised to generate a lot of interest and active discussion. This informa-
tion can be used by product and marketing teams to proactively identify desired product
features for future releases, and to quickly discover issues with existing product features.
Your team has successfully built a model to identify about-to-buzz topics on the forum.
Now you want to explain the project results to the project sponsor, and also to the prod-
uct managers, marketing managers, and support engineering managers who will be
using the results of your model.

Table 12.1 summarizes the relevant entities in our scenario, including products that
are sold by your company and by competitors.

Table 12.1   Entities in the buzz model scenario

Entity	Description
WVCorp	The company you work for
eRead	WVCorp's e-book reader

Table 12.1 Entities in the buzz model scenario *(continued)*

Entity	Description
TimeWrangler	WVCorp's time-management app
BookBits	A competitor's e-book reader
GCal	A third-party cloud-based calendar service that TimeWrangler can integrate with

A disclaimer about the data and the example project

The dataset that we used for the buzz model was collected from Tom's Hardware (tomshardware.com), an actual forum for discussing electronics and electronic devices. Tom's Hardware is not associated with any specific product vendor, and the dataset doesn't specify the topics that were recorded. The example scenario in this chapter was chosen to present a situation that would produce data similar to the data in the Tom's Hardware dataset. All product names and forum topics in our example are fictitious.

Let's start with the presentation for the project sponsors.[1]

12.1 *Presenting your results to the project sponsor*

As mentioned in chapter 1, the project sponsor is the person who wants the data science result—generally for the business need that it will fill. Though project sponsors may have technical or quantitative backgrounds and may enjoy hearing about technical details and nuances, their primary interest is business oriented, so you should discuss your results in terms of the business problem, with a minimum of technical detail.

You should also remember that the sponsor will often be interested in "selling" your work to others in the organization, to drum up support and additional resources to keep the project going. Your presentation will be part of what the sponsor will share with these other people, who may not be as familiar with the context of the project as you and your sponsor are.

To cover these considerations, we recommend a structure similar to the following:

1 Summarize the motivation behind the project, and its goals.
2 State the project's results.
3 Back up the results with details, as needed.
4 Discuss recommendations, outstanding issues, and possible future work.

---

[1] We provide the PDF versions of our example presentations at https://github.com/WinVector/PDSwR2/tree/master/Buzz as ProjectSponsorPresentation.pdf, UserPresentation.pdf, and PeerPresentation.pdf. The directory also includes handouts of these presentations with brief notes, as xxxPresentation_withNotes.pdf.

Some people also recommend an "Executive Summary" slide: a one-slide synopsis of points 1 and 2.

How you treat each point—how long, how much detail—depends on your audience and your situation. In general, we recommend keeping the presentation short. In this section, we'll offer some example slides in the context of our buzz model example.

Let's go through each point in detail.

We'll concentrate on content, not visuals

The discussion in this chapter will concentrate on the content of the presentations, rather than the visual format of the slides. In an actual presentation, you'd likely prefer more visuals and less text than the slides that we provide here. If you're looking for guidance on presentation visuals and compelling data visualizations for presentations, two good books are

- Michael Alley, *The Craft of Scientific Presentations* (Springer, 2007)
- Cole Nussbaumer Knaflic, *Storytelling with Data* (Wiley, 2015)

If you peruse those texts, you'll notice that our bullet-laden example presentation violates all of their suggestions. Think of our skeleton presentations as outlines that you'd flesh out into a more compelling visual format.

It's worth pointing out that the visually oriented, low-text format that Alley and Knaflic recommend is meant to be *presented*, not read. It's common for presentation decks to be passed around in lieu of reports or memos. If you're distributing your presentation to people who won't see you deliver it, make sure to include comprehensive speaker's notes. Otherwise, it may be more appropriate to go with a bullet-laden, text-heavy presentation format.

12.1.1 Summarizing the project's goals

This section of the presentation is intended to provide context for the rest of the talk, especially if it will be distributed to others in the company who weren't as closely involved as your project sponsor was. Let's put together the goal slides for the WVCorp buzz model example.

In figure 12.2, we provide background for the motivation behind the project by showing the business need and how the project will address that need. In our example, eRead is WVCorp's e-book reader, which led the market until our competitor released a new version of their e-book reader, BookBits. The new version of BookBits has a shared-bookshelf feature that eRead doesn't provide—though many eRead users expressed the desire for such functionality on the forums. Unfortunately, forum traffic is so high that product managers have a hard time keeping up, and somehow missed detecting this expression of user needs. Hence, WVCorp lost market share by not anticipating the demand for the shared-bookshelf feature.

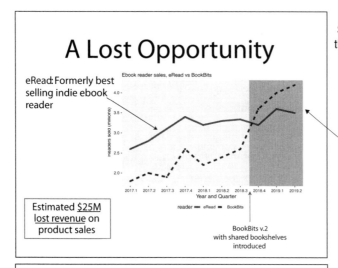

Show the business need that motivated this project: WVCorp lost revenue and market share to a competitor.

Blue solid curve: WVCorp's product (eRead) Green dashed curve: Competitor's product (BookBits)

WVCorp has the information to help address this need, but not enough resources (labor) to use the information effectively.

In a real presentation, use a screenshot of a relevant forum discussion.

Figure 12.2   Motivation for project

In figure 12.3, we state the project's goal, in the context of the motivation that we set up in figure 12.2. We want to detect topics on the forum that are about to buzz so that product managers can find emerging issues early.

Once you've established the project's context, you should move directly to the project's results. Your presentation isn't a thriller movie—don't keep your audience in suspense!

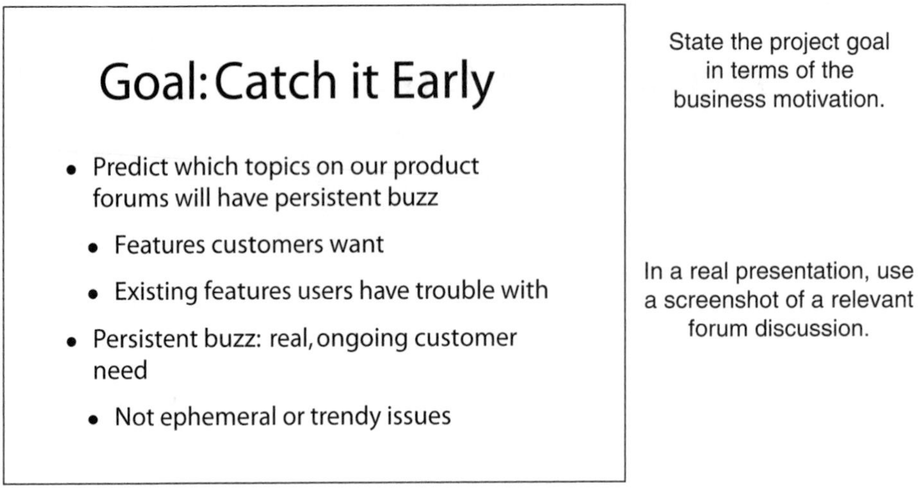

Figure 12.3   Stating the project goal

12.1.2   *Stating the project's results*

This section of the presentation briefly describes what you did, and what the results were, in the context of the business need. Figure 12.4 describes the buzz model pilot study, and what you found.

Keep the discussion of the results concrete and nontechnical. Your audience isn't interested in the details of your model *per se*, but rather in why your model helped solve the problem that you stated in the motivation section of the talk. Don't talk about your model's performance in terms of precision and recall or other technical metrics, but rather in terms of how it reduced the workload for the model's end users, how useful they found the results to be, and what the model missed. In projects where the model is more closely tied to monetary outcomes, like loan default prediction, try to estimate how much money your model could potentially generate, whether as earnings or savings, for the company.

Pilot Study

- Collected three weeks of data from forum
- Trained model on Week 1 to identify which topics will buzz in Weeks 2/3
  - Buzz = Sustained increase of 500+ active discussions in topic/day, relative to Week 1, Day 1
  - Compared predicted results to topics that actually buzzed
  - Feedback from team of five product managers — how useful were the results?

Briefly describe how the project was run

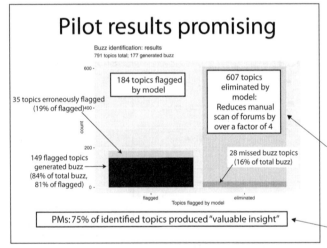

Pilot results promising

Buzz identification: results
791 topics total; 177 generated buzz

600 -

184 topics flagged by model

607 topics eliminated by model:
Reduces manual scan of forums by over a factor of 4

35 topics erroneously flagged (19% of flagged) 400 -

count

200 -

149 flagged topics generated buzz (84% of total buzz, 81% of flagged)   0 -

28 missed buzz topics (16% of total buzz)

flagged   eliminated
Topics flagged by model

PMs: 75% of identified topics produced "valuable insight"

State the results up front.

State the results in terms of how they affect the end users (product managers).

The model reduces the end users' workload by zeroing in on what they need to look at.

Representative end users thought the model's output was useful.

Figure 12.4   Describing the project and its results

12.1.3 *Filling in the details*

Once your audience knows what you've done, why, and how well you've succeeded (from a business point of view), you can fill in details to help them understand more. As before, try to keep the discussion relatively nontechnical and grounded in the business process. A description of where the model fits in the business process or workflow and some examples of interesting findings would go well in this section, as shown in figure 12.5.

The "How it Works" slide in figure 12.5 shows where the buzz model fits into a product manager's workflow. We emphasize that (so far) we've built the model using metrics that were already implemented into the system (thus minimizing the number of new processes to be introduced into the workflow). We also introduce the ways in

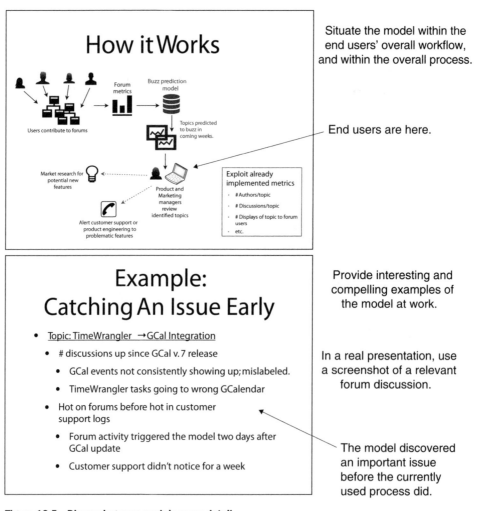

Figure 12.5 Discussing your work in more detail

which the output from our model can potentially be used: to generate leads for potential new features, and to alert product support groups to impending problems.

The bottom slide of figure 12.5 presents an interesting finding from the project (in a real presentation, you'd want to show more than one). In this example, Time-Wrangler is WVCorp's time-management product, and GCal is a third-party cloud-based calendar service that TimeWrangler can talk to. In this slide, we show how the model was able to identify an integration issue between TimeWrangler and GCal sooner than the TimeWrangler team would have otherwise (from the customer support logs). Examples like this make the value of the model concrete.

We've also included one slide in this presentation to discuss the modeling algorithm (shown in figure 12.6). Whether you use this slide depends on the audience—some of your listeners may have a technical background and will be interested in hearing about your choice of modeling methods. Other audiences may not care. In any case, keep it brief, and focus on a high-level description of the technique and why you felt it was a good choice. If anyone in the audience wants more detail, they can ask—and if you anticipate such people in your audience, you can have additional slides to cover likely questions. Otherwise, be prepared to cover this point quickly, or to skip it altogether.

There are other details that you might want to discuss in this section. For example, if the product managers who participated in your pilot study gave you interesting quotes or feedback—how much easier their job is when they use the model, findings that they thought were especially valuable, ideas they had about how the model could be improved—you can mention that feedback here. This is your chance to get others in the company interested in your work on this project and to drum up continuing support for follow-up efforts.

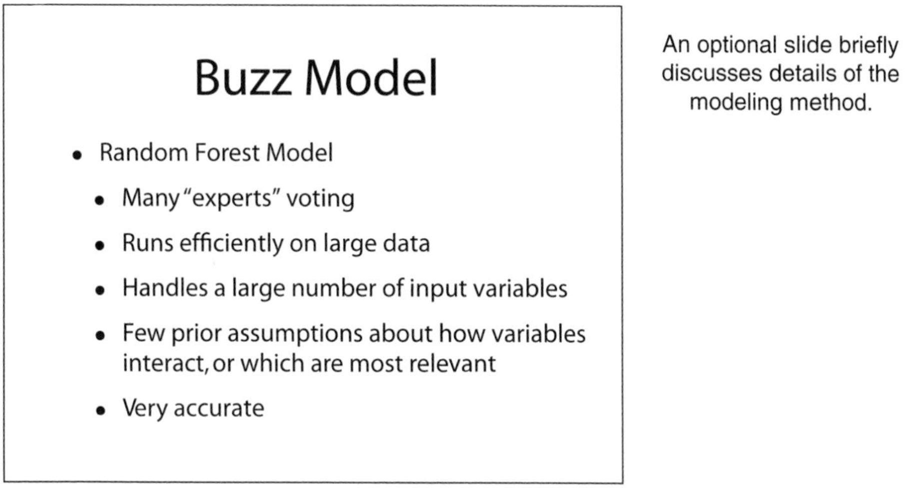

An optional slide briefly discusses details of the modeling method.

Buzz Model

- Random Forest Model
  - Many "experts" voting
  - Runs efficiently on large data
  - Handles a large number of input variables
  - Few prior assumptions about how variables interact, or which are most relevant
  - Very accurate

Figure 12.6 Optional slide on the modeling method

12.1.4 *Making recommendations and discussing future work*

No project ever produces a perfect outcome, and you should be up-front (but optimistic) about the limitations of your results. In the Buzz model example, we end the presentation by listing some improvements and follow-ups that we'd like to make. This is shown in figure 12.7. As a data scientist, you're of course interested in improving the model's performance, but to the audience, improving the model is less important than improving the process (and better meeting the business need). Frame the discussion from that perspective.

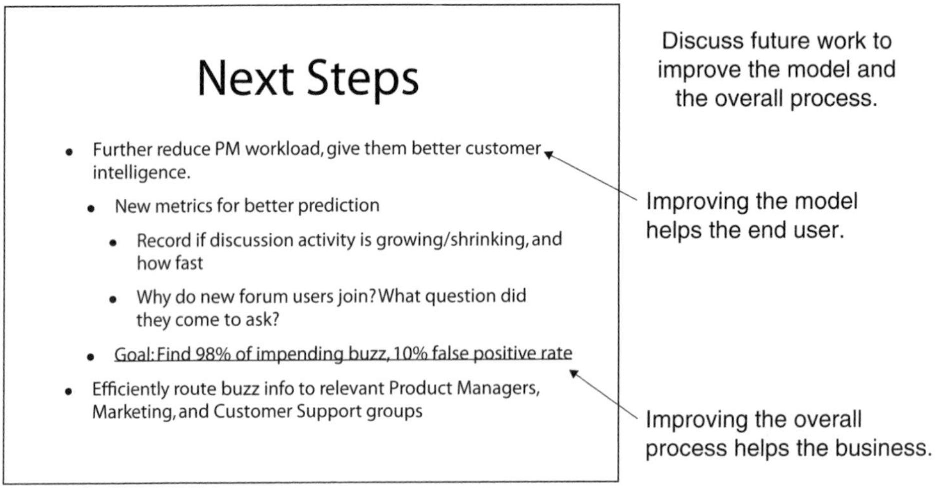

Figure 12.7   Discussing future work

The project sponsor presentation focuses on the big picture and how your results help to better address a business need. A presentation for end users will cover much of the same ground, but now you frame the discussion in terms of the end users' workflow and concerns. We'll look at an end user presentation for the buzz model in the next section.

12.1.5 *Project sponsor presentation takeaways*

Here's what you should remember about the project sponsor presentation:

- Keep it short.
- Keep it focused on the business issues, not the technical ones.
- Your project sponsor might use your presentation to help sell the project or its results to the rest of the organization. Keep that in mind when presenting background and motivation.
- Introduce your results early in the presentation, rather than building up to them.

12.2   *Presenting your model to end users*

No matter how well your model performs, it's important that the people who will actually be using it have confidence in its output and are willing to adopt it. Otherwise, the model won't be used, and your efforts will have been wasted. Hopefully, you had end users involved in the project—in our buzz model example, we had five product managers helping with the pilot study. End users can help you sell the benefits of the model to their peers.

In this section, we'll give an example of how you might present the results of your project to the end users. Depending on the situation, you may not always be giving an explicit presentation: you may be providing a user manual or other documentation. However the information about your model is passed to the users, we believe that it's important to let them know how the model is intended to make their workflow easier, not more complicated. For the purposes of this chapter, we'll use a presentation format.

For an end user presentation, we recommend a structure similar to the following:

1 Summarize the motivation behind the project, and its goals.
2 Show how the model fits into the users' workflow (and how it improves that workflow).
3 Show how to use the model.

Let's explore each of these points in turn, starting with project goals.

12.2.1   *Summarizing the project goals*

With the model's end users, it's less important to discuss business motivations and more important to focus on how the model affects them. In our example, product managers are already monitoring the forums to get a sense of customer needs and issues. The goal of our project is to help them focus their attention on the "good stuff"—buzz. The example slide in figure 12.8 goes directly to this point. The users already know that they want to find buzz; our model will help them search more effectively.

> ## Our Goal:
> ## Catch User Needs Early
>
> - <u>Predict which topics on our product forums will have persistent buzz</u>
>   - Features customers want
>   - Existing features users have trouble with
> - Persistent buzz: <u>real, ongoing customer need</u>
>   - Not ephemeral or trendy issues

Motivate the work from the end user's perspective: help them find useful buzz faster.

In a real presentation, you might use a screenshot of a relevant forum discussion.

Figure 12.8   Motivation for project

12.2.2 *Showing how the model fits user workflow*

In this section of the presentation, you explain how the model helps users do their job. A good way to do this is to give before-and-after scenarios of a typical user workflow, as we show in figure 12.9.

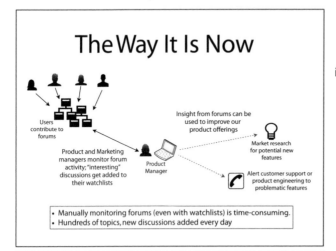

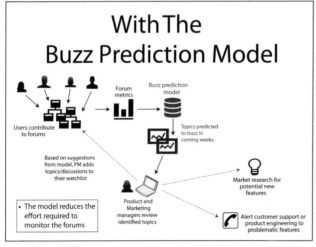

Figure 12.9   User workflow before and after the model

Presumably, the before process and its minuses are already obvious to the users. The after slide emphasizes how the model will do some preliminary filtering of forum topics for them. The output of the model helps users manage their already existing watchlists, and of course users can still go directly to the forums as well.

The next slide (figure 12.10, top) uses the pilot study results to show that the model can reduce the effort it takes to monitor the forums, and does in fact provide useful information. We elaborate on this with a compelling example in the bottom slide of figure 12.10 (the TimeWrangler example that we also used in the project sponsor presentation).

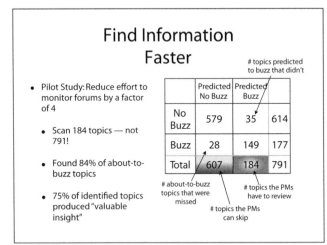

Figure 12.10   Present the model's benefits from the users' perspective.

You may also want to fill in more details about how the model operates. For example, users may want to know what the inputs to the model are (figure 12.11), so that they can compare those inputs with what they themselves consider when manually looking for interesting information on the forums.

Once you've shown how the model fits into user workflow, you can explain how users will use it.

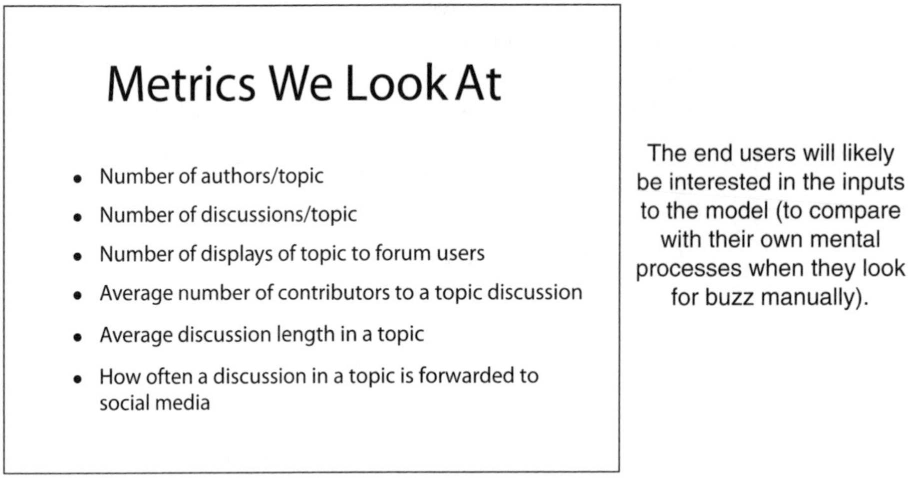

Metrics We Look At

- Number of authors/topic
- Number of discussions/topic
- Number of displays of topic to forum users
- Average number of contributors to a topic discussion
- Average discussion length in a topic
- How often a discussion in a topic is forwarded to social media

The end users will likely be interested in the inputs to the model (to compare with their own mental processes when they look for buzz manually).

Figure 12.11   Provide technical details that are relevant to users.

12.2.3 *Showing how to use the model*

This section is likely the bulk of the presentation, where you'll teach users how to use the model. The slide in figure 12.12 describes how a product manager will interact with the Buzz model. In this example scenario, we're assuming that there's an existing mechanism for product managers to add topics and discussions from the forums to a watchlist, as well as a way for product managers to monitor that watchlist. The model will separately send users notifications about impending buzz on topics they're interested in.

In a real presentation, you'd then expand each point to walk users through how they use the model: screenshots of the GUIs that they use to interact with the model,

Using the Buzz Model

1. Go to https://rd.wvcorp.com/buzzmodel and register.
2. Subscribe to the product category or categories that you want to monitor.
3. Every day, the model will email you links to topics in your categories that are predicted to buzz (if there are any)
4. The links will lead you to the relevant topics on the forum
5. Explore!
6. Add topics/discussions of interest to your watchlist, as usual.
   - We will monitor which topics you mark to assess how effective our predictions are (how useful they are to you).

Showing the users how to interact with the model

In a real presentation, each point would be expanded with step-by-step detailed instructions and appropriate screenshots.

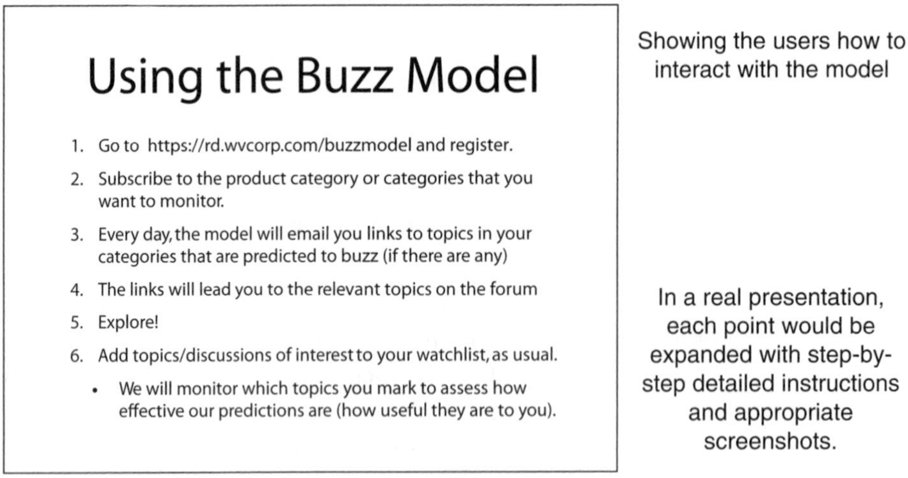

Figure 12.12   Describe how users will interact with the model.

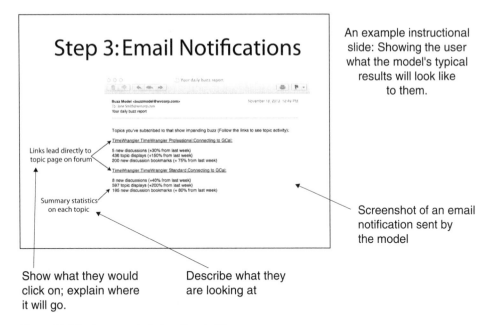

Step 3: Email Notifications

An example instructional slide: Showing the user what the model's typical results will look like to them.

Links lead directly to topic page on forum

Summary statistics on each topic

Screenshot of an email notification sent by the model

Show what they would click on; explain where it will go.

Describe what they are looking at

Figure 12.13   An example instructional slide

and screenshots of model output. We give one example slide in figure 12.13: a screenshot of a notification email, annotated to explain the view to the user. By the end of this section, the user should understand how to use the Buzz model and what to do with the Buzz model's output.

Finally, we've included a slide that asks users for feedback on the model, once they've been using it in earnest. This is shown in figure 12.14. Feedback from users

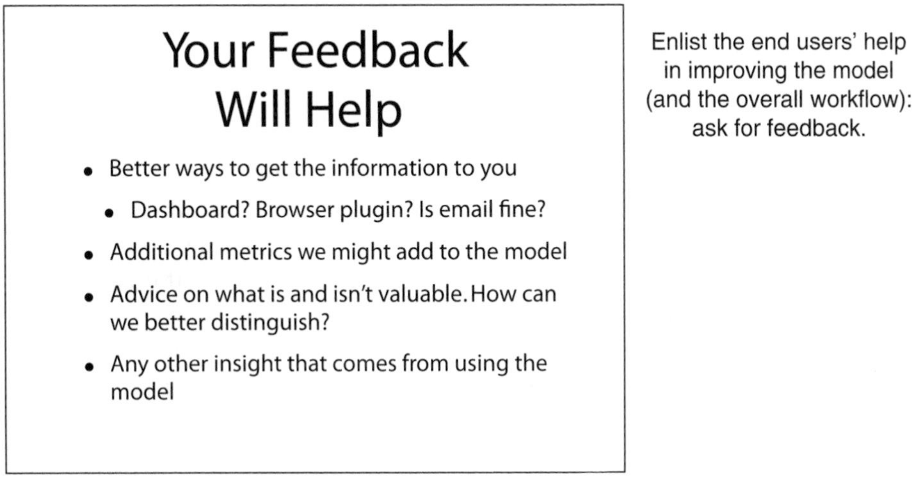

Your Feedback Will Help

- Better ways to get the information to you
  - Dashboard? Browser plugin? Is email fine?
- Additional metrics we might add to the model
- Advice on what is and isn't valuable. How can we better distinguish?
- Any other insight that comes from using the model

Enlist the end users' help in improving the model (and the overall workflow): ask for feedback.

Figure 12.14   Ask users for feedback.

can help you (and other teams that help to support the model once it's operational) to improve the experience for users, making it more likely that the model will be accepted and widely adopted.

In addition to presenting your model to the project sponsors and to end users, you may be presenting your work to other data scientists in your organization, or outside of it. We'll cover peer presentations in the next section.

12.2.4 *End user presentation takeaways*

Here's what you should remember about the end user presentation:

- Your primary goal is to convince users that they want to use your model.
- Focus on how the model affects (improves) end users' day-to-day processes.
- Describe how to use the model and how to interpret or use the model's outputs.

12.3 *Presenting your work to other data scientists*

Presenting to other data scientists gives them a chance to evaluate your work and gives you a chance to benefit from their insight. They may see something in the problem that you missed, and can suggest good variations to your approach or alternative approaches that you didn't think of.

Other data scientists will primarily be interested in the modeling approach that you used, any variations on the standard techniques that you tried, and interesting findings related to the modeling process. A presentation to your peers generally has the following structure:

1 Introduce the problem.
2 Discuss related work.
3 Discuss your approach.
4 Give results and findings.
5 Discuss future work.

Let's go through these steps in detail.

12.3.1 *Introducing the problem*

Your peers will generally be most interested in the prediction task (if that's what it is) that you're trying to solve, and don't need as much background about motivation as the project sponsors or the end users. In figure 12.15, we start off by introducing the concept of buzz and why it's important, then go straight into the prediction task.

This approach is best when you're presenting to other data scientists within your own organization, since you all share the context of the organization's needs. When you're presenting to peer groups outside your organization, you may want to lead with the business problem (for example, the first two slides of the project sponsor presentation, figures 12.2 and 12.3) to provide them with some context.

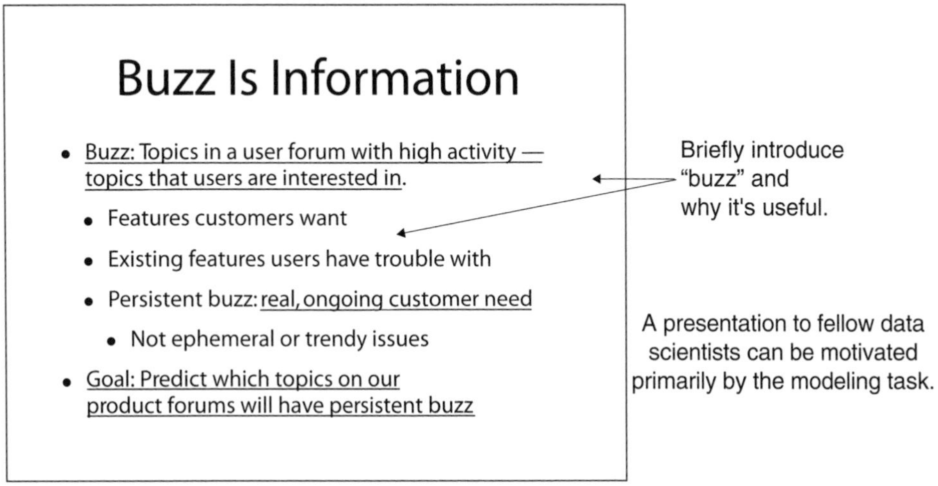

Buzz Is Information

- Buzz: Topics in a user forum with high activity — topics that users are interested in.
  - Features customers want
  - Existing features users have trouble with
  - Persistent buzz: real, ongoing customer need
    - Not ephemeral or trendy issues
  - Goal: Predict which topics on our product forums will have persistent buzz

Briefly introduce "buzz" and why it's useful.

A presentation to fellow data scientists can be motivated primarily by the modeling task.

Figure 12.15   Introducing the project

12.3.2 *Discussing related work*

An academic presentation generally has a related work section, where you discuss others who have done research on problems related to your problem, what approach they took, and how their approach is similar to or different from yours. A related work slide for the buzz model project is shown in figure 12.16.

You're not giving an academic presentation; it's more important to you that your approach succeeds than that it's novel. For you, a related work slide is an opportunity

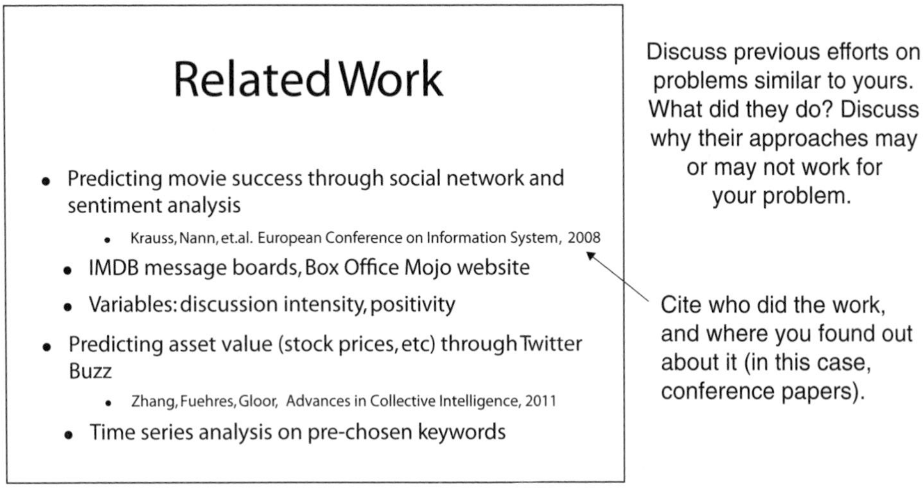

Related Work

- Predicting movie success through social network and sentiment analysis
  - Krauss, Nann, et.al. European Conference on Information System, 2008
- IMDB message boards, Box Office Mojo website
- Variables: discussion intensity, positivity
- Predicting asset value (stock prices, etc) through Twitter Buzz
  - Zhang, Fuehres, Gloor, Advances in Collective Intelligence, 2011
- Time series analysis on pre-chosen keywords

Discuss previous efforts on problems similar to yours. What did they do? Discuss why their approaches may or may not work for your problem.

Cite who did the work, and where you found out about it (in this case, conference papers).

Figure 12.16   Discussing related work

IA 877 3775

to discuss other approaches that you considered, and why they may not be completely appropriate for your specific problem.

After you've discussed approaches that you considered and rejected, you can then go on to discuss the approach that you did take.

12.3.3 *Discussing your approach*

Talk about what you did in lots of detail, including compromises that you had to make and setbacks that you had. This sets context, and builds up the audience's confidence in you and your work. For our example, figure 12.17 introduces the pilot study that we conducted, the data that we used, and the modeling approach we chose. It also mentions that a group of end users (five product managers) participated in the project; this establishes that we made sure that the model's outputs are useful and relevant.

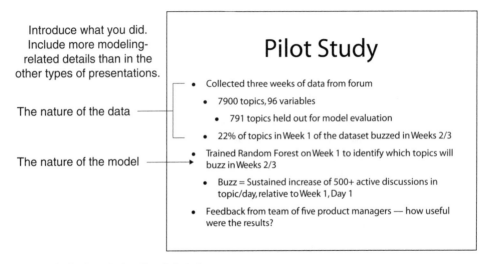

Figure 12.17   Introducing the pilot study

After you've introduced the pilot study, you introduce the input variables and the modeling approach that you used (figure 12.18). In this scenario, the dataset didn't have the right variables—it would have been better to do more of a time-series analysis, if we had the appropriate data, but we wanted to start with metrics that were already implemented in the product forums' system. Be up-front about this.

The slide also discusses the modeling approach that we chose—random forest— and why. Since we had to modify the standard approach (by limiting the model complexity), we mention that, too.

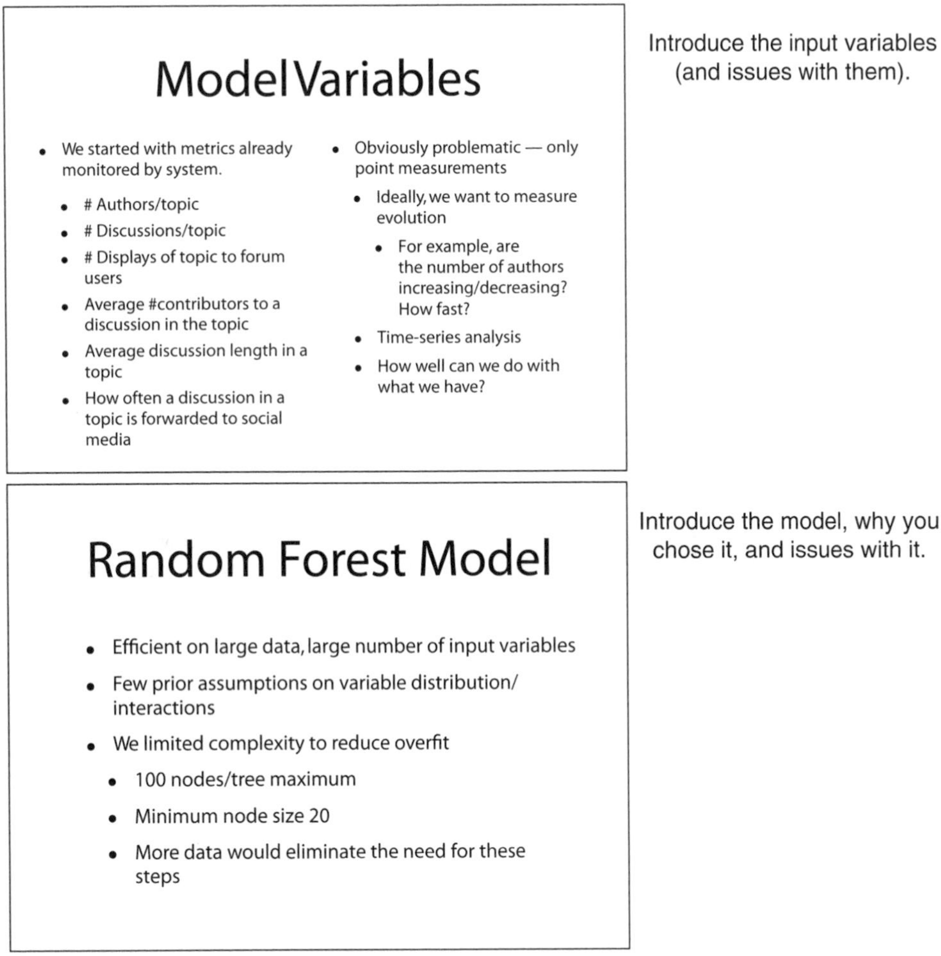

Introduce the input variables (and issues with them).

Introduce the model, why you chose it, and issues with it.

Figure 12.18 Discussing model inputs and modeling approach

12.3.4 *Discussing results and future work*

Once you've discussed your approach, you can discuss your results. In figure 12.19, we discuss our model's performance (precision/recall) and also confirm that representative end users did find the model's output useful to their jobs.

The bottom slide of figure 12.19 shows which variables are most influential in the model (recall that the variable importance calculation is one side effect of building random forests). In this case, the most important variables are the number of times the topic is displayed on various days and how many authors are contributing to the topic. This suggests that time-series data for these two variables in particular might improve model performance.

Results

Show your results: model performance and other outcomes.

- 84% recall, 83% precision
- Reduced manual scan of forums by over a factor of 4
  - From 791 to 184 topics to inspect
- PMs: 75% of identified topics produced "valuable insight"

	Predicted No Buzz	Predicted Buzz	
No Buzz	579	35	614
Buzz	28	149	177
Total	607	184	791

Variable Importance

Discuss other key findings, like which variables were most influential on the model.

- Key inputs:
  - # times topic is displayed to user (num.displays)
  - # authors contributing to topic (attention.level.author)
- Velocity variables for these two inputs could improve model

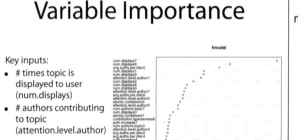

Figure 12.19 Showing model performance

You also want to add examples of compelling findings to this section of the talk—for example, the TimeWrangler integration issue that we showed in the other two presentations.

Once you've shown model performance and other results of your work, you can end the talk with a discussion of possible improvements and future work, as shown in figure 12.20.

Some of the points on the future work slide—in particular, the need for velocity variables—come up naturally from the previous discussion of the work and findings. Others, like future work on model retraining schedules, aren't foreshadowed as strongly by the earlier part of the talk, but might occur to people in your audience and are worth elaborating on briefly here. Again, you want to be up-front, though optimistic, about the limitations of your model—especially because this audience is likely to see the limitations already.

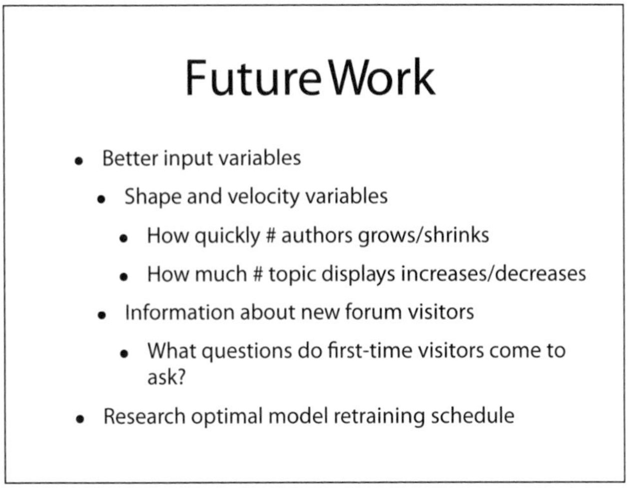

Discuss future work.

Figure 12.20   **Discussing future work**

12.3.5 *Peer presentation takeaways*

Here's what you should remember about your presentation to fellow data scientists:

- A peer presentation can be motivated primarily by the modeling task.
- Unlike the previous presentations, the peer presentation can (and should) be rich in technical details.
- Be up-front about limitations of the model and assumptions made while building it. Your audience can probably spot many of the limitations already.

Summary

In this chapter, you've seen how to present the results of your work to three different audiences. Each of these audiences has their own perspective and their own set of interests, and your talk should be tailored to match those interests. Organize your presentations to declare a shared goal and show how you're meeting that goal. We've suggested ways to organize each type of talk that will help you to tailor your discussion appropriately.

None of our suggestions are set in stone: you may have a project sponsor or other interested executives who want to dig down to the more technical details, or end users who are curious about how the internals of the model work. You can also have peer audiences who want to hear more about the business context. If you know this ahead of time (perhaps because you've presented to this audience before), then you should include the appropriate level of detail in your talk. If you're not sure, you can also prepare backup slides to be used as needed. There's only one hard-and-fast rule: have empathy for your audience.

In this chapter you have learned

- How to prepare a business-focused presentation for project sponsors
- How to prepare a presentation (or documentation) for end users to show them how to use your model and convince them that they want to
- How to prepare a more technical presentation for your peers

appendix A
Starting with R
and other tools

In this appendix, we'll show how you can install tools and start working with R. We'll demonstrate some example concepts and steps, but you'll want to follow up with additional reading.

Section A.1 is something all readers should review, as it shows where to get all of the software support materials for this book. The other sections should be considered on an as-needed basis, as they outline the details of how R works (something the reader may already know), and some specific applications (such as using databases) that may not be needed by all readers. Throughout the book we have tried to avoid teaching things "just in case," but here in the appendixes we supply some things you only "might" need.

A.1 Installing the tools

The primary tool for working our examples will be R, and possibly RStudio. But other tools (databases, version control, compilers, and so on) are also highly recommended. You may also need access to online documentation or other help to get all of these tools to work in your environment. The distribution sites we list are a good place to start.

A.1.1 Installing Tools

The R environment is a set of tools and software that can be installed on Unix, Linux, Apple macOS, and Windows.

R

We recommend installing the latest version of R from the Comprehensive R Archive Network (CRAN) at https://cran.r-project.org, or a mirror. CRAN is the authoritative central repository for R and R packages. CRAN is supported by The R

Foundation and the R Development Core Team. R itself is an official part of the Free Software Foundation's GNU project distributed under a GPL 2 license. R is used at many large institutions, including the United States Food and Drug Administration.[1]

For this book, we recommend using at least R version 3.5.0 or newer.

To work with R, you need a text editor specialized for working with non-formatted (or not-rich) text. Such editors include Atom, Emacs, Notepad++, Pico, Programmer's Notepad, RStudio, Sublime Text, text wrangler, vim, and many more. These are in contrast to rich text editors (which are not appropriate for programming tasks) such as Microsoft Word or Apple Text Edit.

RStudio

We suggest that when working with R, you consider using RStudio. RStudio is a popular cross-platform integrated development environment supplied by the company RStudio, Inc. (https://www.rstudio.com). RStudio supplies a built-in text editor and convenient user interfaces for common tasks such as installing software, rendering R markdown documents, and working with source control. RStudio is not an official part of R or CRAN, and should not be confused with R or CRAN.

An important feature of RStudio is the file browser and the set-directory/go-to-directory controls that are hidden in the gear icon of the file-browsing pane, which we point out in figure A.1.

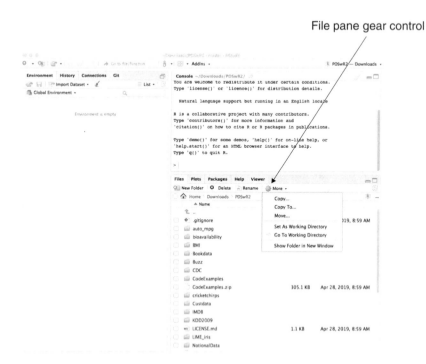

Figure A.1   RStudio file-browsing controls

---

[1]   Source: https://www.r-project.org/doc/R-FDA.pdf.

RStudio is not a requirement to use R or to work through the examples in this book.

GIT

Git is a source control or version management system that is very useful for preserving and sharing work. To install Git, please follow the appropriate instructions from https://git-scm.com.

Data science always involves a lot of tools and collaboration, so the willingness to try new tools is a flexibility one needs to develop.

THE BOOK-SUPPORT MATERIALS

All of the book-support materials are freely available from GitHub: https://github .com/WinVector/PDSwR2, as shown in figure A.2. The reader should download them in their entirety either using `git clone` with the URL https://github.com/WinVector/PDSwR2.git or by downloading a complete zip file by using the "Clone or Download" control at the top right of the GitHub page.

https://github.com/WinVector/PDSwR2

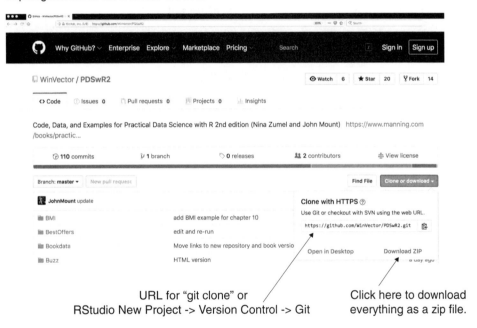

Figure A.2 **Downloading the book materials from GitHub**

Another way to download the book material is to use RStudio and Git. Select File > New Project > Create Project from Version Control > Git. That will bring up a dialog box as shown in figure A.3. You can fill in the Git URL and download the book materials as a project.

GitHub clone URL

Figure A.3   Cloning the book repository

We will refer to this directory as PDSwR2 throughout the book, and all files and paths we mention are either in this directory or a subdirectory. Please be sure to look in this directory for any README or errata files.

Some features of the support directory include these:

- All example data used in the book.
- All example code used in the book. The examples from the book are available in the subdirectory CodeExamples, and also as the zip file CodeExamples.zip. In addition to this, the entire set of examples, rerun and rerendered, are shared in RenderedExamples. (All paths should be relative to where you have unpacked the book directory PDSwR2.)

R PACKAGES

A great advantage of R is the CRAN central package repository. R has standardized package installation through the `install.packages()` command. An installed package is typically not fully available for use in a project until the package is also attached for use by the `library()` command.[2] A good practice is this: any sort of R script or work should attach all the packages it intends to use as a first step. Also, in most cases scripts should *not* call `install.packages()`, as this changes the R installation, which should not be done without user supervision.

---

[2] In R installing a package is a separate step from attaching it for use. `install.packages()` makes package contents potentially available; after that, `library()` readies them for use. A handy mnemonic is this: `install.packages()` sets up new appliances in your kitchen, and `library()` turns them on. You don't have to install things very often, however you often have to turn things back on.

INSTALLING THE REQUIRED PACKAGES

To install the set of packages required to work all the examples in this book, first download the book repository as described previously. Then look in the first directory or top directory of this repository: PDSwR2. In this directory, you will find the file packages.R. You can open this file with a text editor, and it should look like the following (though it may be more up to date than what is shown here).

```
# Please have an up to date version of R (3.5.*, or newer)
# Answer "no" to:
# Do you want to install from sources the packages which need compilation?
update.packages(ask = FALSE, checkBuilt = TRUE)

pkgs <- c(
    "arules", "bitops", "caTools", "cdata", "data.table", "DBI",
    "dbplyr", "DiagrammeR", "dplyr", "e1071", "fpc", "ggplot2",
    "glmnet", "glmnetUtils", "gridExtra", "hexbin", "kernlab",
    "igraph", "knitr", "lime", "lubridate", "magrittr", "MASS",
    "mgcv", "pander", "plotly", "pwr", "randomForest", "readr",
    "readxls", "rmarkdown", "rpart", "rpart.plot", "RPostgres",
    "rqdatatable", "rquery", "RSQLite", "scales", "sigr", "sqldf",
    "tidypredict", "text2vec", "tidyr", "vtreat", "wrapr", "WVPlots",
    "xgboost", "xts", "webshot", "zeallot", "zoo")

install.packages(
    pkgs,
    dependencies = c("Depends", "Imports", "LinkingTo"))
```

To install everything, run every line of code in this file from R.[3]

Unfortunately, there are many reasons the install can fail: incorrect copy/paste, no internet connection, improperly configured R or RStudio, insufficient permissions to administer the R install, out-of-date versions of R or RStudio, missing system requirements, or no or incorrect C/C++/Fortran compiler. If you run into these problems, it is best to find a forum or expert to help you work through these steps. Once everything is successfully installed, R is a self-contained environment where things just work.

Not all packages are needed for all examples, so if you have trouble with the overall install, just try to work the examples in the book. Here's a caveat: if you see a library(pkgname) command fail, please try install.packages('pkgname') to install the missing package. The preceding package list is just trying to get everything out of the way in one step.

OTHER TOOLS

R's capabilities can be enhanced by using tools such as Perl,[4] gcc/clang, gfortran, git, Rcpp, Tex, pandoc, ImageMagick, and Bash shell. Each of these is managed outside of

---

[3] The preceding code can be found as the file packages.R at https://github.com/WinVector/PDSwR2. We could call it PDSwR2/packages.R, which could mean the file from the original GitHub URL or from a local copy of the GitHub repository.

[4] See https://www.perl.org/get.html.

R, and how to maintain them depends on your computer, operating system, and system permissions. Unix/Linux users have the easiest time installing these tools, and R is primarily developed in a Unix environment.[5] RStudio will install some of the extra tools. macOS users may need Apple's Xcode tools and Homebrew (https://brew.sh) to have all the required tools. Windows users who wish to write packages may want to research RTools (https://cran.r-project.org/bin/windows/Rtools/).

Windows users may need RTools to compile packages; however, this should not be strictly necessary as most current packages are available from CRAN in a precompiled form (at least for macOS and 64-bit Windows). macOS users may need to install the Xcode compiler (available from Apple) to compile packages. All of these are steps you probably want to skip until you need the ability to compile.

A.1.2   *The R package system*

R is a broad and powerful language and analysis workbench in and of itself. But one of its real strengths is the depth of the package system and packages supplied through CRAN. To install a package from CRAN, just type `install.packages('nameofpackage')`. To use an installed package, type `library(nameofpackage)`.[6] Any time you type `library('nameofpackage')` or `require('nameofpackage')`, you're assuming you're using a built-in package or you're able to run `install.packages('nameofpackage')` if needed. We'll return to the package system again and again in this book. To see what packages are present in your session, type `sessionInfo()`.

> **CHANGING YOUR CRAN MIRROR** You can change your CRAN mirror at any time with the `chooseCRANmirror()` command. This is handy if the mirror you're working with is slow.

A.1.3   *Installing Git*

We advise installing Git version control before we show you how to use R and RStudio. This is because without Git, or a tool like it, you'll lose important work. Not just lose *your* work—you'll lose important *client* work. A lot of data science work (especially the analysis tasks) involves trying variations and learning things. Sometimes you learn something surprising and need to redo earlier experiments. Version control keeps earlier versions of all of your work, so it's exactly the right tool to recover code and settings used in earlier experiments. Git is available in precompiled packages from http://git-scm.com.

---

[5] For example, we share notes on rapidly configuring R and RStudio Server on an Amazon EC2 instance here: www.win-vector.com/blog/2018/01/setting-up-rstudio-server-quickly-on-amazon-ec2/.

[6] Actually, `library('nameofpackage')` also works with quotes. The unquoted form works in R because R has the ability to delay argument evaluation (so an undefined `nameofpackage` doesn't cause an error) as well as the ability to snoop the names of argument variables (most programming languages rely only on references or values of arguments). Given that a data scientist has to work with many tools and languages throughout the day, we prefer to not rely on features unique to one language unless we really need the feature. But the "official R style" is without the quotes.

A.1.4   *Installing RStudio*

RStudio supplies a text editor (for editing R scripts) and an integrated development environment for R. Before picking up RStudio from http://rstudio.com, you should install both R and Git as we described earlier.

The RStudio product you initially want is called *RStudio Desktop* and is available precompiled for Windows, Linux, and macOS.

When you're first starting with RStudio, we strongly recommend turning off both the "Restore .RData into workspace at startup" and "Save workspace to .RData on exit" features. Having these settings on (the default) makes it hard to reliably "work clean" (a point we will discuss in section A.3. To turn off these features, open the RStudio options pane (the Global option is found by such as menus RStudio > Preferences, Tools > Global Options, Tools > Options, or similar, depending on what operating system you are using), and then alter the two settings as indicated in figure A.4.

Figure A.4   RStudio options

A.1.5   *R resources*

A lot of the power of R comes from its large family of packages, available from the CRAN repository. In this section, we'll point out some packages and documentation.

INSTALLING R VIEWS

R has an incredibly deep set of available libraries. Usually, R already has the package you want; it's just a matter of finding it. A powerful way to find R packages is using *views*: http://cran.r-project.org/web/views/.

You can also install all the packages (with help documentation) from a view with a single command (though be warned: this can take an hour to finish). For example, here we're installing a huge set of time series libraries all at once:

```
install.packages('ctv', repos = 'https://cran.r-project.org')
library('ctv')
# install.views('TimeSeries') # can take a LONG time
```

Once you've done this, you're ready to try examples and code.

ONLINE R RESOURCES

A lot of R help is available online. Some of our favorite resources include these:

- *CRAN*—The main R site: http://cran.r-project.org
- *Stack Overflow R section*—A question-and-answer site: http://stackoverflow.com/questions/tagged/r
- *Quick-R*—A great R resource: http://www.statmethods.net
- *LearnR*—A translation of all the plots from *Lattice: Multivariate Data Visualization with R (Use R!)* (by D. Sarker; Springer, 2008) into ggplot2: http://learnr.wordpress.com
- *R-bloggers*—An R blog aggregator: http://www.r-bloggers.com
- *RStudio community*—An RStudio/tidyverse–oriented company site: https://community.rstudio.com/

A.2   *Starting with R*

R implements a dialect of a statistical programming language called *S*. The original implementation of S evolved into a commercial package called S+. So most of R's language-design decisions can be traced back to S. To avoid confusion, we'll mostly just say *R* when describing features. You might wonder what sort of command and programming environment S/R is. It's a pretty powerful one, with a nice command interpreter that we encourage you to type directly into.

Work clean

In R or RStudio, it is important to "work clean"—that is, to start with an empty workspace and explicitly bring in the packages, code, and data you want. This ensures you know how to get into your ready-to-go state (as you have to perform or write down the steps to get there) and you aren't held hostage to state you don't know how to restore (what we call the "no alien artifact" rule).

To work clean in R, you must turn off any sort of autorestore of the workspace. In "base R" this is done by restarting R with the `--no-restore` command-line flag set. In RStudio, the Session > Restart R menu option serves a similar role, *if* the "Restore .Rdata into workspace on startup" option is not checked.

Working with R and issuing commands to R is in fact scripting or programming. We assume you have some familiarity with scripting (perhaps using Visual Basic, Bash, Perl, Python, Ruby, and so on) or programming (perhaps using C, C#, C++, Java, Lisp, Scheme, and so on), or are willing to use one of our references to learn. We don't intend to write long programs in R, but we'll have to show how to issue R commands. R's programming, though powerful, is a bit different than many of the popular programming languages, but we feel that with a few pointers, anyone can use R. If you don't know how to use a command, try using the help() call to get at some documentation.

Throughout this book, we'll instruct you to run various commands in R. This will almost always mean typing the text or the text following the command prompt > into the RStudio console window, followed by pressing Return. For example, if we tell you to type 1/5, you can type that into the console window, and when you press Enter, you'll see a result such as [1] 0.2. The [1] portion of the result is just R's way of labeling result rows (and is to be ignored), and the 0.2 is the floating-point representation of one-fifth, as requested.

HELP Always try calling help() to learn about commands. For example, help('if') will bring up help about R's if command.

Let's try a few commands to help you become familiar with R and its basic data types. R commands can be terminated with a line break or a semicolon (or both), but interactive content isn't executed until you press Return. The following listing shows a few experiments you should run in your copy of R.

Listing A.1   Trying a few R commands

```
1
## [1] 1
1/2
## [1] 0.5
'Joe'
## [1] "Joe"
"Joe"
## [1] "Joe"
"Joe"=='Joe'
## [1] TRUE
c()
## NULL
is.null(c())
## [1] TRUE
is.null(5)
## [1] FALSE
c(1)
## [1] 1
c(1, 2)
## [1] 1 2
c("Apple", 'Orange')
## [1] "Apple"  "Orange"
length(c(1, 2))
```

```
## [1] 2
vec <- c(1, 2)
vec
## [1] 1 2
```

 # IS R'S COMMENT CHARACTER   The # mark is R's comment character. It indicates that the rest of the line is to be ignored. We use it to include comments, and also to include output along with the results.

A.2.1   *Primary features of R*

R commands look like a typical procedural programming language. This is deceptive, as the S language (which the language R implements) was actually inspired by functional programming and also has a lot of object-oriented features.

ASSIGNMENT

R has five common assignment operators: =, <-, ->, <<-, and ->>. Traditionally, in R, <- is the preferred assignment operator, and = is thought of as a late addition and an amateurish alias for it.

The main advantage of the <- notation is that <- always means assignment, whereas = can mean assignment, list slot binding, function argument binding, or case statement, depending on the context. One mistake to avoid is accidentally inserting a space in the assignment operator:

```
x <- 2
x < - 3
## [1] FALSE
print(x)
## [1] 2
```

We actually like = assignment better because data scientists tend to work in more than one language at a time and more bugs are caught early with =. But this advice is too heterodox to burden others with (see http://mng.bz/hfug). We try to consistently use <- in this book, but some habits are hard to break.

> **MULTILINE COMMANDS IN R**   R is good with multiline commands. To enter a multiline command, just make sure it would be a syntax error to stop parsing where you break a line. For example, to enter 1+2 as two lines, add the line break after the plus sign and not before. To get out of R's multiline mode, press Escape. A lot of cryptic R errors are caused by either a statement ending earlier than you wanted (a line break that doesn't force a syntax error on early termination) or not ending where you expect (needing an additional line break or semicolon).

The = operator is primarily used to bind values to function arguments (and <- can't be so used) as shown in the next listing.

Listing A.2 Binding values to function arguments

```
divide <- function(numerator,denominator) { numerator/denominator }
divide(1, 2)
## [1] 0.5

divide(2, 1)
## [1] 2

divide(denominator = 2, numerator = 1)
## [1] 0.5

divide(denominator <- 2, numerator <- 1)  # wrong symbol <-
    , yields 2, a wrong answer!
## [1] 2
```

The -> operator is just a left-to-right assignment that lets you write things like x -> 5. It's cute, but not game changing.

The <<- and ->> operators are to be avoided unless you actually need their special abilities. They are intended to write values outside of the current execution environment, which is an example of a side effect. Side effects seem great when you need them (often for error tracking and logging), but when overused they make code maintenance, debugging, and documentation much harder. In the following listing, we show a good function that doesn't have a side effect and a bad function that does have one.

Listing A.3 Demonstrating side effects

```
x<-1
good <- function() { x <- 5}
good()
print(x)
## [1] 1

bad <- function() { x <<- 5}
bad()
print(x)
## [1] 5
```

VECTORIZED OPERATIONS

Many R operations are called *vectorized*, which means they work on every element of a vector. These operators are convenient and to be preferred over explicit code like for loops. For example, the vectorized logic operators are ==, &, and |. The next listing shows some examples using these operators on R's logical types TRUE and FALSE.

Listing A.4 R truth tables for Boolean operators

```
c(TRUE, TRUE, FALSE, FALSE) == c(TRUE, FALSE, TRUE, FALSE)
## [1]  TRUE FALSE FALSE  TRUE

c(TRUE, TRUE, FALSE, FALSE) & c(TRUE, FALSE, TRUE, FALSE)
## [1]  TRUE FALSE FALSE FALSE

c(TRUE, TRUE, FALSE, FALSE) | c(TRUE, FALSE, TRUE, FALSE)
## [1]  TRUE  TRUE  TRUE FALSE
```

To test if two vectors are a match, we'd use R's `identical()` or `all.equal()` methods.

> **WHEN TO USE && OR || IN R** `&&` and `||` work only on scalars, not vectors. So *always* use `&&` and `||` in `if()` statements, and never use `&` or `|` in `if()` statements. Similarly prefer `&` and `|` when working with general data (which may need these vectorized versions).

R also supplies a vectorized sector called `ifelse(,,)` (the basic R-language `if` statement isn't vectorized).

R's OBJECT SYSTEM

Every item in R is an object and has a type definition called a *class*. You can ask for the type of any item using the `class()` command. For example, `class(c(1,2))` is *numeric*. R in fact has two object-oriented systems. The first one is called *S3* and is closest to what a C++ or Java programmer would expect. In the S3 class system, you can have multiple commands with the same name. For example, there may be more than one command called `print()`. Which `print()` actually gets called when you type `print(x)` depends on what type x is at runtime. S3 is a unique object system in that methods are global functions, and are *not* strongly associated with object definitions, prototypes, or interfaces. R also has a second object-oriented system called *S4*, which supports more detailed classes and allows methods to be picked based on the types of more than just the first argument. Unless you're planning on becoming a professional R programmer (versus a professional R user or data scientist), we advise not getting into the complexities of R's object-oriented systems. Mostly you just need to know that most R objects define useful common methods like `print()`, `summary()`, and `class()`. We also advise leaning heavily on the `help()` command. To get class-specific help, you use a notation *method.class*; for example, to get information on the `predict()` method associated with objects of class `glm`, you would type `help(predict.glm)`.

R's SHARE-BY-VALUE CHARACTERISTICS

In R each reference to a value is isolated: changes to one reference are not seen by other references. This is a useful feature similar to what other languages term "call by value semantics," or even the immutable data types of some languages.

This means, from the programmer's point of view, that each variable or each argument of a function behaves as if it were a separate copy of what was passed to the function. Technically, R's calling semantics are actually a combination of references and what is called *lazy copying*. But until you start directly manipulating function argument references, you see what looks like call-by-value behavior.

Share-by-value is a great choice for analysis software: it makes for fewer side effects and bugs. But most programming languages aren't share-by-value, so share-by-value semantics often come as a surprise. For example, many professional programmers rely on changes made to values inside a function being visible outside the function. Here's an example of call-by-value at work.

Listing A.5 Call-by-value effect

```
a <- c(1, 2)
b <- a                    Alters a. This is implemented by building an entirely
                          new vector and reassigning a to refer to this new
print(b)                  vector. The old value remains as it was, and any
                          references continue to see the old, unaltered value.
a[[1]] <- 5   ⊲─────┘

print(a)

print(b)   ⊲──────── Notice that b's value is not changed.
```

A.2.2 Primary R data types

While the R language and its features are interesting, it's the R data types that are most responsible for R's style of analysis. In this section, we'll discuss the primary data types and how to work with them.

VECTORS

R's most basic data type is the *vector*, or array. In R, vectors are arrays of same-typed values. They can be built with the `c()` notation, which converts a comma-separated list of arguments into a vector (see `help(c)`). For example, `c(1,2)` is a vector whose first entry is 1 and second entry is 2. Try typing `print(c(1,2))` into R's command prompt to see what vectors look like and notice that `print(class(1))` returns `numeric`, which is R's name for numeric vectors.

R is fairly unique in having no scalar types. A single number such as the number 5 is represented in R as a vector with exactly one entry (5).

> **Numbers in R**
>
> Numbers in R are primarily represented in double-precision floating-point. This differs from some programming languages, such as C and Java, that default to integers. This means you don't have to write `1.0/5.0` to prevent `1/5` from being rounded down to 0, as you would in C or Java. It also means that some fractions aren't represented perfectly. For example, `1/5` in R is actually (when formatted to 20 digits by `sprintf("%.20f", 1 / 5)`) `0.20000000000000001110`, not the `0.2` it's usually displayed as. This isn't unique to R; this is the nature of floating-point numbers. A good example to keep in mind is `1 / 5 != 3 / 5 - 2 / 5`, because `1 / 5 - (3 / 5 - 2 / 5)` is equal to `5.55e-17`.

R doesn't generally expose any primitive or scalar types to the user. For example, the number `1.1` is actually converted into a numeric vector with a length of 1 whose first entry is `1.1`. Note that `print(class(1.1))` and `print(class(c(1.1, 0)))` are identical. Note also that `length(1.1)` and `length(c(1.1))` are also identical. What we call scalars (or single numbers or strings) are in R just vectors with a length of 1. R's most common types of vectors are these:

- *Numeric*—Arrays of double-precision floating-point numbers.
- *Character*—Arrays of strings.
- *Factor*—Arrays of strings chosen from a fixed set of possibilities (called *enums* in many other languages).
- *Logical*—Arrays of TRUE/FALSE.
- *NULL*—The empty vector c() (which always has type NULL). Note that length(NULL) is 0 and is.null(c()) is TRUE.

R uses square-bracket notation (and others) to refer to entries in vectors.[7] Unlike most modern programming languages, R numbers vectors starting from 1 and not 0. Here's some example code showing the creation of a variable named vec holding a numeric vector. This code also shows that most R data types are *mutable*, in that we're allowed to change them:

```
vec <- c(2, 3)
vec[[2]] <- 5
print(vec)
## [1] 2 5
```

> **NUMBER SEQUENCES**   Number sequences are easy to generate with commands like 1:10. Watch out: the : operator doesn't bind very tightly, so you need to get in the habit of using extra parentheses. For example, 1:5 * 4 + 1 doesn't mean 1:21. For sequences of constants, try using rep().

LISTS

In addition to vectors (created with the c() operator), R has two types of lists. Lists, unlike vectors, can store more than one type of object, so they're the preferred way to return more than one result from a function. The basic R list is created with the list() operator, as in list(6, 'fred'). Basic lists aren't really that useful, so we'll skip over them to *named lists*. In named lists, each item has a name. An example of a named list would be created with list('a' = 6, 'b' = 'fred'). Usually the quotes on the list names are left out, but the list names are always constant strings (not variables or other types). In R, named lists are essentially the only convenient mapping structure (the other mapping structure being environments, which give you mutable lists). The ways to access items in lists are the $ operator and the [[]] operator (see help('[[') in R's help system). Here's a quick example.

Listing A.6   Examples of R indexing operators

```
x <- list('a' = 6, b = 'fred')
names(x)
## [1] "a" "b"
x$a
## [1] 6
x$b
```

---

[7] The most commonly used index notation is []. When extracting single values, we prefer the double square-bracket notation [[]] as it gives out-of-bounds warnings in situations where [] doesn't.

```
## [1] "fred"
x[['a']]
## $a
## [1] 6

x[c('a', 'a', 'b', 'b')]
## $a
## [1] 6
##
## $a
## [1] 6
##
## $b
## [1] "fred"
##
## $b
## [1] "fred"
```

Labels use case-sensitive partial match

The R list label operators (such as $) allow partial matches. For example, `list('abe' = 'lincoln')$a` returns `lincoln`, which is fine and dandy until you add a slot actually labeled `a` to such a list and your older code breaks. In general, it would be better if `list('abe'='lincoln')$a` was an error, so you'd have a chance of being signaled of a potential problem the first time you made such an error. You could try to disable this behavior with `options(warnPartialMatchDollar = TRUE)`, but even if that worked in all contexts, it's likely to break any other code that's quietly depending on such shorthand notation.

As you see in our example, the `[]` operator is vectorized, which makes lists incredibly useful as translation maps.

Selection: [[]] versus []

`[[]]` is the strictly correct operator for selecting a single element from a list or vector. At first glance, `[]` appears to work as a convenient alias for `[[]]`, but this is not strictly correct for single-value (scalar) arguments. `[]` is actually an operator that can accept vectors as its argument (try `list(a='b')[c('a','a')]`) and return nontrivial vectors (vectors of length greater than 1, or vectors that don't look like scalars) or lists. The operator `[[]]` has different (and better) single-element semantics for both lists and vectors (though, unfortunately, `[[]]` has different semantics for lists than for vectors).

Really, you should *never* use `[]` when `[[]]` can be used (when you want only a single result). Everybody, including the authors, forgets this and uses `[]` way more often than is safe. For lists, the main issue is that `[[]]` usefully unwraps the returned values from the list type (as you'd want: compare `class(list(a='b')['a'])` to `class(list(a='b')[['a']])`). For vectors, the issue is that `[]` fails to signal out-of-bounds access (compare `c('a','b')[[7]]` to `c('a','b')[7]` or, even worse, `c('a','b')[NA]`).

DATA FRAMES

R's central data structure is the *data frame*. A data frame is organized into rows and columns. It is a list of columns of different types. Each row has a value for each column. An R data frame is much like a database table: the column types and names are the schema, and the rows are the data. In R, you can quickly create a data frame using the data.frame() command. For example, d = data.frame(x=c(1,2),y=c('x','y')) is a data frame.

The correct way to read a column out of a data frame is with the [[]] or $ operators, as in d[['x']], d$x or d[[1]]. Columns are also commonly read with the d[, 'x'] or d['x'] notations. Note that not all of these operators return the same type (some return data frames, and some return arrays).

Sets of rows can be accessed from a data frame using the d[rowSet,] notation, where rowSet is a vector of Booleans with one entry per data row. We prefer to use d[rowSet,, drop = FALSE] or subset(d,rowSet), as they're guaranteed to always return a data frame and not some unexpected type like a vector (which doesn't support all of the same operations as a data frame).[8] Single rows can be accessed with the d[k,] notation, where k is a row index. Useful functions to call on a data frame include dim(), summary(), and colnames(). Finally, individual cells in the data frame can be addressed using a row-and-column notation, like d[1, 'x'].

From R's point of view, a data frame is a single table that has one row per example you're interested in and one column per feature you may want to work with. This is, of course, an idealized view. The data scientist doesn't expect to be so lucky as to find such a dataset ready for them to work with. In fact, 90% of the data scientist's job is figuring out how to transform data into this form. We call this task *data tubing*, and it involves joining data from multiple sources, finding new data sources, and working with business and technical partners. But the data frame is exactly the right abstraction. Think of a table of data as the ideal data scientist API. It represents a nice demarcation between preparatory steps that work to get data into this form and analysis steps that work with data in this form.

Data frames are essentially lists of columns. This makes operations like printing summaries or types of all columns especially easy, but makes applying batch operations to all rows less convenient. R matrices are organized as rows, so converting to/from matrices (and using transpose t()) is one way to perform batch operations on data frame rows. But be careful: converting a data frame to a matrix using something like the model.matrix() command (to change categorical variables into multiple columns of numeric level indicators) doesn't track how multiple columns may have been derived from a single variable and can potentially confuse algorithms that have per-variable heuristics (like stepwise regression and random forests).

---

[8] To see the problem, type class(data.frame(x = c(1, 2))[1,]), which reports the class as numeric, instead of as data.frame.

Data frames would be useless if the only way to populate them was to type them in. The two primary ways to populate data frames are R's `read.table()` command and database connectors (which we'll cover in section A.3).

MATRICES

In addition to data frames, R supports matrices. Matrices are two-dimensional structures addressed by rows and columns. Matrices differ from data frames in that matrices are lists of rows, and every cell in a matrix has the same type. When indexing matrices, we advise using the `drop = FALSE` notation; without this, selections that should return single-row matrices instead return vectors. This would seem okay, except that in R, vectors aren't substitutable for matrices, so downstream code that's expecting a matrix will mysteriously crash at run time. And the crash may be rare and hard to demonstrate or find, as it only happens if the selection happens to return exactly one row.

NULL AND NANA (NOT AVAILABLE) VALUES

R has two special values: NULL and NA. In R, `NULL` is just an alias for `c()`, the empty vector. It carries no type information, so an empty vector of numbers is the same type as an empty vector of strings (a design flaw, but consistent with how most programming languages handle so-called null pointers). `NULL` can only occur where a vector or list is expected; it can't represent missing scalar values (like a single number or string).

For missing scalar values, R uses a special symbol, NA, which indicates missing or unavailable data. In R, NA behaves like the not-a-number or NaN seen in most floating-point implementations (except NA can represent any scalar, not just a floating-point number). The value NA represents a nonsignaling error or missing value. *Nonsignaling* means that you don't get a printed warning, and your code doesn't halt (not necessarily a good thing). NA is inconsistent if it reproduces. `2+NA` is NA, as we'd hope, but `paste(NA, 'b')` is a valid non-NA string.

Even though `class(NA)` claims to be logical, NAs can be present in any vector, list, slot, or data frame.

FACTORS

In addition to a string type called `character`, R also has a special "set of strings" type similar to what Java programmers would call an *enumerated type*. This type is called a *factor*, and a factor is just a string value guaranteed to be chosen from a specified set of values called *levels*. The advantage of factors is they are exactly the right data type to represent the different values or levels of categorical variables.

The following example shows the string `red` encoded as a factor (note how it carries around the list of all possible values) and a failing attempt to encode `apple` into the same set of factors (returning NA, R's special not-a-value symbol).

Listing A.7   R's treatment of unexpected factor levels

```
factor('red', levels = c('red', 'orange'))
## [1] red
## Levels: red orange

factor('apple', levels = c('red', 'orange'))
## [1] <NA>
## Levels: red orange
```

Factors are useful in statistics, and you'll want to convert most string values into factors at some point in your data science process. Usually, the later you do this, the better (as you tend to know more about the variation in your data as you work)—so we suggest using the optional argument "StringsAsFactors = FALSE" when reading data or creating new data.frames.

Making sure factor levels are consistent

In this book, we often prepare training and test data separately (simulating the fact that new data will usually be prepared after the original training data). For factors, this introduces two fundamental issues: consistency of numbering of factor levels during training, and application and discovery of new factor level values during application. For the first issue, it's the responsibility of R code to make sure factor numbering is consistent. The following listing demonstrates that lm() correctly handles factors as strings and is consistent even when a different set of factors is discovered during application (this is something you may want to double-check for non-core libraries). For the second issue, discovering a new factor during application is a modeling issue. The data scientist either needs to ensure this can't happen or develop a coping strategy (such as falling back to a model not using the variable in question).

Listing A.8   Confirming lm() encodes new strings correctly

```
d <- data.frame(x=factor(c('a','b','c')),
                y=c(1,2,3))                      Builds a data frame and linear
m <- lm(y~0+x,data=d)              ◁————————     model mapping a,b,c to 1,2,3
 print(predict(m,
   newdata=data.frame(x='b'))[[1]])   ◁————————  Shows that the
 # [1] 2                                          model gets the
print(predict(m,                                  correct prediction
   newdata=data.frame(x=factor('b',levels=c('b'))))[[1]])  ◁——  for b as a string
 # [1] 2
```

Shows that the model gets the correct
prediction for b as a factor, encoded with a
different number of levels. This shows that
lm() is correctly treating factors as strings.

SLOTS

In addition to lists, R can store values by name in object slots. Object slots are addressed with the @ operator (see help('@')). To list all the slots on an object, try slotNames(). Slots and objects (in particular the S3 and S4 object systems) are advanced topics we don't cover in this book. You need to know that R has object systems, as some packages will return them to you, but you shouldn't be creating your own objects early in your R career.

A.3   *Using databases with R*

Sometimes you want to use R to work with data in a database. Usually this is because the data is already in a database, or you want to use a high-performance database (such as Postgres or Apache Spark) to manipulate data at speed.

If your data is small enough to fit in memory (or you can spin up a large enough computer to make this so, say on Amazon EC2, Microsoft Azure, or Google Cloud), we suggest bringing the data over to R using `DBI::dbReadTable()` and then using `data.table`. Except for the data transfer time, this will be very hard to beat. Note, however, that writing large results back to a database is not fully supported on all R database drivers (sparklyr, in particular, explicitly does not support this).

If you want to work with data in a database (which we usually do for our clients), then we suggest using a query generator such as `rquery` or `dbplyr`. We also believe the idea of thinking in terms of Codd relational operators (or thinking in terms of SQL databases) is very beneficial, so playing around with one of the preceding systems can be well worth the effort.

A.3.1   *Running database queries using a query generator*

Example   *Ranking customer offers*

We are given a table of data keyed by customer names, product names. For each of these key pairs we have a suggested price discount fraction and a predicted discount offer affinity (both produced by some machine learning models, of the type we have been discussing in this book). Our task is to take this table and select the two offers with highest predicted affinity for each customer. The business goal is this: we want to show the customer only these two offers, and none of the others.

To simulate this task, we will take some arbitrary data and copy it from R to a Postgres database. To run this example, you would need your own Postgres database, and copy in your own connection details, including host, port, username, and password. The purpose of this exercise is to give a taste of working with databases from R and a taste of thinking in Codd relational terms (the basis for many data processing systems, including `dplyr`).[9]

First, we set up our database connection and copy some data into this fresh database:

```
library("rquery")

raw_connection <- DBI::dbConnect(RPostgres::Postgres(),
                                 host = 'localhost',
                                 port = 5432,
                                 user = 'johnmount',
                                 password = '')

dbopts <- rq_connection_tests(raw_connection)
db <- rquery_db_info(
```

Uses DBI to connect to a database. In this case, it creates a new in-memory SQLite.

Builds an rquery wrapper for the connection

---

[9] The full example and worked solution are available here: https://github.com/WinVector/PDSwR2/blob/master/BestOffers/BestOffers.md.

```
    connection = raw_connection,
    is_dbi = TRUE,
    connection_options = dbopts)
data_handle <- rq_copy_to(
  db,
  'offers',
  wrapr::build_frame(
    "user_name"   , "product"                          , "discount", "predicted_of
      fer_affinity" |
      "John"    , "Pandemic Board Game"              , 0.1      , 0.8596
                    |
      "Nina"    , "Pandemic Board Game"              , 0.2      , 0.1336
                    |
      "John"    , "Dell XPS Laptop"                  , 0.1      , 0.2402
                    |
      "Nina"    , "Dell XPS Laptop"                  , 0.05     , 0.3179
                    |
      "John"    , "Capek's Tales from Two Pockets",   0.05     , 0.2439
                    |
      "Nina"    , "Capek's Tales from Two Pockets",   0.05     , 0.06909
                    |
      "John"    , "Pelikan M200 Fountain Pen"        , 0.2      , 0.6706
                    |
      "Nina"    , "Pelikan M200 Fountain Pen"        , 0.1      , 0.616
                    ),
  temporary = TRUE,
  overwrite = TRUE)
```

Copies some example data into the database

Now we will solve the problem by thinking relationally. We work in steps, and with experience, we would see that to solve this problem, we want to assign a per-user rank to each offer and then filter down to the ranks we want.

We will work this example using the rquery package. In rquery, window functions are available though the extend() method.[10] extend() can calculate a new column based both on a partition of the data (by user_name) and an ordering of columns within these partitions (by predicted_offer_affinity). It is easiest to demonstrate this in action.

We'll calculate rank() or the order of the data rows.

The ranking will be recalculated for each user (our window partition).

Pipes our data into the execute() method. Notice that we use the wrapr dot pipe.

The window ordering that controls the rank will be from predicted_offer_affinity, reversed (largest first).

```
data_handle %.>%   extend(.,
            simple_rank = rank(),
            partitionby = "user_name",
            orderby = "predicted_offer_affinity",
            reverse = "predicted_offer_affinity") %.>%
  execute(db, .) %.>%
knitr::kable(.)
```

Pretty-prints the results

Translates the operation plan into SQL, sends it to the database for execution, and brings the results back to R

---

[10] The odd name "extend" was chosen out of respect for the source of these ideas: Codd's relational algebra.

```
# |user_name |product                           | discount| predicted_offer_affi
      nity| simple_rank|
# |:---------|:--------------------------------|--------:|--------------------
      ---:|-----------:|
# |Nina      |Pelikan M200 Fountain Pen        |    0.10|                  0.6
      1600|           1|
# |Nina      |Dell XPS Laptop                  |    0.05|                  0.3
      1790|           2|
# |Nina      |Pandemic Board Game              |    0.20|                  0.1
      3360|           3|
# |Nina      |Capek's Tales from Two Pockets   |    0.05|                  0.0
      6909|           4|
# |John      |Pandemic Board Game              |    0.10|                  0.8
      5960|           1|
# |John      |Pelikan M200 Fountain Pen        |    0.20|                  0.6
      7060|           2|
# |John      |Capek's Tales from Two Pockets   |    0.05|                  0.2
      4390|           3|
# |John      |Dell XPS Laptop                  |    0.10|                  0.2
      4020|           4|
```

The question is this: how did we know to use the extend method and what options to set? That requires some experience with relational systems. There are only a few primary operations (adding derived columns, selecting columns, selecting rows, and joining tables) and only a few options (such as the partition and order when adding a windowed column). So the technique can be learned. The power of the theory is that just about any common data transform can be written in terms of these few fundamental data operators.

Now, to solve our full problem, we combine this operator with a few more relational operators (again using the wrapr dot pipe). This time we'll have the result written into a remote table (so no data ever moves to or from R!) and then only copy the results back after the calculation is complete.

Defines our sequence of operations

```
ops <- data_handle %.>%
    extend(.,
           simple_rank = rank(),
           partitionby = "user_name",
           orderby = "predicted_offer_affinity",
           reverse = "predicted_offer_affinity") %.>%
        select_rows(.,
                simple_rank <= 2) %.>%
    orderby(., c("user_name", "simple_rank"))

result_table <- materialize(db, ops)

DBI::dbReadTable(db$connection, result_table$table_name) %.>%
    knitr::kable(.)

# |user_name |product                           | discount| predicted_offer_affinity|
      simple_rank|
```

Marks each row with its simple per-user rank

Selects the two rows with highest rank for each user

Orders the rows by user and product rank

Runs the result in the database, instantiating a new result table

Copies the result back to R and pretty-prints it

```
#  |:---------|:---------------------------|--------:|------------------------
      :|-----------:|
#  |John       |Pandemic Board Game         |     0.10|                 0.8596|
              1|
#  |John       |Pelikan M200 Fountain Pen   |     0.20|                 0.6706|
              2|
#  |Nina       |Pelikan M200 Fountain Pen   |     0.10|                 0.6160|
              1|
#  |Nina       |Dell XPS Laptop             |     0.05|                 0.3179|
              2|
```

The reason we saved the operation plan in the variable ops is because we can do a lot
more than just execute the plan. For example, we can create a diagram of the planned
operations, as in figure A.5.

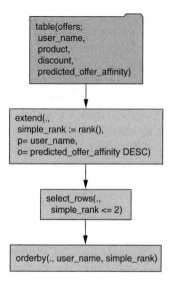

Figure A.5 `rquery` operation
plan diagram

Also—and this is the big point—we can see the SQL that gets actually sent to the database. Without a query planner (such as rquery or dbplyr), we would have to write
something like this SQL:

```
ops %.>%
  to_sql(., db) %.>%
  cat(.)

## SELECT * FROM (
##   SELECT * FROM (
##     SELECT
##       "user_name",
##       "product",
##       "discount",
##       "predicted_offer_affinity",
##       rank ( ) OVER (  PARTITION BY "user_name" ORDER BY "predicted_offer_aff
     inity" DESC ) AS "simple_rank"
```

```
##    FROM (
##      SELECT
##        "user_name",
##        "product",
##        "discount",
##        "predicted_offer_affinity"
##      FROM
##        "offers"
##      ) tsql_17135820721167795865_0000000000
##    ) tsql_17135820721167795865_0000000001
##    WHERE "simple_rank" <= 2
##  ) tsql_17135820721167795865_0000000002 ORDER BY "user_name", "simple_rank"
```

The issue is that relational thinking is productive, but SQL itself is fairly verbose. In particular, SQL expresses sequencing or composition as nesting, which means we read from the inside out. A lot of the grace of Codd's ideas is recovered when we move to an operator notation (such as seen in `dplyr` or `rquery`).

A longer treatment (with more references) of this example can be found here: https://github.com/WinVector/PDSwR2/blob/master/BestOffers/BestOffers.md.

Relational data manipulation thinks in terms of operators, which we briefly touched on here, and data organization, which is the topic of our next section.

A.3.2 *How to think relationally about data*

The trick to thinking relationally about data is this: for every table, classify the columns into a few important themes, and work with the natural relations between these themes. One view of the major column themes is provided in table A.1.

Table A.1 Major SQL column themes

Column theme	Description	Common uses and treatments
Natural key columns	In many tables, one or more columns taken together form a natural key that uniquely identifies the row. Some data (such as running logs) doesn't have natural keys (many rows may correspond to a given timestamp).	Natural keys are used to sort data, control joins, and specify aggregations.
Surrogate key columns	Surrogate key columns are key columns (collections of columns that uniquely identify rows) that don't have a natural relation to the problem. Examples of surrogate keys include row numbers and hashes. In some cases (like analyzing time series), the row number can be a natural key, but usually it's a surrogate key.	Surrogate key columns can be used to simplify joins; they tend not to be useful for sorting and aggregation. Surrogate key columns must not be used as modeling features, as they don't represent useful measurements.

Table A.1 Major SQL column themes *(continued)*

Column theme	Description	Common uses and treatments
Provenance columns	Provenance columns are columns that contain facts about the row, such as when it was loaded. The `ORIGIN-SERTTIME`, `ORIGFILENAME`, and `ORIGFILEROWNUMBER` columns added in section 2.3.1 are examples of provenance columns.	Provenance columns shouldn't be used in analyses, except for confirming you're working on the right dataset, selecting a dataset (if different datasets are commingled in the same table), and comparing datasets.
Payload columns	Payload columns contain actual data. Payload columns may be data such as prices and counts.	Payload columns are used for aggregation, grouping, and conditions. They can also sometimes be used to specify joins.
Experimental design columns	Experimental design columns include sample grouping like `ORIGRANDGROUP` from section 2.3.1, or data weights like the `PWGTP*` and `WGTP*` columns we mentioned in section 7.1.1.	Experiment design columns can be used to control an analysis (select subsets of data, used as weights in modeling operations), but they should never be used as features in an analysis.
Derived columns	Derived columns are columns that are functions of other columns or other groups of columns. An example would be the day of week (Monday through Sunday), which is a function of the date. Derived columns can be functions of keys (which means they're unchanging in many `GROUP BY` queries, even though SQL will insist on specifying an aggregator such as `MAX()`) or functions of payload columns.	Derived columns are useful in analysis. A *full normal form* database doesn't have such columns. In normal forms, the idea is to not store anything that can be derived, which eliminates certain types of inconsistency (such as a row with the date February 1, 2014, and the day of week Wednesday, when the correct day of week is Saturday). But during analyses, it's always a good idea to store intermediate calculations in tables and columns: it simplifies code and makes debugging much easier.

The point is that analysis is much easier if you have a good taxonomy of column themes for every supplied data source. You then design SQL command sequences to transform your data into a new table where the columns are just right for analysis. In the end, you should have tables where every row is an event you're interested in, and every needed fact is already available in a column (which has been called a *model matrix* for a very long time, or a *denormalized table* in relational database terms).

FURTHER DATABASE READING

Our go-to database reference is Joe Celko, *SQL for Smarties,* Fourth Edition (Morgan Kauffman, 2011).

A.4 The takeaway

In our opinion, the R ecosystem is the fastest path to substantial data science, statistical, and machine learning accomplishment. Other systems may have more advanced machine learning capabilities (such as Python's deep learning connections), but these are now also available to R users through an adapter called *reticulate.*[11] No data scientist should expect to work forever in just one language, or with just one system; but we feel R is a good place for many to start.

---

[11] For an example, please see François Chollet and J. J. Allaire, *Deep Learning with R* (Manning, 2018).

appendix B
Important
statistical concepts

Statistics is such a broad topic that we've only been able to pull pieces of it into our data science narrative. But it's an important field that has a lot to say about what happens when you attempt to infer from data. We've assumed in this book that you already know some statistical ideas (in particular, summary statistics such as the mean, mode, median, variance, and standard deviation). In this appendix, we'll demonstrate a few more important statistical concepts that relate to model fitting, characterizing uncertainty, and experimental design.

Statistics is math, so this appendix is a bit mathematical. It's also intended to teach you the proper *statistical nomenclature*, so you can share your work with other data scientists. This appendix covers technical terms you will hear as part of "data science shop talk." You've been doing the data science work; now, we'll discuss tools to talk about and criticize the work.

A *statistic* is any sort of summary or measure of data. An example would be the number of people in a room. *Statistics* is the study of how observed summaries of samples relate to the (unobserved) true summaries of the entire population we hope to model. Statistics help us to describe and mitigate the variance (or variation) of estimates, uncertainty (ranges or estimated ranges of what we do not know), and bias (systematic errors our procedures unfortunately introduce).

For example, if we are using a database of *all* past marketing of our company, this is still at best a sample of all possible sales (including future marketing and sales we are hoping to predict with our models). If we do not account for the uncertainty in sampling (and also from many other causes), we will draw incorrect inferences and conclusions.[1]

---

[1] We like to call machine learning the optimistic view of data and statistics the pessimistic view. In our opinion, you need to understand both of these viewpoints to work with data.

B.1   *Distributions*

A distribution is a description of likelihoods of possible values in a set of data. For example, it could be the set of plausible heights of an adult, American, 18-year-old male. For a simple numeric value, the distribution is defined thus: for a value b, the distribution is the probability of seeing a value x, with x <= b. This is called the *cumulative distribution function* (CDF).

We can often summarize a set of possible outcomes by naming a distribution, and some summary statistics. For example, we can say that if we flip a fair coin 10 times, the number of heads we observe should be binomially distributed (defined in section B.5.7) with an expected mean of 5 heads. In all cases, we are concerned with how values are generated, and getting a bit more detail beyond just a characterization of mean and standard deviation, such as getting the name and shape of the distribution.

In this section, we'll outline a few important distributions: the normal distribution, the lognormal distribution, and the binomial distribution. As you work further, you'll also want to learn many other key distributions (such as Poisson, beta, negative binomial, and many more), but the ideas we'll present here should be enough to get you started.

B.1.1   *Normal distribution*

The *normal* or *Gaussian distribution* is the classic symmetric bell-shaped curve, as shown in figure B.1. Many measured quantities, such as test scores from a group of students, or the age or height of a particular population, can often be approximated by the normal. Repeated measurements will tend to fall into a normal distribution. For example, if a doctor weighs a patient multiple times, using a properly calibrated scale, the measurements (if enough of them are taken) will fall into a normal distribution around the patient's true weight. The variation will be due to measurement error (the variability of the scale). The normal distribution is defined over all real numbers.

In addition, the *central limit theorem* says that when you're observing the sum (or mean) of many independent, bounded variance random variables, the distribution of your observations will approach the normal as you collect more data. For example, suppose you want to measure how many people visit your website every day between 9 a.m. and 10 a.m. The proper distribution for modeling the number of visitors is the *Poisson distribution*; but if you have a high enough volume of traffic, and you observe long enough, the distribution of observed visitors will approach the normal distribution, and you can make acceptable estimates about your traffic by treating the number of visitors as if it were normally distributed.

Many real-world distributions are approximately "normal"—in particular, any measurement where the notion of "close" tends to be additive. An example would be adult heights: a 6-inch difference in height is large both for people who are 5'6" and for those who are 6".

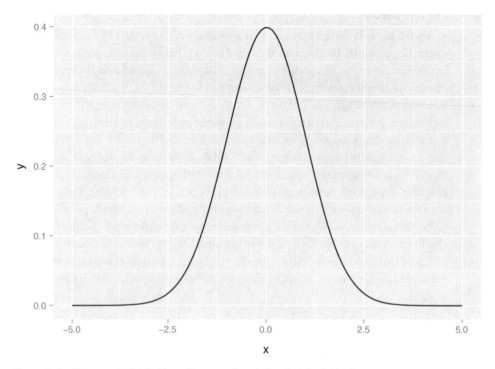

Figure B.1   The normal distribution with mean 0 and standard deviation 1

The normal is described by two parameters: the mean m and the standard deviation s (or, alternatively, the variance, which is the square of s). The mean represents the distribution's center (and also its peak); the standard deviation represents the distribution's "natural unit of length"—you can estimate how rare an observation is by how many standard deviations it is from the mean. As we mention in chapter 4, for a normally distributed variable

- About 68% of observations will fall in the interval (m-s,m+s).
- About 95% of observations will fall in the interval (m-2*s,m+2*s).
- About 99.7% of observations will fall in the interval (m-3*s,m+3*s).

So an observation more than three standard deviations away from the mean can be considered quite rare, in most applications.

Many machine learning algorithms and statistical methods (for example, linear regression) assume that the unmodeled errors are distributed normally. Linear regression is fairly robust to violations of this assumption; still, for continuous variables, you should at least check if the variable distribution is unimodal and somewhat symmetric.

When this isn't the case, you may wish to consider using a variable transformation, such as the log transformations that we discuss in chapter 4.

USING THE NORMAL DISTRIBUTION IN R

In R the function dnorm(x, mean = m, sd = s) is the *normal probability density function*: it will return the probability of observing x when it's drawn from a normal distribution with mean m and standard deviation s. By default, dnorm assumes that mean=0 and sd = 1 (as do all the functions related to the normal distribution that we discuss here). Let's use dnorm() to draw figure B.1.

Listing B.1 Plotting the theoretical normal density

```
library(ggplot2)

x <- seq(from=-5, to=5, length.out=100) # the interval [-5 5]
f <- dnorm(x)                           # normal with mean 0 and sd 1
ggplot(data.frame(x=x,y=f), aes(x=x,y=y)) + geom_line()
```

The function rnorm(n, mean = m, sd = s) will generate n points drawn from a normal distribution with mean m and standard deviation s.

Listing B.2 Plotting an empirical normal density

```
library(ggplot2)

# draw 1000 points from a normal with mean 0, sd 1
u <- rnorm(1000)

# plot the distribution of points,
# compared to normal curve as computed by dnorm() (dashed line)
ggplot(data.frame(x=u), aes(x=x)) + geom_density() +
    geom_line(data=data.frame(x=x,y=f), aes(x=x,y=y), linetype=2)
```

As you can see in figure B.2, the empirical distribution of the points produced by rnorm(1000) is quite close to the theoretical normal. Distributions observed from finite datasets can never exactly match theoretical continuous distributions like the normal; and, as with all things statistical, there is a well-defined distribution for how far off you expect to be for a given sample size.

The function pnorm(x, mean = m, sd = s) is what R calls the *normal probability function*, otherwise called the *normal cumulative distribution function*: it returns the probability of observing a data point of value less than x from a normal with mean m and standard deviation s. In other words, it's the area under the distribution curve that falls to the left of x (recall that a distribution has unit area under the curve). This is shown in the listing B.3.

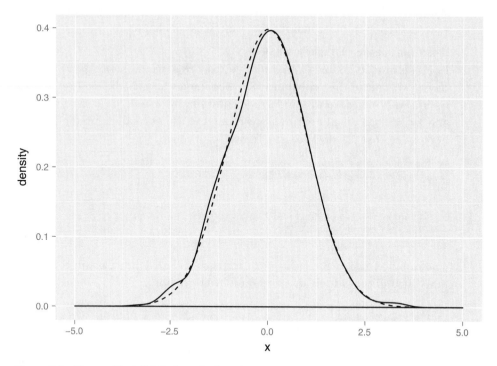

Figure B.2   The empirical distribution of points drawn from a normal with mean 0 and standard deviation 1. The dotted line represents the theoretical normal distribution.

Listing B.3   Working with the normal CDF

```
# --- estimate probabilities (areas) under the curve ---

# 50% of the observations will be less than the mean
pnorm(0)
# [1] 0.5

# about 2.3% of all observations are more than 2 standard
# deviations below the mean
pnorm(-2)
# [1] 0.02275013

# about 95.4% of all observations are within 2 standard deviations
# from the mean
pnorm(2) - pnorm(-2)
# [1] 0.9544997
```

The function qnorm(p, mean = m, sd = s) is the *quantile function* for the normal distribution with mean m and standard deviation s. It's the inverse of pnorm(), in that qnorm(p, mean = m, sd = s) returns the value x such that pnorm(x, mean = m, sd = s) == p.

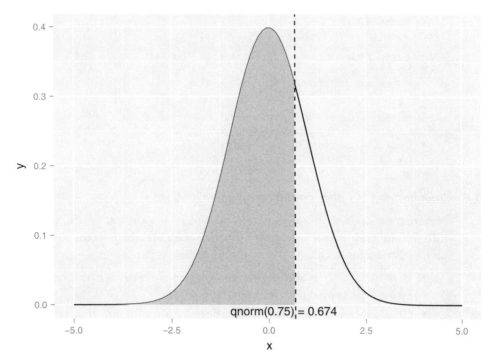

Figure B.3 Illustrating x < qnorm(0.75)

Figure B.3 illustrates the use of qnorm(): the vertical line intercepts the x axis at x = qnorm(0.75); the shaded area to the left of the vertical line represents the area 0.75, or 75% of the area under the normal curve.

The code to create figure B.3 (along with a few other examples of using qnorm()) is shown in the following listing.

Listing B.4 Plotting x < qnorm(0.75)

```
# --- return the quantiles corresponding to specific probabilities ---

# the median (50th percentile) of a normal is also the mean
qnorm(0.5)
# [1] 0

# calculate the 75th percentile
qnorm(0.75)
# [1] 0.6744898
pnorm(0.6744898)
# [1] 0.75

# --- Illustrate the 75th percentile ---

# create a graph of the normal distribution with mean 0, sd 1
x <- seq(from=-5, to=5, length.out=100)
f <- dnorm(x)
nframe <- data.frame(x=x,y=f)
```

```
# calculate the 75th percentile
line <- qnorm(0.75)
xstr <- sprintf("qnorm(0.75) = %1.3f", line)

# the part of the normal distribution to the left
# of the 75th percentile
nframe75 <- subset(nframe, nframe$x < line)

# Plot it.
# The shaded area is 75% of the area under the normal curve
ggplot(nframe, aes(x=x,y=y)) + geom_line() +
  geom_area(data=nframe75, aes(x=x,y=y), fill="gray") +
  geom_vline(aes(xintercept=line), linetype=2) +
  geom_text(x=line, y=0, label=xstr, vjust=1)
```

B.1.2 Summarizing R's distribution naming conventions

Now that we've shown some concrete examples, we can summarize how R names the different functions associated with a given probability distribution. Suppose the probability distribution is called DIST. Then the following are true:

- dDIST(x, ...) is the *distribution function* (or *PDF*, see the next callout) that returns the probability of observing the value x.
- pDIST(x, ...) is the cumulative distribution function that returns the probability of observing a value less than x. The flag lower.tail = FALSE will cause pDIST(x, ...) to return the probability of observing a value greater than x (the area under the right tail, rather than the left).
- rDIST(n, ...) is the random number generator that returns n values drawn from the distribution DIST.
- qDIST(p, ...) is the quantile function that returns the x corresponding to the pth percentile of DIST. The flag lower.tail = FALSE will cause qDIST(p, ...) to return the x that corresponds to the 1 - pth percentile of DIST.

> **R'S CONFUSING NAMING CONVENTION**   For some reason, R refers to the cumulative distribution function (or CDF) as the short term *distribution function*. Be careful to check if you want to use the probability density function or the CDF when working with R.

B.1.3 Lognormal distribution

The *lognormal distribution* is the distribution of a random variable X whose natural log log(X) is normally distributed. The distribution of highly skewed positive data, like the value of profitable customers, incomes, sales, or stock prices, can often be modeled as a lognormal distribution. A lognormal distribution is defined over all nonnegative real numbers; as shown in figure B.4 (top), it's asymmetric, with a long tail out toward positive infinity. The distribution of log(X) (figure B.4, bottom) is a normal distribution centered at mean(log(X)). For lognormal populations, the mean is generally much higher than the median, and the bulk of the contribution toward the mean value is due to a small population of highest-valued data points.

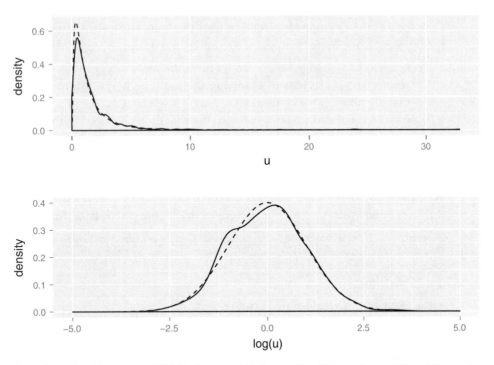

Figure B.4   Top: The lognormal distribution X such that `mean(log(X))` = 0 and `sd(log(X))` = 1. The dashed line is the theoretical distribution, and the solid line is the distribution of a random lognormal sample. Bottom: The solid line is the distribution of `log(X)`.

DON'T USE THE MEAN AS A "TYPICAL" VALUE FOR A LOGNORMAL POPULATION   For a population that's approximately normally distributed, you can use the mean value of the population as a rough stand-in value for a typical member of the population. If you use the mean as a stand-in value for a lognormal population, you'll overstate the value of the majority of your data.

Intuitively, if variations in the data are expressed naturally as percentages or relative differences, rather than as absolute differences, then the data is a candidate to be modeled lognormally. For example, a typical sack of potatoes in your grocery store might weigh about five pounds, plus or minus half a pound. The distance that a specific type of bullet will fly when fired from a specific type of handgun might be about 2,100 meters, plus or minus 100 meters. The variations in these observations are naturally represented in absolute units, and the distributions can be modeled as normals. On the other hand, differences in monetary quantities are often best expressed as percentages: a population of workers might all get a 5% increase in salary (not an increase of $5,000/year across the board); you might want to project next quarter's revenue to within 10% (not to within plus or minus $1,000). Hence, these quantities are often best modeled as having lognormal distributions.

USING THE LOGNORMAL DISTRIBUTION IN R

Let's look at the functions for working with the lognormal distribution in R (see also section B.5.3). We'll start with `dlnorm()` and `rlnorm()`:

- `dlnorm(x, meanlog = m, sdlog = s)` is the *probability density function* (PDF) that returns the probability of observing the value x when it's drawn from a lognormal distribution X such that `mean(log(X))` = m and `sd(log(X))` = s. By default, `meanlog` = 0 and `sdlog` = 1 for all the functions discussed in this section.
- `rlnorm(n, meanlog = m, sdlog = s)` is the random number that returns n values drawn from a lognormal distribution with `mean(log(X))` = m and `sd(log(X))` = s.

We can use `dlnorm()` and `rlnorm()` to produce figure 8.4, shown earlier. The following listing demonstrates some properties of the lognormal distribution.

Listing B.5 Demonstrating some properties of the lognormal distribution

```
# draw 1001 samples from a lognormal with meanlog 0, sdlog 1
u <- rlnorm(1001)

# the mean of u is higher than the median
mean(u)
# [1] 1.638628
median(u)
# [1] 1.001051

# the mean of log(u) is approx meanlog=0
mean(log(u))
# [1] -0.002942916

# the sd of log(u) is approx sdlog=1
sd(log(u))
# [1] 0.9820357

# generate the lognormal with meanlog = 0, sdlog = 1
x <- seq(from = 0, to = 25, length.out = 500)
f <- dlnorm(x)

# generate a normal with mean = 0, sd = 1
x2 <- seq(from = -5, to = 5, length.out = 500)
f2 <- dnorm(x2)

# make data frames
lnormframe <- data.frame(x = x, y = f)
normframe <- data.frame(x = x2, y = f2)
dframe <- data.frame(u=u)

# plot densityplots with theoretical curves superimposed
p1 <- ggplot(dframe, aes(x = u)) + geom_density() +
  geom_line(data = lnormframe, aes(x = x, y = y), linetype = 2)

p2 <- ggplot(dframe, aes(x = log(u))) + geom_density() +
  geom_line(data = normframe, aes(x = x,y = y), linetype = 2)

# functions to plot multiple plots on one page
library(grid)
```

```
nplot <- function(plist) {
  n <- length(plist)
  grid.newpage()
  pushViewport(viewport(layout=grid.layout(n, 1)))
  vplayout<-
    function(x,y) { viewport(layout.pos.row = x, layout.pos.col = y) }
  for(i in 1:n) {
    print(plist[[i]], vp = vplayout(i, 1))
  }
}

# this is the plot that leads this section.
nplot(list(p1, p2))
```

The remaining two functions are the CDF `plnorm()` and the quantile function `qlnorm()`:

- `plnorm(x, meanlog = m, sdlog = s)` is the cumulative distribution function that returns the probability of observing a value less than x from a lognormal distribution with `mean(log(X)) = m` and `sd(log(X)) = s`.
- `qlnorm(p, meanlog = m, sdlog = s)` is the quantile function that returns the x corresponding to the pth percentile of a lognormal distribution with `mean(log(X)) = m` and `sd(log(X)) = s`. It's the inverse of `plnorm()`.

The following listing demonstrates `plnorm()` and `qlnorm()`. It uses the data frame `lnormframe` from the previous listing.

Listing B.6 Plotting the lognormal distribution

```
# the 50th percentile (or median) of the lognormal with
# meanlog=0 and sdlog=10
qlnorm(0.5)
# [1] 1
# the probability of seeing a value x less than 1
plnorm(1)
# [1] 0.5

# the probability of observing a value x less than 10:
plnorm(10)
# [1] 0.9893489

# -- show the 75th percentile of the lognormal

# use lnormframe from previous example: the
# theoretical lognormal curve

line <- qlnorm(0.75)
xstr <- sprintf("qlnorm(0.75) = %1.3f", line)

lnormframe75 <- subset(lnormframe, lnormframe$x < line)

# Plot it
# The shaded area is 75% of the area under the lognormal curve
ggplot(lnormframe, aes(x = x, y = y)) + geom_line() +
  geom_area(data=lnormframe75, aes(x = x, y = y), fill = "gray") +
  geom_vline(aes(xintercept = line), linetype = 2) +
  geom_text(x = line, y = 0, label = xstr, hjust = 0, vjust = 1)
```

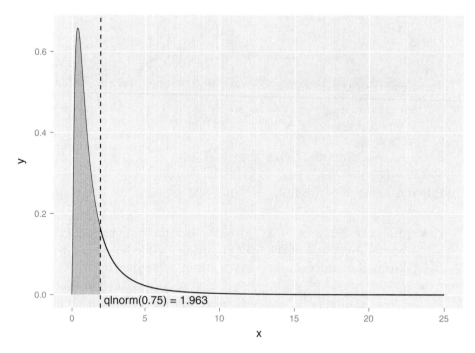

Figure B.5   **The 75th percentile of the lognormal distribution with** `meanlog = 1, sdlog = 0`

As you can see in figure B.5, the majority of the data is concentrated on the left side of the distribution, with the remaining quarter of the data spread out over a very long tail.

B.1.4   *Binomial distribution*

Suppose you have a coin that has a probability `p` of landing on heads when you flip it (so for a fair coin, `p = 0.5`). In this case, the binomial distribution models the probability of observing `k` heads when you flip that coin `N` times. It's used to model binary classification problems (as we discuss in relation to logistic regression in chapter 8), where the positive examples can be considered "heads."

Figure B.6 shows the shape of the binomial distribution for coins of different fairnesses, when flipped 50 times. Note that the binomial distribution is *discrete*; it's only defined for (non-negative) integer values of `k`

USING THE BINOMIAL DISTRIBUTION IN R

Let's look at the functions for working with the binomial distribution in R (see also section B.5.3). We'll start with the probability density function `dbinom()` and the random number generator `rbinom()`:

- `dbinom(k, nflips, p)` is the PDF that returns the probability of observing exactly `k` heads from `nflips` of a coin with heads probability `p`.
- `rbinom(N, nflips,p)` is the random number generator that returns `N` values drawn from the binomial distribution corresponding to `nflips` of a coin with heads probability `p`.

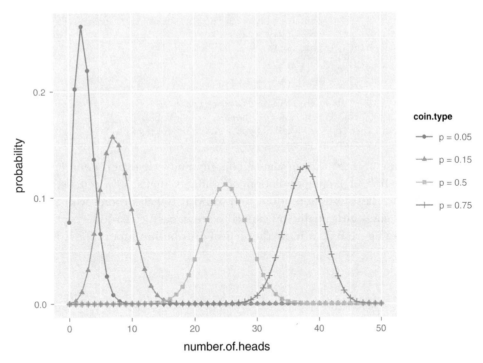

Figure B.6   The binomial distributions for 50 coin tosses, with coins of various fairnesses (probability of landing on heads)

You can use dbinom() (as in the following listing) to produce figure B.6.

Listing B.7   Plotting the binomial distribution

```
library(ggplot2)
#
# use dbinom to produce the theoretical curves
#

numflips <- 50
# x is the number of heads that we see
x <- 0:numflips

# probability of heads for several different coins
p <- c(0.05, 0.15, 0.5, 0.75)
plabels <- paste("p =", p)

# calculate the probability of seeing x heads in numflips flips
# for all the coins. This probably isn't the most elegant
# way to do this, but at least it's easy to read

flips <- NULL
for(i in 1:length(p)) {
  coin <- p[i]
  label <- plabels[i]
```

```
    tmp <- data.frame(number_of_heads=x,
                      probability = dbinom(x, numflips, coin),
                      coin_type = label)
    flips <- rbind(flips, tmp)
}

# plot it
# this is the plot that leads this section
ggplot(flips, aes(x = number_of_heads, y = probability)) +
  geom_point(aes(color = coin_type, shape = coin_type)) +
  geom_line(aes(color = coin_type))
```

You can use rbinom() to simulate a coin-flipping-style experiment. For example, suppose you have a large population of students that's 50% female. If students are assigned to classrooms at random, and you visit 100 classrooms with 20 students each, then how many girls might you expect to see in each classroom? A plausible outcome is shown in figure B.7, with the theoretical distribution superimposed.

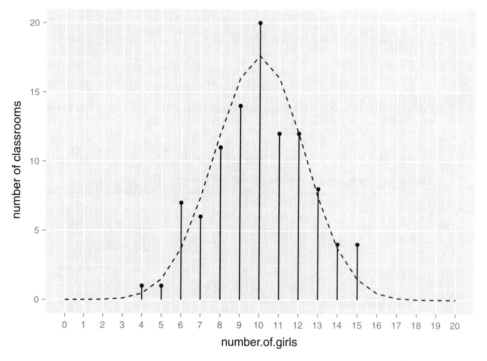

Figure B.7 **The observed distribution of the count of girls in 100 classrooms of size 20, when the population is 50% female. The theoretical distribution is shown with the dashed line.**

Let's write the code to produce figure B.7.

Listing B.8 Working with the theoretical binomial distribution

```
p = 0.5 # the percentage of females in this student population
class_size <- 20 # size of a classroom
numclasses <- 100 # how many classrooms we observe

# what might a typical outcome look like?
numFemales <- rbinom(numclasses, class_size, p)

# the theoretical counts (not necessarily integral)
probs <- dbinom(0:class_size, class_size, p)
tcount <- numclasses*probs

# the obvious way to plot this is with histogram or geom_bar
# but this might just look better

zero <- function(x) {0} # a dummy function that returns only 0

ggplot(data.frame(number_of_girls = numFemales, dummy = 1),
  aes(x = number_of_girls, y = dummy)) +
  # count the number of times you see x heads
  stat_summary(fun.y = "sum", geom = "point", size=2) +
  stat_summary(fun.ymax = "sum", fun.ymin = "zero", geom = "linerange") +
  # superimpose the theoretical number of times you see x heads
  geom_line(data = data.frame(x = 0:class_size, y = tcount),
            aes(x = x, y = y), linetype = 2) +
  scale_x_continuous(breaks = 0:class_size, labels = 0:class_size) +
  scale_y_continuous("number of classrooms")
```

> Because we didn't call set.seed, we expect different results each time we run this line.

> stat_summary is one of the ways to control data aggregation during plotting. In this case, we're using it to place the dot and bar, measured from the empirical data, in with the theoretical density curve.

As you can see, even classrooms with as few as 4 or as many as 16 girls aren't completely unheard of when students from this population are randomly assigned to classrooms. But if you observe too many such classrooms—or if you observe classes with fewer than 4 or more than 16 girls—you'd want to investigate whether student selection for those classes is biased in some way.

You can also use rbinom() to simulate flipping a single coin.

Listing B.9 Simulating a binomial distribution

```
# use rbinom to simulate flipping a coin of probability p N times

p75 <- 0.75 # a very unfair coin (mostly heads)
N <- 1000  # flip it several times
flips_v1 <- rbinom(N, 1, p75)

# Another way to generate unfair flips is to use runif:
# the probability that a uniform random number from [0 1]
# is less than p is exactly p. So "less than p" is "heads".
flips_v2 <- as.numeric(runif(N) < p75)

prettyprint_flips <- function(flips) {
  outcome <- ifelse(flips==1, "heads", "tails")
  table(outcome)
}
```

```
prettyprint_flips(flips_v1)
# outcome
# heads tails
# 756   244
prettyprint_flips(flips_v2)
# outcome
# heads tails
# 743   257
```

The final two functions are the CDF pbinom() and the quantile function qbinom():

- pbinom(k, nflips, p) is the CDF that returns the probability of observing k heads or fewer from nflips of a coin with heads probability p.

  pbinom(k, nflips, p, lower.tail = FALSE) returns the probability of observing more than k heads from nflips of a coin with heads probability p.

  Note that the left tail probability is calculated over the inclusive interval numheads <= k, while the right tail probability is calculated over the exclusive interval numheads > k.

- qbinom(q, nflips, p) is the quantile function that returns the number of heads k that corresponds to the qth percentile of the binomial distribution corresponding to nflips of a coin with heads probability p.

The next listing shows some examples of using pbinom() and qbinom().

Listing B.10   Working with the binomial distribution

```
# pbinom example

nflips <- 100
nheads <- c(25, 45, 50, 60)   # number of heads

# what are the probabilities of observing at most that
# number of heads on a fair coin?
left.tail <- pbinom(nheads, nflips, 0.5)
sprintf("%2.2f", left.tail)
# [1] "0.00" "0.18" "0.54" "0.98"

# the probabilities of observing more than that
# number of heads on a fair coin?
right.tail <- pbinom(nheads, nflips, 0.5, lower.tail = FALSE)
sprintf("%2.2f", right.tail)
# [1] "1.00" "0.82" "0.46" "0.02"

# as expected:
left.tail+right.tail
#  [1] 1 1 1 1

# so if you flip a fair coin 100 times,
# you are guaranteed to see more than 10 heads,
# almost guaranteed to see fewer than 60, and
# probably more than 45.

# qbinom example

nflips <- 100
```

```
# what's the 95% "central" interval of heads that you
# would expect to observe on 100 flips of a fair coin?

left.edge <- qbinom(0.025, nflips, 0.5)
right.edge <- qbinom(0.025, nflips, 0.5, lower.tail = FALSE)
c(left.edge, right.edge)
# [1] 40 60

# so with 95% probability you should see between 40 and 60 heads
```

One thing to keep in mind is that because the binomial distribution is discrete, pbinom() and qbinom() won't be perfect inverses of each other, as is the case with continuous distributions like the normal.

> **Listing B.11 Working with the binomial CDF**

```
# because this is a discrete probability distribution,
# pbinom and qbinom are not exact inverses of each other

# this direction works
pbinom(45, nflips, 0.5)
# [1] 0.1841008
qbinom(0.1841008, nflips, 0.5)
# [1] 45

# this direction won't be exact
qbinom(0.75, nflips, 0.5)
# [1] 53
pbinom(53, nflips, 0.5)
# [1] 0.7579408
```

B.1.5   *More R tools for distributions*

R has many more tools for working with distributions beyond the PDF, CDF, and generation tools we've demonstrated. In particular, for fitting distributions, you may want to try the fitdistr method from the MASS package.

B.2   *Statistical theory*

In this book, we necessarily concentrate on (correctly) processing data, without stopping to explain a lot of theory. The steps we use will be more understandable after we review a bit of statistical theory in this section.

B.2.1   *Statistical philosophy*

The predictive tools and machine learning methods we demonstrate in this book get their predictive power not from uncovering cause and effect (which would be a great thing to do), but by tracking and trying to eliminate differences in data and by reducing different sources of error. In this section, we'll outline a few of the key concepts that describe what's going on and why these techniques work.

EXCHANGEABILITY

Since basic statistical modeling isn't enough to reliably attribute predictions to true causes, we've been quietly relying on a concept called *exchangeability* to ensure we can build useful predictive models.

The formal definition of exchangeability is this: suppose all the data in the world is x[i,],y[i] (i=1,...m). Then we call the data *exchangeable* if for any permutation j_1, ...j_m of 1, ...m, the joint probability of seeing x[i,],y[i] is equal to the joint probability of seeing x[j_i,], y[j_i]. In other words, the joint probability of seeing a tuple x[i,], y[i] does *not* depend on *when* we see it, or where it comes in the sequence of observations.

The idea is that if all permutations of the data are equally likely, then when we draw subsets from the data using only indices (not snooping the x[i,],y[i]), the data in each subset, though different, can be considered as independent and identically distributed. We rely on this when we make train/test splits (or even train/calibrate/test splits), and we hope (and should take steps to ensure) this is true between our training data and future data we'll encounter in production.

Our hope in building a model is that in the unknown future, data the model will be applied to is exchangeable with our training data. If this is the case, then we'd expect good performance on training data to translate into good model performance in production. It's important to defend exchangeability from problems such as overfit and concept drift.

Once we start examining training data, we (unfortunately) break its exchangeability with future data. Subsets that contain a lot of training data are no longer indistinguishable from subsets that don't have training data (through the simple process of memorizing all of our training data). We attempt to measure the degree of damage by measuring performance on held-out test data. This is why generalization error is so important. Any data not looked at during model construction should be as exchangeable with future data as it ever was, so measuring performance on held-out data helps anticipate future performance. This is also why you don't use test data for calibration (instead, you should further split your training data to do this); once you look at your test data, it's less exchangeable with what will be seen in production in the future.

Another potential huge loss of exchangeability in prediction is summarized is what's called *Goodhart's law.* "When a measure becomes a target, it ceases to be a good measure." The point is this: factors that merely correlate with a prediction are good predictors—until you go too far in optimizing for them or when others react to your use of them. For example, email spammers can try to defeat a spam detection system by using more of the features and phrases that correlate highly with legitimate email, and changing phrases that the spam filter believes correlate highly with spam. This is an essential difference between actual causes (which do have an effect on outcome when altered) and mere correlations (which may be co-occurring with an outcome and are good predictors only through exchangeability of examples).

BIAS VARIANCE DECOMPOSITION

Many of the modeling tasks in this book are what are called *regressions* where, for data of the form `y[i],x[i,]`, we try to find a model or function `f()` such that `f(x[i,])~E[y[j]|x[j,]~x[i,]]` (the expectation `E[]` being taken over all examples, where `x[j,]` is considered very close to `x[i,]`). Often this is done by picking `f()` to minimize `E[(y[i]-f(x[i,]))^2]`.[2] Notable methods that fit closely to this formulation include regression, k-nearest neighbors (KNN), and neural nets.

Obviously, minimizing square error is not always your direct modeling goal. But when you work in terms of square error, you have an explicit decomposition of error into meaningful components, called the *bias/variance decomposition* (see *The Elements of Statistical Learning* by T. Hastie, R. Tibshirani, and J. Friedman; Springer, 2009). The bias/variance decomposition says this:

```
E[(y[i] - f(x[i, ]))^2] = bias^2 + variance + irreducibleError
```

Model bias is the portion of the error that your chosen modeling technique will never get right, often because some aspect of the true process isn't expressible within the assumptions of the chosen model. For example, if the relationship between the outcome and the input variables is curved or nonlinear, you can't fully model it with linear regression, which only considers linear relationships. You can often reduce bias by moving to more complicated modeling ideas: kernelizing, GAMs, adding interactions, and so on. Many modeling methods can increase model complexity (to try to reduce bias) on their own, for example, decision trees, KNN, support vector machines, and neural nets. But until you have a lot of data, increasing model complexity has a good chance of increasing model variance.

Model variance is the portion of the error that your modeling technique gets wrong due to incidental relations in the data. The idea is this: a retraining of the model on new data might make different errors (this is how variance differs from bias). An example would be running KNN with `k = 1`. When you do this, each test example is scored by matching to a single nearest training example. If that example happened to be positive, your classification will be positive. This is one reason we tend to run KNN with larger `k` values: it gives us the chance to get more reliable estimates of the nature of neighborhood (by including more examples) at the expense of making neighborhoods a bit less local or specific. More data and averaging ideas (like bagging) greatly reduce model variance.

Irreducible error is the truly unmodelable portion of the problem (given the current variables). If we have two datums `x[i, ]`, `y[i]` and `x[j,]`, `y[j]` such that `x[i, ] == x[j, ]`, then `(y[i] - y[j])^2` contributes to the irreducible error. We emphasize that irreducible error is measured with respect to a given set of variables; add more variables, and you have a new situation that may have its own lower irreducible error.

---

[2] The fact that minimizing the squared error gets expected values right is an important fact that is used in method design again and again.

The point is that you can always think of modeling error as coming from three sources: bias, variance, and irreducible error. When you're trying to increase model performance, you can choose what to try based on which of these you are trying to reduce.

> ### Averaging is a powerful tool
> Under fairly mild assumptions, averaging reduces variance. For example, for data with identically distributed independent values, averages of groups of size n have an expected variance of $1/n$ of the variance of individual values. This is one of the reasons why you can build models that accurately forecast population or group rates even when predicting individual events is difficult. So although it may be easy to forecast the number of murders per year in San Francisco, you can't predict who will be killed. In addition to shrinking variances, averaging also reshapes distributions to look more and more like the normal distribution (this is the central limit theorem and related to the law of large numbers).

STATISTICAL EFFICIENCY

The *efficiency* of an unbiased statistical procedure is defined as how much variance there is in the procedure for a given dataset size: that is, how much the estimates produced by that procedure will vary, when run on datasets of the same size and drawn from the same distribution. More efficient procedures require less data to get below a given amount of variance. This differs from computational efficiency, which is about how much work is needed to produce an estimate.

When you have a lot of data, statistical efficiency becomes less critical (which is why we don't emphasize it in this book). But when it's expensive to produce more data (such as in drug trials), statistical efficiency is your primary concern. In this book, we take the approach that we usually have a lot of data, so we can prefer general methods that are somewhat statistically inefficient (such as using a test holdout set, and so on) over more specialized, statistically efficient methods (such as specific ready-made parametric tests like the Wald test and others).

Remember: it's a luxury, not a right, to ignore statistical efficiency. If your project has such a need, you'll want to consult with expert statisticians to get the advantages of best practices.

B.2.2   A/B tests

Hard statistical problems usually arise from poor experimental design. This section describes a simple, good, statistical design philosophy called *A/B testing* that has very simple theory. The ideal experiment is one where you have two groups—control (A) and treatment (B)—and the following holds:

- Each group is big enough that you get a reliable measurement (this drives significance).

- Each group is (up to a single factor) distributed exactly like populations you expect in the future (this drives relevance). In particular, both samples are run in parallel at the same time.
- The two groups differ only with respect to the single factor you're trying to test.

In an A/B test, a new idea, treatment, or improvement is proposed and then tested for effect. A common example is a proposed change to a retail website that it is hoped will improve the rate of conversion from browsers to purchasers. Usually, the treatment group is called *B* and an untreated or control group is called *A*. As a reference, we recommend "Practical Guide to Controlled Experiments on the Web" (R. Kohavi, R. Henne, and D. Sommerfield; KDD, 2007).

SETTING UP A/B TESTS

Some care must be taken in running an A/B test. It's important that the A and B groups be run at the same time. This helps defend the test from any potential confounding effects that might be driving their own changes in conversion rate (hourly effects, source-of-traffic effects, day-of-week effects, and so on). Also, you need to know that differences you're measuring are in fact due to the change you're proposing and not due to differences in the control and test infrastructures. To control for infrastructure, you should run a few A/A tests (tests where you run the same experiment in both A and B).

Randomization is the key tool in designing A/B tests. But the split into A and B needs to be made in a sensible manner. For example, for user testing, you don't want to split raw clicks from the same user session into A/B, because then A/B would both have clicks from users that may have seen either treatment site. Instead, you'd maintain per-user records and assign users permanently to either the A or the B group when they arrive. One trick to avoid a lot of record keeping between different servers is to compute a hash of the user information and assign a user to A or B depending on whether the hash comes out even or odd (thus, all servers make the same decision without having to communicate).

EVALUATING A/B TESTS

The key measurements in an A/B test are the size of effect measured and the significance of the measurement. The natural alternative (or null hypothesis) to B being a good treatment is that B makes no difference, or B even makes things worse. Unfortunately, a typical failed A/B test often doesn't look like certain defeat. It usually looks like the positive effect you're looking for is there and you just need a slightly larger follow-up sample size to achieve significance. Because of issues like this, it's critical to reason through acceptance/rejection conditions before running tests.

Let's work an example A/B test. Suppose we've run an A/B test about conversion rate and collected the following data.

Listing B.12   Building simulated A/B test data

```
set.seed(123515)          Builds a data frame to store
d <- rbind(          ◁    simulated examples
    data.frame(group = 'A', converted = rbinom(100000, size = 1, p = 0.05)),
    data.frame(group = 'B', converted = rbinom(10000, size = 1, p = 0.055))  ◁
)
```

**Adds 100,000 examples from the A group
simulating a conversion rate of 5%**

**Adds 10,000 examples from the B group
simulating a conversion rate of 5.5%**

Once we have the data, we summarize it into the essential counts using a data structure called a *contingency table*.[3]

Listing B.13   Summarizing the A/B test into a contingency table

```
tab <- table(d)
print(tab)
##      converted
## group     0     1
##     A 94979  5021
##     B  9398   602
```

The contingency table is what statisticians call a *sufficient statistic*: it contains all we need to know about the experiment outcome. We can print the observed conversion rates of the A and B groups.

Listing B.14   Calculating the observed A and B conversion rates

```
aConversionRate <- tab['A','1']/sum(tab['A',])
print(aConversionRate)
## [1] 0.05021

bConversionRate <- tab['B', '1'] / sum(tab['B', ])
print(bConversionRate)
## [1] 0.0602

commonRate <- sum(tab[, '1']) / sum(tab)
print(commonRate)
## [1] 0.05111818
```

We see that the A group was measured at near 5%, and the B group was measured at near 6%. What we want to know is this: can we trust this difference? Could such a difference be likely for this sample size due to mere chance and measurement noise? We need to calculate a significance to see if we ran a large enough experiment (obviously, we'd want to design an experiment that was large enough—what we call *test power*, which we'll discuss in section B.6.5). What follows are a few good tests that are quick to run.

Fisher's test for independence

The first test we can run is Fisher's contingency table test. In the Fisher test, the null hypothesis that we're hoping to reject is that conversion is independent of group, or

---

[3]   The confusion matrices we used in section 6.2.3 are also examples of contingency tables.

that the A and B groups are exactly identical. The Fisher test gives a probability of seeing an independent dataset (A=B) show a departure from independence as large as what we observed. We run the test as shown in the next listing.

Listing B.15 Calculating the significance of the observed difference in rates

```
fisher.test(tab)

##      Fisher's Exact Test for Count Data
##
## data:  tab
## p-value = 2.469e-05
## alternative hypothesis: true odds ratio is not equal to 1
## 95 percent confidence interval:
##   1.108716 1.322464
## sample estimates:
## odds ratio
##   1.211706
```

This is a great result. The p-value (which in this case is the probability of observing a difference this large if we in fact had A=B) is 2.469e-05, which is very small. This is considered a significant result. The other thing to look for is the *odds ratio*: the practical importance of the claimed effect (sometimes also called *clinical significance*, which is not a statistical significance). An odds ratio of 1.2 says that we're measuring a 20% relative improvement in conversion rate between the A and B groups. Whether you consider this large or small (typically, 20% is considered large) is an important business question.

Frequentist significance test

Another way to estimate significance is to again temporarily assume that A and B come from an identical distribution with a common conversion rate, and see how likely it would be that the B group scores as high as it did by mere chance. If we consider a binomial distribution centered at the common conversion rate, we'd like to see that there's not a lot of probability mass for conversion rates at or above B's level. This would mean the observed difference is unlikely if A=B. We'll work through the calculation in the following listing.

Listing B.16 Computing frequentist significance

Signals that we want the probability of being greater than a given q

Uses the pbinom() call to calculate how likely different observed counts are

Asks for the probability of seeing at least as many conversions as our observed B groups did. We subtract one to make the comparison inclusive (greater than or equal to tab['B', '1']).

```
print(pbinom(
    lower.tail = FALSE,
    q = tab['B', '1'] - 1,
    size = sum(tab['B', ]),
    prob = commonRate
))
## [1] 3.153319e-05
```

Specifies the total number of trials as equal to what we saw in our B group

Specifies the conversion probability at the estimated common rate

This is again a great result. The calculated probability is small, meaning such a difference is hard to observe by chance if `A` = `B`.

B.2.3   *Power of tests*

To have reliable A/B test results, you must first design and run good A/B tests. We need to defend against two types of errors: failing to see a difference, assuming there is one (described as test power); and seeing a difference, assuming there is not one (described as significance). The closer the difference in A and B rates we are trying to measure, the harder it is to have a good probability of getting a correct measurement. Our only tools are to design experiments where we hope A and B are far apart, or to increase experiment size. A power calculator lets us choose experiment size.

> **Example   Designing a test to see if a new advertisement has a higher conversion rate**
>
> *Suppose we're running a travel site that has 6,000 unique visitors per day and a 4% conversion rate[4] from page views to purchase inquiries (our measurable goal). We'd like to test a new design for the site to see if it increases our conversion rate. This is exactly the kind of problem A/B tests are made for! But we have one more question: how many users do we have to route to the new design to get a reliable measurement? How long will it take us to collect enough data? We're allowed to route no more than 10% of the visitors to the new advertisement.*

In this experiment, we'll route 90% of our traffic to the old advertisement and 10% to the new advertisement. There is uncertainty in estimating the conversion rate of the old advertisement going forward, but for simplicity of example (and because nine times more traffic is going to the old advertisement) we will ignore that. So our problem is this: how much traffic should we route to the new advertisement?

To solve this, we need some criteria for our experimental design:

- What is our estimate of the old advertisement's conversion rate? Let's say this is 0.04 or 4%.
- What is a lower bound on what we consider a big enough improvement for the new advertisement? For the test to work, this must be larger than the old conversion rate. Let's say this is 0.046 or 4.5%, representing a slightly larger-than-10% relative improvement in conversion to sale.
- With what probability are we willing to be wrong if the new ad was no better? That is, if the new ad is in fact no better than the old ad, how often are we willing to "cry wolf" and claim there is an improvement (when there is in fact no such thing)? Let's say we are willing to be wrong in this way 5% of the time. Let's call this the *significance level*.

---

[4]   We're taking the 4% rate from http://mng.bz/7pT3.

- With what probability do we want to be right when the new ad was substantially better? That is, if the new ad is in fact converting at a rate of at least 4.5%, how often do we want to detect this? This is called *power* (and related to sensitivity, which we saw when discussing classification models). Let's say we want the power to be 0.8 or 80%. When there is an improvement, we want to find it 80% of the time.

Obviously, what we *want* is to be able to detect improvements at sizes close to zero, at a significance level of zero, and at a power of 1. However, if we insist on any of these parameters being at their "if wishes were horses value" (near zero for improvement size, near zero for significance level, and near 1 for power), the required test size to ensure these guarantees becomes enormous (or even infinite!). So as part of setting expectations before a project (always a good practice), we must first negotiate these "asks" to more achievable values such as those we just described.

When trying to determine sample size or experiment duration, the important concept is *statistical test power*. Statistical test power is the probability of rejecting the null hypothesis when the null hypothesis is false.[5] Think of statistical test power as 1 minus a p-value. The idea is this: you can't pick out useful treatments if you can't even identify which treatments are useless. So you want to design your tests to have test power near 1, which means p-values near 0.

The standard way to estimate the number of visitors we want to direct to the new advertisement is called a *power calculation* and is supplied by the R package pwr. Here is how we use R to get the answer:

```
library(pwr)
pwr.p.test(h = ES.h(p1 = 0.045, p2 = 0.04),
           sig.level = 0.05,
           power = 0.8,
           alternative = "greater")

#      proportion power calculation for binomial distribution (arcsine transfo
   rmation)
#
#              h = 0.02479642
#              n = 10055.18
#      sig.level = 0.05
#          power = 0.8
#    alternative = greater
```

Notice that all we did was copy our asks into the pwr.p.test method, though we did put the two assumed rates we are trying to distinguish through the ES.h() method, which converts the difference of rates into a Cohen-style "effect size." In this case. ES.h(p1 = 0.045, p2 = 0.04) is 0.025, which is considered quite small (and therefore hard to measure). Effect sizes are very roughly how big an effect you are trying to

---

[5] See B. S. Everitt, *The Cambridge Dictionary of Statistics* (Cambridge University Press, 2010).

measure relative to the natural variation of individuals. So we are trying to measure a change in the likelihood of a sale that is $1/0.025$ or 40 times smaller than the individual variation in likelihood of a sale. This is unobservable for any small set of individuals, but observable with a large enough sample.[6]

The n = 10056 is the amount of traffic we would have to send to the new advertisement to get a test result with at least the specified quality parameters (significance level and power). So we would need to serve the new advertisement to 10056 visitors to achieve our A/B test measurement. Our site receives 6,000 visitors a day, and we are only allowed to send 10% of them, or 600, to the new advertisement each day. So it would take us $10056/600$ or 16.8 days to complete this test.[7]

Venue shopping reduces test power

We've discussed test power and significance under the assumption you're running one large test. In practice, you may run multiple tests trying many treatments to see if any treatment delivers an improvement. This reduces your test power. If you run 20 treatments, each with a p-value goal of 0.05, you would expect one test to appear to show significant improvement, even if all 20 treatments are useless. Testing multiple treatments or even reinspecting the same treatment many times is a form of "venue shopping" (you keep asking at different venues until you get a ruling in your favor). Calculating the loss of test power is formally called "applying the Bonferroni correction" and is as simple as multiplying your significance estimates by your number of tests (remember, large values are bad for significances or p-values). To compensate for this loss of test power, you can run each of the underlying tests at a tighter *p* cutoff: *p* divided by the number of tests you intend to run.

B.2.4   *Specialized statistical tests*

Throughout this book, we concentrate on building predictive models and evaluating significance, either through the modeling tool's built-in diagnostics or through empirical resampling (such as bootstrap tests or permutation tests). In statistics, there's an efficient correct test for the significance of just about anything you commonly calculate. Choosing the right standard test gives you a good implementation of the test and access to literature that explains the context and implications of the test. Let's work on calculating a simple correlation and finding the matching correct test.

We'll work with a synthetic example that should remind you a bit of our PUMS Census work in chapter 8. Suppose we've measured both earned income (money earned in the form of salary) and capital gains (money received from investments) for 100 individuals. Further suppose that there's no relation between the two for our indi-

---

[6] Effect sizes are nice idea, and have a rule of thumb that 0.2 is small, 0.5 is medium, and 1.0 is large. See https://en.wikipedia.org/wiki/Effect_size.

[7] This is fact one of the dirty secrets of A/B tests: measuring small improvements of rare events such as conversion of an advertisement to a sale (often called "conversion to sale") takes a lot of data, and acquiring a lot of data can take a lot of time.

viduals (in the real world, there's a correlation, but we need to make sure our tools don't report one even when there's none). We'll set up a simple dataset representing this situation with some lognormally distributed data.

Listing B.17 Building synthetic uncorrelated income

```
set.seed(235236)
d <- data.frame(EarnedIncome = 100000 * rlnorm(100),
                CapitalGains = 100000 * rlnorm(100))
print(with(d, cor(EarnedIncome, CapitalGains)))

# [1] -0.01066116
```

Sets the pseudo-random seed to a known value so the demonstration is repeatable

Generates our synthetic data

The correlation is –0.01, which is very near 0—indicating (as designed) no relation.

We claim the observed correlation of -0.01 is statistically indistinguishable from 0 (or no effect). This is something we should quantify. A little research tells us the common correlation is called a *Pearson coefficient*, and the significance test for a Pearson coefficient for normally distributed data is a Student's t-test (with the number of degrees of freedom equal to the number of items minus 2). We know our data is not normally distributed (it is, in fact, lognormally distributed), so we research further and find the preferred solution is to compare the data by rank (instead of by value) and use a test like Spearman's rho or Kendall's tau. We'll use Spearman's rho, as it can track both positive and negative correlations (whereas Kendall's tau tracks degree of agreement).

A fair question is, how do we know which is the exact right test to use? The answer is, by studying statistics. Be aware that there are a lot of tests, giving rise to books like *100 Statistical Tests in R* by N. D. Lewis (Heather Hills Press, 2013). We also suggest that if you know the name of a test, consult B. S.Everitt and A. Skrondal, *The Cambridge Dictionary of Statistics*, Fourth Edition (Cambridge University Press, 2010).

Another way to find the right test is using R's help system. help(cor) tells us that cor() implements three different calculations (Pearson, Spearman, and Kendall) and that there's a matching function called cor.test() that performs the appropriate significance test. Since we weren't too far off the beaten path, we only need to read up on these three tests and settle on the one we're interested in (in this case, Spearman). So let's redo our correlation with the chosen test and check the significance.

Listing B.18 Calculating the (non)significance of the observed correlation

```
with(d, cor(EarnedIncome, CapitalGains, method = 'spearman'))

# [1] 0.03083108

(ctest <- with(d, cor.test(EarnedIncome, CapitalGains, method = 'spearman')))

#
#       Spearman's rank correlation rho
#
#data:  EarnedIncome and CapitalGains
#S = 161512, p-value = 0.7604
```

```
#alternative hypothesis: true rho is not equal to 0
#sample estimates:
#       rho
#0.03083108
```

We see the Spearman correlation is 0.03 with a p-value of 0.7604, which means truly uncorrelated data would show a coefficient this large about 76% of the time. So there's no significant effect (which is exactly how we designed our synthetic example).

In our own work, we use the `sigr` package to wrap up these test results for more succinct formal presentation. The format is similar to the APA (American Psychological Association) style, and `n.s.` means "not significant."

```
sigr::wrapCorTest(ctest)
```

```
# [1] "Spearman's rank correlation rho: (r=0.03083, p=n.s.)."
```

B.3   *Examples of the statistical view of data*

Compared to statistics, machine learning and data science have an optimistic view of working with data. In data science, you quickly pounce on noncausal relations in the hope that they'll hold up and help with future prediction. Much of statistics is about how data can lie to you and how such relations can mislead you. We only have space for a couple of examples, so we'll concentrate on two of the most common issues: sampling bias and missing-variable bias.

B.3.1   *Sampling bias*

Sampling bias is any process that systematically alters the distribution of observed data.[8] The data scientist must be aware of the possibility of sampling bias and be prepared to detect it and fix it. The most effective way is to fix your data collection methodology.

For our sampling bias example, we'll continue with the income example we started in section B.4. Suppose through some happenstance we were studying only a high-earning subset of our original population (perhaps we polled them at some exclusive event). The following listing shows how, when we restrict to a high-earning set, it appears that earned income and capital gains are strongly anticorrelated. We get a correlation of -0.86 (so think of the anticorrelation as explaining about $(-0.86)^2 = 0.74 = 74\%$ of the variance; see http://mng.bz/ndYf) and a p-value very near 0 (so it's unlikely the unknown true correlation of more data produced in this manner is in fact 0). The following listing demonstrates the calculation.

---

[8] We would have liked to use the common term "censored" for this issue, but in statistics the phrase *censored observations* is reserved for variables that have only been recorded up to a limit or bound. So it would be potentially confusing to use the term to describe missing observations.

Listing B.19 Misleading significance result from biased observations

```
veryHighIncome <- subset(d, EarnedIncome+CapitalGains>=500000)
print(with(veryHighIncome,cor.test(EarnedIncome,CapitalGains,
    method='spearman')))
#
#       Spearman's rank correlation rho
#
#data:  EarnedIncome and CapitalGains
#S = 1046, p-value < 2.2e-16
#alternative hypothesis: true rho is not equal to 0
#sample estimates:
#       rho
#-0.8678571
```

Some plots help to show what's going on. Figure B.8 shows the original dataset with the best linear relation line run through. Note that the line is nearly flat (indicating change in x doesn't predict change in y).

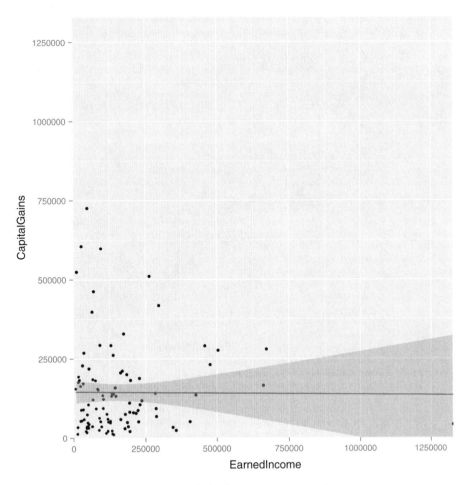

Figure B.8 Earned income versus capital gains

Figure B.9 shows the best trend line run through the high income dataset. It also shows how cutting out the points below the line x+y=500000 leaves a smattering of rare high-value events arranged in a direction that crudely approximates the slope of our cut line (–0.8678571 being a crude approximation for –1). It's also interesting to note that the bits we suppressed aren't correlated among themselves, so the effect wasn't a matter of suppressing a correlated group out of an uncorrelated cloud to get a negative correlation.

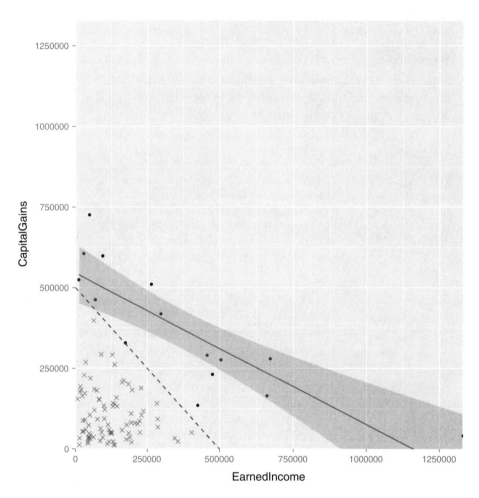

Figure B.9   Biased earned income vs. capital gains

The code to produce figures B.8 and B.9 and calculate the correlation between suppressed points is shown in the following listing.

Listing B.20　Plotting biased view of income and capital gains

```
library(ggplot2)
ggplot(data=d,aes(x=EarnedIncome,y=CapitalGains)) +
    geom_point() + geom_smooth(method='lm') +
    coord_cartesian(xlim=c(0,max(d)),ylim=c(0,max(d)))
ggplot(data=veryHighIncome,aes(x=EarnedIncome,y=CapitalGains)) +
    geom_point() + geom_smooth(method='lm') +
    geom_point(data=subset(d,EarnedIncome+CapitalGains<500000),
        aes(x=EarnedIncome,y=CapitalGains),
      shape=4,alpha=0.5,color='red') +
    geom_segment(x=0,xend=500000,y=500000,yend=0,
      linetype=2,alpha=0.5,color='red') +
    coord_cartesian(xlim=c(0,max(d)),ylim=c(0,max(d)))
print(with(subset(d,EarnedIncome+CapitalGains<500000),
    cor.test(EarnedIncome,CapitalGains,method='spearman')))
#
#        Spearman's rank correlation rho
#
#data:  EarnedIncome and CapitalGains
#S = 107664, p-value = 0.6357
#alternative hypothesis: true rho is not equal to 0
#sample estimates:
#        rho
#-0.05202267
```

Annotations:
- **Plots all of the income data with linear trend line (and uncertainty band)**
- **Plots the very high income data and linear trend line (also includes cut-off and portrayal of suppressed data)**
- **Computes correlation of suppressed data**

B.3.2　Omitted variable bias

Many data science clients expect data science to be a quick process, where every convenient variable is thrown in at once and a best possible result is quickly obtained. Statisticians are rightfully wary of such an approach due to various negative effects such as omitted variable bias, collinear variables, confounding variables, and nuisance variables. In this section, we'll discuss one of the more general issues: omitted variable bias.

WHAT IS OMITTED VARIABLE BIAS?

In its simplest form, omitted variable bias occurs when a variable that isn't included in the model is both correlated with what we're trying to predict and correlated with a variable that's included in our model. When this effect is strong, it causes problems, as the model-fitting procedure attempts to use the variables in the model to both directly predict the desired outcome and to stand in for the effects of the missing variable. This can introduce biases, create models that don't quite make sense, and result in poor generalization performance.

The effect of omitted variable bias is easiest to see in a regression example, but it can affect any type of model.

AN EXAMPLE OF OMITTED VARIABLE BIAS

We've prepared a synthetic dataset called synth.RData (download from https://github.com/WinVector/PDSwR2/tree/master/bioavailability) that has an omitted variable problem typical for a data science project. To start, please download synth.RData and load it into R, as the next listing shows.

Listing B.21 Summarizing our synthetic biological data

```
load('synth.RData')
print(summary(s))
##       week         Caco2A2BPapp        FractionHumanAbsorption
##  Min.   :  1.00   Min.   :6.994e-08   Min.   :0.09347
##  1st Qu.: 25.75   1st Qu.:7.312e-07   1st Qu.:0.50343
##  Median : 50.50   Median :1.378e-05   Median :0.86937
##  Mean   : 50.50   Mean   :2.006e-05   Mean   :0.71492
##  3rd Qu.: 75.25   3rd Qu.:4.238e-05   3rd Qu.:0.93908
##  Max.   :100.00   Max.   :6.062e-05   Max.   :0.99170
head(s)
##   week Caco2A2BPapp FractionHumanAbsorption
## 1    1 6.061924e-05              0.11568186
## 2    2 6.061924e-05              0.11732401
## 3    3 6.061924e-05              0.09347046
## 4    4 6.061924e-05              0.12893540
## 5    5 5.461941e-05              0.19021858
## 6    6 5.370623e-05              0.14892154
# View(s)
```

Displays a date in a spreadsheet-like window. View is one of the commands that has a much better implementation in RStudio than in basic R.

This loads synthetic data that's supposed to represent a simplified view of the kind of data that might be collected over the history of a pharmaceutical ADME[9] or bioavailability project. RStudio's `View()` spreadsheet is shown in figure B.10. The columns of this dataset are described in table B.1.

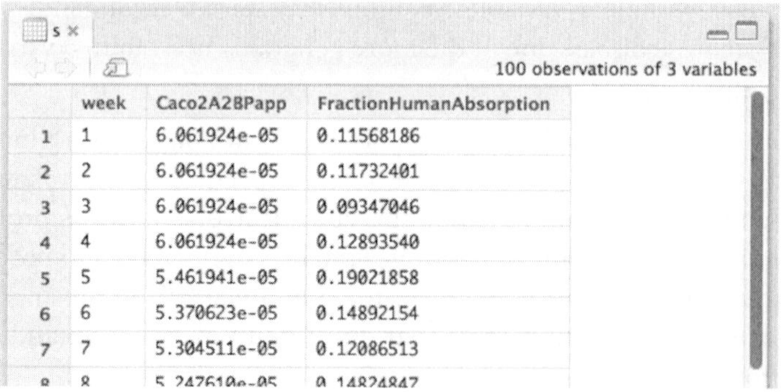

	week	Caco2A2BPapp	FractionHumanAbsorption
1	1	6.061924e-05	0.11568186
2	2	6.061924e-05	0.11732401
3	3	6.061924e-05	0.09347046
4	4	6.061924e-05	0.12893540
5	5	5.461941e-05	0.19021858
6	6	5.370623e-05	0.14892154
7	7	5.304511e-05	0.12086513

Figure B.10 View of rows from the bioavailability dataset

9 ADME stands for absorption, distribution, metabolism, excretion; it helps determine which molecules make it into the human body through ingestion and thus could even be viable candidates for orally delivered drugs.

Table B.1 Bioavailability columns

Column	Description
week	In this project, we suppose that a research group submits a new drug candidate molecule for assay each week. To keep things simple, we use the week number (in terms of weeks since the start of the project) as the identifier for the molecule and the data row. This is an optimization project, which means each proposed molecule is made using lessons learned from all of the previous molecules. This is typical of many projects, but it means the data rows aren't mutually exchangeable (an important assumption that we often use to justify statistical and machine learning techniques).
Caco2A2BPapp	This is the first assay run (and the "cheap" one). The Caco2 test measures how fast the candidate molecule passes through a membrane of cells derived from a specific large intestine carcinoma (cancers are often used for tests, as noncancerous human cells usually can't be cultured indefinitely). The Caco2 test is a stand-in or analogy test. The test is thought to simulate one layer of the small intestine that it's morphologically similar to (though it lacks a number of forms and mechanisms found in the actual small intestine). Think of Caco2 as a cheap test to evaluate a factor that correlates with bioavailability (the actual goal of the project).
FractionHumanAbsorption	This is the second assay run and is what fraction of the drug candidate is absorbed by human test subjects. Obviously, these tests would be expensive to run and subject to a lot of safety protocols. For this example, optimizing absorption is the actual end goal of the project.

We've constructed this synthetic data to represent a project that's trying to optimize human absorption by working through small variations of a candidate drug molecule. At the start of the project, they have a molecule that's highly optimized for the stand-in criteria Caco2 (which does correlate with human absorption), and through the history of the project, actual human absorption is greatly increased by altering factors that we're not tracking in this simplistic model. During drug optimization, it's common to have formerly dominant stand-in criteria revert to ostensibly less desirable values as other inputs start to dominate the outcome. So for our example project, the human absorption rate is rising (as the scientists successfully optimize for it) and the Caco2 rate is falling (as it started high, and we're no longer optimizing for it, even though it *is* a useful feature).

One of the advantages of using synthetic data for these problem examples is that we can design the data to have a given structure, and then we know the model is correct if it picks this up and incorrect if it misses it. In particular, this dataset was designed such that Caco2 is always a positive contribution to fraction of absorption throughout the entire dataset. This data was generated using a random non-increasing sequence of plausible Caco2 measurements and then generating fictional absorption numbers, as shown next (the data frame d that you also loaded from synth.RData is the published graph we base our synthetic example on). We produce our synthetic data that's known to improve over time in the next listing.

Listing B.22   Building data that improves over time

```
set.seed(2535251)
s <- data.frame(week = 1:100)                                    Builds synthetic
s$Caco2A2BPapp <- sort(sample(d$Caco2A2BPapp,100,replace=T),     examples
  decreasing=T)
sigmoid <- function(x) {1/(1 + exp(-x))}
s$FractionHumanAbsorption <-
 sigmoid(
    7.5 + 0.5 * log(s$Caco2A2BPapp) +
    s$week / 10 - mean(s$week / 10) +
    rnorm(100) / 3
    )
write.table(s, 'synth.csv', sep=',',
    quote = FALSE, row.names = FALSE)
```

Adds in Caco2 to the absorption relation learned from the original dataset. Note that the relation is positive: better Caco2 always drives better absorption in our synthetic dataset. We're log transforming Caco2, as it has over 3 decades of range.

Adds in a mean-0 term that depends on time to simulate the effects of improvements as the project moves forward

Adds in a mean-0 noise term

The design of this data is this: Caco2 always has a positive effect (identical to the source data we started with), but this gets hidden by the week factor (and Caco2 is negatively correlated with week, because week is increasing and Caco2 is sorted in decreasing order). Time is not a variable we at first wish to model (it isn't something we usefully control), but analyses that omit time suffer from omitted variable bias. For the complete details, consult our GitHub example documentation (https://github .com/WinVector/PDSwR2/tree/master/bioavailability).

A SPOILED ANALYSIS

In some situations, the true relationship between Caco2 and FractionHumanAbsorption is hidden because the variable week is positively correlated with Fraction-HumanAbsorption (as the absorption is being improved over time) and negatively correlated with Caco2 (as Caco2 is falling over time). week is a stand-in variable for all the other molecular factors driving human absorption that we're not recording or modeling. Listing B.23 shows what happens when we try to model the relation between Caco2 and FractionHumanAbsorption without using the week variable or any other factors.

Listing B.23   A bad model (due to omitted variable bias)

```
print(summary(glm(data = s,
    FractionHumanAbsorption ~ log(Caco2A2BPapp),
    family = binomial(link = 'logit'))))
## Warning: non-integer #successes in a binomial glm!
##
## Call:
## glm(formula = FractionHumanAbsorption ~ log(Caco2A2BPapp),
##     family = binomial(link = "logit"),
```

```
##     data = s)
##
## Deviance Residuals:
##    Min      1Q  Median      3Q     Max
## -0.609  -0.246  -0.118   0.202   0.557
##
## Coefficients:
##                   Estimate Std. Error z value Pr(>|z|)
## (Intercept)        -10.003      2.752   -3.64  0.00028 ***
## log(Caco2A2BPapp)   -0.969      0.257   -3.77  0.00016 ***
## ---
## Signif. codes:  0 '***' 0.001 '**' 0.01 '*' 0.05 '.' 0.1 ' ' 1
##
## (Dispersion parameter for binomial family taken to be 1)
##
##     Null deviance: 43.7821  on 99  degrees of freedom
## Residual deviance:  9.4621  on 98  degrees of freedom
## AIC: 64.7
##
## Number of Fisher Scoring iterations: 6
```

For details on how to read the glm() summary, please see section 7.2. Note that the sign of the Caco2 coefficient is negative, not what's plausible or what we expected going in. This is because the Caco2 coefficient isn't just recording the relation of Caco2 to FractionHumanAbsorption, but also having to record any relations that come through omitted correlated variables.

WORKING AROUND OMITTED VARIABLE BIAS

There are a number of ways to deal with omitted variable bias, the best ways being better experimental design and more variables. Other methods include use of fixed-effects models and hierarchical models. We'll demonstrate one of the simplest methods: adding in possibly important omitted variables. In the following listing, we redo the analysis with week included.

Listing B.24   A better model

```
print(summary(glm(data=s,
   FractionHumanAbsorption~week+log(Caco2A2BPapp),
   family=binomial(link='logit'))))
## Warning: non-integer #successes in a binomial glm!
##
## Call:
## glm(formula = FractionHumanAbsorption ~ week + log(Caco2A2BPapp),
##     family = binomial(link = "logit"), data = s)
##
## Deviance Residuals:
##     Min      1Q  Median      3Q     Max
## -0.3474 -0.0568 -0.0010  0.0709  0.3038
##
## Coefficients:
##                   Estimate Std. Error z value Pr(>|z|)
## (Intercept)         3.1413     4.6837    0.67   0.5024
## week                0.1033     0.0386    2.68   0.0074 **
```

```
## log(Caco2A2BPapp)     0.5689      0.5419     1.05    0.2938
## ---
## Signif. codes:  0 '***' 0.001 '**' 0.01 '*' 0.05 '.' 0.1 ' ' 1
##
## (Dispersion parameter for binomial family taken to be 1)
##
##     Null deviance: 43.7821  on 99  degrees of freedom
## Residual deviance:  1.2595  on 97  degrees of freedom
## AIC: 47.82
##
## Number of Fisher Scoring iterations: 6
```

We recovered decent estimates of both the Caco2 and week coefficients, but we didn't achieve statistical significance on the effect of Caco2. Note that fixing omitted variable bias requires (even in our synthetic example) some domain knowledge to propose important omitted variables and the ability to measure the additional variables (and to try to remove their impact through the use of an offset; see help('offset')).

At this point, you should have a more detailed intentional view of variables. There are, at the least, variables you can control (explanatory variables), important variables you can't control (nuisance variables), and important variables you don't know (omitted variables). Your knowledge of all of these variable types should affect your experimental design and analysis.

B.4   *The takeaway*

Statistics is a deep field with important implications for data science. Statistics includes the study of what can go wrong in modeling and analysis, and if you don't prepare for what can go wrong, it tends to go wrong. We hope you will take this appendix as an invitation for further study. A book we recommend is *Statistical Models: Theory and Practice* by David Freedman (Cambridge Press, 2009).

appendix C
Bibliography

Adler, Joseph. *R in a Nutshell*, 2nd ed. O'Reilly Media, 2012.

Agresti, Alan. *Categorical Data Analysis*, 3rd ed. Wiley Publications, 2012.

Alley, Michael. *The Craft of Scientific Presentations*. Springer, 2003.

Brooks, Jr., Frederick P. *The Mythical Man-Month: Essays on Software Engineering*. Addison-Wesley, 1995.

Carroll, Jonathan. *Beyond Spreadsheets with R*. Manning Publications, 2018.

Casella, George, and Roger L. Berger. *Statistical Inference*. Duxbury, 1990.

Celko, Joe. *SQL for Smarties*, 4th ed. Morgan Kauffman, 2011.

Chakrabarti, Soumen. *Mining the Web*. Morgan Kauffman, 2003.

Chambers, John M. *Software for Data Analysis*. Springer, 2008.

Chang, Winston. *R Graphics Cookbook*, 2nd ed. O'Reilly Media, 2018.

Charniak, Eugene. *Statistical Language Learning*. MIT Press, 1993.

Chollet, François, with J. J. Allaire. *Deep Learning with R*. Manning Publications, 2018.

Cleveland, William S. *The Elements of Graphing Data*. Hobart Press, 1994.

Cohen, J., and P. Cohen. *Applied Multiple Regression/Correlation Analysis for the Behavioral Sciences*, 2nd ed. Lawrence Erlbaum Associates, Inc., 1983.

Cover, Thomas M., and Joy A. Thomas. *Elements of Information Theory*. Wiley, 1991.

Cristianini, Nello, and John Shawe-Taylor. *An Introduction to Support Vector Machines*. Cambridge Press, 2000.

Dalgaard, Peter. *Introductory Statistics with R*, 2nd ed. Springer, 2008.

Dimiduk, Nick, and Amandeep Khurana. *HBase in Action*. Manning Publications, 2013.

Efron, Bradley, and Robert Tibshirani. *An Introduction to the Bootstrap*. Chapman and Hall, 1993.

Everitt, B. S. *The Cambridge Dictionary of Statistics*, 2nd ed. Cambridge Press, 2006.

Freedman, David. *Statistical Models: Theory and Practice*. Cambridge Press, 2009.

Freedman, David, Robert Pisani, and Roger Purves. *Statistics*, 4th ed. Norton, 2007.

Gandrud, Christopher. *Reproducible Research with R and RStudio*, 2nd ed. CRC Press, 2015.

Gelman, Andrew, John B. Carlin, Hal S. Stern, David B. Dunson, Aki Vehtari, and Donald B. Rubin. *Bayesian Data Analysis*, 3rd ed. CRC Press, 2013.

Gentle, James E. *Elements of Computational Statistics.* Springer, 2002.

Goldberg, David. "What every computer scientist should know about floating-point arithmetic." ACM Computing Surveys, Volume 23 Issue 1, pp. 5–48, March 1991.

Good, Philip. *Permutation Tests.* Springer, 2000.

Hastie, Trevor, Robert Tibshirani, and Jerome Friedman. *The Elements of Statistical Learning,* 2nd ed. Springer, 2009.

Hothorn, Torsten, and Brian S. Everitt. *A Handbook of Statistical Analyses Using R,* 3rd ed. CRC Press, 2014.

James, Gareth, Daniela Witten, Trevor Hastie, and Robert Tibshirani. *An Introduction to Statistical Learning.* Springer, 2013.

Kabacoff, Robert. *R in Action,* 2nd ed. Manning Publications, 2014.

Kennedy, Peter. *A Guide to Econometrics,* 5th ed. MIT Press, 2003.

Kohavi, R., R. Henne, and D. Sommerfield. "Practical Guide to Controlled Experiments on the Web." KDD, 2007.

Koller, Daphne, and Nir Friedman. *Probabilistic Graphical Models: Principles and Techniques.* MIT Press, 2009.

Krzanowski, W. J., and F. H. C. Marriott. *Multivariate Analysis, Part 1,* Edward Arnold, 1994.

Kuhn, Max, and Kjell Johnson. *Applied Predictive Modeling.* Springer, 2013.

Lander, Jared P. *R for Everyone.* Addison-Wesley Data & Analytics Series, 2017.

Lewis, N. D. *100 Statistical Tests in R.* Heather Hills Press, 2013.

Loeliger, Jon, and Matthew McCullough. *Version Control with Git,* 2nd ed. O'Reilly Media, 2012.

Magee, John. "Operations Research at Arthur D. Little, Inc.: The Early Years." *Operations Research,* 2002. 50 (1), pp. 149–153.

Marz, Nathan, and James Warren. *Big Data.* Manning Publications, 2014.

Matloff, Norman. *Statistical Regression and Classification: From Linear Models to Machine Learning.* CRC Press, 2017.

———*The Art of R Programming: A Tour of Statistical Software Design.* No Starch Press, 2011.

Mitchell, Tom M. *Machine Learning.* McGraw-Hill, 1997.

Nussbaumer Knaflic, Cole. *Storytelling With Data.* Wiley, 2015.

Provost, Foster, and Tom Fawcett. *Data Science for Business.* O'Reilly Media, 2013.

R Core Team. *R: A language and environment for statistical computing.* R Foundation for Statistical Computing. https://R-project.org/.

———*R Language Definition.* R Foundation for Statistical Computing, 2019. https://cran.r-project.org/doc/manuals/r-release/R-lang.html.

Raymond, Erick S. *The Art of Unix Programming.* Addison-Wesley, 2003.

Sachs, Lothar. *Applied Statistics,* 2nd ed. Springer, 1984.

Seni, Giovanni, and John Elder. *Ensemble Methods in Data Mining.* Morgan and Claypool, 2010.

Shawe-Taylor, John, and Nello Cristianini. *Kernel Methods for Pattern Analysis.* Cambridge Press, 2004.

Shumway, Robert, and David Stoffer. *Time Series Analysis and Its Applications,* 3rd ed. Springer, 2013.

Spector, Phil. *Data Manipulation with R.* Springer, 2008.

Spiegel, Murray R., and Larry J. Stephens. *Schaum's Outline of Statistics,* 4th ed. McGraw-Hill, 2011.

Sweeney, R. E., and E. F. Ulveling. "A Transformation for Simplifying the Interpretation of Coefficients of Binary Variables in Regression Analysis." *The American Statistician,* 26(5), 30–32, 1972.

Tibshirani, Robert. "Regression shrinkage and selection via the lasso." *Journal of the Royal Statistical Society,* Series B 58: 267–288, 1996.

Tsay, Ruey S. *Analysis of Financial Time Series*, 2nd ed. Wiley, 2005.

Tukey, John W. *Exploratory Data Analysis*. Pearson, 1977.

Vapnik, Vladimir N. *Statistical Learning Theory*, Wiley-Interscience, 1998.

———*The Nature of Statistical Learning Theory*, 2nd ed. Springer, 2000.

Wasserman, Larry. *All of Nonparametric Statistics*. Springer, 2006.

———*All of Statistics*. Springer, 2004.

Wickham, Hadley. *Advanced R*. CRC, 2014.

———*ggplot2: Elegant Graphics for Data Analysis (Use R!)*. Springer, 2009.

———*R Packages: Organize, Test, Document, and Share Your Code*. O'Reilly Media, 2015.

Wilkinson, Leland. *The Grammar of Graphics*, 2nd ed. Springer, 2005.

Xie, Yihui. *Dynamic Documents with R and knitr*. CRC Press, 2013.

Zumel, Nina, and John Mount. "vtreat: a data.frame Processor for Predictive Modeling." 2016. https://arxiv.org/abs/1611.09477.

index

Symbols

; (semicolons) 25
:: notation 26
.. notation 119
.() notation 127
.BY list 140
.RData 33
.RDS 33
.tsv (tab-separated values) 33
[,] indexing operator 27, 118
[[]] operator 22, 36, 472–473
@ operator 415, 476
& operator 23, 469
&& operator 23
#' marks 415
%in% operation 23
<- operator 25–26, 468
= operator 25, 468
-> operator 25, 469
| operator 23, 469
|| operator 23
$ operator 472

A

A/B tests 502–506
   evaluating 503–506
     Fisher's test for independence 504–505
     frequentist significance test 505–506
   setting up 503
accuracy evaluation measure 178–179, 184
accuracyMeasures() function 358
additive processes 105
adjusted R-squared 236
AIC (Akaike information criterion) 255
Akismet 178, 180

all.equal() method 470
alpha parameter 264, 269, 271
Apgar test 240
Apriori algorithm 169
apriori() function 347
arcsinh 106
area under the curve (AUC) 189–192, 278
arrange() command 28
arules package 343–351
   apriori() function 347–348
   examining data 344–347
   inspecting and evaluating rules 348–349
   reading in the data 344
   restricting which items to mine 349–351
as.factor() function 230
as.numeric() command 25
assign_cluster() function 339
assignment operators 25
assignments, left-hand sides of 25
association rules 167–169, 340–352
   example problem 342–343
   mining with arules package 343–351
     apriori() function 347–348
     examining data 344–347
     inspecting and evaluating rules 348–349
     reading in the data 344
     restricting which items to mine 349–351
   overview 340–342
asw (average silhouette width) 332, 335
AUC (area under the curve) 278
automatic printing 21

B

bagging classifiers 361
bar areas 68

bar charts
  checking distributions for single variables 66
  checking relationships between two
      variables 76
  with faceting 85
base error rate 17
base package 44
basic analytics 38
baskets 341
Batch method 429
beta regression 237
betas 218
between sum of squares (BSS) 328–329, 332, 415
bias 172
bias variance decomposition 501–502
bids 148
bimodal distribution 61–62
binary variables 230
BinaryYScatterPlot function 75
binomial classification 166
binomial distribution 494–499
bootstrap evaluation 323–325
BSS (between sum of squares) 328–329, 332, 415
Buzz dataset 405–406
buzz scoring 431
by keyword 127

C

C hyperparameter 397, 399
c() operator 34, 36, 471–472
calibration set 108
Calinski-Harabasz (CH) index 328, 330–332,
      335–336
call-by-value effect 471
CamelCase 24
CART trees 361
categorical variables 228, 286
  bar charts for comparing 76
  comparing continuous and 81
  missing data in 92
  using xgboost with 373–375
cbind operator 46, 142
cboot$bootmean 337
cdata::pivot_to_rowrecs() 157
cdata::unpivot_to_blocks 155
cdatapivot_to_rowrecs() function 157
cdataunpivot_to_blocks() function 152
center attribute 104, 317
centering and scaling 101–104
centroid 326
CH (Calinski-Harabasz) index 330, 335–336
char.freq.bang 366
character class 54
character types 25, 36

Character vector 472
Characterizing task 11
chi-squared test 254
chunks 407
class of interest 240
class() method 32, 470
classification 166, 169, 175–185
  accuracy 178–179
  classification problems 165–166
  confusion matrix 176–177
  data preparation for 282–297
    building model 292–297
    mkCrossFrameCExperiment() 290–292
    properly using treatment plan 288–289
    variable score frame 284–288
  defined 11
  F1 181
  precision and recall 179–180
  sensitivity and specificity 181–184
cleaning data 88–98
  domain-specific data cleaning 89
  missing values 91–95
    in categorical variables 92
    in numeric or logical variables 92
    nature of 92–93
    treating as information 94–95
    vtreat package for automatic treatment
      of 95–98
ClevelandDotPlot function 68
client role 5
cluster analysis 167, 312–340
  assigning new points to clusters 338–339
  data preparation 316–318
  distances 313–316
    cosine similarity 315–316
    Euclidean distance 314
    Hamming distance 314
    Manhattan (city block) distance 315
  hierarchical clustering with hclust 319–332
    bootstrap evaluation 323–325
    picking number of clusters 325–332
    principal components analysis 321–322
  k-means algorithm 332–337
    clusterboot() 336–337
    kmeans() function 332
    kmeansruns() function 335–336
cluster stability 324
clusterboot() function 323–325, 331, 335–337
clustering 11, 167, 170, 312
coalescing 121
Codd-style operators 115
coding style 20
coef() function 265
coefficient of determination 187
coefficients 218, 228, 248, 261–262

coefficients(model) function 228, 248
coefs vector 266
collinearity 216, 234
colnames() command 36
git help 422
comma-separated values (CSV) 33
comments
    comment character (#) 21
    writing effective 414
complete cases 301
complete.cases() function 123–124
Comprehensive R Archive Network (CRAN) 19,
        459–460, 464, 466
concatenate operator c() 22–23
conditional transforms 99
confusion matrix 13, 175–177
continuous histograms 64
continuous variables, comparing categorical
        and 81
coord_flip() function 80
copy by value semantics 26
correlation 187
cos() function 378
cosine similarity 315–316
coverage 348
CRAN (Comprehensive R Archive Network) 19,
        459–460, 464, 466
create_pruned_vocabulary() function 206, 213
CRISP-DM (cross-industry, standard, process, for,
        data mining) 6
cross-frame 290, 305–309
    dangers of naively reusing data 306–308
    safely reusing data 308–309
crossFrame element 308
cross-language linkage method, to deploy
        models 429
cryptographic hash, SHA 411
CSV (comma-separated values) 33
cumsum() 23
customer churn 275, 277
customer_data2 dataset 75
cutree() function 320
cv.glmnet() function 265–266, 269–270
cva.glmnet() function 269–270

D

data architect role 6
data collection and management stage 8
data coordinates 158
data dictionary 34, 285
data directory 418
data engineering
    data selection 116–128
        ordering rows 124–128

removing records with incomplete data
        121–124
    subsetting rows and columns 116–121
data transforms 128–133
    adding new columns 128–133
    aggregating 134–137
    multitable transforms 137–149
        combining data from multiple tables
            143–149
        combining two or more ordered data frames
            quickly 137–143
    reshaping transforms 149–158
        data coordinates 158
        moving data from tall to wide form 153–157
        moving data from wide to tall form 149–153
data frames 474
data provenance 111, 411–412
data range problems 56
data refresh 20
data science projects
    roles in 4
        client 5
        data architect 6
        data scientist 5
        operations 6
        project sponsor 4
    setting expectations for 16
    stages of 6
        data collection and management 8
        defining goal 7
        model deployment and maintenance 15
        model evaluation and critique 12
        modeling 10
        presentation and documentation 14
data scientists 5
data selection 116–128
    ordering rows 124–128
    removing records with incomplete data
        121–124
    subsetting rows and columns 116–121
data shaping, reshaping transforms 149–158
    data coordinates 158
    moving data from tall to wide form 153–157
    moving data from wide to tall form 149–153
data transformations 98, 128–133
    adding new columns 128–133
    aggregating 134–137
    centering and scaling 101–104
    log transformations 104
    multitable transforms 137–149
        combining data from multiple tables
            143–149
        combining two or more ordered data frames
            quickly 137–143
    normalization 99–100

data transformations *(continued)*
  reshaping 149–158
    data coordinates 158
    moving data from tall to wide form 153–157
    moving data from wide to tall form 149–153
data tubing 474
data.frame class 28
data.frame() function 26
data.frames 24–25, 29, 114, 118, 476
data.table by argument 155
data.table class
  adding new columns 130–131, 133
  appending columns 142
  appending rows 138
  combining many rows into summary rows
    135–136
  full join 147
  inner join 146
  left join 144–145
  ordering rows 125–127
  removing records with incomplete data 124
  splitting tables 140–141
  subsetting rows and columns 119
data.table package 24, 41, 114, 116, 119–120, 152
data.table::melt.data.table() 152
databases, using with R 477
  running database queries using query
    generator 477
  thinking relationally about data 481
datasets package 117, 154
datatable::dcast.data.table() 157
datatable::melt.data.table() 152
DBI package 43
dbplyr package 114, 477
dcast.data.table() 157
decision surface 200
decision trees 355
degrees of freedom 235
delayed class 240
delegation, to R 29
dendrograms 319
denormalized form 158
denormalized tables 482
density estimation 313
density plots 64
dependent variables 222, 277
deploying models 15, 428
  as HTTP services 431
  by export 433
  using Shiny 430
derived columns 482
design*() methods 305
design_missingness_treatment() function 104,
  300, 309
designTreatments*() function 308

designTreatmentsC() function 284, 288–290,
  297, 300
designTreatmentsN() function 297, 300, 308, 374
designTreatmentsZ() function 300, 309, 374
deviance evaluation measure 194
df.null - df.model 254
dgCMatrix class 207, 371
dim() function 32, 344
disparity in units 317
dissimilarity 313
dist() function 319
distributions 485–499
  binomial distribution 494–499
  lognormal distribution 490–494
  normal distribution 485–489
  other R tools for 499
  R's distribution naming conventions 490
documentation 14
  comments 414
  predicting popularity 405
  R markdown 406
    documenting data and producing model 411
    example 407
    purpose of 409
    technical details 409
  version control
    to explore projects 422
    to record history 416
    to share work 424
document-term matrix 206
domain empathy 6
domain-specific data cleaning 89
dot arrow pipe 121, 129
dot notation 24, 27
dot pipe %.>% 28
dotplots 66
dot-product similarity 398
double density plot 188–189
double-precision floating-point 471
dply::bind_rows 139
dplyr
  adding new columns 131, 133
  appending columns 143
  appending rows 139
  combining many rows into summary rows 136
  full join 147
  inner join 146
  left join 145
  ordering rows 126–128
  removing records with incomplete data 124
  splitting tables 141
  subsetting rows and columns 120–121
dplyr::bind_cols 143
dplyr::filter 120, 124
dplyr::full_join 147

dplyr::group_by 136
dplyr::select 120
dplyr::summarize 136
drop = FALSE argument 27, 118
dtest data frame 230
dummy variables 46, 286, 302

E

edf (effective degrees of freedom) 380–381
effects coding 303
efficiency, statistical 502
elastic net 263, 269–273
end user presentations 447–452
  showing how model fits user workflow 448–449
  showing how to use the model 450–452
  summarizing project goals 447
end-of-statement markers 25
enrichment rate 246
ensemble learning 359
errors 22, 186
Euclidean distance 314–315
evalframe 373
evaluating models 170–195
  classification models 175–185
    accuracy 178–179
    confusion matrix 176–177
    F1 score 181
    precision and recall 179–180
    sensitivity and specificity 181–184
  measures of model performance 174–175
  overfitting 170–174
    K-fold cross-validation 173–174
    testing on held-out data 172–173
  probability models 187–195
    Akaike information criterion 195
    deviance 194
    double density plot 188–189
    log likelihood 192–194
    receiver operating characteristic curve 189–192
  scoring models 185–187
    root mean square error 186–187
    R-squared 187
Excel Spreadsheet (XLS) 33
exchangeability 500
experimental design columns 482
explain() function 199, 201–202
explainers 199
explanatory variables 218, 281
explicit dot notation 120
exploring data for problems
  summary statistics 53
    data range 56
    invalid values and outliers 56

missing values 55
  units 57
visualization and graphics 58
  checking distributions for single variables 60
  checking relationships between two variables 70
exporting models 429
extend() method 478
eXtensible Markup Language (XML) 33–34, 435
extrapolation 220

F

F1 score 181
facets 80, 86
facet_wrap layer 80
facet_wrap() command 82
factor class 54
factor coding 45–47
factor variables 228
Factor vector 472
factors 25–26, 475–476
false negatives (FN) 177, 189
false positive rate 14, 184
false positives (FP) 177
family function 242
filled bar charts 78–79, 85
filter() function 137
Fisher scoring iterations 255–256, 260
Fisher's test for independence 504–505
Fisher's exact test 348
fit_imdb_model() function 207
fit_iris_example() function 198, 369
fixed-width files (FWF) 33
floating-point format 22, 24
FN (false negatives) 177, 189
forecasting 170
FP (false positives) 177
fpc package 323, 335
frequentist significance test 505–506
F-statistic 236
F-test 236, 254, 307
full joins 146–147
function arguments 469
FWF (fixed-width files) 33

G

gam package 379
gam() function 379, 381, 384, 387, 389
GAMs (generalized additive models) 376–389
  extracting non-linear relationships 382–384
  one-dimensional regression example 378–382
  overview 376–378

GAMs (generalized additive models) *(continued)*
 using for logistic regression 387–388
 using on actual data 384–387
gap statistic 332
Gaussian distributions 332
generalization error 170
generalized additive models. *See* GAMs
generalized linear models 237
geom_hex layer 75
geom_histogram layer 63
geom_histogram() command 82
geom_line layer 60
geom_point layer 60, 71
geom_smooth function 73, 75
ggplot() function 60, 107
ggplot2 package 21, 59–60, 66–67, 116, 150
ggpubr package 59
ggstatsplot package 59
Git 428
 installing 461, 464
 starting project using command line 418
 using git diff to compare files from different
  commits 423
 using git log and git status to view progress 419
 using git log to find last time file was
  around 424
 using through RStudio 420
git blame command 422
git clone command 425, 461
git commit command 420
git diff command 423
git help log command 422
git log command 419
git pull command 426
git push command 424, 426
git rebase command 424
git remote add command 425
git remote command 425
git status 419, 425
git tag command 423
glm() function 166, 222, 237, 240, 242–243,
  255–256, 259, 264, 280, 282, 303
glmnet 263–273
 elastic net 269–273
 lasso regression 268–269
 ridge regression 264–268
glmnet method 233
glmnet package 263
glmnet::cv.glmnet() function 264
glmnet::glmnet() function 264
glmnetUtils package 263, 269, 272
goal defining stage 7
gradient boosting models 373
gradient-boosted trees 359, 368–375
 gradient boosting for text classification
  371–373

iris example 369–371
 using xgboost with categorical variables 373–
  375
GROUP BY queries 482
group() function 137
group_by() command 127, 141
grouped data 251

H

Hamming distance 314
hash mark (#) 21
hashes 39
hclust() function 319–332, 334, 336
 bootstrap evaluation 323–325
 picking number of clusters 325–332
  Calinski-Harabasz index 328–332
  total within sum of squares 325–327
 principal components analysis 321–322
head() command 32, 154, 282
help() command 20, 22, 49, 470
help(match) command 145
help(model_support) command 199
help(setwd) command 20, 26
hexbin plots 70, 75, 85
HexBinPlot function 75
hierarchical clustering 313, 319–332
 bootstrap evaluation 323–325
 picking number of clusters 325–332
  Calinski-Harabasz index 328–332
  total within sum of squares 325–327
 principal components analysis 321–322
histograms 62–63, 70
Homebrew 464
homoscedastic errors 379
horizontal offset 177
HTML 407
HTTP services, deploying models as 431
hyperparameters 397, 399
hypothesis testing 17

I

IDE (integrated development environment) 405
identical() method 470
if statements 23
impact 286
impact coding 303–305
implicit printing 21
importance() function 365
imputed value 92
independent variables 218, 222, 277
indicator variables 90, 230, 302–303
infix scalar-valued operators 23

inner joins 145–146
input variables 277
install.packages() command 462
integrated development environment (IDE) 405
interestMeasure() function 348
intermediate values, organizing 27–28
introducing indicators 46
invalid values 56
iris dataset 116–117, 134, 197, 369
itemFrequency() function 345
items 341

J

Jaccard coefficient 323
join command 53
JSON (JavaScript Object Notation) 33

K

k(,) function 398
kernel functions 389–390, 397–399
    defined 397–398
    support vectors 398–399
kernel trick 399
kernlab library 390
k-fold cross-validation 173–174
k-means algorithm 323, 332–337
    clusterboot() 336–337
    kmeans() function 332
    kmeansruns() function 335–336
k-means clustering 168, 313
kmeans() function 332, 338
kmeansruns() function 335–336
knitr 407, 409, 412
    documenting data and producing model
        411–414
        confirming data provenance 411–412
        recording performance of naive analysis 412
        using milestones to save time 413
    technical details 409
        block declaration format 410
        chunk options 410

L

L1 distance 315
L1-regularized regression 263
L2 distance 315
L2-regularized regression 262
Laplace smoothing 305
lasso regression 263, 268–269
LaTeX 407
lattice package 59

layers 60
lazy copying 470
LearnR 466
least squares method 231
left joins 143–145
length() function 32
length-zero vector 23
lhs() function 350
library() command 26, 462, 464
library(pkgname) command 463
lift 348
LIME (local interpretable model-agnostic
        explanations) 195–214
    automated sanity checking 197
    example 197–204
    for text classification 204–207
        explaining predictions 209–214
        representing documents for modeling
            206–207
        training text classifier 208
    how LIME works 200–202
lime package 199, 202
LIME variable importances 367
lime() function 209
line breaks 24–25
line of perfect prediction 223
line plots 70, 84
line wrapping 21
linear combination 217
linear regression 216–237
    building model 221
    finding relations and extracting advice
        228–230
    making predictions 222–228
    PUMS dataset 220–221
    reading model summary and characterizing
        coefficient quality 230–236
        coefficients table 232–235
        original model call 230
        overall model quality summaries 235–236
        residuals summary 230–232
    when assumptions of are violated 219–220
link function 243
lists 22–23, 472
lm() command 218, 221–222, 229, 242, 264, 303,
        381, 476
load() command 33
local interpretable model-agnostic explanations.
        See LIME
loess function, 73
log likelihood 192–194, 253
log transformations 104
logarithmic scale 66
logical vectors 472

logistic regression 11, 176, 216, 237, 240–256
  building model 242
  finding relations and extracting advice
    248–249
  making predictions 243–248
  overview 237
  reading model summary and characterizing
    coefficients 249–256
    deviance residuals summary 250–251
    Fisher scoring iterations 255–256
    original model call 250
    overall model quality summaries 252–255
    summary coefficients table 251–252
  using generalized additive models for 387–388
logit function 240
logit link 243, 387
logit space (link space) 287
logit() 239–240
lognormal distribution 490–494
lognormally distributed monetary amounts 104
log-odds, of probabilities 239
log-scaled density plot 66

M

magrittr package 27
magrittr pipe operator %>% 28, 120, 124
Manhattan (city block) distance 315
mapping problems to machine learning tasks 164
  classification problems 165–166
  grouping 167
    association rules 168
    clustering 167
  problem-to-method mapping 169–170
  scoring problems 166
margins 397
Markdown 407
match() method 23, 145
matrices 475
MAX() function 482
m-dimensional linear model 202
mean squared error 186–187
measurement types 405
Mercer's theorem 398
method chaining 127
mgcv package 379, 388
Microsoft Excel workbooks 33
Microsoft Word 407
missing values 55, 301
missing-value imputation 301
mixture of Gaussians 332
mkCrossFrame*Experiment() method 305
mkCrossFrame*Experiment() methods,
  vtreat's 308

mkCrossFrame*Experiment()/$crossFrame
  pattern 309
mkCrossFrameCExperiment() function 290–292,
  297, 300
mkCrossFrameNExperiment() function 297, 300,
  308, 374
mkExperiment*() methods 305
mk_formula() function 242, 280
mlogit package 166
model deployment and maintenance stage 15
model evaluation and critique stage 12
model matrix 158, 482
model object 222
model performance, determining lower bounds
  on 16
model.matrix() function 300, 302, 374, 474
modeling 10
  evaluating models 170–195
    classification models 175–185
    measures of model performance 174–175
    overfitting 170–174
    probability models 187–195
    scoring models 185–187
  local interpretable model-agnostic explanations
    195–214
    automated sanity checking 197
    example 197–204
    for text classification 204–214
    how LIME works 200–202
  mapping problems to machine learning tasks
    164–170
    classification problems 165–166
    grouping 167
    problem-to-method mapping 169–170
    scoring problems 166
  sampling for 107–111
  trade-offs 246
modeling algorithm 445
model_ridge$lambda.1se 265
model_ridge$lambda.min 265
MongoDB 34
multicategory classification 166
multimodal data 61
multinomial classification 166
multiple comparison bias 173
multiple comparison problems 233
multiplicative process 106
multitable transforms 137–149
  combining data from multiple tables 143–149
    full joins 146–147
    inner joins 145–146
    left joins 143–145
    right joins 145
    rolling joins 147–149

multitable transforms *(continued)*
  combining two or more ordered data frames
      quickly 137–143
    appending columns 142–143
    appending rows 138–139
    splitting tables 139–141
multivariate data matrix 158
mutable data types 472
mutate() function 28, 90, 127, 131

N

NA (not available) values 23–24, 33, 91–95, 475
  in categorical variables 92
  in numeric or logical variables 92
  nature of 92–93
  treating as information 94–95
  vtreat package for automatic treatment of
      95–98
  vtreat variable treatment package 301–302
na.locf() function 121, 131
na.omit() function 123
na_if() function 90
naked repositories 425
named arguments 26
named lists 33, 472
named maps 36
NaN (not a number) 106
narrow data ranges 57
natural key columns 481
NB (nota bene or note well) 415
nchar() function 23
needsSplit 305
NEGATIVE (non-spam). *See* truth mark
negative coefficients 248
negative R-squareds 187
newpt data point 338
n_features parameter 202
N-fold cross-validation 364
no operation (no-op) 23
non-linear combinations 389
nonsignaling 475
–no-restore command-line flag set 466
normal distribution 485–489
normalization (rescaling) 99–100
normalized form 53
not a number (NaN) 106
not available values. *See* NA (not available) values
nota bene or note well (NB) 415
nu hyperparameter 397, 399
null deviance 253
null model 16, 187
NULL values 23–24, 253, 475
NULL vector 472
Numeric vector 472

O

one-hot encoding 286, 300, 302
one-versus-rest classifier 166
operations role 6
operator 22–23, 114, 145, 473
order() function 28
outcome variable 277
outliers 56
out-of-bag samples 364
overfitting 170–174, 235, 255, 262, 364
  K-fold cross-validation 173–174
  testing on held-out data 172–173
overlaid density plot 86

P

package notation 26
payload columns 482
PCR (principal components regression) 261
peer presentations 452–457
  discussing related work 453–454
  discussing results and future work 455–456
  discussing your approach 454–455
  introducing problem 452
permTestAUC() function 295
phi() function 390, 395, 397–399
piped notation 27
pipe-separated (vertical bar) files 33
pivoting 149, 154
plot() function 382
plot(gammodel) function 385
plot_features() function 199, 210
plot_text_explanations() function 210
plumber package 432–433
PMML (Predictive Model Markup Language) 435
Poisson regression 221
POSITIVE (spam). *See* truth mark
prcomp() function 321
precision 14, 177, 179–181, 185, 246
predict() function 222, 243, 265, 322, 382, 388,
      470
predictions 170, 225
prepare() method 283–284, 288, 290, 292, 300,
      308, 374
presentations 14
  end user presentations 447–452
    showing how model fits user workflow
        448–449
    showing how to use the model 450–452
    summarizing project goals 447
  peer presentations 452–457
    discussing related work 453–454
    discussing results and future work 455–456

presentations, peer presentations *(continued)*
  discussing your approach 454–455
  introducing problem 452
  project sponsor presentations 439–446
    filling in details 444–445
    making recommendations and discussing
        future work 446
    stating project results 442
    summarizing project goals 440–441
principal components analysis 321–322
principal components regression (PCR) 261
print() function 32, 470
printing 21–22
probability models 187–195
  Akaike information criterion 195
  deviance 194
  double density plot 188–189
  log likelihood 192–194
  receiver operating characteristic curve
      189–192
problem-to-method mapping 169–170
project sponsor presentations 439–446
  filling in details 444–445
  making recommendations and discussing
      future work 446
  stating project results 442
  summarizing project goals 440–441
project sponsors 4
provenance columns 482
PRTPlot() function 246
pseudo distance 316
pseudo R-squared 187, 194
pseudo-random sample 40
PUMS (Public Use Microdata Sample) data
      38–49
  curating data 39
  examining and conditioning data 42
  factor coding 45–47
  linear regression 220–221
  working with 47–49
p-value (significance) 234–236, 251, 254–255

Q

quasi-separation 256–262
query generators 477
Quick-R 466
quotes 148

R

R 19, 459, 466
  installing 20, 459–460
  installing tools
    book-support materials 461

R package system 462, 464
  required packages 463
primary data types 471
  data frames 474
  factors 475
  lists 472
  matrices 475
  NULL and NA 475
  slots 476
  vectors 471
primary features of 468
  assignment 468
  object system 470
  share-by-value characteristics 470
  vectorized operations 469
programming basics 20
  assignment operators 25
  comment character 21
  data.frame class 28
  delegating to R 29
  factors 25–26
  identifiers 24
  left-hand sides of assignments 25
  line breaks 24–25
  lists 22–23
  NA value 23–24
  named arguments 26
  NULL value 23–24
  organizing intermediate values 27–28
  package notation 26
  printing 21–22
  semicolons 25
  value semantics 26–27
  vectors 22–23
relational databases 37–49
  curating data 39
  examining and conditioning data 42
  factor coding 45–47
  production-size example 38–49
  working with 47–49
resources for 465
  installing R views 465
  online 466
structured data 29
  less-structured data 34
  well-structured data 29
using databases with 477
  running database queries using query
      generator 477
  thinking relationally about data 481
R markdown 406–414
  documenting data and produce model
      411–414
    confirming data provenance 411–412
    recording performance of naive analysis 412
    using milestones to save time 413

R markdown (*continued*)
  example 407
  purpose of 409
  technical details 409
    block declaration format 410
    chunk options 410
RAND command 110
random forests 359, 361–367, 373
  exporting to SQL with tidypredict 434–435
  variable importance 364, 367
randomForest package 432
randomForest() function 361–362, 364–365
ranking tasks 11
raw (unscaled) variables 318
rbind 138
R-bloggers 466
Rcpp package 429, 463
RDF triples 153
reactive programming 431
read.table() function 26, 32–33
read.transactions() function 344
reader package 33
readr package 30
readRDS() command 33
readxl package 37
rebase 426
recall 14, 17, 177, 180–181, 185, 246
receiver operating characteristic curve (ROC) 189–192
record grouping 110–111
rect.hclust() function 319
reference level 44, 221, 228, 303
reference semantics 114
regression modeling, data preparation for 297–299
regression testing 109
regression to the mean 225
regressions 166, 169
regularization 216, 257–273
  example of quasi-separation 257–262
  types of 262–263
    elastic net 263
    lasso regression 263
    ridge regression 262
  with glmnet 263–273
    elastic net solution 269–273
    lasso regression solution 268–269
    ridge regression solution 264–268
relational databases 37–49
  curating data 39
  examining and conditioning data 42
  factor coding 45–47
  production-size example 38–49
  working with 47–49
relations, finding 11

relevel() function 230
remote relation 425
residual deviance 253
residual standard error 235–236
residuals 186, 231
reversion to mediocrity 225
ridge regression 262, 264–268
right joins 145
rm.duplicates = TRUE argument 344
rm() command 222
RMSE (root mean square error) 186, 226–228, 235, 378, 380–381
ROC (receiver operating characteristic curve) 189–190
rolling joins 147–149
root mean square error (RMSE) 186–187, 226–228, 235, 378, 380–381
rownames() function 126
rows 405
roxygen2 R package 415
rquery package 41, 114, 477–478, 481
R-squared 187, 226–228
  adjusted 236
  multiple 236
  pseudo R-squared 254
RStudio 405, 420, 430, 460
  community for 466
  installing 460, 465
  using Git through 420
RStudio Desktop 465
RTools 464
runif() function 109

S

S programming language 466
s() function 380, 382, 386
sample_frac() function 109
sample_n() function 109
sampling 107–111
  creating sample group columns 109–110
  data provenance 111
  record grouping 110–111
  splitting data into training and test sets 108
save() command 33
saveRDS() function 32–33
scale attribute 104, 317
scale() function 102–103, 317, 338–339
scaling 317–318
scatter plots 70, 75, 84
schema documentation 34
scikit-learn, Python 46
score frame 284
scoring 11, 166

scoring models 185–187
  root mean square error 186–187
  R-squared 187
scoring problems 166
scoring residuals 186
sdata data frame 241, 252
se = FALSE argument 73
sensitivity 181, 183–185
sentinel values 56, 64
sepal measurements 197
separable data 397
separation 256
Services method 429
sessionInfo() command 464
set.seed() command 109
setorderv() function 125
setosa 198, 203
setwd() function 26, 31
shadow graphs 78
shadow histograms 86
shadow plots 78, 85
ShadowHist() function 82
ShadowPlot command 79
Shiny tool 430
side-by-side bar charts 76, 85
sigmoid function 239
signed logarithm 106
significance 251
  lack of 252
  testing 17
  vs. goodness of fit 255
sigr package 194, 261
sigr::wrapFTest() function 308–309
silhouette clustering 335
similarity 313
sin() function 378
single-variable models 175
slotNames() 476
slots 476
smoothing 304
smoothing curves 70, 85
SOA (services oriented architecture) 431
soft margin 397
sort() function 348
spam filters 180–181
spam model 176
spam proportion 181–182
sparse matrix 207
specificity 183, 185
split() function 258
sponsor sign-off 5
SQL (Structured Query Language) 33, 434–435
SQL WHEN clause 435
sqldf package 38
sqr_edist() function 338

Stack Overflow R section 466
stack() notation 149
stacked bar charts 76, 79, 85
standard error ribbon 73
statistical efficiency 502
statistical theory 499–510
  A/B tests 502–506
    evaluating 503–506
    setting up 503
  power of tests 506–508
  specialized statistical tests 508–510
  statistical philosophy 499–502
    bias variance decomposition 501–502
    exchangeability 500
    statistical efficiency 502
statistical view of data, examples of
  omitted variable bias 513–518
    example of 514–516
    overview 513
    spoiled analysis 516–517
    working around 517–518
  sampling bias 510–513
statistically efficient estimators 173
statistically significant thresholds 234
stats package 29, 44, 221, 242
str() function 32, 46, 279
str(dTrain) command 279
stringsAsFactors = FALSE argument 26
string-valued (categorical) variable 230
structured data 29–37
  less-structured tabular data 34–37
    examining 37
    transforming 34
  well-structured data in comma-separated values
    format 29
    examining 32
    loading 30
  well-structured data in other data formats 33
structured values 29
subset() function 129, 351
sum(error_sq) (sum squared error) 187
summarize() function 128
summary statistics 38, 53
  typical problems revealed by 54
    data range issues 56
    invalid values 56
    missing values 55
    outliers 56
    units 57
summary() function 26, 32–33, 37, 45, 53–54,
    154, 230, 470
summary(customer_data$marital.stat) command
    67
summary(dpus) command 47
summary(dpus$COW) command 44

summary(dTrain) command 279
summary(model) command 222, 230, 232, 235
summary(model)$coefficients 232
supervised learning 166
support vectors 399
Surrogate key columns 481
SVMs (support vector machines) 389–390,
    392–395, 397, 399–400
  kernel functions 397–399
    defined 397–398
    support vectors 398–399
  overview 395–397
  problem solving with 390–395
    spiral example 390–392
    with good kernels 393–395
    with oversimple kernels 392–393
symbol names (identifiers) 24
syntax error 25
synthetic data points 200

T

table() command 47
tab-separated values (.tsv) 33
tall data form 153
tapply() command 47–48
target class 240
test (holdout) set 108, 177
test data 170
text classification
  gradient boosting for 371–373
  local interpretable model-agnostic explanations
    for 204–207
    explaining predictions 209–214
    representing documents for modeling
      206–207
    training text classifier 208
text2vec package 206
the kernel trick 399
The R Foundation 460
theta angle 316
thin data form 153
tidypredict package 434–435
tidyr solution 152
tidyrgather() function 153
tidyrspread() function 157–158
Times attribute 405
title column 343
TN (true negatives) 177
token column 343
topics 405
total variance 187
TP (true positives) 189
trades 148
training error 170

training set 108, 166
training_prepared data frame 96
train_treated 375
transactions object 340, 344
transform() function 129, 382
treat package for automatic treatment of 95
treatment plans 95, 276, 278, 284
tree-based methods 11, 355–376
  bagging 359–361
  basic decision tree 356–358
  gradient-boosted trees 368–375
    gradient boosting for text classification
      371–373
    iris example 369–371
    using xgboost with categorical variables
      373–375
  random forests 361–367
true negative rate 183
true outcome 225
true positive rate 183
truth mark 177
TSS (total sum of squares) 328
TSV (tab-separated values) 33
two-category classification 166
two-dimensional histograms 75
typeof() command 32

U

unbiased predictors 218
unconditioned transform 99
underscore notation 24
underscore style 24
ungroup() function 137
ungrouped data 251
unimodal distribution 62
units
  cluster analysis 317–318
  unit problems 57
unstack() notation 149
unsupervised learning 167
unsupervised methods
  association rules 340–352
    example problem 342–343
    mining with arules package 343–351
    overview 340–342
  cluster analysis 312–340
    assigning new points to clusters 338–339
    data preparation 316–318
    distances 313–316
    hierarchical clustering 319–332
    k-means algorithm 332–337
unsystematic errors 218
utils package 29, 44
utils::read.table() command 30

V

validation, sampling for 107–111
value semantics 26–27, 114
value.var argument 157
values 91
values in categorical variables 92
values in numeric or logical variables 92
values nature of 92
value_variables_C() method 292, 294
varImpPlot() function 365–366
vectorized operations 23
vectors 22–23, 471
version control 418
  to explore projects 422
    finding out who wrote what and when 422
    using git diff to compare files from different commits 423
    using git log to find last time file was around 424
  to record history 416
    choosing project directory structure 417
    starting Git project using command line 418
    using add/commit pairs to checkpoint work 419
    using git log and git status to view progress 419
    using Git through RStudio 420
  to share work 424
    setting up remote repository relations 425
    using push and pull to synchronize work with remote repositories 426
versioning 418
vertical offset 177
View() command 31–32, 154
visualization and graphics 58
  checking distributions for single variables 60
    bar charts 66
    density plots 64
    dotplots 66
    histograms 62
  checking relationships between two variables 70
    bar charts for two categorical variables 76
    comparing continuous and categorical variables 81
    hexbin plots 75
    line plots 70
    scatter plots and smoothing curves 70
  overview 84

vtreat variable treatment package 95–98, 299–309
  cross-frame 305–309
    dangers of naively reusing data 306–308
    safely reusing data 308–309
  data preparation for classification 282–297
    building model 292–297
    properly using treatment plan 288–289
    variable score frame 284–288
  data preparation for regression modeling 297–299
  dataset 277–282
    bull-in-the-china-shop approach 280–282
    characterizing outcome 279
  impact coding 303–305
  indicator variables 302–303
  missing values 301–302
  phases of 299–301
  purpose of 275
  treatment plan 305

W

with() function 125, 129
wrapr package 28, 242
wrapr pipe 121
wrapr::orderv() 126
WSS (within sum of squares) 319, 325–327, 332
WVPlots library 75, 246
WVPlots package 68, 79

X

xcenter attribute 338
Xcode tools 464
xgb.cv() function 369, 375
xgboost package 198–199, 205–206, 294, 369, 373–375, 395
xgboost() function 286, 293, 370
XLS (Excel Spreadsheet) 33
XLSX 33
XML (eXtensible Markup Language) 33–34, 435
xscale attribute 338

Y

YAML (yet another markup language) 407

Z

zeallot package 205, 258
zoo package 131